305.2
Jen

SCSU Library
Alnwick Castle
Alnwick England
CANCELLED

SCSU
British Studies Prog
Alnwick Castle

adolescence:
theories, research, applications

adolescence:

theories, research, applications

Larry Cyril Jensen

WEST PUBLISHING COMPANY
St. Paul   New York   Los Angeles   San Francisco

Copyediting Joan Torkildson
Design Adrianne Dudden
Composition Master Typographers
Two-color artwork Barbara Hack Barnett

Cover design Delor Erickson

COPYRIGHT © 1985 By WEST PUBLISHING CO.
50 West Kellogg Boulevard
P. O. Box 43526
St. Paul, Minnesota 55164

All rights reserved

Printed in the United States of America

Library of Congress Cataloging in Publication Data

Jensen, Larry C.
   Adolescence: theories, research, applications.

   Bibliography: p.
   Includes index.
   1. Youth. I. Title.
HQ796.J46   1985   305.2′35   84-17231
ISBN 0-314-85251-4
1st Reprint—1985

PHOTO CREDITS

2 Chris Grajczyk. **8** The Bettmann Archive. **11** Monkmeyer Press (Photo Service): Paul Conklin. **13** Stock, Boston: Donald Dietz. **19** EKM-Nepenthe: John Maher. **27** Magnum: Richard Kalvar. **34** Jeroboam: © Frank Siteman MCMLXXXI. **40** The Bettmann Archive. **44** EKM-Nepenthe: Tom Ballard. **46** Stock, Boston: Patrick Ward. **50** UPI/The Bettmann Archive. **51** The Bettmann Archive. **57** Stock, Boston: Hazel Hankin. **64** Renaud Thomas/FPG. **67** © 1970 Black Star: Olive R. Pierce. **71** EKM-Nepenthe: Tom Ballard. **74** EKM-Nepenthe: © John R. Maher. **77** Jeroboam: © 1982 Frank D. Smith. **83** Stock, Boston: Peter Menzel. **88** Stock, Boston: © 1984 Ulrike Welsch. **96** Jeroboam: Evan Johnson. **100** Stock, Boston: © Jean-Claude Lejeune. **104** EKM-Nepenthe: © Cathy Cheney. **105** EKM-Nepenthe: © Tom Ballard. **114** Archive Pictures, Inc.: © Mary Ellen Mark. **117** Stock, Boston: © Arthur Grace. **118** EKM-Nepenthe: © Tom Ballard. **124** Jeroboam: © Kit Hedman. **127** EKM-Nepenthe: © Tom Ballard. **129** EKM-Nepenthe: John R. Maher. **132** Stock, Boston: Michael Hayman. **138** EKM-Nepenthe: John R. Maher. **145** Magnum: © David Hurn. **147** Jeroboam: Bill Aron. **164** Stock, Boston: © Peter Vandermark. **168** Magnum: © Alex Webb. **178** James L. Shaffer. **182** Stock, Boston: © Cary Wolinsky. **190** Stock, Boston: © Peter Southwick. **198** Jeroboam: © 1982 Frank D. Smith. **207** Evan Peskin/FPG. **212** Woodfin Camp & Associates: ©1982 Donna Ferrato. **220** Magnum: David Hurn. **224** Jeroboam: © Evan Johnson. **230** Woodfin Camp & Associates: ©1978 Sepp Seitz. **236** Woodfin Camp & Associates: © 1980 Baron Wolman. **238** Woodfin Camp & Associates: © 1982 Jim Anderson. **246** Woodfin Camp & Associates: © 1983 Lynne Jaeger Weinstein. **248** Woodfin Camp & Associates: © 1980 Jim Anderson. **251** Woodfin Camp & Associates: © Timothy Eagan. **260** Chris Grajczyk. **264** Stock, Boston: Ulrike Welsch. **271** Woodfin Camp & Associates: © 1983 Jim Anderson. **281** Magnum: Sebastiao Salgado, Jr. **287** (left) Jeroboam: Mitchell Payne; (right) Jeroboam: Peeter Vilms. **294** Jeroboam: Kent Reno. **297** Black Star: © 1980 Yves de Braine. **302** Black Star: Lee Lockwood. **311** Jeroboam: © 1981 Bruce Forrester. **317** Magnum: Henri Cartier-Bresson. **321** Jeroboam: Rose Skytta. **328** © Edward Lettau/FPG. **334** Woodfin Camp & Associates: © 1980 Baron Wolman. **344** Photo Researchers, Inc.: © 1984 Joseph Szabo. **352** Magnum: Paul Fusco. **359** Magnum: Paul Fusco. **370** Frost Publishing: American Cancer Society. **376** © Jeffry W. Myers/ *(continued following Subject index)*

This book is dedicated to those of my children who are or have been teenagers and have taught me so much.

Jan
Laury
Kimberly
Darcia
Dena
Shauri
Niko!

ABOUT THE AUTHOR

Professor Larry Cyril Jensen joined the faculty of the psychology department at Brigham Young University in 1965. He has also taught at Michigan State University, the State University of New York at Potsdam, and Utah State University. He received his B.S. and M.S. degrees at Brigham Young University and his Ph.D. at Michigan State University.

Besides writing numerous papers which have been presented at professional meetings, Professor Jensen has authored more than twenty research reports appearing in journals such as *Journal of Developmental Psychology, Journal of Experimental Psychology, Psychological Reports, Journal of Educational Psychology, Journal of Genetic Psychology, British Journal of Social or Clinical Psychology, Education, Psychology in the Schools, Educational and Psychological Measurement.* He has also authored several books, including a text on parenting to be published shortly by Holt, Rinehart and Winston.

Professor Jensen's primary area of research is in youth socialization with a special emphasis on parent-child relationships and moral development.

CONTENTS

Preface xi
Acknowledgments xii

Section One · AN INTRODUCTION 1

Chapter One · Overview of Adolescence 2

Historical Considerations 6
Definitions of Adolescence 11
Perceptions of Adolescence 14
Improving Our Relationships with Adolescents 16
Characteristics of American Youth 18
Recent Background of American Youth 21
Youth in Other Countries 24
Adolescents from Differing Socioeconomic Groups 28

Chapter Two · Theories and Viewpoints of Adolescence 34

The Value of Theories 37
Biological Theories and Viewpoints 39
Psychological and Sociological Theories and Viewpoints 42
Anthropological Theories and Viewpoints 48
Psychoanalytic Theories and Viewpoints 51
Range and Use of Theories 58

Chapter Three · The Developing Self 64

Erik Erikson and Developing a Sense of Identity 68
The Sense of Identity 70
Marcia's Theory of Identity, Role Status, and Research 73
The Self-Concept and Self-Esteem 78
Influences on Self-Esteem and Self-Concept 80
Variations in Self-Concept 89

Section Two · INFLUENCES 95

Chapter Four · Adolescent Peer Relationships 96

Conformity 98
Peer Groups 105
Friendships 111
Adolescent Marriages 115

Chapter Five · The Family 124

Family Organizations 126
Ethnic Family Differences 135
Parental Influence and Discipline 150

Chapter Six · Adolescence and Education 164

Evaluating American Schools 166
Inside the Schools 172
Other Educational Concerns of American Schools 181
Discipline in the Schools 189

Chapter Seven · Biological Influences 198

Puberty and Biological Changes 201
The Effects of Early and Late Maturation 207
Adolescent Body Types 210
The Secular Trend 213
Physical Attractiveness 215
The Onset of Puberty 217
Sex Differences 221
Adolescent Handicaps 222

Chapter Eight · The Media: Music, Video, Television, Film, Literature, and Pornography 230

Music 233
Video 237
Television 241
Films and Television Drama (Soaps) 247
Adolescent Literature 250
Pornography 252

Section Three · BEHAVIORS AND THINKING 259

Chapter Nine · Dating, Love, Sex, and Sex Roles 260

Love, Romance, and Dating 262
Sexual Behavior Development 272
Sexual Behavior Motivation 279
Sex Roles 285

Chapter Ten · Morality, Values, and Religion 294

Development of Moral Reasoning 297
Values 305
Moral Behavior 313
Religion 319

Chapter Eleven · Clinical Problems in Adolescence 328

Mental Health and Stress 332
Hyperactivity 335
Depression or Affective Disorders 340
Neurosis 346
Conversion Reaction 350
Schizophrenia 353
Anorexia Nervosa 358
Suicide 360

Chapter Twelve · Drug Use During Adolescence 370

Adolescent Drug Use 372
Theories of Motivation for Drug Use 389
Prevention and Treatment of Drug Abuse 401

Chapter Thirteen · Juvenile Delinquency   414

Defining the Problem   416
Causes of Juvenile Delinquency   420
Behavior Patterns   428
Prevention and Treatment   433

Chapter Fourteen · Thinking and Intelligence   444

Piaget's Theory of Learning   447
Adolescent Thinking   450
Change in Cognitive Development and Formal Operations   452
The Concept of Intelligence and Intelligence Testing   456

Section Four · THEORIES FOR APPLICATION   469

Chapter Fifteen · Applying Behavioral Theory to Adolescents   470

Behavior Modification Theory   473
Shaping   477
Token Economies   478
Positive Reinforcement and Punishment   487
Special Concerns When Using Behavior Modification with Adolescents   490
Other Approaches   493

Chapter Sixteen · Phenomenological Theory: Application for Building Relationship Skills   500

Phenomenological Theory and its Application   503
Relationship Skills   505
Communication Skills   513
Listening   517
Owning Feelings   518
Empathy   521

Chapter Seventeen · Phenomenological Theory: Application for Building Helping Skills   530

Dealing with Conflict   532
Skills for Helping   536
Phenomenological Practices in Self-Development   553

PREFACE

Having taught courses on adolescence for many years, I have adopted many good textbooks, but my students have always wanted something different. They have wanted a useful textbook! What do they mean by the word *useful?* To understand this word, one must understand the students who enroll in a course on adolescence.

Perhaps the largest block of students come from those enrolled in programs that require a course in adolescence as part of their curriculum (e.g., education, social work, law enforcement, family sciences.) These are students who will be working directly with adolescents and they want material that will help them.

The other large group of students are those who take the course as part of their credit hour requirements for majors in disciplines such as psychology or sociology. These students want research data about adolescence, but also have selected the course because most of them plan to enter a service profession and accordingly want a practical course.

Lastly, there are the older students frequently enrolled in evening and off-campus sections. These are parents, teachers, social workers, pastors, and others working on a day-to-day basis with adolescents. These students ask even more of both the instructor and the text. They almost demand a practical textbook. These students will criticize a solid, comprehensive, and research-oriented text as being a "fine reference book" or a "research manual" but "not something I want to read." I found that these students do not like a text if it reads like a literature review.

With these concerns and students in mind I have tried to create a new kind of text for a course on adolescence without sacrificing a solid research base. To do this, several elements were added. They are:

1. Focus on content that can be applied.
2. Base the content on solid and up-to-date research as much as possible; but be willing to stretch for information that is relevant and timely, even if it has not received a lot of research attention.
3. Include interdisciplinary research and theory.
4. Organize a text around a sound learning and study approach. In this text, meaningful questions are presented at the first of each chapter and then restated throughout the text where content can be found to answer the questions. This provides a more active study approach and a motivational basis for studying the material.
5. Divide the text into four sections based on distinct types of content. The four sections in this text include: introductory concepts and theories, major influences on adolescents, basic descriptions of adolescent behavior and thinking, and an explanation of skills for relating and working with adolescents.
6. Use of case studies to help students relate abstract concepts to their daily lives. The case studies were provided by students after studying earlier drafts of this text.

I have used the early drafts in my classes and found that they were well received. Apparently, the features used to make this a practical and applied text have not resulted in a dilution of perceived depth or accuracy on the part of students using the text. In summary, the inclusion of the features listed above, as well as the basic concept behind this text, is user-oriented. The features enumerated above are based on meeting student needs. The text along with a teacher's manual is designed to focus on meaningful questions about adolescence, to develop skills in helping, and to enable the student to better understand adolescence. It is my hope that students will find this text, along with the associated course, one of their most rewarding, long-lasting, and valuable experiences in higher education.

ACKNOWLEDGMENTS

Thanks and credit are given to Vern Lewis and Scott Kearin, who as research assistants contributed to both the research and the writing for some of the preliminary drafts. Vern Lewis, a doctoral student in clinical psychology, is coauthor of the chapters on drug usage and clinical problems. Scott Kearin, a law student, coauthored the chapter on juvenile delinquency.

For dependable and intelligent assistance in all phases of writing this text, I give thanks to Felicia Barnes. She worked on the library research, rough drafts, permissions, and editing. Her sense of responsibility and her ability to work with deadlines were needed and continue to be appreciated. She has also written the Instructor's Manual that accompanies this text.

The manuscript was prepared by the Faculty Support Center of the College of Family, Home, and Social Sciences at Brigham Young University. The director, Marilyn Webb, through her organization and relating skills, removed most of the frustrations ordinarily associated with manuscript preparation. Typists worked on the manuscript, but the special help of Kim Olson made it possible to meet the manuscript due dates. I wish to thank Paul Bouchard for the thorough and efficient preparation of the index and for doing this work in the time frame allowed.

I give credit and thanks to the students in my classes on adolescence, who read preliminary chapters and provided so many of the examples and cases that enhance the interest level of this text.

Because writing a textbook requires so much time and effort, I first consulted with my wife Janet about the impact of this project with my family. She not only encouraged me at the time, but has since supported my work on a day-to-day basis.

Lastly, I give credit to West Publishing Company for the professional approach they adopted in managing this project, including the extensive review process. The editor, Tom LaMarre, was a pleasure to work with and had the insight to make several key judgements during the reviewing phase. The text was completed under the guidance of Pamela Barnard who exemplified confidence and had a willingness to give help beyond what is ordinarily expected from a production editor.

Larry Cyril Jensen

TO THE STUDENT

Most students studying the adolescent period (e.g., teachers, counselors, social workers, parents, and psychologists) intend to directly or indirectly work with adolescents. The study of adolescence should be both interesting and applicable for these students, with no loss in content, depth, or theory.

The text is divided into four sections, reflecting differences in the type of material presented. Section One is the introduction and consists of three chapters: an overview, theories, and a basic chapter on the self-concept. In Section Two the focus is on influences. These influences include the family, peers, schools, biological factors, and the media. Section Three deals with adolescent behavior and thinking. The topics discussed include dating, love, and sex; values, reasoning, and morals; clinical problems; drug abuse; and juvenile delinquency.

Section Four provides the reader with a presentation of the two most basic and popular theories in contemporary psychology: behaviorism and phenomenology. Each theory is presented and then applied to help the student see how it can be used when working with adolescents. In the last two chapters, applications specifically designed to develop one's ability to counsel and establish positive relationships are presented.

Thus, by studying this text sequentially the student should first become generally aware of adolescents in Section One. In Section Two the major influences can be identified. In Section Three the student should acquire a basic understanding of more specific adolescent behavior and thought. Finally, the student can learn to apply the two major theories as well as acquire skills in developing helping relationships. The four sections of this text provide a general introduction, an understanding of what influences adolescents today, a description of their thinking and behaviors, and an application of the two most basic theories in psychology.

CONTENT OF THIS TEXT

The distinctive feature of this text is the application emphasis. Application is stressed in all chapters. The basic content is primarily theory or research, and is drawn from several disciplines. Adolescence is an interdisciplinary area of study. Psychology has been the discipline most responsible for data, but other academic disciplines such as education, medicine, sociology, and anthropology provide much-needed perspectives and information. Because young people today daily encounter societal change from a rapidly evolving culture, insights from social commentators, pollsters, and the popular press must be considered. Thus, the information presented draws from all these sources, and where possible, the information is related to existing theories and evaluated for potential applications.

In order to move from the underpinnings of research and theory to application, case studies occur throughout the text. Most of these case studies were gleaned from students, using prepublication copies of this text. I have discovered that a study and an examination of actual case studies increases the clarity of research and theory. Case studies also facilitate recall. In reading these case studies students will see how to relate the content to their lives.

HOW TO USE THIS TEXT

The organization of this text departs from the traditional format. It is modeled after a successful and popular text by Dennis Coon. Coon found that by applying the established Survey, Question, Read, Recite, and Review (SQ3R) study method to the format of his text, his students' recall, understanding, motivation, and interest level were increased. A surprising fact is that this study method has been successfully used for more than forty years, but few textbook writers have incorporated the principles of this popular study system. As a graduate teaching assistant more than twenty years ago, I taught a class in effective study using the SQ3R technique and found that the method helped students organize their texts so they could better learn and retain the information. Now I see it is more efficient for the author of a text to do this when he or she writes the book rather than have the students do it on their own. The reader will find each chapter has the following sequential features:

1. Survey: content and questions to be considered

2. Questions: major question headings to be answered as the student reads the chapters

3. Reading: concepts, theory, and research presented in the text

4. Review: content is summarized

The application varies from chapter to chapter as content varies greatly in applicability. The applications are sometimes so obvious that a simple summary is sufficient; other times a separate extension with new content is called for. Regardless, my intent is that the student receive something useful, practical, and applicable by the time he or she has completed the study of each chapter.

adolescence:
theories, research, applications

an introduction

SECTION ONE

1. Overview of Adolescence
2. Theories and Viewpoints of Adolescence
3. The Developing Self

CHAPTER ONE

Overview of adolescence

SURVEY AND QUESTIONS

In this chapter the student will find a general introduction to the field of adolescence. Reading the chapter will provide answers to the following questions:

Historical Considerations

How can one make sense of so many contradictory statements about adolescence?
Have we known from the beginning of civilization that there is a period of adolescence?
Do major changes in society influence adolescents?
Have researchers found similar societal effects on youth during this century?
How did these major changes in society directly influence the definition of *youth*?

Definitions of Adolescence

What are the definitions of adolescence?
What is the psychological definition of adolescence?
What is the sociological definition of adolescence?
Which definition of adolescence is best?
What is the difference between the terms *adolescence, pubescence,* and *puberty?*

Perceptions of Adolescents

Why do the words *adolescence* and *teenagers* cause so much reaction and interest today?
What is the "storm and stress" issue?
Does a large generation gap exist today?
Have adolescents become harder to manage, and do adults need to exercise stronger control and power?

Improving Our Relationships with Adolescents

How can a person work with and relate better to adolescents?
Is teaching a person to enjoy youth possible?
Why are so many negative stereotypes of youth prevalent today?

Characteristics of American Youth

According to recent polls, what are American adolescents really like today?
What are the educational aspirations of American youth?
What are the family aspirations of American youth?
What are the employment aspirations of American youth?
What are the major values and concerns of American adolescents?
What are some of the most alarming facts about today's youth?

Recent Background of American Youth

What were the youth of earlier decades like?
What happened to the serious revolutionary and idealistic youth of the sixties?
What were the youth of the seventies like?

Youth in Other Countries

What are the youth of Europe like today?
What is the cause of the adolescent unrest of the eighties in Europe?
How are Canadian youth described?
What are the youth like in Japan, where respect for tradition is strong?
Do the youth in other Asian countries, like China, tend to accept many traditional values as the Japanese youth do?

Adolescents from Differing Socioeconomic Groups

Are there differences in belief and behavior present among youth from various social classes in the United States?
Are adolescents a minority group?
Do differences of belief between social classes affect actual behavior?
What do these differences in countries, decades, and social classes imply?

No, I'm mixed up very bad. Maybe I oughta get married. Maybe I oughta get stuck into something. Maybe that's my trouble. I'm like a boy. I'm not married. I'm not in business. I just—I'm like a boy. Are you content, Hap? You're a success aren't you? Are you content?

These words, spoken by Biff in Arthur Miller's famous play, *Death of a Salesman*, illustrate several critical issues for the adolescent. Adolescence is a time of great changes—changes, that are almost as sweeping as those of childhood. The adolescent is involved in a search to answer the question, Who am I? The most disconcerting change is that the adolescent has actually become aware of herself. The adolescent now examines and ponders her own development. This self-awareness and introspection is sometimes painful, sometimes delightful, and sometimes an obsession.

Humorist Richard Armour says the following about the adolescent period:

Adolescence is a disease—like the common cold there is no cure for it. Unlike the common cold, nothing can be prescribed such as aspirin, which will give the patient temporary relief. The most that can be done is to give aspirin, along with a shot of whiskey, to those who are lucky enough to have come into contact with the victim—as for treatment of the disease it would be a mistake to put the adolescent to bed, having had such a time of getting him out of it—someday a Dr. Salk will probably come along with a vaccine for adolescents. If so, the only question will be which Nobel Prize he should get—the one for medicine or the one for peace. (Armour 1963, 19)

These two viewpoints, one sympathetic and the other humorous, are joined by a more alarmist viewpoint about adolescence. The following statement by Anna Freud describes the high energy and impulsiveness of this time in our lives:

Aggressive impulses are intensified to the point of complete unruliness, hunger becomes voracity and the naughtiness of the latency-period turns into the criminal behavior of adolescence. Oral and anal interest, long submerged, comes to the surface again. Habits of cleanliness, laboriously acquired during the latency period, give place to pleasure in dirt and disorder, and instead of modesty and sympathy we find exhibitionistic tendencies, brutality, and cruelty to animals...The Oedipus wishes are fulfilled in the form of fantasies and daydreams, in which they have undergone but little distortion; in boys, ideas of castration, and in girls, penis-envy, once more become the center of interest. There are very few new elements in the invading forces. Their onslaught merely brings once more to the surface the familiar content of the early infantile sexuality of little children. (Freud 1946, 159)

This view can also be contrasted with a settled opinion of contemporary adolescents.

Robert Coles, a Harvard psychiatrist, perceives young people as being more level-headed about sex, race, and social classes than earlier generations. He believes that youth are maturing faster and that they are more "worldly wise than their parents were at the same age" (Coles 1976). Surveys also support this conclusion. One such survey states the following:

All our data, including the psychological testing, point in the opposite direction. Adolescents not only adjust well, but, they are also in touch with their feelings and develop meaningful relationships with significant others. (Offer and Offer 1969, 184)

Historical considerations

QUESTION: How can one make sense of so many contradictory statements about adolescence?

Understanding different points of view can be helped by taking a look at several issues. First, one must understand the definition of the word *adolescence* and the history of the concept. For example, some believe that adolescence is simply a social invention used to explain a space in life. Several definitions of adolescence are discussed later in this chapter.

Even more important than the differences in definitions are the differences in theories. Views of adolescence will change depending upon one's preferred psychological theory. One may ask why theory should influence truthful facts. Theories do not actually influence the facts, but they do influence the interpretation of the facts. Theories of adolescence are among the most creative in psychology. The next chapter focuses on these theories.

When presented with two or more conflicting theories, a person almost always asks, "Which is true?" An answer cannot and should not be given to this question. Theories are basically tools used for the discovery of truth. They lead a person to information and knowledge and help him to incorporate, and to make sense out of, too much data. When theories lead to dead ends or are not helpful in interpreting and integrating data, they are modified or sometimes discarded.

The best approach is to become familiar with various theories and then decide which theories seem most useful and accurate. In this text the basic theories of adolescence will therefore be presented as fairly and as impartially as possible. It is for the student to select one or more of the theories for his or her personal use. Before discussing theories further or attempting to define adolescence, however, knowing when this notion of adolescence developed is important.

QUESTION: Have we known from the beginning of civilization that there is a period of adolescence?

Records indicate that adolescence is a relatively recent phenomenon of the twentieth century. Some fascinating books have been published recently that trace the history of childhood. In *The History of Childhood* (1974), Lloyd de Mause argues that from antiquity up until the thirteenth century, parents had not attained the personal, supportive type of relationship with their children that is evident today. In difficult times, parents frequently abandoned children by placing them in monasteries, nunneries, or foster homes, selling them to slavery, or even killing them (de Mause 1974). Author Phillipe Aries (1962) shows that in medieval times, children were not given special status but were treated as miniature adults, which often resulted in their inhumane treatment. Aries says the first written mention of adolescence occurred in a thirteenth century Latin translation of ancient Byzantine writings. However Aries believes that the real roots of the adolescent period began in the sixteenth century academy schools for youth in France, where schools were only for noblemen. Thus until recently, a general and widespread notion of adolescence did not exist. Forty percent of the New England factory workers in 1832 were adolescents (Bakan 1971). These young people went directly from childhood to adulthood with no period in between. The time period of adolescence was lost for these youth. The story of a young English girl around the turn of the century provides an example of this missing life phase:

> [My mother] died when I was 12. And then, being the eldest, I soon had to go out to work. And work, in those days, if you were a country girl, meant service. So at just 13 I left school, and I went on the carrier's cart to Kibworth, about 16 miles away. It seemed like going to the end of the earth. I went to a woman, a Mrs. Pettigrew. She was a widow, and she lived with her bachelor brother who owned a factory in Peterborough, where he made jam, I believe. But there was nothing sweet about either of them. This Mrs. Pettigrew had a grown-up daughter, also a widow—or so they said—and this daughter's little boy lived with them. He was about seven or eight. But they were unkind to me. They must have been delighted in having me, a poor 13-year-old, living in a freezing room at the top of the house. I was like a mouse in a cage. This Mrs. Pettigrew put me in a room that had no window. She said, "Young girls spend too much time dreaming and looking out of windows." It was really a sort of loft. In winter it was so cold I'd wake up with my teeth chattering, and I had to be up before six, getting everything ready for them all. I virtually waited on all four of them. When I stayed down for an evening, I'd have a pile of darning to do; and this Mrs. Pettigrew would come and thrust her hand into the sock I was darning, to make the holes bigger on purpose, so it would make more work for me. I knew it gave her pleasure. I could tell from the way she set me tasks to do. I had to scrub the floors without soap, only a bit of soda, and oh, my hands, all the winter were red and raw. They cracked and bled, all winter long they never healed. It was agony to put them in water. (Senbrook 1982, 63)

Contrasting with this point of view, humane and compassionate conditions have also existed in historical times. For example, one authority describes youth in the ancient Near East:

> Children, the young ones as well as the adolescents, were active participants in the life of families at all levels of society.... In fact, Egyptians seem to have thrived on large families....
> Judging from the number of provisions for the maintenance of children in Hammurabi's law code (ca. 1750 B.C.), the Babylonians also viewed the child as an important constituent of the community.... For example, the purpose of a dowry in Babylonia was to insure a proper upbringing for a woman's children, and the code of Hammurabi also foreshadows modern notions of community property law: "They shall return her dowry to that (divorced) woman and also give her half of the field, orchard and goods so that she may rear her children...." (French 1977, 7).

The history from medieval to modern times in the Western world provides a confused picture of the notion of adolescence. However, the following quotes

The concept of adolescence is a relatively new phenomenon. Years ago, many youth, such as these young boys in the early 1900s, began work as adults at an early age and thus missed the period of adolescence entirely.

by an investigator of this time period provide a historical outline of, and help clarify, some interesting developments:

> The history of the influence of the child in medieval Europe varies enormously according to geographic and temporal locations, but a few generalizations can be hazarded concerning historical developments that help establish a bridge to the philosophers.... Against the background of centuries of unremitting invasions, internal warfare, and famines, the standard measure of success in the medieval period was survival. Under such circumstances, all members of society were rendered equal.... (Bell 1977, 30–31)

A special period of adolescence was thus impossible because the luxury would be impractical in terms of human survival.

By the early twentieth century, evolutionary theory led to a different emphasis. Sociologists and psychologists focused on instincts. The father of adolescent psychology, G. Stanley Hall, held such a viewpoint, and the Darwinian influence is clearly present in his theory, as shown in the next chapter.

Sociologists and psychologists later rejected this biological thinking in the early part of the twentieth century. Children came to be viewed in an entirely different way. John B. Watson's radical behaviorist approach rejected the child's developmental process and instinctual forces along with the entire biological approach. For these twentieth-century social scientists, the environment determined what a person would be.

QUESTION: Do major changes in society influence adolescents?

To answer this difficult question, careful historical analysis is necessary. Some attempts have been made to investigate how changes in society influence youth. One researcher (Greven 1970) studied seventeenth and eighteenth century Handover, Massachusetts. He discovered that rural fathers first exerted great influence over the independence of their offspring through control and division of their land. Their sons' marriages and financial autonomy were thereby delayed. By the third and fourth generation, changes had occurred. Parental control declined due to the scarcity of land and to greater opportunities to leave the farm. Because of these economic changes, adolescents' independence was achieved earlier.

Another town studied was during the founding years of Hamilton, Canada. Studies demonstrated how the transformation of a small town into an industrial and commercial center changed its youth (Katz 1975; Modell, Furstenberg, and Hershberg 1976). During this period of growth, improved school systems, transportation, public services, and employment opportunities were shown to have an effect on the youth: a period of adolescence or semiautonomy began to develop. The previous pattern in this town had been that a boy left home young and entered a world of adults. Katz stated the following:

> Many adolescents must have roamed the city with little or nothing to do, a situation which provided an objective underpinning for the desire felt by adults in this period to devise institutions that would take adolescents off the street. (Katz 1975, 262).

This youth problem was partially solved by rising school enrollment and increased job opportunities.

QUESTION: Have researchers found similiar societal effects on youth during this century?

Research does not clearly show how this century has influenced youth. The effects on youth of the Great Depression of the 1930s, however, is one well-investigated area (Elder 1974). Families from all social classes experienced depression hardships. According to this research, the deprivation of hard times moved youth into adulthood faster than the same youth from homes with less hardship. These deprived youth were more likely to be involved in adultlike work, to aspire to a grown-up status, and to enter marriage and work at an early age. They were said to have more self-consciousness, emotional vulnerability, and desire for social acceptance. Although hardships also reduced their prospects for education beyond high school, this fact neither impaired their attainment in secondary school nor weakened their ambition. Compared with nondeprived young men, young men from hard-pressed families entered adulthood with a more clear idea of their occupational goals, delayed having children, started work at an earlier age, and generally at midlife had a higher occupational rank. Job security was important to them. They also stressed family activity and considered children to be the most important aspect of marriage; they emphasized the responsibility of parenthood and stressed that children should be dependable. Children were expected to help more, and the family was considered to be a support in times of crisis. On the whole, adulthood offered more gratification for men from deprived homes, and they were more likely than the nondeprived men to regard adult years as the best of their lives.

The depression also had an effect upon women. Distressed women were more inclined to favor marriage and family over a career, compared with women who did not have family hardships during adolescence in the depression. The former tended to enter marriage earlier and most frequently dropped out of the labor force after marrying and having their first child. Still, the deprived were no less successful than other women in marrying college-educated men who made their ways to the upper echelons in business and professions. During adulthood, family, children, and homemaking were their priorities when compared with the nondeprived, regardless of educational level or social position.

QUESTION: How did these major changes in society directly influence the definition of youth?

In an excellent in-depth article, "Historical Development of Adolescents in America," the author states:

> The country changed dramatically during the second half of the 19th Century ...by the year 1900 more than a third of the population was living in cities and more than half of the population of the North Atlantic area lived in cities of more than 8,000 persons....The low level of "morality" of the new occupants of the burgeoning cities was a matter of frequent comment. Drinking, sexual immorality, vagrancy, and crime were not only intrinsically threatening to orderliness but were also particularly distressing influences on the young.... As a result of these conditions, three major movements developed, all of which conspired to make a social fact out of adolescence: compulsory (and characteristically public) education, child labor legislation, and special legal procedures for "juvenile." By the explicit citation of a precise chronological age, the legislation associated with these three areas essentially eliminated the vagueness of all previous ideas of the time at which adolescence terminates. Thus adolescence became a period between pubescence, a concrete biological occurrence, and the age specified by law for compulsory education, employment and criminal procedure. (Bakan 1971, 12)

Requiring all children to attend schools through compulsory education laws identified them as persons needing guidance and kept them in school, separating them from employment and the rest of society. By 1914, every U.S. state had passed laws prohibiting the employment of children (usually under the age of fourteen) and restricted the hours of their employment. This set them off from the main labor market, which had not been the case in earlier times. Finally, special legal protection for juveniles identified them as needing special attention, guidance, and family and community support. This eventually resulted in the creation of a separate court system called the juvenile court. In summary, adolescence became a special time resulting from the legal development and the industrialization of the nation. Some scholars regard this notion of adolescence as developing a minority status for this age group.

Definitions of adolescence

QUESTION: What are the definitions of adolescence?

The three basic categories of definitions are the biological, the psychological, and the sociological. These three types of definitions exist because adolescence is usually studied by three groups of scientists: biologists, psychologists, and sociologists. One group of definitions is not better than the others, for they each have strengths and shortcomings.

Consider the biological definitions. Webster's dictionary defines puberty as "the condition of being or in the period of becoming first capable of reproducing sexually." This definition sounds straightforward and easy, but consider its problems. If adolescence is defined as that period of one's life after puberty, what would the criterion be for the end of adolescence? Also, a different age of adolescence for males and females would have to be determined, because girls mature earlier than boys. In addition, the biological definition is confusing, because for girls there is a definite event—the menarche—that reveals a significant and obvious body change, which is followed within one year by fertility. For boys there is no such specific and observable event. Would it be the first ejaculation, a growth spurt, or the appearance of pubic hair? Each could be an arbitrary symbol of adolescence. The biological definition, despite its initial appeal, has many serious shortcomings.

QUESTION: What is the psychological definition of adolescence?

Generally, psychologists define adolescence as that period of life when certain developmental tasks or changes take place in the behavior or the cognitive

The compulsory education laws, which were developed partially out of the need to separate youth from the more distressing influences of city life, helped establish adolescence as a viable period in one's life.

development (or both) of the individual. Later we examine and identify what changes are considered appropriate and important enough to indicate the beginning and end of adolescence. The most famous psychologist to present a psychological definition of adolescence is Robert Havighurst. He calls his psychological dimensions *developmental tasks*. They are:

1. Accepting one's physique and using the body effectively.
2. Achieving new and more mature relationships with peers of both sexes.
3. Achieving a masculine or feminine sex role.
4. Achieving emotional independence from parents and other adults.
5. Preparing for an economic career.
6. Preparing for marriage and family life.
7. Designing and achieving socially responsible behavior.
8. Acquiring a set of values and an ethical system as a guide to behavior, and developing an ideology. (Havighurst 1972)

These criteria are similar to those proposed by other psychologists. Like the biological definitions, however, psychological definitions also have weaknesses, because determining when an adolescent has accomplished each task is difficult, and the tasks are vague and have neither beginning nor end. Also, they may not all be initiated at the same time. For identifying the beginning and ending of adolescence they therefore have limited value.

QUESTION: What is the sociological definition of adolescence?

Sociologists generally define adolescence as a transitional period from the interdependent state of childhood to a self-sufficient state of adulthood. A difficulty is inherent in this definition, for in our society one rarely achieves full self-sufficiency, and everyone in one way or another remains dependent on others. In addition, changing social conditions can affect when a person becomes more independent. For example, during the Vietnam War, the Vietnamese soldiers were often in their early teens yet were assuming adult responsibility. In contrast, many medical students in our culture are unable to earn money, are highly in debt, and rely on their family for support throughout their graduate training. Who then is the adolescent?

Another example of how social conditions can influence the onset of adolescence can be seen in the history of County Clare, Ireland:

> All sons had an equal right to inherit their father's farm, but by the 1930s the land was so heavily populated that farms could no longer be sub-divided. Instead, each farmer picked one son to inherit the farm and then arranged for that son's marriage. They delayed marriage so long that 62% of all males were unmarried between the ages of 30–35, with 42% of the women of the same age unmarried. Twenty-five percent of the males were unmarried by the time they reached 50. Until a man was married he was still [considered] a boy although he might be over 50 years of age. He was even called a boy. (Arensberg 1959, 165–166)

QUESTION: Which definition of adolescence is best?

All definitions have some utility. The biological definition, however, is still generally used for the onset of adolescence, that is, the attaining of sexual maturity. The end of adolescence is usually defined by the sociological definition of achieving at least the beginnings of adult self-sufficiency. For ease of communication, however, particularly between various disciplines, and to facilitate the study of behavior and biological changes, it seems parsimonious to define adolescence chronologically in congruence with our legal criteria. This generally means that adolescence is approximately that period of time between the ages of eleven and nineteen.

The chronological definition is probably a popular resolution to this definition problem. The long title of a primary research journal for the study of adolescence illustrates this solution: *Adolescence: An international quarterly devoted to the psychological, psychiatric, sociological, and educational aspects of the second decade of life.* Perhaps this chronological isolation of a decade of human life is the only way that the various disciplines can be pulled together to study adolescence. Two other major journals rely on the word *youth*: *Youth and Society* and *Journal of Youth and Adolescence.*

QUESTION: What is the difference between the terms *adolescence*, *pubescence*, and *puberty*?

Generally, *adolescence* is a broad term that covers the time period of both pubescence and puberty. *Adolescence* is derived from the Latin verb *adolescere* meaning "to grow into maturity." *Pubescence* is derived from the Latin word *pubescere*, which means "to grow hairy," and *puberty* is derived from *puberta*, which means

Part of the difficulty in establishing a definition of adolescence lies in the fact that each individual develops somewhat differently from all others.

"the age of manhood." Puberty is the point at which sexual maturity is reached, while pubescence is the period of approximately two years preceding puberty. Pubescence, then, corresponds to the period of early adolescence and ends with the appearance of the secondary sex characteristics. The term *youth* is often used to describe the late adolescent years before adulthood; however, as used in this text, "youth" refers to all ages between childhood and adulthood. *Teenager* generally refers specifically to the ages from eleven to nineteen.

Perceptions of adolescents

QUESTION: Why do the words *adolescence* and *teenagers* cause so much reaction and interest today?

Many issues appear to be raised, but we will explore three that have continued as a source of debate and speculation. They are:

1. Adolescence is a period of storm and stress.
2. A generation gap exists.
3. Youth today are becoming harder to manage.

QUESTION: What is the "storm and stress" issue?

In the Old German it was called *sturm und drang*. The belief was that adolescents inevitably underwent great emotional upheavals due to newfound urges. G. Stanley Hall, the father of adolescent psychology, was probably most responsible for popularizing this point of view. The quote from Anna Freud at the beginning of this chapter also emphasizes the stress of new sexual drives that emerge after a long period of childhood latency.

An opposing point of view was taken by anthropologist Margaret Mead, who studied Polynesian cultures. She discovered in Samoa and New Guinea that the typical young woman finds adolescence a peaceful, tranquil, and pleasant phase of life, more pleasant than her childhood or the adulthood to follow. Margaret Mead is also discussed in the theory chapter of this text.

If one accepts the viewpoint of Margaret Mead, the belief is that depending on the culture, the expectations, and the stereotypes, the adolescent period of life can be enjoyable. Some adolescents have a difficult struggle striving for acceptance and belonging during their teenage years, but many others breeze through this period. Possibly the storm and stress issue exists because we have general expectations of adolescence as a period of strain, and we are thus more likely to produce or create that experience for adolescents.

QUESTION: Does a large generation gap exist today?

Writers throughout history have described the emerging generation as wicked and decadent. Consider what Socrates wrote more than two thousand years ago:

> The children now love luxuries; they show disrespect for elders and love chatter in the place for exercise. Children are tyrants, not the servants of their households. They no longer rise when their elders enter the room. They contradict their parents, chatter before company, gobble up dainties at the table, cross their legs, and tyrannize over their teachers. (Socrates)

Does each generation write about the rising generation in the same way? That this may be so can be seen in the following statement describing teenagers in 1864:

> For the last 10 years I have been a close observer of what has passed among the rising generation in this great metropolis [New York], and I cannot suppress the humiliating condition that even pagan Rome, in the corrupt age of Augustus, never witnessed among certain classes of youth a more utter disregard of honor, of truth and piety, and even the commonest decencies of life. (Rogers 1981, 3)

As shown in later chapters, sometimes more similarities exist between adjacent generations than between people of different cultures. Sometimes a swing occurs as in a pendulum, so that youth return to beliefs and values of a previous time. Research shows that fewer differences are present between generations than are commonly purported in popular writing.

QUESTION: Have adolescents become harder to manage, and do adults need to exercise stronger control and power?

Cultural anthropologists have shown that force and power have for a long time been used to keep young people in line. Consider the following statement by one anthropologist:

> Generational conflict was widespread and threatened the very continuance of Samburu society. Like the Azande to the North, the Samburu relied on young warriors to protect their boundaries from the insurrections of cattle raiding enemies. The warriors in the cattle camps were denied all access to girls as were the Azande but they were forced to remain bachelors for many years while their elders accumulated wives, often including girlfriends of the warriors.... The resentment of the young increased, as they saw the elders accumulate wives and wealth at their expense. When the elders found more and more reason to delay their decision that the most senior grade of warriors be allowed to marry, this resentment boiled over.... As a result, warriors sometimes rebelled with cattle raids that provoked retaliation, with brawls that threatened social solidarity...when this disrespect included adultery with the young wives of the elders, the elders' wrath was especially great...the elders bullied and wheedled and in desperation evoked the curse—the magical force they possessed which was believed capable of bringing illness or death to its target—the warriors. (Spencer 1965)

The logic behind this example may be that if one is using power to control a youth's behavior, then as the youth becomes stronger, controlling him with power is going to be more difficult. As children move from childhood to adolescence, they continue to grow intellectually, socially, and physically. Adults will eventually lose in power struggles with adolescents. One author feels such practices actually make it harder for youth to be acceptable:

> We are entangled in stereotypes about young teenagers, stereotypes so negative that we would find them offensive were they racial, religious, or ethnic. Such stereotyping of the young...co-opts our sensibilities and blinds us to the realities of adolescence. (Ligsett 1979, 2)

Thus, this third issue may in essence be a result of how adults socialize youth. Too often traditional methods of force and power cause rebellion and a loss of behavior control. Other methods of relating have been shown to be more successful.

Improving our relationships with adolescents

QUESTION: How can a person work with and relate better to adolescents?

Some basic concepts about adolescents, if well understood, can lead to insight into dealing with adolescents. These types of understandings are presented in the first part of this textbook.

Being successful also requires having skills in behavior management, communication, and dealing with conflict. The skills in behavior management include techniques to strengthen desirable behaviors and to weaken undesirable behaviors. The skills in communication include ways to talk and to listen effectively.

A group of essential skills is how to resolve conflict. Because adolescents progressively want more autonomy and are in opposition to the control being gradually diminished by adults, conflict is inevitable. When considering the history of humankind, one can see that in order to survive, humans have had to devise ways to address and resolve conflict in peaceful ways. These methods of conflict resolution have had important international implications and are currently more important worldwide than in any other era. Nations negotiate treaties, have arms limitations, and resolve differences in ways other than war or direct confrontation. These types of conflict resolution skills can be applied to dealing with adolescents and are presented in later chapters.

Another element that is helpful in being successful with adolescents may be surprising. This element is to enjoy the adolescent—a statement that may sound presumptuous. How can one be told to enjoy something or someone, or be taught to enjoy it? Knowing that the enjoyment of youth is important may influence personal motivation and help people to develop that appreciation. Consider the following research. Robert Sears, Eleanor Maccoby, and Harry Levin performed one of the finest child-rearing studies ever undertaken in the United States. They sought to identify parenting techniques that influence personality development by interviewing 379 mothers of kindergartners and rating each mother on 150 different child-rearing practices. Twenty-five years later, a research team headed by David C. McClelland interviewed and tested many of those children, who were then thirty-one years old with, in most cases, children of their own. They were able to identify successful, happy, and responsible adults and to compare the child rearing they received with that of other adults who had not become as successful.

They concluded that practices such as breast-feeding, toilet training, and spanking are not as important as believed. How parents feel about their children is critical. "Mother's warmth" was found to be the key determinant of adult maturity. A positive outcome resulted when a mother liked her child and enjoyed playing with the child, rather than when she considered her child a nuisance or a burden. Children of affectionate fathers were also more likely as adults to show tolerance and understanding than were children of other fathers. These researchers concluded:

How can parents do right by their children? If they are interested in promoting moral and social maturity in later life, the answer is simple: they should love them, enjoy them, want them around. They should not use their power to maintain a home that is only designed for the self-expression and pleasure of adults. (McClelland, Regaldo, Constantian, and Stone 1978)

One nineteen-year-old student, who considered the child rearing of her parents to have been successful, related the following to this author:

There were many times I didn't understand my father. But I knew he loved me, although he never told me. How? He spent time with me and seemed to enjoy it. I decided at a young age he enjoyed being a dad.

Contrast the previous comment with this less fortunate story, also told to the author by one of his students:

My mother was an overworked woman with several children and didn't seem to enjoy any of them. She complained a lot, spanked and slapped them around daily and made comments such as, "Maybe when you kids are grown, I'll be able to have nice things again."

QUESTION: Is teaching a person to enjoy youth possible?

Some beliefs and some situations will influence and increase the enjoyment of adolescents. First, if people were to believe that youth are positive and that they are naturally programmed to be social and likable, then people would tend to enjoy youth more. When someone has a positive view and sees adolescents as basically good and wholesome, then they are likely to believe that adolescents also have the capacity to be empathetic, kind, and understanding. They will then be more trusting and relaxed in their relationships with adolescents, and will enjoy them more.

Second, being close to a child-oriented culture is important. In some cultures the prevailing view is that youth are an impediment to happiness. If by choice, chance, or accident a person lived in that culture and all the people around them believed this about youth, enjoying adolescents might be more difficult. By contrast, if someone were to relate with others who have child-oriented ways of life, they would find that it would be much easier to enjoy teenagers.

Third, being skilled in relating with youth and in managing behavior will help. People enjoy the things that they do well. For example, consider athletics. Those who pick up a sport more quickly than others (e.g., those who are able to make more baskets, run a little farther, or hit a ball further) start to like and to enjoy that sport more. The same principle is true when working with youth. People who are skilled, effective, and efficient in dealing with adolescents, will find that they like them more. In part, studying this material is a step toward improving such skills.

Fourth, one needs to have realistic and reasonable expectations of youth. Some adults have such high goals that youth are certain to become frustrated when they inevitably fail to meet those goals. Youth are by nature imperfect and are going to make mistakes. Unrealistic goals are often set by adults who are meeting their own identity needs through their children. For example, many a frustrated father, unable to meet his own life goals, wants his child to be the athlete, the musician, the business executive, or the leader that he never was. The parent and the child will rarely feel successful in this situation. Adolescents have a hard enough time meeting their own expectations, let alone the unrealistic expectations of their parents. My hope is that this book will assist the student in determining reasonable goals and expectations.

QUESTION: Why are so many negative stereotypes of youth prevalent today?

Some negative stereotypes of youth continue to exist today. Author Phillip Rice (1981) has identified and discredited some of these erroneous and questionable stereotypes. The false stereotypes he identifies are: pampered, irresponsible, hedonistic, immoral, cynical, rebellious, and rude. In his text, he refutes these stereotypes and presents data showing their inaccuracies. For example, using poll data, he shows that most youth truly want, and respond to, moderate amounts of discipline. Another example is that most youth honestly believe that having a good job is important to a person, and that they expect to work as adults. Rice states that adults often produce misconceptions about youth because of their own resentment and dislike of adolescents. He points out that youth sometimes (1) remind adults of things that adults would rather forget, (2) present a threat to the security and status of adults, (3) elicit jealousy and envy, and (4) cause adults to be fearful of losing control.

Characteristics of American youth

QUESTION: According to recent polls what are American adolescents really like today?

Here is a sample of results from several polls. One Gallup Youth Survey (1980) reported that one-fourth of the teenagers surveyed did not think that their parents were strict enough, while the majority thought their parents' discipline methods were about right. The majority also thought that they were getting along well with their parents. In another survey, 87 percent of the boys and 89 percent of the girls had a lot of respect for their parents as people (Sorenson 1973). A number of polls over the years have basically shown that in modern U.S. society, no generation gap exists between the young people and the adults. Kandel (1974) found that in the basic questions of future life goals, fundamental behavior codes, and core values, adolescents seem to be responsive to parental influence. On some issues involving immediate gratification, such as marijuana use, smoking, drinking, cheating, and musical tastes, adolescents are more responsive to their peers. In general, for the majority of adolescents, no generation gap exists, and adolescent behavior seems to be basically in line with that proposed by adults. The youth of the late seventies and early eighties are apparently fairly traditional and have conventional aspirations.

In the UNESCO report, "Youth in the 1980s," American youth of the eighties are shown to carry an increasingly heavy economic and idealistic burden:

> The result of this is a generation of youth facing the 1980s with few ideological or compartmental resources for innovation or even protest. The effect of

these circumstances so far has been remarkable. Young people are making substantial sacrifices to pursue career choices, child-rearing, even in the pursuit of increasingly costly levels of higher education. (Forstenzer 1981, 70–71)

Two researchers (Crowley and Shapiro, 1982a, 1982b) recently reported survey findings about the aspirations of youth in the *Journal of Youth in Society*. They looked at adolescent aspirations for education, families, and employment. In general, they found that the majority of youth have a healthy, positive, and strong motivation in all three areas.

QUESTION: What are the educational aspirations of American youth?

Crowley and Shapiro conclude that virtually all American youth aspire to complete at least high school, and nearly two-thirds want to go to college. Also surprising was their conclusion that educational aspirations do not vary greatly by sex or race. In educational aspirations, an equality closer to social ideals is present. The researchers found, however, that the level of parental education is a powerful influence on the educational expectations of youth.

Also important was religion. For example, youth of both sexes who are raised Jewish have higher educational expectations than do Protestant youth. Frequency of attendance at religious services is positively and quite significantly related to higher educational aspirations (Crowley and Shapiro 1982a, 391-422).

Most of the negative stereotypes of youth fail to recognize and give credit to the positive aspirations that many youth have today.

QUESTION: What are the family aspirations of American youth?

Crowley and Shapiro found the two-child family is the dominant ideal, and differences between males and females are minimal among whites. On the other hand, minority group males want children less than minority females do. The minorities are less likely to prefer the two-child ideal and are more likely to favor larger families. Youth identified as Protestants, Catholics, and Jews have higher expected family size ideals than those not identified with a religion. Of interest is that the recent increase of female-headed households may harbor an important social implication for the future. Young women brought up by female heads of households are less favorably disposed to traditional patterns of family roles.

QUESTION: What are the employment aspirations of American youth?

When asked what they would like to do at age thirty-five, 85 percent of the young men and 66 percent of the young women said that they would like to be working. Most of the young men did not know exactly what they would be doing, while one-fourth of the young women expected to be working at home. Crowley and Shapiro found that the aggregate vocational aspirations of youth today are strongly oriented toward high status and white-collar jobs. They stated:

> Comparisons of the work expectations of female youth in 1979 with their counterparts in the late 60s reveal a dramatic increase in the proportion of young women who expect to be employed as adults, and a shift in their aspirations toward high status jobs....individuals from better educated families expecting to obtain significantly more education and aspiring to higher status occupations....(Crowley and Shapiro 1982b, 33)

Religious involvement and sex role traditionally are consistently related to higher educational and occupational aspirations. On the other hand, early marriage and parenthood are consistently associated with lower educational expectations and lower occupational aspirations, particularly for young women (Crowley and Shapiro 1982b).

QUESTION: What are the major values and concerns of American adolescents?

One general answer to this question comes from a survey of teenagers, conducted by Jane Norman and psychiatrist Dr. Myron Harris (Norman and Harris 1981). Using a large sample and questionnaires with some in-depth interviews, they concluded that teenagers' values are basically conventional and similar to those of their parents. Youth understand the importance of the rules and responsibilities that their parents give them. In this research Norman and Harris found that adolescents' most common concern is not nuclear war, friends, or getting a good job, but losing their parents' approval. When asked what they wanted most out of life, they reported: (1) to be loved, (2) to be healthy, and (3) to do the kind of work they really like. One teenager said, "I think the majority of us are all right; I wish adults wouldn't give us such a bad name."

The major concern is not sex, drinking, drugs, or parents—but school. Young people report great pressure to succeed, and schooling seems to be their way to achieve success.

The problem that was rated most serious by 240 adolescents in a four-year high school was physical appearance, followed in order by careers, grades, future schooling, present employment, parents, independence, peers, sexual impulses, siblings, alcohol, extracurricular activities, smoking, and drugs (Eme, Maisiak, and Goodale 1979). Students intending to go straight to work rather than to college were less worried about grades, future schooling, and extracurricular activities. Eme's study confirms that during adolescence is when physical appearance seems to assume its greatest importance in our culture. The largest concern about physical appearance (and, in this case, sexual impulses as well) occurred among freshmen. This finding is expected, since freshmen are closer to the onset of puberty than are other age groups, and may not have learned dress and grooming skills.

The finding that careers, grades, future schooling, present employment and parents occupy positions of second, third, fourth, fifth, and sixth in adolescent importance, suggests that the youth of today are serious and conventional.

QUESTION: What are some of the more alarming facts about today's youth?

Research supports the popular view that adolescents today may be more involved with sex, drugs, and alcohol. Youth today engage in more early sexual activity than did the youth of the past. One-third of thirteen- to fifteen-year-olds say that they have had intercourse. Alcohol and drugs are also areas of concern. Fifty-three percent of thirteen- to fifteen-year-olds and 78 percent of sixteen- to eighteen-year-olds say they drink whiskey, beer, or wine occasionally. One-quarter of the high schoolers admit that they drink more than once a week (Norman and Harris 1983). These issues are discussed in more detail in later chapters.

QUESTION: What were the youth of earlier decades like?

Recent background of American youth

The youth of the fifties have been characterized as escapist or uncommitted, and the youth of the sixties have been described as rebellious. Both generalizations seem to be at least partially accurate. The popular movie *American Graffiti* portrays the lighthearted and carefree spirit prevalent during the fifties. Another popular portrayal, the television show "Happy Days" with the Fonz and Richie, is also somewhat accurate. The fifties was a decade of full employment and prosperity following a weary recovery from war. Every segment of society was touched by the good times, and it was not until the sixties that issues of social justice became acute and rebellious countercultures came into being.

More has been written about the sixties' youth than any other era's youth, probably because of the occurrence of a youth counter culture that reached its apex late in the sixties. Some of the sixties' youth demanded basic changes in our culture and presented a threat to the established way of life. The intensity of this youth movement centered on the Vietnam War, civil rights, and equality. Also at issue were permissive premarital sexual behavior, nonmarital cohabitation, and changes in dress and appearance. Examining popular press reports about the youth during the sixties is interesting. In one issue of a national newsmagazine, the following incidents were reported during the peak of student turmoil:

> Terrorism by student mobs is creating turmoil on U.S. campuses... Disorders brought chaos for days to Columbia University in New York City. Rampaging students seized and vandalized the office of the university president....
>
> At Boston University on April 24, about 300 Negro students took over the Administration Building to enforce demands for an expanded Negro Scholarship Program....
>
> A demonstration at Trinity College, Hartford, Connecticut, marked by a 24-hour sit-in at the administration building, had the same objective and ended with similar concessions by the college....
>
> A 42-hour strike at the University of Oregon was called off when the University administration agreed to give students a voice in selecting a new president....
>
> At Colgate University, Hamilton, New York, hundreds of students joined by some faculty members seized control of the administration building and held it for five days....
>
> The administration building of the University of Michigan at Ann Arbor was taken over by Negro students on April 9, the day of the funeral of Rev. Dr. Martin Luther King, Jr. All entrances were blocked....
>
> At Bowie State College in Bowie, Maryland, where the student body is largely black, students seized the administration building and subsequently brought a shutdown order....
>
> At Stanford University, Palo Alto, California, officials bowed to the demands of the Black Student Union....
>
> At the University of California, Berkeley, for years a center of turmoil, a student-faculty study commission called for revolutionary changes which give undergraduates a much expanded role in student government. *(U.S. News & World Report* 1968, 65)

Ironically, the high quality of American youth, their enrollment, and their performance in the Vietnam War are reported later in the same issue of this press report. Also it should be considered that turmoil was instigated and conducted by less than 15 percent of the student age group, according to one researcher (Yankelovich 1974).

QUESTION: What happened to the serious revolutionary and idealistic youth of the sixties?

One researcher finds that many activists of the early sixties have continued in social change activities:

> Activists are concentrated in the knowledge and human service industry; they participate in change-oriented, voluntary organizations, and have resisted the potential moderating influence of nuclear family commitments. Their political behavior reflects a radical commitment to political and economic changes in the United States and [to a] participation in both institutional and noninstitutional politics. (Fendrich 1974, 115)

Another researcher reports differently:

> Former radicals now seek peace, personal fulfillment, and a sense of community through religious (and quasi-religious) teachings and fellowship...[they] practice Transcendental Meditation, maintain organic food diets, share personal troubles in encounter groups, and get high on Jesus. (Frier and Porter 1975, 12)

Thus, the exact outcome of the sixties youth is still unclear, but the trauma and strong activity of the sixties apparently has had a relatively lasting influence on the adolescents of that era and perhaps even upon the youth of the seventies.

QUESTION: What were the youth of the seventies like?

The students of the seventies have been called the self-centered generation, characterized as pragmatic in their outlook and oriented toward careers and financial security. Accordingly, they are seen to be concerned about the economy and interested in finding their own place in the established society rather than creating a better society.

> There seems to be less visible alienation among youth of the 70s than there were among youth of the late 60s. Present-day youth have come to be included in the societal decision-making processes, which may be a result of youth trying to make it within the existing social system...having been included in the decision-making process at college campuses and society in general, and having an array of alternative lifestyles at their disposal, youth of the mid 70s may have fewer reasons to experience the type of alienation which was manifest in the counter-culture youth of the 60s. (Time 1974, 84–85)

Compared with the youth of the sixties the youth of the seventies have some distinctive personal and vocational characteristics:

> (a) Yesterday's college students struggled for, and fought for, increased student rights; the present-day youth inherits their rights. (b) Yesterday's students asked for *in loco parentis;* but today's youth assume their inalienable rights for social and personal freedom. (c) Youths of the past had a sure future of employment; today's youth does not have such a bright economic future. (d) The past student was idealistic; the present student is pragmatic. (e) The past student was achievement oriented; the present student is security oriented. (f) The past student believed life should adjust to him; whereas the present student is more willing to adjust to life. (Ballswick and Ballswick 1980, 691)

In a book called *The New Morality,* Daniel Yankelovich (1974) convincingly amassed a large amount of data to show some rather marked changes between the youth of the sixties and those of the early seventies. The differences, he felt, were largely due to the unique events of the sixties and thus were unlikely to recur. The unusual events included the Kennedy presidency, the civil rights movement, city riots and burnings, the assassination of the two Kennedys and Martin Luther King, the Vietnam War, and the draft. The differences are summarized in Box 1-1. Yankelovich states:

In the mid-1960s we identified a subgroup of college students as "Forerunners." This group—never a majority of the college population—struggled to live by a new set of post-affluent values. We were struck by two motivations that seemed to enjoy exceptional strength among the so-called Forerunner students: one was private, directed toward personal self-fulfillment; the other was public, directed toward a vision of what a just and harmonious society might be....

They rejected economic well-being as an indispensable source of the freedom and dignity of the individual. They derided society's definition of education as the royal road to success and achievement. They belittled the efforts of the average person to cope with the economic harshness of everyday life and his struggle to stand on his own two feet and retain some measure of autonomy within the complex conditions of modern life. They professed beliefs that seemed to flout faith in marriage, work, family, patriotism, democracy, competition, and equality of opportunity. They downgraded traditional American aspirations for more material comfort—more money, more education, more leisure, and more opportunities for one's self and one's children. They challenged established authority in the larger society in every one of its forms—the law, the police, the universities, the elected officials, the professions, the corporate structure. (Yankelovich 1974, 9–10)

Yankelovich states that he was amazed with the rapidity of the process of transferring these values from a small minority to a majority of youth in the next decade. Nevertheless, even though many of the values were accepted by the youth of the seventies, their style and way of life is seen as dissimilar.

Youth in other countries

QUESTION: What are the youth of Europe like today?

At least one account indicates there is considerable unrest among European youth today (*Newsweek* 1981). Large groups of youthful vandals and demonstrators have been reported throughout Europe, particularly in Germany and Britain. During 1981, German police arrested 1,590 youthful demonstrators who had caused more than $5 million worth of property damage. Some of the youths in Great Britain have been even more vicious, focusing their wrath on, and physically assaulting, minority groups of West Indian, Pakistani, and Asian descent. Besides rioting and vandalism, this unrest is partially due to the current 40 percent jobless rate among European people under twenty-five years of age. Other forms of undesirable behavior have been reported: resignation, alcoholism, drug abuse, and suicide are increasing sharply among the youth. Another European country, Switzerland, reports that 102 people, most of them young, died of heroin overdoses last year.

According to *World Press Review* (December 1981), at least 15 percent of the young in East Germany are troubled. While most of their young people are members of the youth organization called the Free German Youth, the troubled minority want rock music and Western clothes; they drink heavily and commit acts of vandalism, and abuse. The first "punks" have even been sighted in the streets of Berlin. Some maintain that while their behavior rarely takes the form of personal violence, they are apparently the first stages of revolt and protest.

Note, however, that this is the view portrayed in popular media. As with the youth of the sixties, a minority may cause this attention, but the issues they represent may provide insight into the feelings of the present or future majority.

BOX 1-1 COMPARISON OF YOUTH IN THE LATE SIXTIES AND THE EARLY SEVENTIES

Late 1960s	Early 1970s
The campus rebellion is in full flower.	The campus rebellion is moribund.
New life-styles and radical politics appear together: granny glasses, crunchy granola, commune living, pot smoking, and long hair seem inseparable from radical politics, sit-ins, student strikes, protest marches, and draft card burnings.	An almost total divorce takes place between radical political and new life-styles.
A central theme on campus: the search for self-fulfillment in place of a conventional career.	A central theme on campus: how to find self-fulfillment within a conventional career.
Growing criticism of America as a "sick society."	Lessening criticism of America as a "sick society."
The women's movement has virtually no impact on youth values and attitudes.	Wide and deep penetration of women's liberation precepts is under way.
Violence on campus is condoned and romanticized; many acts of violence are committed.	Violence-free campuses; the use of violence, even to achieve worthwhile objectives, is rejected.
The value of education is severely questioned.	The value of education is strongly endorsed.
A widening generation gap appears in values, morals, and outlook, dividing young people (especially college youth) from their parents.	The younger generation and older mainstream America move closer together in values, morals, and outlook.
A sharp split in social and moral values is found within the youth generation, between college students and the noncollege majority. The gap within the generation proves to be larger and more severe than the gap between the generations.	The gap within the generation narrows. Noncollege youth has virtually caught up with college students in adopting the new social and moral norms.
A new code of sexual morality, centering on greater acceptance of casual premarital sex, abortions, homosexuality, and extramarital relations, is confined to a minority of college students.	The new sexual morality spreads both to mainstream college youth and to mainstream working-class youth.
The challenge to the traditional work ethic is confined to the campus.	The work ethic appears strengthened on campus, but is growing weaker among noncollege youth.
Harsh criticisms of major institutions, such as political parties, big business, the military, etc., are almost wholly confined to college students.	Criticism of some major institutions are tempered on campus, but are taken up by the working-class youth.
The universities and the military are major targets of criticism.	Criticism of the universities and the military decrease sharply.
The campus is the main focus of youthful discontent: noncollege youth are quiescent.	Campuses are quiescent, but many signs of latent discontent and dissatisfaction appear among working-class youth.
Much youthful energy and idealism are devoted to concern for minorities.	Concern for minorities lessens.
The political center of gravity for college youth: left/liberal.	No clear-cut political center of gravity: pressures in both directions, left and right.
The New Left is a force on campus: the number of radical students grows.	The New Left is a negligible factor on campus: the number of radical students declines sharply.
Concepts of law and order are anathema to college students.	College students show greater acceptance of law and order requirements.
The student mood is angry, embittered, and bewildered by public hostility.	Few signs of anger or bitterness are evident, and little overt concern with public attitudes toward students.

Source: Daniel Yankelovich, *The New Morality* (New York: McGraw-Hill), 3.

QUESTION: What is the cause of the adolescent unrest of the eighties in Europe?

Finding an authoritative source to answer this question is difficult but the popular press cites economic reasons as a possible cause, including unemployment and a housing shortage (*World Press Review* July 1981). According to a recent German poll, at least a quarter of a million youths want an alternative culture where they can organize themselves into a different economic society modeled after the North American Indian tribal societies. A German sociologist, Horst Richte, states:

> Today's young express fear and desperation derived from a lack of prospects for the future. They try to affirm an identity through protest....
>
> Still, a profound identity crisis seems to lie at the root of their attitudes. Many middle and working class young have rejected the traditional values of the family and material wealth without finding valid alternatives. (*World Press Review* July 1981, 59)

QUESTION: How are Canadian youth described?

In Canada, another phenomenon is being observed. Instead of choosing violence and protest as an expression of rebellion, some young people are shunning responsibility and work. A number of professionals have tried to describe this Canadian phenomenon. Dr. Stewart Find, head of child psychiatry at the University of British Columbia, estimates that one out of ten children in the province will need psychiatric attention during adolescence. Dr. Sal Levine, head of psychiatry at Toronto Sunny Brook Hospital, observes:

> What these 1980s kids represent is the first firing of a generation that bespeaks the self-indulgent decade, the human potential movement. It is a generation that has turned inward and is more interested in itself than in other people. (*World Press Review* 1982a)

Again, the press reports do not constitute information based on substantial research, but they can identify basic issues, concerns, and behaviors. Because Canada and Europe are close to the United States culturally, considering more distant places such as Asia may be more revealing.

QUESTION: What are the youth like in Japan where respect for tradition is strong?

The social environment of Japanese youth has changed vastly in the past twenty years. Adolescents are much more affluent than they were a generation ago. A survey (Seizaburo 1982) showed that about 70 percent of eighth-grade youth own a radio-cassette recorder, 70 percent own a watch, and 30 percent a camera. About 20 percent own guitars, calculators, telescopes, and microscopes. Ten percent to 15 percent own a videotape recorder, a television set, or a stereo.

Besides the trend toward economic affluence, a trend toward urbanization and the nuclearization of the Japanese family is evident. Over three-quarters of the Japanese population live in a city. Most Japanese adolescents live with

Friendships have been found to be a major concern of Japanese college students.

their parents and perhaps one sibling in a city with a population of 300,000 or more. The traditional extended family with a household business is becoming a thing of the past. At the same time, the traditionally strong discipline of the Japanese has ebbed, and the home has become a place of relaxation. Because families are small, adolescents receive the more or less undivided attention of their parents and are often free to do as they please.

An interesting feature of modern Japanese adolescents is their satisfaction with the status quo. The vast majority of adolescents live with their parents, enjoy living at home, and are not troubled by family quarrels. A survey of fifteen- to twenty-three-year-olds asked them, "Do you have any trouble or problems in your family or home life?". Forty-nine percent answered, "None at all," while 40 percent said, "Not many." Eighty-six percent said they often, or at least occasionally, consulted with their mothers, and 58 percent said they often, or at least occasionally, consulted with their fathers. Only 13 percent of the Japanese youth today said that they felt a great deal of dissatisfaction with society in general. Nearly 50 percent felt dissatisfaction or had no complaints at all.

The largest generation gap in Japan is in the area of sexual morality. Although under 30 percent of the Japanese in their sixties approve of premarital relations, almost 80 percent of the Japanese in their twenties approve of it. The Japanese media floods young people with information concerning love and sex. Perhaps as a result of this, one of three eighteen- to twenty-two-year-olds believes in living together before marriage. One adolescent in ten is also sympathetic to homosexuality, while three out of four strongly oppose it.

Japanese college students say that their greatest interests are in leisure- and school-related affairs. Friendships are their most major concern, followed by hobbies and recreation, studies, sports, and love. Friendships seem to make life worth living for the Japanese. When asked "What is important to you?" 81 percent of the college students in the Tokyo-Yokohama area answered, "Friends" (Seizaburo 1982)

QUESTION: Do the youth in other Asian countries, like China, tend to accept many traditional values as the Japanese youth do?

Yes. A team of American social scientists visited Communist China and were surprised at how well the Chinese youth readily accepted the adult culture. Adolescent life is highly structured with little freedom of choice. For example, the programs youth will be in at school and the specific courses they will take are specified. They are not even allowed to browse through the library or to learn what they voluntarily choose. Exceptional students have artistic, literary, and cultural advantages open to them, but these advantages are still highly structured. The schools, parents, and the government all work hand in hand in developing the programs for youth; for example, government cultural agencies reinforce traditional values, especially those of service, self-reliance, and self-control.

Chinese youth still maintain strong family ties, even though families are now asked to support and to advocate the official position of the school and government. The youth in China are expected not only to participate in school, but also to learn the practical ways of the world. When students graduate from high school, they must labor in a factory or on a farm for at least two years before they can attend a university. In general, adolescent acceptance of this way of life occurs smoothly with little or no protest. (Kessen 1975).

The examples of Japan and China illustrate how youth will tend to accept a structured and planned organization within a culture. The structured pattern in China is the only pattern these youths have known. This indicates the strong influence of the controlling environment in influencing behavior.

Adolescents from differing socioeconomic groups

QUESTION: Are there differences in belief and behavior present among youth from various social classes in the United States?

In general, the answer is yes; differences are reported throughout this text on adolescence. As the student reads this text, he or she should try to be sensitive to the differences between the youth from differing social, racial, and economic groups. Unfortunately, almost all the popular information about adolescence in our culture is based on research with white middle-class subjects.

Sociologists Bahr, Chadwick, and Strauss (1979) consider a community to be people who view themselves as belonging together and as different from outsiders. They share a common life-style and territory. This exclusiveness gives members security, but it is achieved at a price. Members of the community must behave in certain ways and maintain a distinctive life-style, or they will lose their identity. These communities are particularly important to disadvantaged minorities, for they give the disadvantaged minority a defense for, and maintenance of, their self-esteem in the face of negative treatment by powerful outside forces. Part of the survival of the community depends on the rejection of ideas from the outside. Perhaps an illustration of a community can be seen by considering the following quote from an eighteen-year-old in Spanish Harlem (New York):

> But, man, ever since I was a little kid, this was my block, the block of the fellow who live in it. It was our property and we govern it and we make our own laws and no outsider or no people who don't live in the block can tell us what to do. But, man, they don't understand, they are living in some kind of dream. Their standards and ideas don't belong on this block because we have been made to feel we are different, like we don't fit, like we don't belong any place but on our own crummy little block. And there is nobody up here who's going to listen until the white man lets us become a part of his society outside, and I don't mean just a couple of guys who are really exceptional, who have got a lot of brains, but I mean everyone who can make it. (Hammer 1964, 22)

QUESTION: Are adolescents a minority group?

The effects of being a minority have been studied from the perspective of ethnic and racial minorities. The dynamics of minority and majority groups is known to be an important factor in minority behaviors. For example, rebelliousness can be a result of minority frustration. Viewing adolescence as a minority group may shed light on the conflicts between adolescents and adults. By several definitions, adolescents do seem to qualify as a minority group. For example, they suffer various disadvantages at the hands of another group, group characteristics are socially visible, and they are a self-conscious group. They do not choose this identity status, for it is conferred upon them. Adolescents could therefore be viewed as a minority group, and this recognition could help adults to avoid needlessly adversarial relationships with adolescents.

QUESTION: Do differences of belief between social classes affect actual behavior?

One author of an earlier adolescent text, strongly emphasized the social class differences in behaviors stating:

> The excessively disorganized (or at least non-middle class) family structure of the poor has been documented again and again, both among Afro-American and white populations....The incidence of so-called matrifocal or matrilinear families is very high, particularly among the Afro-American poor. For example, 43 percent of the Black children in an inner city population with which the author is now working come from fatherless homes. Since the situation is so common, it cannot be considered pathological. But its existence is bound to result in very real problems for children and adolescents who aspire to succeed in middle class terms, since they will [not] have ground rules. (McCandless 1970, 111–12).

In another text entitled *Children,* McCandless (1967) describes social class differences. Some values are supported more by the middle class than by the lower class. These values include the following: (1) belief in God, (2) cleanliness, (3) thrift, (4) belief in intellect before emotion, (5) avoiding the expression of strong emotions, (6) inhibition upon the avenues for expressing aggression,

(7) control and restraint over sexual behavior, (8) clean and correct language, (9) temperance, (10) honesty, (11) hard work and self-discipline, (12) belief that one's duty is virtuous in itself, and (13) faith in learning for learning's sake.

These differences are not clearly documented by research, although McCandless identifies them as becoming apparent during his professional experience working within the lower-class social groups. For example, he uses logic to show that the lower-class emphasis upon emotion rather than reason is caused by the belief that reasoning breeds a delay in action, and hence reduces the intensity of effective behavior. He also shows that lower-class members statistically attend and affiliate less with churches, and verbally indicate less commitment to formal religion. Regarding cleanliness, he points out that many lower-class persons find it hard to afford a level of cleanliness that is typical of the middle class. Sharing bathrooms, and the lack of soaps, toiletries, hot water, laundry facilities, and wardrobes, force cleanliness to be relegated to a low priority. The next value difference—thrift—occurs because one must have money to save money. One must also have faith in a dependable world of the future to be motivated to save money. The poor have neither. McCandless states:

> Reason has never won a street fight, or enabled him to get the biggest share of the can of beans, served to keep his father from beating his mother when he got drunk. (McCandless 1967, 583)

While the middle-class family believes that learning for learning's sake is good and that their children should go to college even if they do not need to for economic reasons, the lower class is more skeptical of those possessing higher degrees, sophisticated language, and purported intellect. Too much learning is viewed with suspicion. Perhaps this is because learning is an activity that is often not available to them. Because learned persons are usually outside their culture and hence are inaccessible, lower-class people are said to be suspicious of what the learned person is really like. In summary, McCandless states:

> We tend to condemn, reject, and exclude those whose values differ from ours; this tragic state of affairs quite generally characterizes relations between lower-class children and middle-class teachers. The failure of teachers to understand such youngsters probably retards the education of at least one-fourth of a nation. (McCandless 1970, 593)

These differences given by McCandless can be argued and likely are in a state of flux, but they do illustrate the need to be aware of social class differences when trying to understand adolescent behavior.

QUESTION: What do these differences between countries, decades, and social classes imply?

The differences and fluctuation strongly suggest that adolescent behavior is markedly influenced by culture and expectations. A wiser approach is to study the principles that govern behavior rather than to memorize descriptive statements about what youth are like. This is reviewed in the next chapter, in which theories of adolescence are presented.

The differences between adolescents given in this chapter are only a sampling of the more salient differences among youth groups that are discussed in this text. For example, adolescents from Indian, black, Japanese, Chinese, Filipino, Mexican, Puerto Rican, Vietnamese, and American families are described in the chapter dealing with the effects of the family on adolescent behavior.

My hope is that the comparison of youth from different eras, countries, and social classes presented in this introduction will provide a broader perspective upon which to evaluate the validity and usefulness of theories and behavioral management skills that are presented in this text.

Summary

Adolescence is a relatively recent phenomenon of the twentieth century. Children were often treated inhumanely and were placed in monasteries or even sold into slavery at times. Adolescence as a distinct entity became a general reality in the sixteenth-century and continued to be refined until our own century, when it became a social fact.

The three basic categories are the biological, the psychological, and the sociological. The biological definition is reflected by Webster's dictionary. For example, adolescence begins with "the condition of being or in the period of becoming first capable of reproducing sexually." The psychological definition of adolescence emphasizes the period of time when certain developmental tasks or changes take place in the behavior or the cognitive development (or both) of the individual. The sociological definition of adolescence stresses the idea of adolescence as a transitional period from the dependent state of childhood to a self-sufficient state of adulthood.

The three common issues about adolescence were said to be:

1. Adolescence is a period of storm and stress.
2. A generation gap exists.
3. Youth today are becoming harder to manage.

Margaret Mead has discovered from her research in Samoa that adolescence can be an enjoyable part of life, depending upon the culture, the expectations, and the stereotypes involved.

Throughout history, writers have consistently described the "rising generation" as wicked and decadent. People tend to see new generations as being different; however, the generations may be much more similar than they can perceive. Sometimes more similarities exist between adjacent generations than between people of different cultures.

The majority of today's adolescents have respect for their parents as people. Adolescents seem to be responsive to parental influence regarding life goals, fundamental behavior codes, and core values. Most young people also tend to have healthy, positive, and strong motivations relative to their educational, familial, and employment aspirations. In addition, when asked what they want most out of life, most adolescents respond that they desire (1) to be loved,

(2) to be healthy, and (3) to do the kind of work they really like.

The fifties was a decade of full employment and prosperity following a weary recovery from war. The youth of the fifties portrayed a lighthearted and carefree generation. Society was touched by the good times, and it was not until the sixties that issues of social justice became acute and rebellious countercultures came into focus. The intensity of the sixties youth movements centered on social justice, civil rights, and equality. The youth of the seventies tended to be self-centered, pragmatic, and oriented toward careers and financial security.

European adolescents appear to be having an experience similar to that which characterized American youth of the sixties. Large groups of youthful vandals and demonstrators have been reported throughout Europe. Asian youth seem to be more traditional and contented with society, although they still have some problems.

Adolescents who come from different social groups tend to differ and members of one group often have difficulty identifying with and communicating to members of other groups. In general, the differences indicate the strong effect of culture or learning on adolescent behavior.

References

Arensberg, C. 1959. *The irish countryman*. Gloucester, Mass.: Petersmith.
Aries, P. 1962. *Centuries of childhood*. New York: Knopf.
Armour, R. 1963. *Through darkest adolescence*. New York: McGraw-Hill.
Bahr, H., B. Chadwick, & J. Strauss. 1979. *American ethnicity*. Lexington: Heath.
Bakan, D. 1971. Twelve to sixteen: Early adolescence. In *Studies in adolescence: a book of readings,* edited by R. Grinder, 3d ed. 3–15. New York: MacMillan, 1975.
Ballswick, J. K., & J. Ballswick. 1980. Where have all the alienated students gone? *Adolescence* XV (59): 691–97 (Fall).
Bell, R. 1977. History of the child influence: Medieval to modern times. In *Child effects on adults,* ed. R. Bell and L. Harper. New York: Lawrence Erlbaum.
Crowley, J., & D. Shapiro. 1982a. Aspirations and expectations of youth in the United States. *Journal of Youth in Society* 13 (4): 391–422 (June).
_____. 1982b. Aspirations and expectations of youth in the United States. *Journal of Youth in Society* 14(1): 32–58 (September).
de Mause, L., ed. 1974. *The history of childhood*. New York: Knopf.
Elder, G. H. 1974. *Children of the great depression*. Chicago: Univ. of Chicago Press.
Eme, R., R. Maisiak, & W. Goodale. 1979. Seriousness of adolescence problems. *Adolescence* XIV (53): 94–97 (Spring).
Fendrich, J. M. 1974. Activists 10 years later: A test of generational unit continuity. *Journal of Social Issues* 30 (3): 95–118.
Forstenzer, T. 1981. In *Youth in the 1980s*. New York: United Nations Press.
French, V. 1977. History of the child's influence: Ancient mediterranean civilizations. In *Child effects on adults,* ed. R. Bell and L. Harper. Hillsdale, N.J.: Erlbaum.
Freud, A. 1946. *The ego and the mechanisms of defense*. Trans. C. Baines. New York: International Univ. Press.
Frier, P., & J. Porter. 1975. Jewish radicalism in transition. *Society* 12:2.
Gallup Youth Survey, 1979. 1980. In *Opinion roundup,* public opinion questionnaire (August).
Greven, P. J. 1970. *Four generations: Population, land, and family in colonial Handover, Massachusetts*. Ithaca, N.Y.: Cornell Univ. Press.
Hall, G. S. 1916. *Adolescence*. New York: Appleton-Century Crofts.
Hammer, R. 1964. Report from a Spanish Harlem fortress. *New York Times Magazine,* 5 January, 22.
Havighurst, R. J. 1972. *Developmental task and education*. 3d ed. New York: McKay.

Kandel, D. B. 1974. Inter- and Intra-generational influences on adolescent marijuana use. *Journal of Social Issues* 30: 107–35.
Katz, M. B. 1975. *The people of Hamilton, Canadian west: Family and class in a mid-19th century city*. Cambridge: Harvard Univ. Press.
Kesson, H. 1975. *Childhood in China*. New Haven, Conn.: Yale Univ. Press.
Ligsett, J. S. 1979. Adolescent development: Myths and realities. *Children Today* 8 (5): 2–7.
McCandless, B. R. 1967. *Children*. 2d ed. New York: Holt, Rinehart & Winston.
_____. 1970. *Adolescence: Behavior and development*. Hinsdale, Ill.: Dryden Press.
McClelland, D. A., Regalado, R. D. Constantian, & C. Stone. 1978. Making it to maturity. *Psychology Today* 12: 42 (June).
Modell, J., F. F. Furstenberg Jr., & T. Hershberg. 1976. Social change and the transition to adulthood in historical perspective. *Journal of Family History* 1: 7–32 (Autumn).
Newsweek. 1981. Europe's Dead End Kids. 27 April, 52.
Norman, J., & M. Harris. 1981. *The private life of the American teenager*. Rawson, N.Y.: Wade.
Offer, D., & J. B. Offer. 1969. *From teenager to young manhood*. New York: Basic Books.
Rice, P. 1981. *The adolescent: Development relationship and culture*. Boston: Allyn & Bacon.
Rogers, D. 1981. *Adolescents and youth*. New York: Prentice-Hall.
Seizaburo, S. 1982. Growing up in Japan. *Japan Echo* 9, special issue.
Senbrook. 1982. *Working class childhood*. London: Camelot Press.
Sorenson, R. C. 1973. *Adolescent sexuality in contemporary America*. New York: Abrams.
Spencer, P. 1965. *The Samburu*. Berkeley: Univ. of California Press.
Time. 1974. Education. 23 September, 84–85.
U.S. News & World Report. 1968. Anarchy spreads on U.S. colleges. 6 May, 66.
World Press Review. 1981. Youth on rampage. July, 59.
_____. 1981. Discontent among German youth. December, 42.
_____. 1982. The 80s: Lost generations. January, 34–36.
Yankelovich, D. 1974. *The new morality*. New York: McGraw-Hill.

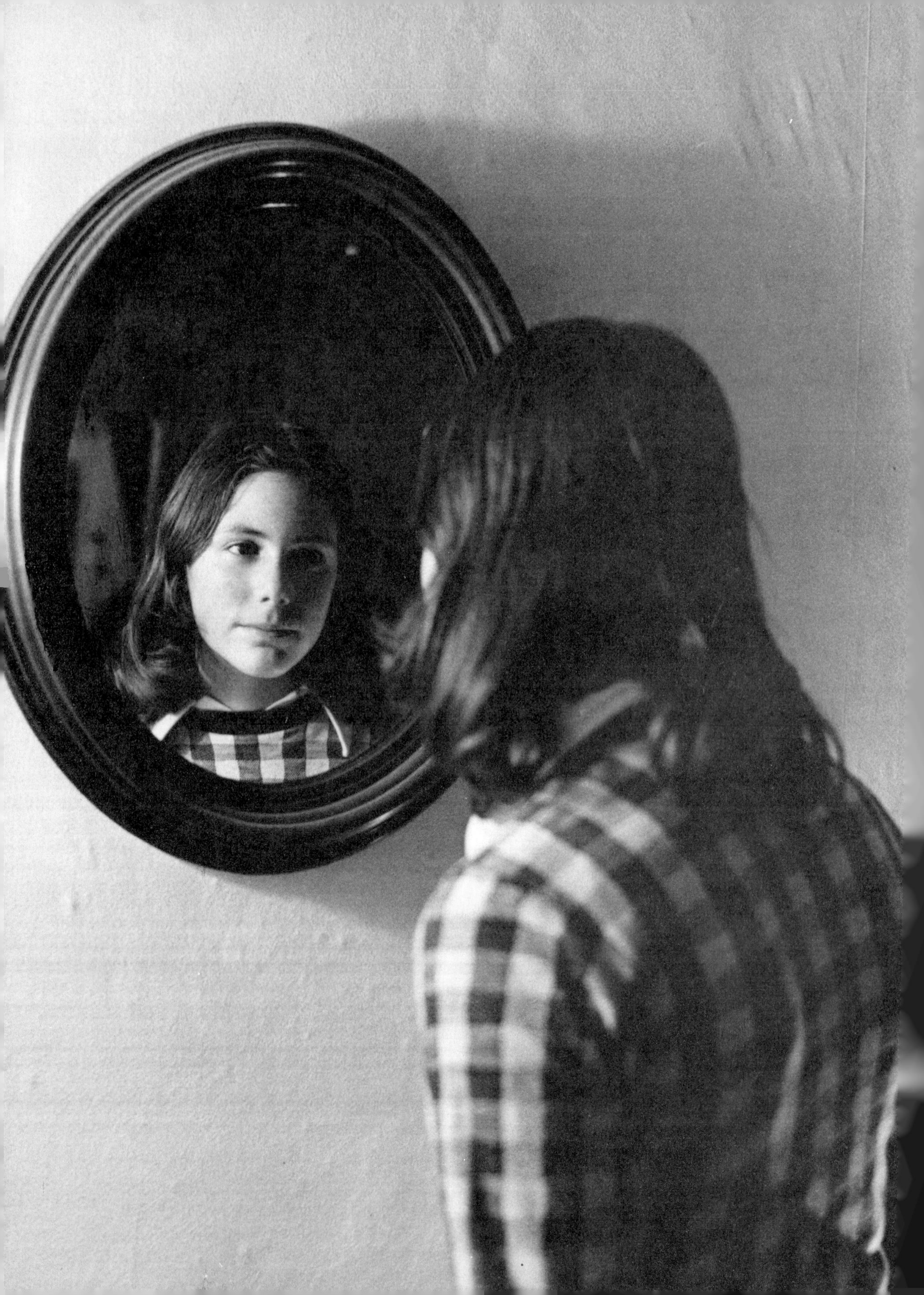

CHAPTER TWO

Theories and viewpoints of adolescence

SURVEY AND QUESTIONS

In this chapter the student will find a general introduction to the field of adolescence. Reading the chapter will provide answers to the following questions:

The Value of Theories

Why should students want to learn a lot of theories?
How can theories help students plan ways to work with others?
Why is a theory practical?

Biological Theories and Viewpoints

　G. Stanley Hall
What is a practical application of Hall's theory?
　Arnold Gesell
What does Gesell specifically say about adolescence?
What implications does Gesell's theory have for working with the adolescent?

Sociological Theories and Viewpoints

　Allison Davis
Does each society have its own ideas as to what is desirable?
　Robert Havighurst
What are the developmental tasks?
What is the practical application of Havighurst's theory?
　James S. Coleman
What is the importance of knowing there is a youth culture?
What are the implications of knowing that schools differ in the extent to which peers value academics?

Anthropological Theories and Viewpoints

　Ruth Benedict
　Margaret Mead
What are some other examples of socioenvironmental rather than biological influences?
What are the implications and practical applications of Margaret Mead's theory?

Psychoanalytic Theories and Viewpoints

Sigmund Freud
What are the three elements of each personality?
Can the id, ego, and superego live in harmony?
What are the defense mechanisms?
Where do Freud's ideas about going through stages fit in?

Anna Freud
What is the practical application of Anna Freud's theory?

Petro Blos
What are Petro Blos's ideas on the three phases of adolescence?

Range and Use of Theories

How do professionals use these theories of adolescence?
Are the theories presented in this chapter all that are important for understanding adolescents?

"I want facts, not theories." So goes a common expression. Most students become disenchanted with theories; they find them long, difficult, complicated vague, and too abstract. Theories seem scary and useless. My hope is that this chapter will change that point of view; students will find that it is written from their perspective rather than from that of the researcher or theoretician. Theories are useful for guiding the researcher and scholar. For this purpose they should be detailed and precisely stated. From the point of view of the student, teacher, parent, or practitioner, however, the value and use of a theory is quite different. These individuals judge a theory on its practicality, pragmatism, and usefulness. To be practical and useful, the theory must first be easily understood. Therefore, in this chapter, elements of theories that can assist students in practical application will be pointed out and clarified.

The value of theories

QUESTION: Why should students want to learn a lot of theories?

To answer this question, consider the findings of a researcher, Beckman, who investigated motivations for being a parent (Beckman 1978). She found that a frequently expressed reason for wanting to have children is that watching children grow and develop is fun. Theories can help students enrich their observations of life. They can help students enjoy watching adolescents grow and develop because they provide something to look for and examine. A theory is like asking a friend, "What is your idea on why adolescents seem to dress alike, and why do they change their language so that it is different from mainstream society?" The answer the friend gives will essentially be personal theory. Students' opinions are also miniature theories; we all have ideas and speculation. Certainly, miniature theories lack precision and breadth compared with those of a scholar. No one need be afraid of theories, however, for theories are simply "a way of binding together a multitude of facts so that [you] may comprehend them all at once" (Kelly 1955).

Statements like "spare the rod and spoil the child," "all children need is love," and "adolescence is a time when one needs to experiment with life" are theoretical. They are not theories, however, and may more accurately be described as viewpoints. Some of the scholars described in this chapter are not really theorists, but do present a small concept or a significant viewpoint. Readers who believe one or more of these statements should look at the world and see if their observations fit the statement. In this way students will become more intelligent observers of life and will be able to better interpret personal observations in daily living. A statement attributed to Charles Darwin says, "All observations must be for or against some point of view to be of value."

From a student's point of view, knowing theory should

1. Make personal observations more interesting and exciting,
2. Help to perceive and comprehend more when observing life,
3. Help students to better understand other theories,
4. Help to intelligently and successfully formulate personal theories, and
5. Help students to more intelligently plan ways to work with adolescents.

QUESTION: How can theories help students plan ways to work with others?

First, each theory emphasizes a unique perspective toward life. To illustrate this point, assume that someone is trying to help a troubled adolescent. If she prefers a theory like Erik Erikson's, which focuses on the development of self-concept and personal identity, her first hunch as to why the youth is troubled would be that he has an inadequately developed self-concept or may lack self-esteem. If, however, her theory is a behavioral one that emphasizes the strong influence of the controlling environment, she may try to determine what events in this troubled youth's life have caused him to respond in the way that he does. She might look for parents, teachers, or friends who have rewarded him for acting in a troubled way. If she prefers a stage-type theory, she would assume that the adolescent is likely going through a stage, and then try to determine what particular stage he might be going through presently. She would here tend to be patient and accepting of his troubled behavior, believing that he would soon outgrow the stage.

These three examples correspond to types of theories that students will read about in this chapter. The first example stresses the psychodynamic and psychological experiences typical of adolescents. The second example illustrates the learning and social anthropological theories that emphasize the controlling environment. The third represents the biodevelopmental theories that maintain that growth patterns can be observed and are the controlling elements of adolescent behavior. These considerations together help explain why one prestigious American psychologist, Kurt Lewin, once said, "Nothing is so practical as a good theory."

QUESTION: Why is a theory practical?

A theory is practical because it performs three basic functions:

1. It allows us to organize observations and to deal meaningfully with large amounts of data.
2. It helps us to see relationships between facts and information that we would otherwise not see.
3. It stimulates our curiosity to try to confirm or reject different points of view (Shaw and Costenzo 1970).

"Facts" change in almost every discipline. For example, ideas and facts in basic physics are continually updated and supplemented with new information. In the practical application of physics, as in all disciplines, facts and theories are used hand in hand. In the behavioral sciences, theories are especially necessary and useful in making practical recommendations. The basis for this statement rests on the greater complexity of the subject matter in the behavioral sciences. The controlling variables in the physical sciences can often be specified and regulated. Many of the variables in human behavior cannot be specified or controlled, (e.g., variables such as intelligence, motivation, past learning, psychological time, sensitivity to external stimuli, and culture). Psychological "facts" from one era, sample, or culture are likely to be different in other settings. For example, the effects of physical punishment as a means of discipline are not the same in 1970 as they were in 1910, nor are the effects of punishment the same on both sexes, on both the Joneses and the Smiths, or on individuals from both the United States and Samoa. Information about the effects of punishment is much harder to generalize than is information about the weight and strength of steel or the boiling and freezing temperatures of saline water.

Because the data of behavioral sciences are more elusive and difficult to study than the physical sciences, students of the behavioral sciences have an especially great need to formulate and use theories. Theories are more easily applied and are more useful than unorganized and uncorrelated facts. Whether the subject is molecular action or self-identity and defensiveness, it will be more interesting and understandable to students if they have a meaningful and appropriate theory at their disposal. Accordingly, the most important and interesting theories about the adolescent are now to be presented. Included are the writings of some scholars who could not be formally classified as theorists but whose writings have had a significant impact on contemporary thought. Their writings can be called viewpoints. The listing of theories or views presented in this chapter is not exhaustive, and many theorists, such as B. F. Skinner, Lawrence Kohlberg, Jean Piaget, David Ausubel, and Erik Erikson, are presented in other chapters. We begin by studying the first American theory of adolescence, proposed by Stanley Hall.

G. STANLEY HALL

Biological theories and viewpoints

G. Stanley Hall (1844–1924) is considered the father of the psychology of adolescence. In a two-volume work (Hall 1916), Hall proposed the theory of recapitulation: All individuals during their development retrace the history of humanity. Thus, each person lives symbolically through all of the progressive periods of humankind:

1. Infancy (0–4 years). The child crawls and enacts the animal stage of the human race, when the species was still on four legs. During this period, sensory development is dominant, and the child acquires motor skills that are necessary for self-preservation. Parents can observe their young children walking on their hands and knees around the floor, picking up objects, putting them in their mouth, and tasting them. Infants have little concern about cleanliness and are interested in how things feel and taste.
2. Childhood (4–8 years). This is the period that symbolizes the era of the savage, when hunting and fishing were the main activities of humans. At this stage, children play hide-and-seek, use toys, play cowboys and indians, play in caves, and build forts and hiding places. They especially enjoy camping and living outdoors.
3. Youth (8–12 years). Another term for this stage is *preadolescence*. This is a representation of the age of human semibarbarianism that existed several thousand years ago. The child develops the ability to work together with others and is susceptible to discipline, routine training, and drills. Hall felt that this is a golden hour for teaching discipline, reading, drawing, manual training, music, and languages. He believed that if children pass through this stage without drill and training, they can never be fully trained without heavy handicap and loss. In summary, this optimum teaching period can never be successfully duplicated again.

4. Adolescence (12–25 years). Hall called this the period of *strum und drang*, a German phrase meaning "storm and stress." This is a period of emotional upheaval, suffering, passion, and rebellion against adult authority. This symbolizes modern civilization, and as the human race has recently made great advances, so too does the human individual now make rapid changes in growth during adolescence.

QUESTION: What is a practical application of Hall's theory?

If humans go through these stages that are biologically innate, trying to alter or change the inevitable emergence of these stages is useless. The environment has little influence, and appropriate parental and educational tasks should be to allow the child to fully experience each natural stage. Parents should be lenient and permissive, providing children with the appropriate experiences for each of the stages. For example, infants should be allowed to roam freely, to taste, to smell, and to touch at will. Young children in turn should be given learning lessons in things which they are most adept. Adolescents should be understood and accepted for their mood swings and powerful feelings of exuberance, gaiety, euphoria, and depression. Adolescents can be allowed to choose solitude when they are disappointed and depressed. They should be allowed to criticize and

G. Stanley Hall (1844–1924), who is considered the father of the psychology of adolescence.

challenge adult authority. Hall firmly believed that if human civilization is to be advanced, adults should supply their children with the appropriate educational experiences they need during the period of adolescence; before adolescence it is too early, and after adolescence it is too late.

ARNOLD GESELL

Arnold Gesell (1880–1961) was a popular writer on human development. His most widely read book was entitled *Youth: The Years from 10 to 16* (Gesell and Ames 1956). As with Hall, Gesell believed that development is basically biological in nature. Gesell presents a description of behaviors typical of children at various ages, and thus his theory is called a "normative" theory. His emphasis is on an intrinsic, biological regulating mechanism that he calls maturation. For him, biology determines the order and appearance of behaviors. The environmental factor, which he calls "acculturation," is not as important as the biological factor.

QUESTION: What does Gesell specifically say about adolescence?

For Gesell, the adolescent's central task is the discovery of self. This self, however, is basically the outcome of natural developments due to biological maturation. Unlike Hall, Gesell does not see adolescence as a time that necessarily involves the storm and stress syndrome. Gesell is specific in his descriptions of typical behavior. For example, he writes about sixteen-year-old girls: "Girls instinctively stress interpersonal relationships in describing their future husbands" (Gesell and Ames 1956, 253). In his book he carefully describes the behaviors typical of each age period from ten through sixteen and establishes the normative behavior for each of these years. The normative behaviors include their activities and interests, emotions, interpersonal relations, philosophical outlook, ethical sense, school life, self, self-care and routines, and "outgoingness." An example of the specific descriptions given by Gesell are the following statements regarding an individual's growing sense of self during the years ten through sixteen:

> **Ten**... is self-contained, relaxed, direct, easy in his give-and-take.
>
> **Eleven** is more tense, questing, and egocentric; he searches and tests himself by conflict with others.
>
> **Twelve** is in better balance; accepts others; sees both them and himself more objectively; but unevenly fluctuates from childish to more mature attitudes.
>
> **Thirteen** withdraws and inwardizes in order to focus more deeply upon his own thoughts, moods, and images in a manner reminiscent of Seven.
>
> **Fourteen**, more outgoing, and seeks to find himself by comparing himself to others, by matching and by imitation; he is less inwardly centered.
>
> **Fifteen** withdraws not physically but mentally to meditate, and to explore his own nature in relationship to ideas, ideals, and the opinions of others.
>
> **Sixteen** is more at ease and circulates more freely among age-mates and adults; seems more independent and self-reliant (Gesell and Ames 1956, 356).

I believe that these fine distinctions are best used as general examples and not as practical applications to individual cases. Accurately describing each age group in such precise terms is impossible. Gesell admits that his age descriptions are only general norms, and he devotes one chapter to trying to show how to interpret norms carefully. Gesell's work makes interesting reading, but it does not yield many basic principles that can be applied to, or that sharpen, our understanding of the adolescent.

QUESTION: What implications does Gesell's theory have for working with the adolescent?

Parent-educators should choose what to teach a child based on the child's natural level of development and not on what *they* think the child should learn. Gesell feels that the natural right of all children is to have the experiences that he found typical at each age level, and thus he argues that we should not try to alter the natural, normal course of a child's development. The characteristics he finds normative at each level should be allowed and encouraged. He makes specific practical suggestions. For example, fifteen-year-olds usually show a craving for independence that makes them rebel against school. Gesell suggests that this age group participate in community experiences. A teacher can motivate fifteen-year-olds best by presenting information that will help them achieve further independence.

Again, I find it difficult to establish the credibility of Gesell's specific descriptions. Gesell's implications for education, although sometimes valuable, are not necessarily consistent with his own normative descriptions of each age group. Still, Gesell's theory has been presented because it has been so popular; his books have been purchased for years at almost every supermarket, bookstore, and drugstore.

Psychological and sociological theories and viewpoints

ALLISON DAVIS

Allison Davis (1944) believes that adolescents become what their culture expects of them; that is, their personalities are shaped by the ideas, beliefs, values, and norms that their culture teaches them. This is called the process of becoming socialized. Davis feels that adolescents are motivated, as are all people, by punishment, threats, and the withdrawal of love. Adolescents adopt some forms of behavior and inhibit other forms because of socially imposed motivation. This motivation is what he calls "socialized anxiety."

Davis noticed that anxiety can be too strong. If it is too strong, it can have a disorganizing and an inhibiting effect. Davis called this "neurotic anxiety." In appropriate amounts, however, anxiety motivates people toward responsible, normal behavior as defined by their society.

QUESTION: Does each society have its own ideas as to what is desirable?

This is true, and it becomes one of the verifications of Davis's theory. Davis noticed that middle- and lower-class cultures expect different things from their adolescents; middle-class cultures value prestige, social position, success, status, and conventional morality. Lower-class cultures value the attainment of more immediate rewards, such as sexual and recreational pleasures. Lower-class children are discouraged from seeking long-term rewards in place of immediate pleasures. Indeed, they learn from trial and error that they are not likely to receive the long-term rewards even if they should seek them. Thus, lower-class youth do not feel as much anxiety as middle-class youth do from social pressures to achieve acceptance, prestige, status, and schooling.

If this theory is essentially correct, then the most important consideration in understanding adolescents is to look carefully at what their social class and culture emphasize for adolescent development. Also important is considering the amount of rewards, punishments, stress, and anxiety used to motivate children. To understand adolescents, one must understand their culture.

ROBERT HAVIGHURST

Similar to Allison Davis's theory of social anxiety is Robert Havighurst's concept of "developmental tasks." In his book *Developmental Tasks and Education* (1972), Havighurst identifies and emphasizes developmental tasks that are midway between individual needs and societal demands. These tasks are for an individual to acquire certain skills, knowledge, functions, and attitudes at certain stages of life. Readers may recall that these developmental tasks were listed in Chapter 1. The completion of the tasks is determined by individual maturation level, by personal effort, and by society's expectations. Once adolescents accomplish one of these tasks, they are ready to work on a harder task ahead of them. If they fail at any one developmental task, however, the result is a lack of adjustment, increased anxiety, social disapproval, and an inability to handle the other tasks.

Handling and mastering the tasks falls in a definite sequence; each task is a stepping stone for the next one. Some of these tasks have a biological basis and must be accomplished within a specific time limit. If the tasks are not completed when they should be, the individual may not be able to accomplish them at a later date, and the accomplishment of all subsequent tasks will be in jeopardy as well. To know the right time to accomplish each of the tasks, three factors need to be considered: physical maturity, social pressures, and motivation.

QUESTION: What are the developmental tasks?

The following is a brief description of each of the developmental tasks:

1. *Accepting one's physique and using the body effectively.* Typically, adolescents are self-conscious about their physical bodies, especially as they reach sexual maturity. Much of their time is spent worrying about their appearance, and they often compare their appearance with that of others. At this stage, adolescents must learn to accept their physiques and their individual patterns of growth. They must also learn to take care of their bodies and to use their bodies effectively in the home, at school, in sports, and so on.

One common characteristic of adolescents is their heightened awareness of their physical appearance. In the first of Havighurst's developmental stages, adolescents must learn to accept their physiques and to use their bodies effectively.

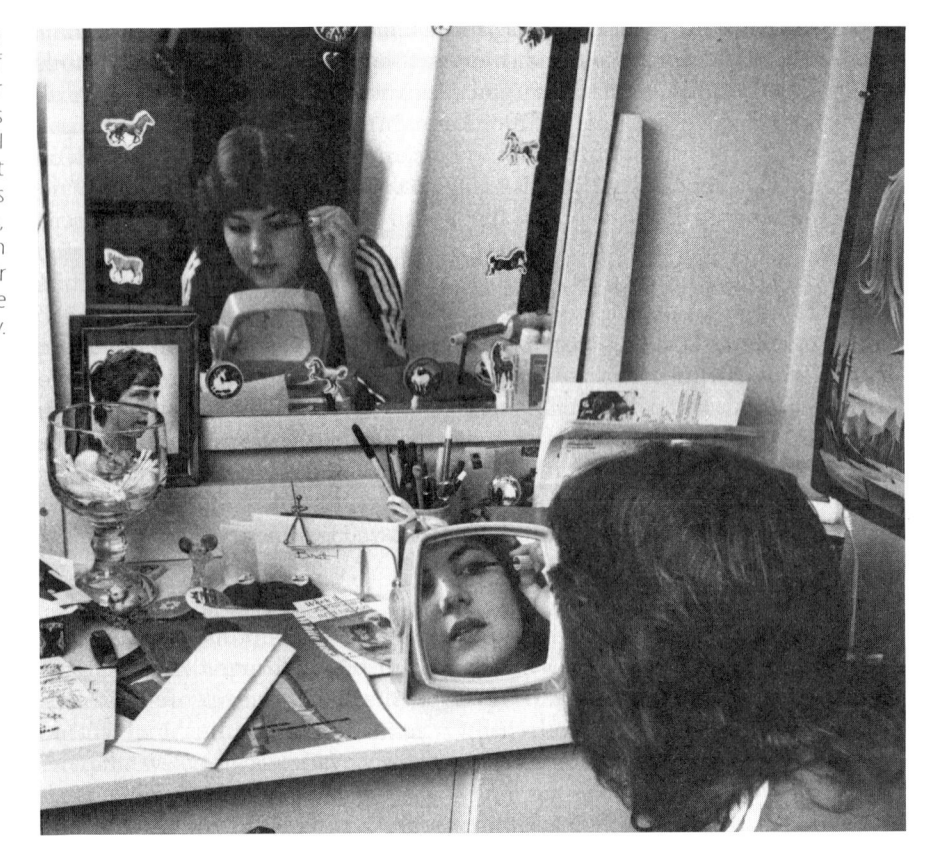

2. *Achieving new and more mature relationships with age-mates of both sexes.* During prepuberty, most children's friends are of the same sex, but during adolescence friendships are established with those of the opposite sex. This task is difficult because of the pressures felt for sexual intimacy and experience, and because group social skills are complex and involve members of both sexes.

3. *Achieving masculinity and femininity.* No one takes formal classes in how to become a man or a woman, but all are expected to behave in a manner appropriate to their designated sex. Masculine and feminine roles in Western culture have undergone rapid changes, and it is hence difficult for adolescents to learn what an appropriate sex role is and then to perform it in a clear-cut way.

4. *Achieving emotional independence.* During childhood, parents are expected to meet the child's physical, social, and emotional needs. Children also depend upon parents for love, tenderness, and praise. During adolescence, young people try to become more self-sufficient, which often creates some psychological and familial conflict. This conflict must be resolved to achieve a healthy, orderly pattern of attaining independence.

5. *Preparing for an economic career.* In a complicated society such as ours, selecting, training for, and succeeding in a career is difficult. Preparing for a career also includes preparing for a particular style of life. In more primitive cultures, choices are often not even available.

6. *Preparing for marriage and family life.* Although many of our youths marry during adolescence, society generally asks them to postpone this task until the end of adolescence. Preparing for marriage includes the development of attitudes, social skills, emotional maturity, and other personal-social attributes that will make a marriage work. Formal as well as informal guidance and learning are necessary. In our society, although other forms of living together are available, the mode and general expectation is for marriage and family life.

7. *Desiring and achieving socially responsible behavior.* At this stage, adolescents must accept society's values, rules, and norms. This includes normal participation in community life and in local, state, and national governments. Nevertheless, within the range of normal participation, adolescents must find a place in society that gives meaning to their lives and, at the same time, serves as a contribution to the community of humanity in which they live.

8. *Acquiring a set of values and an ethical system as a guide to behavior—developing an ideology.* Living in a complicated society requires individuals to successfully resolve a number of value and moral dilemmas. Therefore, adolescents should be able to study, analyze, and compare society's value systems with their own morals and ideals.

QUESTION: What is the practical application of Havighurst's theory?

This particular theory is useful because it comprehensively identifies the areas in which adolescents may be excelling and the areas in which they may be having problems. The theory also shows the importance and influence of each particular culture in which an adolescent resides. Most developmental tasks are probably common to all cultures, but some tasks will vary from culture to culture in the way they are achieved. In almost all cultures some form of these tasks will need to be met, even though they may be handled in different ways.

JAMES S. COLEMAN

Although he did not intend to develop a formal theory of adolescence, James S. Coleman should be mentioned in this chapter because of the impact of his ideas. He has been prolific in conducting large-scale studies of American youth (Coleman 1960, 1961, 1965) and has served on national panels to discuss the role of schools, youth, and society. His theory could be called the "youth culture theory," since he is probably the first writer to identify and successfully popularize the significance of a youth culture that has evolved within our society. He identifies several recurring characteristics of a youth culture.

A youth culture is described as inward looking in the sense that the culture itself is the important criterion for personal evaluation. Youth cultures give their members guidance, approval, and a frame of reference. Adolescents need close relationships with others to receive love, security, and support. Because a need for autonomy also exists at this age, adolescents respect those who maintain and increase their autonomy by challenging adult cultures. In youth cultures, there is a concern for and an identification with the role of underdog, which influences political affiliation and the acceptance of heroes and models. Members of a youth culture are interested in the idea of change in general, which stems from their self-perception as outsiders and their hope to achieve a better position in life by changing society. Coleman states that

> Youth are segregated from adults by the economic and educational institutions created by adults. They are deprived of psychic support from persons of other ages, a psychic support that once came [to them as children] from the family. They are subordinate and powerless in relation to adults, and "outsiders" [in relation to the] dominant social institutions. Yet they have money, they have access to a wide range of communications media, and control of some, and they are relatively large in number. (Coleman et al. 1974, 125)

QUESTION: What is the importance of knowing there is a youth culture?

It is important to recognize how membership in a youth culture affects the way adolescents will relate to society (e.g., their political alignment, preference for the underdog, choice of heroes, styles, music, idols).

A second important aspect of Coleman's theory that has practical implications is the emphasis on the role of an adolescent's peers. To discover the importance of peers, Coleman studied ten midwestern high schools that represented both large and small enrollments. Students were asked, "How would you most like to be remembered in school?" The most common answer was "a star athlete" for boys and "most popular" for girls. Coleman found, in a number of ways, that popularity and peer acceptance were the driving motivational forces within the

This high school homecoming king and queen illustrate the tremendous influence and importance popularity and peer acceptance play in the high school youth culture.

high school culture. He also found that athletics and good looks were more important than academic achievement. Adolescents gave academic achievement a low priority on a scale of desired traits. When Coleman asked what it took to become popular or to get into a "leading crowd," he discovered the following answers:

> What does it take to get into the leading crowd within these schools? This is another way of asking what the dominant values are in these adolescent cultures. According to the adolescents themselves, it takes a lot of things; academic success is not one of them. It takes athletic prowess, knowing how to dance, owning a car, having a good reputation, or liking to have fun. It takes being a good date, liking parties, and often not being a prude (for girls) or a sissy (for boys). Good grades and intelligence are mentioned, but not very often, and not as often as the other items. (Coleman 1965, 19)

To Coleman, this strong peer culture with its associated dominant values has a negative effect on adolescent academic performance. Coleman hypothesized that the more peers stress academics, the more competition should exist for grades, and the most capable students will ordinarily get the best grades. A somewhat reversed trend should occur in schools where the peer group devalues academics; not everyone will make an effort to get good grades, and a number of moderately capable students may receive the best grades.

Coleman found this to be the case. Among excellent students at one of the high schools, about 20 percent of the boys mentioned good grades as a means of getting into the leading crowd. At another of the schools, only about 6 percent of the boys mentioned grades. At schools in which good grades were relatively influential in delivering peer status, the A and A minus students were usually the ones with the highest measured IQs. At the schools in which academics were de-emphasized by the peer culture, the students with the highest measured IQs were not necessarily the ones getting the highest grades—more overachieving students were getting the best grades.

QUESTION: What are the implications of knowing that schools differ in the extent to which peers value academics?

Coleman answers this question by stating:

> These results are particularly intriguing, for they suggest ways in which rather straightforward social learning theory [can]...be used in organizing the activities of high schools in such a way that adolescent subcultures would encourage, rather then discourage, the channeling of energies into directions of learning. One might speculate on the possible effects of city-wide or state-wide "scholastic fairs" composed of academic games, and tournaments between schools and school exhibits to be judged. (Coleman 1960, 347)

Coleman also found that adolescents' social classes and family backgrounds influence their achievement in the schools. This includes parents' educational achievements, the physical possessions in their homes, and parents' interest in their children.

Coleman is disturbed that so much socialization takes place within the school and not within the context of the family and the work institutions, which have been traditional places of socialization. This is serious because adolescents now remain in school for longer periods of time then ever before in the history of humankind. In addition, Coleman shows that adolescents are no longer passive but are active in defining the social fabric in which they live; at school they develop their own activities, newspapers, clubs, social affairs, and so on (Coleman 1961).

Coleman feels that high schools are partly responsible for the strong peer influence in American society today. At school, adolescents are with each other for the majority of each day, which provides a locus for many of their activities and social reinforcements. Adolescents develop and give social reinforcements because they do not have any material reinforcements to dispense. Some of the most powerful social reinforcements are in the form of status and acceptance.

The importance of these findings for adolescents indicates that society, to be successful, should seriously and carefully look at the power, the strength, and the source of the youth culture. Scholars and practitioners who deal with adolescents cannot afford to overlook this variable; for this reason it is discussed elsewhere throughout this text.

Anthropological theories and viewpoints

RUTH BENEDICT

Ruth Benedict (1847–1948) made two scholarly contributions that have a direct application to the understanding of adolescence. The first is *Patterns of Culture* (Benedict 1950), and the other is "Continuities and Discontinuities in Cultural Conditioning" (Benedict 1938). Ruth Benedict's theory shows how the patterns of a given culture affect individual development. Individual biological development should be a gradual and continued process, moving from infantile dependence to adult independence. In most cultures a continuous process allows this growth to occur. This is called *continuity,* but in some cultures, such as in the United States, the difference between a child and an adult is somewhat arbitrary and is maintained by contrived social and legal considerations. This abrupt change from one mode of relating (childhood) to another (adulthood) creates *discontinuity,* and discontinuity in turn causes problems and difficulties. An example of one such discontinuity is society's emphasis on sexlessness during childhood as contrasted to its emphasis on sexuality in adulthood. In our society children are screened and shielded from sexual information on subjects like intercourse, sexual perversion, childbirth, breast-feeding, and most forms of sexual intimacy. In more "continuous" societies, however, like the one in Samoa, youth have a continuous opportunity to learn about the sexual aspect of life from birth to adulthood. Hence, Samoan adolescent development is a relatively gradual, continuous process void of radical interruptions, interferences, and restrictions.

The opposite is true in America, where many experiences are shielded from children and then rapidly exposed to them during the adolescent years. Childhood ways of handling sexual issues in behavior, thoughts, and attitudes must be unlearned in adolescence and adulthood. What was inhibited during childhood becomes suddenly encouraged during adolescence.

Benedict specifically identified three areas of role discontinuity: the sexual role, varying from inactive to active; the responsible role, varying from nonresponsibility in youth to responsibility in adulthood; and the dominant-submissive role, varying from submissiveness during youth to dominance during adulthood. Most of these discontinuities take place during the adolescent years and are the major cause of the stress that adolescents feel in American society.

MARGARET MEAD

Margaret Mead (1901–1978) followed a similar pattern of reasoning as Ruth Benedict in comparing other cultures with our own. Her most popular books are the *Coming of Age in Samoa* (Mead 1950) and *Growing up in New Guinea* (Mead 1953).

Mead was most concerned with the adolescent girl. She found that the Samoan pattern of child rearing did not show the discontinuity found in America. In her visits to Samoa, she found that life for the Samoan was unhurried, casual, and without deep feelings. The Samoan girls' sexuality was a contrast to the sexual discontinuity in American adolescents. In the United States, childhood sexual experiences are restricted and inhibited. Until marriage, sex is considered wicked. After an American wedding, sensuality is expected. Margaret Mead points out that young girls frequently cannot perform sexually until they unlearn their inhibitions against thinking and acting sexually. In contrast, the Samoan girl does not have to unlearn anything about sex. She has had many opportunities to experiment and to become familiar with sex from an early age. She has observed and indulged in masturbation and sexual adventures. Practically no sexual repression has occurred during her life. As a result, Mead points out, sexual maladjustment during marriage is essentially unknown in Samoa.

Margaret Mead confirms Ruth Benedict's notions that societies have either continuity or discontinuity, and that the storm and stress of adolescence occurs in those societies which have the discontinuity. Mead, along with Benedict and other cultural anthropologists, assumes that social and cultural environments play the key role in an adolescent's adjustment and pattern of behavior. These researchers tend to disregard biological factors and assume a high plasticity in human responsiveness.

QUESTION: What are some other examples of socioenvironmental rather than biological influences?

Consider the example of menstruation among adolescent girls. Different societies treat a menstruating girl in vastly different ways. These are socioenvironmental influences (and not biological influences) in the lives of adolescent girls. Margaret Mead points out that an Indian tribe in northern California held the attitude that a menstruating girl was dangerous to the village because she could dry up the well and scare the game. In contrast to this attitude, another tribe in north central California (the Yuki Indians) emphasized the goodness of a menstruating girl. The tribe believed that through certain rituals, such as by lying quiet, the girl could increase the food supply. Among Sioux Indians, a menstruating girl's observation of symbolic rituals and taboos supposedly increased her chances for a career and a happy life. She lived in a hut away from other people and performed acts of magic. On the Gilber Islands, a menstruating girl was considered susceptible to enemy

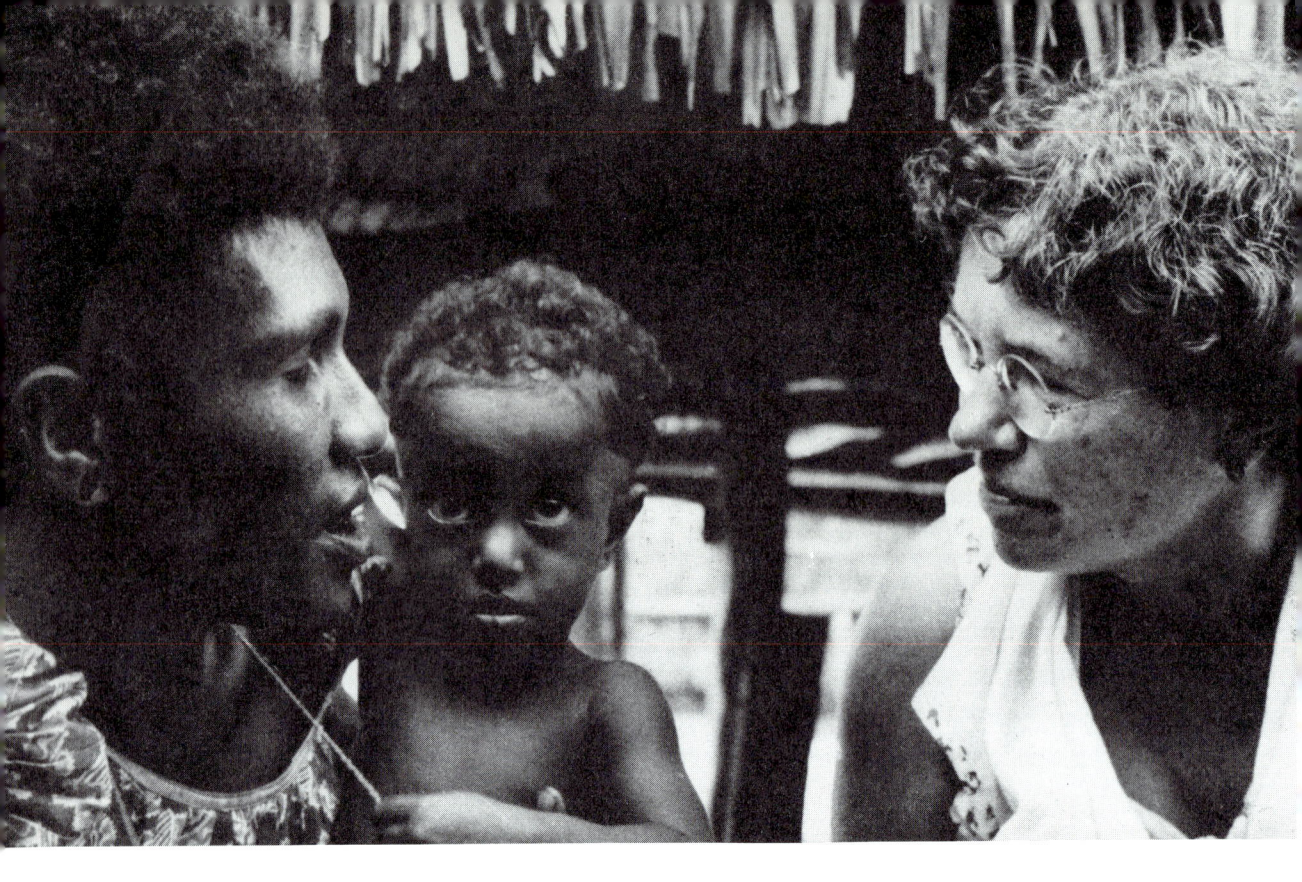

Anthropologist Margaret Mead (1901–1978) emphasized the need for continuity in a society. Here she is shown with a Manus mother and child in 1953 during a visit to the Admiralty Islands.

magic. She could protect herself only sitting still and facing west. In Samoa, no taboos or rituals were connected with menstruation. The Apache Indians would have their priests kneel before a girl to obtain a blessing of her touch when she first menstruated (Mead 1952). In summary, the different socioenvironmental influences that each of these cultures represent caused adolescent girls to respond in different ways to their menstruation.

QUESTION: What are the implications and practical applications of Margaret Mead's theory?

First, when adolescents experience a difficulty, one should look to the culture to discover the problem. For example, in the United States, adolescents suffer stress, strain, anxiety, and excessive emotionality. Margaret Mead feels that with social planning, the contradictions and difficulties of physical and social puberty could be eliminated. Mead sees more problems in the way our society is developing. For example, children are expected to act adultlike at an early age, but they are also expected to remain dependent and receive extended education for a number of years. She sees a logical contradiction between expectations for adult behavior and the need to remain dependent with extended educational demands. Mead believes that junior high schools are another problem area. Young males, who are physically immature compared with their female counterparts, are placed into the same classrooms with them. Thus, young males must associate with females to whom they are neither psychologically nor physiologically ready to relate. They feel inadequate and learn to distrust their own male companions as competitors in the dating process.

Margaret Mead believes that males and females depend upon each other too soon, both socially and intellectually. She also feels that our cultural emphasis on consumption, especially the consumption of sex, places an unjust demand on the adolescent boy, who has strong sexual desires yet has not learned how to control them. His sexual desires conflict with the moral code of society that restricts his sexual activity until marriage. This is an example of the logical contradictions Mead found in our culture to explain adolescent difficulties.

SIGMUND FREUD

No one person has had a greater impact on psychology than has Sigmund Freud (1856–1939). Freud's psychoanalytic theory has important implications for adolescent personality and behavior development. Freud stressed biological factors as the basis for motivation, purporting that three elements are in each personality, and two strong drives or instincts called the life and death instincts. The life instinct is sex, and the death instinct is aggression. These two powerful motivating forces—sex and aggression—become especially pronounced during adolescence. Adolescent instincts of sex and aggression are often governed by the use of defense mechanisms, all of which also become highly operative during the adolescent years.

Freud believed that the personality has a three-part structure: the id, the ego, and the superego. The id provides the most basic motivational force. Urges

Psychoanalytic theories and viewpoints

Sigmund Freud (1856–1939), the founder of psychoanalytic theory. Freud's work has important implications for adolescent personality and behavior development.

emerging from the id seek immediate satisfaction, often in an irrational manner; the id has been referred to as the "pleasure principle." Freud emphasized that drives—even those of infants—are primarily sexual. Infant sexual impulses, however, are only energies desiring gratification through erogenous zones. Not until adolescence do sexual desires become closer to the popular notions of sexuality.

The ego develops to help delay the discharge of impulses until the appropriate environmental conditions are present. The ego has been termed the "reality principle." The ego is in contact with the external world and serves as an executive, considering safety and self-preservation in seeking socially appropriate means of expressing impulses and releasing tension.

The third part of the mental structure is the superego. The superego is a product of parental influence and society's morals. The superego has been termed the "conscience"—the judge between good and bad. The superego seeks a perfect ideal by desiring only socially acceptable behavior.

QUESTION: Can the id, ego, and superego live in harmony?

No. Readily apparent is that conflict between these three parts is both inevitable and continuous. Biological urges (the id) are restricted from being expressed by societal and environmental restraints (the ego and superego). These restraints become internalized in the adolescent, and the warfare continues internally. Freud implied that this dynamic interaction between biological urges and environmental restraints during the first few years of life determines the course of personality development. The libido (a fixed quantity of sexual energy) is present at birth and provides the source of mental energy. Society and the superego control that energy.

Conflict between the energy of the id and the controlling influence of the superego is the source of anxiety. Neurotic anxiety occurs when people fear that their instincts are uncontrollable and will cause them to behave in a socially unacceptable fashion, resulting in punishment. Moral anxiety occurs when people feel guilty about unacceptable acts or thoughts. Anxiety produces a state of painful tension, and if this anxiety cannot be effectively dealt with through realistic means, the individual will resort to the use of unrealistic or overly used defense mechanisms. These defense mechanisms are all commonly used during adolescence and are important for understanding adolescent behavior.

QUESTION: What are the defense mechanisms?

Defense mechanisms hide the internal conflict between the id, the ego, and the superego from oneself and others. They become pronounced during adolescence and are summarized in the following:

Repression means to forget, or to eject from consciousness, threatening memories and impulses that might have objectionable consequences. For example, aggressive impulses are repressed by the ego because their expression would be punished by society.

Suppression means to consciously, rather than unconsciously, forget something because of discomfort or fear. An example of suppression occurs when adolescents deliberately refuse to face a responsibility. Rather than think about something unpleasant, they simply put it out of their minds. Another illustration of suppression is that adolescents tend to quickly forget the warnings on labels that state, "This product is harmful to your health."

Projection means to attribute one's own unacceptable impulses to others. For example, people who experience considerable anxiety over sexual impulses may attribute these impulses either to another person or to the environment. By focusing attention on "sexually permissive" friends, people avoid anxiety by not admitting the strength of their own sexual desires; they may simply say, "Everyone is doing it."

Reaction-formation refers to replacing unacceptable impulses by their opposites. For example, individuals who are frightened by their own pornographic obsessions might openly denounce pornography and even crusade against it.

Sublimation means to redirect anxiety-producing sexual impulses toward socially acceptable ends. To illustrate, adolescents who fear their sexual impulses might divert their energies to athletics.

Regression means to return to an earlier behavior, one that is usually childlike and immature. This frequently occurs when individuals suddenly face new stress. In these situations people often return to earlier patterns of behavior that have proven successful for them in the past. These patterns of behavior might even include having a temper tantrum at age sixteen.

Rationalization means to explain and to justify one's actions with words that are logical but nevertheless untrue. The statement is usually not a conscious lie but rather a self-deception. Rationalization is probably the most common defense mechanism used by adolescents. If we assume, as psychoanalysts do, that there is an unconscious component of motivation, then rationalization clearly is a continuous activity for all of us, because our conscious motives explain only part of our behavior. Our behavior serves unconscious purposes as well as conscious ones. Our unconscious purposes remain unconscious, or even repressed, because they conflict with the self-structure. Rationalization is the process of making these conflicts appear to be consistent or perhaps even nonexistent.

For example, imagine a young man who asks a girl for a date. His friend suggests he is asking for a date with this particular girl because she is known as a "heavy petter." If the adolescent *does* feel sexually attracted to her, and yet does not want to see himself as sexy, he may indignantly insist he is dating this girl because—and *only* because—he wants to discuss the lecture they both attended.

If defense mechanisms become inadequate, or are pathologically adhered to, neurotic anxiety results. Neuroses often have their roots in adolescence, even though symptoms might not emerge until years later.

QUESTION: Where do Freud's ideas about going through stages fit in?

Freud theorized that the child passes through five stages of personality development: the oral, anal, phallic, latency, and genital stages. The first three stages occur during the first five or six years of a child's life; the last two stages during late childhood and throughout adolescence.

During each of these stages, libidinal energy is focused on erogenous zones that characterize each particular stage. Traumatic experiences during any stage, in the form of overindulgence or deprivation, may produce a fixation in an individual's personality development. If fixation occurs, the individual will develop a character structure that is built around the unresolved conflicts of the fixated stage.

Oral Stage: During the first year of life, the focus of sexual pleasure is in the mouth. Gratification is achieved through sucking, biting, and chewing, and infants are dependent upon others for the care and satisfaction of their needs. If children's needs at this stage are frustrated, they will fixate at the oral stage. When these children become adults, they will probably be dependent upon others, be friendly and generous, and yet feel that the world owes them a living. Depending upon at what point in the oral stage children fixate, and upon whether the fixation is due to frustrated needs or overindulgence, these children may later become gullible, sarcastic, or argumentative.

Anal Stage: When children are about one to three years of age, the focus of their pleasure shifts to the anal functions of elimination and retention. As children face parental attempts to force them to complete their toilet training, a conflict between parental demands and anal pleasures develops. If children view their feces as a possession, toilet-training conflicts may be the foundation for a host of attitudes about possessions and valuables. If parental demands for toilet training are overly harsh, children may develop excessively clean, shy, shameful, or impulsive tendencies. If parental demands are realistic, and children resolve their toilet-training conflicts with ease, these children will develop a healthy degree of self-control. Difficulties in the conflict resolution process may result in an adult personality with tendencies toward aggression, hostility, stinginess, and stubbornness.

Phallic or Oedipal Stage: When children are about four years of age, the genital region becomes the focus of pleasure. Conflict in this stage arises out of what Freud termed the Oedipus and Electra complexes, for males and females respectively. The Oedipus complex occurs when a young boy who sexually desires his mother experiences a competitive fear of his father. The boy believes that his father is jealous and might hurt him. This fear is sufficiently anxiety provoking to cause the child to give up sexual longings for his mother and to identify with his father. This identification is instrumental in facilitating the young boy's superego development. Identification occurs when the child incorporates his father's attitudes and values; through this process of sexual desire, fear, and identification, proper sex role and moral development is achieved.

The Electra complex is a somewhat similar, but reversed, process. A young girl comes to identify with her mother as she forces longings for her father out of her consciousness. Again, this complete identification process is necessary for proper sex role and moral development.

Psychoanalysts believe that the oral, anal, and phallic or Oedipal stages are the most significant stages in an individual's life. These stages largely determine the kind of personality that an individual will have as an adult.

Latency and Genital Stages: The latency and genital stages occur from the ages of six to twelve, and after puberty, respectively. During latency, the strong id is temporarily suppressed and children are less buffeted by sexual-aggressive forces than they were during earlier stages. This stage is a tranquil period of development during which much cognitive learning takes place. Then, all of the energy not released during latency (the childhood years from six to twelve) explodes, and the personality experiences "storm and stress."

Although Freud's theory has several important implications for adolescent personality development, many of the most useful applications of psychoanalytic theory are not from Freud at all but from other scholars who have extended Freud's theories and applied them specifically to adolescence. Anna Freud and Petro Blos are two such psychoanalysts.

ANNA FREUD

Anna Freud (1895–1983) views adolescence as a time of increased libidinal or sexual energy, which is associated with biological maturation (Freud 1946). She states that genital feelings, sexual objects, and sexual goals become the primary focus of libidinal energy. One psychoanalyst, describing this aspect of psychoanalysis, was very graphic:

> Picture an adolescent now poised at the brink of adulthood. Racked by sexual desire, frustrated by outer prohibitions and inner inhibitions; desperately longing for independence yet fearful of isolation; eager for responsibilities yet fraught with anxieties about inferiority; flooded by irrational impulses yet committed to rules of propriety, he is hopelessly and helplessly confused and an enigma to everyone and himself. (Gustin 1961, 83)

Anna Freud warns of two extreme consequences that are possible as a result of this increased libidinal energy. First, a new surge of instinctual energy can make the id so strong that it dominates the ego. This would take the form of extreme hedonism. In this case, the adolescent is impulsive, has a low tolerance for frustration, and has continuous demands for self-gratification. The other potentially negative consequence is that the ego may respond in a rigid, defensive manner to the rise in libidinal energy. If this occurs, the ego may, for example, reject or deny all aspects of sexual instincts within the individual. The two extremes here are actually defense mechanisms called asceticism and intellectuality. Asceticism is a mistrust of personal instincts and a refusal to engage in any form of pleasurable activity.

Intellectuality is a preoccupation with the abstract—ideas about friendship, love, marriage, and so on. A preoccupation with abstract entities is an attempt by the ego to gain control of threatening instincts. Anna Freud writes:

> The abstract intellectual discussions and speculations in which young people delight are not genuine attempts at solving the tasks set by reality. Their mental activity is rather an indication of a tense alertness for the instinctual processes and the translation into abstract thought of that which they perceive. The philosophy of life which they construct—it may be their demand for revolution in the outside world—is really their response to the perception of the new instinctual demands of their own id, which threaten to revolutionize their whole lives. Their ideals of friendship and undying loyalty are simply a reflection of the disquietude of the Ego when it perceived the evanescence of its

new and passionate object-relations. The longing for guidance and support in the often hopeless battle against their own powerful instincts may be transformed into ingenious arguments about man's inability to arrive at independent political decisions. We see then that instinctual processes are translated into terms of intellect. But the reason why attention is thus focused on the instincts is that an attempt is being made to lay hold of and master them on a different psychic level. (Freud 1946, 177–78)

Adolescents who use this defense mechanism will often repeat, discuss, and read about topics that are linked to sexuality. In this situation, the real threat that the adolescent feels is that the ego may be overwhelmed.

QUESTION: What is the practical application of Anna Freud's theory?

Perhaps a primary application of her theory is to help identify asceticism and intellectuality as defense mechanisms used by struggling youths to help them cope with their sexual desires. Indeed, adolescents are often observed engaging in extreme forms of asceticism. This is especially true among males as they attempt to deny feelings of tenderness, pain, or sensitivity. As a second application of her theory, Freud also emphasizes the importance of providing an outlet for the sexual energy that is associated with biological maturity. Generally speaking, a psychoanalyst should try to rectify adolescent problems due to excessive sexual energy by finding more acceptable outlets for the pent-up energy rather than through encouraging the use of exaggerated defense mechanisms.

Psychoanalysts also believe that creativity is a type of adolescent defense. The most obvious and common form may be the extensive writing in a diary that was not in existence prior to puberty and which will have few empty places after these tempestuous years. Poetry is another creative behavior that seems to flourish and informally die at the end of this age period.

PETRO BLOS

While Sigmund Freud and Anna Freud emphasize a defense-oriented perspective toward coping, Blos points out the importance of coping behaviors that result from the evolution of a psychodynamic coping system for adolescents (Blos 1962). He believes that coping is an active effort by persons to resolve stress and to create new solutions to problems. The need for coping is sometimes the result of mental conflict and at other times is caused by environmental pressures. The process of coping consists of three abilities:

1. The ability to gain and process new information
2. The ability to control emotions
3. The ability to move freely in one's environment

Petro Blos thinks that students must consider three phases of adolescent adaptation. He believes that people can teach adolescents to have better coping skills. These coping skills can effectively help young people to progress through the three stages of adolescence.

For example, during early adolescence, children can be encouraged to form friendships by having an inviting and supportive home environment in which they can have friends join them in play. During middle adolescence, parents can help plan activities for mixed groups (e.g., parties and barbeques), which help youths become more familiar and comfortable with members of the opposite sex. During late adolescence, parents can provide their teenagers with opportunities to develop empathy (e.g., through modeling and moral reasoning discussions), which can help replace their egocentrism with more outwardly directed thoughts.

QUESTION: What are Petro Blos's ideas on the three phases of adolescence?

The three phases are (1) early adolescence, (2) middle adolescence, and (3) late adolescence. Most early adolescents experience conflicts as a result of biological motivations. These adolescents are surprised by their thoughts and impulses; they are unprepared for the biological changes within their bodies. They quickly become interested in the opposite sex. Almost every fantasy is potentially sexual in nature. They become easily distracted and quickly stimulated, and they maintain a high erotic sensitivity. According to Blos, even a sweep across the arm of a preadolescent shoulder can stimulate erotic fantasies or instant penile erection. This supersensitivity to stimulation, combined with a disintegrating ego control, makes it difficult for youths at this stage to learn from and respond to adults. Early adolescence is also a period of interpersonal development as youths desperately search for new love attachments to escape confusion, loneliness, and isolation.

During the middle adolescent period, a young person desires friendships. Often, the youth's interest in a friend is a narcissistic desire to admire and love another person who possesses some quality that the adolescent can vicariously obtain through friendship. Middle adolescence is also a stage that is characterized

These high school band members could be seen to illustrate one accomplishment characteristic of late adolescence: the stable interest in intellectual functions.

by confusion. As a result of this confusion, adolescents often fluctuate between sensitivity and coarseness, gregariousness and solitude, optimism and pessimism, idealism and materialism, indulgence and asceticism. Blos feels that it is during this period that male adolescents must definitely renounce their Oedipus strivings. As this is accomplished, youths feel an increased need to belong and to have attachments to age-mates of the opposite sex.

Late adolescence is a period of consolidation. It is characterized by five major accomplishments: (1) an interest in intellectual functions becomes stable, (2) the ego seeks to incorporate new people and new experiences, (3) an irreversible sexual identity is formed, (4) the egocentrism of childhood is replaced by a balance between thoughts of oneself and thoughts about others, and (5) a wall separating the adolescent's public and private selves is established. Notwithstanding these major changes in late adolescence, Blos believes that one does not achieve an integrated, consolidated, and comfortable sense of self until adulthood.

Range and use of theories

QUESTION: How do professionals use these theories of adolescence?

The following example, drawn from a popular textbook on adolescence, illustrates how theories assist and give direction to practical application:

> The senior authors' work with an adolescent some years ago in a Midwestern mental-health clinic exemplifies how theoretical orientations can influence one's understanding of a social problem and point to possible ways to approach it. A young man, whom we shall call Miguel R., was referred to the clinic by his school's psychologist. A broadly based intervention team from the school district and from the clinic met to discuss the problems underlying Miguel's behavior and decide what might be done for him. The team consisted of two teachers, a psychologist, a psychiatrist, a social worker, a physician, and a child-developmental specialist. The following is an abbreviated case history of Miguel R:
>
> Miguel R. is 15 years old. He is bilingual. His reading ability is at the sixth-grade level, though psychological examinations have indicated that he is of normal intelligence. He has a long history of problems with peer and family relationships, and he shows signs of hostility, aggression, and high levels of anxiety. After he and his family came to the United States from Cuba, his parents were divorced. His father disappeared, and his mother committed suicide. Miguel has been placed in two foster homes and Boys Town (a Catholic orphanage). Recently he has been quarrelsome with his teachers, has been fighting with his peers, has been caught stealing, and is known as a chronic liar. However, Miguel is not without some good points. He has a strong interest in wood working and is skilled in making furniture. He also paints outstanding portraits using Spanish themes. Miguel does have two friends. Unfortunately, both of these boys engage in frequent vandalism and aggressive behavior. Miguel has reached the point where his teachers are refusing to work with him. Foster-home care has become impossible. Boys Town is unsure whether it can continue caring for him unless his conduct improves.
>
> Using the wealth of information in Miguel's files, the results of a medical examination, and an extensive interview with Miguel, the members of the intervention team made the following comments. They illustrate how varying theoretical perspectives lead to varying ways of approaching a particular prob-

lem. Due to space limitations, only a few of each professional's comments are reproduced here.

The social worker

"After reviewing Miguel's case, I have come to the inescapable conclusion that he faces endless conflict with his past and present family members. He appears to find little or no warmth in the concept of home or even of friends." The social worker was guided in his judgments by the importance of understanding parent/child conflict and peer relations from a sociological perspective.

The physician

"My examination indicates that while Miguel is physically healthy, he is quite small for his age. Given his stature, I am concerned about his image among his peers. He referred to his size himself during the examination." The physician recognized that physical size can play a role in understanding peer relations. Drawing upon a biosocial perspective, he shared his concerns about the potential implications for assuming responsible roles in the school or with peers.

The teachers

"Is it possible that given Miguel's I.Q., the school has let him down? We see him as capable of average performance for a 15-year-old, yet his reading ability is well below average. The bilingualism may have created a problem. Perhaps by placing him in an educational program that recognizes his bilingual ability and reinforces the use of either language, we can motive him to work harder in school."

The teachers were drawing upon elements of social-learning theory when they suggested that it might be possible to motivate Miguel through recognizing his bilingual abilities. This strategy might enhance a sense of self-efficacy and mastery of skills. The teachers also recognized the utility of reinforcement in changing behavior.

The psychologist and the psychiatrist

Both of these professionals focused on the same issues, personal adjustment and psychological defenses. As the psychologist put it: "It seems clear that Miguel has put between himself and others a wall of defenses against the possibility of losing yet another significant person in his life. Perhaps we need to help him come to understand that even though he has lost others, he is capable of loving and being loved."

Both mental-health professionals recognized from psychosocial and psychoanalytic perspectives that a history of loss and a fear of losing others can create a myriad of psychological defenses that create interpersonal conflict. These perspectives helped in understanding why Miguel finds himself in conflict with almost everyone around him.

The child-development specialist

"I can't help wondering whether Miguel has developed a sense of initiative or an understanding of who he is. Through continual placement and replacement, he has lost a sense of continuity with his past. He knows he must move on from one placement to the next. He seems confused about who he is as a person and isolated from any truly significant relation with others." Drawing upon a psychosocial perspective, the child developmentalist saw Miguel as having failed to resolve several major life-stage crises and as stuck in a vicious cycle of nonproductive behavior.

Summary

The members of the intervention team all examined the same material on Miguel, but their different theoretical orientations brought them to different, though related, conclusions. Each perspective offered important and useful insights into working with Miguel. Taken together, they offered a meaningful way to address his problems systematically, and the team decided to use a multidimensional approach to therapy. (Adams and Gullotta 1983, 51–53)

QUESTION: Are the theories presented in this chapter all that are important for understanding adolescents?

No. Conspicuously omitted are some of the most popular theorists, like B. F. Skinner, Erik Erikson and Jean Piaget. These theorists have more general theories and deserve a more in-depth analysis than would be possible in this survey chapter. Accordingly, each of these theorists is included in a single chapter. For instance, in the next chapter Erik Erikson is highlighted because of his emphasis on achieving a sense of identity during adolescence. Piaget is discussed in the chapter on thinking, and Lawrence Kohlberg in the moral reasoning chapter.

In the final section, the two broad classes of theory, behaviorism and phenomenology, are described and applied. Adaptations of phenomenological theory are used to form the basis of the final chapters, which were written to help develop skills for successfully relating with adolescents.

Summary

The biological theories of Hall and Gesell illustrate the importance of biologically determined behavior patterns.

G. Stanley Hall's theory of recapitulation claims that all individuals, from birth until death, reenact in their own lives the history of humankind's progress and development throughout the ages. Adolescence, which represents the great changes and the emotional upheaval of modern civilization, is called a period of *strum und drang*—a German phrase that means "storm and stress."

Hall believes that each stage of an individual's life involves unique opportunities and unique challenges. Parents should provide their children with the support and experience they need at each stage. Infants should be allowed immense freedom to touch, to smell, and to taste as many things as possible; they should also be allowed great freedom of mobility to explore their environment. Preadolescents should be taught and trained extensively; this stage is the optimal time to help them learn how to work with others and to help them establish behavioral routines. Adolescents should be allowed a time and place for solitude as they work through their own mood swings and emotionality.

Arnold Gesell's normative theory describes particular behaviors that are specific to each year of an adolescent's development. The normative behaviors that he describes for each age group include their activities and interests, emotions, interpersonal relations, and philosophical outlooks.

Gesell finds that children will, if not hindered, follow a normal, natural course of development, and parents should concentrate on providing children with the experience they need at each level of motivation. For example, parents should encourage their fifteen-year-old to participate in community activities to help fulfill the adolescent's craving for independence.

The sociological theories of Davis, Havighurst, and Coleman emphasize the importance of examining socioeconomic classes, cultures, norms, and expectations to determine how adolescents will act.

Allison Davis believes that adolescents become what society expects them to become. Society uses the threat of punishment and the withdrawal of love to motivate adolescents and to modify their behavior. This motivation creates within adolescents a feeling of socialized anxiety.

Davis's theory can be applied to family and community structures. On the family level, parents can adjust their discipline and behavioral demands on adolescents to maintain a healthy level of socialized anxiety. They can prevent neurotic anxiety in adolescents by allowing them some freedom to choose their own alternatives to specific behaviors. On the community level, programs can be implemented to teach and motivate adolescents who are in discouraging environments. Affirmative community efforts can encourage adolescent programs and development within cultural norms.

Robert Havighurst believes that individuals must accomplish certain tasks at specific stages of their own personal development. These tasks consist of acquiring certain skills, knowledge, functions, and attitudes. Individuals must accomplish each task at an optimum age, or they will have difficulty accomplishing all subsequent tasks.

Havighurst believes that we should study our culture to determine what specific tasks are required of adolescents. A list of developmental tasks can then be used to identify and isolate areas in which an adolescent may be having problems.

James Coleman emphasizes the existence of youth cultures that actively and effectively influence adolescents. Youth cultures help determine adolescent political alignments and choice of heroes, styles, music, and idols.

Coleman feels that schools and communities should use the power and resources of youth cultures to motivate and guide adolescents. Leaders of youth cultures can be invited to participate in community leadership committees. Then as native members, they can influence and be influenced by community norms and expectations. This can motivate the entire youth culture to participate more in community affairs.

The anthropological theories of Benedict and Mead show that adolescence in America is not the same as adolescence in all other countries.

Ruth Benedict's theory states that an individual's development should be a gradual process from infancy to adulthood. If discontinuities—abrupt and traumatic changes—occur that disrupt this gradual process, the individual's growth will be distorted. An example of one common discontinuity is the change in society's sexual expectations for adolescents. Society withholds sexual information from children and bombards them with provocative and stimulating material when they reach adolescence. This abrupt change increases the difficulties of adolescent adjustment.

Benedict believes that parents and educators should try to prevent adolescent role discontinuity in three major areas: sex, responsibility, and independence. Our present culture requires adolescents to make abrupt transitions from sexlessness to sexuality, from dependence to independence, and from submissiveness to dominance. Adolescence would be much less stressful if young people could be allowed to make these changes slowly, safely, and smoothly.

Margaret Mead believes that the discontinuities that Benedict describes do exist in several Western cultures. These discontinuities, especially relative to sexual roles and expectations, cause stress, strain, anxiety, and excessive emotionality among our youth.

Mead feels that social planning could eliminate much of the stress, strain, anxiety, and excessive emotionality of Western youth. For example, sexual education should be taught to children at an early age and should be continued throughout adolescence. This education might help young people to gradually be aware of and adjust to their sexuality. Adolescent boys should also have less intimate interaction with girls of the same age. Our society today prematurely places them in situations in which they must depend on each other socially and intellectually. In addition, Western culture could stop emphasizing the consumption of sex. The abundance of sexual materials in today's society makes it difficult for adolescents to understand and control their sexuality.

The theories of Sigmund Freud, his daughter, Anna, and Peter Blos all emphasize the inevitable stress that will exist when adolescents mature physically and are confronted with the emergence of sexual desires.

Sigmund Freud's theory states that personalities are composed of three elements: the id, the ego, and the superego. These three personality components deal constantly with two strong drives within each individual—a life instinct (sex) and a death instinct (aggression). The id operates on the pleasure principle and seeks immediate and constant gratification of the two drives. The ego operates on the reality principle and seeks to control the id, to preserve the self, and to find socially appropriate means of expressing the two drives. The superego is the conscience and serves to judge between good and evil.

Defense mechanisms are used to hide internal conflict between the id, the ego, and the superego from the conscious self and from other individuals. If defense mechanisms become inadequate or are irrationally adhered to, neurotic anxiety results.

Anna Freud extended her father's theories and applied them specifically to adolescence. She believes that sexual or libidinal energy increases dramatically during adolescence. Individuals often try to cope with this energy by using defense mechanisms, especially asceticism and intellectuality.

Sigmund and Anna Freud's theories can be applied to the field of adolescent development in several ways. For example, parents should help adolescents cope with their biological maturity and should recognize ineffective defense mechanisms for what they are. When adolescents exhibit excessive rationalization, regression, projection, asceticism, intellectuality, or any other defense mechanism, parents should help them become aware of their behavior, understand their biological processes, accept their feelings and fears, and channel their libidinal energy into socially acceptable outlets.

Petro Blos's theory describes the importance of coping behaviors that adolescents use to resolve stress and to create new solutions to problems. The coping process consist of three abilities:

1. The ability to gain and process new information
2. The ability to control emotions
3. The ability to move freely in one's environment

Early adolescence is a period of dramatic increases in sexual awareness and stimulation. Middle adolescence is a period of intense emotional fluctuations and desire for intense friendship. Late adolescence is a period of consolidation.

References

Adams, G., & T. Gullotta 1983. *Adolescent life experiences*. Monterey, Calif.: Brooks/Cole.
Beckman, L. 1978. The relative rewards and costs of parenthood and employment for employed women. *Psychology of Woman Quarterly* 2:3.
Benedict, R. 1938. Continuities and discontinuities in cultural conditioning. *Psychiatry* 1: 161–67.
_____. 1950. *Patterns of culture*. New York: New American Library
Benedict, R., & C. Standler, eds. 1954. *Readings in child development*. New York: Harcourt Brace Jovanovich.
Blos, P. 1962. *On adolescence: A psychoanalytic interpretation*. New York: Free Press.
Coleman, J. S. 1960. The adolescent subculture and academic achievement. *American Journal of Sociology* 65:337–47.
_____. 1961. *The adolescent society*. New York: Free Press.
_____. 1965. *The adolescent and the schools*. New York: Basic Books.
_____. 1972. How do the young become adult? *Review of Educational Research* 42:431–39.
Coleman, J. S., R. H. Bremner, C. R. Burton, J. B. Davis, P. H. Eichorn, Z. Grilichos, J. F. Kett, N. B. Ryder, Z. B. Doering, & J. M. Mays. 1974. *Youth: Transition to adulthood*. Chicago: Univ. of Chicago Press.
Davis, A. 1944. Socialization and the adolescent personality. In *Adolescence, yearbook of the National Society for the Society of Children for the Study of Education* 43, pt. 1.
Freud, A. 1946. *The ego and the mechanisms of defense*. Trans. C. Baines. New York: International Univ. Press.
Freud, S. 1953. *A general introduction to psychoanalysis*. Trans. Wonn Riviere. New York: Permabooks.
Gesell, A., & L. B. Ames. 1956. *Youth: the years from 10 to 16*. New York: Harper & Row.
Gustin, J. C. 1961. The revolt of youth. *Psychoanalysis and the Psychoanalytic Review* 98:83.
Hall, G. S. 1916. *Adolescence*, vols. 1 and 2. New York: Appleton-Century-Crofts.
Havighurst, R. J. 1951. *Developmental tasks and education*. New York: Longmans, Greene.
_____. 1972. *Developmental tasks and education*. 3d ed. New York: McKay.
Kelly, G. A. 1955. *The psychology of personal constructs*. New York: Norton.
Mead, M. 1950. *Coming of age in Samoa*. New York: New American Library.
_____. 1952. Adolescence in primitive and modern society. In *Readings in social psychology*, ed. G. E. Swanson, T. Newcomb, E. L. Hartley. New York: Holt, Rinehart & Winston.
_____. 1953. *Growing up in New Guinea*. New York: New American Library.
Shaw, M. E., & P. R. Costenzo. 1970. *Theories of social psychology*. New York: McGraw-Hill.

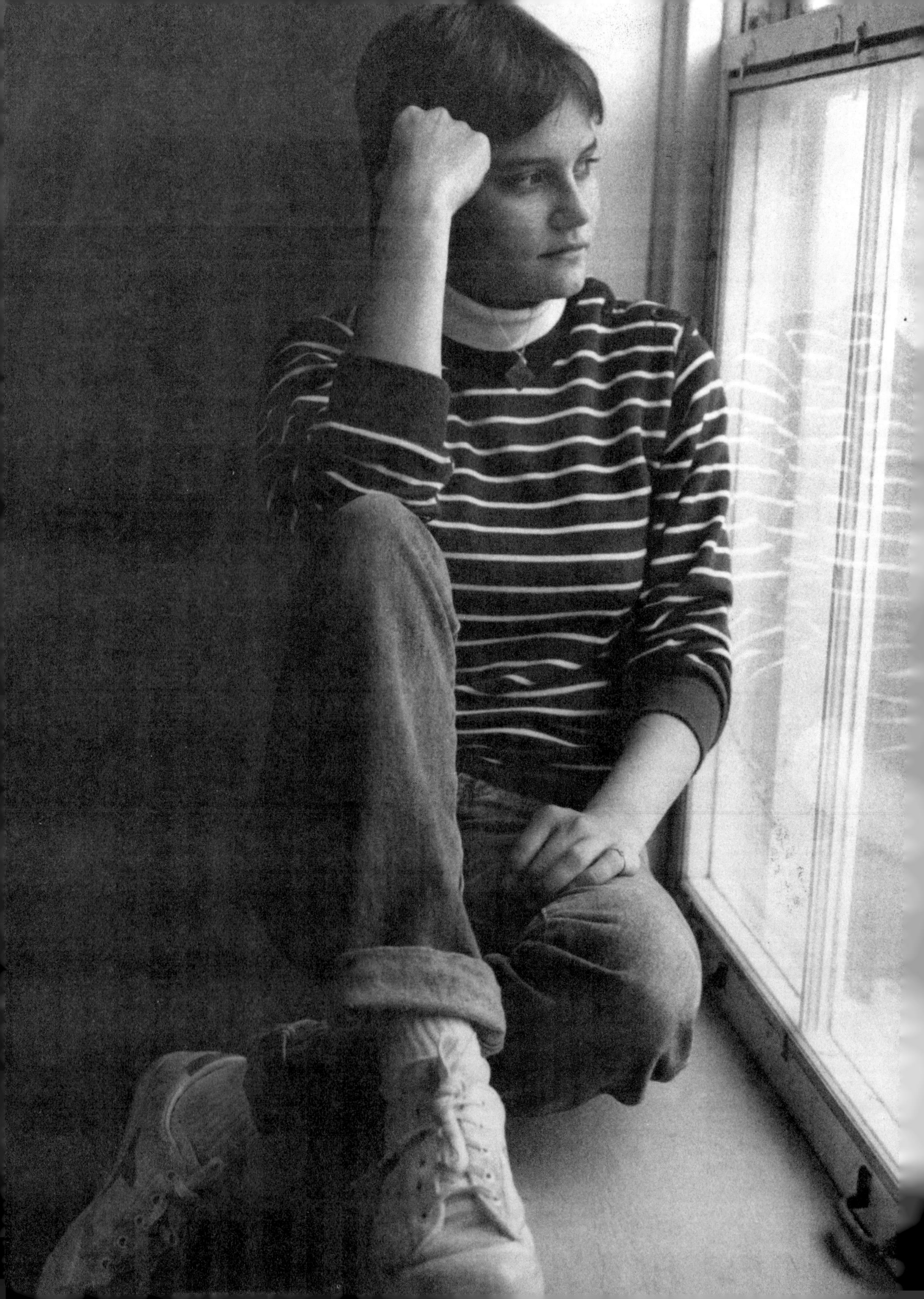

CHAPTER THREE

The developing self

SURVEY AND QUESTIONS

In this chapter the student will find a general introduction to the developing self. Reading the chapter will provide the answers to the following questions:

Erik Erikson and Developing a Sense of Identity

Are all of the developmental tasks accomplished during adolescence?
What are the preadolescent tasks?

The Sense of Identity

What is the adolescent task of finding a sense of identity?
What causes an adolescent to seek an identity?
How do adults influence adolescent development?
What is role diffusion?
Does an individual have ample time *before* the onset of adolescence to develop a sense of identity?

Marcia's Theory of Identity, Role Status, and Research

When does identity development take place?
Are there sex differences in the development of identity?
What causes the particular identity state of each adolescent?
Are different achievements of identity status related to development in other personality areas?
Is the resolution of an identity crisis related to personal and interpersonal adjustment?
What are some applications of the findings about identity states?

The Self-Concept and Self-Esteem

What are the definitions of the words *self, self-concept, self-esteem, self-image,* and *identity?*
How can these terms describing the self be applied to a specific example?
What causes adolescents to be on opposite poles of self-esteem and self-concept?

Influences on Self-Esteem and Self-Concept

What are the parental practices that result in high self-esteem?
What influences the development of a positive self-concept?
Do personal accomplishments improve one's self-concept?
Can people increase their self-concept and self-esteem?

Variations in Self-Concept

Can self-concept have both positive and negative elements?
Can an individual's self-concept and behavior differ from situation to situation?

In high school, I had a coach I loved very much. He cared deeply about us and wanted us to know how important we each were. In fact, the entire team was close, and most all of us looked out for each other.

Our team had had two relatively good years, but this year—my senior year—we were having only a mediocre season. During the last game, which was against our rival, we were being beaten at half-time, 28–7, and it didn't look good. None of us were looking forward to the half-time talk by the coaches.

When we walked into the locker room, we were surprised. The coach explained how much each of us was worth and how we needed to realize that we were important. He choked up and told us that we would be important to him for the rest of his life, that he would always be there to help any of us whenever we needed that help. He then went around the locker room and shook each of our hands and told us individually how important we were to him.

When we went out of the locker room, we didn't feel any "rah-rah" but only a quiet reassurance that we were important people. We ended up playing above our potential and winning 42–28, just because we knew that we meant something to someone.

The power and significance of what we think about ourselves repeatedly turn up in stories such as these. This is particularly true for the adolescent years, when youth are daily struggling with the question, Who am I?

Erik Erikson, a popular neopsychoanalyst who stresses the importance of acquiring an identity during adolescence.

Erik Erikson and developing a sense of identity

This chapter will focus on the self. The work of the influential theorist Erik Erikson is presented first.

Erik H. Erikson's (1902–) ideas about youth and the self are best presented in his book *Childhood and Society* (Erikson 1963). Erikson took Freud's five psychosexual development stages, and reformulated and expanded them into a sequence of eight psychosocial stages. Erikson believes that personality slowly progresses through each of these eight stages. At each stage a specific developmental task must be accomplished to ensure normal development. The successful accomplishment of each developmental task is measured on a continuum. The more completely individuals accomplish each task, the greater chance they will have for a healthy personality. There is a specific and critical time for individual achievement of each task.

The eight developmental bipolar tasks that Erikson describes are shown in Table 3–1.

TABLE 3–1 Erikson's Psychosocial Stages of Man as they correspond with Freud's stages

Period of Time	Erikson's Stages	Freudian Stages	Description
Infancy	Basic trust vs. mistrust	Oral	Parents must maintain an adequate environment—supportive, nurturing, and loving—so that the child develops basic trust.
Years 1–3	Autonomy vs. shame or doubt	Anal	As the child develops bowel and bladder control, he or she should also develop a healthy attitude toward being independent and somewhat self-sufficient. If the child is made to feel that independent efforts are wrong, then shame and self-doubt develop instead of autonomy.
Years 3–5½	Initiative vs. guilt	Phallic	The child must discover ways to initiate actions on his or her own. If such initiatives are successful, guilt will be avoided.
Years 5½–12	Industry vs. inferiority	Latency	The child must learn to feel competent, especially when competing with peers. Failure results in feelings of inferiority.
Adolescence	Identity vs. role confusion	Genital	A sense of role identity must develop, especially in terms of selecting a vocation and future career.
Early adulthood	Intimacy vs. isolation		The formation of close friendships and relationships with the opposite sex is vital to healthy development.
Middle adulthood	Generativity vs. stagnation		Adults develop useful lives by helping and guiding children. Childless adults must fill this need through adoption or other close relationships with children.
Later adulthood	Ego integrity vs. despair		An adult will eventually review his or her life. A life well spent will result in a sense of well-being and integrity.

Source: Adapted from J. P. Dworetzky, *Introduction to child development* (St. Paul: West Publishing, 1981) 42.

Erikson purposely uses the term *sense of*, because the affective feelings of having accomplished or having failed to accomplish a particular stage are the most important determining factors in development in succeeding phases (Maier 1965, 30).

QUESTION: Are all of the developmental tasks accomplished during adolescence?

No. Only one of these tasks must be completed during the adolescent period of life. If previous tasks have not been met and mastered by then, however, they too will need to be accomplished, or the adolescent's growth will be hindered. Let us briefly look at preadolescent tasks.

QUESTION: What are the preadolescent tasks?

Erikson describes a *sense of trust* as the cornerstone for all future personality development. The critical time for the development of a sense of trust is during the first year of life. A sense of trust is twofold: It is a basic belief in the security of one's environment, and it is a basic confidence in one's self, in one's capacity, and in one's ability to cope with urges. Maier (1965, 31) believes that this feeling of trust arises from "a feeling of physical comfort and a minimum experience of fear or uncertainty. . . . In contrast, a sense of mistrust arises from unsatisfactory physical and psychological experiences." Once people achieve a sense of trust, they will willingly face new experiences in life.

When children reach the second year of life and have learned to trust their environment and themselves, they then begin to realize they have minds and wills of their own. They should now develop a *sense of autonomy* rather than shame and doubt. A sense of autonomy shows that children are discovering that they are people in their own right and that they are gaining self-esteem and confidence in their abilities to confront the world. Parents must grant freedom to children in certain areas and yet must exercise control in other areas lest children experience shame and doubt. Shame is the feeling of self-consciousness and incompetence in the eyes of others. Children can easily experience shame if parents do not safeguard them from adventuring into areas where they cannot physically and mentally perform adequately.

At the age of four to five, children engage in another task, that of achieving a *sense of initiative* instead of a sense of guilt. During the previous stage (gaining a sense of autonomy), children were trying to discover that they were people in their own right with wills of their own. At this stage (gaining a sense of initiative), they become concerned with bringing their autonomy under conscious control. In explaining this stage, Erikson says:

> Initiative adds to autonomy the quality of undertaking, planning and attacking a task for the sake of being active and on the move, where before [the stage of initiative] self-will more often than not inspired acts of defiance. (Erikson 1963, 255)

Achieving this sense of initiative is necessarily important because it is the motivational basis for all future acts that an individual undertakes.

Two major aspects of the sense of initiative are appropriate sex role development and conscience development. Up to this point in children's lives, their parents have played a major role in whatever the children attempted to do, and have been telling them what is right and wrong. During the stage of initiative, however, children's own consciences begin to develop, and help direct them in deciding what is right or wrong. When children do not obey their parents or heed this inner voice, they experience guilt. The development of the conscience occurs at a time when people outside children's immediate families are for the first time having significant relationships with the children.

Starting about the age of six and continuing until the age of twelve, children experience critical conflict between a *sense of industry* and a sense of inferiority. Children have previously been involved only in initiating projects. Children at this stage are often busy doing and making things, such as making model airplanes, collecting stamps, and learning to prepare foods. The child now "wants to be engaged in real tasks that he can carry through to completion."

During this period of life, the importance of family members diminishes and the importance of peers increases. Peers become the measuring rod for success, and children at this age are often heard to make comments such as, "I can do something better than Jane," "I'm in the best reading group," or "I've got more stamps in my collection than any of the other kids."

These tasks to be achieved before adolescence are presented to identify what should have taken place. Frequently they have not been resolved and so must be dealt with during adolescence. For most youth they have been successfully completed, and so the central issue of adolescents is the task of achieving an identity.

The sense of identity

QUESTION: What is the adolescent task of finding a sense of identity?

Erikson believes that adolescents must accomplish the specific task of developing a *sense of identity* in place of identity confusion. Sawrey and Telford (1963), who interpret Erikson's theory, define identity as having three parts: (1) the development and maintenance of a feeling of "inner sameness and continuity," which is matched by the sameness and continuity of one's meaning for others, (2) a conviction that the individual's way of achieving personal and vocational goals (and receiving appropriate recognition for such) is a successful variant of the way other significant people in the individual's culture achieve the same goals, and (3) the feeling that one is learning effective social skills to deal with a tangible future, and the feeling that one is developing a unique personality within an understood social context.

QUESTION: What causes an adolescent to seek an identity?

Individuals can achieve a sense of identity through various processes. All of the processes require adolescents to explore and to perhaps temporarily commit themselves to various philosophies, vocations, or religions. Before individuals can make a final commitment to a specific identity, they must integrate their personal needs, inherent abilities, identifications with significant people, and previous roles.

Our society, with no definite initiation of adolescents into the adult world, provides what Erikson calls "a psychological moratorium," or as Maier describes it, "an authorized delay of adulthood" (1965, 57). During this moratorium, adolescents have time to work through their problems of achieving a sense of identity. In an effort to resolve their problems, adolescents often overidentify with stereotyped groups and fasten on petty similarities of dress and gesture to assure themselves that they belong. Youth in a particular social group can then be intolerant and even cruel to people who are not in their group—that is people who are "different." Erikson warns that such behavior in youth should not be severely condemned by adults, because it helps adolescents to find their identities. Adolescent intolerance toward others who are "different" gives them some measure of security that there is something that they are not. A second way that adolescents overidentify is through "falling in love." This love is often not physical in nature, but involves a lot of thought and conversation, and is based on a great deal of romanticism and idealism. Erikson (1963, 262) believes that adolescent love is "an attempt to arrive at a definition of one's identity by projecting one's diffused ego image onto another and seeing it thus reflected and gradually clarified." This is why so much of young love is conversation.

QUESTION: How do adults influence adolescent development?

Adolescents select certain adults who become meaningful to them—often teachers, social leaders, or parents. The adolescent's selection of such adults is based not so much on social function but on the particular role they are playing during this time of confusion in the adolescent's life. Adults, especially parents who want to be influential in helping their adolescents, should allow them the freedom to try out different roles, mentally and behaviorally. Erikson describes the results of *not* granting young people the freedom to experiment with different roles:

> Should a child feel that the environment tries to deprive him too radically of all the forms of expression which permit him to develop and to integrate the next step in [his] ego identity, he will defend it with the astonishing strength encountered in animals who are suddenly forced to defend their lives. And indeed, in the social jungle of human existence there is no feeling of being

Adolescents often select certain adults who become meaningful to them. It is easy to see how a coach, for example, could greatly influence self-concept as well as adolescent development.

alive without a sense of ego identity. Deprivation of identity can lead to murder. (Erikson 1968, 437)

During this stage, parents must be able to talk with their teenagers, for talking has a special significance to adolescents. Adults and parents should also refrain from labeling youth with negative terms such as "delinquents" or "lazy-good-for-nothings," even though the youth might be temporarily exhibiting such behavior. Labeling only forces adolescents to accept a negative identity, even if their problem behavior is only a temporary trial.

If adolescents integrate the many influences in their life (e.g., personal desires, peers, family), they will achieve a sense of identity and will find themselves. If they cannot integrate the parts of their personality, they will feel a sense of role diffusion.

QUESTION: What is role diffusion?

A character in Arthur Miller's *Death of a Salesman* describes role diffusion when he says, "I just can't take hold, Mom. I just can't take hold of some kind of life." Another text gives an example illustrating the psychodynamics of a man who also suffers from role diffusion. It depicts the influence of experience on early adolescence:

> In the course of growing up, Mr. Orchard had developed imperfect identifications with several people important to him, and he had been unable to achieve that kind of integration we describe as identity. His close attachment to his mother had been interrupted by her death when he was 12; he longed for closeness to his father but his father was away from home a great deal until his early adult life. The third influence upon him was an aged, religious grandfather who took much responsibility for him after his mother's death, but who was too old to be a good identification figure. Who did Orchard think himself to be? He was like his mother in her hard-working, gentle ways. He was like his father in caring for artistic work, but with a certain debonair irresponsibility. His religious conflicts derived in part from his grandfather. (Hilgard 1957, 450)

Youth who have successfully accomplished the preadolescent developmental tasks and who have achieved a sense of identity will now be able to find their place in society. As Erikson describes it, adolescents have achieved continuity between that which they have come to be during the long years of childhood and that which they promise to become in the anticipated future.

QUESTION: Does an individual have ample time *before* the onset of adolescence to develop a sense of identity?

No. Erikson believes that the sense of identity must be achieved during adolescence in order for the person to be wholly integrated:

> The wholeness to be achieved at this stage I have called a sense of inner identity. The young person, in order to experience wholeness, must feel a progressive continuity between that which he has come to be during the long years of childhood and that which he promises to become in the anticipated future; between that which he conceives himself to be and that which he perceives others to see him [as] and to expect of him. Individually speaking, identity includes, but is more than, the sum of all the successive identifications

of those early years when the child wanted to be, and was often forced to become, like the people he depended on. Identity is a unique product, which now meets a crisis to be solved only in new identification with age-mates and with leader figures outside of the family. (Erikson 1968, 87)

Erikson's notion of a sense of identity is a much more pervasive concept than simply learning about the self as one would experience during childhood. An identity includes a number of factors:

1. A definite sense of self-definition, which is like the self-concept
2. The presence of commitments to goals, values, and beliefs
3. The existence of activities directed toward the implementation of the commitments
4. The consideration of a range of identity alternatives
5. The development of self-acceptance
6. A sense of personal uniqueness
7. Confidence in one's personal future

Erikson believes that the development of a true identity is so profound that individuals may consider themselves to have been "born again" (Erikson 1958). The term *born again* is used to describe a psychological growth crisis—a second birth—that some individuals undergo during development of their identities. The twice-born undergo a crisis in which their adult personality is formed through personal choices during adolescence. Other individuals are called "once-born" and experience no difficulty in fitting into society with their childhood identifications.

A number of pencil and paper tests have been developed to measure identity. They include: Ego Identity Scales (Rosmussen 1961, 1711–12), Inventory of Psychosocial Development (Constantinople 1969, 357–72), and Identity Achievement Scale (Simmons 1970, 241–44). In almost all of these tests, people are asked to report on their own identity development by responding to statements in the test.

Many theorists do not use written tests but instead prefer to derive their conclusions about an individual's identity from clinical interviews or semi-structured interviews. This is true of J. E. Marcia, an influential researcher in the field who has focused on the study of identity.

Marcia's theory of identity, role status, and research

James Marcia expanded Erikson's basic idea that the progressive formation of a sense of identity occurs during the transition from adolescence to adulthood. (Marcia 1967, 1980; Marcia and Waterman 1982)

Marcia believes that the classification system should involve four identity states:

1. *Identity achievement* is a period of crisis followed by a person's development of firm commitments.
2. *Moratorium* is a crisis during which a person is actively seeking ways to arrive at acceptable choices.

3. *Foreclosure* occurs when a person has never experienced a crisis but is still committed to goals, values, and beliefs developed during childhood from authoritarian figures.
4. *Diffusion* takes place when individuals who do not have firm commitments are not actively trying to form them. They may or may not have been in a crisis; they have not resolved their identity.

Like Marcia, other researchers have been concerned about when identity development takes place, if there are sex differences in the development of identities, and what causes the particular identity state of each adolescent: achievement, moratorium, foreclosure, or diffusion (Marcia 1980, 348–58).

QUESTION: When does identity development take place?

Prior to high school, youths have relatively little interest in their identities. Even during high school, less identity development takes place than what is commonly believed (Marcia 1980). Not until college are the greatest adolescent gains in identity formation made. College environments provide a range of experiences that instigate and develop identity issues and provide choices for their resolution. College experiences seem to clearly facilitate the formation of identities. For example, seniors generally have stronger personal identities than do freshmen. Although college environments facilitate personal identity development (especially in the area of vocational plans), they often undermine traditional religious beliefs without providing alternative belief systems. This means that, at least on the issue of belief systems, college students tend to have less foreclosure and more identity diffusion. Most change takes place between the ages of eighteen and twenty-one (Stark and Traxler 1974; Marcia 1980, 180).

The college experience provides an optimal environment for the identity achievement among older adolescents.

During the adult years, individuals tend to strengthen their previously formed identities rather than form new identities.

College environments apparently cause the strongest identity changes to take place. Individuals in moratorium are the least stable and are the most likely adolescents to change. Identity achievement and foreclosure states are more stable in the areas of religious beliefs and political ideology. The basic notions of Marcia and Erikson confirm the belief that although people experience some identity development during early adolescence, the greatest identity development seems to occur during late adolescence.

QUESTION: Are there sex differences in the development of identity?

Some researchers believe that sex differences in this area "exist" (Newman and Newman 1978, 157–66). They believe that for a boy to achieve a sense of identity, parents must relate to him warmly, responsively, and with clear and consistent acts of limit setting and discipline. This approach will cause the boy to distinguish between himself and his parents while still reacting positively to them. For girls, a warm parent-child relationship is also important, but strong discipline simply overemphasizes her dependency and causes her to be excessively acquiescent. To become autonomous, girls must be rewarded for their efforts to be independent. A small amount of conflict in the home can help girls develop moral judgment and progress toward independent thinking, but discipline that is too strict may be unhealthy. In contrast, a more harmonious family helps boys develop a mature, moral view.

This study by Newman and Newman should not be used to justify conflict in the home, but it does indicate that some identity confusion may be good because it permits change and helps prevent premature foreclosure. For both males and females, identity achievement is associated with good coping and adjustment capabilities. Among males, the greatest behavioral difficulties occur for those in the foreclosure and identity diffusion states; however, this is not true for females.

QUESTION: What causes the particular identity state of each adolescent?

Marcia (1980) carefully studied this issue and found that adolescents in identity diffusion of both sexes are more distant from their families than are adolescents in other identity states. The parents of young people in identity diffusion are perceived by their youth as being indifferent, inactive, detached, not understanding, and rejecting. Foreclosure is usually found in families where parents are possessive and directive toward their sons while supportive and encouraging of their daughters. Sons in a foreclosure state are often more willing to involve their families in making more important life decisions than are sons in other identity states. Both sexes in moratorium and identity achievement states tend to have critical attitudes toward their parents and to be in conflict with them. Sons in the moratorium and identity achievement states do not usually turn to their families for help in making important decisions, because of tension and ambivalence. Adolescents with an identity achievement status tend to be more strongly influenced by their same-sex parent than by their parent of the opposite sex. Current research is not conclusive regarding family stability as a possible determinant of identity states (Marcia 1980). A cautious interpretation would be that family disorganization is related to identity diffusion.

Other research on families (Kohn 1959 1969; Douvan and Adelson 1966; Goode 1970; Blum et al. 1972) has shown that working-class parents are more restrictive and tradition oriented in their approach to child rearing. Parents in middle and upper classes have more permissive attitudes toward the needs and desires of their children (Laufer 1971) tend to emphasize the quality of independence in their children. In contrast, working-class adults are often intolerant of their children's "exploration of alternatives," which in turn influences identity status. In addition to the social class differences between their parents, adolescent experience with blue-collar work instead of prolonged education may alter the frequency and duration of their identity states.

QUESTION: Are different achievements of identity status related to development in other personality areas?

Apparently so, although research on this issue is so recent that reaching specific conclusions is impossible. Adams and Fitch feel that it may be necessary for adolescents to obtain a higher level of ego functioning before they can move out of the identity diffusion status. Other studies, although they are hard to interpret systematically, have yielded interesting information regarding identity states. For example, poetry writing is more frequent among people who have obtained identity achievement. Another interesting finding is that those youth who have had full-time employment are more likely to achieve an identity status than those who have not had full-time employment. (Adams and Fitch 1981) It is likely that the employment helps establish a definite identity.

QUESTION: Is the resolution of an identity crisis related to personal and interpersonal adjustment?

Studies have shown that resolution of an identity crisis is an important determinant of adjustment and behavior. Peer adjustment (Block 1961), authoritarian personality traits (Marcia 1967), and alienation and delinquency (Erikson 1968) have been related to the outcome of identity crises. Researchers have also found that decision-making styles (Waterman and Waterman 1974), moral behaviors (Podd 1972), styles of relating to other people (Donovan 1975), cognitive styles, sex role identities (Schenkel 1975), and "intimacy versus isolation crises of young adulthood" (Orlofsky, Marcia, and Lasser 1973) are all related to the resolution of identity crises.

QUESTION: What are some applications of the findings about identity states?

If one assumes that achieving an identity status is a desirable goal, then knowledge of foreclosure, moratorium, and diffusion states can help parents understand adolescents and can assist them in guiding adolescents to achieve their sense of identity. Parents can expect a child entering adolescence to be in a diffusion state, except for a few children who are in a state of foreclosure. Assisting children to achieve their identity, particularly in the areas of vocation, religion and values, and ideology, would benefit their development. However, a direct imposition of adult opinions and beliefs is not advisable. Youths must be given enough time, as well as sufficient freedom of choice, to explore and try out ideas in order to find themselves. Children from affectionate families with relatively high levels of organization may not experience a crisis stage and may rapidly approach, achieve, and maintain a foreclosure status.

Simply being aware of the psychological processes and developments that occur in adolescence (just as knowing the movements of the current helps a river captain to navigate) helps adults understand how they can relate more effectively to adolescents.

The natural course of psychological development is often hard to see at any particular point in time, but in retrospect becomes much clearer. One student writes about her brother, who had identity confusion. She notes that this confusion is often mistaken for delinquency:

> My brother, Jim, may be such a case. As I look back at Jim's developmental years, I see many of the "symptoms" Erikson described. Jim tried out several roles during his secondary educational years. He went the sports route (wrestling and football), he dabbled in the arts (music), and eventually succumbed to peer pressure and experimented with alcohol and pot. He resented authority figures during that period, be they educational, ecclesiastical or parental, and he worked hard at avoiding them, though never in total open rebellion. But Jim was not comfortable or happy with any of these roles—especially the last.

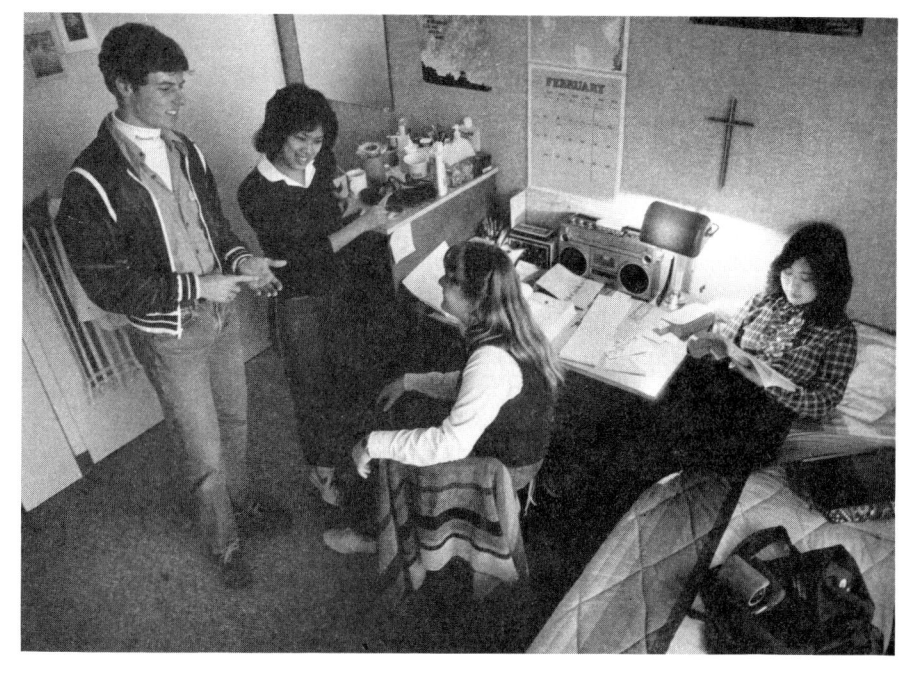

Identity is related to achievement and social skills, both of which may be discovered by an individual for the first time in a post-high school setting.

It wasn't until Jim went away to college and was almost forced by the unfamiliar situation to establish himself as an individual that he found his niche and became happy.

A significant point is that identity states may not be completed during adolescence and must then be resolved during adulthood. Further, the process of achieving an identity status is not always unidirectional. Some adolescents may go from foreclosure to diffusion or from an achieved identity to moratorium. Lastly, parents and teachers are always searching for criteria, categories, and other ways to better understand the adolescent world; the status states of Marcia may be useful in understanding adolescents who are in diffusion, moratorium, or identity states.

The self-concept and self-esteem

QUESTION: What are the definitions of the words *self*, *self-concept*, *self-esteem*, *self-image*, and *identity*?

Although the use of terms defining the person lacks consistency, and complete definitional consensus is impossible, some distinctions and definitions seem both defensible and practical:

1. *Self:* The self has been defined as "that part of one's personality of which one is aware" (Rice 1981, 198). Basically, the self is one's awareness—the agent that acts. It is the part of a person that directs and initiates action.
2. *Self-Concept:* "The self-concept refers to how adolescents view themselves" (Santrock 1983, 377). In general, it is opinion, belief, or what you think about yourself.
3. *Self-Esteem* is the emotional evaluation that adolescents make about themselves; it is generally in the form of approval or disapproval. Self-esteem refers more to *feelings* about oneself, while the self-concept refers more to intellectual beliefs about oneself (Coopersmith 1967).
4. *Self-Image* is more temporary and subject to change than is the self-concept or self-esteem (Turner 1968).
5. *Identity* is a broad term used to describe the general components of a total personality, which may include diverse elements such as religion, values, and vocation. Answers to questions like, Who am I?, Where am I going?, and What kind of career will I pursue? are dependent upon the sense of identity (Santrock 1983, 383).

The self-concept and self-esteem have generally been measured using pencil and paper tests. These self-reports have been standard assessment procedures in psychology. For a sample listing of tests measuring the self-concept and self-esteem, one should consult reference sources such as *Measures of Social Psychological Attitudes* (Robinson and Shaver 1983). The authors list more than thirty tests to measure aspects of the self. In most cases a statement is made about the self, and respondents are asked to indicate their agreement with the statement. For example, in the Tennessee Self-Concept Scale (Fitts 1965) the following statements are made:

I am satisfied with my moral behavior.

I am as sociable as I want to be.

These questions are then rated as:

Completely False	Mostly False	Partly False Partly True	Mostly True	Completely True
1	2	3	4	5

A higher score would indicate higher self-esteem and would yield separate self-esteem scores in categories such as physical, moral, family, and social self.

QUESTION: How can these terms describing the self be applied to a specific example?

Imagine two adolescents, David and Clem. David comes from a successful family, one that expects him to achieve and excel in what he does. He has outstanding abilities and has earned excellent grades throughout his schooling. He is over six feet tall, is good looking, and is on the high school football team. He has also distinguished himself in other athletic events and in his part-time job after school. David is well liked, has a good value system, and is highly motivated. He is, however, somewhat ill at ease in large social groups and is hesitant when speaking in public. Around girls he blushes easily and is not confident. He is somewhat reluctant to assert himself at a task unless he is sure he is qualified and capable of successfully accomplishing it. In groups of his age-mates, he is a little quiet, not argumentative, and is cheerful and congenial. This style results in little confrontation between him and his peers.

Clem is very different. He comes from a large, happy, working-class family. Clem is large for his age, but not particularly well built or physically attractive; he does not perform well in athletics. Clem also has a difficult time learning hard subject matter, and his grades are marginal. Clem is well liked and more sociable than David. He is at ease with members of the opposite sex, and enjoys joking and having the companionship of same-sex age-mates. He has been in trouble for minor delinquency that resulted from running around with a group of older high school dropouts.

Clem is at ease when talking with people and represents himself well. He is not afraid to give his ideas on any topic and is forward when discussing his grades with teachers. He expects his teachers to defend their position for not having given him higher grades. He speaks out in class, often to get attention, but also to present what he feels are the correct points of view, especially on social issues and sports.

ANALYSIS OF CASE STUDY

The likelihood is that David, despite his abilities and physical attributes, does not have as secure a self-esteem as does Clem. His feelings about himself may cause him to be easily embarrassed, shy, and less assertive. Clem seems to have an inner security and confidence that allows him to feel at ease in his world. He even feels confident in areas in which he is not particularly competent, such as in the area of grades.

David, however, appears to have a more positive *self-concept* than does Clem.

David probably would describe himself as handsome, a good athlete, and intelligent. Clem's beliefs and opinions about himself are likely to be less positive. Persons observing both David and Clem, however, notice that Clem's self-esteem (his feelings about himself) is higher than that of David's.

This short case description of David and Clem does not permit an in-depth analysis of their identities. A longer description might provide answers to questions like the following:

What beliefs do Clem and David have?

What kind of vocation or work will they eventually choose?

Do they accept themselves the way they are now, or do they expect to change?

The *self-images* that David and Clem project to others will at times be high or low, depending on the current feedback that they receive from others. The likelihood is that Clem, because of his higher self-esteem, could handle more negative criticism than could David.

QUESTION: What causes adolescents to be on opposite poles of self-esteem and self-concept?

That is a complex question. One possible answer is that when Clem compares himself with his ideal self, the difference may not be great. His ideal self may not be as high as David's, and he may be able to accept himself as an average student and nonathlete and still feel comfortable. For David, the difference between his self-description and his description of his ideal self is large. Incidently, one method used to measure a positive self-concept is to ask adolescents to describe themselves and then describe their ideal selves. If frequent and large differences occur between the self and the ideal self, then the person is believed to have lower self-esteem.

Influences on self-esteem and self-concept

Stanley Coopersmith, who wrote a popular book entitled *The Antecedents of Self-Esteem* (Coopersmith 1967, 96–106), studied boys having high self-esteem and compared them with boys having low self-esteem. When investigating the parents of these children, he found that the low self-esteem children had parents who more frequently used physical punishment or the withholding of love as a means of discipline. High self-esteem youth had parents who used management techniques that emphasized strict and consistent discipline coupled with parental interest and concern for the child. Coopersmith's conclusion was that the most effective parenting minimizes punishment and avoids criticism and withdrawal of love.

QUESTION: What are the parental practices that result in high self-esteem?

An author of one textbook wrote the following guidelines for parents to develop or foster self-esteem:

1. Separate disapproval of the act from the disapproval of the child. Instead of saying "I am going to punish you because you are bad," say "I am upset about what you did."
2. Punishment should never be harsh or injurious to a child; don't physically punish a child while you are angry. Also remember [that] to give a child the message, "I don't love you right now," can be more painful than spanking. (Coon 1983, 386)

He also states:

What summary statements and conclusions can we make about the conditions associated with the developments of high self-esteem? . . . Most general statements about the antecedents of self-esteem can be given in terms of three conditions: Total or nearly total acceptance of the child by their parents, clearly defined and enforced limits, and respect and latitude for individual action that exists within the defined limits. (Coon 1983, 386)

These conclusions by Coon make the puzzle about why Clem has more self-esteem than David a little more understandable. Possibly David's parents were critical of him as he was growing up, and gave their love only when David excelled or met their expectations. The long-term impact of conditional or unconditional love that occurs over years and years of living together in a family setting is exceptionally forceful. Also possible is that David's parents were less likely than Clem's to clearly establish what they would accept and would not accept regarding personal behavior. Lastly, Clem's parents may have given him more respect and latitude for individual actions within the limits they imposed. Over a period of years, Clem may have been treated so that he experienced much individual freedom and was not fearful of failure; he knew basically what he could do and could not do without fearing the loss of love. This made him a more self-assured and confident individual, even though he lacked most of the attributes in which David far surpassed him.

Another factor should be considered when talking about self-esteem. A number of researchers have found that parents with high self-esteem also tend to have children with high self-esteem (Bateson 1944; Sears 1957). The reason for this is generally explained by the concept of identification. These theorists believe that children identify with their parents and thus acquire parental attributes, which would include the attribute of high self-esteem. The relationship between parents' self-esteem and their children's is one of modeling; parents with low self-esteem model low self-esteem attitudes and behaviors for their children, and their children imitate their example through the normal processes of learning (Coopersmith 1967, 242).

Peers, extended relatives, teachers, and friends may also be influential in directly influencing an adolescent's self-esteem. Although these groups of individuals are often not the primary sources of self-esteem for adolescents, they can still encourage them to have healthy levels of self-esteem by giving them unconditional love and acceptance. Unfortunately, these groups usually tend to give conditional love to adolescents.

QUESTION: What influences the development of a positive self-concept?

Apparently more variables are involved in the formation of self-concept than in the formation of self-esteem. The focus of research has been placed on variables other than the family to explain self-concept:

> A large variety of seemingly unimportant factors exerts a powerful effect on the adolescent's developing self-concept. The individual's name is one such factor. Nicknames and labels have been associated with maladjustment or superior adjustment. . . . Clothing among adolescents is much more than a protective covering . . . it is sometimes an expression of individuality. It can reveal a "self" that is concerned with its physical appearance, preoccupied with it, or unconcerned, a self that is deliberately and ruggedly non-conformist, or an approval-seeking that is uni-sexual, an active self, a quiet self, a happy self, a sad self. (LeFrancois 1981, 190)

Unquestionably, peer acceptance, rejection, and popularity influence one's self-appraisal (Staub 1979, 237–38). Peers can make critical contributions to the development of one's self-concept, as shown in the following young girl's statement.

> Throughout my adolescence I relied much on my friends to discuss my problems and aspirations. I felt that they would understand me better because I was able to confide in them things that to this day I cannot discuss with my parents. I basically had two or three close friends with whom I could deeply confide. Two of these friends were girls and I could see in them the way I thought a female was supposed to act. One of these girls went astray from many of her values/goals. By observing her mistakes, I tried to improve myself and keep close to my standards.
>
> The third friend was male and we were/are closer than I was with the former two. I attribute this to the fact that I did not feel intimidated by him as I did with most girls. There was not any competition between us.

In discussing other factors influencing self-concept, one author writes:

> The sense of self is modified by various factors including experiences with the body; for instance, the early maturer who feels out of place and extremely self-conscious. Indeed, adolescents cannot forget their bodies; the body is the external presentation of one's self to the world, and other persons continually remind one of it. Therefore, adolescents seek endlessly to modify the physical image of themselves to conform to and support the picture they wish to present to others. (Rogers 1978, 21)

QUESTION: Do personal accomplishments improve one's self-concept?

Yes, overt behavioral success does have an effect, at least superficially, upon an individual's self-concept. One student describes this:

I noticed that with myself, when I'm doing well in school my perception of myself is quite favorable. I also know that when I'm doing badly in school my self-image really takes a dive. That's a short example but it illustrates how this attitude of how I perceive myself is contingent upon my accomplishments.

I know from my working with retarded children, that their self-image is enhanced by the reinforcements (social praise, attention, etc.) they receive after accomplishing a certain task successfully. I think that is one of the reasons for the Special Olympic games for the retarded. It's to give them "success" experiences to help them see that they can successfully achieve certain tasks.

On the other hand, I caution against believing that this type of behavioral success will result in basic changes in an adolescent's self-esteem. Recall, for example, the case of David and Clem. One can see how David could acquire a positive self-concept due to his clothing, handsome appearance, athletic ability, grades in school, and so on, and yet still have a weak self-esteem. Perhaps this is because some variables tend to influence the self-concept, and other variables tend to influence the self-esteem.

Additional factors that influence the development of the self-concept include parental interest, parental concern, family social class, and even personal physical handicaps. Often discussed is the effect of a divorced home, but the research is not clear on this issue. Apparently the divorced family is not the problem, but

The self-concept more than self-esteem is influenced by achievement. Parental interest and concern in this achievement can also influence the development of the self-concept.

rather the quality of interpersonal relationships that are frequently associated with broken families (Rice 1983, 203–7). F. Philip Rice states, referring to the self-esteem of young girls,

> Late adolescent girls who feel close to their mothers tend to see themselves as confident, wise, reasonable, and self-controlled. Those who feel distant from their mothers tend to perceive themselves in negative terms: as rebellious, impulsive, touchy, and tactless. (Rice 1983, 205)

The self-concept is seemingly influenced by a variety of informational sources and behavioral accomplishments, whereas self-esteem is influenced more by the general way a person is treated.

QUESTION: Can people increase their self-concept and self-esteem?

Two different approaches may be used depending upon whether people want to enhance and improve their self-esteem or whether they want to improve their self-concept. Increasing and enhancing one's self-esteem apparently requires a longer period of time than that required to improve one's self-concept. Change results primarily from being treated with unconditional love and living in a secure world. Developing a more healthy self-esteem may require years; establishing healthy, long-term, permanent interpersonal relationships may be necessary.

The self-concept, on the other hand, may be more modifiable through educational experiences and situational accomplishments, changes, and achievements. For example, it may be possible to improve individual self-concept by providing adolescents with encouragement, by helping them achieve specific accomplishments, or by providing them with positive feedback through small-group discussions and short-term therapy.

Improving one's self-concept may be a preliminary stepping stone toward enhancement of self-esteem. The need for improving the self-concept can be seen in the case of the following young boy:

> "What is your favorite sport?" I began with a smile.
> "Baseball," he answered unsmilingly, "but I don't play very well."
> "What is your next favorite?"
> After considerable thought he answered, "Ice skating, but I am not very good at it." He gave a weary sigh.
> "What is your best friend's name?" I asked, hoping to touch a happier interest area.
> "Chuck, but he moved away. None of the other guys seem to like me."
> (Berne and Savary 1981, XV)

This child probably categorizes himself as unsuccessful in both sports and friendships. Undoubtedly, his self-esteem is weak and in jeopardy.

A psychologist who has studied ways to help children feel self-confident and resilient, provides the following insights into the development of self-confidence, self-concepts, and self-esteem:

1. Pointing out to children where they have excelled and praising their accomplishments help them through hard times.

2. What the child sees mirrored in her parents' eyes eventually becomes her self-portrait.
3. Without the basic trust that comes from a consistent nurturing household, attempts to bolster self-esteem rest on shaky foundation.
4. Realistically high expectations communicate to children that they are competent people, capable of doing well at age-appropriate tasks. Conversely, the children of parents who make few demands or maturity show little self-reliance. . . . Children interpret the lack of expectations as not caring and devaluing; they feel as if their parents are saying, we cannot ask anything of you. . . .
5. Older children become secure the more they can do for themselves and the greater the demands placed upon them for self-reliance. (Bernstein 1982, 54)

As a guide to assist parents to develop self-esteem and healthy self-concepts in their children, two child development specialists wrote the following:

1. Parents are the first and most important teachers.
   a. Parents serve as the primary models for the developing behaviors.
   b. Parents are powerful models because of the intimate relationship which exist between parent and child.
   c. One learns effectively when someone shows/demonstrates how to do a task.
   d. A relationship of trust, closeness, and openness must be built as a foundation before teaching through direct instruction will be effective.
2. A person is not born with a self-concept; it emerges through experiences and interactions with significant others. . . .
3. One needs to first feel a sense of belonging, competence and worth.
   a. A child feels a sense of belonging as he attaches himself to the parent and begins to make himself like the parent.
   b. Parents can help develop competencies by giving direct instructions and creating opportunities for success experiences to occur.
   c. One receives confirmation that he is of value and worth by the verbal and physical expressions of love which his parents show him.
4. A vital part of self-concept development consists of positive self-referent language such as "I can do it."
   a. An internal system of self-referent praise is a means of maintaining a positive self-concept.
   b. The commends one makes about himself reveal his inner feelings of self-worth.
5. Encouragement is directed at helping the youth feel worthy.
   a. Encouragement is the process of focusing on assets and strengths in order to build self-confidence and feelings of worth.
   b. Encouragement is valuing and accepting one as he is (not putting conditions on acceptance).
   c. Encouragement is pointing out the positive aspects of behavior.
   d. Encouragement is showing appreciation for effort and improvement (rather than requiring perfection and achievement).
   e. Encouragement is not praise associated with competition. It should be reserved for things accomplished and well-done. (Egelund and Vance 1980, 14)

To illustrate how a short-term experience can influence the self-concept, the following account of a young girl is presented:

When I was in Junior High, I had very little self-concept and self-esteem. I had a hard time relating to most kids my age. The image of myself was so low that anytime anyone would look at me wrong, I would just start crying. I hated myself and I wouldn't go anywhere. I didn't hang around other people because I was sure they hated me. I never got involved in anything or had a boyfriend.

At the start of my freshman year, my brother sat me down and really talked to me. He told me that I was worth a lot and that I shouldn't let people push me around. He told me to stand up and be a person. That year he made me run for student body treasurer and I won. He helped me a lot and I became aware of myself. I developed a positive concept of self. I began to be aware that I did have worth. I started fixing my hair more. I began to be asked out all the time and even went so far as to run for New Mexico State President of Future Homemakers of America. I learned how really important it is to have a good self-concept and image. It made a big difference in my life.

Roger P. Coplen and James D. MacArthur (1982) have developed a program to enhance and strengthen internal sources of self-esteem. (See Tables 3–2 and 3–3 to contrast the external versus internal supports of self-esteem.) They believe that "human beings often typically seek *outside* sources of approval, acceptance, affirmation, validation, and direction." Seeking outside (external) sources of personal strength has a tendency to create weaknesses within individuals, along with an inability to be self-reliant. As adolescents seek feelings of worth and love, they at times tenaciously embrace external "sources" of these feelings, which are unfortunately inaccurate and inadequate:

They think success is love. They think money, clothes, cars, or things are love. They think sex is love. They think drug-trips are love. They think crime is love. They think super-activity is love. It's a long list of right and wrong things, but all done for wrong reasons. Where does this leave you? Out of which list have you experienced most of your love supplies? The real love list will make you feel genuine, very happy, and super secure. The cheap substitutes will make you nervous, afraid, phony, showy, trapped, confused, distant, cold, dependent, weak and so on and so on. (Coplen and MacArthur 1982, 107)

TABLE 3–2 A Popular View of Self-Worth, Self-Esteem, and Self-Concept

Externals	Internals (Self-Worth)	How I Feel about What I See, or Self-Esteem	Self-Concept
Physical "Me"	Personal value	Shaky, questionable,	Consists of all that I
Social "Me"	Fundamental worth	and unstable	am aware of:
Intellectual "Me"	as a human being	Conditional	Knowledge
Emotional "Me"	Feelings of being	Negotiable	Insights
The perceived "Me"	lovable and	Transitory	Feelings
The ideal "Me"	capable	Fluctuating	My place in
"I" am not in full	"I" am at the mercy		humanity (roles)
control—heredity	of my externals		Is positive as long as
and environment	"I" am what "I" do		my externals hold
have their inputs	(performance)		up and my internals
			don't "crash"

Source: Adapted from Roger D. Coplen and James D. MacArthur, *Developing a Healthy Self-Image* (Provo, Utah: Brigham Young University Press, 1982).

TABLE 3-3 A Different View of Self-Worth, Self-Esteem, and Self-Concept

Internals (Self Worth)	Externals	How I Feel about What I See, or Self-Esteem	Self-Concept
Personal value	Physical "Me"	Highest level achieved when my thoughts, feelings, and behaviors match my internal identity	Consists of all that I am aware of: Knowledge Insights Feelings My place in humanity (roles) Will remain positive as long as my vision is clear and my externals serve "Me"
Fundamental worth as a human being	Social "Me"		
Feelings of being lovable and capable	Intellectual "Me"		
Serves as anchor to personal identity	Emotional "Me"		
The "diamond"	The things "I" do (performance)		
Internal identity	The perceived "Me"		
"I" am in control	The ideal "Me"		
The real "Me"	"I" am not in full control—heredity and environment have their inputs		
(I am lovable and capable)		(vision)	

Source: Adapted from Roger D. Coplen and James D. MacArthur, *Developing a Healthy Self-Image* (Provo, Utah: Brigham Young University Press, 1982).

Eventually, many individuals discover that they cannot develop feelings of worth, lovableness, self-esteem, or a strong sense of identity simply by relying on external circumstances or by "earning" it. David Burns of the University of Pennsylvania Medical School clarifies this:

> And what, in the final analysis, is the source of genuine self-esteem? This, in my opinion, is the most important question you will ever confront.
>
> First, you cannot earn worth through what you do. Achievements can bring you satisfaction but not happiness. Self-worth based on accomplishments is a "Pseudo-esteem," not the genuine thing! My many successful but depressed patients would all agree. Nor can you base a valid sense of self-worth on your looks, talent, fame, or fortune. Marilyn Monroe, Mark Rothko, Freddie Prinz, and a multitude of famous suicide victims attest to this grim truth. Nor can love, approval, friendship, or a capacity for close, caring human relationships add one iota to your inherent worth. The great majority of depressed individuals are in fact very much loved, but it doesn't help one bit because self-love and self-esteem are missing. "So," you may be asking with some exasperation, "How do I get a sense of self-worth?" (David Burns in Coplen and MacArthur 1982, 17)

Coplen and MacArthur feel that worth is innate and that within each and every human being is a genuine source of self-worth and self-esteem. This source of worth comes with understanding the basic nature of every individual. Abraham Maslow briefly described this basic nature:

> We have, each one of us, an essential inner nature which is instinctoid, intrinsic, given, "nature," which tends strongly to persist. . . . This is "raw material" rather than the finished product. This inner core shows itself as natural inclination, propensities or inner bent. This raw material very quickly starts growing into a self as it meets the world outside and begins to have transaction with it. Each person's inner nature has some characteristics which all other selves have (species-wide) and some which are unique to the person (idiosyncratic). The need for love characterizes every human being that is born. (Maslow 1968, 3)

Adolescents can discover what their real sources of worth are as they learn to internalize the fact that all individuals have worth simply because they are alive and exist. Each specific person also has numerous unique combinations of qualities that seem to persist regardless of the external circumstances (e.g., sensitivity, kindness, appreciation for beauty, desire for happiness). By understanding these concepts, adolescents can develop internal feelings of self-esteem and worth that will persist regardless of the successes or failures they experience in life:

> Being internal in nature we already [have] personal value and fundamental worth and we ought to put our basic, internal identity *into* our external world and make them (externals) serve us. When we *make* our externals serve us and maintain an accurate vision of our internal identity, we have two sources of feeling more lovable and capable (self-esteem) so that as we grow older and/or lose control of our externals, we can still maintain a certain level of value because we *see* our internal nature. (Coplen and MacArthur 1982, 112)

Variations in self-concept

QUESTION: Can an individual's self-concept and behavior differ from situation to situation?

Mark Snyder, a professor of psychology at the University of Minnesota, has developed a theory and a test of "self-monitoring" (Snyder 1981). In his research, he found that some people have an ability to carefully monitor their own performance and to strictly adjust their behavior in order to regulate their impact on other people. He believes that professional actors, lawyers, salespeople, confidence artists, and politicians are skilled at adapting their mannerisms and behavior to influence others. Snyder also feels that these people seek out the information about the best mode for their self-presentation. This can be used for good or bad. He points out that a high self-monitoring orientation may be purchased at the cost of having one's actions reflect and communicate little about one's real attitudes, feelings, and disposition:

> I believe that high self-monitoring individuals and low self-monitoring individuals have very different ideas about what constitutes a self and that their notions are quite well suited to how they live. High self-monitoring individuals regard themselves as rather flexible and adaptive people who tailor their social behavior shrewdly and pragmatically to fit appropriate conditions. They believe that a person is whatever he appears to be in any particular situation: "I am the me, the me I am right now." This self-image fits very well . . . by contrast, low self-monitoring individuals have a firmer, more single-minded idea of what their self should be. They value and strive for congruence between "who they are" and "what they do" and regard their actions as faithful reflections of how they feel and think. For them, a self is a single identity that must not be compromised for other people or in certain situations. (Snyder 1981, 223)

This whole concept of self-monitoring and changing behavior raises questions as to which type of person is desirable. From one perspective, the high self-monitoring person could be called flexible; on the other hand, the high self-monitoring person could be called an expedient person who has not achieved a stable self-identity.

QUESTION: Can self-concept have both positive and negative elements?

Yes, and sometimes large differences are present in the self-concept between separate personal characteristics. Consider the following account:

> As I was growing up my mother often instilled in me good ideas about myself. She told me that I was fun, nice, and had a great personality. She also instilled within me some bad ideas as well. She always told me that I was overweight, had a fat nose, had thin weepy hair, and had pimples. Subsequently, I gained a good self-concept as far as personality went, but a poor self-concept physically. I always thought I was ugly growing up. Luckily I felt pretty good about my personality and so I felt halfway good about myself. It took a long time of comparing myself to others and getting other opinions before I came to the realization that I wasn't as ugly as I had previously thought. Even now, sometimes I will think I have a fat nose or something like that. Those concepts have stuck with me all these years.

Summary

Erikson, a neo-psychoanalyst, developed a sequence of eight psychosocial stages through which every individual must pass. During each stage, a particular developmental task must be accomplished to ensure that the individual gains a healthy, normal personality. The eight stages are as follows:

1. Sense of trust versus mistrust
2. Sense of autonomy versus shame and doubt
3. Sense of initiation versus guilt
4. Sense of industry versus inferiority
5. Sense of identity versus identity diffusion
6. Sense of intimacy versus isolation
7. Sense of generativity versus stagnation
8. Sense of integrity versus despair

The first four stages should be resolved before adolescence. At the onset of adolescence, each person enters the fifth stage and must develop a sense of identity rather than a sense of identity diffusion.

Our society allows individuals an opportunity to develop a sense of identity by providing them with a psychological moratorium—"an authorized delay of adulthood." During this time, adolescents can work through their problems as they try to achieve a complete identity. During the moratorium, significant adults have a tremendous influence upon the development of adolescent identities. These adults can help adolescents by giving them the freedom to experiment with different roles and by actively listening to their concerns, opinions, and dreams.

If youths have successfully accomplished all of the preadolescent developmental tasks, and if they can integrate the different parts of their personality during adolescence, they will be able to achieve a sense of identity. Erikson believes that when an individual gains a sense of identity, he feels continuity between that which he has come to be during the long years of childhood and that which he promises to become in the anticipated future. If the individual fails to gain a feeling of identity, a sense of role diffusion will develop.

James R. Marcia, a researcher who prefers to measure identity through the use of clinical interviews, has expanded Erikson's concept of identity formation into four identity states: (1) identity achievement, (2) moratorium, (3) foreclosure, and (4) diffusion. Most individuals make the greatest gains in their identity formations during late adolescence, especially if they are in a college environment.

Identity development is often closely related to ego functioning. In other words, as an individual's personality matures, the person may be more capable of progressing toward a sense of identity. The resolution of the identity crisis and the achievement of a sense of identity in turn affect many other variables, such as peer adjustment, decision-making styles, cognitive styles, sex role identities.

Several terms are frequently used in discussions about personality and identity: (1) *self*, "that part of one's personality of which one is aware," (2) *self-concept*, the opinions and beliefs that adolescents have about themselves, (3) *self-esteem*, the emotional evaluation adolescents make about themselves, (4) *self-image,* a temporary self-concept, and (5) *identity,* the general components of a total personality.

Various factors can influence individual self-esteem. Social class is one such factor. Other factors that influence personal identity development include family, the type of discipline parents use, and the quality of long-term relationships the person has with other individuals.

Various social factors can also influence the development of a positive self-concept. They include, among others, an individual's name, nicknames and labels, dress and grooming, peer acceptance, experiences with the body, behavioral successes, educational experiences, and situational accomplishments.

Self-concept and self-esteem vary somewhat from situation to situation and from year to year. Also, most individuals have self-concepts that reflect some positive opinions as well as some negative opinions about themselves. People who are high self-monitors tend to have the most fluctuating self-concepts and feelings of self-esteem.

References

Adams, G. R., & S. A. Fitch. 1981. Ego states and identity status development: a cross-lag analysis. *Journal of Adolescence* 4: 163–71.
Agrawal, P. 1978. A cross-cultural study of self-image: Indian, American, Australian, and Irish adolescents. *Journal of Youth and Adolescence* 7(1):107–16.
Bateson, G. 1944. Cultural determinants of personality. In *Personality and behavior disorders,* vol. 2, ed. H. J. McVicker. New York: Ronald Press.
Berne, P. H., & L. M. Savary. 1981. *Building self-esteem in children.* New York: Continuum Publishing.
Bernstein, A. C. 1982. Feeling great. *Parents,* September, 51–56.
Block, J. 1961. Ego identity, role variability, and adjustment. *Journal of Consultation and Psychology* 25:362–97.
Blum, R. H. 1972. *Horatio Alger's children.* San Francisco: Jossey-Bass.
Cahoon, O. W., A. H. Price, & A. L. Scoresby. 1979. *Parents and the achieving child.* Provo, Utah: Brigham Young Univ. Press.
Combs, A. W., et al. 1974. *The professional education of teachers.* 2d ed. Boston: Allyn & Bacon.
Constantinople, A. 1969. An Erikson measure of personal development in college students. *Developmental Psychology* 1:357–72.
Coon, D. 1983. *Introduction to psychology.* St. Paul, Minn.: West Publishing.
Coopersmith, S. 1967. *The antecedents of self-esteem.* San Francisco: Freeman.
Coopersmith, S., & W. H. Freeman. 1968. Studies in self-esteem. *Scientific American* 218:96–106.
Coplen, R. D., & J. D. MacArthur. 1982. *Developing a healthy self-image.* Provo, Utah: Brigham Young Univ. Press.
Dinkmeyer, D., & G. D. McKay. 1976. *Parents' handbook; systematic training for effective parenting.* Circle Pines, Minn.: American Guidance Services.
———. 1976. *Systematic training for effective parenting.* Circle Pines, Minn.: American Guidance Services.
Donovan, J. M. 1975. Identity status and interpersonal style. *Journal of Youth and Adolescence* 4:37–56.
Douvan, E., & J. Adelson. 1966. *The adolescent experience.* New York: Wiley.
Dworetzky, J. P. 1981. *Introduction to child development.* St. Paul, Minn.: West Publishing.
Egelund, R., & J. Vance. 1980. A guide to assist parents in the development of positive self-concepts in young children. Unpublished manuscript, via personal communica-

tion to author, Brigham Young University, Provo, Utah. Abridged and edited.
Erikson, E. 1958. *Young man Luther*. New York: Norton.
_____. 1963. *Childhood and society*. 2d ed. New York: Norton.
_____. 1964. *Insight and responsibility*. New York: Norton.
_____. [1952] 1966. A healthy personality for every child. Reprint. *Healthy personality for your child*, no. 337–1952. U.S. Department of Health, Education, and Welfare. Children's Bureau. Washington, D.C.: U.S. Government Printing Office.
_____. 1968. *Identity, youth, and crisis*. New York: Norton.
Felker, D. W. 1974. *Building positive self-concepts*. Minneapolis, Minn.: Burgess Publishing.
Fields, A. B. 1981. Perceived parent behavior and the self-evaluations of lower-class black male and female children. *Adolescence* 16 (64): 919–32 (Winter).
Fitts, W. 1965. *Tennessee self-concept scale*. Nashville, Tenn.: Counselor Recording and Tests.
Frazier, D. J., & R. R. Deblaasie. 1982. A comparison of self-concept in Mexican American and non-Mexican American late adolescents. *Adolescence* 17(66):327–33 (Summer).
Fromm, E. 1956. *The art of loving*. New York: Bantam Books.
Goode, E. 1970. *The marijuana smokers*. New York: Basic Books.
Greene, L. B. 1928. The minority psychology of adolescents: A concept for adult equanimity and rationality. *Adolescence* 17(67):585–603 (Fall).
Hilgard, F. R. 1957. *Introduction to psychology*. New York: Harcourt Brace Jovanovich.
Jones, E. E. 1979. Personality characteristics of black youth: A cross-cultural investigation. *Journal of Youth and Adolescence* 8(2):149–58.
Kanter, D., & W. Lehr. 1975. *Inside the family: Toward a theory of family process*. New York: Harper & Row.
Kohn, M. L. 1959. Social class and parental values. *American Journal of Sociology* 64:387–97.
_____. 1969. *Class and conformity: A study in values*. Homewood, Ill.: Dorsey.
Laufer, R. S. 1971. Sources of generational consciousness and conflict. *Annals of the American Academy of Political Science* 395:80–94.
LeFrancois, G. 1981. *Adolescence*. 2d ed. Belmont, Calif.: Wadsworth.
Maier, H. W. 1965. *Three theories of child development*. New York: Harper & Row.
Marcia, J. E. 1967. Ego identity status: Relationship to change in self-esteem, general maladjustment, and authoritarianism. *Journal of Personality* 1:118–33.
_____. 1980. Identity and adolescence. In *Handbook of adolescent psychology*, ed., J. Adelson. New York: Wiley.
Marcia, J. E., & A. S. Waterman. 1982. Identity development from adolescence through adulthood: An extension of theory and a review of research. *Developmental Psychology* 18(3):348–58.
Maslow, A. H. 1968. *Toward a psychology of being*. 2d ed. Princeton, N.J.: D. Van Nostrand.
Newman, B. M., & P. R. Newman. 1978. The concept of identity: Research and theory. *Adolescence* 13(49):157–66.
Newsweek. 1970. Psychoanalyst Erik Erikson and the search for identity. 21 December, 84.
Orlofsky, J. L., J. E. Marcia, & I. M. Lasser. 1973. Ego identity status and the intimacy versus isolation crisis of young adulthood. *Journal of Personal Sociology and Psychology* 27:211–19.
Podd, M. H. 1972. Ego identity status and morality: The relationship between two developmental constructs. *Developmental Psychology* 6:497–507.
Rice, P. 1981. *The adolescent*. Boston: Allyn & Bacon.
Robertson, I. 1977. *Sociology*. New York: Worth.
Robinson, J. P., & P. R. Shaver. 1973. *Measures of social psychological attitudes*. Ann Arbor: Survey Research Center, Institute for Social Research.
Rogers, D. 1978. *Adolescence: A psychological perspective*. Monterey, Calif.: Bookscomb.
Rosmussen, J. E. 1961. An experimental approach to the concept of ego identity as related to character disorder. *Dissertation Abstracts* 22: 1711–12, university microfilms no. 61–3723.
_____. 1964. Relation of ego identity to psychosocial effectiveness. *Psychology Report* 16:815–25.
Santrock, J. W. 1983. *Adolescence: An introduction*. Dubuque, Iowa: Brown.
Sawrey J., & C. Telford. 1963. *The dynamics of mental health: Psychology of adjustment*. Boston: Allyn & Bacon.

Schenkel, S. 1975. Relationship among ego identity status, field-independence, and traditional femininity. *Journal of Youth and Adolescence* 4:73–82.

Sears, R. R. 1957. Identification as a form of parental development. In *The concept of development*, ed. D. B. Harris. Minneapolis: Univ. of Minnesota Press.

Simmons, D. D. 1970. The development of an objective measure of identity achievement status. *Journal of Protective Techniques and Personality Assessment* 34:241–44.

Snyder, M. 1981. The many needs of the self-monitor. In *Human development*, annual editions, ed. H. Fitzgerald. Guilford, Conn.: Dushkin.

Stark, P. H., & A. H. Traxler. 1974. Empirical validation of Erikson's theory of identity crisis on late adolescence. *Journal of Psychology* 4(84):25–33.

Staub, E. 1979. *Positive social behavior and morality*. New York: Academic Press.

Turner, R. H. 1968. The self-conception in social interaction. In *The self in social interaction*, ed. C. Gordon & K. J. Gergen. New York: Wiley.

Waterman, A. S., P. S. Geary, & C. K. Waterman. 1974. A longitudinal study of changes in ego identity from the freshman to the senior year at college. *Developmental Psychology* 10:387–92.

Waterman, C. K., & A. S. Waterman. 1974. Ego identity status and decision styles. *Journal of Youth and Adolescence*, 387–92.

Worley, S. E. 1967. Parents are also teachers. *Childhood Education* 43: 10–15.

SECTION TWO

influences

4 Adolescent Peer Relationships
5 The Family
6 Adolescence and Education
7 Biological Influences
8 The Media: Music, Video, Television, Film, Literature, and Pornography

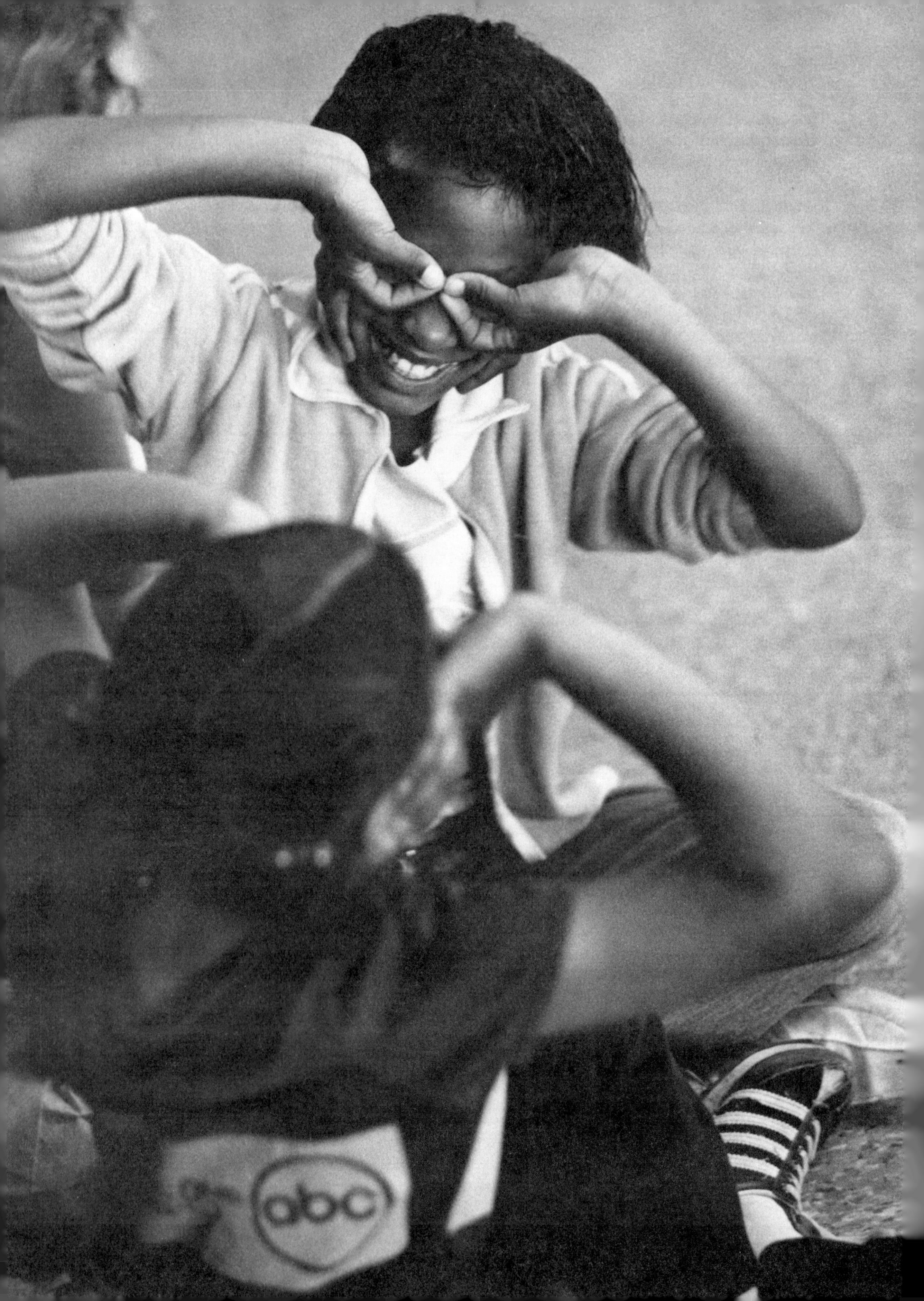
abc

CHAPTER FOUR

Adolescent peer relationships

SURVEY AND QUESTIONS

This chapter deals with peer group influences and relationships in adolescence. Reading the chapter will provide answers to the following questions:

Conformity

Is there a difference between the basic values of peers, adolescents, and their parents—that is, a generation gap?
Are peer-oriented youth at a disadvantage?
What causes acceptance and popularity within the peer group?
How important is physical attractiveness in adolescent peer relationships?

Peer Groups

Are there different types of peer groups?
What are the characteristics of different cliques?
Why do adolescents often speak differently from adults?
Is conformity to the peer group good or bad?
What is anticonformity?
What is other-conformity?
How does independence differ from anticonformity and other-conformity?
Why is peer group experience important?
How can recognizing this importance help adults relate to adolescents?

Friendships

Do the findings regarding the peer group apply to friendships?
What is the importance of friends during adolescence?
Is there a difference between boys and girls in their friendships?
Are friendships and peer group experience important for later development?

Adolescent Marriages

What are the causes of adolescent marriages?
What attitudes do peers and parents have toward adolescent marriages?
What problems do teenage parents face?
How important is parental support to an adolescent marriage and pregnancy?

Conformity

At age 12 I was in junior high school and I was beginning to feel pretty old and pretty smart. My parents were old people who had lost touch with the new generation of kids. I knew about the generation gap and used it to explain any differences that existed between my parents and me. During this time the girls at school were all wearing barrettes in their hair. I, of course, wanted to be in vogue with the rest of the group so I put my hair back in barrettes. The only problem was that my bangs were not long enough and I looked awful wearing my hair that way. My mother told me I looked hideous with my hair that way but I wouldn't listen—she was old and couldn't relate to the new generation so I ignored her and continued to wear my hair that way, despite the continual warnings of how awful it looked from my mother. I finally grew out of that phase and when I look back at pictures of me I can hardly believe I wore it like that. What you can be convinced to do to be part of the group as a youth always amazes me.

Adolescents frequently go through this type of conformity experience during the adolescent years. A similar account was given by the following student as she reflected on her experience as an adolescent:

> When I was in junior high school I felt a great desire to fit in. It was really important that you wore just the right kind of clothes. If you didn't you were looked down on and sometimes teased. I remember my mother would make me clothes and they would just sit in our closet because they weren't what everyone else wore. I also remember rolling up my skirts when I got to school so I wouldn't feel different. One of my friend's mother wouldn't let her wear tennis shoes so she snuck them to school and then put them on. You had to have your Levis a certain way with frayed bottoms and split up the side or inserts. Your hair had to be worn a certain way. If you were too skinny or too big busted or too small busted you weren't cool. Now that I look back on that time in my life I don't see how I stood it or really understand why I felt such a need to be like everyone else and accepted by them.

Researchers have found an increase in conformity and an increasing power by the peer group as one approaches adolescence (Asubel 1958; Cambell 1964; Stone and Schultz 1968; Coleman 1980). A closer look at what is happening, however, indicates that a reversal of the trend occurs at approximately age twelve or thirteen, with a continuing decrease in conformity to peer pressure (Costanzo and Shaw 1966; Iscoe, Williams, and Hardy 1963; Costanzo 1970). Figure 4–1 illustrates this trend. Note, however, that while conformity decreases, it is still high during the adolescent years.

Costanzo states:

> [T]he suggestibility of the child to peer influence increases with age into pubescence, after which the efficacy of peer influence and decent public conformity decline with increasing age. The ability of the peer group to influence a child's behavior increases in function and increases the child's involvement with this group, and decreases with the adolescent's gradual disengagement from his peer group. Naturalistic and experimental observations of peer interaction support the notion that children become increasingly oriented to and involved with the peer group between middle childhood and pubescence. . . . On the

Figure 4-1 Percentage of conformity as a function of age level (N = 36 per age level)

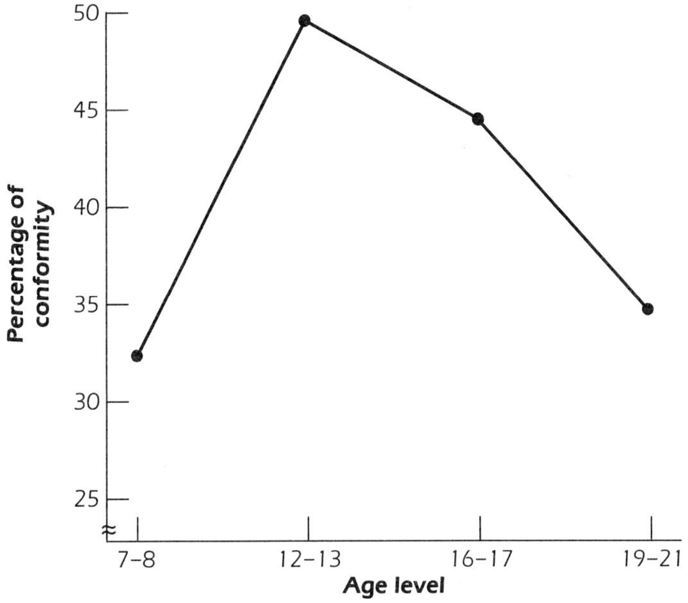

Source: P. R. Costanzo, "Conformity Development as Reproach or Self-Blame," *Journal of Personality and Social Psychology* 14: 368 (1970).

other hand, as a child moves into late adolescence, factors such as enhanced personality identity, increased social competence, and more firmly rooted social self-esteem merges countervailing forces against the influence of the group. The observed decreases in conformity during ages 13–21 [see Figure 4–1] should not be viewed as a simple reduction in the importance of the peer group, for this interpretation defies both logic and findings of experimental investigation which dealt with conformity. Rather, a more likely interpretation is that the importance of self increases relative to the importance of the group. Therefore, the adolescent and young adult become more able to resist pressures of the group. (Costanzo 1970, 370)

Nonetheless, during the junior high school years (ages twelve, thirteen, and fourteen), the powerful effect of the peer group is felt most strongly and in some cases has a tragic effect on youth, especially those with weak identities. In considering her past, one student aptly characterizes this strain between the group and her developing sense of identity:

I know with myself the first group I attached myself to in high school was a group whose morals, opinions, thoughts and goals were very different from my own. But to be an accepted member of this group I was to accept these ideals and goals. It took me two years to convince myself that my group wasn't me. Through high school I went to attach myself to several different groups,

The years of greatest conformity are during the early years (12–15) of adolescence. It is during these years that the effects of a peer group are felt most strongly.

finding out that these groups weren't me. Some groups had some of my ideals and goals but none had all of them. It took me well into college to realize that I had my own feelings and goals and opinions and these were just as valid and good as anyone else's. I finally figured out that my own identity would never be item for item the same as any one group of friends, or any one person for that matter, and that that was OK. I think we need to teach our adolescents that groups are great to be in. It gives them people to associate with but I think more importantly is that they realize their opinions and feelings will differ from their groups and that this is OK—that is their identity.

One would be hard pressed to find a group of people who have less personal freedoms than American junior high school youth. Their peer group dictates the color and style of clothing, even to within one inch of the length of trousers or skirts. Also, deviance from the established preference in music or food is criticized within the clique or crowd. Fortunately, this extreme pressure for conformity gradually decreases. The dependence in conformity is especially important for low-status youth (Harvey and Rutherford 1960). In review of the effects of age on conformity, one author states:

To conclude, we can be very confident in saying conformity is at its height among the early adolescent group but that it diminishes significantly from about 14 or 15 on up. Girls, under some circumstances at least, appear to be more conforming than boys are, although the differences between the sexes are not unduly large. Conforming is affected by status in the peer group as well as by self-blame, and it would undoubtedly by of interest to examine its relation to other personality variables. Evidently, by middle adolescence some individuals are beginning to see that there are advantages to be gained from independence, and the number of persons taking such a view clearly increases rapidly from this age onward. (Coleman, 1980, 424)

QUESTION: Is there a difference between the basic values of peers, adolescents, and their parents—that is, a generation gap?

One approach to answer this question has been to compare the attitudes of high school and college adolescents with those of their parents (Leonard and Pendarf 1971; Meisels and Canter 1971; Leonard et al. 1972; Weinstock and Leonard 1972). In general, when groups of adolescents and parents have significant differences, they generally deal with amount of difference rather than direction of differences. That is, instead of being opposites, the difference between parents and youth is in terms of how strongly they feel about something. These researchers conclude that there is little evidence of major discrepancies between adolescents and their parents. When different they are usually on more superficial items (e.g., dress and language), but on the more fundamental issues, differences between parents and youth are minimal.

One of the best explanations for the difficulty in drawing conclusions about the prevailing belief in a generation gap appears in a popular textbook. The authors give four points to consider in attempting to understand this false dichotomy: (1) There is much overlap in values between parents and peers; (2) in areas where parents lack conviction or belief, youth are more likely to turn toward peers for opinion and backing; (3) the tendency and desire and need to conform vary greatly from individual to individual; and (4) the personality, maturity, family relationships, and type of family from which an adolescent comes all need to be considered (Conger and Peterson 1984, 303–4).

Furthermore, homes where positive emotions are expressed and felt between parents and youth were homes in which youth did not worry about choosing between parents and peers (Larsen 1972a 1972b). Thus the generation gap and the perceived antagonism between parents and peers are more popular stereotypes than fact. In most instances parents and peers will agree because of the common background and culture.

Peer-oriented and peer-dominated youth generally come from homes in which parents are not as salient. Researcher Urie Bronfenbrenner pointed out that the peer-oriented child is more a product of parental disregard than of the attractiveness of the peer group. Conforming children turn to their age-mates less by choice than by default from the vacuum left by the withdrawal of parents and adults. The lives of such youths are filled with the undesired—and possibly undesirable—substitute of a ruling peer group (Bronfenbrenner 1970, 96).

QUESTION: Are peer-oriented youth at a disadvantage?

At least one researcher has found negative correlates (Larsen 1983). He states:

> The peer oriented youth generally had a lower self evaluation than more adult oriented youth. They tended to see themselves as more antisocial "meanor"

and were more pessimistic. As might be expected they did not value achievement and academic work as much as adult oriented youth.

Perhaps the nature of peer activities in part explains this. According to this research their peer activities were less social involving; teasing others, playing hooky, listening to records, parties, and even crime.

In a related study it was found that among 75 adolescents in a Chicago high school found that peer activities were more open, free, and fun, with more joking. However, these adolescents who spent more time with friends than with family showed poorer school performance and undermined variability. The research concluded that while friendship interactions are experienced more positively they have negative components. They feel the constant and sometimes negative feedback within the family is desirable.

The mixture of discouragement and encouragement that a family provides keeps those remaining in its orbit on the track towards adulthood. (Larsen 1983, 747)

The ironic element in this discussion is that the adult-oriented youth often emerge as having greater acceptance by the peer group. Components of family experience enhance self-confidence and independence, leading to more peer acceptance (Purnell 1970).

Another complication of this issue is that the parents of adult-oriented youth seem to have the attributes commonly associated with good parenting. Parents of adult-oriented adolescents were considered to be more loving, involved, and better companions, yet they delivered more discipline (Condry and Simon 1974).

QUESTION: What causes acceptance and popularity within the peer group?

Two significant studies (Coleman 1960, 1961; Horowitz 1967) conclude that popularity in both sexes is related to personality, sociability, and athletic ability. Other studies have shown that physical attractiveness is positively correlated with popularity (Coleman 1960, 1961; Cabior and Dokecki 1973). A survey conducted by Sebald (1981) found that primary emphasis is placed on peer conformity as a condition for popularity. Forty-seven percent of the teenagers who were interviewed stressed the importance of conforming in attitude, clothing, speech, actions, and interests of peers. The significance of conformity as related to peer acceptance is illustrated in the following experience:

> I went to a private Catholic school, and when I was in seventh grade there were two major groups of girls. There were the "good," those who didn't smoke, drink, read pornography, or "make-out" with the guys; and the "bad," those who did all the things the "good" girls didn't do. Everyone pretty much belonged to one group or the other, but each girl had to behave in character or she was no longer "accepted" in that group.

The study by Sebald showed that teenagers who placed the most emphasis on popularity not only were influenced by their peers but also received some pressure from their parents. As a whole, adolescents have an urgent need for acceptance and popularity, which often causes pressure and stress in varying degrees. Adults, rather than adding to this stress, could better help the adolescent build self-esteem and self-confidence. This can be done by providing the adolescent with structured guidance as well as freedom of choice.

One study found that conformity was the most commonly cited way to become popular (Sebald 1981). The results of the survey are presented in Table 4–1.

TABLE 4–1 Answers and Percentage Distribution for Males and Females in 1976 to the Question, What Is Expected of a Teenager by His or Her Friends in Order to be Popular with Them?

	Males	Females	Average
1. Conformity (in activity, argot, attitude, dress, interest)	37	55	47
2. Being friendly, courteous, and getting along with others	40	40	40
3. Being yourself, being an individual	18	20	19
4. Good personality	10	20	14
5. Sense of humor, being cheerful, being fun to be with	11	12	11
6. Being cool	11	8	9
7. Helping, caring, and taking an interest in others	0	17	8
8. Being trustworthy, honest	11	5	8
9. Good looking	4	10	7
10. Having money	4	0	2
11. Good reputation	2	2	2
12. Not being gay	0	4	2
13. Keeping up with fashions	0	2	1
14. Antiestablishment behavior	2	0	1

Source: Hans Sebald, "Adolescent Concepts of Popularity and Unpopularity, Comparing 1960 with 1976," *Adolescence* 16(61): 189 (Spring 1981).

Again, adolescents stressed the importance of doing the same things, talking the same way, holding the same attitudes, dressing in the same style, and demonstrating the same interests. This was found to be true especially among girls.

QUESTION: How important is physical attractiveness in adolescent peer relationships?

The importance of attractiveness is illustrated in this recollection:

> I can remember the feelings of intense elation and excitement upon having a date with a girl who was generally and unanimously considered by myself and my peers to be what was termed an "absolute fox."
>
> There was never any doubt cast as to her more apparent virtues exemplified in face and figure which in high school often prove to be much more influential over the lesser requirements of intelligence, character or personality.

Studies have shown that peer conformity is an important condition for popularity within the peer group.

Possessing attractiveness is not a sufficient condition to ensure one's popularity and most people are not at the extremes. Other variables do operate to influence popularity, but meeting societies pattern of physical beauty has been found to be a powerful determinant.

Studies conducted by Langlois and Stephan (1977), Dion (1973), Kleck, Richardson, and Ronald (1974), Miller (1970), and Lerner and Lerner (1977) all indicate that physical attractiveness is positively related to positive peer relations. Adults and children believe that attractive children engage in more socially desirable behaviors than do unattractive children and are selected as potential friends (Dion 1973; Lerner and Lerner 1977). A variety of experiments have also shown that attractiveness is an important indication of how well students will be liked by others (Styczymski and Langlois 1977).

The evidence is inconclusive as to what age children begin to discriminate differences in facial attractiveness, but Cavoir and Lombardi (1973) distinguish age six as the point at which children begin to use similar or common criteria in judging physical attractiveness. Research demonstrates that an individual's physical attractiveness does affect others' reactions to the individual (Dion and Berscheid 1974) and that attractive children are liked more and are perceived as being smarter than unattractive children. Attractive children apparently have a distinct sociometric advantage over their less attractive counterparts, both socially and in the classroom (Dion 1973; Langlois and Stephan 1977).

Conforming to society's pattern of physical beauty can sometimes be an active learning process.

Peer groups

QUESTION: Are there different types of peer groups?

The answer to this question requires some definitions. First consider a clique. One author defines a clique in this way: "A clique comes into existence when two or more persons are related one to another in minimum fellowship that involves 'going places and doing things'" (Hollingshead 1949). Cliques are usually unisexual and are in most cases easily identified by their members. A strong in-group and out-group orientation exists in that cliques are not permeable and membership is selected, restricted, and definite. In the following case study, a student recalls her first real encounter with this orientation:

> When I first moved into a new small town, I learned what cliques were all about. There was a very strong line as to who was in the clique and who was out. The people in the clique were nice to me only as much as they *had* to be and no more. There was no question in anyone's mind as to who was in and who was out.

A clique should be distinguished from a gang in that a gang is much larger and its membership more formal. Cliques often refer to middle-class culture, whereas gangs refer to lower-class culture and are often deviant, or at least connote deviance. Both gangs and cliques demand compliance and deliver sanctions to members who deviate (McGovern 1967). A crowd is the least formal of these categories and is usually a combination of cliques. Whereas intimate relationships are present within cliques and gangs, crowds are more temporary, informal, and action oriented. The different functions of each can be explained in the following way:

> Cliques and crowds perform different functions for their members. The clique, smaller in size (with an upper limit in one study of nine members), permits

and encourages a far higher degree of intimacy and group cohesion than the larger crowd. The limited membership of cliques makes possible the strong cohesion which characterizes them. (Conger and Peterson 1984, 334)

This function is contrasted with the larger crowd which is often a way of responding to institutions or other crowds. A crowd may serve the collective needs of individuals, especially social needs for they provide a selection of other individuals to associate with (Durphy 1963, 235).

QUESTION: What are the characteristics of different cliques?

Perhaps the high school provides the best example of cliques that can and do receive distinctive labels. One investigation (Riester and Zucker 1968) found that one group could be called "collegiates." This group had the upwardly mobile, middle-class, socially active, all-American students. Another group was called the "leathers." These were persons on the fringe of acceptable society. A third group received the names of "beatniks," "hippies," and "freaks" during the time the study was conducted. Other groups were the "quiet kids," who independently did their own thing and sometimes did not participate in a group, and the "intellectuals," who as a group studied a lot and were serious about academic pursuits. There were also the "going steady kids," who spent considerable time with dates, with other couples, or in romantic activities.

These names and types of cliques continue to exist, although the names change. More popular names today are "heads" or "potheads," "cowboys" and "kickers," "jocks," etc. These terms refer to individual groups and to individual students. In an increasingly complex world, this type of classifying or stereotyping (or both) is likely an attempt to simplify one's understanding of the social world rather than as a means to display classical prejudice. Nevertheless, membership does require conformity to the group's general standards of behavior, appearance, and even language.

QUESTION: Why do adolescents often speak differently from adults?

Language can play a special function of keeping one group separate from another. One scholar has suggested that there is one form in the language for adults, another in the language for peers (Lewis 1963).

The slang of the adolescent usually identifies the youth as culturally distinct, and it expresses values and norms, approval, hostility, and other attitudes. Language can reinforce the adolescent position as independent from adults. Notice that when adults and larger communities adopt the slang words used among adolescents, the adolescents are quick to discard the words and find others. It is as if there is a perpetual changing of language to keep oneself separate and distinct from the adult culture. Notice how fast adolescents stopped using the words "cool" or "far out" as soon as they became popular with the general adult society. The importance of allowing adolescents to use terms and language of their own is that it allows uniqueness of the adolescent. Adults who attempt to mimic and adopt adolescent language patterns are likely to be viewed with suspicion unless the person has high credibility and credentials within the youth culture based on other criteria. Knowing that adolescents use unusual language to set them apart suggests that the use of this language by teachers and parents would be interpreted as an encroachment on adolescents' freedom to be distinct and separate.

QUESTION: Is conformity to the peer group good or bad?

Making an impartial statement about the word *conformity* is difficult. Ordinarily, conformity has a negative connotation. Conformists tend to be viewed as bad people—weak willed, mindless, spineless, without convictions. On the other hand, nonconformists are viewed as good people who have the courage to stand up for personal conviction in the face of group pressures and who do their "own thing" regardless. Whether one is a conformist or nonconformist depends upon which group one is being compared with. Conformity to one group may imply nonconformity to a rival group.

A person's trying to judge conformity as good or bad can also be affected by the labels chosen to describe the behavior. Consider the following observation by social psychologist Elliot Aronson:

> Words do carry evaluative meaning—thus, to be called an individualist or a nonconformist is to be designated, by connotation, as a "good" person: the label evokes an image of Daniel Boone, standing on a mountain top with a rifle slung over his shoulder, the breeze blowing through his hair, as the sun sets in the background. To be called a conformist is somehow to be designated as an "inadequate" person: it evokes an image of a row of Madison Avenue admen with grey flannel suits, porkpie hats, and attache cases, looking as though they had been created by a cookie cutter, and all saying simultaneously, "Let's run it up the flagpole and see if anyone salutes."
>
> But we can use synonymous words that convey very different images. For "individualist" or "nonconformist," we can substitute "deviate;" for "conformist," we can substitute "team player." Somehow, "deviate" does not evoke Daniel Boone on the mountain top, and "team player" does not evoke the cookie-cutter-produced Madison Avenue adman. (Aronson 1976, 12).

Perhaps wiser is to give the benefit of the doubt to youth and to allow and support a certain amount of conformity as part of the developmental process. Again, research indicates that the conformity will lessen beginning around age thirteen. In addition, the conformity is usually over nonsignificant elements such as hairstyle, clothing, and sometimes language.

Various reasons underlie behavior *not* in agreement with a norm. Three terms are useful: anticonformity, other-conformity, and independence. Independence does not necessarily mean nonconformity, but most people tend to equate it with nonconformity.

QUESTION: What is anticonformity?

The term *anticonformity* refers to what is commonly called "rebellion." Whereas true conformity involves going along with a group, anticonformity involves going against the group just because the group is doing it.

Anticonformists are as dependent on group norms as are true conformists; the difference is that for anticonformists the norms communicate what *not* to do rather than what to do. Like true conformists, the anticonformists must be aware of what is acceptable to the group. They respond by doing something different. That a conflict be present between the norm and anticonformists' preferences is not necessary; they may actually seek to widen the gap between themselves and the group. They are like the adolescent described as being so contrary that if drowned, searchers would have to look for the body upstream. If this seems a bit extreme, consider the following statement by Mao Tse-tung: "We should support whatever the enemy opposes, and oppose whatever the enemy supports" (Mao Tse-tung, 1972).

People who are aware that the fashion is long hair, and who therefore get theirs cut short, show anticonformity. This reaction describes the behavior of some leaders of rebel movements in the United States. During the early sixties they wore long hair to symbolize rejection of "establishment" norms. Then, by the early seventies, when longer hair had become more acceptable, the symbolic rebellion lost its visibility. They cut their hair because long hair was no longer a sign of rebellion.

QUESTION: What is other-conformity?

The term *other-conformity* refers to a failure to conform to the norms of one group because of a conformity to the norms of another group. Sometimes the person we call a "nonconformist" is merely conforming to a different set of norms from the ones we are using as a reference, as the following observation suggests:

> Those who violate the norms of the mainstream of society are deviates in an ethical and legal sense. But, psychologically, they are no exceptions to the general rule. Psychologically, the great bulk of such violators, including anarchists, most delinquents, and many criminals, are acting in conformity with the rules of the game standardized in their own give-and-take, or in groups of their own choosing. These rules they consider as their own. They are the binding ones for them. (Sherif and Sherif 1964, 296)

Much of the nonconforming behavior among the so-called hippies of the late 1960s and early 1970s may have been other-conformity. Though their behavior did not conform to many prevailing social norms, many of them appeared to be dependent on the norms of their own groups, conforming strongly to hippie norms of dress, speech, and behavior. Teenagers may be viewed by adults as nonconformists because of behavior deviating from adult norms, when actually they are yielding even more to peers' norms than the adult conformist is to adult norms.

QUESTION: How does independence differ from anticonformity and other-conformity?

Both types of nonconformity we have discussed—anticonformity and other-conformity—need group norms. They are forms of conformity, neither one representing independence. Independent people are those who think for themselves. These individuals do not ignore the norm; rather, they evaluate it for intrinsic merits. Compliance or deviation from a norm depends on whether the independent person thinks that norm is right or wrong, appropriate or inappropriate. This person may sometimes appear to be a conformist and sometimes a nonconformist, as was recognized by this student:

> I can remember someone in my high school who was independent. She wore what was "in" only if she liked it, and kind of created her own style. She was confident and really seemed to know where she was going. She did what she wanted to.

Independence actually differs from the common point of view. In one sense, independence and true conformity may be in opposition: A true conformist does not display nonconforming behavior. In another sense they are compatible: An individualist *can* display conforming behavior (Hollander and Willis 1967).

This view of independence also differs from the view that the independent person is indifferent to group norms. The norms are not irrelevant, but they will not be the critical factor that they are to the anticonformist and to the other-conformist.

On the behavioral level, anticonformity, other-conformity, and independence may sometimes appear the same—people deviating from a norm. As with conforming behavior, however, a better understanding of nonconforming behavior occurs when we consider the underlying motive and intention. For example, parents and teachers who frequently associate adolescent deviance with anticonformity would do well to consider the possibility that teenagers might be complying with peers' norms, or even showing independence by rejecting an adult norm because they do not agree with it.

QUESTION: Why is peer group experience important?

As the last chapter pointed out, Erik Erikson believed that adolescence is a time of psychosocial moratorium, during which freedom is given to allow young people to learn about their world and to try out new roles. As one student put it, "Adolescence is when you try out your future life-style. It is kind of like trying on hats until you find something that fits." Teenagers at this age can learn how to relate socially with other members of their world. Friends, cliques, crowds, and peer groups all play their part and are necessary for this experimentation; they do make a significant difference in the adolescent's development. Certainly there are hazards, difficulties, and disadvantages, but social experience is both necessary and inevitable (Boyce and Jensen 1978, 147).

Although positive effects from the peer group and social interaction are the rule, they need not always be the case. Peer interactions can obstruct the process of discussion and can compromise rather than promote it. Often the weight of peer opinion allows less, not more, freedom in selecting and considering various points of view. Groups that dictate a limited range of thought or opinion are a hindrance rather than a help in facilitating growth of moral reasoning.

Bronfenbrenner's studies (Bronfenbrenner 1962, 1967, 1968, 1970; Garbarino and Bronfenbrenner 1976) show surprising differences between children from the United States and the USSR. In regard to the opposition between adult and peer standards, Bronfenbrenner (1967) found that in the United States, when youth are led to believe that parents will inspect their answers, they give more prosocial responses. When they believe peers will inspect their answers, however, they give more antisocial answers. In the Soviet Union children do not do this, giving more toward the prosocial end of the dimension for both parents and peers.

In another study, Beloff and Temperley (1972) found that twelve-year-old Scottish children are peer-oriented in their answers on this same test; they prefer answers that would seem undesirable in the context of the society's values. The researchers concluded that popular children are informal leaders in the school environment, and they provide a hidden curriculum for other pupils that contradicts the teacher-approved or culturally approved social values. This suggests that the power of the pupil in this setting to reinforce other students effectively may be as great as that of the teacher.

The power of peers is again illustrated in a study by Berkowitz and Walker (1967). University students were tested to see if laws and peer opinions could influence their judgment of morality and social action. Three groups were formed. One group was told that laws existed, defining actions as legal or illegal. The second group was told that a peer group approved or disapproved of the behavior, and a control group received no influence. The following indicates the type of problems posed:

> A man who is drunk in a public place is acting in an immoral manner even if he is not disorderly.
> A person is *not* in the wrong morally if he allows someone else to borrow his car without checking this individual's license.
> The person who borrows money for the purpose of betting is not doing anything morally wrong even if he does not inform the lender why he wants the money.
> The individual who sees another person attempting to commit suicide and does not try to help him is acting immorally himself.
> People should be willing to overlook failures in the manners and unpleasant habits of other people.
> It is always important to finish anything that you have started.
> I would never let a friend down when he expected something from me.
> (Berkowitz and Walker 1967, 415)

The study found that both knowledge of the law and knowledge of peer opinions led to greater shifts in judgment than were found in the control group. Moreover, peer opinion was found to cause a greater change than belief in the existence of legal sanction. The students were influenced more by peers than by knowledge of the law.

QUESTION: How can recognizing this importance help adults relate to adolescents?

As parents, teachers, and other people who work with adolescents become aware of this strong peer influence and its effects on adolescents (both positive and negative), it will help them gain a greater sensitivity to the needs of youth and an ability to meet those needs. For example, when adults understand that adolescents have an urgent need to belong, and also realize that clothing and actions are important criteria to belonging, then they become more sympathetic toward teenagers. One student described how her mother handled this phase in her children's lives:

> I think that my mother has especially been wise, maybe it is because of all her experience (there are 12 children in my family) and she is aware of the teen peer pressure and the need to belong to groups that each of us has felt. I realize that she is wise enough to understand that most often it is unlikely that conforming to a peer group at the adolescent period will result in a permanent conforming personality. Many times this takes a lot of patience on her part. With my older brothers she'd buy them new Levis and they'd rip them up the sides and fray the bottoms. Now with my younger brothers she buys them the Ocean Pacific and Lightening Bolt shirts and they cut them off at the chest, rip the sleeves out of their sweatshirts, etc., but she seems to take it all with a grain of salt and even jokes with them about it. I really think it's a wise way to handle it. At least it's worked with my brothers.

Adults can also be aware of the acute and keen pressure placed on adolescents by the peer group. By most conventional standards of wisdom, good taste, and sensibility, the extreme conformity expected of the twelve- to thirteen-year-old age group is unacceptable, but nevertheless, it is real in the lives of children this age. Adults can assist by helping youth dress and behave within the bounds acceptable to the peer group. When this is not possible, adults should be understanding of the stress and possible rejection that youth will experience.

Friendships

QUESTION: Do the findings regarding the peer group apply to friendships?

No, the formation and duration of friendships seem to function differently than do conformity to and membership in the peer group (Conger and Peterson 1984, 336). For example, friendships apparently become increasingly more stable and important until late adolescence, rather than tapering off during early adolescence (Horrocks and Baker 1951). These researchers did find that fluctuations always occurred in friendships, even though they became more stable.

An in-depth study of adolescent friendships found that friendships have at least three stages and that the motivations for friendships vary for each stage (Douvan and Adelson 1966, 192). In stage one, for eleven- through thirteen-year-olds, friendships center on activity rather than on friendship through personal relations. Friends are people with whom things can be done, but there is not an emphasis on depth or relating.

In stage two, age fourteen through sixteen, the stress and motivation for friends are on security. A friend at this stage should be loyal and trustworthy, someone who will not betray the friendship. Adolescents of this age need someone who is going through the same problems at the same time. They become dependent on having someone else with whom to share their experiences. Friends also provide emotional support and confidence.

In stage three, seventeen years and older, the emphasis is on personality and mutual interests. Appreciation for individual differences is greater, and the friendships are now relaxed with less stress.

A study comparing the age differences in motivation and psychological bases for friendship can be seen in Table 4–2.

TABLE 4–2 Percentage Incidence Distributed by Grade Levels for Friendship Expectation Dimensions

Dimension	Onset	1	2	3	4	5	6	7	8
Help—friend as giver	2	5	12	14	7	14	25	33	35
Common activities	2	3	7	32	52	24	40	60	60
Propinquity	3	7	5	9	12	12	20	38	32
Stimulation value	3	2	3	12	23	30	51	52	61
Organized play	3	2	0	15	26	9	10	17	20
Demographic similarity	3	0	3	7	35	15	15	10	23
Evaluation	3	2	5	13	13	17	33	21	30
Acceptance	4	3	0	5	9	9	18	18	38
Admiration	4	0	0	5	23	17	24	32	41
Incremental prior interaction	4	2	7	4	10	10	17	32	34
Loyalty and commitment	5	0	0	2	5	10	20	40	34
Genuineness	6	0	3	0	2	5	12	19	32
Help—friend as receiver	6	2	5	3	5	2	12	13	25
Intimacy potential	7	0	0	0	0	0	0	8	20
Common interests	7	0	0	5	7	0	5	30	19
Similarity—attitudes and values	7	0	0	0	0	2	3	10	8

Source: B. J. Bigelow and J. J. LaGaiqa, "Children's Written Descriptions of Friendships," *Developmental Psychology* 2:858 (1975).

As can be seen in Table 4–2, friendships serve different needs at different ages, becoming increasingly more stable and mature with age (Bigelow and LaGaiqa 1975, 858).

QUESTION: What is the importance of friends during adolescence?

Probably the characteristic of adolescents most often observed is their strong attachment to their friends. Some have referred to it as a period of life in which the basis of sociability is established. Friends are important to adolescents because they fulfill many of their needs, such as feeling important, feeling secure, and having status. What any person gets out of friendship is an individual matter and varies from person to person and place to place. Of all the factors affecting friendship, probably propinquity, opportunity to spend time together, and mutual satisfaction of psychological needs are most important. The ability to share friendships tends to grow with age. Friendships generally are more stable and fluctuate less with increasing age, although such stability is affected by one's environment. Friendships provide initial opportunities to interact with age-mates.

Friendships allow the adolescent a chance to develop social behavior and to control antisocial behaviors. They provide important assistance in the development of both skills and interests, and enable the adolescent to relate to others with similar problems and values. Even more important for the adolescent is that peer groups form the basis for the important and enduring heterosexual relationships that are essential for adult life. The following statement by Douvan and Adelson reflects empathy for the adolescent and illustrates the need for peer interaction:

> [H]e is in the process of breaking (or recasting) his ties to the family and desperately needs the support, approval and security, as well as the norms, of a peer group. He is discovering, and trying to interpret and control, a changed body, and with it new and frightening impulses, and so requires both the example and communion of peers. He is about to crystallize an identity, and for this needs others of his generation to act as models, mirrors, helpers, testers, foils. (Douvan and Adelson 1966, 192)

Many adolescents are insecure, oversensitive, tempestuous, and somewhat unstable. Many are still rebelling against adult authority and are seeking emotional emancipation from parents. Infatuations often develop at this stage, usually with an older teen or adult. These relationships may center on a dependency to escape home rather than on a healthy, interpersonal give-or-take typical of genuine friendships. One of the dangers at this point is that these close relationships sometimes lead to early marriages, which is discussed later in this chapter.

Another legitimate concern is overconformance to peer culture in U.S. society. Overcompliance with adolescent peer groups may result in a kind of conforming personality, the mass person with whom disagreement with prevailing norms and opinions becomes impossible. The adolescent peer culture is ordinarily less mature and lacks the meaningful traditions and values that emerge only over long time periods. In many cases, adolescent peer groups are cruel to their members, such as in deviant subcultures and gangs. An advisable approach is to give adolescent groups considerable freedom, but to emphasize respect for rules, norms, and values evolved through tradition and reason.

QUESTION: Is there a difference between boys and girls in their friendships?

In reviewing the research on this question, Coleman (1980) states:

> In summary, we cannot say that friendship is more or less important for one or the other of the sexes. What is clear, however, is that girls have more anxiety about this relationship, particularly in middle adolescence, and it seems probable that Douvan and Adelson (1966) are correct in pointing to the differing socialization processes as well as the high value that girls place on intimacy and dependency as the causes of this discrepancy. In addition and closely interconnected, we have seen that friendship is likely to have a somewhat different meaning for boys and girls. Although the boys lay stress on relationships that are action-oriented, for girls the satisfaction of emotional needs tends to be predominant. (Coleman 1980, 414)

To illustrate the importance of friendships for females, the following account is provided:

> When I made the transition from junior high to senior high school I found the entire ordeal frightening and unsettling. Many of my junior high friends

went to a different high school due to boundary rules and I felt a need to establish an identity with the "in" groups as quickly as possible. Despite the fact that a very small percentage of sophomores were admitted to either group I auditioned for and desperately wanted to be identified with "The Drill Team(!!)" and the elite jazz vocal group. I didn't make either group and I was devastated. I had to join the sophomore chorus and I hated it. I went through quite an unhappy adjustment period and had an acute confidence crisis. Fortunately things all evened out. I made friends where I was, I fell "in love," and by my junior year I felt happy about where I was, who I was, and who I was doing it with. I also auditioned again and made the groups I tried for in my junior year. What the groups thought of me was very important to me at the time.

QUESTION: Are friendships and peer group experience important for later development?

Some researchers believe that they are. In examining the long-term effects of poor peer relations, Roof, Sells, and Goldman (1972) found that they are linked to later development of neurotic and psychotic behavior. During adolescence the peer group provides the opportunity for reversing and comparing ideas and actions. This includes a large range of tasks that adolescents must face, such as dating, school, personal relating, success, and friends. Adults are often critical and the adolescents feel inhibited, but among persons of their own age they can work out their personal problems with more confidence and perhaps less stress. The seriousness of this is seen in the following example:

Friendships during adolescence are important in that they enable adolescents to relate to others with similar problems and values.

Three girls that I went to school with had very poor peer relations because they were heavily picked on. One of the girls did in fact drop out of school after becoming pregnant. Of the remaining two, one was pretty much scarred for life (so it seemed) emotionally because even in high school she was considered an outcast. The other girl did make out all right and adjusted through the years. I don't know how she did it. Perhaps it was some teacher who took time out to help her socially. It could have been parents who helped her to cope with her problems.

In the adolescent's life, peer interaction and friendships are apparently critical. Peers and friendships are there not only for enjoyment but also to facilitate healthy adjustment. Deficiencies in peer interactions can result in many difficulties and adjustment problems, some severe. The role of friend is perhaps more important than acceptance by the larger peer group. Research does find some negative effects of peer groups in terms of producing demands and conformity, whereas establishing friendships has not shown any adverse effects. Noticing when adolescents do not have adequate friendships, and in many cases assisting the adolescent in establishing needed friendships, is important.

Adults can help adolescents establish friendships by pointing out to them personal characteristics and mannerisms that may be hindering the establishment of friendships.

Of all peer relationships and experience, none is more significant in our culture and for the participating adolescent than marriage. Although our culture does not condone or support marriages during the teen years, they are increasing. Teenage marriages face a unique set of problems for which resolutions have not been found.

Adolescent marriages

QUESTION: What are the causes of adolescent marriages?

A large proportion of high school marriages result from pregnancy. One segment of the population—girls under fifteen years of age—has more births than in any previous generation. In 1975 the birthrate for this group was one birth per 700 girls (Brown 1978). One in every five deliveries in the United States is to a teenager. Although the birthrate for girls from fourteen to seventeen has remained fairly constant according to Brown, the birthrate among older groups has declined. These statistics indicate that the number of teenage parents is increasing, in contrast to what is occurring on the average nationwide. This disproportionate increase is not merely a result of illegitimate children or pregnancies leading to marriage. Studies correlating age at marriage to birth of the first child have shown that the younger a couple are when they marry, the sooner they will have children (Rice 1979).

Another reason for marriage was indicated by a couple who married fairly young because both wanted to leave stressful family environments. Wedlock to them was a way to escape controversy and to exercise independence. Similar reasons include getting married to satisfy dependency needs or to make the desired transition to adulthood. The couple's feelings for each other are also a basis for such decisions, but impatience and a limited understanding of one's needs may contribute to the decision to marry early.

QUESTION: What attitudes do peers and parents have toward adolescent marriages?

Perhaps one of the greatest problems that teenage parents face is found in this quote by Lewis and Lewis (1980):

> The greatest enemy of young marriages is the fact that from the beginning we anticipate their failure. Almost no one—neither the friends of the young couple, nor their parents, teachers and employers expect a very young marriage to grow in stability and happy mutuality.

Social ostracism is even more evident, however, if the teenage parent is *not* married. Teenage parents are pushed into a limbo state; they are no longer treated as children, yet they are not granted adult status. Recalling her adolescent years, one student describes her feelings about the girls in her peer group who married in tenth grade:

> During the last week of school two of the girls in my class eloped with their boyfriends. One of them ended up getting married. The other one—well, her parents wouldn't give their permission, and they even pressed charges against the young man. I noticed how quickly and how thoroughly my own and my friend's feelings about these two girls changed. I didn't want to even see the girl who didn't get married, because though I felt sorry for her, I was also very uncomfortable with the whole situation. A little later on I went to visit the girl who did get married and found that I was still uncomfortable. I wasn't sure how to act. She wasn't one of the gang anymore. She and her husband were a unit, and I was an outsider.

Adults and peers can be of help to teenage parents by being encouraging and optimistic rather than judgmental. With less social rejection, the transition to marriage and parenthood would not be as difficult. The transition to parenthood is troublesome in any marriage. Birth of the first child is a crisis whether the child was planned or unplanned, or whether the marriage is "good" or not (LeMasters 1967).

QUESTION: What problems do teenage parents face?

Some of the social problems that teenage parents face were mentioned earlier. Emotional and financial problems are also involved. Many teenagers of seventeen and eighteen are still searching for an identity. Erik Erikson's "identity crisis" is probably the most frequently quoted term when referring to adolescent development. This development is complicated by pregnancy and marriage. If an identity crisis is not handled, an inability to establish stable sex and occupational roles will result. A stable identity, understanding and wisdom, maturity, or whatever it is termed, seems to be a product of certain experiences resulting in part from the aging process.

In a general sense, many teenage parents have not had the opportunity to develop a certain maturity that helps them endure marital and parental obstacles and difficulties. Early parenthood also interferes with completion of school and economic self-support. These interruptions can and often do produce problems concerning finances, living quarters, and child rearing decisions.

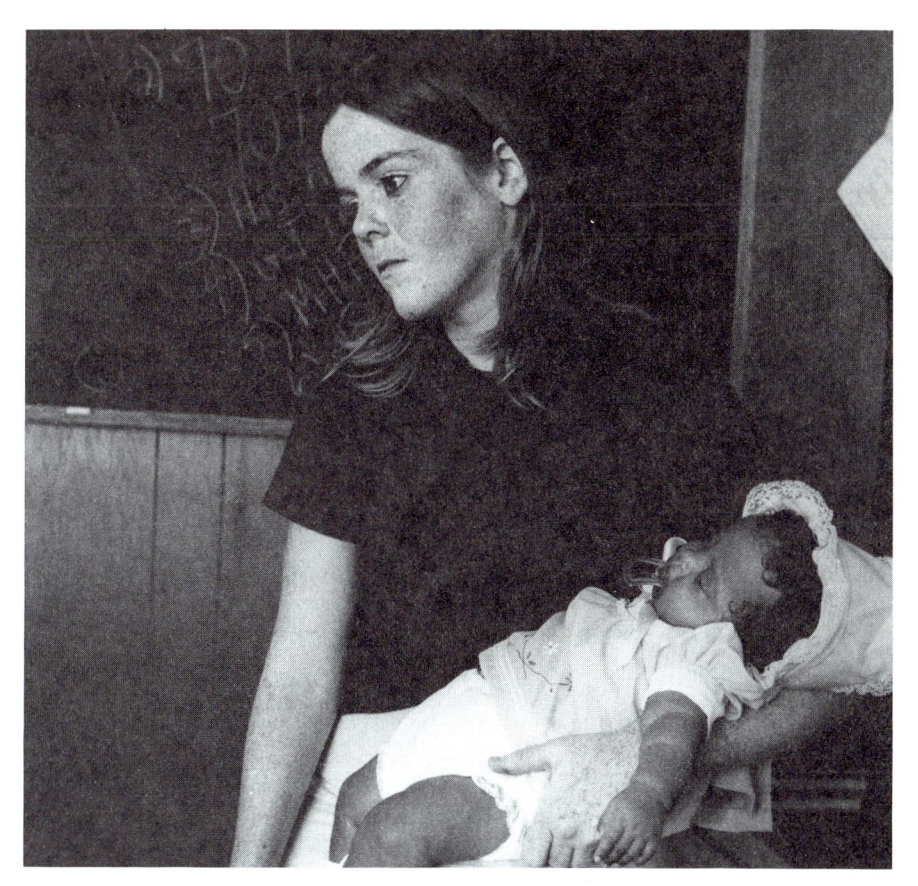

In addition to the social and financial obstacles that are common for the young unmarried mother, she may also have to deal with a search for her identity.

FINANCIAL DIFFICULTIES

Education and economic security are closely related when considering the financial status of teenage parents. Education is often interrupted to earn money. Unless the father is highly skilled in a particular trade, lack of education prevents adequate support for three family members—perhaps one reason why statistics often show that couples who marry at early ages more often become divorced.

Many unmarried mothers do not receive adequate support through assistance from the child's father. Two additional sources of economic aid—family and public—are therefore used heavily. Public assistance is often necessary regardless of whether the mother receives economic support from the child's father or from her own parents. Presser (1980) found that 86 percent of unmarried mothers in her study were residing in households that received public assistance.

Since financial problems may be implicated in divorce in any family, it is not surprising that so many early marriages result in divorce. Many pregnant teenagers do not get married in the first place.

LIVING QUARTERS

A large number of teenage mothers live with relatives. This arrangement is related to our previous discussion on financial difficulties. Young unmarried mothers simply cannot afford to make it on their own. This is the case even when married; one study found that 43 percent of the currently married mothers were also living with relatives one year after delivery (Furstenberg 1980). Furstenberg found that age was not an important factor in making the decision to remain at home. Rather, the decision to continue with school was important.

An accepting and supportive parent may be the single most important factor in successful adjustment for a pregnant adolescent.

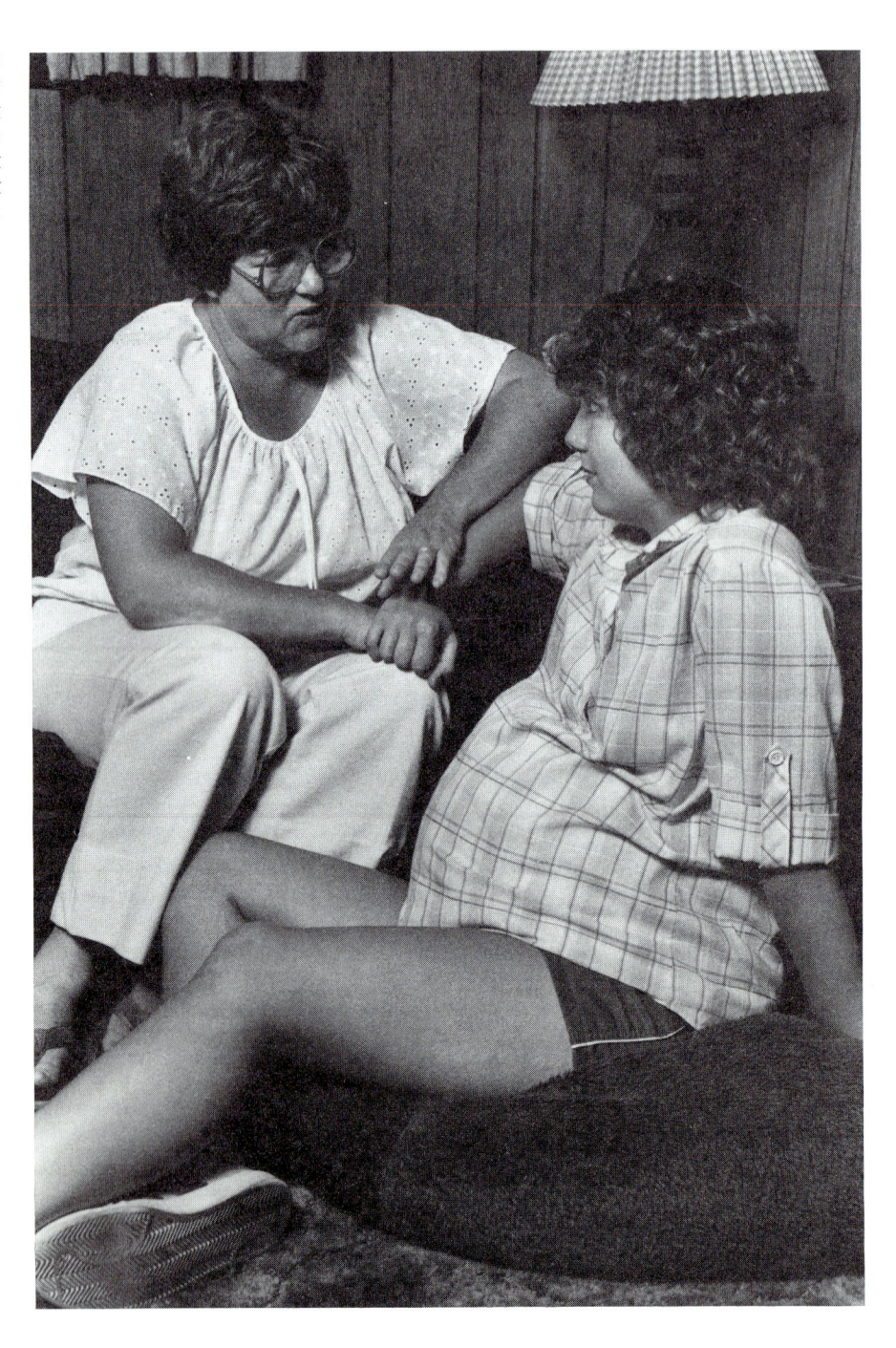

If the mother continued her education after becoming a parent, she was significantly more likely to live with parents than those who dropped out of school.

QUESTION: How important is parental support to an adolescent marriage and pregnancy?

A friend of mine is almost 18 and has a two-year-old son. She is not married and lives with her parents. She works every day to support herself and the baby, and seems to enjoy raising her child; she is happy. Having a child has matured her outlook on life. She feels good that it happened to her for she has grown so much and has started back on the right path.

The young girl described was fortunate because of the support she received. Unwed mothers who continue to live at home are assisted financially and have a greater chance of continuing their education. In addition, the infant has a better chance of receiving adequate discipline, love, and acceptance. To make the best of difficult situations, whether in a teenage marriage or a peer group experience, an accepting, patient adult is perhaps the major factor in successful adjustment.

Assistance in child care is probably responsible for some mothers living at home. Moving out of a parent's home not only reduces economic assistance in the form of room and board but also reduces the chance that relatives are available to help care for the child (Furstenberg 1980).

Summary

As a child approaches adolescence, peer group influence increases. As the child moves into late adolescence, peer influence decreases. The powerful effect of the peer group reaches its peak during the junior high school years. Twelve-thirteen-, and fourteen-year-olds feel a strong pressure to conform to the peer group preference in clothing, food, and language. Research has found, however, that in general, no major differences exist between values of peers, adolescents, and their parents.

A number of factors contribute to acceptance and popularity within the peer group. Physical attractiveness influences popularity, although such things as personality, sociability, and athletic ability have been found to influence popularity as well.

Conformity is another condition for popularity. The word *conformity* has a negative connotation, because conformists are often regarded as people who do not have their own convictions, as people who are easily swayed. Nonconformists are seen as people who stand up for themselves, who have their own ideas and convictions.

To conform to some things, a person must be nonconforming to others. A choice is still involved. Determining whether conformity is good or bad is therefore difficult. Many variables are concerned, and much depends on each particular situation. A certain amount of conformity is part of the developmental process.

One of the areas affected by conformity is the language of the adolescent. Adolescents often speak differently from adults and use slang as a way to assert their independence. Unusual language lends uniqueness to adolescents.

Nonconformity refers to behavior that is *not* in agreement with a norm. The three terms connected with nonconformity are anticonformity, other-conformity, and independence. Anticonformity involves going against what the group is doing. To *not* do what the group is doing, the anticonformist must know what is acceptable to the group.

Failure to conform to the conditions of one group because of conformity to another group is called other-conformity. Anticonformity and other-conformity need group norms, whereas independent people rely on their own thinking. They evaluate the norms and choose to comply or deviate, depending on their concept of right or wrong.

One of the difficulties that faces adolescents in peer group interaction is caused by the existence of cliques—small, unisexual groups of people in which membership is selected, restricted, and definite. Cliques receive labels that usually describe the major distinguishing feature of that particular group, such as "intellectuals," "potheads," and "jocks."

Findings regarding conformity and membership in the peer group do not apply to friendships. The formation and duration of friendships function differently. Whereas peer influence decreases with age, friendships become increasingly more stable.

Friendship may have a different meaning for boys and girls. The former stresses action-oriented relationships, while the latter gives more importance to the satisfaction of emotional needs. Friendships and peer group experience are important for later development. Studies have shown a connection between poor peer relations and the later development of neurotic and psychotic behavior.

Friendships and group experience are important in a person's growth and development. They are important not only for enjoyment but also for healthy adjustment.

Friendship is perhaps more important than acceptance by a larger peer group that could have adverse effects, especially on adolescents with weak identities. Friends are important to adolescents because they fulfill many of their needs, such as feeling important and secure. They also provide initial opportunities to interact with other people. Through friendships the adolescent develops social behavior and controls antisocial behavior. The adolescent is able to relate to others with similar problems and values.

One problem that a large number of adolescents face is that of early marriage. A large proportion of these marriages are due to pregnancy. Some adolescent marriages are based on a desire to leave stressful family environments, to escape controversy and exercise independence, to satisfy dependency needs, or to make the transition to adulthood. The couple's feelings for each other are also a basis for the decision to marry.

One of the greatest problems that teenage parents have is social ostracism and the negative attitudes that expect such marriages to fail. Often adults and peers are not sure how to categorize teenage parents; they are no longer treated as children, but they are not yet granted full adult status. Teenage parents face not only social problems but also emotional and financial problems.

Adolescents have not yet developed the maturity that is necessary to endure and overcome marital and parental difficulties. Early parenthood interrupts education. Often neither the father nor the mother is skilled in a particular trade. Financial responsibilities are often difficult for teenage parents.

Parental support is probably the major factor in helping young parents adjust properly to their new roles. An accepting, patient parent is important to an adolescent in any difficult situation, whether it is a teenage marriage or a peer group experience.

Although difficulties and disadvantages are associated with peer influence, social experience is necessary and inevitable. With sympathetic guidance and support from adults, peer interaction can have the needed positive effect on adolescent development.

References

Aronson, E. 1976. *The social animal*. 2d ed. San Francisco: Freeman.
Asubel, B. P. 1958. *Creating problems of child development*. New York: Blume & Stratton.
Beloff, H., & K. Temperley. 1972. The power of the peers: Bronfenbrenner's moral dilemmas in Scotland. *Scottish Educational Studies* 4:3–8.
Berkowitz, L., & N. Walker. 1967. Laws and moral judgments. *Sociometry* 30:410–22.
Bigelow, B. J., & J. J. LaGaiqa. 1975. Children's written descriptions of friendships. *Developmental Psychology* 2:857–58.
Blood, R., & M. B. Blood. 1978. *Marriage* 3d ed. New York: Free Press.
Boyce, D., & L. Jensen. 1978. *Moral reasoning*. Lincoln: Univ. of Nebraska Press.
Bronfenbrenner, U. 1962. Soviet methods of character education: Some implications for research. *American Psychologist* 17:550–64.
———. 1967. Response to pressure from peers versus adults among Soviet and American school children. *International Journal of Psychology* 2:199–207.
———. 1968. The changing Soviet family. In *The role and status of women in the Soviet Union*, ed. D. R. Brown. New York: Teachers College Press, Columbia University.
———. 1970. *Two worlds of childhood: U.S.A. and U.S.S.R.* New York: Russell Sage Foundation.
Brown, J. 1978. Teenage pregnancies are increasing. *Searching for alternatives to teenage pregnancy* (pamphlet).
Cabior, M., & P. R. Dokecki. 1973. Physical attractiveness, perceived attitude similarity, and academic achievement as contributed to interpersonal attraction among adolescents. *Developmental Psychology* 9:44–45.
Cambell, J. B. 1964. Two relations in childhood. In *Review of child development research*, vol. 1, ed. M. Hoffman & L. Hoffman. New York: Russell Sage Foundation.
Cavoir, N., & D. A. Lombardi. 1973. Developmental aspects of judgment of physical attractiveness in children. *Developmental Psychology* 8(1):67–71.
Coleman, J. C. 1980. Friendship and peer group in adolescence. In *Handbook of adolescent psychology*, ed. J. Adelson. New York: Wiley.
Coleman, J. S. 1960. The adolescent sub-culture and academic achievement. *American Journal of Sociology* 65:337–47.
———. 1961. *The adolescent society*. New York: Free Press.
Condry, W. W., & M. L. Simon. 1974. Characteristics of peer- and adult-oriented children. *Journal of Marriage and the Family* 36:543–54.
Conger, J. J., & A. C. Petersen. 1984. *Adolescents and youth*. New York: Harper & Row.
Costanzo, P. R. 1970. Conformity development as reproach or self-blame. *General Principles of Psychology* 14: 356–64.

Costanzo, P. R., & M. E. Shaw. 1966. Conformity as a function of age level. *Child Development* 27:967–75.
Dion, K. K. 1973. Young children's stereotyping of facial attractiveness. *Developmental Psychology* 9(2):183–88.
Dion, K. K., & E. Berscheid. 1974. Physical attractiveness and peer perception among children. *Sociometry* 37(1):1–12.
Douvan, E., & J. Adelson. 1966. *The adolescent stage*. New York: Wiley.
Durphy, D. C. 1963. The social structure of adolescent peer groups. *Sociometry* 26:230–46.
Epstein, A. S. 1979. Pregnant teenagers' knowledge of infant development. Paper presented at the biennial meeting of the Society for Research in Child Development, San Francisco, March.
Furstenberg, F. F. 1980. Burdens and benefits: The impact of early childrearing on the family. *Journal of Social Issues* 36:64–87.
Garbarino, J., & U. Bronfenbrenner. 1976. The socialization of moral judgment and behavior in cross-cultural perspective. In *Moral development and behavior: Theory, research, and social issues,* ed. T. Lickona, 70–83. New York: Holt, Rinehart & Winston.
Harris, S. 1966. Non-conformists may be slaves. *Deseret News,* 24 February.
Harvey, O. J., & J. Rutherford. 1960. Status in the informal group. *Child Development* 31:377–85.
Hollander, E. P., & R. H. Willis. 1967. Some current issues in the psychology of conformity and nonconformity. *Psychological Bulletin* 68:62–76.
Hollingshead, A. B. 1949. *Camptown youth*. New York: Wiley.
Horrocks, J. E., & M. Baker. 1951. The study of the friendship fluctuations of pre-adolescents. *Journal of Genetic Psychology* 78:131–44.
Howard, M. 1975. *Only human*. New York: Seabury Press.
_____. 1978. How can classroom teachers help? *Today's Education,* February–March.
Iscoe, I., M. Williams, & J. Hardy. 1963. Modification of children's judgment by a single group technique: A normative developmental study. *Child Development* 44:963–78.
Kleck, R. E., S. A. Richardson, & L. Ronald. 1974. Physical appearance cues and interpersonal attraction in children. *Child Development* 45:305–10.
Langlois, J. H., & C. Stephan. 1977. The effects of physical attractiveness and ethnicity on children's behavioral attributions and peer preferences. *Child Development* 48:1694–98.
Larsen, L. E. 1972a. The influence of parents and peers during adolescence. *Journal of Marriage and the Family* 34:67–74.
_____. 1972b. The relative influence of parent-adolescent affect in predicting the salience hierarchy among youth. *Pacific Sociological Review* 15:83–102.
Larsen, R. 1983. Adolescents' daily exposure with family and friends in contrasting opportunity systems. *Journal of Marriage and the Family* 45(4):739–51.
LeMasters, E. E. 1967. Parenthood as crisis. *Marriage and Family Living* 19:352–55.
Leonard, R. N., & J. Pendarf. 1971. Attitudes of adolescents and adults towards contemporary issues. *Psychology Reports* 28:139–45.
Leonard, R. N., C. Schroeder, N. Witzer, & A. Weinstock. 1972. Attitudes of high school students and their parents towards contemporary issues. *Psychology Reports* 41:255–58.
Lerner, R. M., & J. V. Lerner. 1977. Effects of age, sex, and physical attractiveness on child-peer relations. *Developmental Psychology* 13(6):585–90.
Lewis, H. R., & M. E. Lewis. 1980. *The parent's guide to teenage sex and pregnancy*. New York: St. Martin's Press.
Lewis, N. 1963. *Language, body, personality in infancy and childhood*. New York: Basic Books.
Mao Tse-tung. 1972. *Quotations from Chairman Mao Tse-tung*. Peking: Foreign Languages Press.
McGovern, J. D. 1967. The adolescent and his peer group. In *Counseling the adolescent,* ed. A. A. Schneider and contributors. San Francisco: Chandler.
Meisels, M., & F. N. Canter. 1971. On the generation gap. *Adolescence* 6:523–30.
Miller, A. G. 1970. Role of physical attractiveness in impression formation. *Psychonomic Science* 19(4):241–43.
Presser, H. B. 1980. Sally's corner: Coping with unmarried motherhood. *Journal of Social Issues* 36:107–29.

Purnell, R. F. 1970. Socioeconomic status and sex differences in adolescent reference-group orientation. *Journal of Genetic Psychology* 116:233–39.

Rice, F. P. 1979. *The adolescent—development, relationships, and culture.* Boston: Allyn & Bacon.

Riester, A. E., & R. H. Zucker. 1968. Adolescent social structure and behavior. *Personnel and Guidance Journal* 46:304–12.

Roof, N., S. B. Sells, & N. N. Goldman. 1972. *Social adjustment and personality development in children.* Indianapolis: Univ. of Indianapolis Press.

Sebald, H. 1981. Adolescent concepts of popularity and unpopularity, comparing 1960 with 1976. *Adolescence* 16(61):187–93 (Spring).

Sherif, M., & C. W. Sherif. 1964. *Reference groups, explorations into the conformity and deviation of adolescents.* New York: Harper & Row.

Stone, L. J., & J. Schultz. 1968. *Childhood and adolescence.* New York: Random House.

Styczymski, L. E., & J. E. Langlois. 1977. The effects of familarity on behavioral stereotypes associated with physical attractiveness in young children. *Child Development* 48:1137–41.

Thompson, G. G., & J. E. Horrocks. 1947. A study of the friendship fluctuations of urban boys and girls. *Journal of Genetic Psychology* 70:53–63.

Weinstock, A., & R. N. Leonard. 1972. Attitudes of late adolescents and their peers towards contemporary issues. *Psychology Reports* 40:239–44.

133

CHAPTER FIVE

The family

SURVEY AND QUESTIONS

In this chapter the student will find a general introduction to the role of the family in the lives of adolescents. Reading the chapter will provide answers to the following questions:

Family Organizations

How significant are parents in the lives of their adolescents?
Have major changes occurred in family life and stability that would diminish the effectiveness of the family for modern youth?
What have researchers found about the effects of employed mothers on their children's development?
What have researchers found about the effects of a one-parent family?
What has research shown about the effects of divorce on adolescent development?
How can adolescents be helped to cope with divorce?
Do large differences exist in the family experience for adolescents living in different socioeconomic and racial groups?

Ethnic Family Differences

Are family difficulties associated with minority groups?
The black family?
The American Indian family?
The Chinese-American family?
The Puerto Rican-American family?
The Mexican-American family?
The Japanese-American family?
What does research say about family differences among ethnic groups?

Parental Influence and Discipline

What effects do parental types have on their children?
What are the adolescent's reactions to attempted parental control and influence techniques?
What is the optimal amount of emotional control in the family?

> Since I was six years old, I have lived in foster homes and previous to that I lived with my single-parent family. When I was 15, I was sent to live with the family that eventually adopted me when I was 18 years old.
>
> By the time I had reached this family, I had acquired all those stereotyped traits that we pin on children raised in foster homes because of divorce. I was aloof, overly independent, introverted, scared, not willing to interact socially, etc. I was your textbook case of all that befalls a person raised under the circumstances I was.
>
> During my high school years, this family really got involved in my "rehabilitation." We did not seek professional help but we were active in a layman's therapy program. My foster parents and foster brothers and sisters all participated in helping me overcome my problems. It became a family problem and not my individual problem. Each person took the responsibility upon himself to see that I adjusted properly.
>
> Since all my family was involved, I felt needed and loved. I took a more active part in our family and our activities. They seemed to make the space for me to move into their family and be accepted. My brothers helped me athletically, my sisters aided me socially and my parents supplied support and the discipline I never had.
>
> My example has a happy ending; I turned out somewhat OK. Many others like me have not made it. I was lucky to have been placed in a foster home where the entire family got involved to help me overcome all the obstacles that I accumulated over the years. I believe that if more families would get involved in the individual member's problems, there would be many more happy ending stories like mine.

This young man's appreciation for the family is obvious, and the feeling of belonging that he acquired in his home is used to illustrate the power of a family experience. Others who have not experienced this type of home may fail to realize the comfort, support, and security that one can feel on a day-to-day basis. Home can be a place where one does not fear failure, where fun and work are shared, a place where we really learn to live.

Despite some extremely pessimistic reports about the future of the family, the institution appears to be alive and well, and is continuing to grow. (Bachman, Johnson, and O'Malley 1981, Norback 1980, Norman and Harris 1981) A recent survey (Kenting 1983, 24–36) of over 200,000 youthful respondents throughout the United States reported the following conclusions, showing that a positive view of home life exists in the United States.

1. Sixty-nine percent indicate that maintaining close contact with family members and other relatives is very important.
2. Eighty-seven percent say that having at least one meal together is a top priority.
3. Love, compansionship, and shared goals are the most important reasons for marriage.
4. Forty-eight percent are very satisfied with the way their children are "turning out," and 44 percent are "mostly" satisfied.
5. Fifty-four percent said if they had to do it all again, they would have the same number of children, and 24 percent would have more children.

Studies show that many adolescents and their parents share a surprising degree of agreement on many traditional values.

These judgments indicate a positive regard for the family context in the mid-1980s. Concerns are also shown, however:

1. Eighty percent feel that family life is in trouble, the greatest threat being an absence of religious experiential foundations.
2. Forty-one percent feel "America is a worse place to raise children than it was five years ago."
3. Forty-seven percent feel moral decay is the greatest threat to family life.
4. Twenty-eight percent say crime and social disorder are the greatest threats to family life.

In the previous survey, 83 percent of the respondents say they generally spend free time at home, and 65 percent spend more time at home than they did five years ago. Although this study cannot be used as solid evidence, the large positive regard for the family illustrates the importance of this institution in the lives of youth. Other research will verify the importance of parents in the lives of adolescents.

QUESTION: How significant are parents in the lives of their adolescents?

Cited in the chapter on peers is research showing that the family has considerable influence on adolescents, even compared with peers. Additional evidence supports this research. For example, in a study of rural Minnesota high schools, students were asked who was the most important reference point in their lives: family, school friends, or someone else. Over three-fourths indicated their parents were primary; school friends received less than 10 percent of the answers (Ostlund 1957). Other evidence shows that political attitudes of teenagers closely follow the voting patterns of their family (Lipset 1957). The same is true of religious preferences (Putney and Middleton 1961).

Interpreting the results of several national surveys conducted through the eighties, one set of authors concluded that, "there was in the late sixties and early seventies—and still remains—a rather surprising degree of agreement among both parents and their young regarding the validity of such traditional values as self-reliance, hard work, and the importance of the family—the extent of the differences often appears to have been exaggerated, at least in the case of the average adolescent and his or her parents." (Conger and Peterson 1984, 207–208)

Perhaps the following statement points out the significance and endurance of the strong parental ties over American youth:

> Indeed, if there is to be continuity between generations, there must be some sharing of basic values between parents and youth. That such continuity exists is shown by the simple fact that—"American society has survived over time." Moreover, there is remarkable agreement as to what American values are or have been and agreement upon their stability through more than 150 years. Such stability could hardly be evident if adolescents rebelled and rejected the basic values of a preceding generation. (Bealer, Willits, and Maida 1969, 487)

QUESTION: Have major changes occurred in family life and stability that would diminish the effectiveness of the family for modern youth?

Let us first discuss the changes in family. The ideal two-parent stable family that lasts forever has definitely become less common. The 1978 census estimated that 20 percent of children under eighteen are living with only one parent. The trend is expected to increase, with approximately 45 percent of all children born in 1978 to experience a form of death, divorce, or separation sometime during their first eighteen years of life. (U.S. Department of Commerce 1979) The form or types of family organizations are likely to change in the future. Adolescents are more frequently growing up in two-parent families where both parents work outside the home (Ramey 1978). One report states that 60 percent of married women are employed outside the home (Sussman 1978).

QUESTION: What have researchers found about the effects of employed mothers on their children's development?

Researchers have found little difference between children of employed and home-based mothers (Wallston 1973; Query and Kuruvilla 1975; Dellas, Vaier, and Enihobich 1979; Marotz-Badden et al. 1979; Hoffman 1974). This finding is surprising when one considers that the primary caretaker is absent from home for eight hours a day. An early research report relating maternal employment to juvenile delinquency (Glueck and Glueck 1957) pointed out that employed mothers did produce a strong negative effect on their children.

The lack of difference between children of employed and home-based mothers may result from several factors. Not surprisingly, in studies where the criteria were school achievement, grades, and IQ scores, the effects of maternal employment outside the home were minimal, as other variables contribute more powerfully to these types of scores. Maternal employment may be most keenly felt in hard-to-research areas such as emotional security, social adjustment, and type and direction of motivation. Also, the employed mother may be different from the home-based mother in a number of ways. Middle- and upper-class mothers are more likely to work outside the home (Chadwick and Bahr 1983). These mothers likely have homes offering compensating experiences to balance the negative effects of outside employment. Employed mothers may also provide a different type of model, one that is hardworking, successful, and independent. These attributes may, in part, compensate for the absence of adequate supervision. Studies have shown that employed mothers spend less time with adolescents than do home-based mothers (Walker and Woods 1972).

In a recent review article on maternal employment and children, Elsie Smith warns that failing to find a difference in research does not mean that no difference exists:

> Yet, equally clear, research that states there is no compelling evidence of harmful effects of maternal employment—without having to sound empirical evi-

The emotional effects of maternal employment on children are hard to measure and further research needs to be done before conclusions can be drawn.

dence to support such a position—is just as wrong. A more reasonable summary of the research on maternal employment might be: For the vast majority of infant and preschool children (meaning those who do not have optimal care arranged through a university), we simply do not know what the effects of maternal employment are. (Smith 1981, 197)

Quotes from an excellent review article can also be used to show that those who find no difference in research of maternal employment must consider other factors:

By the same token, studies showing no effects do not necessarily demonstrate that maternal employment is irrelevant. It is possible that the wrong effects were sought, or the studies were inadequate, or the research did not examine the particular group or specific conditions that might have revealed an effect. (Hoffman 1979, 860)

Research also shows that the reason for working outside the home makes a difference; e.g., does the mother *want* to be employed outside the home? Because of these difficult, confounding factors in conducting research in this area, definite statements will apparently have to wait pending further research that includes more subtle social and emotional characteristics and more research control.

QUESTION: What have researchers found about the effects of a one-parent family?

In general, one-parent families refer to father-absent families, since more than 80 percent of single parents are women. Again, interpreting research and drawing definite conclusions in this area are difficult. For example, one-parent families have had a higher-than-normal representation of delinquent children (Greer 1974). Blaming the delinquency on the one-parent family would be a mistake, however. A number of other factors can explain this finding. Parents of delinquents may be more likely to divorce, separate, or simply to desert the family. Life trauma and poor family relationships may be more common; therefore, the effects of a one-parent family may be due to the missing parent, to changes that result in the remaining parent, to low economic conditions of the home, or to altered relationships between family and outside influences such as church, school, state, and extended family (Brandwein, Brown, and Fox 1974; Lind 1974; Weller and Luchtorhand 1983).

As in the case of the employed mother, the father-absent home may produce more subtle effects that are not found in general, group-administered paper and pencil tests of psychological adjustment, personality, IQ scores, and school grades. Hetherington (1972) conducted an insightful and interesting study that illustrates this assertion. The study focused on three groups of adolescent girls. One group came from families in which both mother and father were present, and the two experimental groups were from father-absent homes. In one experimental group the father had died; in the other, the parents had separated or divorced. Instead of taking tests, these girls were interviewed and observed. When the interviewer was male, the daughters of divorced mothers typically sat closest to the interviewer. In contrast, daughters of widowed mothers sat in the farthest chair. When the interviewer was female, no consistent pattern was found. Daughters of divorced mothers were more likely to engage in attention- or proximity-seeking behaviors. They engaged in more eye contact with the male interviewer, sprawled loosely in their chairs, and were more relaxed and open. They reported more contact with members of the opposite sex, spent more time in the "male" part of the recreation center, and tended to press closely to the stag line at dances. The researchers studied these girls into young adulthood. Daughters of divorcées tended to marry younger men who frequently had drug problems or inconsistent work histories. Daughters of widows tended to marry men with a more puritanical makeup. Daughters of widows and divorcées reported more sexual adjustment problems than daughters of widowers (Hetherington, Cox, and Cox 1977).

The conclusions of a study such as this should not be taken too literally. The study is cited here, however, to point out that real and preferred effects of employed mothers or single-parent families may be found in studies in which cases are closely examined. The previous study used observational research to identify subtle but important differences in development. Logically, when change occurs in established or traditional models of family life, some problems should arise as a result of these disruptions.

QUESTION: What has research shown about the effects of divorce on adolescent development?

Emotional strains and problems are definitely associated with divorce, especially for the adolescent male residing in these families. As in other studies, however, the trauma effect does not seem to create a long-lasting, permanent impairment. As in the previous two areas, most reports of disturbance or differences are found in clinical settings. Differences found also include a higher frequency of delinquent behavior and depression. This delinquency includes sexual activity and drug use (McDermott 1970; Sugar 1970; Morrison 1974).

Apparently one of the problems of divorce is the deterioration of parental skills and general home climate (Wallerstein and Kelly 1976). Children from divorced homes seem to have lower self-esteem and also devalue their families (Parish and Dostal 1980). Others experience serious emotional disturbances such as anger, depression, and so on. (Anderson and Anderson 1981; Curran 1981).

Some researchers believe the effects of divorce have been overstated or that their research has not shown detrimental effects (Burchinal 1964; Reinhard 1977). One possibility for the difference of opinion may be that divorce affects males and females differently (Grossman, Shea, and Adams 1980). One research team (Slater, Stewart, and Linn 1983) found that males from disrupted homes had higher self-esteem sooner, but that the females had lower self-esteem and suffered more from the effects of family disruption. The researchers concluded:

> For the male teenager, more friction was found in intact homes than in disrupted homes. Perhaps males who live with both parents find themselves in competition with their father or see their father as limiting their move toward independence. Since custody is more frequently awarded to the mother, these sources of friction may be alleviated when the father moves out of the house. Females, on the other hand, who had experienced parental separation or

Divorce may force a new lifestyle on a family as the result of a changed economic situation. The family stress that may result from this and other changes influence each child differently.

divorce, reported more conflict than the male group. Females whose parents were still married felt the least amount of friction within their homes. . . . The ability to adapt to a new lifestyle without negative self-concepts or perceptions of their family environment is central to a healthy adjustment. Future efforts should be aimed at identifying the factors which facilitate the adjustment process. (Slater, Stewart, and Linn 1983, 940–41)

QUESTION: How can adolescents be helped to cope with divorce?

One researcher (Lupenitz 1979) found that children received support in other institutions, such as schools, Boy Scouts or Girl Scouts, and sport activities. There they received attention and caring that were missing at home. For others, withdrawing and steering clear of home were ways of avoiding the conflict. Friends also supply help at these times, because young people are less inclined to confide in parents for fear of being used in emotional arguments.

Some of these techniques can be seen in the following account of a young girl who had experienced divorce in her home:

> When my parents finally made the decision to get a divorce, I was relieved that the ever-present shadow was finally faced. I agreed with my parents and supported their decision, and when my grandmother asked us to pray that my parents

would get back together I did not. My parents conflicted in all areas including religious, political, and general way of life. Together their lives were frustrating and unsuccessful, for their goals were different and neither could achieve.

Though I supported my parents, I remained somewhat distant from the central conflict, for it was not mine, but rather my parents' separation. My ability to cope with the situation and keep it from becoming a crisis in my own life was due to my somewhat self-centeredness. I had my own goals and I was determined to achieve them. My parents appreciated my attitude and both supported me and did all to make sure I was successful according to my own standards. My brothers and sisters somewhat resented my aloofness, but later realized that they too must make the same separation.

I love both sets of parents and consider myself a member of two families. It is as if I lead two completely different lives, which allows me to see life from different viewpoints, and thereby determine how I myself would like to live. I would not change this situation for a different life. I love the way I live and all my families.

When a family breaks down as in separation and divorce, an important step is for the community to provide assistance. This assistance may be formal in the way of counseling. Counseling should stress that divorce is not a reflection on adolescents personally, and that although the parents divorce each other, they do not divorce their children, and satisfying moments are to be experienced in the years ahead with their parents.

QUESTION: Do large differences exist in the family experience for adolescents living in different socioeconomic and racial groups?

How large the social class differences are in this area is debatable, but they can be identified. In this section of the chapter we will try to look at some differences between adolescents from different ethnic groups. Because most minority and distinguishable ethnic groups are predominantly members of lower socioeconomic status, considering differences between social classes is one approach. Although accurately classifying socioeconomic status is difficult, it is possible to classify based on income level, type of occupation (e.g., professional, business owner, skilled or unskilled labor), the type of neighborhood in which one lives, and so on. Some generalizations and social class differences in child rearing that hold across race and culture are summarized by Maccoby (1980) after viewing the literature. She states:

1. Lower-SES parents tend to stress obedience, respect, neatness, cleanliness, and staying out of trouble. High-SES parents are more likely to stress happiness, creativity, ambition, independence, curiosity, and self-control.

2. Lower-SES parents are more controlling, power-assertive, authoritarian, and arbitrary in their discipline, and they are more likely to use physical punishment. Higher-SES parents are more democratic and tend to be either permissive or authoritative. . . . They are more likely to use induction (that is, point out the effects of a child's actions on others, or ask the child how she or he would feel in the other's place) and to be aware of and responsive to their children's perspectives.

3. Higher-SES parents talk to their children more, reason with them more, and use more complex language.

4. Higher-SES parents tend to show more warmth and affection toward their children. (Maccoby 1980, 400)

From a sociologial perspective, LeMasters and DeFrain (1983) identified the relationship of parenting with social class. According to these authors, one-fifth of all Americans are rearing their children at poverty level (1983, 88), which results in a number of detrimental conditions that low-income parents have to cope with in raising their children. Many of the people in this poverty classification are single-parent women. One-third of women who are divorced and not remarried fall below the poverty line, even after counting alimony, child support, and so on. Thirteen percent of divorced men are also categorized as such. The problems associated with child rearing at the poverty level include high birth rates, slum neighborhoods, inferior employment, inadequate parental education, poor health, unstable marriages, and inadequate legal services. The following are excerpts of the statements about each problem:

1. High birth rates—"This means that, in addition to their other handicaps, poverty parents are struggling with more children per parent than any other social class group in the society."

2. Slum neighborhoods—"In their study, *Beyond the Melting Pot,* Nathaniel Glazer and Daniel Patrick Moynihan document the various behavioral difficulties that have been endemic in certain slum areas of New York City, regardless of whether the area was inhabited by Italians, blacks, Irish, or Puerto Ricans. . . . [T]he fact remains that rearing children in a slum area is a challenge that most parents would be happy to escape."

3. Inferior employment—"Low-class mothers are more likely to seek outside employment if it is available; and, if they find it, the working hours, the wages, and the conditions of employment are less than ideal. Low income black mothers in Chicago, for example, according to St. Clair-Drake and Horace Cayton in *Black Metropolis,* are likely to be domestic servants, commuting long distances between suburbs and working long hours, six days a week, with little or no vacation time off."

4. Inadequate parental education—"These lower-class parents do not usually have a high school education. . . . Some of them cannot read or write. All this means that they face almost insuperable handicaps in trying to understand the world they and their children live in, to say nothing of trying to cope with that world."

5. Poor health—"Any person who has ever been a parent knows what it is like to try to take care of children when the parent is not feeling well, and the situation is no different when trying to cope with an adolescent youngster under similar circumstances. In over 150 parent discussion groups conducted by the writers in the past several years, ill health is one of the items most often cited by fathers and mothers for not being able to live up to their own standards of parental performance."

6. Unstable marriages—"One of the crucial factors for the parental team seems to be a stable marriage. If so, there appears to be evidence that marital instability rates are highest at the low-income level. . . . There also seems to be evidence that desertion rates are higher at the lower-class level. To this list must be added the fact that the absent-father syndrome is more common of low-income levels. All of this adds up to

the fact that poverty parents are more than normally plagued with marital problems as they struggle to rear their children."

7. Inadequate legal services—"Numerous studies have demonstrated that low-income parents and their children do not receive their share of justice in America. Children in the poverty groups are more apt to be arrested for minor offenses in the community; they receive relatively poor legal defense; and when convicted the children of poverty families tend to receive more severe punishments; if they end up in jail, their parents can't see them very often because they can't afford to pay bus fare to and from the correctional center. . . . Government legal services for the poor are under constant attack by conservative enemies in the community, and budgets are so miniscule that programs sometimes have to put in more time on new clients because they can't take care of old clients." (LeMasters and DeFrain 1983, 91–94)

Ethnic family differences

QUESTION: Are family difficulties associated with minority groups?

Not exactly. Minority groups often include middle-class, lower-middle, and upper-middle-class groups, as well as those in a high socioeconomic position. These low socioeconomic conditions are pointed out so that in a discussion of minority group family behavior we can have the perspective of knowing that a close relationship exists between identifiable social class and ethnic family structure and problems (Thornburg 1975; Clark 1981; LeMasters and DeFrain 1983).

To illustrate minority group differences in the family experience, the following discussions will be based on statements taken from an excellent book entitled *Culture and Childrearing,* edited by Ann Clark. The following descriptions are quotes, but have been abridged, reordered, and adapted with permission from the publishers. The reader should consult the original source for more comprehensive coverage and documentation. Each chapter of *Culture and Childrearing* was written by an author who is a member of a minority group and also a professional in the field. Excerpts from these chapters are presented because the authors were raised into the culture and can provide a more idiographic description. The writings are more sensitive, touching, and revealing than can be found by interpreting statistical facts about a group of people. Caution is urged, however, not to draw inferences about specific individuals from these general group findings which describe only patterns of life styles.

The first is a discussion of the black family and youth, and is prefaced by an insightful and touching description of the writer's parents:

> I, Betty Greathouse, am a Black American woman, wife, mother, friend, and university professor. Yes, I am a very diverse, complex, and yet simple human being. This is so because of the myriad of people, places, and things that have touched me.
>
> My parents, Oliver and Mae Lizzie Harris, had the greatest impact on my life. Without them, I would not be! Dad and Mama made quite a team. I was never quite sure which of them was the head of the family. Mama was hardly a castrating quarterback, nor was she the water-girl; sometimes decisions were made by my father and on other occasions Mama had the last word. They just seemed to know when it was their turn to carry the ball.

My appreciation for education, work, flexibility of roles, and religion was acquired from my parents. Dad worked two jobs and my mother worked outside of the home, also. He worked as a truck driver and yard man; she worked as a domestic worker, cleaning motels and houses. My parents wanted to provide a good home and education for their seven children.

Dad, who had a fourth-grade education, not only talked about the importance of a Black person getting an education; he would sit down with me and a big old 5-cent tablet with primary grade spacing and go over my "times," as he called them. (Greathouse 1981, 78)

THE BLACK FAMILY

In spite of racism and poverty, the Black family—the institution that is primarily responsible for the socialization of Black children—has been able to not only survive, but has indeed moved to a higher level of existence and humanity. This survival, this progress, is due largely to the strengths of the Black family. Our experiences and review of the literature on Black families reveal that at least five major strengths of the Black family have been functional for its survival, development, and stability: namely, strong kinship bonds, strong work orientation, adaptability of family roles, strong achievement orientation, and religious orientation.

One of the most salient differences between the socialization of young Black males and the females is in their sex education. Females seem to receive a more thorough orientation to sex within the family and at an earlier age than the males. Also, often when parents are giving advice to males, it is limited to their double standard attitude. Boys are advised not to "mess around with girls," but at the same time it is emphasized that messing around is natural for boys.

The same-sex peer group's influence on the Black male peaks during the adolescent period. Within this group he obtains the bulk of his sex education and sex-role behaviors. Among his friends he hones his verbal skills—rapping, jiving, and playing the dozens to a fine art. Jiving, playing the dozens, and the use of slang are techniques utilized for a variety of purposes, such as maintaining one's status in "the group," reaffirming one's identity as being Black, isolating non-Blacks, having fun, or putting down a brother. . . . The tone and the quality of his words are significant. He must remember to use a different rap for lower-class females than middle-class females.

One of the most difficult problems facing Black parents is assisting the adolescent deal with his or her sexuality. While all parents must contend with this problem, the myths and stereotypes associated with Black sexuality make the task more difficult. Both boys and girls can be entrapped in trying to live up to the image of sexual prowess. . . .

It is purported that Black girls are often socialized to be independent, disciplined, and puritanical. In contrast to Black boys, there seems to be some evidence that there are fewer social conformists among Black females at an early age. On the other hand, Black boys have frequently been socialized to be obedient and compliant, not to be too ambitious or aggressive. Historically, parents have been fearful for the safety of the son. Today, there is emphasis on survival and ethnic pride. Racism is seldom tolerated and more apt to be confronted.

Today, within the Black community, males are socialized to be strong, aggressive, and independent. A boy who seems "weak" is often reprimanded and ridiculed by his father and other adults including his mother and older sisters and peers. While Black males and females are encouraged to get an education, the Black male frequently emulates professional athletes and is subtly encouraged by parents and the community to develop athletic and physical prowess. They view sports as a vehicle to a successful future and physical prowess as an indication of "maleness.". . .

The high unemployment and limited opportunities for Black adolescent males have a negative effect on their ability to gain independence, to have access to higher education, and to even subsist. Hence, a young Black male's identity is often in jeopardy.

The conditions under which many young Black males live are largely responsible for an increase in the use of drugs and the kind of crime rate that goes with it. It's all built into the kind of despair and lack of projection —"who gives a damn?" Fortunately, a number of Black youths are able to find jobs, complete their education, and establish successful careers. This success is largely due to the Black child's high resilience and survival skills. . . .

Black girls' conceptions of what kind of women they eventually are to become are influenced also by their associations with older sisters, mothers, grandmothers, aunts, and a variety of other role models. They frequently select a model who has been successful. Success is measured among lower-class Black females by the degree to which one can take care of oneself and assist others in the family. Black middle-class girls are socialized to define a successful model as one who has a college education and a professional job—such as teaching. In fact, to insure that their young Black girls continue to value a college education and professional job, many Black parents send them to the "best" Black college in the South.

The start of menstruation for any adolescent female is a major developmental event. Many traditional "preventive" health care practices to be carried out during the cycle are taught to young girls by their mothers, grandmothers, and significant others. Girls are strongly admonished not to wash their hair, take tub baths, go swimming, or submerge their feet in water. Cleanliness is stressed, however.

The anticipation of womanhood is symbolized by certain acquired characteristics that are felt to result in independence. One of these characteristics of independence is shown in the belief of some lower-class Black adolescents that having a baby will help them to achieve a certain kind of responsibility, and consequently womanhood, that they could not otherwise enjoy. . . .

Working outside the home is one means of acquiring some semblance of independence. Owing to the historically high unemployment rate among Black youth, this route often does not provide the desired payoff.

The strongest concept of womanhood for the young Black female is that of how she has to play a strong role in the family. Another major conception is that she will probably have to work to help her mate support a family. Few Black girls grow up expecting to stay home and care for the children, but anticipate that they will work outside the home. Indeed, they are socialized to be strong because they more than likely will have to use their resourcefulness.

Learning how to relate to members of the opposite sex is also part of the preparation for womanhood. Relating to boys appropriately is a skill learned within the same-sex peer group early in life. Boys become sexual persons at an earlier age for the lower-class Black girl than for the middle-class Black girl and her White counterparts. Also, heterosexual relationships, such as dating, develop at an early age in the communal setting of Black social relationships.

While young Black male adolescents are becoming more and more adept at the technique of rapping, the female is learning to discriminate between a guy who is "for real" and one who has a "weak rap." When the male makes a ploy to develop a relationship of varying degrees of sexual intimacy, she may agree to participate or decline. Her decision will be influenced by her peer group, degree of internalization of parental values, religion, and her self-selected goals. Black girls who engage in premarital sex tend to be more critical of parental control and to feel that their parents do not understand the needs and problems of adolescents. Some young Black females told Joyce Ladner that some reasons for participating in premarital sex are that they perceive it as (1) a substitute for other areas of gratification that could not be fulfilled through ordinary channels, (2) an attainment of a sense of belonging and feeling needed, (3) a system of exchange (sex for gifts), and (4) an indication of being a woman.

Black parents urge their daughter to remain chaste until adulthood. However, more emphasis is placed on the practical consequences of premarital sex (pregnancy), rather than on the religious stance—sex relations before marriage are sinful. (Greathouse 1981, 78–92)

In the following sections other ethnic families are discussed. Next is the American Indian family.

THE AMERICAN INDIAN FAMILY

Discipline was and is extraordinarily permissive and mild by non-Indian standards. Shame and ridicule were ordinarily effective in achieving the desired behavior. Traditionally, corporal punishment was rarely used. However, as a last resort, some tribes utilized traditional scratching as a behavior control for especially obstreperous youth. This was done by painfully raking a sharp-toothed object on the arm or upper body and was administered by a maternal male relative, usually the child's uncle. As part of discipline, Indian children were taught not to cry out at night. This was a precautionary protective measure for the welfare and benefit of the tribe, especially if they were being hunted and a child's cry would reveal their hiding place. Many Indian families feel their children are competent to care for themselves at an early age and older children are often given supervisory responsibilities for younger children. Some non-Indians label this as objectionable neglect and child abuse, and it may conflict with the non-Indian society's child care standards and the laws, resulting in removal of the child from his family. . . .

Indian societies, like all societies, have formal and informal sex mores and taboos. In most tribes there were few inhibitions or restrictions regarding the intermingling of the sexes up to the age of puberty. Bodily functions were accepted as a normal everyday part of living and sex play and body curiosity by children were not subjected to shaming or disciplinary punishment. When an Indian child reached puberty, ceremonial recognition was and is still given in many tribes. The individual boy in many tribes would go on a specially planned vision quest to an isolated place in the woods or upon a mountain that would have special meaning and give spiritual direction to his future life. The vision might convey a special name or a guardian spirit, or give him some supernatural power related to his future destiny. It was a part of an expected maturing process that tested and reinforced his tribal identity.

Unfortunately modern Indian life has failed to develop a satisfactory maturational substitute for today's Indian youth, and this is often reflected tragically in a lack of purpose and direction, high incidence of alcoholism, drug abuse, school under-achievement and dropping-out, and suicide. Current suicide rates among Indian youth have reached epidemic proportions. The seriousness of this is demonstrated by the 1974–76 age-adjusted suicide rate among Indians, which is 2.1 times as high as the overall United States.

Prior to the onset of puberty, Indian girls were instructed by the older women of the tribe in their responsibilities as a wife and mother. At puberty there usually were symbolic ceremonies in which she played a leading role signifying her attainment of adulthood with its attendant rights and responsibilities. One example of such a ceremony is the Apache "Gahns" (sometimes called "Mountain Spirits"). It is an event sponsored by the girl's family, with many sacred and social meanings. Today, such ceremonies are becoming rare, primarily because of the prohibitive expense of feeding the many friends and spectators, plus the fees for the medicine men/women and singers. Many Apache families feel they can no longer afford such an expensive ceremony that may no longer be appropriate or necessary in a modern Indian society. . . .

Dating was generally unrestricted among Indian youth, but was primarily within one's own tribe. There were usually no tribal class distinctions and one could date and marry anyone except for the incest prohibitions relating to members of one's own clan.

A modern phenomenon regarding dating has developed as a result of the intertribal mix found in the student bodies of the Bureau of Indian Affairs (BIA) boarding schools. It is not unusual to find not only intertribal friendships but marriages resulting when students from different tribes meet. Today, there is apparently little concern by young Indians for observing the traditional incest prohibitions for taboos regarding intertribal dating and marriage within the same clan. However, such intertribal marriages do present some unique legal and social problems for the husband, wife, and their off-spring. Tribal membership requirements usually allow individual membership in only one tribe, that is, an Indian can only be a voting member and receive benefits from one tribe. Unfortunately, the quantum of "Indianness" of the children from the intertribal marriage may become diluted to such an extent as to make them ineligible for membership in either one or both of their parents' tribes. It may in effect make them non-Indians. This tribal membership restriction may also create familial divisiveness with serious problems relating to tribal loyalty and family allegiance in a family that may already have serious adjustment problems.

Another problem of family relationships results from the fact that traditionally many tribes were matriarchal and the children belonged to their mother's clan and took their mother's surname. All tribal rights emanated from this maternal relationship. Today, this may create friction in estate settlements and parental and sibling relationships. The most important man in matriarchal tribes for an Indian child may not be his natural father but his mother's oldest brother. Not only was this uncle responsible for parental training and discipline, but he introduced the child to the clan and sponsored his initiation into important tribal societies. He was an effective father surrogate and role model, but one without legal sanction from the non-Indian society.

It is expected that the Indian youth will be different, and he is encouraged to be independent. In particular, Indian boys are reared to be physically daring and impetuous. If he does not perform an occasional controversially defiant act, he will be less acceptable as a son, brother, friend, or sweetheart. Indian boys are reared to be proud and are expected to a degree to resist outside behavior controls. They have certain familial obligations, but their primary behavior models often come from peers. A major problem with this adolescent peer emulation is that with extra time on their hands, in a relatively unsupervised setting away from the family, such as boarding schools, adolescent acting out and testing may lead to dangerous antisocial experimentation in prohibited areas such as truancy, drugs, alcohol, and premarital sex. This behavior is usually nonviolent. In many Indian communities, this type of behavior is abetted by poverty, isolation, alcoholism, and in many cases the apparent permissiveness found in traditional family controls of the extended Indian family. . . .

Social erosion in Indian cultures has resulted in Indian family relationships changing significantly in recent years. One major change has been in the role and function of the extended family. Instead of being an available viable resource of support and self-sufficiency, it has become an anomalous, impermanent structure for retreat and withdrawal for those individuals who are insecure. Another important change in Indian family life has been in the weakening of the relationship and role of the Indian father to his children. He no longer has marketable skills and knowledge to teach and is not a positive role model for his children to emulate. Male youths tend to turn to their brothers and peers for support and role models. There are also new roles and relationships between females, with only token gestures toward traditionally important relationships. Special importance and status are given to the obtaining of a non-Indian education and successful and well-paid employment. (Farris and Farris 1981, 61–64)

THE CHINESE-AMERICAN FAMILY

Parents feel totally responsible for their child's behavior, which is considered a reflection on them. If a child misbehaves, he has not received proper training at home. Sollenberger relates an incident in which the teacher sent home a note reporting an infraction of the rules by a Chinese pupil. The father personally went to the school the next day to apologize to the teacher for *his* failure in the proper upbringing of his child. Such action on the part of the father would probably be rare today; more likely the child would be chastised at home and the parent would remind him of the shame he has brought to the family name. "One person's disgrace results in shame to the entire family" and similar admonitions are repeated early to the young Chinese.

Education has always been stressed as a means of achievement and continues to be an important value. Immigrant children were told to "study hard, then life will be easier for you than it is for us." Implicit in statements made nowadays is a similar chain of events: if you study hard you can go to college, which will help you get a better job, resulting in more income and a higher standard of living. American schools have reinforced this by stressing academic achievement, effort, and good conduct. They also indicate models of famous people who have earned their fame by this behavior.

The absence of overt parental praise and reward has been identified as a childrearing practice designed to teach a child humility. Young's study confirmed this and also found that reward for desired behavior was not totally lacking. Mothers were unable to describe positive incentives for good behavior, but they acknowledged that substantial recognition from peers, teachers, and relatives served as encouragement. Non-verbal indicators of pleasure, such as a slight affirmative nod or the glimpse of a smile on the parent's face, are obvious to the child from an early age. The absence of a scolding may also serve as positive reinforcement to the Chinese child. Immigrant parents preferred to give material rewards, such as money or a food treat, rather than praise. Modern parents give material rewards and in addition are more generous in verbal praise.

Verbal communication has increased between Chinese children and their parents. Immigrant families had stilted, formal contacts, which were commands or scoldings. The child remained within hearing range of an adult and was ignored as long as he did not exhibit rough behavior or unnecessary loudness. Children did not speak unless they were spoken to. Chinese families today have more small talk and children voice their opinions in discussions.

Parents convey the importance of certain values verbally and through their actions. First-generation parents were strict authoritarians and their commands were never questioned. "If my parents disapproved, it was wrong," was a guideline for second-generation children. Hard-working parents demonstrate through their own actions their belief that diligence is a desirable trait and leads to success. Industrious parents reiterate to their children, "We work hard so you can have this and even better. You must also work hard to maintain what you have and strive to improve."

Spanking and scolding are common methods of punishment. Immigrant families were accustomed to beatings with a bamboo rod from either parent but modern families spank or threaten spankings. Shaming or lecturing are other usual forms of punishment. The young child may be temporarily removed from the social life of the family or deprived of privileges or objects. Rarely is the child ridiculed. Undesired behaviors are disobedience, aggressiveness, fighting, messiness, and poor school work. Desired behaviors are obedience, sharing, noncompetitiveness among siblings, and achievement, especially in school work.

Chinese children are incorporated early and relatively fully into the daily life of the family. They are taught that everyone works for the welfare of the family, so they, too, must be useful at an early age. They are assigned specific chores not only to demonstrate that their help is needed at home, but as proper training for their future life. The children are given a great deal of responsibility at a comparatively young age. Older children are responsible for teaching and supervising younger children and assisting with food preparation. Older siblings are encouraged to set the example for younger ones by giving up pleasure or comfort in favor of someone else, to give in during a quarrel, and to politely refuse in favor of someone else. Although given responsibility for tasks at home, the Chinese child is not encouraged to have independent activity outside the home or with other non-family children until late childhood.

The young child is dependent on his parents for food, shelter, clothing, and other aspects of his physical existence, as well as his emotional security. As he grows older and ventures outside the family and home, his parents are insistent upon knowing details about his friends. Peers are carefully screened and the child is not allowed playmates who exhibit undesirable traits or behavior. Other Chinese children of similar economic and social status are highly encouraged as associates.

Chinese children enjoy playing, but it is not overtly encouraged by their parents. Little girls in China did not play with dolls because they were regarded as having magical powers. In the Chinese language, the word "doll" comes from the same root word as "idol" or "fetish." "Dolls were used as ritual objects to be held during confinement or placed as a temple offering when one hoped for the birth of a child." Exuberant physical activity is not highly valued among traditional parents, who prefer games and puzzles that challenge the mind. . . .

Contemporary Chinese-American youths are more vocal than those of previous generations. They are less hesitant to champion a cause, speak out, protest, or demonstrate against what they deem inequities or injustices. A youthful political activist related being ostracized more by his own family than by outside society. "They didn't throw me out, they just iced me and then surrounded me, that really did the job."

Those interviewed described some of the acculturative changes that they observed. The young adults are no longer pressured to date only Chinese. Social interaction among people of different racial backgrounds is acceptable; the Chinese no longer need to band together for protection. These young adults want to perpetuate certain aspects of their heritage. They want their children to learn the cultural ways and the tradition that binds them. They also want their children to experience the closeness, sense of belonging, and acceptance that is part of the extended family. (Char 1981, 154–57)

THE PUERTO RICAN-AMERICAN FAMILY

Puerto Rican adolescents on the Mainland grow up with many of the same ideals as their Anglo-Saxon counterparts. They are expected to be responsible, care for themselves, pursue their studies, and go on to college or pursue a trade. The latter expectations, however, are intermingled with many of the traditional Puerto Rican ideals, resulting in added conflicts between parent and child. Here parents become increasingly conscious of the dilemma involved in raising a Puerto Rican child in an American society. The child who is already going through the identity crisis typical of early adolescence must deal as well with his Puerto Rican versus his American identity. The child's experiences outside the home teach him that he is an American, while his experiences at home teach him that he is a Puerto Rican. In school he is discouraged from speaking Spanish; at home he is expected to use his native language. The conflict widens as the independence and self-assertion that is taught in school is viewed by his parents as defiance and revolt against parental authority.

The Puerto Rican male approaches adolescence with aspirations of becoming an independent man. Parents, however, continue to demand respect and adherence to parental authority far into adulthood. The parent likes to see his son grow into a responsible adult, yet feels that the child should not override parental authority. Dependency is especially encouraged by the mother, who continues to cater to the young man's tastes in food and continues to clean up after him. He is expected to do well in school and to either enter some sort of career or obtain a good paying job. The Puerto Rican child is taught from an early age that he must work hard to realize his goals.

Males generally begin dating at an earlier age. Parents prefer to know the dating partner, but will not object if this is not the case. He is expected to date several girls before he makes a decision to marry. The marriage choice should preferably be someone of the same culture, but other cultures are very well accepted into the Puerto Rican family. The son is expected to bring the girl home to meet his parents. Several visits by the girl prior to marriage are expected so that the parents can get to know her. Conversations may revolve around the girl's family background. An instant bond is often formed if the girl or her family are from the parent's home town. This is often followed by having the girl's parents meet the boy's parents, bringing the relationship to a more serious plane.

Independence to a degree is more accepted in the male than it is in the female. The son is allowed to be absent from the home for longer periods without causing much alarm on the part of the parents. The female who does the same can disrupt an entire household.

As has been previously mentioned, the female is as a rule overprotected. Although expected to be successful in school and career, she is expected to remain close to home while realizing these goals. The father is especially protective of his daughter, often imposing excessive restrictions on her. The female is expected to be more dependent on the parents. It is almost mandatory that dating partners be introduced to the parents. The marriage partner here should, again, preferably be of Hispanic background to facilitate communication between him and the girl's parents. Boys dating the daughter are customarily scrutinized by the parents, whether or not they are steady partners, in order to determine the daughter's degree of safety with the individual. Although chaperonage has become rare, the traditional belief in male aggression and female weakness prevails in many Puerto Rican homes. Women are still often seen as "incapable of defending themselves against male sexual aggression, while men are incapable of internally imposed self-discipline." When a female begins to see a certain partner on a steady basis, he is expected to visit her home frequently and to be conversant with the girl's family.

Interpretations of the marriage relationship vary in the Puerto Rican culture. Ideally, a period of engagement should be followed by a formal wedding ceremony and reception. It is important to the parent that the daughter wear a white gown with crown and veil so that society may see that she is chaste and respectable. In many families, however, the common law marriage is accepted. This is particularly the case in those families where financial conditions do not allow for a formal wedding. Although the young adult is granted the freedom to choose the marriage partner, family opinion tends to have a great influence on the relationship. Pressure from either of the two families is often enough to create discord in the marriage.

Attitudes toward sex and the adolescent also vary. As a rule, sexual activity should not occur outside marriage. The female is expected to be a virgin at the time of marriage, but this is not stressed for the male. The adolescent will most often obtain his sex education in school and from his peers. The mother and daughter continue to be the ones who discuss sexual matters in the home. The father continues to be passive and the son excluded almost completely from home discussion in this area.

The parent's involvement in the child's health care is mostly geared toward nutrition, physical illness, and emotional problems if some appear to exist. Although many parents continue their all-out effort to continue the child's preventive health care, the child's resistance results in less stress in this area at this time. Parents are often more involved in dealing with the conflicts that arise during this stage of development. Parents who were accustomed to an obedient and respectful child may now be faced with what they see as a rebellious and disrespectful teenager. Many parents may experience feelings of failure during this period. Father, in particular, may experience a threat to his authority and self-esteem when his son's interests and opinions differ from his own. These differences may be great between a father who has seen his youth in Puerto Rico and a son who is seeing his on the Mainland.

Parents prefer that their children remain in the home until they marry. A son's or daughter's decision to obtain a separate apartment may be offensive to the parents, who feel that they are no longer appreciated or respected. When marriage does occur the family appears to go through a period of adjustment, during which frequent visiting takes place between the couple and their parents. Families still often reside in close proximity to each other.

The ultimate dream of the Puerto Rican parent is to see his children attain educational and professional success, establish a stable marital relationship, and bring forth grandchildren. Grandchildren are seen as a reward for the years of striving to raise their children properly. (Lacay 1981, 222–24)

THE MEXICAN-AMERICAN FAMILY

Adolescence is a difficult age for most children and parents. The Chicano parent and adolescent are no different. In the traditional family puberty is treated quite differently for boys and girls.

The male is allowed much more freedom and usually has a strong peer group that he identifies with. The male adolescent spends a lot of time outside the home with the boys or what is frequently referred to as the *palomilla*. The word means moths that gather around a light at night. Palomillas are not to be confused with gangs found in some urban areas. Gangs are more frequently associated with violence, and fights over property or "turf." There is much being written about gangs and some organizations are working towards turning them into something positive for themselves and the community. Many feel that gangs are a result of weakening of the Chicano family caused by urban pressures and weakening of family roles. This is a phenomenon that will not be dealt with in this chapter.

Many of the traditional practices once followed by Chicano families are now changing in response to pressure put on parents by their sons and daughters.

The palomilla, then, is a harmless peer group that serves a need for the Chicano male. This is where he receives his sex-education, and not surprisingly most of the discussions center around girls. There is not much discussion in the home in regard to sex education. Any discipline the boy might get will be given by his father. It is at this time that the father becomes a very strong authority figure. At the present time there is much revolt by young males against their fathers. It is difficult for the father to maintain his traditional role when his children are being exposed to different values in the society.

The Chicana adolescent faces a similar struggle with her mother in regard to dating practices. When a Chicana girl has her fifteenth birthday she is given a very special birthday party. If her parents can afford it, they give a large party with food, drink, and music. This occasion is called a Quinceanera and is equivalent to a coming-out party or debut. With the Chicano movement and the rededication to the culture, Quinceaneras have increased in popularity. The girl usually dresses in a white dress (like a bride), carries flowers and is accompanied by fourteen couples to a church service. Middle-class acculturated parents who are trying to hang on to parts of their cultural heritage are also having Quinceaneras for their daughters. In Mexico this meant that a girl was ready to be courted in her home. Although some Chicano families still hold on to this tradition, most have been forced to relax their standards by the young girls who are rebelling against this authority. The old and new generations are clashing and parents are no longer able to keep young Chicanas within the confines of the home. In some urban areas, they are even going out into the streets and forming their own social clubs, much like the palomillas of the teen-age male. They are challenging the traditional male-female relationship, which has given them very little flexibility in their roles. At the same time many Chicanas are advancing changes that advocate positive cultural values. This is not true of all families and many still maintain extremely strict rules of conduct for the daughter. Mothers and daughters continue to be close in most cases, with the daughters doing many of the household chores and caring for the younger children.

Menstruation is viewed as a necessary evil. Many girls are still not prepared for it, although with sex education in the schools this is much less likely to happen. The theory of hot and cold applies to menstruation; many cold foods are avoided during this time. Sour foods, such as lemons and pickles, are avoided as are chilled drinks. These are thought to cause menstrual pain and to coagulate the blood. Many herbs are used for the relief of menstrual cramps, with the most common being mint tea, chamomile, and cumin. A girl is taught to take it easy on those days and to avoid bathing or shampooing her hair. This restriction, along with the one after delivery, seems to be disappearing. Chicano girls see Anglo girls taking a shower and nothing happens, so they try it.

Most parents want their children to do better than they did in a career goal. A study of Hoope and Leon on coping and non-coping parents showed that parental aspirations for children in coping families were high. They attached a high value to education and saw it as a means for the children to do better in life than they had done. They at least desired that their children finish high school, as most of the parents had to drop out of school for reasons of family finance or illness. The non-coping families in the study had lower aspirations for their children, including in education. According to this study neither group of parents voiced higher hopes for sons than for daughters, as had been expected.

Fifty percent of our informants felt that they wanted their children to go to college, while the other fifty percent said they wanted their children to finish high school. Most parents indicated that it would be the child's choice and that they would accept average grades if that is all that the child could do. (Ehling 1981, 206–7)

THE JAPANESE-AMERICAN FAMILY

When the child begins to socialize outside of the family, much emphasis is placed on interpersonal harmony and avoidance of conflict. Quarreling outside of the family is looked upon as a very serious behavior. To maintain the social control within the family, "giri" or a child's moral obligation toward others and his family is stressed. Children are trained to restore harmony after a quarrel on their own initiative, without adult intervention, particularly when the conflict involves other families. . . .

Finally, the child is trained to conform to the norms governing his prescribed role. Role behavior is defined by his sex, age, and birth order.

Sex differences in response to manners and etiquette are stressed within the Japanese culture. Such differences between the two sexes, however, have been recognized in other cultures and are one of the important conditions upon which cultures have been built.

Meredith reported that in the traditional Japanese culture, good behavior for the sexes was defined primarily in terms of obedient, conforming, and responsible conduct. The prolongation of customs, such as Girl's and Boy's Days, in acculturating Japanese groups, reinforces differential sex role behavior. For the female, particular emphasis is placed on poise, grace, and control. For the male, stress is placed on manliness, determination, and the will to overcome all obstacles in the path to success.

The influence of early socialization experiences and maternal attitudes toward differential treatment of the sexes plays an important role. For example, modesty is stressed more in the rearing of girls. The female quickly learns to be modest of her nude body and to sleep straight with her legs together. Boys, on the other hand, are allowed a greater amount of freedom.

The culture further reinforces sex differentiation with terms and phrases in its language. Feminine words are reserved for only females and masculine words are reserved for only males.

In terms of age, the older brothers and sisters are consistently told to set good examples for their younger siblings. The older siblings are also taught to indulge the younger children. When there are quarrels, the mother will likely ask the older child to give in to the younger one. "Why not lose to win?" is a common phrase. The rationale for this phrase is that if the older child gives up his toy to the younger child, the baby will be satisfied and turn to some-

Adolescents whose families have more than one ethnic background, may be influenced and stand to benefit by the traditions in those different backgrounds.

thing else; then the older child will have won back his toy even as he relinquished it. "To lose to win" becomes an arrangement greatly respected in the Japanese life, even through adulthood.

Benedict noted that in large families "the alternate children are united by closer ties. The oldest will be the favored nurse and protector of the third child and the second of the fourth. The younger children reciprocate."

Role discipline increases when the child reaches school age. The child is repeatedly instructed to obey his teachers and not to bring shame to the family. He is encouraged to develop a strong sense of belonging and total commitment to the group of which he is a part, and is instilled with the motivation for status identification and role performance. . . .

Like parents of other cultures, Japanese parents manipulate the pleasure and pain directly felt by their children. The Japanese child is rewarded materially with candies, toys, or other special treats and punished by being deprived of them for his misbehavior. Physical punishment, such as pinching or light hitting, is also used. The most severe physical punishment used is "moxa," which is regarded as a medicinal technique for curing.

> This is the burning of a little cone of powder, the moxa, upon the child's skin. It leaves a lifelong scar. Cauterization by moxa is an old, widespread Eastern Asiatic medicine, and it was traditionally used to cure many aches and pains in Japan too. It can also cure tantrums and obstinacy. A little boy of six or seven may be "cured" in this way by his mother or grandmother. It may even be used twice in a difficult case but very seldom indeed is a child given the moxa treatment for naughtiness a third time. It is not a punishment in the sense that "I'll spank you if you do that" is a punishment. But it hurts far worse than spanking, and the child learns that he cannot be naughty with impunity.

A Sansei recalls the use of moxa as a child:

> When I was very young, I remember my grandfather threatening to yaito (burn) my older sister with senko (cone-type incense) for using her left hand. Or he at times would set the lighted senko on the table if we failed to finish our food. . . .

Sex education for the young Nisei female was very restrictive. Even after marriage, she was urged not to read books on sex and believe that she was capable of sexual satisfaction.

The continuation of the restrictive attitudes toward information on sex over generations was illustrated in Kitano's studies on parental childrearing attitudes among a sample of Issei and Nisei. The studies disclosed that both generations fostered dependency and were sexually repressive of their offspring.

Similarly, in 1966 Connor conducted a study on family bonds, maternal closeness, and the suppression of sexuality among groups of Issei, Nisei, and Sansei living in Sacramento. The responses from the three generations of Japanese Americans were matched with similar scores obtained from similar Caucasian American groups. . . . The Japanese Americans also scored higher on areas concerning nuturance, affiliation, succor, abasement, and order; they had lower scores on dominance, autonomy, and heterosexuality, and suppression of sexuality. Connor suggested that the lower scores on heterosexuality appear to be part of the larger pattern of maternal closeness and strong family ties, and not an isolated phenomenon. This also suggests that while considerable acculturation has occurred, the lower scores among the Sansei reveal a preservation of sexual repressive attitudes from their immigrant grandparents.

The interrelation between suppression of sexuality and strong family ties and close emotional bonds with the mother is further supported in writings by Caudill and Doi and DeVos. Both works indicate that Japanese mothers strive to foster dependency needs in their offspring and then utilize these dependency needs to manipulate the behavior of the child. The dependency needs and maternal closeness thereby lead to a suppression of sexuality. . . .

Current Japanese-American parental attitudes toward adolescent dating seem to fall within the same realm as those of a large number of other American parents. Their attitudes and patterns vary from family to family.

In general, during the period prior to dating, when a child begins to socialize outside of the family, Japanese-American parents prefer that their child associate with peers from his own ethnic group. They are, however, quite accepting when their child associates with peers from other ethnic groups.

Although attitudes toward interracial dating have relaxed through the years, particularly after World War II, parents still seem to place a strong emphasis on their ethnicity and in group dating. The attitudes prevail until marriage. A recent study indicated that there is a preference for in-group marriage, even for those who married out of the group, although it was not a major issue. It is noteworthy to mention that while the incidence of interracial marriages have steadily increased in recent years, there is still a high rate of in-group marital patterns. . . .

As previously noted, throughout Japan's recorded history, high standards of excellence have been emphasized. Such standards were highly emphasized in the Issei's childhood and were one of the values that they brought with them from Japan. (Sodetani-Shibata 1981, 128–33)

QUESTION: What does research say about family differences among ethnic groups?

Most research has focused on the two largest minority groups, blacks and Mexican Americans. In general, differences in family style apparently are present, which are independent and separate from socioeconomic or social class differences. Separating the effects of family from the general effects of the social milieu is difficult, and as one can see by reading the preceding accounts of family life, among different racial groups the prevailing values, attitudes, and cultural traditions are different. The reader is also cautioned about generalizing these general group behavior patterns to individuals, as the within-group variance is almost always greater than the between-group variance in psychological characteristics.

In addition, the family constantly evolves as it adjusts to new conditions. This has been particularly true in modern America, where change rather than continuity has been typical and part of the culture. What conclusions have been drawn are therefore almost certain to change. Being aware of differences in the new past, however, allows one to more intelligently interpret differences in the present and in the future. Among Mexican Americans, for example, the patriarchial extended family has been the tradition over years, but in modern times the nuclear family has evolved as and is proving to be the most efficient and durable in mainstream American society. Not surprisingly, the Mexican family feels strange as it evolves toward the American model. One researcher (Derbyshire 1968) noted this coming together. His opinion is that the strong male patriarchial family exists only because the females allow it. He states, "Females frequently verbalize the satisfaction that their husband's and father's position in the family promotes family respect out of deference to his loss in status in Anglo culture."

Although the black family has been unique in that the stresses resulting from slavery and economic oppression still produce an impact, a larger number of black families also live within the poverty level and are subject to social, educational, and political disadvantages. In trying to explain the special circumstances surrounding black families, one text author writes:

> The mother is a frustrated object to many black adolescents. It is not the intent of the mother to neglect or mistreat her children; on the contrary, she usually has strong maternal feelings, is excessively protective, and has every hope of being a good provider. The child or adolescent's perception may be somewhat different. Children often relate stories of frustration, discipline, cruelty, cursing, and a general attitude among kids that the mother hates them. (Thornburg 1975, 81, 237–38)

The strong matriarchal dominance is also viewed by this same author as causing another type of problem among lower-class black boys. He states:

> Lower-class black boys must declare their masculinity in the most direct ways they know. Easy of all, avoidance of women, whom they view as trying to emasculate them; scorn for middle-class standards, including the striving for academic achievement; and hatred for authority. . . . They quickly assume the attitude that educational and cultural pursuits are feminine concerns and therefore not for them. They regard women teachers as desexualized automatons, for whom they have either contempt or pity. Men teachers are often suspected as being not quite "right," especially male white teachers, since liberal males especially lower-class ones, perceive white men as being somewhat feminine anyway. (Thornburg 1975, 239)

These types of concerns strongly suggest that it is important to be acquainted with factors in family life that influence adolescents from different racial subgroups. We have stressed that change is constantly occurring. Again, the family is the strongest single influence in our culture, even though it may have been weakened and altered with the changing times of the twentieth century.

Parental influence and discipline

Beginning with the work of an earlier theorist, three dimensions of parental behavior can be identified (Becker 1964). These three dimensions are seen in Figure 5–1. The warmth versus hostility dimension is defined at the warm end by accepting, affectionate, approving, understanding, child-centered, frequent use of explanations, positive response to dependency behavior, high use of reasons in discipline, high use of praise in discipline, low use of physical punishment, and (for mothers) low criticism of husband. The hostility end of the dimension is defined by the opposite characteristics.

The restrictiveness versus permissiveness dimension is defined at the restrictive end by: many restrictions and strict enforcement of demands in the areas of sex play, modesty behavior, table manners, toilet training, neatness, orderliness, care of household furniture, noise, obedience, aggression to siblings, aggression to peers, and aggression to parents.

Anxious emotional involvement versus calm/detached is defined at the anxious end by high emotionality in relation to child, babying, protectiveness, and solicitousness for the child's welfare.

Examination of Figure 5–1 demonstrates, as Becker pointed out, that the only difference between democratic and indulgent parents is the amount of emotional involvement (anxiety). The same difference is found between organized effective and overprotective, rigid controlling and hostile authoritarian, and neglecting and anxious neurotic.

Figure 5–1 *Classification System for Parent Types*

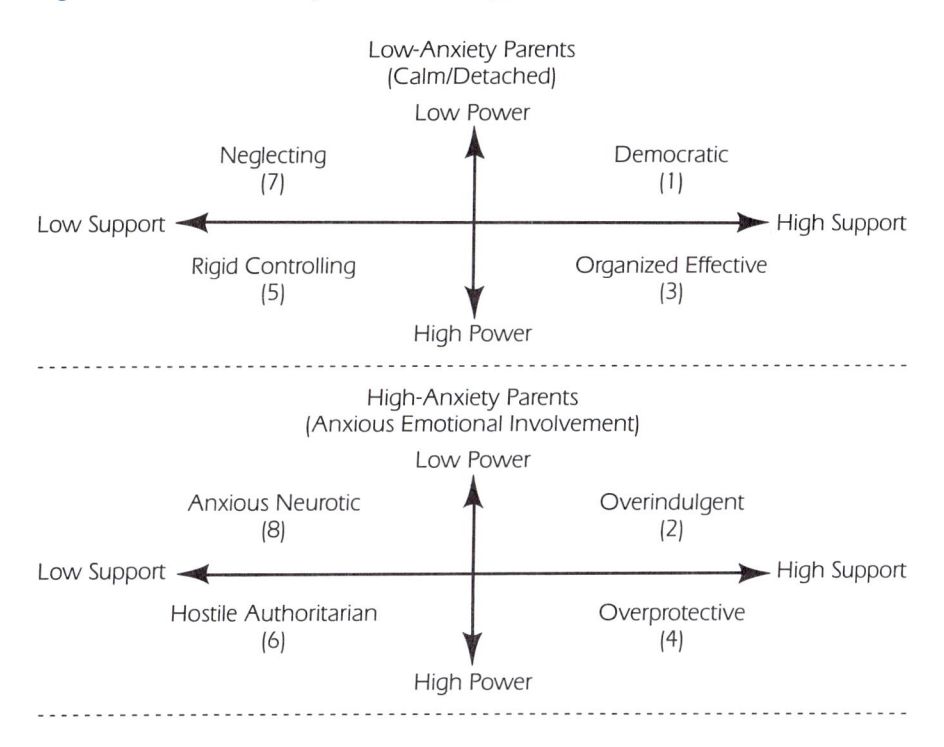

```
                Low-Anxiety Parents
                 (Calm/Detached)
                    Low Power
                        ▲
       Neglecting      │      Democratic
          (7)          │         (1)
Low Support ◄──────────┼──────────► High Support
     Rigid Controlling │    Organized Effective
          (5)          │         (3)
                        ▼
                   High Power
- - - - - - - - - - - - - - - - - - - - - - - - -
                High-Anxiety Parents
            (Anxious Emotional Involvement)
                    Low Power
                        ▲
     Anxious Neurotic   │     Overindulgent
          (8)          │         (2)
Low Support ◄──────────┼──────────► High Support
   Hostile Authoritarian │     Overprotective
          (6)          │         (4)
                        ▼
                   High Power
- - - - - - - - - - - - - - - - - - - - - - - - -
```

Source: Adapted from W. L. Becker, "Consequences of Different Kinds of Parental Discipline," in *Review of Child Development*, vol. 1, edited by M. L. Hoffman and L. W. Hoffman (New York: Sage Foundation, 1964), 175.

Parent types can thus be described as follows:

		Affection	*Authority*	*Worry*
1.	Democratic	High support,	Low power,	Low anxiety
2.	Indulgent	High support,	Low power,	High anxiety
3.	Organized effective	High support,	High power,	Low anxiety
4.	Overprotective	High support,	High power,	High anxiety
5.	Rigid controlling	Low support,	High power,	Low anxiety
6.	Hostile authoritarian	Low support,	High power,	High anxiety
7.	Neglecting	Low support,	Low power,	Low anxiety
8.	Anxious neurotic	Low support,	Low power,	High anxiety

Anxiety in parents results from many factors, either those directly related to their role as parents or those not connected with their parental role. A mother may be afraid she is not adequately prepared to be a mother. A father may be afraid of what his child will do if he does not let the child know (regularly) who is the boss. A father may be a tyrant with his children because he feels threatened about losing his job at the factory. A mother may be indulgent because she does not want the neighbors to think she is a cruel person.

QUESTION: What effects do parental types have on their children?

Now that we have briefly discussed the three dimensions of support, power, and anxiety, let us describe and discuss the characteristics of the parent types presented in Figure 5-1. The following is a more in-depth discussion based on the general research findings in this area. (See Schaeffer 1959, Becker 1964, Maccoby 1980, and Baumrind 1971). Since the majority of research is related to the four parent types centering on the high-support axis (over-protective, organized effective, democratic, and indulgent), most of our discussion will focus on these types. First, however, the four types that have low support as a common bond (neglecting, rigid controlling, anxious neurotic, and hostile authoritarian) are described.

PARENTS LOW IN LOVE-SUPPORT

Neglecting parents with low support, low power, and low anxiety are characterized by a lack of concern for their children. They are usually hedonistic and tend to leave children to their own devices. A significant percentage of delinquents come from this type of parent. These parents lack warmth and are either neglectful in exercising parental control or highly inconsistent in the use of discipline. Children raised by overly hostile and restrictive parents are more likely to internalize their own angry feelings. They usually exhibit aggressive and poorly controlled behavior.

Rigid controlling parents are those who have low support, high power, and low anxiety. They are both restrictive and hostile and tend to produce counter-hostility in their children. Under such conditions, children tend to become neurotic. These children are socially withdrawn, shy, anxious, and highly self-punishing because they cannot express their hostility behaviorally. This combination of low support, high power, and low anxiety fosters resentment and is generally experienced as turmoil.

Anxious neurotic parents are those with low support, low power, and high anxiety. They transfer their anxiety to their children. They were probably the product of rigid controlling or hostile authoritarian parents themselves. Their anxieties are focused inward. They believe the world is out to get them. Children from these homes are motivated toward antisocial behavior; they are socially aggressive and punitive.

Hostile authoritarian parents are those with low support, high power, and high authority. Like rigid controlling parents, they are restrictive and punitive. Their authoritarianism, however, is primarily a result of anxiety. They are generally frustrated people who try to appease their feelings by striking out at their children. The children of hostile authoritarian parents in general tend to be like those from rigid controlling homes—specifically, socially withdrawn and self-punishing.

PARENTS HIGH IN LOVE-SUPPORT

It is often said that it makes no difference what you do to or with children as long as you love them. However, the literature reveals that highly supportive, highly anxious parents at either end of the power dimension are undesirable. One type, overprotective parents, tend to smother their children with love, while the other parent type is highly supportive but exerts little control over the child.

Overprotective parents with high support, high power, and high anxiety focus their control on their children's behavior. They are quick to respond to a child's misbehavior. They use the threat of withdrawal of love and other emotional tactics in controlling their child's behavior. Some of these methods may seem irrational, but are more effective than physical punishment. Overprotective parents usually set high standards for their children. Their children are compliant and dependent on their parents for approval. They often have strong consciences to protect themselves from a withdrawal of love.

Indulgent parents are those with high support, low power, and high anxiety. They set few limits or restrictions. They are quick to remove obstacles from the child's life, but they exert little control. They tend to be warm, supportive, and unconditionally accepting. The children from indulgent homes are extremely independent. They are frequently aggressive, not only toward their peers but also toward their parents and other adults. Due to minimal limits on behavior and an unconditional acceptance of the child, the child does not develop a typical conscience, being uncompliant and mischievous.

The two remaining parent types, democratic and organized effective, are better than the other six parent types. Both democratic and organized effective parents are low in anxiety and high in support or love, although the organized effective parent uses high power assertion, while the democratic parent uses power sparingly. They will be discussed in more detail.

Democratic parents are those with high support, low power, and low anxiety. They are warm and supportive of their children, and like indulgent parents, use little power and assertion. Behavior limits and ground rules are mutually accepted, set by parents and children. Characteristics of the democratic family is the family council with equal say and power. Democratic and indulgent parents differ as a function of anxiety or emotional involvement. Indulgent parents act in fear, while democratic parents express confidence in their children and reflect an attitude of cooperation.

Democratically raised children are creative and highly independent. Their independence is founded on confidence as opposed to rebellion—expressed by the child from an indulgent home. These children are socially outgoing and accepting of others. Their sense of achievement is based on a self-rewarding structure. Their conscience is usually based on a golden rule philosophy with respect for the rights of others. Democratically raised children are typically friendly, like to do their "own thing," and allow others the same privilege.

They have been assigned attributes such as being rowdy and lacking obedience and submissiveness.

The organized effective parent has high support, high power, and low anxiety. Their parent-set limits are structured, but unlike the overprotective parent, fewer limits are imposed. These limits are rationally selected for the child's benefit. Organized effective parents are not as intense in response to misbehavior. They are methodical in choosing a course of action, basing their decision on what is best for the child. Organized effective parents set high standards of excellence for their children; they push them to operate at the peak of their abilities. Organized effective parents are confident, warm, supportive, and success-oriented people.

The characteristics of organized effective children are like those of their parents. They have high achievement striving and are responsible. They lack the independence and creativity of children from more democratic families. Organized effective children have a strong conscience and are compliant and respectful to persons in power or authority. In short, they are more the model child as prescribed by our Western civilization.

These descriptions are summaries of the most salient points from the research. Risk is involved in too much oversimplification. Nevertheless, these basic findings provide a general picture of how parental behaviors influence adolescents.

QUESTION: What are the adolescent's reactions to attempted parental control and influence techniques?

Some research (Smith 1983) has indicated that moderate parental control is directly related to socially acceptable behavior in children and adolescents. Smith (1983) contends that there is a need for more differentiation of the influence techniques used by parents in trying to exert control over their children's lives. Smith feels that parental influence may be divided into five categories, ranging from strict influence where children are given no choice to suggestions from parents that allow children to make their own choices. He also studied the overall amount of control the parent tries to use (e.g., the amount of rules parents use to govern the child's behavior).

His primary concern was adolescent reactions to parental use of power and control. These reactions are separated into categories of compliance or noncompliance and acceptance or resentment of the desired behavior. Smith found compliance is related to the amount of control that parents attempt. Interestingly, the relationship is different with maternal control than with paternal control. Smith explained that due to sex role conceptions adolescents hold, a high level of control seems to be more appropriate for men than women. Another explanation is that mothers use more attempted control, but this causes more resistance.

The strength of the parent's command also seems to influence compliance. Adolescents seem more likely to comply when their parents give a strong command during a disagreement. Although adolescents comply, however, they seemingly do not accept their parent's response. Internal acceptance was found to be inversely related to strength of command.

The implication from this article is that the best approach is to exert only a moderate amount of control over adolescents lives, setting only a few rules and restrictions. Then at a time of an important disagreement or questions, a strong command should be given, and the adolescent will tend to comply with less resentment. Smith states:

> Either of the two preceding explanations of why compliance and attempted control are curvilinearly related in the maternal but not in the paternal analysis would suggest that very high levels of attempted parental control could, by generating resistance, reduce offspring compliance in "most important" disagreements. Perhaps this is the reason why the vast majority of the parent respondents attempt to exercise no more than a moderate amount of overall control over their adolescent offspring. Most of the parents may realize that moderate overall control will maximize the probability of compliance in important situations.
>
> Turning from overall attempted control to specific parental influence techniques, the findings clearly show that offspring behavioral compliance is minimized, but that emotional acceptance is maximized, by the technique labeled persuasion, which lacks the element of parental command. Apparently, either qualified or unqualified command is more likely than persuasion to result in expressions of resentment by offspring but also is more likely to result in compliance. Since compliance, in "important" disagreements, is probably more important to parents than emotional acceptance, it is not surprising that persuasion without command was employed by only a small minority of parents in what they regarded as their "most important" disagreements with their offspring. (Smith 1983, 541)

QUESTION: What is the optimal amount of emotional control in the family?

A highly respected child psychologist, Eleanor Maccoby at Stanford University, points out the importance and necessity of parental help in achieving emotional control:

> Studies of undercontrolled adolescents have shown that their parents have neglected both disciplinary and teaching functions and that the parents were conflicted about their own values. One of the major accomplishments of normal childhood is the acquisition of controls over impulsive behavior. (Maccoby 1981, 200)

Not all psychologists would agree with this emphasis. During the previous decades psychology has stressed the importance of self-expression to the point of "letting it all hang out."

One study describes a group of boys who were overcontrolled from adolescence into adulthood. They were unable to accept and handle emotions. The study found that their parents were also inhibited and repressive toward their children's displays of anger. Strong pressure existed for compliance toward rigid demands. The demands were enforced by making the adolescents feel guilty if they did not comply. Their family life was reported to be authoritarian and joyless. For the ideal maturation of the adolescent, a healthy balance of control and full emotional expression must be present (Block 1971).

The following case illustrates the importance of the family and that the home can be a safe place to handle a new and difficult feeling. Home can provide a haven from frightening, disintegrating emotions. A young women received this kind of support from her home:

> Richard and I had dated all summer and then when we came back to college he started dating someone else. I felt like I had been used for his "summer fling." This breakup was extremely hard on me because I had never fallen in love with someone enough to feel like I could marry him as I did with Richard.
>
> The depressed, rejected, low feelings I was having were not just going to leave in a couple of days. I had never felt so depressed in my whole life. Everything I saw, everything I heard, touched or thought reminded me of Richard. I spent more hours of the day on my knees and crying than anything else.
>
> The best way I could handle the whole situation was to leave it. So I withdrew from school and went home. . . . Those negative feelings lasted from September to December and luckily my family was considerate enough to let me have my time and not get on my case about being down. I had to find my own way out.
>
> It took time to overcome my feelings but once I did, I felt like I was ready to tackle the world again.
>
> Now that I've been through the experience and it's over, I know I can handle things like that and I can overcome the hurt, rejection, and depression that I felt.

One way to resolve differences of emphasis is to recognize the role of change, vacillation, and balance in daily family life. This is especially true of emotions. The following study bears upon this issue, showing the need for both positive and negative affective states.

The National Institute of Mental Health and the National Opinion Research Center at the University of Michigan developed tests for mental health (Bradburn and Noll 1969). They wanted to study what caused happiness and psychological well-being. They used a test called the Affect Balance Scale, which measured psychological well-being as the difference between the scores on the positive and negative feelings items in the test. They found that people who report many feelings are not happier than those who report fewer; the proportion is what determines happiness. Although negative emotions will inevitably occur in everyone's world, the ratio or balance of positive or negative is important for healthy psychological growth. Little evidence supports the contention that negative emotions or feelings have a beneficial impact. The emotions of hate, anger, resentment, rage, and jealousy have not been shown to be helpful, beneficial, or necessary. At best, they are inevitable and must be dealt with. Positive emotions, however, enhance adolescent development and personal-social adjustment. What can adults do?

The how and when to begin helping children handle emotions is easy. The key is to begin with the general emotional tone. Box 5–1 provides ten suggestions for achieving emotional balance.

> **BOX 5-1   TEN SUGGESTIONS FOR ACHIEVING EMOTIONAL BALANCE**
>
> 1. Share your emotions with teenagers so that they can see how you handle strong feelings. In this way, will they learn to label and identify emotions.
> 2. Listen to and accept the feelings of adolescents. The need to have help is vital. If adolescents have no one to talk to, or if they are criticized for having these feelings, then they will be forced to deal with them alone—often unsuccessfully.
> 3. Emphasize the positive rather than the negative emotions. Although negative emotions are to be accepted and expressed, we seek positive emotions for ourselves and for others. Abundance of positive feeling is the key to the good life.
> 4. Encourage the expression of feelings. In this way, teenagers have a safe place for emotional learning.
> 5. Work toward achieving emotional control. On the issue of overcontrol and undercontrol, the more serious error is to be unable to control emotions. In this case, emotions will rule the person and personal freedom will be jeopardized.
> 6. Deal with unwanted emotions when they first appear. Handling weak emotions when they first appear is easier than coping with full-blown negative emotions.
> 7. Avoid overcontrol and suppression of feelings by accepting teenagers' feelings and by being less demanding.
> 8. Create a balance with a dominance of positive effect. The balance is one with an abundance of positive feelings.
> 9. Take the initiative by setting the tone with a positive attitude. Not only will this result in a more pleasant response from youth, but also you will be better able to handle their feelings and will serve as an example.

To summarize the importance of a positive home to assist troubled youth, the following conclusions have been offered:

> How best may adults help tame the turmoil in youth's troubled breast? How can a youth whose defenses are as hard as a bulletproof vest be approached? The most important aspect of helping adolescents is prevention—eliminating conditions that would threaten their mental health and structuring environments conducive to positive emotions. In contrast to this positive approach, there is an abundance of negative advice. There are long lists of evils to avoid, such as emotional deprivation, overprotection, and severe discipline; usually the "don'ts" greatly outnumber the "dos." The positive side of counseling has been somewhat neglected, and the calmer phases of emotional life are little investigated and less understood. Nevertheless, enough of the positive approach is known to prove effective if put to work.
>
> Adolescents need assured and steady contact with persons of integrity and kindness, partly to offset the mass media's steady diet of emotionally distorted situations. Positive emotions are often neglected in favor of moods of hate, violence, jealousy, and passion. (Rogers 1981, 117)

Summary

The family has considerable influence on adolescents, even compared with peers. Attitudes of teenagers closely follow the patterns of their family in basic values. According to surveys, the family appears to be an institution that is alive and well, and is continuing to grow.

However, changes have occurred in family life and stability. The two-parent stable family has become less common. One-parent families are on the rise, due to death, divorce, or separation, and the trend is expected to increase. Also, adolescents are more frequently growing up in two-parent families in which both parents work outside the home.

While researchers have found little difference between children of employed and home-based parents, the effects of maternal employment may be most felt in hard-to-research areas such as emotional security, social adjustment, and type and direction of motivation.

The one-parent family is usually a father-absent family, since more than 80 percent of single parents are women. Although one-parent families have a higher-than-normal representation of delinquent children, the one-parent family is not necessarily to blame. Logically, when disruption or change occurs in established or traditional models of family life, some problems arise.

Emotional strains and problems are associated with divorce for the adolescent, but the trauma does not appear to create a permanent impairment. A higher frequency of delinquency and depression (including sexual activity and drug use) is reported among adolescents with divorced parents. These adolescents seem to have lower self-esteem and devaluate their family. Research continues to document and find effects of family disruption.

Adolescents can be helped to cope with divorce. They can receive support and attention from other institutions. Friends can also help. An important step is for the community to provide assistance such as in the way of counseling.

Differences exist in the family experience for adolescents living in different socioeconomic and racial groups. Lower socioeconomic status parents stress different things and tend to have different disciplinary methods. The problems associated with child rearing at the poverty level include higher birth rates, slum neighborhoods, inferior employment, inadequate parental education, poor health, unstable marriages, and inadequate legal services.

These types of difficulties are not always associated with minority groups. Minority groups often include middle-class, lower-middle, and upper-middle-class groups, as well as an occasional high socioeconomic position. Ethnic groups, however, have different cultural aspects that affect the type of family experiences an adolescent may have.

The five major strengths of the black family are strong kinship bonds, strong work orientation, adaptability of family roles, strong achievement orientation, and religious orientation. A difficult problem facing black parents is assisting adolescents in dealing with their sexuality. The myths and stereotypes associated with black sexuality make the task more difficult.

Today, black boys have been socialized to be strong, aggressive, and independent. Emphasis is on survival and ethnic pride. Although black males and females are encouraged to get an education, the black male is also encouraged to develop athletic and physical prowess.

Black girls are socialized to be independent and disciplined. Success is measured among lower-class black females by the degree to which she can take care of herself and assist others in the family. Few black girls grow up expecting to stay home and care for the children; they anticipate that they will work outside the home.

Many Indian families feel their children are competent to care for themselves at an early age. Older children are often given supervisory responsibilities for younger children.

Indian societies, like all societies, have formal and informal sex mores and taboos. Ceremonial rites and recognitions that were part of a maturing process tested and reinforced the youth's tribal identity. Modern Indian life has failed to develop a substitute for today's Indian youth, which has resulted in a lack of purpose and direction, and a higher incidence of alcoholism, drug abuse, school underachievement and dropping out, and suicide.

Tribal traditions are no longer kept in many cases, due to friction created because of modern values. Social erosion in Indian cultures has resulted. The relationship and role of the Indian father to his children have been weakened. Special importance and status are given to the obtaining of a non-Indian education and well-paid employment.

Parents in the Chinese-American family feel totally responsible for their child's behavior, which is considered a reflection on them. Education is stressed as a means of achievement. Verbal communication has increased between Chinese children and their parents. Parents convey the importance of values verbally and through actions.

Spanking and scolding are common methods of punishment. Chinese children are incorporated early and relatively fully into the daily life of the family. They are given choices and responsibilities.

Social interaction among people of different racial backgrounds is acceptable. A closeness, a sense of belonging, and acceptance are part of the extended family.

Puerto Rican adolescents on the mainland grow up with many of the same ideals as their Anglo-Saxon counterparts, mingled with many of the traditional Puerto Rican ideals. Children who are already going through the identity crisis typical of early adolescence must also deal with their Puerto Rican versus American identity.

Puerto Rican children are taught from an early age that they must work hard to realize their goals. Parents like to see their children grow into responsible adults, yet they feel that children should not override parental authority.

Males generally begin dating at an early age. The marriage choice should preferably be someone of the same culture, but other cultures are well accepted into the Puerto Rican family.

As a rule, the female is overprotected. She is expected to remain close to home and to be more dependent on the parents. Although chaperonage has become rare, parents scrutinize the boys dating the daughter to determine the daughter's degree of safety with the individual.

As a rule, sexual activity should not occur outside marriage. The female is expected to be a virgin at the time of marriage, but this is not stressed for the male. Parents prefer that their children remain in the home until they marry.

The ultimate dream of Puerto Rican parents is to see their children attain educational and professional success, establish a stable marital relationship, and bring forth grandchildren.

In the traditional Mexican-American family, puberty is treated quite differently for boys and girls. The male is allowed much more freedom and usually has a strong peer group that he identifies with—frequently referred to as the *palomilla*. Little discussion takes place in the home in regard to sex education.

The Chicana girl is given a special party on her fifteenth birthday, if her parents can afford it. This occasion is called a Quinceanera. In Mexico this meant that a girl was ready to be courted in her home.

Parents are no longer able to keep young Chicanas under the confines of the home. They are challenging the traditional male-female relationship. Mothers and daughters remain close, with the daughter doing many of the household chores and caring for the younger children. Most parents, however, want their daughters as well as their sons to do better than they did in a career goal.

In the Japanese-American family emphasis is placed on interpersonal harmony and avoidance of conflict both inside and out of the family. Children are also trained to conform to the norms governing their prescribed role, which is defined by sex, age, and birth order. High standards of excellence are emphasized.

Sex differences in response to manners and etiquette are stressed. The culture reinforces this differentiation with terms and phrases in its language—feminine words only for female, masculine for male.

Older siblings are to set good examples and indulge the younger children. Children are taught to be obedient. Japanese parents, like parents of other cultures, manipulate the pleasure and pain directly felt by their children, using rewards and punishments. The most severe physical punishment is "moxa"—burning a little cone of powder upon the child's skin.

Japanese mothers strive to foster dependency need in their offspring and then use these needs to manipulate the child's behavior. The dependency needs and maternal closeness lead to a suppression of sexuality.

Current Japanese-American parental attitudes toward adolescent dating are similar to American parents. Japanese-American parents prefer their children to associate with peers from their own ethnic group, but are accepting when their children associate with peers from other ethnic groups. The incidence of interracial marriages has steadily increased in recent years.

Separating the effects of family from the general effects of the social milieu is difficult. The family constantly evolves as it adjusts to new conditions, especially in modern America, where change rather than continuity has been typical. Still, the family is the strongest single influence in our culture.

Researchers have found meaningful dimensions of parental behavior. Neglecting parents are characterized by a lack of concern for their children. They lack warmth and are inconsistent in their use of discipline. A large percentage of delinquents result from this type of parent. Children in this climate exhibit aggressive and poorly controlled behavior.

Rigid controlling parents are restrictive and hostile. Children under such conditions tend to become neurotic, socially withdrawn, shy, anxious, and self-punishing.

Anxious neurotic parents transfer their anxiety to their children. They believe that the world is out to get them and view their children as symbols of their inability to function as a normal parent. Children from these homes are socially aggressive and punitive.

Hostile authoritarian parents are restrictive and punitive as a result of anxiety. They are generally frustrated people who strike out at their children. Their children are compliant and dependent, and often have strong consciences.

Indulgent parents set few limits or restrictions. They are warm, supportive, and unconditionally accepting. Their children are independent and frequently aggressive toward peers and parents, as well as being noncompliant and mischievous.

Democratic parents are warm and supportive and use little power and assertion. Rules and mutually accepted by parents and children. Parents express confidence in their children and have an attitude of cooperation. Their children are creative and highly independent due to confidence rather than rebellion. These children are socially outgoing and friendly.

Organized effective parents set structured limits, rationally selected for the child's benefit. They push their children to operate at the peak of their abilities. They are confident, warm, supportive, and success oriented. Their children reflect the characteristics of their parents. They are responsible and achieving but lack independence and creativity. They have a strong conscience and are respectful of authority.

These classifications by researchers, although not absolute, provide information on parental influence on adolescents. Achieving the optimal amount of family control is difficult to establish. A special need exists for emotional control, but a balance between control and freedom and between expression of positive and negative emotions is required.

References

Anderson, H. W., & G. S. Andersen. 1981. *Mom and Dad are divorced but I'm not.* Chicago: Nelson Hall.
Bachman, J., L. Johnston, & P. O'Malley. 1981. *Monitoring the future: Questionnaire responses from the nation's high school seniors 1980.* Ann Arbor, Mich: Institute for Social Research, University of Michigan.
Baumrind, D. 1971. Current patterns of parental authority. *Developmental Psychology Monographs* 4 (1), pt. 2.
Bealer, R. C., F. K. Willits, & P. R. Maida. 1969. The rebellious youth cultures. In *Issues in adolescent developmental psychology,* ed. B. Rogers, 484–98. New York: Appleton-Century-Crofts.
Becker, W. L. 1964. Consequences of different kinds of parental discipline. In *Review of Child Development,* M. L. Hoffman & L. W. Hoffman. vol. 1, ed. New York: Russell Sage Foundation.
Block, J. H. 1971. *Lives through time.* Berkeley, Calif.: Bancroft Books.
Bradburn, N. M., & C. F. Noll. 1969. *The structure of psychological well-being.* Chicago: Aldine.
Brandwein, R., C. Brown, & D. Fox. 1974. Women and children last: The social situation of divorced mothers and their families. *The all-American family:* 498–514 (August).
Burchinal, L. 1964. Characteristics of adolescents from unbroken, broken, and reconstituted families. *Journal of Marriage and The Family* 26:44–51.
Char, E. 1981. The Chinese American. In *Culture and childrearing,* ed. A. Clark, 154–57. Philadelphia: Davis.
Clark, A., ed. 1981. *Culture and childrearing.* Philadelphia: Davis.
Congor, J., & A. Peterson. 1984. *Adolescence and youth* 3d. New York: Harper and Row.
Curran, B. F. 1981. Divorce in clinical practice. *Journal of Family Practice* 12:471–76.
DeLamater, J., & P. MacCorquodale. 1979. *Premarital sexuality: Attitudes, relationships, behavior.* Madison, Wis.: Univ. of Wisconsin Press.
Dellas, M., E. Vaier, & C. Enihobich. 1979. Maternal employment and selected behaviors and attitudes of pre-adolescents and adolescents. *Adolescence* 14:579–89.
Derbyshire, R. L. 1968. Adolescent identity crisis in urban mexican-americans in East Los Angeles. In *Minority group adolescence in the United States,* ed. E. B. Brady. Baltimore: Williams & Wilkins.
Ehling, M. 1981. The Mexican American. In *Culture and childrearing,* ed. A. Clark, 206–7. Philadelphia: Davis.
Farris, E., & L. Farris. 1981. The American Indian. In *Culture and childrearing,* ed. A. Clark, 61–64. Philadelphia: Davis.

Fisher, J. 1980. Reciprocity, agreement, and family style in family systems with disturbed and nondisturbed adolescents. *Journal of Youth and Adolescence* 9(5):391–410.

Glass, J. C., Jr. 1972. Premarital sexual standards among church youth leaders: An exploratory study. *Journal for the Scientific Study of Religion* 11 (4):361–67.

Glueck, S., & E. Glueck. 1957. Working mothers and delinquency. *Mental Hygiene* 41:327–52.

Greathouse, B. 1981. The black American. In *Culture and childrearing,* ed. A. Clark, 78–87. Philadelphia: Davis.

Grossman, S. M., J. Shea, & G. Adams. 1978. Effects of parental divorce during childhood on ego development and identity formation of college students. *Journal of Divorce* 1:341–59.

Hetherington, E. 1972. Effects of father absence on personal development in adolescence bodies. *Developmental Psychology* 7:313–23.

Hetherington, E., M. Cox, & R. Cox. 1978. The aftermath of divorce. In *Mother-child, father-child relations,* ed. J. H. Stevens, Jr., & M. Matthews. Washington, D.C.: Naeyc.

Hoffman, L. 1974. Effects of maternal employment on the child—A revealing research. *Developmental Psychology* 10:204–28.

———. 1979. Maternal employment. *American Psychologist* 34(10):859–65.

Hopkins, J. R. 1977. Sexual behavior in adolescence. *Journal of Social Issues* 33 (2):67–85.

Jensen, L. 1981. *The psychology of parenting.* Provo, Utah: independent study, Brigham Young University, 85–87.

Jensen, L., & M. Kingston. 1985. *Parenting.* New York: Holt, Rinehart & Winston.

Jessor, S. L., & R. Jessor. 1974. Maternal ideology and adolescent problem behavior. *Developmental Psychology* 10 (2):246–54.

———. 1975. Transition from virginity to nonvirginity among youth: A social-psychological study over time. *Developmental Psychology* 11 (4):473–84.

Jessor, R., & S. L. Jessor. 1977. *Problem behavior and psychosocial development: A longitudinal study of youth.* New York: Academic Press.

Kenting, K. 1983. What's happening to American families? A report from more than 200,000 readers. *Better Homes and Gardens* :24–36, pt. 2 (July).

Kinsey, A. C., W., Pomeroy, & C. E. Martin. 1948. *Sexual behavior in the human male.* Philadelphia: Saunders.

Lacay, G. 1981. The Puerto Rican in mainland America. In *Culture and childrearing,* ed. A. Clark, 222–23. Philadelphia: Davis.

LeMasters, E., & J. DeFrain. 1983. *Parents in contemporary America.* Homewood, Ill.: Dorsey.

Leon, G. 1974. *Case histories of deviant behavior.* Boston: Holbrook.

Lind, D. 1974. *The father: His role in child development.* Monterey, Calif.: Brooks/Cole.

Lipset, S. M. 1957. *Political man.* Garden City, N.Y.: Doubleday.

Lupenitz, D. 1979. Which aspects of divorce affect children? *Family Coordinator* 28:79–85.

Maccoby, E. E. 1981. *Social development: Psychological growth and the parent-child relationship.* New York: Harcourt Brace Jovanovich.

Maccoby, E. 1980. *Social development.* New York: Harcourt Brace Jovanovich.

Mahoney, E. R. 1980. Religiosity and sexual behavior among heterosexual college students. *Journal of Sex Research* 16(1):97–113.

Marotz-Badden, R., B. R. Adams, N. Bueche, B. Munro, & C. Munro. 1979. Family form or family process? Reconsidering the deficit family model approach. *Family Coordinator* 28:5–82.

McDermott, D. J. 1970. Divorce and its psychiatric sequelae in children. *General Psychiatry* 23:421–27.

Mirande, A. M. 1968. Reference group theory and adolescent sexual behavior. *Journal of Marriage and the Family* 30:572–77.

Morrison, J. 1974. Parental divorce as a factor in childhood psychiatric illness. *Comprehensive Psychiatry* 15(2):95–102.

Norback, C. 1980. *The complete book of American surveys.* New York: New American Library (Signet).

Norman, J. M. Harris. 1981. *The private life of the American teenager.* New York: Rawson, Wade.

Ostlund, L. A. 1957. Environment-personality relationships. *Rural Sociology* (March).
Parish, T., & J. Dostal. 1980. Evaluation of self and parent produced by children from Utah, divorce, and reconstituted families. *Journal of Youth and Adolescence* 9:347–51.
Parish, T., J. Dostal, & J. Parish. 1981. Evaluation of self and parents on a function of intactness of family and family happiness. *Adolescence* 16(61):203–13.
Putney, S., & R. Middleton. 1961. Rebellion, conformity, and parental-religious ideologies. *Social Metre* (June).
Query, J. M., & T. Kuruvilla. 1975. Male and female adolescence achievement and maternal employment. *Adolescence* 10:350–56.
Ramey, J. 1978. Experimental family forms—The family of the future. *Journal of Marriage and the Family* 1:1.
Reinhard, P. 1977. The reaction of adolescent boys and girls to the divorce of their parents. *Journal of Clinical Child Psychiatry* 6(2):21–23.
Rogers, D. 1981. *Adolescents and youth*. 4th ed. Englewood Cliffs, N.J.: Prentice-Hall.
Rohrbaugh, J., & R. Jessor. 1975. Religiosity in youth: A personal control against deviant behavior. *Journal of Personality* 43(1):136–55.
Schaeffer, E. S. 1959. A circumplex model for maternal behavior. *Journal of Abnormal and Social Psychology* 59:226–35.
Schulz, B., G. W. Bohrnstedt, E. F. Borgatta, & R. R. Evans. 1977. Explaining premarital sexual intercourse among college students: A causal model. *Social Forces* 56(1):148–65.
Slater, E., S. Krista, & M. Linn. 1983. The effects of family disruption on adolescent males and females. *Adolescence* 18(72):940–41.
Smith, E. 1981. The working mother: a critique of the research. *Journal of Vocational Behavior* 19:191–211.
Smith, T. 1983. Adolescent reactions to attempted parental control and influence techniques. *Journal of Marriage and the Family* 2:533–41.
Sodetani-Shibata, A. E. 1981. The Japanese American. In *Culture and childrearing*, ed. A. Clark, 128–33. Philadelphia: Davis.
Sorensen, R. 1972. *Adolescent sexuality in contemporary America*. New York: World Publishing.
Sugar, N. 1970. Children of divorce. *Pediatrics* 46:588–95.
Sussman, N. B. 1978. New family forms and lifestyles. In *Family core dying or developing*, ed. D. Reiss. New York: Plenum.
Thomas, L. 1973. The relationship between premarital sexual behavior and certain personal and religious background factors of a sample of university students. *American College Health Association Journal* 21(5):460–64.
Thornburg, H. 1975. *Development in adolescence*. Monterey, Calif.: Brooks/Cole.
U.S. Bureau of the Census. 1979. Population profile of the United States: 1978 population characteristics. *Current population reports*, ser. P-20, no. 336. Washington, D.C.: U.S. Government Printing Office, April.
Walker, K., & M. Woods. 1972. *Calling news for clear family members*. Ithaca: Cornell Univ.
Wallerstein, J., & J. Kelly. 1976. Effect of parental divorce: Experiences of the child in late latency. *American Journal of Psychiatry* 46:256–69.
⸺. 1980. *Surviving the breakup: How children and parents cope with divorce*. New York: Basic Books.
Wallston, B. 1973. The effects of maternal employment on children. *Journal of Child Psychology and Psychiatry* 14:81–95.
Weller, L. & Luchterhand. 1983. Family relationships of "problem" and "promising" youth. *Adolescence* 18(69):94–113.
Zelnick, M., J. F. Kantner, & K. Ford. 1981. *Sex and pregnancy in adolescence*. Beverly Hills, Calif.: Sage.

GEOMETRY

CHAPTER SIX

Adolescence and Education

SURVEY AND QUESTIONS

This chapter will acquaint the reader with the educational standards of American schools, how students feel about the schools, and why some drop out. It will also discuss the differences between private and public schools, vocational education, and discipline in schools. Reading the chapter will provide answers to the following questions:

Evaluating American Schools

How valid is the conclusion by the NCEE that immediate reform is needed in our educational system?
Is there evidence that attending high school has positive effects?
What do students think of secondary public schools?
What is the general public's attitude toward public schools in the eighties?
What is the major problem in the public schools?

Inside the Schools

At the high school level, do courses vary among racial groups and between males and females?
What are the main causes of dropping out of school?
What are the signs that indicate that a student may be likely to drop out?
How do private schools compare with public schools?
What is the role of the schools in influencing desegregation?
Do other countries, such as the Soviet Union, have higher educational standards than the United States, especially in math and science?
Do some advocate a movement away from education that stresses the basics?
What is a typical classroom like in American schools?
Are smaller schools and classes more effective?
Does a single high school culture exist?
Is the role of athletics overstressed in American public schools?
Do subcultures exist within the general school culture?
What about students who do not fit in the school culture?

Other Education Concerns of American Schools

Exactly what is vocational education?
Is vocational education effective in preparing youth for the labor market?
Other than teaching the basics and vocational education, which goals are important for public schools?
Can morals be taught in public schools?
Is sex education needed in public schools?

Discipline in the Schools

What can be done to prevent violence in the schools?
What are some specific actions to help with discipline in the classroom?

> About 13 percent of all 17-year-olds in the United States can be considered functionally illiterate. Functional illiteracy among minority youth may run as high as 40 percent.
> Average achievement of high school students on most standardized tests is now lower than 26 years ago when Sputnik was launched.
> Over half the population of gifted students do not match their tested ability with comparable achievement in school.
> The College Board's Scholastic Aptitude Tests (SAT) demonstrate a virtually unbroken decline from 1963 to 1980. Average verbal scores fell over 50 points and average mathematics scores dropped nearly 40 points.
> College Board achievement tests also reveal consistent declines in recent years in such subjects as physics and English.
> Both the number and proportion of students demonstrating superior achievement on the SATs (i.e., those with scores of 650 or higher) have also dramatically declined.
> Many 17-year-olds do not possess the "higher order" intellectual skills we should expect of them. Nearly 40 percent cannot draw inferences from written material; only one-fifth can write a persuasive essay; and only one-third can solve a mathematics problem requiring several steps.
> There was a steady decline in science achievement scores of U.S. 17-year-olds as measured by national assessments of science in 1969, 1973, and 1977. (NCEE 1981)

The recently appointed National Commission on Excellence in Education reported these alarming statistics (NCEE 1981). The NCEE was appointed by the United States secretary of education to evaluate the state of public education in the nation's public and private schools and colleges and universities. The commission concludes that our whole nation is at risk due to our educational system and that immediate reform is needed. The NCEE further states that these statistics and their interpretation by experts show only the surface dimensions of the difficulties we face.

Evaluating American schools

QUESTION: How valid is the conclusion by the NCEE that immediate reform is needed in our educational system?

These figures primarily focus on only one aspect of schools. During this century, schools have been called upon to do much more than teach the basics. Public schools have been asked to (1) assist with vocational and job training, (2) help with integration of racial groups, (3) help individuals adjust and develop a positive self-concept and personal-social skills in relating with others, (4) develop citizenship and civic thinking, (5) model appropriate behavior and provide social experience within school settings, such as clubs, extracurricular activities, and athletics, (6) assisting in developing adjustment with the peer group, and (7) occupy the time of adolescents who are unable to be placed in the job market and whose free time places a burden on parents and the community.

Compared with these functions of the school, the NCEE statistics relate to only one part of the overall responsibilities that society has placed on its public schools. Even considering these statistics, however, the American Association of School Administrators gave the following statement about the accuracy of the report:

In fact, the statistics the Commission has chosen to use may be somewhat outdated. The decline in S.A.T. scores, according to the College Board, has stabilized and appears to be reversing. Students have taken an increasing number of academic courses in each of the last six years. Many states have already adopted stricter graduation standards. Many local student districts are also raising expectations for students.

As the report points out, American schools educated a larger proportion of our 17-year-olds than any other educational system in the world. And it is important to remember that the average citizen is "better educated and more knowledgeable than the average citizen of a generation ago—more literate, and exposed to more mathematics, literature, and science." According to the United Nations, the U.S. has one of the highest literacy rates in the world. (AASA 1983, 14)

Each year a larger percentage of our youth population attends secondary schools. In 1900, only 11 percent of the nation's high-school-age youth attended high school, and in 1930 the figure was 51 percent. Today the figure is closer to 90 percent. This increased enrollment undoubtedly results in a larger percentage of students who score low on intelligence tests, which therefore lowers the overall scores. The increased enrollment also pressures the educational system to offer a variety of programs for a more heterogeneous student body.

QUESTION: Is there evidence that attending high school has positive effects?

Yes. First let us compare effects of course work on test scores (Shaycoft 1967). One research team compared responses to national surveys that were conducted in the early fifties, late fifties, early sixties, and late sixties. At each time period, the four age groups were compared. Comparisons were made for each age group that had been educated at different periods of time. The researchers found that for all four periods, more education was associated with a greater amount of knowledge in both academic and public affairs. Students who completed high school were more highly informed than those who had completed only elementary school. This finding held true no matter how old the students were when they were tested or when they attended school.

This study indicates that the way to evaluate public education is to compare students who attend school with students who do not. Using this criterion is an indisputable way to measure the success of our public schools.

For the first time in nineteen years, the average nationwide scores have risen for both the verbal and the mathematics sections of the Scholastic Aptitude Test (SAT). The rise was slight, and the National College Board believes it reflects the improvement in American schools. The average scores rose from 1981 to 1982 by two points (on the verbal portion, and by one point on the mathematics portion). The executive director of research and development for the College Board states that "In 1981, the scores were stable. This year they're up. The trendline is important here. I could be wrong, but I'm optimistic that from what I know is going on in American education, they'll go up next year too" (Cameron 1982, 1).

Interpreting these score changes is difficult. One interpretation is that the schools have made grading stiffer, have increased enrollments in more difficult courses, and have given more coaching to students on how to take the SAT.

Roger Farr of Indiana University gives another explanation:

> A lot of the decline was probably due to the pain of expanding to a lot of kids previously excluded from the test. It took time for that change to be absorbed, and the scores are starting to go up as those students become more like the middle-class kids who used to be the only ones taking the SAT. (Farr 1982, 2)

QUESTION: What do students think of secondary public schools?

In large public opinion polls it has been reported that a majority of students thought the schools were doing A- or B-grade work and that seventy percent of the students thought teachers were doing an excellent job (Hobart 1979; Proctor 1979).

In another study, 2,100 teachers and 13,000 twelfth-grade boys in eighty-seven high schools throughout the country were surveyed about fourteen goals and objectives in their school (Johnson and Bachman 1976). Students and teachers thought greater emphasis could be placed on almost all of the educational objectives. One exception was that they thought athletics was overstressed. The students felt that teachers place slightly too much emphasis on the proportion of seniors who go to college, and they tended to think that too much stress was placed on order and quiet. The teachers' ideals were slightly higher than those of the students, but in general the perceptions of both teachers and students were similar and positive.

Yankelovich (1974) found that two-thirds of his sample of high school students were satisfied that they were obtaining an adequate education. In a pool

Despite much criticism of public education by those outside of schools, many students themselves give the education they are receiving and the public schools a relatively high rating.

of over 22,000 students, Miller (1976) found the majority thought their education at the end of high school had been important, relevant, and stimulating.

The Gallup Organization for *Newsweek* (1983) conducted the most recent and illuminating study, in which 523 persons were interviewed. When asked, "How well would you say your high school prepared you for college?" 28 percent said very well, 32 percent said fairly well, 27 percent said adequately, 10 percent said poorly, and only 3 percent said that their high school prepared them very poorly for college. The same people were also asked to grade their individual teachers for competence using the A–F grade scale. Eighty-two percent responded with an A or B rating of their teachers, while the total percentage breakdown by the respondents was as follows: 12 percent rated their teachers an A, 60 percent rated them a B, 24 percent gave them a C, 3 percent a D, and 1 percent rated the teachers they had in high school an F. (Arena 1983) Taken together these findings indicate that students are generally satisfied with schools. This conclusion may not be surprising, as students have little else with which to compare their school. Dissatisfaction and criticism of the school, however, may originate from outside the school rather than from within.

Most of the criticism of school comes from the outside and is focused on deficiencies in teaching the basics, whereas those criticisms that come from within the schools and from teachers and students focus on concern for prosocial needs and meeting individual differences in areas like adjustment, social relating, and so on.

The amount and type of schooling influence all these developmental tasks and even personal enrichment. The experience in school will influence attitudes, behavior, and opportunities for the future. Data from the National Longitudinal Survey of Youth Labor Market Experience provide a national sample of 12,700 young men and women age fourteen to twenty-one. The following findings are reported. Ten questions were asked. After each question notice the percentage of youth who thought that the statement was somewhat or very true.

1. It is easy to make friends at this school. 95%
2. Most of the teachers are willing to help with personal problems. 79%
3. Most of my classes are boring. 52%
4. I don't feel safe at this school. 11%
5. Most of my teachers really don't know their subject well. 91%
6. You can get away with almost anything at this school. 26%
7. My school work requires me to think to the best of my ability. 84%
8. At this school, a person has the freedom to learn what interests him or her. 88%
9. This school offers good job counseling. 80%
10. Overall satisfaction with school. 88%

(Rumberger 1982, 449–68)

With the exception of Question 3 and 5, these attitudes toward school are positive. The findings were similar for males, females, blacks, hispanics, and whites.

QUESTION: What is the general public's attitude toward public schools in the eighties?

This data has been collected annually since 1970, using a Gallup poll *(Phi Delta Kappan* 1982). Table 6–1 extracts and presents the following conclusions from the 1982 survey:

TABLE 6–1 Public Attitudes Towards the Public Schools

Students are often given the grades A, B, C, D, and Fail to denote the quality of their work. Suppose the *public* schools themselves, in this community, were graded in the same way. What grade would you give the public schools here—A, B, C, D, or Fail?

National Totals

Ratings Given the Public Schools	1982 %	1981 %	1980 %	1979 %	1978 %	1977 %	1976 %	1975 %	1974 %
A rating	8	9	20	8	9	22	13	13	18
B rating	29	27	25	28	27	28	29	30	30
C rating	33	34	29	30	30	28	28	28	21
D rating	14	12	12	11	11	11	19	9	6
Fail	5	7	6	7	8	5	8	7	5
Don't know	11	10	18	18	15	19	14	13	20

Ratings Given the Public Schools

By Parents with:	A %	B %	C %	D %	Fail %	Don't Know %
Children in public schools	11	38	31	13	6	1
Children in nonpublic schools	13	25	39	13	9	1
No children in school	7	25	34	14	5	15

How about the public schools in the nation as a whole? What grade would you give the public schools nationally—A, B, C, D, or Fail?

	A %	B %	C %	D %	Fail %	Don't Know %
Public schools in this community	8	29	33	14	5	11
Public schools in the nation	2	20	44	15	4	15

	National Totals %	No Children in School %	Public School Parents %	Nonpublic School Parents %
A rating	2	2	3	—
B rating	20	20	20	21
C rating	44	44	44	48
D rating	15	15	15	15
Fail	4	3	5	2
Don't know	15	16	13	14

	Public Schools in the Nation	
	1982	1981
	%	%
A rating	2	2
B rating	20	18
C rating	44	43
D rating	15	15
Fail	4	6
Don't know	15	16

Public Schools in the Nation

Further breakdowns:	A	B	C	D	Fail	Don't Know
	%	%	%	%	%	%
National Totals	2	20	44	15	4	15
Sex						
Men	2	20	47	15	4	12
Women	3	20	42	14	3	18
Race						
White	1	20	46	16	3	14
Nonwhite	8	22 ± 37 9		6	18	
Age						
18–29 years	2	24	47	14	2	11
30–49 years	2	18	47	15	5	13
50 and over	4	18	40	14	4	20
Community size						
1 million and over	1	20	44	12	5	18
500,000–999,999	1	22	44	14	6	13
50,000–499,999	3	23	43	17	2	12
2,500–49,999	4	21	45	14	4	12
Under 2,500	3	15	45	14	4	19
Central city	3	23	39	15	4	16
Education						
Grade school	9	17	33	10	6	25
High school	2	24	43	14	3	14
College	1	15	52	18	3	11
Region						
East	2	22	46	12	4	14
Midwest	2	16	51	16	3	12
South	3	22	39	14	3	19
West	3	19	41	18	4	15

The surveys have generally found that no significant change has occurred in recent years. More than one-third of those sampled give the schools a high rating, and one-sixth give a low rating. The lower ratings come primarily from adults who do not have children in the schools. The report states, "[T]hose who know most about the schools hold a better opinion of them than do those who do not have firsthand knowledge. The public schools, as an American institution, have an image problem" *(Phi Delta Kappan* 1982, 39).

QUESTION: What is the major problem in the public schools?

In eight of nine Gallup polls from 1969 to 1977 on attitudes toward schools, discipline was named as a major problem (See Table 6–1 for the 1982 opinions).

Apparently, the safety of teachers has become a major problem, as they have been physically attacked in classrooms (Rosow 1979). One reviewer believes that to cope with this problem, distinguishing between normal and seriously disturbed students is important (Kindsvatter 1978). For normal students, the expectation is that occasional discipline problems will occur, and normal methods of dealing with them will be successful. Important is distinguishing between the normal child and the child with severe emotional problems that cannot be dealt with in the normal way.

In the latter part of this chapter, a summary of how to discipline in the school is outlined.

Inside the schools

QUESTION: At the high school level, do courses vary among racial groups and between males and females?

The differences in courses taken in school vary more between males and females than among racial groups. In general, females take more courses in foreign languages, and males take more in mathematics. Female take their vocational courses in home economics and business, while males take theirs in business and trades. Little or no difference exists between race and gender groups in programs identified as general programs (50 percent), college preparatory (33 percent), and vocational (15 percent).

Even though 94 percent of fourteen- to seventeen-year-olds were enrolled in high school in 1978 compared with 11 percent in 1900, some evidence indicates that dropping out may be increasing. For whites the proportion in 1978 was 10 percent, for blacks 15 percent, and for Hispanics 23 percent. For blacks and whites the dropout rate was higher among males, but females had the highest dropout rate for Hispanics. The high dropout rate may appear to conflict with the data that show a positive evaluation of the school experience by those enrolled. The reasons why students drop out of school provide one possible resolution for this discrepancy (Rumberger 1982).

QUESTION: What are the main causes of dropping out of school?

The three basic reasons are (1) family background, (2) nonschool factors, and (3) experiences within school.

Females, especially blacks, give marriage and pregnancy as reasons for leaving school. Males often leave because they do not like school. Forty percent of Hispanic males drop out for economic reasons, home responsibility, good job offers, or financial difficulties. Other reasons include lack of ability, poor grades, and expulsions or suspensions. Again, these reasons can be grouped into family background factors, nonschool factors such as work and economic reasons, and experiences within school, such as criticism, poor grades, and expulsion.

Above-average ability and high-educational, high-occupational aspirations increase the likelihood of finishing high school, while pregnancy and childbearing decrease the chances (Masters 1969; Weight and Moore 1978).

A listing of specific reasons why students drop out would include the following problems: Poor reading ability, severe retardation, low and failing marks, inability to get along with teachers, misconduct in school, low I.Q. or mental retardation, apathy and lack of motivation, feeling that school is irrelevant, emotional and social maladjustment, pregnancy and marriage, and the need to work, among other reasons.

Negative reactions are common among people who leave school. They often retreat into the world of crime and drugs, or they become part of a counterculture. The counterculture group is often antagonistic toward the main goals of society, and this results in crime—selling drugs, vandalism, robbery, assault. Dropouts may retreat to drugs or a counterculture because of feelings of personal inadequacy and the belief that they do not have the ability to succeed. When this happens, dropouts do not have the guidelines and the conventional encouragement and models needed for success in our complicated society. By dropping out, youth also lose the encouragement and motivation to become successful people. All adolescents need encouragement and assistance in coping with the complicated world they live in. When they are no longer in school, however, society does not have a successful way to reach them (Mackey 1977).

QUESTION: What are the signs that indicate that a student may be likely to drop out?

Signs can be combined with other knowledge to indicate who is likely to drop out of school. The indicators are numerous. Apparently, persons from low socioeconomic status are more prone to withdraw from school because they lack positive parental influence and examples. In addition, teachers are often prejudiced against youth from low socioeconomic families. Black and other minority students have a higher dropout rate than whites. Even within socioeconomic classes, family relationships are important. Youth from unhappy homes with problems will more frequently drop out. Youth from broken homes are twice as likely to leave school early. Youth who drop out are likely to be more immature and less adjusted. This lack of adjustment also applies to social adjustment and peer relations. Youth are often socially isolated and unhappy with their friendships in school. In general, financial necessity is not as important as the other reasons for dropping out of school. For females, pregnancy is the most frequent reason reported (Rice 1981, 489–592).

QUESTION: How do private schools compare with public schools?

Comparisons generally use performance on tests but other criteria can be considered. Such criteria include disciplinary climate, academic demands, student behavior, homework, student attendance, in-school behaviors, and social development.

In looking at basic intellectual achievement, James Coleman (1982) found the levels of achievement for public school students are approximately the same as those found in Catholic and other private schools overall. He found that level of achievement depended on the type of school and factors within the school, and not on whether it was a private, Catholic, or public school. Public schools enroll 90 percent of the total high school population and have an average of 750 students per school. Catholic schools have only 6 percent of the population and average about 500 students. Other types of private schools enroll 3 and 4 percent and average only about 150 students. The student-teacher ratio is lower for the smaller private schools. Partially because of the student-teacher ratio, smaller class size, and the homogeneous nature of the students, students in the Catholic and other private schools show far fewer problems than those in public schools.

The most serious argument against the private school concept is that the private school will draw off the most talented and economically affluent from the public school system. This would move the public school system toward an unequal system comprised of the less advantaged, with an elite group going to private schools. Also, if governmental support is given to the private schools in the form of tax credits or vouchers, then the economic base of the public school would be weakened, and providing a comparable quality of education would be more difficult. In addition, strengthening the private school system would result in more whites attending private schools, thus moving toward school segregation, which our society has worked hard to eliminate for the last twenty-five years. A related criticism is that the private schools would often be religious in nature, and direct or indirect governmental support of an institution advocating a religion would be unconstitutional. From the point of view of the public schools, the best students would be pulled away and the rejects retained. The public schools are in a position where they must educate everyone, and they would therefore become a receptacle for the disadvantaged, slow learners, students with behavioral problems, and others difficult to educate. This bears on the question of racial segregation; the public school has been assigned a role to reduce rather than to increase racial division.

QUESTION: What is the role of the schools in influencing desegregation?

In 1954 the Supreme Court made the landmark decision directed toward providing equal educational opportunity for all citizens. In essence, this decision stated:

> Separate education facilities are inherently unequal. . . . To separate [black children] from others of similar age and qualifications solely because of their race generates a feeling of inferiority as to their status in the community and may affect their hearts and minds in ways unlikely ever to be undone. *(Brown v. Board of Education)*

To achieve this goal, schools were ordered to desegregate, and schools comprised primarily of one race based on geographic boundaries were combined with other schools via busing of children.

To evaluate the successes of this goal, a report was issued in which the investigator concluded that the role and action of the federal government were essential. He states:

> In school districts . . . schools have been grudgingly desegregated only after federal courts have demanded that action be taken, and only in the face of bitter local opposition. . . . Nor has a court-ordered process of pupil desegregation been swift and steady. Rather, it has been slow and sporadic. (Bendette 1981)

The report contends that it was and is essential that the government maintain a role in pushing for equal educational opportunities for all citizens, but the author believes that local and state governments will have to assist if this approach is to be successful. The problem at the local and state level is that middle-class whites have moved to the suburbs leaving a predominantly black school system in the city. The closing down of the dual school system in the South caused black elementary and secondary school personnel to lose their jobs first, thus changing school staffing.

A serious criticism is that even when the schools are integrated, no program is instituted to promote interracial harmony and understanding among the children so that they can live and work in an optimal manner:

> Experience, observation, and reading of the literature leads me to the gloomy conclusion that the typical desegregated school, tragically, is a place in which integration has yet to occur, if one defines the integrated school as a place where students of different races generally understand and appreciate each other and benefit equally from all facets of their educational program. (Bendette 1981, 36)

A correction of this problem will occur only when parents and the public insist that the schools help youth live and fulfill the ideals of our society. The teaching profession also needs to function as an advocacy group and use its talents to bring this goal about.

QUESTION: Do other countries, such as the Soviet Union, have higher educational standards than the United States, especially in math and science?

In his testimony to the Senate Subcommittee on Science, Technology, and Space, a University mathematics professor contended that the Soviet Union had developed programs during the last fifteen years that created a dangerous gap between our educational standards and those of the Soviet Union. He showed that American students spend less time studying mathematics and science courses, that fewer courses are required, and that the curricula of the Soviets are superior. A closer look shows that some question exists regarding the extent to which Soviet students outside urban areas and elite institutions receive this demanding mathematics and science instruction. Soviet educators and teachers have a difficult time teaching. Widespread dissatisfaction is present among students, teachers, parents, and even some members of the USSR Academy of Sciences. In addition, Russian students spend less time studying their own language, literature, history, and the social sciences (Rotberg 1983).

QUESTION: Do some advocate a movement away from education that stresses the basics?

In general, critics of American schools point out that in sciences, math, and the basics, America does not fare as well as some other countries. But some argue against returning to the basics:

> Anyone trained in education knows there is a difference between skills and an ability to use those skills. When skills are learned in isolation the connection

between them and their use is tenuous. Creative teachers prefer to employ various instructional techniques so that children can integrate subject matter into their lives. Educational theories have long held that repetitive drill in basic skills not connected to comprehension or composition is the least efficient way to educate and in some instances is even counterproductive. (Shine and Goldman 1980, 197)

Perhaps the most critical statement against pushing youth to achieve in the basics is by the popular child psychologist David Elkind in his book *The Hurried Child:*

> The effects on young people of these management approaches is the opposite of what was intended. The high school dropout rate, which had been level for the past ten years, was on the rise again—particularly in those states, such as Connecticut, New York, and New Jersey, that have introduced management systems. At the other end of the spectrum, the emphasis on early identification of children with potential learning problems forces children to think of themselves as defective before they have a chance to show what they can do. . . . The pressure has had other effects as well. What schools teach children, more than anything else, is that the end result, or grade, is more important than what the grade is supposed to mean in the way of achievement. Children are much more concerned with grades than what they know. . . . Even more discouraging is the dishonesty and cheating that are forced by the overemphasis on testing. If it is a grade you get, rather than what you know that counts, then the most important thing to do is to get the highest grade. . . . If young people are treated as products, as worth only as much as they score on a test, then they need to have no more ethical scruples than any other industrial product would have. Treated as objects, young people can hardly be held either ethically or morally accountable. (Elkind 1981, 55)

QUESTION: What is a typical classroom like in American schools?

One researcher (Sirotnik 1983), who interpreted data collected in over one thousand elementary and secondary classrooms through the 1976–78 school years, paints a discouraging picture. He found that the majority of class time consists of teachers lecturing to the class and students working on written assignments. He compared this arrangement with research throughout the century and found that the pattern has remained unchanged since 1900.

This pattern is in contrast with what is considered most effective in modern methods of education. Consider the researcher's statement:

> Consider again the modal classroom picture presented here: a lot of teacher talk, a lot of student listening, unless students are responding to teachers' questions or working on written assignments; almost invariably closed and factual questions, little corrective feedback and no guidance; and predominantly total class instructional configurations around traditional activities—all in a virtually affectless environment. It is but a short, inferential leap to suggest that we are implicitly teaching dependence upon authority, linear thinking, social apathy, passive involvement, and hands-off learning. (Sirotnik 1983, 29)

A study of four hundred eminent people found that three-fifths of them expressed dislike of school and schoolteachers. For these gifted people, their homes were most instrumental in setting their motivation. In speaking about their homes, the authors stated that there was a love of learning and an exuberance and drive towards goals in their parents (Goertzel and Goertzel 1962).

These youth, who were later to become eminent people, possibly found the lecture and rote learning of the typical classroom frustrating. This frustration likely resulted from their need for accomplishment and desire for self-direction, as well as from the more commonly noted intellectual boredom. To the motivated youth with a keen intellect, the constraints and restraints of passive-lecture schooling are certain to be discouraging.

To integrate these findings and negative statements about the classroom experience with the positive overall evaluation of the school, one must keep in mind the difference between the parts and the whole when evaluating a problem.

While learning does takes place, the passive-lecture mode of learning is apparently deficient and a severe problem. In an age of technological achievement, the slowness and ineptness applied to the educational process are surprising. Perhaps contrasting the horse-and-buggy lecture with other forms of cognitive stimulation creates the negative evaluation. The media also have a powerful effect, which is discussed in another chapter.

Another problem frequently cited as a hindrance to learning in the schools is the large size of the schools and classes.

QUESTION: Are smaller schools and classes more effective?

Although students in smaller schools participate in more extracurricular activities and are able to be included in more leadership positions (Barker and Gump 1964), the answer to this question is still open. The U.S. Office of Education (1974) found that small classes did not always improve academic performance. Another researcher states:

> Students individually select different subjects every year or every semester, and find themselves with a different group of peers in almost every course. As a result there are no classes in the traditional sense, no small, coherent communities of children who go through high school together. . . .
> I have described aspects of the size and the organizational structure of high schools which reduce human conduct and have a negative influence on the sense of community, the development of relationships, and the formation of personal identity. They are part of the progress and the malaise of our time, and it seems unlikely that we could modify them substantially. (Schmiedeck 1979, 191–96)

This assessment does point out a problem in forming close relationships in the public schools today. Other groupings take place in which youth having common interests band together, such as athletics, band, drama, or even some cliques. These smaller groups, however, are not as continuous and stable as would be a traditional class of about thirty children who get to know one another day after day.

One of the problems faced by many public schools is the high student-teacher ratio that sometimes exists. School counselors, such as the one these boys are waiting to see, may be able to fill in the gaps caused by this high ratio.

QUESTION: Does a single high school culture exist?

An early investigation by James Coleman (1961) studied ten different high schools from different socioeconomic and geographic areas. Coleman found that the school assumed a much more important role in socialization of youth than what occurred in previous times, and that the schools have displaced families and work as a basic source of adolescent upbringing. He believes this youth culture has resulted in youth functioning according to their own rules rather than those given by the church or by the family.

Coleman asked high school boys and girls what they would like to be remembered as after high school. Boys preferred to be remembered as athletes rather than as scholars. Boys in leading crowds rarely considered themselves intellectuals, whereas people who were not in intellectual crowds or who were in no crowd at all considered themselves intellectuals. The same pattern emerged for girls. They did not desire a scholarly image. Coleman's research implies that in the youth culture, social and athletic aspects of high school life are considerably more important than academics.

QUESTION: Is the role of athletics overstressed in American public schools?

A number of people have criticized the emphasis placed on interscholastic athletics (Coleman 1965; Burnett 1969; Solberg 1970). These critics believe that athletics has almost become a tail that wags the dog, and that considering the amount of time and expenditure, the returns are not meaningful or significant. The principal objective is that athletics serves only a few students, and in the past these students have all been male. In recent years, federal legislation has moved schools to enact interscholastic athletic programs for females.

Title IX of the 1972 Educational Amendments Acts prohibits any educational program that practices sex discrimination from receiving federal funds. Nevertheless, only a small part of the student body participates in athletics. Furthermore, the emphasis on winning and competitiveness may not be desirable, as our discussion in a later part of this chapter indicates.

Athletics seems to benefit those who do participate. For example, athletics assists in popularity (Rehberg 1969). The successful athlete also becomes a model for other students which benefits both the athlete and others. Rehberg's logic shows that successful athletes have increased self-esteem, which then transfers to academic work and helps in their scholastic performance. Athletes may also receive greater quality and quantity of counseling, which therefore enables them to crystalize their future goals and adjustment. Achievement in athletics requires some of the same characteristics that lead to success in other areas, such as hard work, motivation, and higher goals of personal performance. The athlete is also easily accessible to an adult coach, who can assist with the process of socialization.

One of the reviewers for this text states that the negative effects of existing high school athletics outweigh the positive, because:

> Sex discrimination is not the only problem. Nor is the limited number of students who participate. There are other...and more important...reasons, such as: does an obsession with athletics interfere with a student's interest in academics? In my experience with college students the answer is yes . . . the cheers of the crowds are seductive. The excitement of playing . . . with the crowds cheering (even with a small crowd of fans cheering) . . . field hockey, football or soccer become much more important to them than their studies of history or biology or psychology. The small-group atmosphere and social and emotional support by the coaches, team members, bolstered by the fans, the intense, often warm, intra-group interactions, become much more meaningful to them because each is important within that group. In contrast, the classroom is impersonal . . . the learning is impersonal and their places within the classroom are impersonal . . . unless students are highly motivated to learn, they are easily seduced by the cheering, excitement, and small-group support. The goals are clear and tangible, in contrast to the more abstract goals of the classroom. Competitive athletic events distract them from their primary task of learning, becoming well-educated, and responding to academic norms.

QUESTION: Do subcultures exist within the general school culture?

One researcher (Cohen 1979) found that three separate subcultures exist, which he calls the fun, the academic, and the delinquent. The fun culture is similar to the general culture that Coleman (1961) describes. According to Cohen, the students value popularity, sports, and involvement in fun school activities. The academic subculture, however, stresses academic achievement, and its members usually attain academic achievement and then go to college. In this culture, students spend more time at home and are less interested in their friends and in dating. The delinquent subculture is characterized by more dating, friends, and semilegitimate behavior such as drinking and smoking. The members spend a lot of time away from home. This group does not desire to go to college, and the members emphasize cars and clothes. Cohen found that membership in a subculture does not depend on socioeconomic status or race, but more on the style of relating values.

To determine how students are oriented, one can look toward their acceptance by the leading peer crowd, to the type of values they hold, or to their motivation to achieve (Gordon 1971). From the categories, one can derive the typical labels applied, such as "brain," "grind," or "curve breaker." These students have high achievement orientation, but do not enjoy as much peer acceptance. Others who have high motivation and high peer acceptance have been called "big wheels," "politicos," or "student council types." Identifying features of their general high school culture as well as features of these subcultures is not difficult for high school students. Similar subcultures seem to continue generation after generation, although the names change.

QUESTION: What about students who do not fit in the school culture?

Persons who have lower motivations or antisocial values could also be categorized, and are often overlooked in the general school culture (Bereiter 1973). Bereiter identifies the common life-style of youth who go directly into marriage or working-class employment and are not highly involved in the intrastructure of the school. Bereiter also identifies a delinquent type, which includes those adolescents who are unwilling to forgo immediate rewards to obtain the long-term payoffs of education. The researcher's argument is that these non-college-bound youth should be accommodated in the public schools, that they should not be forced into a model designed only for those seeking advanced degrees. Bereiter feels that college youth are allowed an unrestricted adolescence or a moratorium during which they can find themselves. The only requirement society places on them is that they accomplish the hurdles of grades, class attendance, and so on. Unfortunately, others are not provided this luxury, and Bereiter believes that society should help them in some way. They should be provided a way to explore the world, travel, audit courses, or do what they want without having to worry about academic obligations. Bereiter even suggests that the government pay these students a grant to do these things, which they would pay back with their future earnings. This concept is provocative and unlikely to be implemented. Nevertheless, it fits with Erikson's theory of the need for a moratorium sometime during adolescence in order to find oneself.

For some students, Bereiter believes that a service corps experience is a way to provide the adolescent with relevant and meaningful work experience. The adolescent could work on a conservation project or become a roving musician or travel guide. For low wages, youth can be hired to do worthwhile and potentially meaningful things to enhance society. This employment is not long-term, but provides work until the assumption of adult work roles. In many cases, this experience occurs after high school but before the student has entered the work force. At this time, students are usually not married and have little or no family obligations. Vocational education is the solution that most educators prefer.

Vocational training is probably the key area on which Bereiter focuses as an option. He believes that schools should give more job-skill training, especially in industries in which youth will be employed, such as plants, factories, and businesses. These institutions may do a better job in job-skill training than the school can. Bereiter suggests that the government assist this private segment in their educational efforts. In recent years, some of his suggestions have been followed. Bereiter's ideas are novel because they are presented as options to the high school experience and they allow even sixteen-year-olds to make decisions about the kind of experience they prefer at this stage of their life.

QUESTION: Exactly what is vocational education?

Perhaps the best way to explain vocational education is to look at the persons involved. More than ten million vocational education students are eighteen years or younger and still attending school. Minority students make up 24 percent of total enrollment, which is about 4 percent more than would be predicted from their proportion in the general population. Approximately 51 percent are female and 48 percent are male. More than 400,000 students have handicaps, but most of these students are mainstreamed into the regular programs. About 30 percent of the students come from the lowest socioeconomic group, and 12 percent come from the highest.

Vocational programs either are of a general nature designed to provide a foundation for career decisions, or are specific to provide skills for occupational areas. Our society's goal is to provide occupational training for all youth, and the public school setting has received a mandate to provide the necessary skills for graduates to be employable (Ausubel, Montemayor, and Svajian 1977). Perhaps the largest of these programs is consumer/homemaking, a program that more than 3.3 million people focus on to improve family life and to develop decision-making, interpersonal, and technical skills. This program is of a general vocational nature. This category includes prevocational programs with related instruction, and employability skills programs. Vocational education is growing but still does not meet today's needs, as partially evidenced by the growing problem of unemployment in the United States (Bottoms and Dopra 1983).

QUESTION: Is vocational education effective in preparing youth for the labor market?

In an analysis of the research to date, with a grant from the Carnegie Foundation, Alan Weisberg, president of Community Systems Association, presents a troubled picture (Weisberg 1983). He found some limited evidence that the secondary vocational program does keep people in school, reducing dropouts.

Other educational concerns of American schools

The scope of vocational education is often underestimated. Skills, such as the ones this girl is acquiring in a welding class, can provide a foundation for an individual to make future career decisions.

His main concern, however, is with the comprehensive high schools; Weisberg feels they are inferior to vocational schools in their ability to offer quality programs. Even though the students may be kept in the schools, he does not feel that job-specific skills, when taught in the comprehensive classroom, are sufficent. He says that labor market projections call for fastest growth in services, finance, and trade, with the greatest number of new jobs in health services, computers, repair of business and industrial machines, banking, secretarial services, and recreation. He thinks employees will need to develop strong general skills, not job-specific skills, which are learned in short-term, on-the-job training. He finds that female graduates of business and office programs fare better in the labor market than female graduates who have been in general programs in the comprehensive high schools, but that these initial benefits drop off with time. No comparable benefits show up for male graduates of vocational programs. When considering postsecondary training, Weisberg maintains that it is the number of years of school, not the type of school, that influences employment. He cites research showing that comprehensive high schools are consistently inferior to area vocational schools in their ability to offer high-quality programs. This difference is because of the vocational schools' greater depth of programming, their ability to employ more experienced staff, the higher priority placed on vocational training, and their closer ties with business and industry. The negative finding is that the vocational facilities are usually unavailable in central cities where minority populations are concentrated. Weisberg concludes that considerable discrimination results because of the training.

With such a high percentage of the population attending high schools, the schools are obligated to help youth. Weisberg suggests that they:

1. Improve the quality of their basic skills offerings, such as improving literacy and other basic skills,
2. Expand and improve job counseling and placement services, and
3. Provide more opportunities for structured supervised work experiences, especially for non-college-bound youth.

QUESTION: Other than teaching the basics and vocational education, which goals are important for public schools?

In general, schools perform three other functions in addition to instruction in the so-called basics and vocational education. The first is to communicate the values and morals of the culture. The second—somewhat particular to the United States and its pluralistic society—is to create successful acculturation or a melting pot of different people. The third function is to foster personal-social development. A controversial area is sex education, which could also be considered as another function.

In a review of the history of moral education, Jensen and Knight (1981) show that throughout history, a major function of schools has been to teach morals. Thirty-three percent of the parents surveyed in 1981 wanted morals taught in the schools, and they were particularly troubled with discipline. In *Moral Education,* Jensen and Knight describe a number of approaches to teaching moral education and the varied approaches that could be and have been applied to this problem. A philosophy and a method of teaching morals and values in the schools may be developed in the near future.

Regarding the melting pot function, people have immigrated to the United States in unprecedented numbers from diverse parts of the world during the last century and the first part of the twentieth century. People who had been traditional enemies were soon living peaceably in the same city. The success of this American experiment in uniting diverse people into a common nation where they could peacefully and successfully work and live together has been partly credited to attendance at public schools (Friedenberg 1959).

While early American schools originally were conceived to teach reading the Bible, their role of teaching skills for success in the marketplace has increased multifold. Finally, the importance of the schools in social development has been noted in recent decades (Coleman 1961). Schools have been increasingly changed to provide a social system to develop personal growth and self-development. Clubs, activities, counseling, dances, and other programs to help the student flower have been important components of the educational experience (McCandless 1970, 259). To illustrate the importance general society places on this function, consider the following quote:

> The students want to discover who they are and the school wants to help them make something of themselves. They want to know where they are; the school wants to help them get somewhere. They want to learn how to live with themselves; the school wants to teach them to get along with others. They want to learn what is right for themselves; the school wants to teach them responses that will earn them rewards in the classroom and the social situation. *(Life* 23 May 1969)

QUESTION: Can morals be taught in public schools?

Several objections have been raised regarding the teaching of morality in public schools; a serious objection is that instruction in morals is prohibited by law constitutionally. In a review of court cases on this question, the governor of Maryland appointed a commission to recommend a program of values education in the public schools. His attorney general's opinion was that no violation of the First Amendment was involved. Cases show that this position is substantiated (English 1982). The need and precedent of morals being taught in the school is expressed in a small book called *Moral Education: Historical Perspectives* (Jensen and Knight 1981). The authors state:

> Certainly citizenship, respect for the flag, obedience to local, state, and federal law are openly taught in the United States public schools. Values, attitudes, and virtues associated with democracy are advocated, for example, the dignity of each individual, respect for life, the right of private property, the need for citizen participation in government can be openly taught. . . . In general, it is unclear what aspects of morality public schools may include and what aspects of morality must remain with the family and religion. (Jensen and Knight, x)

The type and amount of moral education does vary, and American educators have developed several strategies for teaching morals and values in the schools at the present time. In the chapter on moral reasoning and values, the moral education programs based on Kohlberg's theory and on value clarification are presented. At the present time, there are several popular approaches to moral education. The first approach is the hidden curriculum with no specific content. The teacher simply incorporates moral education with other subject matter. The second approach is teaching traditional values with direct instruction, rewards for appropriate behavior, and modeling (Wooden 1972). The third approach is Kohlberg's cognitive approach designed to help facilitate moral thinking (Kohlberg 1969, 1978). Other approaches include curriculum developed by social studies specialists, applying philosophy to moral situations (Shaver and Larkins 1973). These approaches generally seek to develop scientific or rational skills for solving moral problems. Another approach is values clarification based on a humanistic understanding of people. Essentially, students acquire skill in learning to clarify the values they have (Roths, Harmin, and Simon 1966). Most of the approaches propose no absolute values; they primarily teach a skill or a process rather than specific content.

QUESTION: Is sex education needed in public schools?

The following statements by an advocate of sex education sum up his feelings about the need for adolescent sex education:

> Since sexuality is at the heart of adolescence consciousness, one isolated course is only the start of a program that might help them achieve full integrity as sexual being. As they experience their own developing sexuality, they are faced with confusing adult behavior and values, and they are manipulated by this sex exploitation of virtually every advertisement they see. They are desperate for information and serious dialogue that will help them grow into sexually healthy persons. Without this opportunity, the strong ones will evolve their

own codes, contemptuous of a society that simultaneously titillates and represses. Those who are less strong will remain confused. Many will slip into behavior that is harmful to themselves and others. (Brick 1981, 38)

Bruno Bettelheim, a reknowned psychiatrist, expresses an opposite opinion:

In my opinion, sex education is impossible in the classroom. Sex education is a continuous process and begins the moment you are born. It is in how you are bathed, how you are diapered, how you are toilet trained, and respect for the body, and the notion that bodily feelings are pleasant and that bodily functions are not disgusting. . . . How you feel about sex comes from watching your parents live together, how they enjoy each other's company, the respect they have for each other, not from what they do in bed with each other. . . . I think even such classes are a danger and that they are implicated in the increase in teenage sex and teenage pregnancies. You cannot have sex education without saying that sex is natural and that most people find it pleasurable. Sex education cannot teach respect. (Bettelheim 1981, 28–44)

Despite protests both pro and con, sex education continues to be presented in a diluted form in the public schools. As taught today, it satisfies neither the advocate nor the foe and will likely continue as a compromise to both.

A Gallup poll (Norback 1980) discovered that 84 percent of teenage youth and 77 percent of adults wanted sex education courses taught. In another study (Hunt 1970), 1,500 adolescent girls were polled, and 98 percent wanted sex taught in the schools. They did not think that discussion of physical intimacy would provoke curiosity or sexual experimentation. They wanted to know more about female reproductive systems, the menstrual cycle, and philosophical and scientific issues including premarital sex, abortion, birth control, sex drives, masturbation, homosexuality, impotence, virginity, and the nature of the orgasm.

Evidence suggests that students do need more information about sexual behavior and that many have definite misconceptions about the cause and control of pregnancy (Sorenson 1973). Although the present (1983) federal administration has announced opposition for federal participation and development of sex education programs, the need will continue, especially since most youth report that school is a primary source of information (Athamasiou 1973).

Still, the most telling and convincing arguments for the need of sex education in the school come from individual accounts or case studies that illustrate the problems that young people face in obtaining accurate information. The following is one such case:

I can still recall my first lesson in sex education. It is one I doubt I will ever forget. It occurred at my grandmother's house. I used to go to my grandmother's and stay with her on weekends.

I arrived at my grandmother's house at the usual time, but I noticed that my aunt—who was never married and still lived with my grandmother—wasn't anywhere around. I dearly loved my aunt and missed her when she wasn't there. So I asked my grandmother, "Grandmaw, where is Aunt Dorothy?"

She answered, "She's in the hospital."

Worriedly I asked, "In the hospital, what's wrong with her?"

"Nothing's wrong with her," she responded, "she just had a baby."

I couldn't believe it; I didn't even know she was pregnant; I just thought she was fat. The impact of the news I had just received along with the circumstances surrounding the situation began to arouse my curiosity as to where babies come from. The curiosity grew until I decided to pose the question to my grandmother. So I approached my grandmother and asked, "Grandmaw, where do babies come from?"

By her response you would have thought a nuclear bomb had exploded. She became overtly hysterical and screamed at me over and over, "Mercy sakes young-in don't ask me, ask your mother!"

The critical element to the success of sex education is to unite parents and schools. To do this a bridge must be built between the two groups. One way to accomplish this is to focus on the social context into which sexual behavior fits, namely and traditionally, the family.

In testimony before the U.S. Senate Labor, Health, and Human Services Subcommittee, Dr. Terry Olson stated:

First of all, it may be naive to think that putting sex education in the schools is going to solve the problem. At best, public schools are a secondary influence in an adolescent's world, while the primary influences on adolescents in our country remain the family and the peer group. However, if the entire population of teenagers is to be addressed, doing so through the school system is logical, but such attempts to influence teenage behavior should link the secondary influence of the schools with the primary influence of the parents. (Olson 1980, 1)

To accomplish this objective, Dr. Olson proposes that the content be taught within the context of family life, as depicted in Figure 6–1.

Figure 6–1   Placing Sex Education in a Correct Prospective

○ Total Family Interaction   ○ Sex Education

Incorrect: The divorcing and enlarging of sexual behavior from total family interaction.

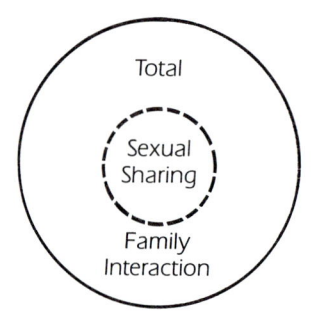

○ Total (Sexual Sharing) Family Interaction

Correct: Acknowledging sexual expression as an integral part of family dynamics.

(Source: Adapted from Olson, T. D. 1980, 3.)

Olson, in explaining Figure 6–1, states that:

> Sex is exalted to a status external to the family and is enlarged in scope from realistic family interactions. By discussing sex as if it were a legitimate activity irrespective of family commitments is to prostitute the role sexual expression can and does play in the family context. Moreover, to dwell on sexual expression independent of the family context is to make it appear larger as related to the background of total human experience than it really is. (Olsen 1980, 3)

The top half of Figure 6–1 depicts how the problem is typically seen in sex education, while the lower half of the figure illustrates a more accurate appraisal of the relationship. One family life specialist has developed a table depicting what might be effectively taught within the family context at different age periods. Table 6–2 outlines his program.

TABLE 6–2 A Teaching Program for Sex Education

The following table contains some information about developmental stages of children and some suggestions for what to teach during each of four stages. Also shown are some suggested ways to teach children.

First Concepts in Childhood

Developmental Stages of Children's Understanding	Concepts That Parents Can Teach	Suggested Ways To Teach
About 0–7 years of age, children are curious and think about objects and their physical properties, such as shape, texture, size, and color. Children also organize ideas into concepts (i.e., what parts do boys and girls have?) They want to know about sensations associated with objects.	1. Teach about body parts using correct terms and differences between males and females. 2. Teach when to talk about parts of the body and when not to talk (i.e., at home with parents and not in primary class). 3. Teach concepts of modesty and how wonderfully our bodies are made. 4. Begin principles of conception, pregnancy, and child prenatal growth.	1. Use baths or showers and children's questions as times to teach about the body. 2. Verbally explain times it is best to talk. 3. Use examples and positive comments about your own body and child's body to teach modesty and self-respect. 4. Use reading material about prenatal growth and childbirth. Use own pregnancy if appropriate. 5. Be loving, touch, and give affection.

Emotional Control and Prepuberty Physical Development

Developmental Stages of Children's Understanding	Concepts That Parents Can Teach	Suggested Ways To Teach
From ages 7–11 children learn preliminary logical thinking, social skills, achieving a sense of relationships to other people, and learning to control emotions associated with personal life and social contracts.	1. Teach about conception (sperm and egg unite) and reproduction. 2. Reinforce the need to talk openly with parents about questions children might have.	1. Initiate conversation to learn about what a child knows. Reinforce your need to have a child talk to you. 2. Respond to questions as asked.

Emotional Control and Prepuberty Physical Development (continued)

	3. Use social systems to teach modesty and appropriate conversation. 4. Help children learn to control their emotional impulses, avoid extreme or uncontrolled displays, be loving, learn to touch, and give affection.	3. When children exhibit extreme emotions, focus on the need to manage their impulses by sitting on a chair until calm, cooling off in a bedroom, and talking about children's feelings. Emphasize that children are responsible for controlling the expression of their emotions.

Developmental Stages of Children's Understanding	Concepts That Parents Can Teach	Suggested Ways To Teach
Age 11–15 1. Increased interest in the body and in relating a person's body to such things as popularity, athletic skill, and attraction to opposite sex. 2. Increased awareness of physical changes and comparing themselves with others. They notice voice change, breast development, height, and hair on the body. 3. Increased self-consciousness about appearance and ability to relate how they look to other things, such as others' respect and social values. 4. More importance is given to opinions of peers. 5. Children experience strong sexual desire for the first time. 6. Children can mentally see the logic behind reasons; they perceive cause and effect relationships.	1. Teach about the changes that occur in puberty (i.e., menstruation, rapid growth that can be related to poor coordination, widening of shoulders and narrowing of hips for boys, widening of hips for girls, enlargement of breasts for both boys and girls, development of body hair under arms, in pubic area, and on boys' face and arms). 2. Teach that good looks do not make a good person and one must develop good values, standards of personal conduct, and modesty. 3. Teach social skills (e.g., how to make friends, how to talk with others, and achievement) so that popularity can be achieved on some basis other than physical attraction. 4. Teach that individuals go through puberty at different rates—some early, some later, some rapidly, some slowly. 5. Teach how hormones change in the menstrual cycle and how they increase and decrease sexual desire.	1. Obtain good reading and other information to use with your family (elementary schools will have a good filmstrip). 2. Reinforce changes in children as positive by paying positive attention to their growth (e.g., "you sure have broad shoulders"). 3. Create teaching times during which children are told how puberty affects boys and girls. 4. Share some of your own experiences with puberty and its changes. 5. Initiate numerous conversations to ensure development of positive attitudes about the body, social success, and personal standards. 6. Frequently ask what ideas your children have about themselves.

Late Adolescence

Developmental Stages of Children's Understanding	Concepts That Parents Can Teach	Suggested Ways To Teach
Age 15–18 1. Children can observe how they relate to others. 2. Reasons and ideas must appear logical to be accepted. 3. Perceived ability to make their choices is necessary for development of personal values. Attempts to force ideas will evoke resistance. 4. Social success increases in importance, especially attention from the opposite sex. Personal esteem is closely tied to feelings of being socially successful. 5. Children require abundant positive emotional support from parents. 6. Although children can understand correct principles, most have difficulty acting according to what they believe.	1. Teach relationship of sex as a commitment to another person in marriage. 2. Reinforce that too much sexual involvement too early cheapens and can ruin the companionship. 3. Teach that physical attractiveness used to increase popularity will achieve temporary results. Personality and social skills will result in more permanent success. 4. Explain how to hold expressions of intimacy within appropriate limits according to the state of responsibile and legal commitment. 5. Convey that well-managed sexual desire is a major part of preparing for success in marriage.	1. Share personal experiences showing correct choice. 2. Ask children to tell you their decisions about premarital sex. 3. Emphasize positive affection, sex, and relationships with others. 4. Express confidence, support, and love. 5. Avoid critical comments about their looks, choices, or actions. Instead, focus on desirable things you want them to do.

Discipline in the schools

With the rising amount of violence in the schools and the public condemnation of violence, the concern is that the American high schools are moving toward a kind of anarchy. Educators Dececco and Richards state, "American high schools are drifting towards a kind of anarchy, faster than most people realize. Too many schools are angry places in which every rule is questioned and conflict is a norm" (DeCecco and Richards 1975, 5). They cite statistics to support these views. For example, vandalism costs as much as textbooks, assaults on teachers rose 77 percent during a three-year period in the seventies, assaults on students rose 85 percent, robberies 36 percent, and rapes and attempted rapes 40 percent.

QUESTION: What can be done to prevent violence in the schools?

Without question, the most important element is to have a strong administration, adequate staff, and sufficient disciplinary programs at the school community level, so that persons engaging in these types of acts are apprehended, appropriately disciplined, and dismissed from school until acceptable behavior is assured. This must be done at the school level. The individual parent or teacher, however, cannot wait until the administration of a school changes policy, but must deal with the individuals on a day-to-day basis and without delay.

QUESTION: What are some specific actions to help with discipline in the classroom?

Glasser (1978) believes that the direct confrontation of the child who is disorderly is not the long-term solution. He believes the answer is to give students a stake in the schools. They need to be involved in school activities and to somehow become able to be successful in school activities and to make passing grades. They need to have the basic skills, they need to be accepted in school, and they should also have subject matter that is meaningful to them. All individuals should have programs that are meaningful and that fit their learning abilities. When students break rules, however, Glasser recommends action or disciplines. Because discipline in the schools has become a serious concern, programs have been developed to establish discipline in the classroom.

While a number of programs for effective discipline in the schools have been developed, we present in detail only one of these programs, which is a system of discipline and has recommendations borrowed from several other techniques (Wilcox 1982). Because the program is short and practical, it is paraphrased with permission. The material is presented to serve as a useful set of recommendations for anyone to use when teaching or working with adolescent groups. The following are fourteen principles of the program:

1. *Decide if you are experiencing difficulty in controlling the entire class or whether just one, two, or a few students are causing the trouble.* If it is the latter case, then modify the following suggestions so you can work with offending students and not with the whole class.

2. *Take time to make friends with your students.* Put all books aside for a day or two. Play some fun, parlor-type games, like, "Twenty Questions," "What

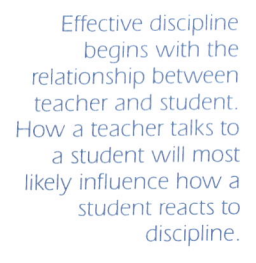

Effective discipline begins with the relationship between teacher and student. How a teacher talks to a student will most likely influence how a student reacts to discipline.

would you do if. . . ?'' Work in some activities where you and the students learn about interests and hobbies shared by each other. Ask students to write about their most unique experience. Write a paper yourself. William Glasser recommends that the teacher arrange students in a circle, and then give them every opportunity to express themselves. Each day, go out of your way to be smiling, kind, and friendly.

3. *Listen to the way you talk to your students.* Haim Ginnott (1972) states that, "A wise teacher talks to students the way he does to visitors at his home." Treat every student in your class with respect and courtesy. Use "I messages" in talking with your students. "I need your attention" is more acceptable than "You need to listen to me." "I feel sad when you hand in such untidy work" does not seem so hurtful as "You always give me such sloppy work!" The last chapter describes how to use these messages.

4. *Involve your students in helping you plan class work for the days and weeks ahead.* Start by asking what they dislike about your subject and the way you have been teaching it. Do not be defensive.

5. *Involve your students in helping you decide class rules.* If you see the need, use your students to help you make rules for proper behavior. William Glasser advocates the use of the class meeting to discuss and make class rules. The "Glasser Circle" is now used in many schools by teachers who are trying to involve their students in setting norms and formulating class rules.

6. *Catch students being good, and praise them for it.* After class rules are made, catching class members being bad is easy, but try not to do it. Catching the students being good is a major suggestion. Teachers tend to ignore good behavior by taking it for granted, but they commonly punish students who disrupt.

7. *Verbally attack improper actions, not the students themselves.* Some situations will occur in which students may do something to arouse your anger and thwart your intention to ignore their bad behavior. For these situations, the basic principle is to attack the improper actions and not the students themselves.

8. *Bargain with the students for appropriate behavior.* Use the "Premack principle" by making something the students want to do contingent upon their doing something they do not want to do. For example, you might say, "If you do ten math problems in the next half hour, you can have fifteen minutes for free reading."

An effective way to identify rewards and privileges for uses as bargaining agents is to observe spontaneous student behavior during "free" class time or to ask students to specify activities that they find enjoyable. Further suggestions for using this method are given in the chapter on behaviorism.

9. *Ask small favors of your worst offenders.* If David is one of your worst offenders, when he comes into the classroom say something like, "It's good to see you, David. Would you please do me a favor and take this down to the office?" The principle is that we tend to like those whom we serve, so try to get the worst offenders involved in doing small favors.

10. *Invite your worst offenders in for private interviews.* If David's disruptive behavior has not improved after your efforts to make him your friend, then it is time for a private interview with David, wherein you follow the steps of reality therapy (Glasser 1965). The following are the steps you might follow:

a. Ask him what he did, to make sure you are both talking about the same problem.

b. Then ask him to make a value judgment about whether what he was doing was helping him succeed in your class—whether it was helping him learn the subject material or whatever.

c. If David makes an appropriate value judgment, ask him to make a plan for improving his behavior, and commit him to follow that plan.

d. Get him to agree to his plan, follow through, and accept no excuses for failure.

11. *In a private interview, threaten your worst offenders with a logical consequence.* When you present logical consequences, make sure it is an immediate consequence and not hurtful (Dreikurs and Grey 1968). Also be sure that you are willing to follow through with the consequence you have chosen. Once you make the threat, you cannot back away from it.

As always, most suggested procedures have exceptions. Safety is one concern that overrides all others. If David breaks a safety rule, threatening his own or another's safety, it is not the time to be gentle and go through all of the steps 1 through 12. When a safety rule is broken, a predetermined consequence ought to follow, and David should have to deal promptly with the predetermined consequence.

12. *Try isolation for your worst offenders.* Although isolation can be thought of as a logical consequence, it is a severe consequence that should be used only as a last resort. Isolation has the added benefit of making normal classroom routines seem more attractive to the misbehaving students. Find a place where David can be isolated from other students, or, with the cooperation of the principal, find another place in the school. William Glasser recommends an SOS room (supervised-optional-study room that serves as an in-school suspension room) taught by a substitute teacher.

13. *Refer obstinate offenders to the principal or to whoever is in charge of school discipline.* Now is the time to threaten suspension from school for a brief time. This threat must be made by the person in charge. Work with parents so that the experience of staying at home is as unpleasant as possible. If David cannot be helped to make it in school, he will have to stay home, which means either a home tutor or going to the final step.

14. *Refer persistent offenders to juvenile court or to an alternative school.* This is the last step. Taking this step, however, is far better than having someone disrupt the classroom. Offenders cannot learn more responsible behavior if they are allowed to remain in the classroom after all the things you have tried.

The fourteen steps are described in more detail by the following authors: Glasser 1965; Dreikurs and Grey 1968; Glasser 1969; Ginnott 1972; Gordon 1974; Glasser 1978; and Wilcox 1982.

The issue of discipline can be approached in a more direct and powerful way using behavior modification principles, as presented in Chapter 15. One popular approach based on behavior modification is called assertive discipline. This approach was developed by Lee and Marlene Canter (1976). They give creative and insightful ways to discipline that focus on behavior control. In the years to come, more programs to handle discipline in the public schools will undoubtedly be developed. Long-term solutions will basically incorporate changes at the sociocultural and institution levels. The fourteen suggestions given, however, will have a positive short-term impact.

Summary

The United States secretary of education recently appointed the National Commission on Excellence in Education to evaluate the state of public education in the nation's public and private schools. The NCEE reported alarming statistics from which they concluded that our educational system needs immediate reform.

These statistics, however, relate to only one part of the overall responsibilities of the public schools. The American Association of School Administrators stated that some of the statistics used by the Capital Commission were outdated. They also cite the observation made by the United Nations that the United States has one of the highest literacy rates in the world. Another possible explanation of the NCEE statistics is that increased enrollment lowers the overall scores on intelligence tests and puts a strain on the educational system.

Attending high school has positive effects, as shown in surveys that found that subjects who completed high school were more highly informed than those who had completed only elementary school. The average nationwide scores have also risen on both the verbal and the mathematics sections of the Scholastic Aptitude Test.

The findings from various studies that have been conducted indicate that in general, students in the United States are satisfied with schools. Apparently, dissatisfaction and criticism may originate from outside the school rather than from within.

Evidence indicates that dropping out of school may be increasing. The three basic reasons for people dropping out of school are family background, non-school factors such as work and economic reasons, and experiences within school, such as criticism, poor grades, and expulsion.

One researcher found that since 1900, the majority of class time in American schools has consisted of teachers lecturing to the class and students working on written assignments. The passive-lecture and role learning of the typical classroom can be frustrating and discouraging, especially to the motivated youth with a keen intellect.

Students in smaller schools are generally able to participate more in extracurricular activities and leadership. Studies have shown, however, that small classes do not always improve academic performance. Schools assume an important role in socialization of youth.

Some advocates call for a movement away from education that exclusively stresses the basics. One suggestion is that creative teachers employ various instructional techniques so that children can integrate subject matter into their lives.

Other than teaching the basics and vocational education, three functions that schools provide include communicating the values and morals of the culture, creating a melting pot of different people, and fostering personal-social development.

Vocational education programs either are of a general nature designed to provide a foundation for career decisions, or are specific to provide skills for occupational areas.

Athletics has been emphasized in the American public school. This emphasis has drawn both negative and positive responses. Some critics believe that considering the amount of time and expenditure, the returns are not meaningful or significant.

Discipline is the most serious concern in the public schools. The most important element in preventing violence in the schools is to have a strong administration, adequate staff, and sufficient disciplinary programs so that offenders are apprehended, appropriately disciplined, and dismissed from school until acceptable behavior is assured. One program for effective discipline offers fourteen suggestions that grow progressively less gentle and more assertive.

References

American Association of School Administrators. 1983. *The excellent report: Using it to improve your schools.* Arlington, Va.: AASA.

Arena, J. 1983. How good was high school: on campus. *Newsweek:* 22 (Nov.)

Athamasiou, R. 1973. A review of public attitudes on sexual issues. In *Contemporary sexual behavior: Critical issues in the 1970s* ed. J. Zubin & J. Money, 361–90. Baltimore: Johns Hopkins Univ. Press.

Ausubel, D., Montemayor, & Svajian. 1977. *Theory and problems of adolescent development.* 2d ed. New York: Grune & Stratton.

Barker, R. G., & P. V. Gump, 1964. *Big school, small school: High school size and student behavior.* Stanford, Calif.: Stanford Univ. Press.

Bendette, F. 1981. Major school desegregation problems. *Integrated Education* 19 (3–6):35 (Summer).

Bereiter, C. 1973. *Must we educate?* Englewood Cliffs, N.J.: Prentice-Hall.

Bettelheim, B. 1981. Our children are treated like idiots. *Psychology Today:* 28–44 (July).

Bottoms, J., & P. Dopra. 1983. A perspective on vocational education today. *Phi Delta Kappan:* 348–50 (January).

Brick, P. 1981. Sex education belongs in school. *Educational Leadership* 38:390–391 (February).

Brown v. *Board of Education,* 347 U.S. 483(1954).

Burnett, J. H. 1969. Ceremony, rites, and economy in the student system of an American high school. *Human Organization* 28: 1–10.

Cameron, R. 1982. *Education summary.* Croft-Nei (November).

Canter, L., & M. Canter. 1976. *Assertive discipline.* Los Angeles: Canter & Associates.

———. 1983. *Assertive discipline for parents.* Los Angeles: Canter & Associates.

Cohen, J. 1979. High school subcultures and the adult world. *Adolescence* 14: 491–502.

Coleman, J. 1961. *The adolescent society.* New York: Free Press.

———. 1965. *Adolescence and the schools.* New York: Basic Books.

———. 1982. Public schools, private schools, and the public interest. *American education* 18:17–22 (January–February).

Dececco, J. P., & A. K. Richards. 1975. Civil wars in the high schools. *Psychology Today* 9(6):51–52.

Dreikurs, R., & L. Grey. 1968. *Logical consequences: A new approach to discipline.* New York: Hawthorne Books.

Elkind, David. 1981. *The hurried child, growing up too fast, too soon.* Reading, Mass.: Addison-Wesley.

English, R. 1982. The revival of moral education. *American Education* 18:6–7 (January–February).

Farr, R. 1982. *English summary.* 2 (December).

Friedenberg, E. Z. 1959. *The vanishing adolescent.* Boston: Beacon Press.

Ginnott, Haim. 1972. *Teacher and child.* New York: Macmillan.

Glasser, W. 1965. *Realty therapy: A new approach to psychiatry.* New York: Harper & Row.

———. 1969. *Schools without failure.* New York: Harper & Row.

———. 1978. Disorder in our schools: Causes and remedies. *Phi Delta Kappan* 59:331–33 (January).

Goertzel, V., & M. Goertzel. 1962. *Cradles of eminence.* Boston: Little, Brown.

Gordon, C. 1971. Social characteristics of early adolescence. *Daedalus* 100:931–60.

Gordon, T. 1974. *TET: Teacher effectiveness training.* New York: Wyden.

Hobart, T. Y. 1979. Polls show student support of teachers and schools. *New York State Teachers* 20:4 (April).

Hunt, M. 1970. Special sex education survey. *Seventeen:* 94.

Jensen, L., & R. Knight. 1981. *Moral education: Historical perspectives.* Washington, D.C.: Univ. Press of America.

Johnson, L. D., & J. G. Bachman. 1976. Educational institutions. In *Understanding adolescents: recent development in adolescent psychology,* 3d ed., ed. J. P. Adams, 290–315. Boston: Allyn & Bacon.

Kindsvatter, R. 1978. A new view of discipline. *Phi Delta Kappan* 59(5):322–25.

Kohlberg, L. 1969. The cognitive developmental approach to socialization. In *Handbook of socialization theory and research,* ed. D. Goslin, 347–480. Chicago: Rand McNally.

———. 1978. Revisions in the theory and practice of moral development. In *New directions for child development: Moral development,* ed. W. Damon. San Francisco: Jossey-Bass.

Langway, L. 1980. Sex education 101 for the kids—and parents. *Newsweek,* 1 September, 50.

Life. 1969. Schools. 23 May, 14.

Mackey, J. 1977. Strategies for reducing adolescent alienation. *Educational leadership* 34:449–52.

Masters, S. H. 1969. The effect of family income on children's education: Some findings on inequality of opportunity. *Journal of Human Resources* 4:158–75. (Fall).

McCandless, B. 1970. *Adolescence: Behavior development.* New York: Holt, Rinehart & Winston.

Metcalfe, L., ed. 1981. *Values education: Rationale, strategies and procedures, 41st yearbook.* Washington, D.C.: National Council for the Social Studies.

Miller, D. D. 1976. What do high school students think of their schools? *Phi Delta Kappan* 57:700–702.

National Commission on Excellence in Education. 1981. *A nation at rest: The emparitus for educational reform.* Washington, D.C.: U.S. Government Printing Office.

Norback, C., ed. 1980. *The complete book of American surveys.* New York: New American Library.

Olson, T. D. 1980. *Sex education: What and who.* Adapted from a presentation to the White House Conference on Families. Washington, D.C.

———. 1984. Sex education. Department of Family Sciences, Brigham Young University, Provo, Utah, personal communication with author.

Phi Delta Kappan. 1982. 14th Annual Gallup poll of the public's attitudes toward the public schools. *Phi Delta Kappan* 64:37–49 (September).

Proctor, P. 1979. Gallup poll: What your kids really think about school. *Parade,* April, 4–5.

Rehberg, R. A. 1969. Behavioral and attitudinal consequences of high school interscholastic sports: A speculative consideration. *Adolescence* 4(13):69–88.

Rice, P. 1981. *The adolescent.* 3d ed. Boston: Allyn & Bacon.

Rosow, J. M. 1979. The work place: A changing scene. *Vocational Education* 54(2):22–25.

Rotberg, I. 1983. Some observations on the reported gap between American and Soviet educational standards. *American Education* 19:9–12 (January–February).

Roths, L. E., M. Harmin, & S. B. Simon. 1966. *Values and teaching: Working with values in the classroom.* Columbus, Ohio: Merrill.

Rumberger, R. W. 1982. *Youth in society* 13(4):449–70 (June).

Schmiedeck, R. A. 1979. Adolescent identity formation in the organizational structure of high schools. *Adolescence* 14:191–96.

Scoresby, L. 1985. *Teaching children about sex and reproduction.* Department of Family Sciences, Brigham Young University, Provo, Utah. Personal communication with author.

Shaver, J. P., & A. G. Larkins. 1973. *The analysis of public issues programs.* Boston: Houghton Mifflin.

Shaycoft, N. F. 1967. Contigrowth during high school. *Project Talent,* bulletin 6.

Shine, W. A., & N. Goldman. 1980. Governance by testing in New Jersey. *Educational Leadership* 38:197–98 (December).

Shovlin, D. W. 1967. The effects of the middle school environment and the elementary school environment upon sixth grade students. Ph.D. diss., University of Washington.

Sirotnik, K. 1983. What you see is what you get—Consistency, persistency, and mediocrity in classrooms. *Harvard Educational Review* 53:16–31 (February).

Solberg, J. R. 1970. Interscholastic athletics—Tail that wags the dog? *Journal of Secondary Education* 45:238–39d.

Sorenson, R. C. 1973. *Adolescent sexuality in contemporary America: Personal values and sexual behavior, ages 13–19.* New York: Abrams.

U.S. Office of Education. 1974. *National evaluation of project follow through.* Washington, D.C.: U.S. Government Printing Office.

Weight, L. J., & K. A. Moore. 1978. The impact of an early first birth on young women's educational attainment. *Social Forces* 56: 845–65. (March).

Weisberg, A. 1983. What research has to say about vocational education and the high schools. *Phi Delta Kappan* 64:355–59. (January).

Wilcox, R. T. 1982. Discipline made gentle. *College of Education Review* 2(1):10–14. Provo, Utah: Brigham Young Univ. Press.

Wooden, J. 1972. *They call me coach.* New York: Bantam Books.

Yankelovich, D. 1974. *The New Morality.* New York: McGraw Hill.

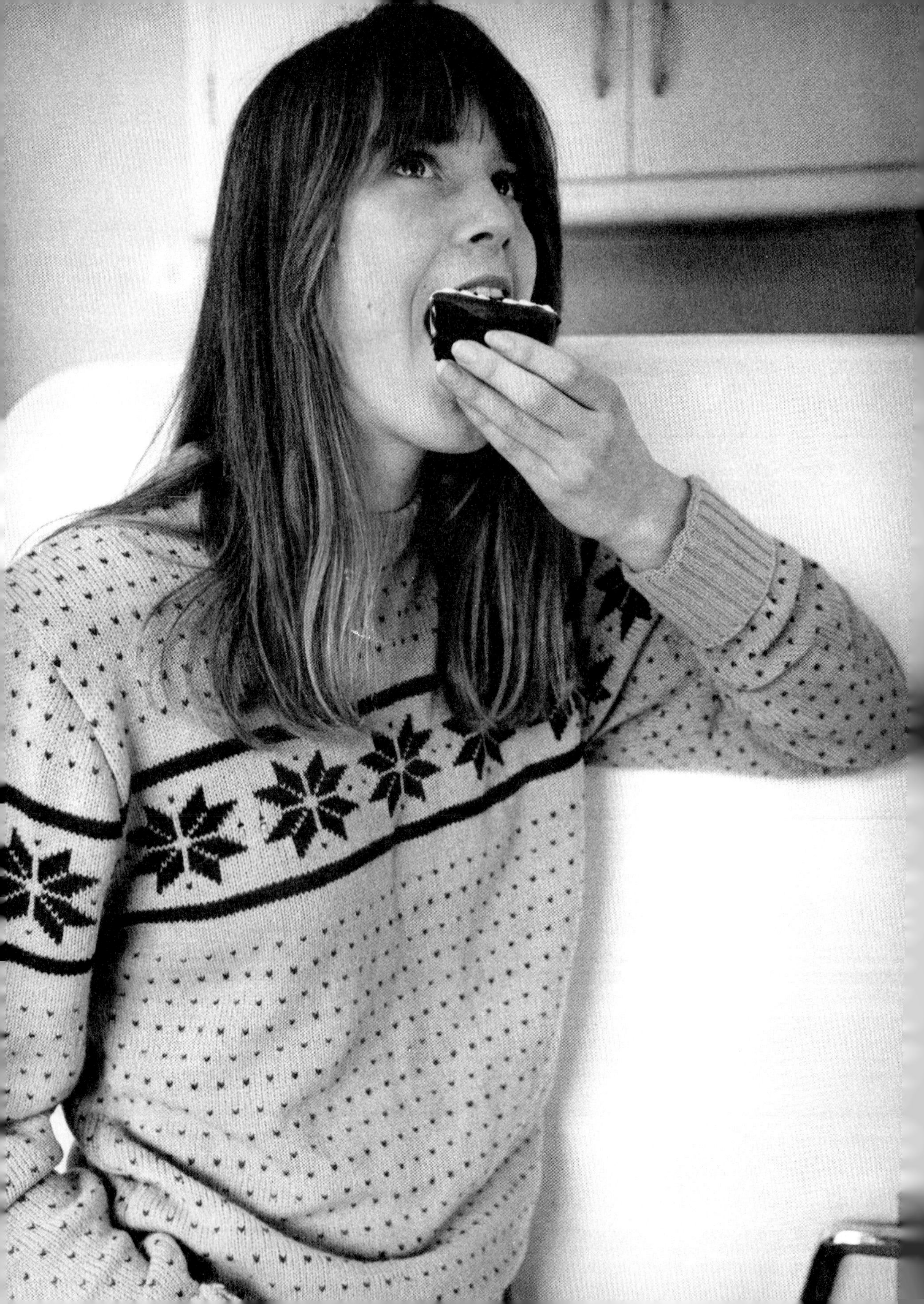

CHAPTER SEVEN

Biological influences

SURVEY AND QUESTIONS

In this chapter the student will find the following subjects discussed and the related questions answered:

Puberty and Biological Changes

What are hormones?
What are the sex hormones?
In the study of adolescence, what are the practical effects of this information on bodily development and function?
How do sociocultural factors biologically influence the adolescent?

The Effects of Early and Late Maturation

What are the effects of being an early-maturing versus a late-maturing adolescent?
Why do early-maturing boys have an advantage over those who mature later?
Have all researchers concluded that maturing early is advantageous?
What are the findings for early- and late-maturing girls?
Why are early-maturing girls at a disadvantage?

Adolescent Body Types

How important is body size and shape for the adolescent?
How can a person's body build have an impact on personality and temperament?
What are the practical implications of knowing an adolescent's body type?

The Secular Trend

Do adolescents today have better body builds and physiques than in previous generations?
Why does this secular trend occur?
What are the implications of the secular trend?

Physical Attractiveness

What is the relationship between an adolescent being overweight or underweight and the adolescent's self-esteem and behavior?
How important is physical attractiveness to adolescents?
What are some explanations for the negative ways in which unattractive people are often treated?

The Onset of Puberty

What is the importance of the menarche for girls?
What is the best way to introduce information about the menarche to a young girl?

What are initiation rites?
Do females have initiation rites similar to those found for males?
What is the significance of initiation rites?

Sex Differences

Do the psychological differences between men and women have a biological base?
Are there other explanations as to why males are more aggressive than females?

Adolescent Handicaps

Does a biological handicap have an especially powerful effect on the developing adolescent?
What can be done to help the handicapped adolescent cope?
Does the handicapped adolescent place an extra burden and stress on parents?

Puberty and biological changes

I remember junior high. I remember Jana. In the 7th grade Jana had the body of a fully developed, voluptuous woman. She had the mind of a child and of course we as her envious peers didn't know that and wouldn't have believed it for a minute had we been told. We simply assumed that along with physical maturity came mental and emotional maturity and thus we looked up to her and tried as best we were able to copy her. Along with her striking physical features came "life in the fast lane." She wore figure-hugging clothes, adopted sophisticated make-up and hair styles, smoked, drank, eventually got caught up in drugs and associated with men much older than herself—mainly GI's from the nearby Army base.

During our 9th grade year she changed schools and it was many years before I came in contact with her again.

When I met Jana again in the 12th grade I found a very mixed up, burnt out young woman. We talked. She had no idea of who she really was, what she wanted, where she was going or how to change.

This account of Jana illustrates how biological factors (early development and inherited physique in this case) can interact with cultural factors to influence an individual's social and emotional development.

Early in adolescence, biological changes commonly referred to as puberty make a profound impact on the psychological, social, and emotional development of individuals. Indeed, according to psychoanalytic authors, puberty is the most critical event of adolescence because of the resurgence of the id (Freud 1946, 1958; Freud [1905] 1953; Bols 1962).

Individual physiological growth tends to be relatively constant from birth to adulthood. The period of puberty is more complex. A dramatic change occurs in body chemistry, not only in the direction of growth but also in the types of change that take place. Boys and girls become men and women through the changes in sexual characteristics. The profound physical changes that occur during puberty are primarily caused by substances called hormones.

QUESTION: What are hormones?

Hormones are chemical substances produced and distributed in the human body that interact with individual body cells. Their interaction with the body cells causes different groups of cells to change in structure and function. In brief, hormones cause the body to act differently. Hormones are part of the special endocrine glandular system in the body. Endocrine glands are classified as ductless glands because they transfer the chemical they produce (hormones) directly into the blood, where they are then distributed throughout the body. The entire endocrine system itself is composed of several small glandular systems that interact with each other in highly complex ways. In this chapter, the endocrine system is described as simply as possible. More complex physiological descriptions, such as how hormones are produced in other body tissues or what happens when they are introduced from outside the body, are beyond the scope of this text. The first step to understanding this system is to consider the pituitary gland.

The pituitary gland controls hormonal levels. The hypothalamus, a portion of the brain stem, controls the pituitary gland. Hormones cause changes in body appearance, functions, and behavior. Some of the changes that may be observed in both males and females are displayed in Figure 7–1. This figure refers only to the most salient changes in the development of male and female sexual characteristics.

The age during which these changes typically occur are displayed in Figure 7–2. Sexual changes that are directly related to reproduction capabilities are called primary sexual characteristics; other biological changes that are not associated with the reproductive organs are called secondary sex characteristics. Puberty typically begins two years later for boys than for girls. The genetically based hormonal systems will cause boys to eventually end up taller and heavier than girls, to have more facial and bodily hair than girls, and to have greater muscular strength. The hormones will also determine reproductive functions and body shapes.

Figure 7–1 Observable Effects of Sex Hormones

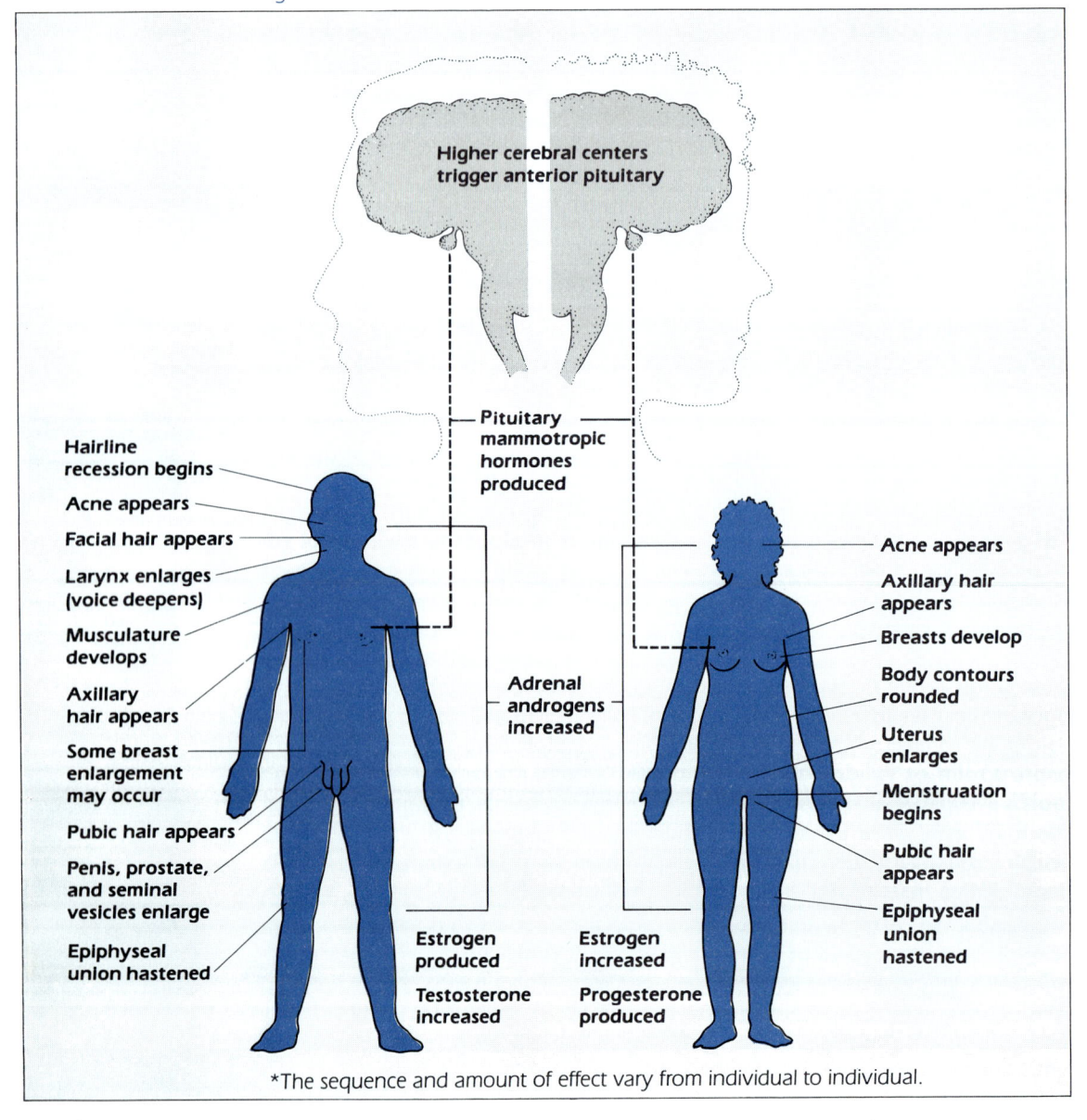

Higher cerebral centers trigger anterior pituitary

Pituitary mammotropic hormones produced

Male:
- Hairline recession begins
- Acne appears
- Facial hair appears
- Larynx enlarges (voice deepens)
- Musculature develops
- Axillary hair appears
- Some breast enlargement may occur
- Pubic hair appears
- Penis, prostate, and seminal vesicles enlarge
- Epiphyseal union hastened

Adrenal androgens increased

Estrogen produced
Testosterone increased

Female:
- Acne appears
- Axillary hair appears
- Breasts develop
- Body contours rounded
- Uterus enlarges
- Menstruation begins
- Pubic hair appears
- Epiphyseal union hastened

Estrogen increased
Progesterone produced

*The sequence and amount of effect vary from individual to individual.

Figure 7-2 Sequence of Changes During Puberty

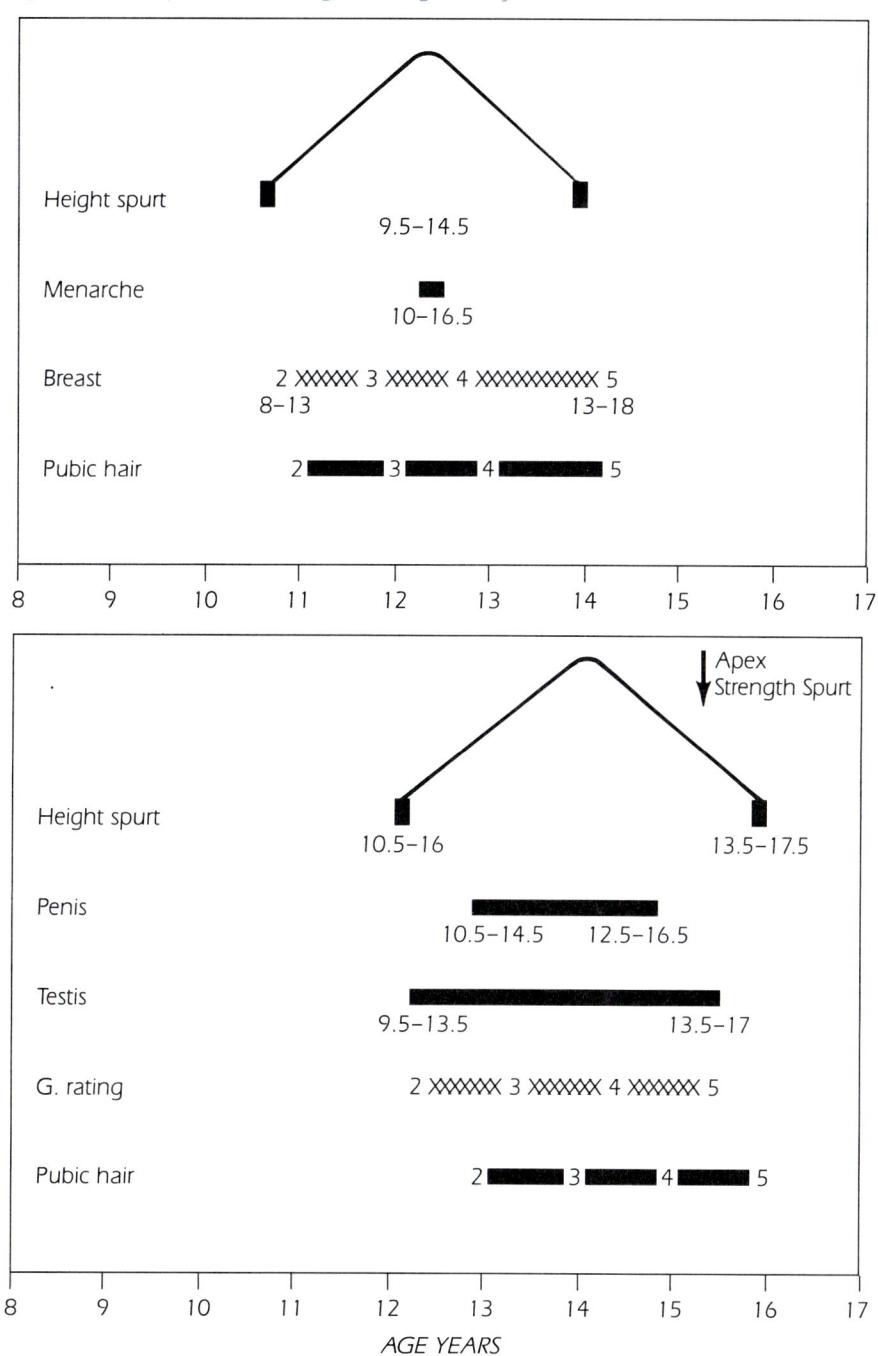

Girl:
- Height spurt: 9.5–14.5
- Menarche: 10–16.5
- Breast: 2 — 3 — 4 — 5; 8–13 to 13–18
- Pubic hair: 2 — 3 — 4 — 5

Boy:
- Apex Strength Spurt
- Height spurt: 10.5–16 to 13.5–17.5
- Penis: 10.5–14.5 to 12.5–16.5
- Testis: 9.5–13.5 to 13.5–17
- G. rating: 2 — 3 — 4 — 5
- Pubic hair: 2 — 3 — 4 — 5

AGE YEARS

The biological approach to adolescence: Biological change and psychological adoption. Schematic sequence of events at puberty. An average girl (upper) and boy (lower) are represented. The range of ages within which each event charted may begin and end is given by the figures placed directly below its start and finish.

Source: Adapted from Tanner 1974.

The sexual physiological changes that have been discussed thus far are controlled and regulated by the sex hormones. Table 7–1 depicts the sequence for males and for females.

TABLE 7–1 Stages of Sexual Development

Males	Females
1. Testicular enlargement	1. Preadolescent
2. Scrotal changes	2. Breast development
3. Sexual hair	3. Sexual hair
4. Penile and testicular enlargement	4. Menarche

Source: Adapted from F. P. Heald and W. Hung, "Enducing Control of the Adolescent Growth Spurt," in *Adolescent Endocrinology,* edited by F. P. Heald and W. Hung (New York: Appleton-Century-Crofts, 1973).

QUESTION: What are the sex hormones?

Androgens are thought of as male sex hormones, and estrogens are considered female sex hormones. Both types of hormones are produced to some degree by both sexes, and their appearance is a gradual process. The hormones need time to fully initiate the reproductive capabilities that will follow. For example, sperm may not be completely viable immediately after a male's first emission, and ovulation fertility does not develop for one or two years after the menarche (Apter and Vihko 1977). Box 7–1 outlines the specific functions of the sex hormones. For the study of adolescence, the hormones testosterone and estrogen produce the effects of greatest importance.

QUESTION: In the study of adolescence, what are the practical effects of this information on bodily development and function?

Although every adolescent undergoes certain biological changes and becomes more sexually mature, significant facts about adolescent physical development should be considered:

1. Boys mature about two years later than females.

BOX 7–1 HORMONAL ACTION IN MALES AND FEMALES

The Role of Hormones in Shaping Organs and Integrating and Regulating Behavior

1. Gonadotrophic hormones:
cause development of the gonads.
are responsible for mating and child-caring behaviors.
maintain functional integrity of the gonads to include sperm production and ova maturation.

2. Testosterone:
causes maturation of penis, prostrate, and other male genitals.
is responsible for increased sex drive at puberty and [for] aggression.
maintains sperm production and secondary sex characteristics.

3. Estrogen:
causes maturation of ovaries, uterus, and other female glands.
is responsible for child-caring behaviors.
maintains cervical secretions and female secondary sex characteristics.

Adapted from Dusek 1977, Table 3–1, p. 35.

2. Adolescent development and performance are controlled biochemically, and at least partially explain adolescent behavior.

3. The internal biochemical interaction is extremely complex and is not fully understood at this time.

In the *Handbook of Adolescent Psychology,* Peterson and Brandon (1980) point out that biological changes of puberty have both a direct and an indirect effect on adolescent behavior and personality development. This effect is seen in Figure 7–3.

In explaining the Figure 7–3, Peterson and Brandon point out that the *direct* effect is probably weaker than previously supposed:

> A review of the research on hormone-behavior relationships suggests that there is some evidence for hormone effect, though this evidence is weaker than popularly believed. . . . In summary, the evidence for direct hormonal effects is less than overwhelming. We must note, however, that the previously inadequate state of endocrine methodology has made it impossible until recently to obtain hormone measurements precise enough to relate to psychological valuables. Further research may demonstrate more relationship. (Peterson and Brandon 1980, 133–34)

Figure 7–3   How Biological and Cultural Factors Interact to Influence the Individual

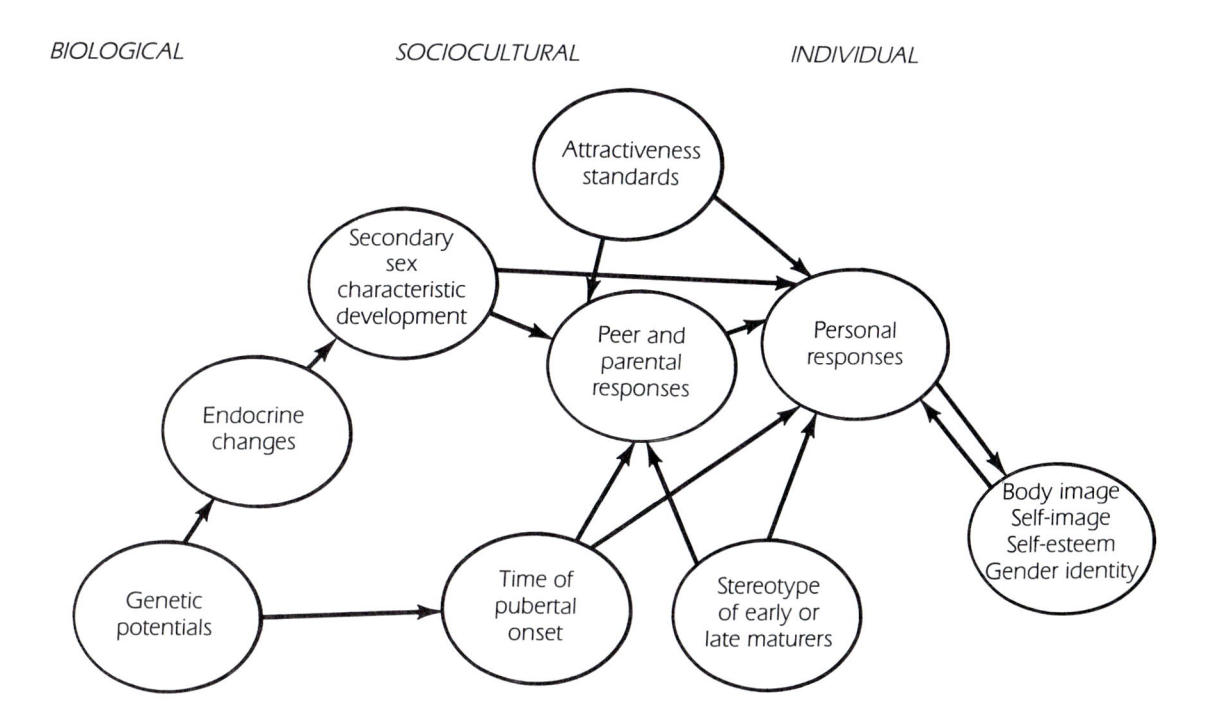

Hypothetical model for biopsychosocial development over the life cycle. Hypothetically important paths between pubertal changes and psychological responses.
Source: Peterson and Brandon 1980, 147.

These authors then describe the powerful yet *indirect* role that hormones have on the psychological behavior and personality development of youths. They call this influence the mediated effects model. Figure 7–3 illustrates the relationship between the biological and the sociocultural mediating factors on individual behavior.

QUESTION: How do sociocultural factors biologically influence the adolescent?

The following documented statements from Peterson and Brandon clarify their description of how factors interact to influence biologically based behaviors:

> [P]rior learning from early socialization experiences connected with parental and cultural attitudes toward the genitals, internal taboos or prohibitions relating to the management of physical tensions, and the nature of prior exposure to adults' sexual behavior—all may result in motivational residues and affectively charge patterns of thought and feeling that influence contemporaneous patterns of adaptions to puberty. (Peterson and Brandon 1980, 137)

They also point out the importance of parental and peer attributions:

> The literature on adolescent body image . . . and on psychological consequences of early or late maturation . . . indicate the importance of parental and peer environments as influential variables in the adolescent's acceptance or satisfaction with body change. Changes in height, weight, complexion and secondary sex characteristics have significant social stimulus value. . . . Parents and peers may communicate positive or negative evaluation of the adolescent's appearance by many overt and covert means. (Peterson and Brandon 1980, 137)

Quoting from another researcher (Fabrega 1972), Peterson and Brandon give two explanations of how these effects take place, and assemble a substantial body of evidence illustrative of the fact that "(1) culture groups differ considerably in the significance they attribute to bodily events, and (2) these normative evaluations may influence both how these biological events are noticed and included within a person's subjective experience, and whether these categorizations give rise to the experience of anxiety or conflict." (Peterson and Brandon 1980, 138).

Goethals (1971) has discussed the importance of social controls as moderating variables and the role of social organization in the regulation of sexual behavior. In all societies, some structuring of adolescent sexual activities takes place. This structuring ensures the continued functioning of the basic social institutions and culture. Peterson and Brandon state:

> With regard to the nature of these controls, there are remarkable variations among cultures both in the amount and type of sexual behavior that is permissible and the consistency of the society's standards as development proceeds (and thus in the developmental continuities and discontinuities imposed upon the individual). (Peterson and Brandon 1980, 139)

Sociocultural factors interact with biological ones to influence social behavior. Thus, adolescents from different generations, such as these from the early 60s, will likely behave somewhat differently according to changes in the sociocultural climate.

These quotes from Peterson and Brandon illustrate their contention that the effects of puberty are influenced and mediated by both environmental and individual conditions. Perhaps the best demonstration of this interaction and the powerful effect of biological processes on adolescent behavior can be seen when studying the effects of being an early-maturing or a late-maturing adolescent.

The effects of early and late maturation

QUESTION: What are the effects of being an early-maturing versus a late-maturing adolescent?

The answer to that question depends upon the sex of the adolescent. The Oakland Growth Study found that early-maturing boys appear more relaxed and attractive to adults, and are more popular with their peers than late-maturing boys. By late adolescence, early maturers display less dependency and have more self-confidence than do the late maturers. The early-maturing boys are also more likely to assume leadership positions in high schools, especially among working-class youth. Early-maturing boys tend to score significantly higher on socialization and dominance scales, and are more adept at making a good impression than are late maturers. These findings have been consistently reported and have become a well-accepted statement on early-maturing versus late-maturing boys (Jones and Bailey 1950; Mussen and Jones 1957; Jones 1965; Clausen 1975).

QUESTION: Why do early-maturing boys have an advantage over those who mature later?

Males tend to base status, esteem, and acceptance on physical achievements. Therefore, a logical assumption is that boys who are taller, heavier, stronger, and quicker, due to both muscular and skeletal development, tend to excel in activities that in turn give them self-esteem and confidence. Early-maturing boys often do well in situations requiring physical confrontation as well as in athletics in general. Early-maturing boys also are similar in height and weight to females of their same age (who have matured an average of two years ahead of most males). These early-maturing males are more appealing to the opposite sex because of their size and weight, while the opposite is true for the late-maturing boy.

Figure 7–4 shows the great differences between boys age fifteen and girls age thirteen. The boy in the upper-left corner is extremely less mature biologically than the girl in the lower-right corner.

Figure 7–4 Differences Between Selected Males at Age 14.75 and Females at Age 12.75

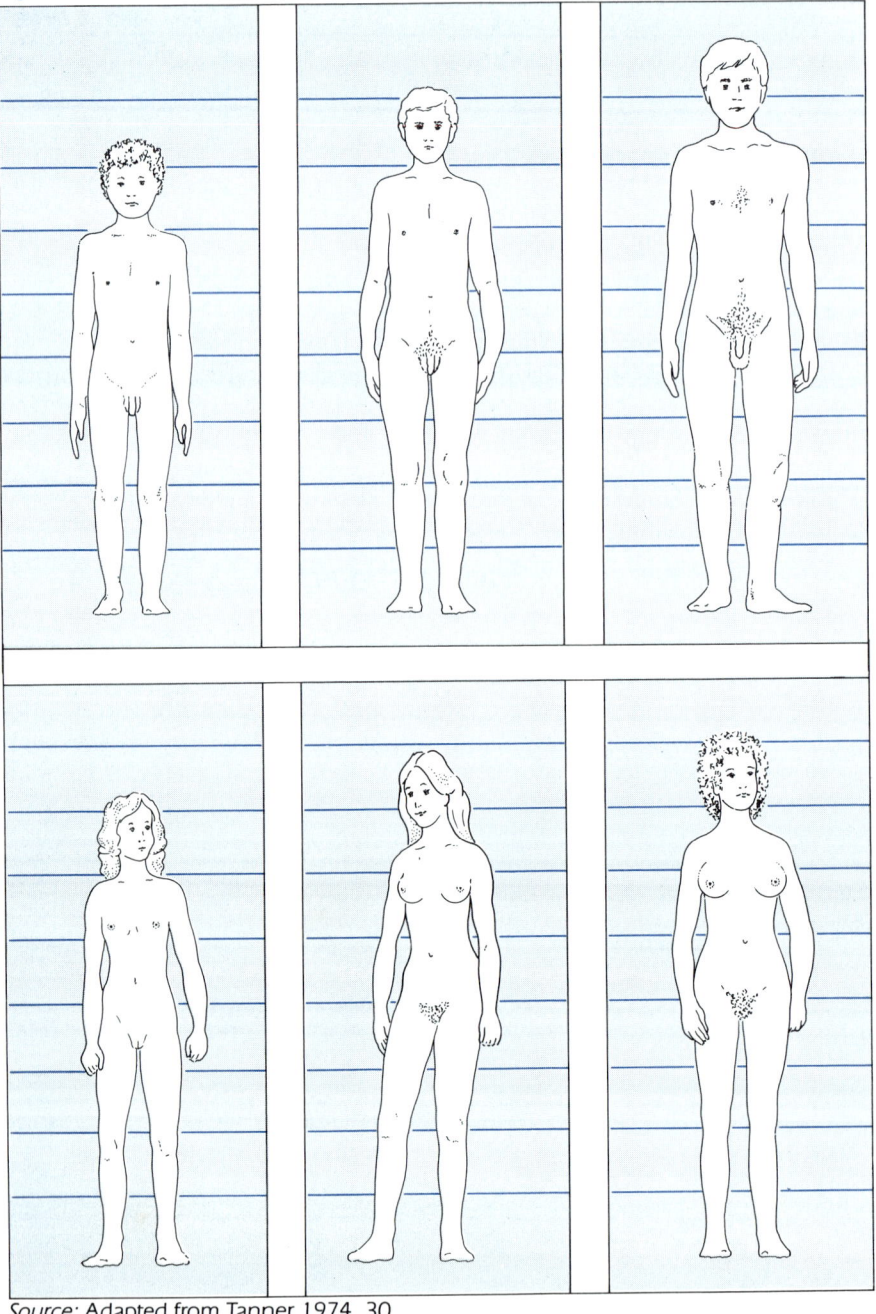

Source: Adapted from Tanner 1974, 30.

QUESTION: Have all researchers concluded that maturing early is advantageous?

No. For example, one researcher found that at age thirty-eight, little difference could be found between previously early and late adolescent maturers (Clausen 1975). Lack of differences in adulthood, however, does not mean that early maturation is not advantageous in adolescence. One case study, which may be an exception, shows a positive outcome in later life and illustrates how an individual might benefit from being a late-maturing male:

> John was a late maturer. In his high school, athletics were greatly stressed and as it was such a small school almost all the boys were involved. John said it was hard for him because he could not play any sport very well and was smaller and less coordinated than were his friends. Because of this, John found other interests, became a leader in school government, and was elected class president. This helped him overcome many of his inferiority feelings. He went steady for most of his high school period and felt maybe this was a form of security for him.
>
> In his college years John grew and matured, and his coordination greatly improved. This helped him to feel more accepted by girls.
>
> John feels that his late maturation influenced the direction his life took. He is more interested in the arts than most of the boys from his age group and school. He developed his leadership abilities and other talents rather than spending most of his time in sports. He found it made him a stronger person, and it also made him develop an identity without relying on physical characteristics.

This case study excerpt possibly supports the findings that show late-maturing males score higher in sociability and participative eagerness, possibly as compensation for late maturation.

Another researcher (Peskin 1967) found that early maturers tend to be more somber, anxious, submissive, less exploratory, and less intellectually curious than late maturers, and that late maturers usually display no such tendencies. Despite some exceptions, however, the socioemotional advantages clearly lie with the early-maturing male.

QUESTION: What are the findings for early- and late-maturing girls?

In general, the findings reported for girls are different from that for boys. Some researchers consider early-maturing girls to be at a disadvantage. In the Oakland Growth Study, Jones and Mussen (1959) found that early-maturing girls had "little influence on the group and seldom obtained a high degree of popularity, prestige, or leadership. They were seen as . . . submissive, listless or indifferent in social situations and lacking in poise" (492). These researchers described late-maturing girls as more outgoing, confident, and assured, with more leadership ability. A later study of this same data found that social class moderated the effects of early maturers. For middle-class girls early maturation was positively related to self-confidence on the California Personality Inventory Scale, but for working-class girls early maturation resulted in less confidence.

The general finding favoring the late-maturing girls was later reported in the Berkeley Guidance Study (Peskin 1973). The following case study illustrates the differences faced by one early-maturing girl:

> Lisa developed earlier than a lot of girls, including me. Because of this she was more confident than many of the other girls in our grade. She quickly made many friends and became somewhat of a leader among them. She also had boyfriends years older than her because she was tall and looked older than she really was.
>
> From maturing so early and being set as the leader, I think this caused her to be forced into forming an identity too early. She soon became tired of the things her same-aged peers were doing because she had already experienced those things through hanging around older people a lot.
>
> She identified herself as a leader so when we got into high school, she got tired of it quickly. She decided to graduate early so that she could work more and go to college as older people did. But after she graduated from high school, the "new life" was not as neat as she thought it would be. She soon joined the Navy, supposedly for six years, but was out of there in one year. Her next experience was to move in with her fiancé. That also didn't work out.

Peskin found that early-maturing girls experience more crises, loss of control, and unrest during adolescence. They have stronger tempers, more introverted and less social personalities, and wider ranges of behavior. Most of these differences, however, are negligible by age thirty. For both boys and girls, early and late maturing apparently has more of an effect during adolescence and may not continue into later life.

QUESTION: Why are early-maturing girls at a disadvantage?

In part, the reasons for a late-maturing girl having an advantage over an early-maturing girl may be the opposite of those given for a boy. The late-maturing girl is more similar to males of her own age in size, weight, and perhaps subtle sexual characteristics. In addition, girls may be more self-conscious and aware of secondary sex characteristics and bodily size. The early-maturing girl may feel uncomfortable with more adult and womanly body proportions. In addition, she is even more out of phase with males her same age.

Margaret Mead said that males and females should not be placed together in a social, emotional, and particularly a dating sexual context during puberty, partially because of this biological difference in rate of maturation. These harmful effects may be particularly pronounced in the early-maturing girl and in the late-maturing boy. Margaret Mead was also a stong critic of the coeducational junior high school. The difference in body size and shape alone may be a significant factor in young adolescent male-female relationships.

Adolescent body types

QUESTION: How important is body size and shape for the adolescent?

One set of researchers (Cortés and Gatti 1965, 1966, 1970) studied adolescence and the relationship of body build to personality. They used the traditional three categories to identify body shapes: mesomorphic, endomorphic, and ectomorphic. In general terms, the mesomorphic build is broad at the shoulders, narrow at the hips, tall, muscular, and athletic in appearance. The endomorphic build is much heavier than the mesomorphic and has a fatty appearance. The ectomorphic build is thin and tall.

Cortés and Gatti ranked the individuals as they compared in all three categories, because few people fit clearly into one category or another. Those people who *did* fit more clearly into a single category tended to have personality and temperament traits that were strongly related to their body builds. One Cortés and Gatti study of one hundred high school boys and girls discovered that the relationship of body build to personality style was especially strong among the girls. They found that endomorphs rated themselves as more kind, relaxed, warm, and softhearted; mesomorphs as confident, energetic, adventurous, and enterprising; and ectomorphs as detached, tense, shy, and reserved. In another study (1966), the same researchers found that twenty prison inmates who had committed serious crimes were mostly mesomorphic. This correlation between the mesomorphic body build and criminality also seems to exist among juvenile delinquents (Cortés and Gatti 1965, 1966). Table 7–2 displays the temperament traits that the researchers found for all three body builds.

TABLE 7–2 Traits Associated with Body Type

Viscerotonia-Endomorphy (Circular Type)	Somatotonia-Mesomorphy (Triangular Type)	Cerebrotonia-Ectomorphy (Linear Type)
1. Dependent	Dominant	Detached
2. Relaxed	Assertive	Tense
3. Calm	Confident	Anxious
4. Kind	Aggressive	Considerate
5. Love of comfort	Love of risk	Love of privacy
6. Extrovert of affect	Extrovert of action	Introvert
7. Extensive rapport	Enduring rapport	Intensive rapport
8. Cheerful—depressed	Even—explosive	Hypersensitive—apathetic
9. Self-satisfied	Self-assured	Self-centered
10. Soft-tempered	Quick-tempered	Gentle-tempered
11. Complacent	Irascible	Reflective
12. Amiable	Talkative	Reserved
13. Warm	Active	Cool
14. Affected	Reckless	Suspicious
15. Tolerant	Energetic	Inhibited
16. Generous	Enterprising	Restrained
17. Forgiving	Outgoing	Precise
18. Needs people when disturbed	Need action when disturbed	Needs solitude when disturbed
19. Stress on being	Stress on doing	Stress on perceiving
20. Lets things happen	Makes things happen	Watches things happen

Source: J. B. Cortés and F. M. Gatti, "Physique and Motivation," *Journal of Consulting Psychology* 30:433(1966), Table 1, and J. B. Cortés and F. M. Gatti, "Physique and Self-Description of Temperament," *Journal of Consulting Psychology* 29:433–34(1965).

Expectations and stereotypes some people have of certain body types may have an impact on an adolescent's personality and temperament.

QUESTION: How can a person's body build have an impact on personality and temperament?

Perhaps the most popular and defensible explanation is that individuals with different body types are treated differently by their peers, family, and friends. Investigations seem to support this contention. People often have favorable views and high expectations of mesomorphs and less favorable attitudes and negative, stereotyped views toward ectomorphs and endomorphs (Lerner 1973). In addition to expectations and stereotypes, the likelihood is that mesomorphic individuals are more apt to excel at sports at a young age when physical skills are more prestigious. For example, one student wrote about himself:

> I was able to start high school before my 13th birthday. At this time I was already 5'9" or 5'10" and weighed close to 200 lbs. I was a boy in a young man's body. As I went through high school, especially in sports, I was treated and talked to as someone much older than I was.

QUESTION: What are the practical implications of knowing an adolescent's body type?

One implication deals with the process of stereotyping. Classifying people with distinct body builds into personality types involves stereotyping, which is inaccurate for some people and which forces other people into molds that they do not fit. Parents, teachers, and caretakers of youth can understand that general research findings and blanket observations may not apply to individual adolescents. A wise approach is to be aware of stereotypes and to reexamine them;

otherwise, adolescents with certain bodily characteristics will receive even more differential treatment on the playground, in the classroom, and on the streets. Giving overly favorable treatment to mesomorphs simply because of their physical appearance is a mistake. Also wise is realizing that a person's self-concept is influenced by what others think; therefore, ectomorphs and endomorphs may be more vulnerable to low self-esteem and self-concepts due to the negative expectations that other people have of them.

Another implication is that contemporary U.S. culture, especially the media, presents ideal stereotypes that are to be copied. This attitude is a double-edged sword. Not everyone can have a Cheryl Tiegs or Farrah Fawcett physique, yet every female is subtly urged toward this ideal. Adolescents are often acutely aware of the discrepancy between cultural ideals and what they are. Adolescents need to know that they are worthy of being valued and prized as human beings without possessing the popularized body builds. In addition, when adolescents want to change their image, as they almost certainly will wish to do during the many years of their growing up. A helpful and willing adult can effectively assist them to understand this motivation and how to deal with it. An understanding adult can assist endomorphs (with an obese body type) in diet counseling or exercising. This may include instructing the adolescents on how to diet, helping the adolescents determine what their eating problems are, and assisting them to learn how to cope with the problems. Adults can help ectomorphs to eat a more nutritious diet and to exercise more rigorously, to obtain athletic skills, and to train so that their athletic skills will be developed.

The secular trend

QUESTION: Do adolescents today have better body builds and physiques than in previous generations?

Yes. This tendency for earlier maturation and an increase in body size is called the secular trend, and refers to the fact that each generation tends to mature earlier and be larger in size and weight than the previous generation. Some dramatic evidence of this trend can be seen when considering the following quote:

> The knights' armor in medieval European castles serves as powerful illustration of the secular trends since the armor seem to be to fit average ten- to twelve-year-old American boys of today. The seats of the famous LaScala Opera House in Milan, Italy, which was constructed in 1776–1778, were 13 inches wide. Thirty years ago most states outlawed seats that were less than 18 inches wide. In 1975, comfortable seats will need to be 24 inches wide. (Muss 1970, 271)

One comprehensive review of this trend estimated the relative growth rate of males during an eighty-year period. They found that from 1870 to 1955 the North American white male at age 15 years became taller by 5.2–6.2 inches (Meredith 1963, 85). The change has occurred more in the *rate* of maturation than in the total amount of change. In other words, adolescent growth seems to occur earlier and be completed sooner for adolescents today. This is particularly true when considering the onset of puberty. The age for first menstruation (menarche) has consistently declined for the past hundred years. One researcher states:

The main conclusion is perfectly clear: girls have experienced menarche progressively [earlier] during the past 100 years by between 3 or 4 months per decade. On this basis, puberty is obtained 2½ to 3½ years earlier today than it was a century ago. (Tanner 1968, 24)

Figure 7–5 shows that this trend has occurred in almost all Western countries.

Figure 7–5 Age of First Menstrual Period Across Several Decades in Six Countries

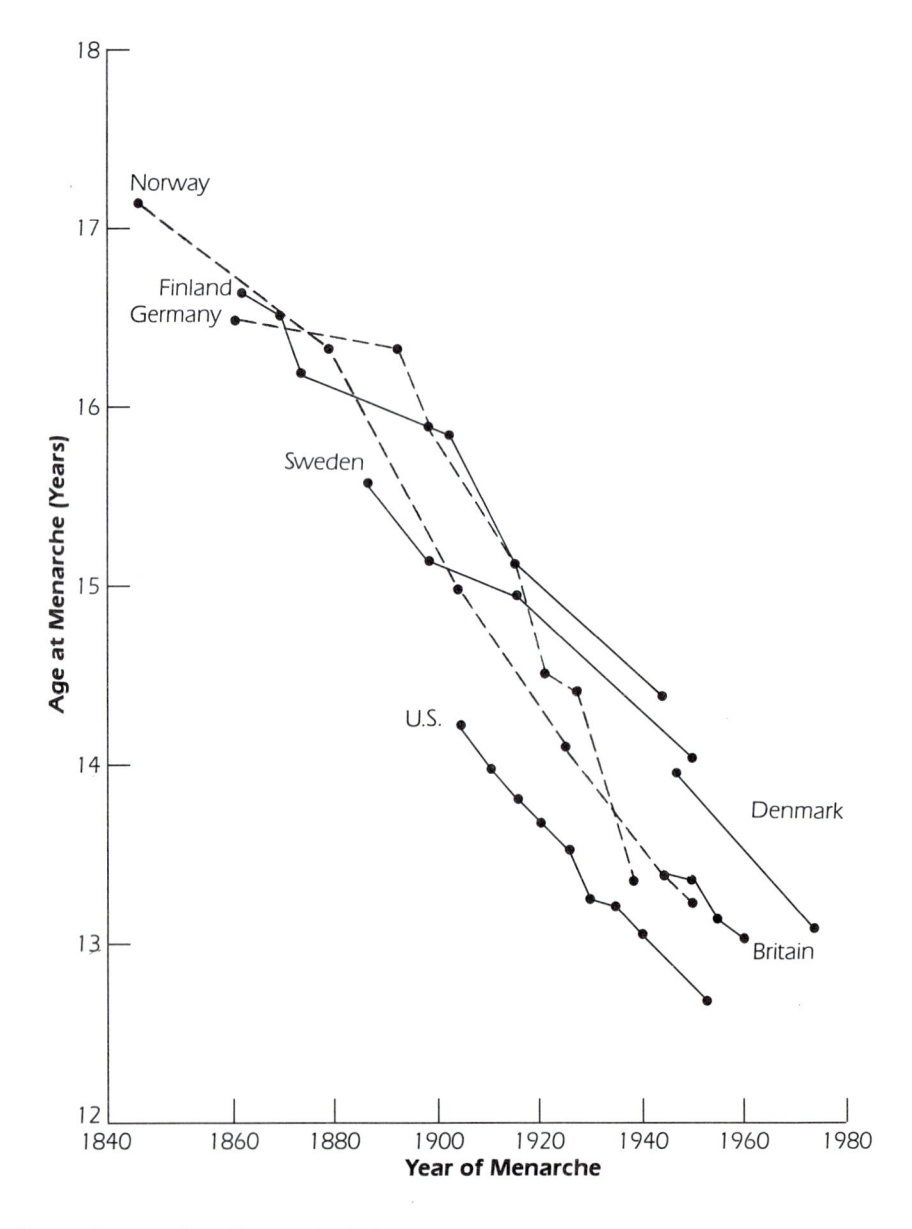

Source: Adapted from Tanner 1968, 26.

QUESTION: Why does this secular trend occur?

Two major explanations account for why the secular trend occurs. The first involves nutritional and health care improvements. Research has shown that the greatest increase in the rate of earlier menarche has occured for lower-class girls whose nutritional improvements during the hundred-year period were greatest. More affluent girls had a 2.8 month per-decade decrease, while lower-class girls had a 5.4 month per-decade decrease in the age of first menstruation (Tanner 1968). In studying the height and weight of Russian boys over a forty-year period, researchers found that the secular trend was interrupted during the years 1940–45 when an acute food shortage occurred in Russia. The secular trend seems to be stronger in countries where there is adequate diet and health care rather than where there is malnutrition (Frish and Revelle 1969).

The second explanation of the secular trend is genetic in nature. The genes controlling stature may partially dominate so that offspring tend to be taller than the average height of their parents. Increasing the variety of "height genes" in a population should lead to an increase in average adult height. This indeed occurs when individuals marry outside of their immediate family and community. This "outbreeding" has been on the increase with each succeeding generation as communication, transportation, and world economics cause people to move. This effect can be seen in the following quote:

> Sons of parents who are from different Swiss villages were taller than the sons of parents from the same village. . . . The average degree of outbreeding that takes place in the last century can account for 0.8 inches increase in height per generation. (Jensen 1969, 229)

The data suggest, however, that effects have leveled off, especially earlier onset of menarche (Bullough 1981).

QUESTION: What are the implications of the secular trend?

World athletic records continue to fall and be broken with each succeeding generation. Geneticists point out, however, that at some point the heterozygous characteristics resulting from a wider range of intermarriage will saturate the world's societies, and gains will level off. Perhaps other attributes of a person behave similarly to the physiological characteristics of decreasing average onset of puberty and adolescent height. Not surprisingly, IQ, athletic skills, and verbal comprehension may also be influenced by the heterozygous effect. In that case, society can expect increasingly higher achievements in many areas of performance and better health with each generation. The nutritional explanation of the secular trend implies that to assist human development, adequate nutrition as well as health care should be maintained and increased when possible.

QUESTION: What is the relationship between an adolescent being overweight or underweight and the adolescent's self-esteem and behavior?

Physical attractiveness

This question was partially answered in an investigation involving one thousand fifteen- to sixteen-year-old students who were categorized as overweight, underweight, or average. In summarizing their study, researchers Hendry and Gillies stated:

> As reflected in their own body estimates, underweight adolescents may have considered their bodies to be less "deviant" than overweights. Yet awareness of their "inadequacy" [caused] them to shun the heterosexual setting and turn to the mass media for solace. Although there appeared to be widespread enjoyment by adolescents of actual sports and games, the experiences within school sports and teachers' expectations of differing body types appeared to reinforce the quite separate feeling of self-depreciation of underweight and overweight adolescents. Thus the current study has provided further evidence of the social importance of physical attractiveness by stressing the relative value of possessing an average physique and pointing out the various effects of adolescents possessing an overweight or underweight physique in certain social and educational encounters. (Hendry and Gillies 1978, 192)

QUESTION: How important is physical attractiveness to adolescents?

Research indicates that physical attractiveness is one of the most powerful influences upon adolescent popularity, peer acceptance, and self-evaluation. In one study, subjects judged and rated photographs of anonymous individuals in terms of their physical attractiveness and their perceived popularity. The researchers concluded that "physical attractiveness and popularity are strongly correlated. The findings thus far have revealed a high correlation between these two variables from age six to college age" (Cavior and Dokecki 1973). Gerald Adams, who has extensively investigated the effects of physical attractiveness, points out that it is one of the most powerful variables that influences adolescents. Attractiveness has an impact upon an adolescent's social relationships, self-perceptions, personality development, social behavior, and life experiences. Attractive individuals are generally thought of in positive terms: positive, warm, friendly, successful, independent, and intelligent. People also tend to behave differently toward attractive individuals. They are more helpful and cooperative with attractive persons than they are with unattractive persons. The difference in perception and treatment has long-range consequences. Attractive individuals appear to be better adjusted socially, to have higher self-perceptions and more healthy personality attributes, and to have more positive social behavior. Attractive people are also more capable of resisting peer pressure (Adams 1977a, 1977b, 1981; Adams and Crossman 1978).

QUESTION: What are some explanations for the negative ways in which unattractive people are often treated?

The differential treatment that unattractive people receive can be explained in perhaps three ways. Basically, unattractive people illicit anxiety simply because they are different. These feelings of anxiety and discomfort that some people feel when looking at an unattractive person cause them to terminate the social interaction. Ending the conversation results in the elimination of the anxiety. Because of this, unattractive people would be less conversed and may feel rejected at the frequent abrupt closure of their social encounters. Unattractive people also tend to notice that other people occasionally stare at them. This may cause unattractive people to prematurely terminate their social encounters.

Another explanation for differential treatment is that individuals may actually prolong encounters with attractive people, and cause attractive people to put their best side forward. One study demonstrated this phenomenon. Male students were told that they were to have a telephone conversation with either an attractive or an unattractive female. The females were unaware of which condition—attractive or unattractive—they were assigned to. The conversations between the males and females were recorded and analyzed. The researchers found that women who were randomly selected for the attractive category became adept in their conversation, while the women in the unattractive condition progressively became socially ineffective. The researchers concluded that when others view us as attractive, they may do subtle things that encourage us to become confident and skillful. If we are viewed as unattractive, however, we are treated in such a manner that it causes our social behavior to deteriorate. We become what others expect us to become (Snyder, Tanke, and Berscheid 1977).

The onset of puberty

QUESTION: What is the importance of the menarche for girls?

The *menarche* is the name given to a girl's first menstruation. Its most important impact is the influence it has on the young girl's sense of herself as a female, which in turn affects her future identity and adult sexuality (Kestemburg 1961, 1967; Ritvo 1971). The experience assures a young girl that her body is female and confirms her womanhood. Because young girls want to be accepted by their peers and to be like them, it is not surprising that girls who have an exceptionally early or late menarche may experience problems. In one study, early menarche was a disadvantage to girls in the sixth grade but an asset to those in junior high (Faust 1960).

An early menarche can be a problem for a young girl in that she is socially and emotionally unprepared for the event, and is also less likely to be counseled and advised by parents and friends. Consider the following account of a girl who began her menarche two months before her tenth birthday:

> I can remember not having any idea what was happening to me. I was scared and didn't tell anyone for two days. I can remember not knowing what could be causing the bleeding but hoping it would stop. I can remember looking at other girls and wishing I were normal like them. Now that I think about it, I almost felt guilty about my condition. . . . Finally, my mother found the underpants I had cleverly stashed away . . . and she and my father explained why a girl has a menstrual cycle. I can remember feeling very relieved that I wasn't going to die. (Koff, Rierdan, and Sheingold 1982, 7)

In one study (Koff, Rierdan, and Sheingold 1982), the objective was to discover if the timing and preparation for a menarche had a significant effect upon an individual:

> What is apparent from our data is that more adequate preparation is associated with a more positive experience with menarche. Knowledge of the anatomy and physiology of menstruation and the mechanics of menstrual hygiene are

two important aspects of adequate preparation. Preparation for menarche is important for all girls, but assumes an especially critical role for the girl who is young at the time of her menarche. It is clear from our data that early menarche imposes special disadvantages. Early maturers experience menarche more negatively than do average or late maturers. (Koff, Rierdan, and Sheingold 1982, 7)

QUESTION: What is the best way to introduce information about the menarche to a young girl?

Some individuals have suggested that a custom is needed in our society to make the menarche a positive experience. A major obstacle to a custom, however, is the anxiety and self-consciousness that may exist even within individual families over this event. Although almost all concerned adults would like to help adolescents deal with menstruation, they are unable to do so because of their own feelings about the subject and because no established way exists for dealing with this event. Some writers suggest that if a standard and understood custom were established surrounding the menarche, the experience would be brought out into the open, and a way would be provided for people to deal more comfortably and expectedly with the event (Weideger 1976; Logan, Calder, and Kohen 1980).

A survey asking mothers, girls, and female psychologists what would be the best way to observe such a tradition of menarche found that the girls thought that such a tradition should involve more than one person. The preference of these mothers, daughters, and psychologists was to limit participation in the tradition to the mother and the father rather than include other members of the family, nuclear or extended. Expressions and messages like the following statements to be given the young girl regarding her menarche received almost unanimous agreement (93 percent or more, for mothers and daughters): "Congratulations, our little girl is growing up." "Something special has happened." "It is a special time."

The type of activity preferred most by mothers was a toast, and the activity preferred most by girls was an embrace. One-third of the girls surveyed preferred some type of gift, such as flowers or a charm for a charm bracelet. The researchers collected a number of anecdotes describing the experience in different families. One of the most positive was the following:

> At last I can pass on the experience of a high school friend to many others. My friend's mother had died when she was eleven, but I suppose her older sister clued her in on the reason for menstruation. She figured her father ought to know, so she shyly told him. Being a somewhat reticent man, he acknowledged and nothing more—until she returned from school that day to find her room *filled* with flowers from him. I have often thought of this loving gesture of a quiet father. (Logan, Calder, and Kohen 1980, 268)

The researchers liked this story because it included a man in the event. No medical or hygienic focus is placed on what is happening. There is simply a positive emotional response that is plain and simple. The young girl's privacy has not been offended, and a tangible gift is involved.

QUESTION: What are initiation rites?

Although no parallel development to the menarche event occurs for males, some cultures observe events that are landmarks for entering adulthood. These events are called *initiation rites* and are primarily directed toward young boys who are entering manhood.

In an article called "The Function of Male Initiation Ceremonies at Puberty," severe and difficult rites are shown to exist in some cultures worldwide for young boys as an entrance requirement into manhood. These rites include the infliction of pain, isolation from women, strenuous trials of manliness, and even genital operations. Consider one such rite:

> When a boy is somewhere between ten and sixteen years of age, he is sent by his parents to a "circumcision school" which is held every four or five years. Here in company with his age-mates he undergoes severe hazing by the adult males of the society. The initiation begins when each boy runs the gauntlet between two rows of men who beat him with clubs. At the end of this experience, he is stripped of his clothes and his hair is cut. He is next met by a man covered with lion manes and is seated upon a stone facing this "lion man." Someone then strikes him from behind and when he turns his head to see who has struck him, his foreskin is seized and in two movements cut off by the "lion man." Afterwards he is secluded for three months in the "yards of mysteries," where he can be seen only by the initiated. It is especially taboo for a woman to approach these boys during their seclusion, and if a woman should glance at the leaves with which the circumcised covers his wound, and which form his only clothing, she must be killed.
>
> During the course of his initiation, the boys undergoes six major trials: beatings, exposure to cold, thirst, eating unsavory foods, punishment and threat of death. On the slightest protest he may be severely beaten by one of the newly initiated men who is assigned to the task by the older men of the tribe. (Whiting, Kluckhohn, and Anthony 1958, 360)

These authors point out that in strongly *matriarchal* cultures, the initiation rites serve as a solution to psychological separation problems experienced by boys entering manhood. In mother-child households with long post-partum sex taboos—both customary in many societies—the boy often has a strong emotional dependence upon the mother and feelings of hostility toward the father. Incestuous desires for the mother and rivalry with the father are socially disruptive. Therefore, boys are required to undergo difficult, painful, and visible initiations into manhood. After the initiations, there is no question of their identity and allegiance. An interesting speculation is that a similar type of initiation rite may exist in subcultures within our own society (e.g., the lower-class minority groups) where no strong father image is present. In these cases, adolescents often have to undergo a type of initiation ceremony. For example, this kind of initiation rite could be the basis of some socialized juvenile delinquency and youth gang membership. Gang memberships usually require a test of strength and endurance, and a rejection of anything feminine, sensitive, and soft. The initiation is also usually supervised and directed entirely by older males.

QUESTION: Do females have initiation rites similar to those found for males?

The researcher who speaks with the most authority on this subject says that there are initiation rites for females (Brown 1963, 1969). An example of a strong female initiation rite is the following:

> When a girl first menstruates, she is confined to a special part of the house for eight days. She remains in seclusion particularly to avoid the spirits of the river and the forest. These would be offended by her condition and they would cause her to sicken and die. The girl is dressed in old clothes in order to be unattractive to the spirits, and her diet is restricted rather severely. During these eight days, she is expected to spin cotton to be used in making a hammock for a member of her family. At the end of her seclusion, an elderly couple noted for industry, arrives at the home of the girl before sunrise. The girl is bathed. Then a small tuft of cotton is placed in the palm of her hand, and a fire set to it. She must remove the cotton rapidly from hand to hand to avoid getting burned. This ritual is done because her hands must always be busy. Next her hand is placed in a bowl of large, biting ants. She must not show pain. The ants are to remind her always to be industrious like the ant. Were a lazy person to attend this part of the ceremony, the girl would also become lazy. The girl is then dressed, painted, and adorned with jewelry. Guests arrive and there is drinking, dancing, and singing. When she has washed her hands in grated manioc, she is free once more to move around the village, to take her daily bath in the river, and to work in the household. (Brown 1975, 41)

Such rites, Brown found, are observed in societies in which the girl continues to live in the household of her parents after marriage. The initiation

Puberty initiation rites are formalized in some cultures with actual ceremonies. Here a young Apache girl celebrates with her tribe in the traditional Apache Sunrise dance. Ceremonies such as these are becoming increasingly rare.

symbolizes a necessary status change for the girl, although she remains in the same residence that she has known since childhood. Also, these rites take place in societies where the women must make a strong contribution to the society's fight for survival. The culture must ensure that the girl will be a hard worker. These female initiation rites also take place in societies where there are problems in achieving one's sex identity.

QUESTION: What is the significance of initiation rites?

It is important for young people to know both publicly and privately that they are true members of their respective sex and that they can assume the appropriate sex behavior for that culture. In societies where there is some confusion about sex roles, as in our own society, having an initiation rite might be important if individuals were reluctant or confused about their sex role and sex identity. Juvenile delinquency might be a misguided attempt by a male to establish himself as a man and not be considered a "sissy" or "feminine." The same may be true for females. Young people who have a problem clearly defining their sex role need an acceptable way to clearly identify, accept, and adopt their appropriate sex role. This would eliminate both the societal and personal motivation for an adolescent to engage in undesirable, painful, and antisocial initiation rites.

QUESTION: Do the psychological differences between men and women have a biological base?

Sex differences

In one extensive review of the psychological differences between men and women, MacCoby and Jacklin (1974) conclude that most of the "differences" between men and women are probably the result of stereotypes. These stereotyped differences might include the beliefs that women are more social, more suggestible, have lower self-esteem, and have less achievement motivation than do men. The authors conclude, however, that some genetically based psychological differences seem to be present between the sexes. For example, men and women have different average levels of tactile sensitivity and fear. Girls also seem to be more compliant and less dominant than are males. Girls tend to excel in verbal ability, while boys score higher on spatial and quantitative items in intelligence tests. The greatest difference between men and women appear to be in the area of aggression. Males are usually more aggressive than females.

The author of this text feels that current evidence indicates that women have more empathy than do men. Melvin Konner (1983) strongly believes that a definite biological difference exists between men and women. He reviews the research of other scholars in the area, showing that males differ from females at birth. Males have greater strength while girls show greater skin sensitivity, more reflex smiles, more taste sensitivity, more searching movements, and so on. He stresses the role of hormones in influencing masculine behavior, showing that castration has been used to reduce aggressiveness in both humans and animals. Konner also cites research (Konner 1983) showing that for male prison inmates the higher their testosterone level, the earlier they tended to be initially arrested. A correlation also exists between their testosterone levels and their observed aggressive behavior. Konner also believes that gender differences may be due to variance in brain structures, which in turn interacts with hormonal influences.

QUESTION: Are there other explanations as to why males are more aggressive than females?

Social psychologists tend to emphasize the environment as one of the most influential factors in almost all behavior including aggressiveness. In almost every society, men typically occupy and control the dominant prestigious positions. Is this a coincidence, or do hormone differences account for gender variations in aggressiveness, which in turn leads to dominance in leadership? This question has several possible answers:

1. It is possible that testosterone directly gives rise to an aggressive nature. One study (Money & Erhardt, 1972) found that girls whose mothers received testosterone during pregnancy played more aggressively than other girls. However, no direct relation has yet been demonstrated between testosterone level and aggressiveness in humans (Huber, 1974). Further, there does not seem to be any good theory of *how* testosterone might directly affect aggressiveness.

2. It is possible that the effects of testosterone on aggressiveness are not so simple. For instance, it may be that testosterone affects musculature, which affects success or failure in sports, which in turn rewards or punishes competition and aggressiveness, which finally generalizes to other life activities. Strong adolescents (especially boys) learn that by playing aggressively they can win in sports, and they adopt a competitive style in other things they do. Other explanations, involving causal chains between testosterone and aggressiveness, are also conceivable.

3. It is possible that parents believe that boys should be competitive and girls cooperative and so reward their children for "sex-role appropriate" behavior and punish "inappropriate" behavior. This *sex-role socialization*, rather than testosterone, may be responsible for early differences in competitiveness that are evident in boys and girls. (Stang 1981, 92)

Adolescent handicaps

QUESTION: Does a biological handicap have an especially powerful effect on the developing adolescent?

Estimates indicate that more than 200,000 children are born with some form of handicap, defect, or deformity each year (Brown 1972). The number of handicapped adolescents is even larger than this figure, since many problems develop during childhood. Adolescence is a time when children are experiencing new feelings, roles, and expectations, and are struggling to find themselves. A biological handicap certainly makes this process more difficult. Studies of handicapped adolescents show that the handicap affects more than what is immediately obvious. For example, blindness affects more than vision. A group of researchers state that

> blindness, for example, [is] more than vision. It is the rare blind individual who does not have any initial problems in dealing with the handicap, or who is not deprived of some educational or occupational opportunities. A handicap pervades all aspects of a person's functioning. Coupled with the *strum und drang* of adolescence, a handicap exacerbates the problems associated with that period of development. (Abramson, Asch, and Mash 1979, 558)

The three problem areas for handicapped adolescents are acceptance, independence, and expectations. Handicapped adolescents are more likely to behave in ways that are objectionable, and this behavior therefore results in more rejection of what they would normally receive (Edgerton 1967). Sensing a lack of acceptance and then acting out to achieve acceptance is self-perpetuating. Abramson, Asch, and Mash state that

> handicapped adolescents find rejection a far more prevalent phenomenon than acceptance. They therefore do not know how to make friends, are not socially acceptable, and may have inadequate or inaccurate self-concepts. This syndrome of rejection places additional stress on the handicapped adolescents. (Abramson, Asch, and Mash 1979, 558)

As the world becomes more complex, independence for anyone is difficult. Handicapped adolescents have an especially hard time dealing with social condition and stereotypic attitudes. Family, school, and institutional attitudes often foster dependence in the handicapped. The dependence of handicapped children sometimes brings comfort to the parents because it provides them with a "means of service" (Telford and Sawrey 1977).

Expectations for the handicapped are difficult to set accurately. They may be either too high or too low. If set too high, the adolescent fails and suffers the consequences:

> The final dialectic finds many handicapped youths in a no-win situation. Parents, peers, teachers, and employers may expect more from the adolescent than he is actually capable of providing, thus creating an opportunity for the youth to fail. Also likely is that the significant others will expect too little, thereby not challenging the individual and causing him to perform at a lower level than is possible. A compromise between expectation and performance is essential. (Abramson, Asch, and Mash 1979, 561)

QUESTION: What can be done to help the handicapped adolescent cope?

Three suggestions can help a handicapped adolescent to cope: modeling, role playing, and self-instruction. Modeling is undoubtedly the most worldwide and traditional method of teaching. Both live models and filmed models are effective. Role playing involves the recreation of social situations in which the individual takes the part of different characters in each situation. These situations are continually repeated from the perspective of different roles. Role playing helps adolescents develop confidence without having to prematurely face problem tasks at which they might fail.

Self-instruction, however, may be the overall best method to help handicapped adolescents cope with social, emotional, and vocational aspects of their life. An illustration shows specifically how self-instruction takes place:

1. An adult model first performs the task while talking to himself out loud (cognitive modeling).
2. The child then performs the same task under the direction of the model's instruction (overt external guidance).

One problem area for handicapped adolescents is acceptance. To overcome a sense of rejection and to act out to achieve acceptance by others can be a significant step for a handicapped adolescent.

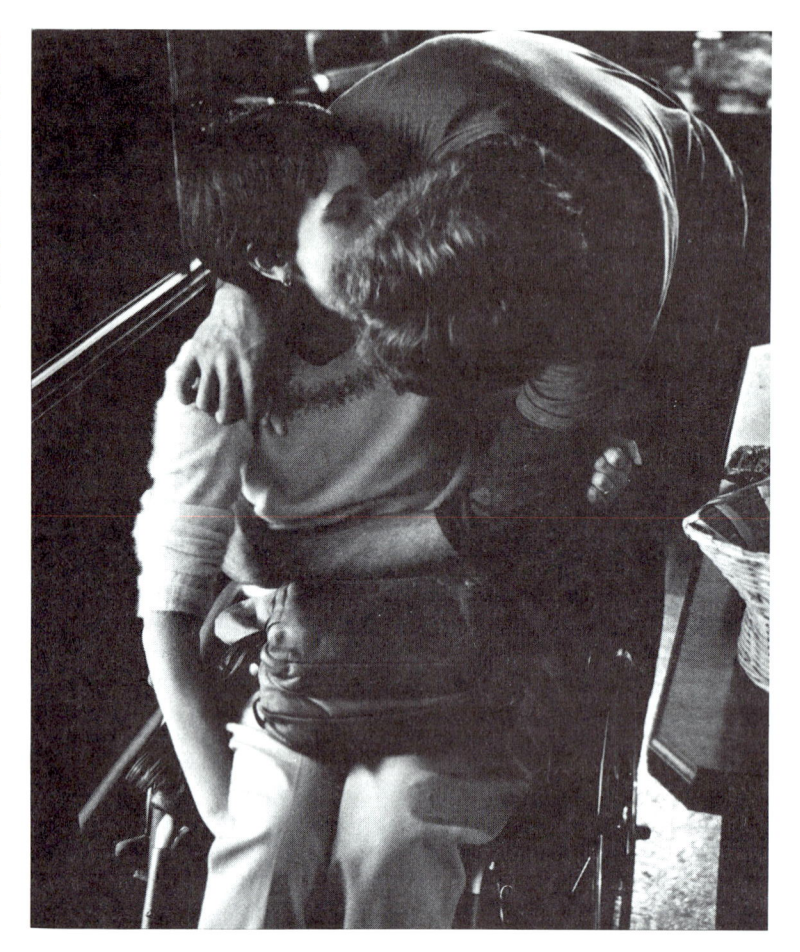

3. The child next performs the task while instructing himself aloud (overt self-guidance).
4. The child then whispers the instructions to himself as he goes through the task (faded overt self-guidance).
5. The child performs the task while guiding his performance via private speech (covert self-instruction) (Mahoney 1974, 186).

Handicapped adolescents need more practice and training in order to learn how to cope with stress that will inevitably occur. This training should take place during late childhood and early adolescence. Being actively involved in the teaching process is important for parents and concerned adults.

QUESTION: Does the handicapped adolescent place an extra burden and stress on parents?

In an article entitled "Counseling with Parents of Handicapped Adolescents," Christensen and DeBlassie (1980) feel that handicapped adolescents do create stress for parents:

> The presence of a handicapped adolescent child in the home also presents a stressful situation for the marriage. This is primarily due to the failure [of the spouse] to communicate what they think and feel about the child and each other, and to ask for each other's support.
>
> Family activities may be curtailed due to the amount of care the child needs and because the parents may become frustrated and despondent over this loss. Many parents feel guilty about having fun, yet these very parents need to have some enjoyment in life. The time they take for fun and a vacation, for example, makes for a more tolerant home situation and thus greatly enhances the home life for the child. (Christensen and DeBlassie 1980, 401)

Parents of handicapped children often develop psychological or mental defenses that are unhealthy (Cutler and Miller 1971). The first defense is to insist that their child is normal. Parents often deny that the child's condition exists, and try to push their child into educational and societal situations that are beyond the child's ability. A second defense is to accept that something is wrong but to hold to a diagnosis that is unrealistically hopeful. Sometimes parents will unrealistically believe that the child can be improved, and will search for unavailable treatments. Third, some defensive parents overly accept the diagnosis. They seem to say, "We know that our child has this condition, we know all about it, and accept it. We are doing everything possible to help him. You can and may not tell us anything." This helps the parents to survive at the present time, but it does not lead to constructive improvement in the conditions needed by the child or the parents themselves. That parents of handicapped children should seek counsel seems advisable:

> The disabled child needs a stable environment in which to grow emotionally, particularly during the adolescent stage of development. But his/her mere presence produces a highly charged emotional atmosphere. The literature indicates that any child reflects the emotional and social adjustment patterns of the parents, and this appears to be magnified for the ill or the handicapped. . . . This points to the need for good communications and education within the family structure—for the benefit of the parents as well as the child. Marriage counseling has been shown to be beneficial in helping parents to learn better ways of communicating with and supporting each other. Through such counseling the parents can learn that they do not need to be super-parents, providing care and attention 24 hours a day. (Christensen and DeBlassie 1980, 402)

Summary

Puberty, the most critical event of adolescence, involves biological changes caused by hormones. Hormones are chemical substances produced and distributed in the human body that interact with individual body cells. Androgens are thought of as male sex hormones, and estrogens are considered female sex hormones. Hormones cause changes in body appearance, functions, and behavior, especially in the development of male and female sexual characteristics. Puberty typically begins two years later for boys than for girls. Biological changes of puberty affect adolescent behavior and personality development.

The effects of puberty are influenced by both environmental and individual conditions. Early-maturing boys have an advantage over late maturers, as they often do well in athletics and are more appealing to the opposite sex. Early-maturing girls, however, are at a disadvantage because they are out of phase with males their own age, and they may feel uncomfortable with more adult body proportions.

The three traditional categories to identify body shapes are mesomorphic (broad at shoulders, narrow hips, tall, muscular, athletic appearance), endomorphic (heavier than mesomorphic and having a fatty appearance), and ectomorphic (thin and tall). Research has found that personality and temperament traits are strongly related to body builds.

Individuals with different body types are treated differently by their peers, family, and friends. A person's self-concept is influenced by what others think. An understanding adult can assist adolescents who want to change their image.

The tendency for earlier maturation and an increase in body size is called the secular trend, and refers to the fact that each generation tends to have larger physiques than the previous generation. Two major explanations for this tendency are nutritional and health care improvements, and genetics.

Physical attractiveness is one of the most powerful influences upon adolescent popularity, peer acceptance, and self-evaluation. Attractive individuals are generally thought of in positive terms. They appear to be more socially adjusted and more capable of resisting peer pressure. Unattractive people are often treated in negative ways, due to feelings of anxiety and discomfort people have when looking at them.

Menarche is the name given to a girl's first menstruation. The experience assures a young girl that her body is female and confirms her womanhood. Girls who have an exceptionally early or late menarche may experience problems. An early menarche can be a problem for a girl who is socially and emotionally unprepared for the event.

Males do not experience a similar process, but they do undergo initiation rites to manhood in some societies. Females also have initiation rites. It is important for young people to know that they are members of their respective sex and that they can assume the appropriate sex behavior for that culture.

Some researchers conclude that most of the "differences" between men and women are probably the result of stereotypes. Some genetically based psychological differences also seem to be present between the sexes.

A biological handicap makes adolescence more difficult. The three problem areas for handicapped adolescents are acceptance, independence, and expectations. Three suggestions for helping a handicapped adolescent to cope are modeling, role playing, and self-instruction. Being actively involved in teaching handicapped adolescents how to cope with stress is important for parents and concerned adults. Parents who develop unhealthy psychological or mental defenses due to a handicapped child should seek counsel.

References

Abramson, M., M. Asch, & W. Mash. 1979. *Handicapped* 14(55): 558 (Fall).

Adams, G. R. 1977. Physical attractiveness, personality and social reactions to peer pressure. *Journal of Psychology* 896: 287–96.

———. 1977. Physical attractiveness: Towards a developmental social psychology of beauty. *Human Development* 20: 217–39.

———. 1981. Physical attractiveness. In *In the eye of the beholder, contemporary issues in stereotyping*, ed. A. C. Miller. New York: Praeger.

Adams, G. R., & S. M. Crossman. 1978. *Physical attractiveness: A cultural imperative*. Rosen Heights, N.Y.: Libra.

Apter, D., & R. Vihko. 1977. Sermon pregnenole, progesterone, 17-hydroxypeogestone, testosterone, and 5-dehydrotestosterone during female puberty. *Journal of Clinical Endocrinology and Metabolism* 45: 1039–48.

Bols, P. 1962. *On adolescence: A psychoanalytic interpretation*. New York: Free Press.

Brown, D. L. 1972. *Developmental handicaps in babies and young children, a guide for parents*. Springfield, Ill.: Thomas.

Brown, J. K. 1963. A cross-cultural study of female initiation rites. *American Anthropologist* 65: 837–55.

———. 1969. Female initiation rites: A review of the current literature. In *Issues in adolescent psychology*, ed. D. Rogers, 74–86. New York: Appleton-Century-Crofts.

———. 1975. Adolescent initiation rites: Recent interpretation. In *Study in adolescence*, 3d ed., ed. R. Grinder, 40–51. New York: Macmillan.

Bullough, V. L. 1981. Age at menarche: A misunderstanding. *Science* 213: 365–66.

Cavior, N., & P. Dokecki. 1973. Physical attractiveness, perceived attitudes in similar areas and academic achievement as contributors to interpersonal attraction among adolescents. *Developmental Psychology* 9: 44–54.

Christensen, B., & R. DeBlassie. 1980. Counseling with parents of handicapped adolescents. *Adolescence* 15(58): 400–407 (Summer).

Clausen, J. A. 1975. The social meaning of differential, physical, and sexual maturation. In *Adolescence and the life cycle*, ed. S. E. Dragastin & G. H. Elder, Jr. New York: Halsted Press.

Cortés, J. B. 1966. Physique and maturation. *Journal of Consulting Psychology* 30: 408–14.

Cortés, J. B., & F. M. Gatti. 1965. Physique and self-description of temperament. *Journal of Consulting Psychology* 29: 432–39.

———. 1966. Physique and motivation. *Journal of Consulting Psychology* 30: 308–14.

———. 1970. Physique and propensity. *Psychology Today* 4: 42–44, 82–84.

Cutler, A. B., & E. A. Miller. 1971. The interpretative and summing up process with parents during and after diagnostic studies of children. In *Counseling parents of the ill and the handicapped*, ed. R. L. Nolan, 62–77. Springfield, Ill.: Thomas.

Dusek, J. B. 1977. *Adolescent development and behavior*. Chicago: Science Research Associates (IBM).

Edgerton, R. B. 1967. *The cloak of confidence: Stigma in the lives of the mentally retarded*. Berkeley: Univ. of California Press.

Fabrega, H. 1972. The study of disease in relation to culture. *Behavioral Science* 12: 183–203.

Faust, M. S. 1960. Developmental maturity as a determinant in prestige of adolescent girls. *Child Development* 31: 173–74.

Freud, A. 1946. *The ego and the mechanisms of defense*. New York: International Univ. Press.

———. 1958. Adolescence. In *Psychoanalytic study of the child*, vol. 13, ed. R. S. Eissler, New York: International Univ. Press.

Freud, S. [1905] 1953. The transformation of puberty. Reprinted in *The standard edition of the complete psychological works of Sigmund Freud*, (vol. 7), ed. J. Strachey. London: Hogarth.

Frish, R. E., & R. Revelle. 1969. The height and weight of adolescent boys and girls at the time of peak velocity of growth in height and weight: Longitudinal data. *Human Biology* 41: 536–99.

Goethals, G. W. 1971. Factors affecting permissive and nonpermissive rules regarding premarital sex. In *The sociology of sex: A book of readings*, ed. J. M. Henslin. New York: Appleton-Century-Crofts.

Heald, F. P., & W. Hung. 1973. Endocrine control of the adolescent growth spurt. In *Adolescent endocrinology,* ed. F. P. Heald and W. Hung. New York: Appleton-Century-Crofts.

Hendry, L. D., & P. Gillies. 1978. Body type, self-esteem, school, and leisure: A study of overweight, average, and underweight adolescents. *Journal of Youth and Adolescence* 7(2): 181–95.

Huber, J. 1974. A review of *The inevitability of patriarchy* by S. Goldberg. *American Journal of Sociology* 80: 567–68.

Jensen, A. R. 1969. Reducing the heredity-environment uncertainty. *Harvard Educational Review* 39: 209–43.

Jones, M. C. 1965. Psychological correlates of somatic development. *Child Development* 36: 899–911.

Jones, M. C., & N. Bailey. 1950. Physical maturing among boys is related to behavior. *Journal of Educational Psychology* 41: 129–48.

Jones, M. C., & P. H. Mussen. 1959. Self-conceptions, motivation and interpersonal attitudes of late and early maturing girls. *Child Development* 29: 491–501.

Kestemburg, J. S. 1961. Menarche. In *Adolescents: Psychoanalytic approach to problems and therapy,* ed. S. Lorand and H. I. Schneer. New York: Hoeber.

———. 1967. Phases of adolescence, part 1 and 2. *Journal of American Academy of Child Psychiatry* 6: 426–63, 577–611.

Koff, E., J. Rierdan, & K. Sheingold. 1982. Memories of menarche: Age, preparation, and prior knowledge as determinants of additional menstrual experience. *Journal of Youth and Adolescence* 2(1): 1–9.

Konner, M. 1983. She and he. In *Human development,* annual ed., ed. H. Fitzgerald & T. Carr, 238–43. Guilford, Conn.: Dushkin.

Lerner, R. M. 1973. The development of personal space schemata to our body build. *Journal of Psychology* 84: 229–35.

Logan, D. D., J. Calder, & B. Kohen, 1980. Toward a contemporary tradition for menarche. *Journal of Youth and Adolescence* 9(3): 263–69.

MacCoby, E., & C. Jacklin. 1974. *The psychology of sex differences.* Stanford, Calif.: Stanford Univ. Press.

Mahoney, M. J. 1974. *Cognition and behavior modification.* Cambridge, Mass.: Ballinger.

Meredith, H. D. 1963. Change in the stature and body weight in North American boys during the last 80 years. In *Advances in child development and behavior,* vol. 1, ed. L. P. Lipsitt & C. C. Spiker, 69–114. New York: Academic Press.

Money, J., & A. Erhardt. 1972. *Man and women: boy and girl.* Baltimore: Johns Hopkins Univ. Press.

Muss, R. E. 1970. Adolescent development and the secular trend. *Adolescence* 5: 267–84.

Mussen, P. H., & M. C. Jones. 1957. Self-conceptions, motivation and interpersonal attitudes of late and early maturing boys. *Child Development* 28: 243–56.

Peskin, H. 1967. Pubertal onset and ego functioning. *Journal of Abnormal Psychology* 72: 1–15.

———. 1973. Influence of the developmental schedule of puberty and early development. *Journal of Youth and Adolescence* 2: 273–90.

Peterson, A., & T. Brandon. 1980. Biological approach to adolescence. In *Handbook of adolescent psychology,* ed. J. Adelson. New York: Wiley.

Ritvo, S. 1971. Adolescent to woman. In *Female psychology: Contemporary psychoanalytic views,* ed. H. P. Blum. New York: International Univ. Press.

Snyder, M., E. Tanke, & E. Berscheid, 1977. *Journal of Personality and Social Psychology* 35: 656–66.

Stang, D. 1981. *Introduction to social psychology.* Monterey, Calif.: Brooks/Cole.

Tanner, J. M. 1962. *Growth at adolescence.* Springfield, Ill.: Thomas

———. 1968. Earlier maturation in men. *Scientific American* 218: 21–27.

———. 1972. Sequence, tempo and individual variations in growth and development of boys and girls ages 12–16. In *12–16: Early adolescence,* ed. J. Kagan & R. Coles. New York: Norton.

———. 1974. Sequence and tempo in the somatic changes in puberty. In *Control of the onset of puberty,* ed. M. N. Grobaugh, G. D. Grave, & F. E. Mayer. New York: Wiley.

Telford, C. W., & J. M. Sawrey. 1977. *The exceptional individual.* 3d ed. Englewood Cliffs, N.J.: Prentice-Hall.

Weideger, P. 1976. Menstruation and menopause: The physiological myth and the reality. New York: Knopf.

Whiting, J. M., R. Kluckhohn, & R. C. Anthony. 1958. The function of male initiation ceremonies at puberty. In *Readings in social psychology,* ed. E. MacCoby, T. M. Newcomb, & E. Hartley, 359–70. New York: Holt, Rinehart & Winston.

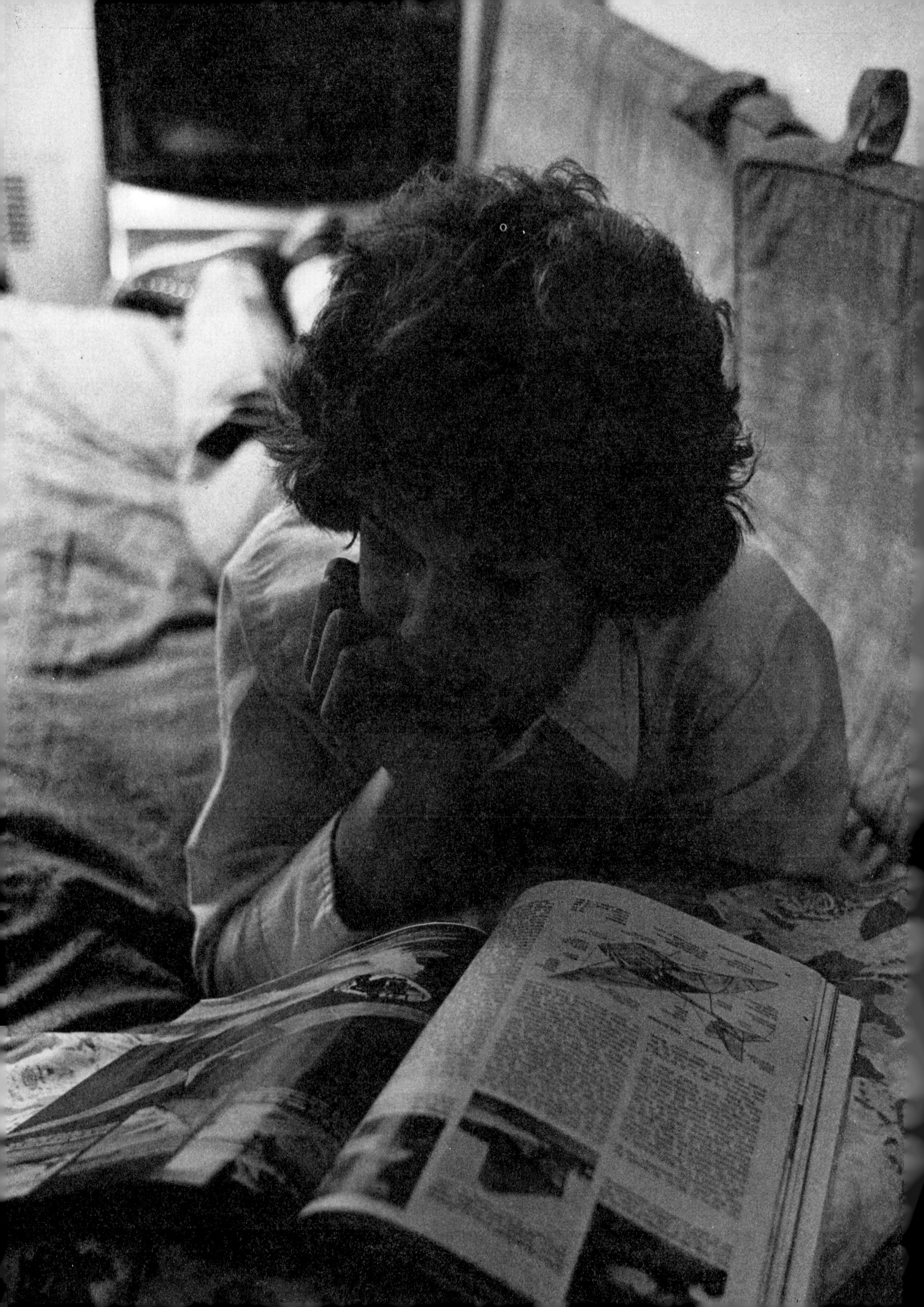

CHAPTER EIGHT

The media: music, video, television, film, literature, and pornography

SURVEY AND QUESTIONS

In this chapter the following topics will be presented and the related questions answered:

Music

Is there a distinctive youth culture with homogeneous tastes in music, movies, and recreation?
How similar are adolescent musical preferences?
What factors determine musical preferences?
Does popular music positively affect youth behavior?

Video

What is the size and impact of the video industry on adolescents?
What makes adolescents want to spend their lunch money, allowances, and job earnings in an arcade?
Is a price being paid for this computer wizardry?
What happens in a video game?

Television

How significant is television in the lives of youth?
Are there age differences in television viewing?
Are there socioeconomic and racial differences in television viewing?
Is intelligence level correlated to television viewing?
Does television influence youth behavior?
What do researchers say about effects of television viewing?
Is there evidence that television positively affects youth?
What can be done to minimize the negative effects and enhance the positive effects of television?

Films and Television Drama (Soaps)

What accounts for the popularity of film fantasy among adolescents?
Are adolescents in search of heroes?
What accounts for the popularity of films like *The Rocky Horror Picture Show*?
Are the effects of soaps similar to that of films?

Adolescent Literature

Does youth literature influence adolescent behavior?
How strong an effect can literature have on adolescents?

Pornography

Does involvement with pornographic material increase sex crimes?
What type of material is sexually stimulating to females?

Jeff was an impressionable 13-year-old with no definite musical preference the summer that 17-year-old cousin Tim came to stay. Tim had a magnetic quality that fascinated Jeff; he was different from any of the more conservative boys Jeff had grown up with. Tim had long, golden hair, a penchant for smoking marijuana, and was lead singer in a rock and roll band. By the end of the summer, Jeff's hair was shoulder length, he was turning his friends on to the wonders of "pot," and he was an avid fan of such rock and roll groups as Rush, Blue Oyster Cult, and Kiss.

Jeff's infatuation with long hair and marijuana was relatively short-lived, but his love affair with rock music intensified. Although Rush remained his favorite group, he also became a fan of "harder" groups such as Black Sabbath, Iron Maiden, and AC/DC. He believed that most of these groups were involved in the occult, in witchcraft, in black magic, and/or in Satan worship. Jeff got tickets to Black Sabbath's concert. He was alternately repelled and fascinated by elaborately made-up and tattooed lead singer Ozzy Osbourne, who is noted for his grotesque stage antics, such as biting the heads off bats and doves. Jeff was amazed at the tense atmosphere in the concert hall, but he was nonetheless drawn into the intensity of the moment. He purchased a black "Mob Rules Tour" T-shirt (the words appear to be scrawled in red, dripping blood), which he wore to gain the shocked and disapproving glances of his parents at home.

Jeff developed a fascination with the skulls and crossbones insignia, collecting posters, candleholders, etc., emblazoned with the ill-boding design.

When he turned 18, he rented his own apartment, which he decorated with his skull collection and satanic emblems. Jeff believes the music does not affect him.

In this chapter the word *media* is defined broadly to cover the visual, auditory, and printed means of communication and influence. Singled out for attention are music, television, film, literature, video, and pornography. These topics are frequently discussed when researchers look for influences on the adolescent's mind and behavior. Many believe a distinct youth culture exists, which can be identified by its preferences for distinct components of the general culture or media.

Music

QUESTION: Is there a distinctive youth culture with homogeneous tastes in music, movies, and recreation?

In James Coleman's influential study *The Adolescent Society* (Coleman 1961), the author suggests that pop music was partly responsible for the formation of a distinctive youth culture in the postwar years. From this perspective, pop music was thought to unite young people and to separate them from the adult generation. At least one research team (Larson and Kubey 1983) feels that the music component of youth culture, in the unstructured, fluid sense, is more an expression of the personality of youth. Can one, however, speak of the adolescent masses as though no differences exist among adolescents of different ages, sexes, social classes, and other factors? This question is discussed in the next section.

QUESTION: How similar are adolescent musical preferences?

Recent research seems to show that the adolescent audience for pop music and other activities is less homogeneous than was formally thought. Even in Coleman's study, when Elvis Presley was the hero of the "teenage revolt," the majority of adolescents favored the more conventional Pat Boone. Ethnic and social differences in tastes have not been swept away by the pop music media. Presley's fans, for example, were mainly adolescents from working-class families. A Michigan study done in 1972 showed that white middle-class high school students tended to favor social protest songs, while white working-class students tended to favor "Top 40 hits," and black adolescents preferred rhythm and blues (Robinson and Hirsch 1972). Middle-class adolescents' preference for progressive rock, characterized by innovative performance, has been explained in terms of the middle-class values of individuality and intellectualism. Working-class adolescents' preference for Top 40 and soul music, with its strong dance beat, has been explained in terms of the opportunity provided for public display of physical competence and group unity (Murdock and Phelps 1973). Musical tastes seemingly tend to define youth subcultures, and these subcultures tend to correspond with class background.

QUESTION: What factors determine musical preferences?

A recent study of Canadian high school students showed that a number of factors, including age, sex, social class, commitment to school, and delinquency, affect adolescent tastes in pop music. The strongest relationship found was that between delinquency of many working-class students who reject school activities, and a preference for heavy metal music. The association between rock music and delinquency, however, should not be overstated. The majority of adolescents do not favor heavy rock, but prefer mainstream Top 40 pop music. By and large, these students endorse the values of the school culture and are not looking for symbols of rebellion. A spectrum of rock music, ranging from Top 40 to progressive rock to heavy metal, seems to correspond with varying degrees of involvement with school and society. Pop music may be a symbolic reflection of the satisfactory and unsatisfactory social experiences of different groups of high school students (Tanner 1981, 1–13).

Heavy rock music is distinguished by great amplification and is dominated by guitar riffs rather than by extended solos. On stage, heavy metal groups adopt a tough, aggressive—even violent—stance. Some argue that the essence of "proletarian rage," heavy rock's appeal, rests on the music's ability to mirror other largely working-class adolescent core values and focal concerns—collective action and physicality, for example. The rebellious overtones of heavy rock are most clearly demonstrated when we examine its relationship with self-reported delinquency. We find that adolescents high in delinquent involvement appear more likely than adolescents low in delinquent involvement to favor heavy rock—30 percent to 13 percent (Tanner 1981, 9). (See Table 8–1.)

TABLE 8-1 Favorite Type of Record by Delinquency, Controlling for Social Class (Percentages)

	Middle Class			Working Class		
	Delinquency			Delinquency		
Type of Record	Low	Medium	High	Low	Medium	High
Top 40	67 (97)	64 (42)	55 (39)	68 (53)	76 (38)	57 (29)
Progressive	10 (15)	18 (12)	13 (9)	12 (9)	4 (2)	2 (1)
Heavy	14 (20)	15 (10)	25 (18)	10 (8)	16 (8)	35 (18)
Miscellaneous	8 (12)	3 (2)	7 (5)	10 (8)	4 (2)	6 (3)
Total	(144)	(66)	(71)	(78)	(50)	(51)

Source: J. Tanner, "Pop Music and Peer Groups: A Study of Canadian High School Students' Responses to Pop Music," *Canadian Review of Sociology and Anthropology* 18:9 (February 1981).

$x^2 = 9.0$ N/2; $x^2 = 18.8$ significance .01

Notes: N in parentheses. REPRINTED FROM THE CANADIAN REVIEW OF SOCIOLOGY AND ANTHROPOLOGY, Volume 18:1 (1981), by permission of the author and the publisher.

QUESTION: Does popular music positively affect youth behavior?

Studies have shown that music can have positive effects. One such study indicates that music influences helpfulness. Four groups of young people were put in four different rooms and given a questionnaire to determine their mood state at the time. During the next seven minutes each group either listened to music that was soothing, stimulating, or aversive, or sat in silence. After the seven minutes, the groups were again given the mood questionnaire. The woman doing the testing then told them she needed their help in participating in another research project, but that they would not be able to get class credit for it as they had in the previous experiment. They were given paper on which to indicate whether they would be willing to help her out by participating. The soothing music was found to have brought a mood of calmness and contentment, the stimulating music brought on a joyful, delighted mood, and the aversive music brought on an annoyed, irritated, angry mood. Furthermore, those who listened to the soothing music were significantly more likely to help than were those in any other group.

This study shows that music does affect our moods, emotions, and behavior. This being so, the converse may also hold: Aversive music must have an effect on the moods and feelings of adolescents, and soothing music may have a positive influence on both moods and behavior (Fried and Berkowitz 1979).

The role of music in influencing adolescent behavior may not be overstated. Although empirical evidence is lacking, the composer of the music for *Where the Red Fern Grows* describes precisely how music exerts an influence:

> Music has been called the universal language. It is a language more powerful than words, for it is the language of emotion. Words communicate ideas; music communicates feelings. While words get stuck in the thinking part of our brains, music sails through to reach the innermost corners of our emotional being. And it is our emotions and feelings which really govern our lives and our actions. This is precisely why music is such a wonderful, dangerous, exhilarating, exciting power.

As an example: While writing music for the film *Where the Red Fern Grows*, I encountered a problem. The entire story was built around a boy's love for his two dogs, and the audience needed to feel that love in order for the film to work. But on the bare celluloid, that important emotion was missing. I composed a tender love theme to fill that void. From the first time the dogs appeared as cute, cuddly little puppies to the end of the show when they died, the theme or one of its variations was played every time they appeared on the screen. Suddenly the flat images on strips of celluloid had emotional life! The audience wept.

Perhaps music communicates emotions so effectively because, more than any other single art form, it possesses the properties of human emotions. For instance, a person may feel elated or depressed for long periods or may experience either emotion with the speed of thought. His emotions have velocity. They may build to a peak. They have intensity. . . . When asked to explain jazz, Louis Armstrong said, "If you have to explain it, forget it." Either you feel it or you don't. Music is as near to pure emotion as any art form can come. It makes us feel deeply, and therein lies its great power. (DeAzevedo 1982, 37–38)

That the economic base of modern pop music is the teenage group can be seen in the following statement of *Billboard*, the international news weekly of music and home entertainment. In describing today's radio format, which focuses on "hot hits," *Billboard* stated:

> The music, though, is uniformly "mass appeal." Designed to reach listeners in the 12–49 age group, with an emphasis on the 18–34 core demographic, the format pumps the hits, from Michael Jackson to the Stray Cats to the Police. (*Billboard* 1983, 1)

It's not clear just how much and in what ways popular music influences adolescents, although it is known that they form pop music's economic base.

With the exception of the electronic video game industry, the economic base of the music industry relies upon young people more than any other industry does.

Video

QUESTION: What is the size and impact of the video industry on adolescents?

The significance of the video industry can be understood if one considers the amount of money spent on video games. The quarters for arcade machines have amounted to $20 billion in one year. This would result in more than 75,000 person years devoted to the machines within one year. If one includes the consoles that hook up to home television sets and the associated cassettes, the $20 billion is more than all the take from the casinos in Nevada and the movie industry, with combined television revenues and all receipts of the major league baseball, basketball, and football games *(Time* 1982).

The estimate is that 80 percent of that sum was spent by teenagers. Nine out of every ten teenagers have tried an arcade game at least once, and experts agree that it takes an investment of between twenty and fifty dollars to master any game enough for it to be fun. The drain on teenagers' time and money is one reason why communities are passing ordinances restricting electronic game playing by teenagers.

Critics of electronic games argue that besides squandering time and money, video games glorify violence and encourage compulsive gambling. Gamblers Anonymous warns against electronic games on the grounds that compulsions can begin in children as young as ten, and some psychiatrists are seeing adolescents who play home video games and they believe the games have become an escape from human contact. Video arcades are not social halls. The concentration required by the game makes socializing almost impossible *(Time* 1982).

A contrasting point of view is presented in a recent article on adolescents and video games (Panelas 1983). The author states that a similarity exists between the video arcade and the traditional social and pool halls:

> Throughout most of this century, there has existed a variety of small-scale commercial establishments, such as pool halls, soda shops, and pinball arcades, that have provided teenagers with a modicum of autonomous social space. In these places, teenagers can meet peers, relieve boredom, act on their emerging sexual identities, and institute cultural practices that build peers into a stable, if temporary, form of social organization. Many of these institutions have been built around some form of interpersonal competition such as the game, and have provided mechanisms for establishing hierarchies of performance and organized ways of reenacting the group's struggle for leadership. (Panelas 1983, 62)

An understanding of the video game phenomenon will likely require a longer time perspective from that available in the mid-1980s. If the home market element of the video game becomes dominant, then researchers will of necessity conclude that the social component was less important, or vice versa.

QUESTION: What makes adolescents want to spend their lunch money, allowances, and job earnings in an arcade?

The "vid-kids" most frequent response is that they enjoy the challenge of the games. One teenager explained, "It is a challenge to myself, and when I get a high score, I feel happy" *(Newsweek* 1981, 90). When a game is no longer challenging, the teenager calls it "boring" and moves on to another game. "You get tired because you get too good, and you can't find no competition. So you switch to another machine." Some more philosophical adolescents explain that video games can relieve anger, that instead of blowing up at their parents or teachers, they can take it out on Asteroids. Still others say that it is a refuge from loneliness. "But when you start to think you are a loser, you come here and get 4,000 at Space Invaders, and you ain't a loser anymore" *(Newsweek* 1981, 90). Players can brag of their accomplishments, and if they are all-time high scorers or top scorers of the day, electronic games will display their names and scores. This latter motivation is supported in the conclusion of an article called "Youth in the Electronic Environment":

One theory behind the intense popularity of video games is that they provide a sense of accomplishment and self-confidence for those who are not skilled in athletics.

But there is another sense in which the electronic environment is a symbolic environment. Possession and/or competence confers symbolic status. Being "television wise" brings prestige on the playground just as being skilled at electronic games wins deference in the arcades. An important question in need of research attention concerns the symbolic value of being heavily immersed in this electronic environment. Are there "information haves" and "information have-nots"? Are there feelings of being deprived because one has not seen a particular R-rated pay-TV movie or played the latest video game? (Ellis 1983, 10)

Consider the report given to the author by one of his senior students investigating this topic:

> It has always been a mystery to me how so many people could be hooked on video games with the addiction of a chronic gambler. I have a younger sister who spends every cent she earns on video games. She constantly does odd jobs around the house to earn money, all of which goes into the games. I also have a brother-in-law who doesn't dare go near a game room for fear of leaving with empty pockets.
>
> What is it about these games that are so addictive? How does one become addicted? I decided to answer these and other questions with hands-on experience.
>
> My first experience with a video game—Donkey Kong—was a reluctant and embarrassing one. It was a long while before I could amass enough courage to approach one of the machines; I was sure everyone in the place was watching, I slipped a quarter quickly from my pocket and into the machine, so far, so good. I then proceeded to push the button that activates the game. Immediately after pushing the button I experienced one of the most embarrassing moments of my entire life. The game began—as most do—with a musical prelude that I was sure could be heard over the entire game room; and I knew if people weren't looking before they certainly were now. I just stood there like a statue, my eyes straight forward and my face a deep color of red. Finally, after what seemed an eternity, the prelude stopped and the game began.
>
> The first game was a disappointment to say the least. It was over in less than a minute. I didn't even get past the first level. I wondered, "Is this all there is?" "How can anyone get addicted to this?" Although I didn't understand at first I didn't give up. Then, after several games, I began to gain a little insight into the answers to my questions; I had finally made it past the first level. After having done this I experienced a feeling of great accomplishment.
>
> That was the first day; each following day I went to the game room and each day I became a little more skilled in playing, and each day I played longer than the day before. It didn't take long before my experiment turned into an obsession. I went to the game room every chance I got; I used the experiment as an excuse to play the game.
>
> I knew I was hooked and I didn't quite know how to get myself unhooked.

Electronic games may increase teenagers self-confidence. Many adolescents who are not accomplished at sports or other popular pastimes can gain a sense of mastery from electronic games. Success on electronic games can be measured in many ways—mastering the machine, bettering one's personal best, or beating a friend—so everyone can experience a sense of accomplishment. Furthermore, since aptitude on electronic games may decrease with age, ten-year-olds could beat their parents. The significance of electronic games for adolescents becomes transparent. These types of psychological benefits might not be verbalized by the teen, but may be the basis for the popularity of this powerful electronic medium. Although many feel that electronic games are something of an addiction, "It might be naive to think that most of the time and the money spent on these video games would be channeled into something productive if video games disappeared."

Video games have many positive influences and potential benefits. They give adolescents across social classes experience with computer-related skills. Some educational consultants feel that we have a generation who, thanks to electronic games, can easily approach the computer. The potential for learning important skills through electronic games is so great that the Pentagon has asked Atari consultants to help the army create a top-table tank gunnery game for training purposes *(Newsweek* 1981).

Many have pointed out that computer-related skills may place the vid-kids in an enviable position in the future. A final conclusion is probably premature, but electronic games may be the best antidote yet developed against future shock. According to John McCarthy, the dean of artificial intelligence at Stanford, the computer revolution will not really begin until the computer terminal is a commonplace item in the home (Hilts 1983). If McCarthy is correct, then the computer revolution awaits a generation who will be as comfortable with the computer terminal as previous generations were with the television.

QUESTION: Is a price being paid for this computer wizardry?

Some fear that a high price may indeed be involved. In an essay entitled "Pacman as Playmate," the point is expressed succinctly: "The machine's demands—its pace, its fixed program—virtually eliminate daydreaming, invention, and fantasy, all cited by Freud, Erikson, and others as significant benefits of true play" (Logan 1983, 58). Author Logan points out adolescents who play electronic games do not freely choose or create their own objectives and methods using their own imagination. The electronic game also removes the element of chance, as anyone who has mastered an electronic game well knows. Masters of electronic games know precisely when a belt of asteroids will appear on the screen and threaten their spaceship. Although this knowledge undoubtedly leads to a sense of mastery and a certain kind of self-esteem, the sense of mastery belongs only to those who are willing to submit to a machine's fixed program. Although Logan does not suggest a conspiracy against individuality, she does suggest that the machines' limited, canned programs will nurture few apostates, heretics, innovators, prophets, or conscientious objectors.

QUESTION: What happens in a video game?

In one study, researcher Paula Smith (1981), a child psychologist with Fisher-Price Toys Company, summarizes facts common to almost all video games:

1. Played on the machine's terms
2. Player must use his own resources to improve his game
3. Uses eye-hand coordination
4. Preset speed controls
5. Feature light and noise
6. Rarely a second chance
7. Players rarely win
8. Machines improve as the players do
9. Difficult to determine age appropriateness
10. Two-dimensional illusions

Smith concludes that although there are negative aspects to video games, electronic games stimulate individuals. As individuals return to better past scores, they improve in beneficial skills. Despite the negative effects, Smith argues that the overall benefits from playing electronic games are great. Musical games can teach children to associate musical tones with colored keys. They are believed to encourage children to develop musical interests that might not have been learned. Most games improve spatial perception and encourage quick decision making and responsiveness in players (Smith 1981).

The impact of video games on youth is still to be assessed. The games may prove to be a passing fad that will give way. The appeal of video games is still a mystery. Could it be for the sense of mastery, as mentioned in the earlier study? Could it be escapism or the meeting of psychological needs? The following example illustrates the latter:

> I walked into the video room and my objective was to pick out one person and have an interview.
>
> The video game that I was most impressed with is called Q-bert. So any person who was to play on this machine first, I was going to talk to. A lady about 21 or 22 years old came in and changed $10 into quarters. She immediately went over to Q-bert and began to play. She seemed really tense and upset. Then she would just burst out laughing. The main objective of Q-bert is to get him to jump from square to square without getting eaten. Also the video player is of course the one who is in control. The player also has to make sure he doesn't jump off of the edge. If he goes off of the edge Q-bert makes a cute little sound (i.e., ohhh).
>
> From watching this lady, she would do really good and then she would intentionally make him go off of the edge. She would just burst out laughing. So I started laughing with her. When she totally poured out her life story to me, telling me how her boyfriend just dumped on her, she said, "I pretend Q-bert is Tony (her boyfriend) and make him go off the edge. I wish it was really him instead!" She spent $10 pretending to kill her boyfriend and had a lot of fun doing it whether it be sane or not.

Television

QUESTION: How significant is television in the lives of youth?

According to George Comstock (1978), a foremost scholar and researcher in the area, when it comes to having power in influencing youths' beliefs, values, and behaviors, television should be given the status of parents and teachers as a socialization agent. During the 1970s the amount of television watching by older children went as high as an average of six hours a day (Friedrich and Stein 1973). Children apparently spend more time per year watching television than they do in any other activity except sleeping; these activities include parents and school. How much time children spend in front of the TV depends on a number of factors, such as age, race, socioeconomic status, educational level, and intelligence. These factors are considered separately.

QUESTION: Are there age differences in television viewing?

In a book describing the relationship between teen behavior and television, Schwartz (1982), points out that teens watch approximately twenty-three hours of television per week, and that on a typical evening close to 100 million people are viewing. Children and adolescents are viewing continuously up to the late night shows, and a small percentage continue viewing past that time. Other research has indicated that students in junior high school spend more than an hour each day longer in television viewing than high school students do (Chaffee, McLeod, and Atkin 1970).

The highest number of hours of viewing is during early adolescence (age eleven to fourteen). One reviewer (Rubin 1977) voices a concern that at this age, adolescents often do not adequately differentiate reality from what is seen on television.

QUESTION: Are there socioeconomic and racial differences in television viewing?

In general, results show that there are differences in the viewing habits of children in different social classes (Blood 1961; Greenberg and Dominick 1969). Teams of scientists working with children of different ages have reported that children of lower socioeconomic status watch more television than do children of higher socioeconomic status. Among teenagers and adults, socioeconomic status viewing patterns were found to be quite similar.

Among young children, race and ethnic background seem to have no effect upon the amount of time spent in television viewing, but at lower ages, some definite differences are present. Results of one study showed that Mexican-American sixth and tenth graders, especially girls, watch more often than do their Anglo peers. Low-income black teenagers watch over six hours per day, while same-age low-income whites watch only four and a half hours per day.

Similar results have been found among fourth- and fifth-grade students. Researchers have also pointed out that "although race is usually associated with socioeconomic status (black children are more likely to be low in social class), these differences appear regardless of economic background (Lyle and Hoffman 1972).

QUESTION: Is intelligence level correlated to television viewing?

One possibility is that those who watch more television are likely to have higher IQs. The reasoning is that children who are exposed to the various types of material that appear on television are likely to learn more. In a general sense, however, studies have found that children with high IQs spend less time watching television than do those with lower IQs. First-grade students who were rated in the bottom third of their classes by their teachers watched more television than did children in the middle and upper thirds of the classes. No differences were noted among the sixth-grade students, but in the tenth grade, the pattern was again more similar to that found among first graders. Students from higher socioeconomic classes, however, score higher on IQ tests, so the prior results do not necessarily mean that viewing television is the *cause* of the relationship (Lyle and Hoffman 1972).

QUESTION: Does television influence youth behavior?

Perhaps the most dramatic evidence is provided by case studies of crimes committed by persons shortly after having watched televised depictions of the same crimes. *The Early Window* (Liebert, Spraklin, and Davidson 1982) is an excellent book that points out the power of the media in influencing negative and antisocial behaviors. The following compelling examples are provided in the book:

> After all these years and dozens of major studies, what can be concluded about TV violence and children? Andison (1977) pooled the findings of all 67 studies conducted between 1956 and 1976 on the relationship between TV violence viewing and aggressive behavior. The final tally was 77% of the studies revealed an association, 20% no results, and about 3% an inverse association (i.e., TV violence decreases aggression). Andison found a relationship between the scientific method used and the type of effects reported. Only 13% of the experiments reported no differences or inverse associations, whereas about 30% of the surveys and field experiments yielded such outcomes. However, a relationship between TV violence viewing and aggressive behavior was found consistently across methods, age of subjects, measures of aggression, and time period and country of investigation. (Liebert, Spraklin, and Davidson 1982, 128)

Television may also influence sexual behavior and attitudes. In a study investigating the effects of television viewing, Sprafkin and Silverman (1981) found that the following mean number of sex acts per hour had increased from 1975 to 1978 to reach a level that was disturbing. Their findings were:

Kissing	from 3.32 to 7.30
Hugging	2.65 to 4.96
Nonaggressive touching	68.07 to 62.35
Suggestiveness (physical)	.79 to 2.75
Suggestiveness (verbal)	1.27 to 10.82
Intercourse (physical)	0 to 0
Intercourse (verbal)	.04 to .90
Intercourse (implied)	0 to .43
Aggressive touching (physical)	5.33 to 6.17
Aggressive touching (verbal)	.15 to .74

These trends are likely to continue. In a later study these same researchers demonstrated that adolescents, even twelve-year olds, comprehend the large number of sexual suggestions depicted. (Sprafkin and Silverman 1980)

Research such as this substantiates the belief that television influences teens' attitudes and behavior. In general, the research has focused on the negative effects of TV viewing.

QUESTION: What do researchers say about the effects of television viewing?

Early in the 1970s the U.S. Surgeon General's Advisory Committee on Television and Children's Aggression set up a panel of experts, approximately half of them from the academic community and half from the TV industry. After extensive review of all of the literature and research to date, the panel issued an extended report. In general, their statements were vague, and no definite conclusion was drawn. In part, this result was because of the mixture of committee members and their prior affiliations. Two members of the committee, Robert Liebert and John Neale, stated outside the official publication that the evidence clearly showed a relationship between viewing violence on television and aggressive behavior among young people (Liebert and Neale 1972). They extracted the following from the Surgeon General's report:

> As matters now stand, the weight of the experimental evidence from the present series of studies, as well as from prior research, suggests that viewing filmed violence has an observable effect on some children in the direction of increasing their aggressive behavior. . . . (109)
>
> On the basis of these findings, and taking into account their variety and their inconsistencies, we can tentatively conclude that there is a modest relationship between exposure to television violence and aggressive behavior or tendencies, as the latter are defined in the studies ahead. (U.S. Surgeon General 1972, 178)

Liebert and Neale also state in their article that "a substantial component (of aggressive behavior at age 19) can be predicted better by the amount of television violence which a child watched in the third grade than by any other causal variable measured, and reinforces the contention that there is a cause-and-effect relationship between violence content of television and overt aggressive behavior" (Liebert and Neale 1972, 60).

Certainly more than violence can be learned if one considers the research on the effects of imitation or modeling. Studies of observational learning demonstrate that such exposure can change varied behaviors, such as children's willingness to aid others (Rosenhan and White 1967), their ability to display self-control (Bandura and Mischel 1965), and the learning of language rules (Liebert et al. 1969). Observation of others can increase learning of unfamiliar behaviors (Coates and Hartrup 1969), increase sharing (Bryan and Walbeck 1970), and decrease fear (Bandura and Menlove 1967; Hill, Liebert, and Mott 1968).

Even though an effort has been made to reduce television violence, the most popular show of 1983–84, "The A-Team," was also the top show for violence, with thirty-nine violent acts per hour beating out the previous year's winner, "The Fall Guy," which had thirty-eight violent acts per hour *(Forcast* 1983, 36).

Officials of the major networks have occasionally justified violence on television, because the "bad guy" is always punished for his violent behavior. The typical plot will show the bad guy going about his crimes. He then almost succeeds only to be caught in the final scene. The hero may then destroy him, walk off with the girl, and vacation in the sun.

Most young people, as well as many adults, tend to accept factual information in films. Many teenagers see the gangster type of personality as living a glamorous life and getting more fun out of life. The problem in viewing content here is that the "bad guys" spend 90 percent of the time living it up, and only in the last few minutes of the program does fate catch up with them as the "long arm of the law" is redeemed from its previously minor role. Many young people realize they might get caught, but indicate that crime would nevertheless be worth it. Is the glamorized life of the criminal as depicted on the screen so appealing that teenagers feel crime is worthwhile even if they got caught?

Let us imagine a young boy sitting in front of the TV early in the evening, watching a typical program. What type of person is he likely to see in the most important roles? Who is most likely to have the greatest effect on his learning and acceptance of what he sees?

The most powerful group on television is the white American male; fully half of all leading television characters fall into this category. He is usually young, middle-class, and unmarried. He is often the playboy type and seldom seems to be held down by any real or everyday type of work. He is likely to be involved in violence—especially as an aggressor rather than as a victim. He is also less likely than the other characters to be punished for his aggression (Gerbner 1972).

QUESTION: Is there evidence that television positively affects youth?

The answer to this question is yes. Most studies on the effects of television on behavior have centered on the violent and what we would call the more negative areas. Television, however, also exhibits examples of sharing, helping, cooperation, and general altruistic behavior. With particular regard to young children, two programs have been found to have prosocial effects as well as general educational potential. These two programs are "Sesame Street" and "The Electric Company," which combine a variety of methods to teach and entertain children in a way that is acceptable to parents.

Born out of the government-sponsored Children's Television Workshop, "Sesame Street" began in 1969. Combining general entertainment material, including animation, with carefully planned educational material designed to foster both practical and intellectual skills, the program has been received and discussed enthusiastically by both children and parents as well as critics. "The Electric Company" made its first appearance in the following years and has enjoyed a similarly good response.

The Educational Testing Service, a highly respected, unbiased educational assessment company, evaluated the efforts of viewing "Sesame Street" (Bogatz and Ball 1972). Children who watched "Sesame Street" were found to improve in several aspects of mental development. The areas included counting, alphabet recognition, vocabulary, sounds of letters, and so on. The more the children watched the program, the greater was the gain; in many areas the changes were great. Children viewing the programs at home seemed to improve as much as, if not more than, those viewing the program at school. In addition, the positive effects seemed to apply to a wide range of individual differences—male, female, white, black, and Spanish, high versus low amount of time viewing, and children from disadvantaged as well as advantaged homes.

Bogatz and Ball feel that similar positive effects also result from watching "The Electric Company," although they were unable to provide as firm an empirical base for their conclusions.

Basically unresearched are the effects of many types of television programming, such as news, broadcasting, and talk shows, for their effect on young people. One recent study was able to show that sports television programs were related to the incidence of prosocial behavior in adolescence. Television sports clips were shown to ten- to thirteen-year-olds and to fourteen- to seventeen-year-olds after the clips had been edited to focus on prosocial behavior. A third set of children viewed sports shows with neutral contact. Prosocial behavior was measured on the playground and was defined as any action directed toward others that was encouraging, consoling, or enhancing the other person. The effect was positive and lasted up to three weeks for some viewers (McCabe and Moriarity 1977).

In the future, other studies will likely show beneficial effects from this powerful medium. In the meantime, those concerned with the well-being of adolescents are generally concerned with minimizing the negative effects and maximizing the positive.

QUESTION: What can be done to minimize the negative effects and enhance the positive effects of television?

To answer this question, one might summarize the negative effects that investigators generally mention. The first negative effect is that television directly influences antisocial actions, such as teaching criminal or violent behavior. Second, television provides antisocial models. Third, television may remove the child away from other activities that are more beneficial, such as reading, sports, clubs, and so on. Fourth, many experience a conflict with the values and sex mores presented on TV. Last, the low level of logic and moral reasoning presented is generally criticized. Box 8–1 presents one set of recommendations to assist parents or other caretakers in positively influencing the impact of TV in the family setting.

Most studies done on the effects of television on behavior tend to emphasize the negative influences, but one study has shown that sports programs on television may influence the development of prosocial behavior.

> **BOX 8-1   STEPS TO MEDIATE THE EFFECTS OF TELEVISION IN THE FAMILY CONTEXT**
>
> Parents can implement some practices to make television a positive influence in the family setting:
>
> 1. Program selection. Obtain a programming guide at the beginning of the week and work out a viewing program. Allow participation in this family planning to encourage responsible decision making.
> 2. Discuss highlights of positive and negative programs. The importance of discussion and counteropinion becomes important when viewing programs known to have negative content. An ideal time to discuss is during commercial breaks. If the material is too volatile and controversial, waiting a day or two before discussion may be better. At the appropriate time, refer back to the program. Even commercials can be discussed. Adolescents take special delight in identifying adult deception and hypocrisy.
> 3. Provide alternative activities. By providing games, family outings, athletic events, reading hours, or even a night of cooking in the kitchen, parents can reduce the need for TV watching.

Films and television drama (soaps)

One expert states that "today the two media are inextricably linked . . . it is unrealistic to speak of the screen as a feature-picture industry; it is a television and movie industry" (Lindey 1981, 796). The support for the industry is young. Fifty percent of America's motion picture audience is under the age of twenty-five (Lindey 1981). A quick scan of the top ten all-time movie money-makers confirms this figure. *Star Wars* hit the top of the list with a gross of $185,138,000. It was followed by *The Empire Strikes Back, Jaws, Grease, Raiders of the Lost Ark, The Exorcist, The Godfather, Superman, The Sound of Music,* and finally *The Sting*. The list differs only slightly from the list of all-time film rental champs provided by *Variety* in 1981.

Stephen Handzo (1982) wrote an article on the 1981–82 film season for *The Hammond Almanac,* emphasizing the youth and adolescent appeal. Even Disney, long known for young children's favorite movies, produced an adolescent film, *Tron,* which was aimed at video game fans. The producers know what appeals to youth, and they go after it (Handzo 1982, 857).

QUESTION: What accounts for the popularity of film fantasy among adolescents?

Bruno Bettelheim (1981) feels that the popularity of fantasy works in the attraction of films. In many films, such as *Star Wars* and *The Empire Strikes Back,* adolescents see the struggle between good and evil depicted. Fantasy is especially important to adolescents because they are trying to decide what kind of people they want to be. By elevating and simplifying the war of good against evil, fantasy gives the adolescent's life an added meaning. Fantasy also helps adolescents to work through the deep anxiety of real-life problems and yet not be overwhelmed by their anxiety. Bettelheim believes that this problem is especially acute for adolescents, because books for youth reflect few of the crucial problems of the day. In children's books, characters are seldom angry and do not fight or suffer. Since the characters that children read about are usually always happy and seldom worry, children begin to believe that something is terribly wrong with their own family and personal life. Such misconceptions may make the

The popularity of such movies as *Rocky* and *Chariots of Fire*, especially among youth, would seem to emphasize the need of adolescents to identify with a hero-model.

flight into fantasy even more appealing. This may be less of a concern as more books for youth now deal with realism.

QUESTION: Are adolescents in search of heroes?

Film writer and producer Peter Greenburg remarked that Americans are desperately in search of true heroes in the movies. In most American films, people manage to cope or survive, but they do not excel. In search of a true hero, adolescents have been attracted to gang movies like *The Warriors* and to remakes of old heroes such as the *Lone Ranger, Tarzan,* and *Superman.* The popularity of the British film *Chariots of Fire* is also largely due to the presentation of a hero who possesses strength, conscience, and a goal greater than himself. This search for heroes is in part a reaction to the sad, cynical tendency of Americans to destroy their heroes. Adolescents witness the exposing of corruption in politics, law, medicine, and religion, and so are prepared to embrace pure, mystic heroes such as those in the *Star Wars* series or *Indiana Jones (Center Magazine* 1982).

QUESTION: What accounts for the popularity of films like *The Rocky Horror Picture Show*?

Films like *The Rocky Horror Picture Show* have a peculiar kind of appeal to adolescents. Far from depicting a valient hero, *Rocky Horror* makes fun of conventional mores, values, and attitudes. Some of the characters are extraterrestrial, as in fantasy, but they are also extremely eccentric and often sadomasochistic. The film blends science fiction with horror, rock and roll, and satire. Despite *Rocky Horror*'s R rating, one study found that nearly 20 percent of the audience was under seventeen years of age. Two-thirds were either high school or college students. Nearly two-thirds of those interviewed had seen *Rocky Horror* at least once before. Now in existence are an international *Rocky Horror* fan club, a *Rocky Horror* official poster book, and a *Rocky Horror Picture Show* official magazine. When asked what they thought of the film, however, the adolescents generally thought that it was "not a terrific film." Why then are some adolescents repeatedly attending the movie?

Austin (1981) explains that the popularity of the film is truly a cult phenomenon. He defines a cult film as a "motion picture which is exhibited on a continuing basis, usually at midnight, and which gathers a sizeable repeat audience" (Austin 1981). He traces the cult film phenomenon to the 1960s, during which Roger Corman's monster and motorcycle movies attracted a repeat, middle-class, adolescent audience. Austin's study shows that what attracts adolescents to the film is the audience. What distinguishes the audience for *Rocky Horror* is their level and frequency of interaction, both with the movie and with each other. Young people prepare to attend *Rocky Horror* by bringing props and by dressing like one of the film's characters. Props are used to imitate characters as well as to throw around the theater. Perhaps the popularity of *Rocky Horror* is due to its becoming, quite by accident, a teenage social event (Austin 1981).

Although pornography could be discussed next in connection with what has been called the crude youth market, the spending power of the youth group has been capable of orienting an entire segment or economic industry.

Youth are the key to the movie industry. The movie industry has changed with the population over the last few years; its ties with television are now inseparable.

QUESTION: Are the effects of soaps similar to that of films?

Of particular interest is the popularity of soaps among youth. No clear explanation has been provided for the appeal of these programs to young people, although the most plausible is that soaps provide an inside look into adult life that is not available to growing children during childhood. If one considers that adults basically hide their inner feelings and activities from children, then a logical assumption is that when adolescence emerges, a keen interest will be taken in what adult life is really like. This assumption is compatible with the theories presented in Chapters 2 and 3, which state that adolescents are searching for identity, and is also compatible with the concept which states that abstract reasoning first becomes the dominant mode during adolescence. Youth want to know about right and wrong, deceit and honesty, and related abstract or conceptual issues. Soaps provide an inside look (even if unrealistic) into the adult mind; they see behind locked doors and secret chambers. For many, soaps provide the first chance to see the frailties, deceptions, and hypocrisies of the adult.

Susan Lang (1982) comments on the viewing of soap operas as a possible influence on the sexual values and behavior of adolescents. She cites that about

10 million Americans view soap operas daily, with an increasing proportion of the audience being school- and college-age students. She fears that the viewers may believe that the television portrayals of life are accurate representations of reality, and may adapt the values, life-styles, and sexual behaviors shown on the program. According to Lang, these programs encourage behaviors that are unacceptable and detrimental to our society (Lang 1982).

The popularity of soaps may also be a result of our impersonal society, wherein personal and emotional feelings are hidden. In the soap opera, feelings are not only brought to the surface but also discussed in detail. Where else in our society do discussions of personal feelings, fears, and ambitions take place, openly and freely presented for public scrutiny? This openness is seen in popular films that bear a strong resemblance to soaps, and to some extent, it is also seen in adolescent literature.

Adolescent literature

Although certain novels have been popular among youthful readers, not until the 1950s were large numbers of books written specifically for teenagers. These early 1950s novels were restricted in vocabulary, themes, and type of characters presented. The characters were usually upper-middle-class whites. The novels generally dealt with home life, dating, careers, athletics, and cars, were noncontroversial, and generally supported prevailing values and morals. During the 1960s writers introduced basic issues that adolescents face, such as drugs, alcoholism, sexuality, pregnancy, rape, racism, and generational conflicts (Watson 1974).

QUESTION: Does youth literature influence adolescent behavior?

One researcher (Culp 1975) studied how literature affects adolescents' attitudes, values, and behavior. She found that about four-fifths of her subjects were somewhat influenced by what they read. The degree of influence was directly proportional to how much they read. Novels seemed to be the form of literature that was most influential. The students classified themselves according to the degree of influence. Half the students believed themselves to have been moderately influenced, one-fourth to have been only slightly influenced, and another one-fourth to have been strongly influenced. The influence seemed to be in the areas of self-image, awareness of moral and ethical issues, sensitivity to others, and awareness of social problems. Culp found that the characters and content of the literature read were of such diversity that generalizing was difficult.

Another researcher, W. B. Lukenbill (1981), studied the actual content of contemporary adolescent novels in terms of family relationships and how the novels may serve as sources of information about, or even models of, social behavior and family living. The study focused only on novels with substantial parent-adolescent relationships. The books were chosen from the following recognized sources of classic book titles: *The Junior High School Library Catalog, The Senior High School Library Catalog, Booklist, Hornbook Magazine, School Library Journal,* and *Children's Books in Print.* Families and their interpersonal relationships were rated according to the J. M. Lewis (1978) model of family structure and parenting behavior. On a graduated scale rating families from highly functional to highly dysfunctional, the average family as portrayed in the contemporary adolescent novel functioned slightly below the medial level. In other words, the literary family is not particularly healthy although not completely pathological. In general, the trend in this fiction is toward realism rather than idealism.

An important and often overlooked aspect of youth literature is humor and the various purposes that it serves. In one study, Don L. F. Nilsen and Allen Pace Nilsen (1981) explored several aspects of humor. Adult and teenage humor often differ because young people have had less experience in various facets of life and can closely relate only to those aspects with which they have come in contact. Teenagers therefore do not find political allusions nearly as amusing as parodies of home environment and the school world.

The Nilsens suggest that teenagers enjoy a certain grossness in their literary humor because they are leaving the world of innocent childhood, and one way to show this change is to avoid anything sweet or poetic in their speech. The broadening of horizons is also manifested in young people's interest in the strange and unusual. Books such as the *Guinness Book of World Records* and *The People's Almanac* become popular in adolescence, because youth are exploring limits.

Whether literature has a significant influence and serves as a socializing medium or whether it merely reflects society and current cultural mores is still largely unknown.

QUESTION: How strong an effect can literature have on adolescents?

The following case study is presented to show the power and influence that literature can have on an adolescent. The case study is based on a personal interview with a twenty-four-year-old white female university student from an upper-middle-class family:

Some adolescents have a voracious appetite for reading and can be greatly influenced in their behavior by what and how much they read.

From a very early age her parents, both educators, read good literature to her beginning with nursery rhymes and then progressing to classical children's works. Here earliest recollections are of *Hans Christian Andersen's Fairy Tales,* Rudyard Kipling's *Just So Stories,* and then Bible stories. She learned to read at a very young age and rapidly grew to love books. She continued to read and be read to by her parents through the first part of grade school.

In the fourth grade having made a recent move and having difficulty making new friends she began to spend more and more time reading. Significant books she remembers during this period are *James and the Giant Peach, Charlie and the Chocolate Factory, The Hardy Boys* mystery series, Edgar Rice Burrough's adventure stories (especially his Tarzan series), *Rifles for Watie* and *Where the Red Fern Grows.* She also had great interest in books about the early explorers of this continent, the taming of the West, Indians, animals, nature, archaeology, sports, the Civil War, and World War II.

Science fiction, Alistair MacLean's adventure stories, and self-improvement books characterized her junior high and early high school years. During high school she began to show interest in books with more social import such as George Orwell's *1984.* Short stories with their quick, concise punch occupied much of her reading time. She also remembers being fascinated by the Irving Stone biographies of Van Gogh, Lincoln, Michelangelo, and Jack London. Religion books, along with many of the classics *(Moby Dick, The Iliad and the Odyssey, Great Expectations,* and Shakespeare's *Hamlet* and *Twelfth Night)* became common fare.

As a college student leisure reading has become less a part of her life as studies and other responsibilities occupy most of her time. The books that have had sufficient impact as to be remembered and noted are the Tolkien trilogy, James Herriott's light and delightfully entertaining books, James Michener's *Centennial,* and some philosophy and religion books.

She now feels that what she has read has had a significant impact on her life and how she has viewed the world. She believes that her personality and basic interests have caused her to choose and read the books that she has, but also that her reading about these subjects has reinforced and intensified these interests. Books have broadened her point of view by giving her vicarious access to people, places, and experiences, both real and fictitious, that she wouldn't have had otherwise. She has gained from reading what would have taken years of direct experience to gain. Through literature as well as many personal experiences she has been exposed to many creative and intelligent minds and to many diverse personalities and situations. This has given her greater insight and understanding of human nature and the world.

Admittedly, this woman's voracious reading habits are not typical, but nevertheless reading is a significant activity among adolescents of all social classes and can have a powerful influence on youth's behavior. For some, like this woman, literature may rival the major media sources.

The media of video, music, television, film, and literature are all extremely potent influences on young people's behavior and activities. These influences can be long lasting, influencing fundamental values, beliefs, and thinking.

Pornography

The commanding officer of the Philadelphia Police Department's Juvenile Division stated, "My men and I have questioned hundreds of . . . juveniles involved with pornography, and we believe . . . that this material acts as an aphrodisiac resulting in rapes, seductions, sodomy, indecent assaults, and indecent exposure" (Clor 1969, 40). Although this statement reflects a common view, is it accurate?

QUESTION: Does involvement with pornographic material increase sex crimes?

Terrence Thornberry and Robert Silverman (1970) looked for empirical data that might either support or disclaim such a viewpoint. They examined the nature of juvenile offenses and the mention of experience with pornography in individual case records. From a sample of 436 juveniles they found that 92 percent of the offenses had no sexual implication, 4 percent implied some sexual activity usually involving incorrigibles or runaways, and 4 percent were classified as specifically sexual offenses. Testimony before various congressional committees had led the researchers to believe that they would find mention of pornography in the records of juvenile delinquents. However, no mention whatsoever was made of any type of erotic material in any of the records, even though each juvenile had undergone psychiatric diagnosis—the details of which were included in their records. Thornberry and Silverman believe that even though the psychiatric staff did not systematically inquire into this area, pornography is apparently not the key element or important enough to spontaneously appear in a probing examination of the background and circumstances of juvenile offenses. The possible effects of pornography are discussed later. Most consumers of pornography are men, and since almost all sex crimes are committed by men against women, one might easily conclude that pornography causes such sex crimes. Females and pornography are not as frequently studied (Nawy 1973).

Pornography can be considered in two ways. Behaviorists could point out that sex roles are learned, so pornography teaches men to be violent toward women. If this position is correct, pornography would produce an effect. Psychoanalysts on the other hand could argue pornography cannot change our fundamental sexual nature, but it can help resolve inner conflicts by providing a means of releasing anger without hurting anyone. In this case, pornography would be beneficial. Few data, however, support this position.

The word *pornography* is difficult to define. The President's Commission on Obscenity and Pornography (1970) examined the effects of a variety of sexually explicit materials and concluded they were not harmful to individuals or to society, and could not distinguish between portrayals of genital intercourse between consenting adults and violent and more explicit depictions of sadomasochism and rape. The study has since been strongly criticized (Gray 1982). Gray discusses the influence of pornography in the context of aggression toward women.

Studies have shown that males become more aggressive after viewing pornography if they are already angered (Gray 1982). Gray states that pornography can also be a tool for validating a deeper anger toward women. If superficially induced anger puts men in touch with a deeper anger, particularly validated by pornography, then pornography becomes more dangerous than we might otherwise believe (Gray 1982, 394). Research has indicated that under certain conditions, exposure to erotic forms of media presentations *can* facilitate aggressive behavior (Donnerstein, Donnerstein, and Evans 1975; Baron and Bell 1977; Donnerstein and Hallam 1978).

QUESTION: What type of material is sexually stimulating to females?

Females tend to be aroused when erotic stimuli evoke feelings and fantasies of emotional involvement and romantic love. Patricia Schiller (1970) studied the media that might evoke this feeling of romantic love and examined how they might affect sexual behavior. Schiller gathered data from a school for pregnant adolescents and also from females attending a junior college. First, the females' reading habits were studied. Of the college women, 31 percent had not read any book in the past four years they considered pornographic. Forty-four percent of them had not been exposed to hard-core or "pulp" erotica, but had found some of the more widely circulated books sexually provocative. Thirty percent of the college women reported reading no magazines they considered pornographic. Ninety-five percent of the magazines considered pornographic by the rest of the women were either *Playboy,* romance, or confession magazines.

The pregnant schoolgirls, however, read almost no erotic books. They did little reading of any kind. Most of them reported reading about sex scandals and romances in the popular confession magazines found in their homes.

The research found that music seems to have a greater influence on female behavior. None of the pregnant schoolgirls and only 14 percent of the junior college women reported that records had *never* stimulated erotic feelings. The schoolgirls especially claimed that the rhythms and lyrics often brought on romantic feelings that were arousing and sometimes led to sexual activity. Both groups listened to a great deal of music with the theme of romantic love and found it sexually stimulating.

For the adolescent schoolgirls, television was the greatest influence; many indicated that their first sexual intercourse occurred in front of a TV. They generally had trouble maintaining conversation with boys, so television and caressing were welcome substitutes. Romantic scenes on TV evoked feelings of love, and the associated erotic response facilitated more and more physical contact.

The college women, however, indicated that television had little erotic impact on them, but considered movies to have the greatest effect of all the media. The researcher noted that the schoolgirls had much less opportunity to go to the movies.

The schoolgirls showed no interest in, and often showed actual disgust with, dirty stories and pictures of nude males. Fifty-seven percent of the college women indicated that clothing or manner of dress would not arouse them unless some erotic feelings were already present.

The results of this study suggest that females do not respond to erotic stimuli as strongly as do males. The more common forms of mass media (e.g., movies, TV, and music) with romantic content seem to have the greatest effect on young females sexually.

The prior information illustrates the difficulty of accurately interpreting the research on pornography and erotic material. Since no consensus exists among experts, establishing firm conclusions is not possible. The effects of pornography may occur in ways not expected. For instance, pornography may not influence sex crimes among youth, but may have more subtle effects on attitudes, motivations, or values. Soft-core pornography may have a more powerful effect than the hard-core, explicit variety. This appears to be especially true among females, who seem to be more aroused sexually by popular music and even television. Until further research is done, a logical conclusion is that erotic material and pornography likely have some impact on impressionable adolescents, although the exact response cannot be satisfactorily identified.

Summary

Recent research indicates that the adolescent audience for pop music and other activities is less homogeneous than was formerly thought. Musical tastes tend to define youth subcultures, and subcultures tend to correspond with class background. A recent study of Canadian high school students showed that a number of factors, including age, sex, social class, commitment to school, and delinquency, affect adolescent tastes in pop music. The majority of adolescents do not favor heavy rock but rather mainstream Top 40 pop music. A spectrum of rock music, ranging from Top 40 to progressive rock to heavy metal, seems to correspond with varying degrees of involvement with school and society. Another finding indicated that adolescents high in delinquent involvement tend to favor heavy rock. Other research found that music both positively and negatively affects moods, emotions, and behavior of adolescents.

The size and impact of the video industry is best understood by considering the amount of money spent on video games. Twenty billion dollars have been spent in quarters for arcade machines. Eighty percent of this sum was spent by teenagers, and nine out of every ten teenagers have tried an arcade game at least once. When asked why they play video games, most adolescents answer that they enjoy the challenge of the game. Many parents feel that electronic games are something of an addiction and that they take adolescents away from their studies. Some communities have expressed their concerns by passing ordinances restricting electronic game playing by teenagers. Others, however, feel that video games are an asset rather than an impediment, particularly in the areas of education and learning. Their conclusion is that video games have the potential to be used or abused.

The impact of television on the lives of youth is best understood by considering the amount of time spent in viewing television. Children spend more time per year watching television than they do in any other activity except sleeping; these activities include parents and school. Among young children, race and ethnic background seem to have no effect upon the amount of time spent in television viewing, but older Mexican-American teenagers, especially girls, watch more TV than their Anglo peers. Low-income black teenagers watch over six hours per day, while same-age low-income whites watch only four and a half hours per day. Another finding is that children with high IQs spend less time watching television than do those with lower IQs. On the topic of TV violence, research suggests that viewing TV violence has an observable effect on some children in the direction of increasing their aggressive behavior. Studies have found that television directly influences antisocial actions, such as teaching criminal or violent behavior. Television also provides antisocial models and removes the child away from other activities that are more beneficial, such as reading, sports, and clubs. Although bad examples of behavior are shown on TV, also exhibited are examples of sharing, helping, cooperation, and general altruistic behavior. Positive effects of TV are found in educational shows that greatly benefit those youth who watch. As with other media, TV can be used or abused. Evidence indicates, however, that TV viewing is presently more abused than used.

Research has found that films and soaps are used by adolescents to search for their identity. Youth want to know about right and wrong, deceit and honesty, and related abstract or conceptual issues. Soaps and films provide an inside look into the adult mind; adolescents use these media to understand themselves better by observing the actions of the characters in the films and soaps. Like TV, however, films and soaps can produce positive or negative results.

Adolescent literature has had a significant influence—both positive and negative—on the attitudes, values, and behavior of adolescents. The influence seems to be in the areas of self-image, awareness of moral and ethical issues, sensitivity to others, and awareness of social problems.

The media—video, music, television, and literature—all produce negative and positive influences on youths' behavior and activities.

Although the research is inconclusive, hard-core and soft-core pornography apparently has the potential for influencing adolescent behavior. Also clear is that the more common elements of the media (film, television, movies, and magazines) are sexually stimulating to females.

References

Andison, F. S. 1977. TV violence and viewer aggression: accumulation of study results 1956–1976. *Public Opinion Quarterly* 41: 314–31.

Austin, B. A. 1981. Portrait of a cult film audience: The Rocky Horror Picture Show. *Journal of Communication* 31(2): 43–54 (Spring).

Bandura, A., & F. L. Menlove. 1967. Factors determining vicarious extinction of avoidance behavior through symbolic modeling. *Journal of Personality and Social Psychology* 5: 16–22.

Bandura, A., & W. Mischel. 1965. Modification of self-imposed delay of reward through exposure to live and symbolic models. *Journal of Personality and Social Psychology* 2: 698–705.

Baron R., & P. Bell. 1977. Sex arousal and aggression by males: Effects of types of erotic stimuli and prior provocation. *Journal of Personality and Social Psychology* 35: 79–87.

Bettelheim, B. 1981. Our children are treated like idiots. *Psychology Today:* 28–44 (July).

Billboard. 1983. The youth market. *Billboard* 3 September: 1.

Blood, R. 1961. Social class and family control of television viewing. *Merrill-Palmer Quarterly* 7: 205–22.

Bogatz, G. H., & S. Ball. 1972. *The first year of "Sesame Street": An evaluation.* Princeton, N.J.: Educational Testing Service.

Bradley, I. 1972. Effect on student musical preference of a listening program in contemporary hard music. *Journal of Research on Music Education* 20: 344–52.

Bryan, J., & N. Walbeck. 1970. Preaching and practicing generosity: Children's actions and reactions. *Child Development* 41: 329–53.

Center Magazine. 1982. American movies and the American character. Vol. 15(3): 47–64 (May–June).

Chaffee, S. H., M. McLeod, & C. Atkin. 1970. Parent-adolescent similarities in television use. Paper presented at the meeting of the Association of Education and Journalism, Washington, D.C.

Clor, H. M. 1969. *Obscenity and public morality.* Chicago: Univ. of Chicago Press.

Coates, B., & W. Hartrup. 1969. Age and verbalization in observational learning. *Developmental Psychology* 1: 556–62.

Coleman, J. 1961. *The adolescent society.* New York: Free Press.
Comstock, G. A. 1978. The impact of television on American institutions. *Journal of Communication* 21: 12–28 (Spring).
Culp, M. B. W. 1975. A study of the influence of literature on the attitudes, values and behavior of adolescents. Ph.D. diss., Florida State University. *Dissertation Abstracts International* 36 (June 1976), 7915–1916-A.
DeAzevedo, L. 1982. *Pop music and morality.* Salt Lake City, Utah: Embryo Books.
Donnerstein E., M. Donnerstein, & R. Evans. 1975. Erotic stimuli and aggression: Facilitation or inhibition? *Journal of Personality and Social Psychology* 32: 237–44.
Donnerstein E., & J. Hallam. 1978. Facilitating effects of erotica on aggression against women. *Journal of Personality and Social Psychology* 36: 1270–77.
Ellis, G. 1983. Youth in the electronic environment. *Youth and Society* 15(1): 10–12.
Forcast. Top Shows: 1983–84. *Forcast* (October 1983).
Fried, R., & L. Berkowitz. 1979. *Music hath charms . . . and can influence helpfulness.* Silver Spring, Md.: Scripta.
Friedrich, L. K., & A. H. Stein. 1973. Aggressive and prosocial T.V. programs and the natural behavior of preschool children. *Monograph for the Society for Research and Child Development* 38(4), serial no. 151.
Gerbner, G. 1972. Violence in television drama: Television and symbolic functions. In *Media content and control.* Vol. 1 of *Television and social behavior,* ed. G. A. Comstock, E. A. Rubenstein, & J. P. Murray, 28–187. Washington D.C.: U.S. Government Printing Office.
Gray, S. 1982. Exposure to pornography and aggression toward women: The case of the angry male. *Social Problems* 29(4): 387–97.
Greenberg, B., & J. Dominick. 1969. Television behavior among disadvantaged children. In *CUP research report.* Department of Communication, Michigan State University.
Handzo, S. 1982. In *The Hammond almanac,* ed. M. Bacheller.
Hill, J. H., R. M. Liebert, & D. E. Mott. 1968. Vicarious extinction of avoidance behavior through films: An initial test. *Psychological Reports* 22: 192.
Hilts, P. 1983. The dean of artificial intelligence. *Psychology Today:* 28 (January).
Jensen, L. C. 1981. Parents can learn to make television work for children. *Mesa Tribune,* 18 December.
Lang, S. S. 1982. Soap operas distort students' views of reality. *Human Ecology Forum* 12: 7–10 (Spring).
Larson, R., & R. Kubey. 1983. Television and music: Contrasting media on adolescent life. *Youth and Society* 15(1): 13–31.
Lewis, M. 1978. The adolescent and the healthy family. In *Adolescent psychiatry: Developmental clinical studies,* vol. 6, ed. S. C. Feinsteine & P. L. Gloraschini. Chicago: Univ. of Chicago Press.
Liebert, R. M., & J. M. Neale. 1972. TV violence and children's aggression: Snow on the screen. *Psychology Today* 5: 38–40.
Liebert, R. M., R. D. Odom, J. M. Hill, & F. L. Huff. 1969. Effects of age and rule familiarity on the production of modeled language constructs. *Developmental Psychology* 1: 108–12.
Liebert, R. M., J. N. Sprafkin, & E. S. Davidson. 1982. *The early window: effects of television on children and youth.* 2d ed. New York: Pergamon Press.
Lindey, A. 1981. *On entertainment, publishing and the arts,* vol. 2, 2d ed. New York: Borgman.
Logan, M. 1983. Pacman as playmate. *Psychology Today* :58 (January).
Lukenbill, W. B. 1981. Family systems in contemporary adolescent novels: Implications for behavior information modeling. *Family Relations* 30: 219–27 (April).
Lyle, J., & H. R. Hoffman. 1972. Children's use of television and other media. In *Television in day to day life: Patterns of youth.* Vol. 4 of *Television and social behavior,* ed. E. A. Rubenstein, G. A. Comstock, & J. P. Murray, 129–256. Washington D.C.: U.S. Government Printing Office.
McCabe, A. E., & R. Moriarity. 1977. A laboratory/field study of television violence and aggression in children's sports. Paper presented at the biannual meeting of the Society for Research in Child Development, New Orleans, March.
Murdock, G., & G. Phelps. 1973. *Mass media and the secondary school.* London: Macmillan.

Natural History. 1982. It's like, good training for life. November, 71.

Nawy, H. 1973. In the pursuit of happiness? Consumers of erotica in San Francisco. *Journal of Social Issues* 29: 147–61.

Newsweek. 1981. Invasion of the video creatures. 16 November, 90.

Nilsen, D. L. F., & A. P. Nilsen. 1981. An exploration and defense of the humor in young adult literature. *Journal of Reading:* 58–65 (October).

Panelas, T. 1983. Adolescence and video games. *Youth and Society* 15(1): 51–65.

President's Commission on Obscenity and Pornography. 1970. *Report of the President's Commission on Obscenity and Pornography*. Washington, D.C.: U.S. Government Printing Office.

Robinson, J. P., & P. Hirsch. 1972. Teenage response to rock-n-roll protest songs. In *The sounds of social changes*, ed. R. S. Denisoff & R. A. Peterson. Chicago: Rand McNally.

Rosenhan, D., & G. M. White. 1967. Observation and rehearsal as determinants of pro-social behavior. *Journal of Personality and Social Psychology* 5: 424–31.

Rubin, A. M. 1977. Television usage, attitudes, and viewing behaviors of children and adolescents. *Journal of Communication* 21: 355–64.

Schiller, P. 1970. Effects of mass media on the sexual behavior of adolescent females. In *Report of the President's Commission on Obscenity and Pornography*. Washington, D.C.: U.S. Government Printing Office.

Schwartz, M. 1982. *T.V. and teens*. Reading, Mass.: Addison-Wesley.

Silverman, L. T. & J. N. Sprafkin. 1980. Adolescents' reactions to televised sexual innuendos. Report prepared for the American Broadcasting Companies, Inc., April 1980.

Smith, P. 1981. The impact of computerization on children's toys and games. *Journal of Children in Contemporary Society* 14(1): 73–82 (Fall).

Sprafkin, J. N. & L. T. Silverman. 1981. Update: physically intimate and sexual behavior on prime-time television: 1978–79. *Journal of Communication* 31(1): 34–40.

Tanner, J. 1981. Pop music and peer groups: A study of Canadian high school students' responses to pop music. *Canadian Review of Sociology and Anthropology* 18: 1–13 (February).

Thornberry, T. P., & R. A. Silverman. 1970. Exposure to pornography and juvenile delinquency. In *Report of the President's Commission on Obscenity and Pornography*. Washington, D.C.: U.S. Government Printing Office.

Time. 1982. Games that play people. 18 January, 50.

U.S. Surgeon General's Advisory Committee on Television and Children's Aggression. 1972. Television and growing up: The impact of televised violence. Washington, D.C.: U.S. Government Printing Office.

Watson, J. 1974. A study of adults' reaction to contemporary junior novels reflecting adolescents' interests in reading about aspects of peer and nonpeer relationships. Ph.D. diss., Michigan State University. *Dissertation Abstracts International* 35(1974), 3785-A University Microfilms 74-27, 503.

SECTION THREE

behaviors and thinking

9 Dating, Love, Sex, and Sex Roles
10 Morality, Values, and Religion
11 Clinical Problems in Adolescence
12 Drug Use During Adolescence
13 Juvenile Delinquency
14 Thinking and Intelligence

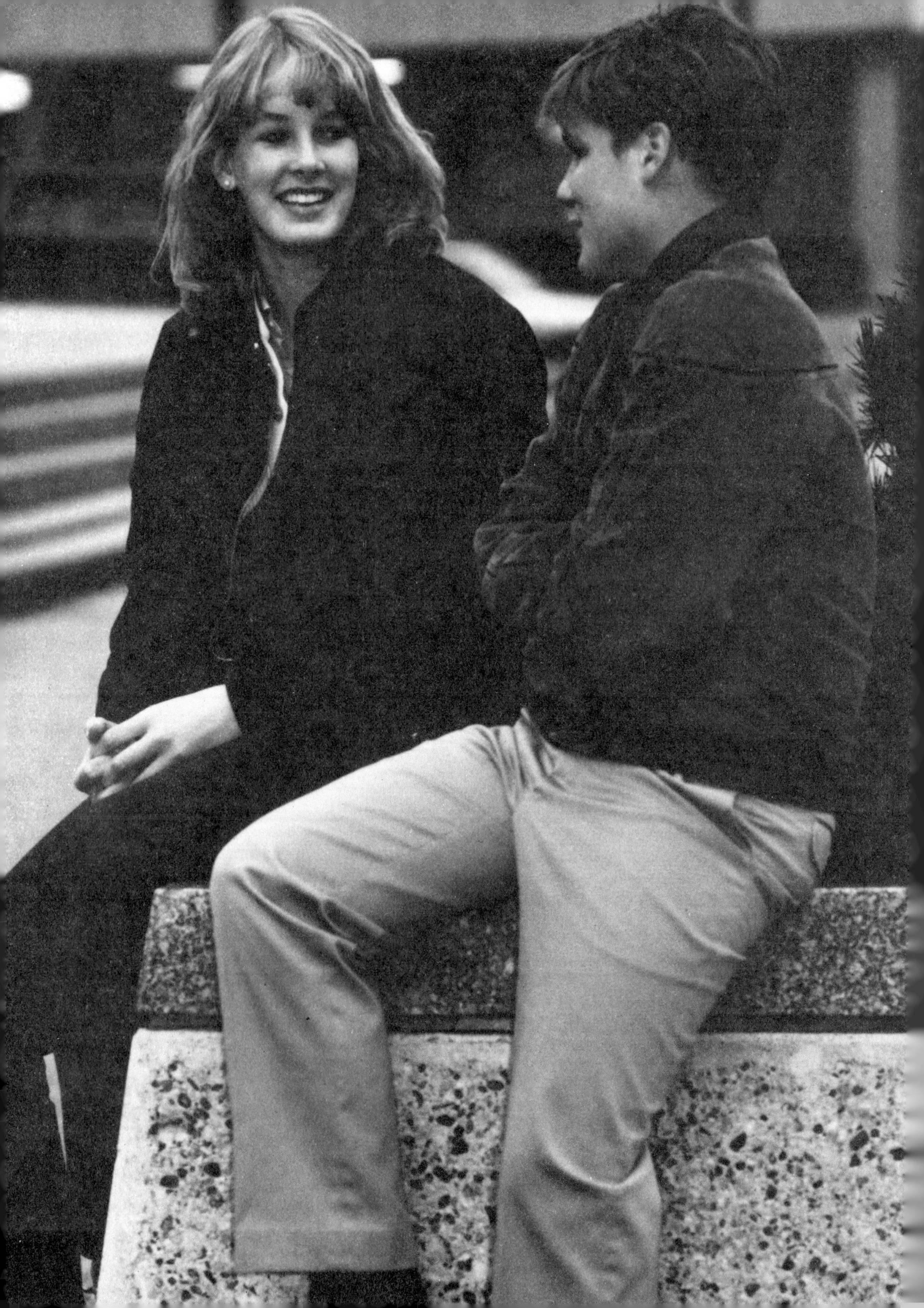

CHAPTER NINE

Dating, love, sex, and sex roles

SURVEY AND QUESTIONS

This chapter deals with the development of adolescent dating, love, and sexual behavior, and the factors that influence these areas, such as religiosity and parental and peer influence. Reading the chapter will provide answers to the following questions:

Love, Romance, and Dating

What does it mean for a teenage boy when he falls in love?
What is love?
What is romance?
Is adolescent "puppy love" genuine?
How does dating influence an adolescent's social relationships?
Why do adolescents date?
When do adolescents begin to date?

Sexual Behavior Development

Does sexual maturation provide motivation for dating?
What are some theories of sexual development?
How do social factors influence the type or direction of sexual motivation?
What are the main factors that influence development of sexuality in adolescents?
Can sexual behavior be increased or decreased?
What are the types and what is the extent of adolescent sexual behavior?

Sexual Behavior Motivation

Has a sexual revolution occurred?
Are indications of a sexual revolution primarily among females?
What is the relationship between religiosity and premarital sexual activity?
Do parents influence the adolescent's outlook on sexual behavior?
What is the role of peers in influencing sexual behavior?

Sex Roles

How do sex roles develop?
What personality characteristics are associated with each sex role?
What is androgyny?
Should a person try to become androgynous?
As sex roles change and overlap, are there any negative aspects of becoming androgynous?

Love, romance, and dating

A boy in love—in case you haven't experienced the phenomenon close up—is one of the most confused, contradictory, and foolish human beings you'll ever meet. A boy in love is a great deal like a puppy chasing his tail. Dizzy, excited, and having a wonderful time, even if he's not exactly sure why.

When a guy's in love, he's often unwilling to admit how much he's enjoying himself. He probably won't even realize he is in love until long after everyone around him is certain of it.

His friends, of course, being boys, will kid him. So may his family. But the boy will always deny being in love, even when you look at his notebooks and find her name scribbled dozens of times. His mind often wanders from English and physics to the land of Cupid, where—though his mouth may deny it—the heart and writing hand want to be.

Why are boys like that? Why so absurd and blind? After all, they're human aren't they? (Having been one, I speak with some authority; boys are human—most of the time.)

The answer, I believe, is that boys aren't quite sure it's all right to be in love. They believe being in love is unmanly, in the same way playing the violin or taking ballet lessons can be considered unmanly. "Give me a football," they think, pounding their chests as sweet love sweeps over them. "Give me my mitt." Being in love, they tell themselves, is for girls. . . .

. . . The first time I felt that way was the summer after my junior year. I was seventeen and lucky enough to be in Strasbourg, France, working in a biochemistry lab and studying French. Allison was a year younger than I was and part of a teen tour. She had long straight brown hair and blue eyes; I remember her as very beautiful. . . .

That's how I felt the entire three weeks we shared. Spinning, dizzy, and too excited to fall asleep at night. Then it was time for her teen tour to leave for Italy. She spent departure day crying. Being a boy in love, I didn't cry at all. We kissed good-bye, her baby blues red and swollen, my brown eyes a little bit bright. Embracing, we felt grown-up, and we promised to write.

Her bus left. As I walked alone to our park to spin again on the carousel, I remember thinking, "So this is what it means to be in love. This glowing, almost burning sensation inside—isn't it wonderful?" (Goodman 1983, 14–18)

"Right at the top of things we don't want to know is why a man falls in love with a woman," stated Senator William Proxmire as he ridiculed the spending of 84,000 federal dollars by two psychologists who were studying romance (*Newsweek* 1980, 89). Much more than $84,000 is now being spent to study love, romance, sex, and other related behaviors. What has already been found is fascinating and perhaps may prove to be some of the best-spent money in improving our general happiness and life satisfaction. In particular, a better understanding of sex, love, and romance is needed for adolescents who encounter these powerful forces for the first time in their lives. The psychological and adjustment problems associated with the emotions of love are particularly acute for teenage boys, as illustrated by the preceding quote from a popular youth magazine.

QUESTION: What does it mean for a teenage boy when he falls in love?

Eric Goodman (1983), who portrays the young male in the opening quote, provides some interesting insights into teenage boys in love, their behavior, and concepts on the topic of love.

Generally, teenage boys will find it difficult to admit to themselves, friends, and family members that they are truly in love. To them, the novelty of love feelings is strange. They have probably never felt this way before, mainly because they think these feelings run contrary to the rough, tough, masculine image they are working to display to themselves and to those around them. Their pride and ego are large but fragile, and admitting their love to themselves and others may cause humiliation, brought on by peer teasing and joking, as well as personal disappointment at not living up to desired expectations. These feelings are illustrated in the following interview:

Q. "When did you first fall in love?"
A. "I was about 16."

Q. "How did you know it was love?"
A. "I don't know—we liked each other a lot and wanted to spend time together."

Q. "Did being in love influence your behavior?"
A. "Quite a bit, I remember talking on the phone every night for hours. Then at school, I had to be right next to her whenever we were in public —another funny thing was sharing lockers at school—any couple who were going steady shared the same locker, so we did. Also, I wasn't able to spend as much time with my 'buds' as I did before.

Q. "Was it this kind of behavior that made you think you were in love?"
A. "Yea, I guess so, but we felt a lot for each other anyway."

Q. "How did your male friends feel about you being in love?"
A. "I don't know, we never talked about it."

Q. "You didn't tell your friends that you were in love?"
A. "No way, never, they would have thought I was out of my mind."

Q. "So, you were embarrassed to be in love?"
A. "No, you just don't tell your friends about your personal relationships and things like that, it's not cool."

Q. "Did you tell your family?"
A. "No, they knew we were dating, but that's it."

Q. "Why didn't you tell them?"
A. "They would have thought I was a silly young boy who was simply infatuated."

Q. "Looking back now, do you think you were really in love?"
A. "No, not really, we thought we were though, but we were too selfish and domineering to each other—at least I was."

Q. "What do you mean, domineering?"
A. "Well, I wanted her always to be around when I wanted her to be, and I didn't want her to make friends with other guys. I wanted her to think I was the only one."

Q. "Overall was it a good relationship?"
A. "Yes, but I think when we started talking love the relationship suffered."

Q. "Why was that?"
A. "Well, I guess because we tried to make commitments and promises that both of us were too immature to make—we didn't understand what those commitments meant. We weren't ready for that kind of life."
Q. "If you had truly been in love, what would have been a more appropriate behavior to display towards your girlfriend?"
A. "First, I would have made certain that she had her freedom, to date, make friends and do anything she wanted. Also I would have made sure that loving her didn't interfere with the relationships I had with other people. I think I would have relaxed more, not be so serious like I was" (Elliot 1983).

Young men often find themselves in this love bind for two major reasons. The first one deals with social influences upon the young man's developing identity: "It's unmanly to be in love." Extremely important to the typical teenage boy are many masculine characteristics and behavioral patterns. Love, however, seems incompatible with becoming a man. As Goodman stated, boys think love "is for girls." The second reason why boys struggle with their identity during love relationships is due to the power game. Stereotypically, being a man means to have power or control. Love threatens this ideology as the boy now finds himself in the power of someone else. Supposedly, the young man loses the power game and with it a part of his manliness.

The teenage boy who finds himself in this crisis will experience many growing pains before he is mature enough to see that loving is as natural for men as it is for women. Society could be blamed for this confusing circumstance if

Teenage boys especially may experience some psychological adjustment problems when they fall in love for the first time because of the conflict in stereotypical roles that may occur.

young males cannot socially prepare boys to accept and experience feelings of love, caring, and tenderness, which are vital to developing identities.

QUESTION: What is love?

Perhaps the most objective answer to this question has been given by Zick Rubin (1973), who developed a short test to measure love and liking. He found that these were two separate emotions or experiences. The following sample questions from two tests will provide a better understanding of each of these emotions:

LOVE SCALE AND LIKING SCALE ITEMS

Love Scale

1. If _____ were feeling bad, my first duty would be to cheer him (her) up.
2. If I were lonely, my first thought would be to seek _____ out.
3. When I am with _____, I spend a good deal of time just looking at him (her).

Like Scale

1. I think that _____ is unusually well-adjusted.
2. I have great confidence in _____'s good judgment.
3. _____ is the kind of person whom I myself would like to be (Rubin 1973, 217).

A large number of dating couples took the test, with the scale ranging from 0 to 9. A zero indicated the statement was not at all true, and a high score indicated it was definitely true. They completed the test for a person to love and date, and also for their relationship with one of their friends. The average scores are presented in Table 9–1.

Looking at the scores, one can see that liking and loving are both high for men and women, but less for friends, especially for males: "Loving for men may often be channeled into a single opposite sex relationship, whereas women may be more able to express attachment, caring, and intimacy in other relationships as well" (Rubin 1973, 221).

Rubin was able to predict that men and women who scored higher on the love scale spent more time gazing into other's eyes, and also found that six months later a link was present between love and maintenance of the relationship. Rubin's findings, however, were complicated by another factor. He found love scores were good predictors if both partners were romantics, which means that they strongly believe in love and support statements such as, "People should marry whomever they love, regardless of social position," and disagree with statements such as "Economic security should be carefully considered before selecting a marriage partner," or "One should not marry against the serious advice of one's parents." Nonromantics are more practical people and

TABLE 9–1 Average Love and Liking Scores for Dating Partners and Same-Sex Friends

	Women	Men
Love for partner	90.57	90.44
Liking for partner	89.10	85.30
Love for friend	64.79	54.47
Liking for friend	80.21	78.38

Source: Z. Rubin, *Liking and Loving* (New York: Holt, Rinehart and Winston, 1973), 221.

consider factors such as similarity, personality, and economic security to be more important than love. When both partners scored were nonromantics, no correlation existed between their love scores and whether their relationship had flourished.

As a beginning to the understanding of love, distinguishing between loving and liking is important, as well as recognizing that some people place much higher value on the experience of love (romantics), while to others the experience is considerably less important (nonromantics).

QUESTION: What is romance?

A practical way to answer this question is to look at the items on a romanticism test. This examination will assist in the understanding of romanticism and will also serve as a self-assessment. Box 9–1 is a romanticism scale. Surprisingly, men tend to score higher on romanticism.

Evidence that men are more romantic is sometimes indirect, but researchers have tended to support this notion. In one group of 700 young lovers, the findings were that males fall in love earlier than females and are more certain of

---

BOX 9-1   ROMANTICISM SCALE

	Agree	Disagree		Agree	Disagree
*1. Lovers ought to expect a certain amount of disillusionment after marriage.	___	___	6. A girl should expect her sweetheart to be chivalrous on all occasions.	___	___
*2. True love should be suppressed in cases where its existence conflicts with the prevailing standards of morality.	___	___	7. A person should marry whomever he loves regardless of social position.	___	___
			8. Lovers should freely confess everything of personal significance to each other.	___	___
3. To be truly in love is to be in love forever.	___	___	*9. Economic security should be carefully considered before selecting a marriage partner.	___	___
*4. The sweetly feminine "clinging vine" girl cannot compare with the capable and sympathetic girl as a sweetheart.	___	___	*10. Most of us could sincerely love any one of several people equally well.	___	___
			11. A lover without jealousy is hardly to be desired.	___	___
5. As long as they can at least love each other, two people should have no trouble getting along together in marriage.	___	___	*12. One should not marry against the serious advice of one's parents.	___	___

If you agreed with items 3, 5, 6, 7, 8, or 11 (the items without an asterisk), give yourself one point per item. If you disagreed with items 1, 2, 4, 9, 10, or 12 (the items with an asterisk), give yourself one point per item.

Hobart found that men had a considerably more romantic view of male-female relationships than did women. On the average, women agreed with about four of the romanticism items; on the average, men agreed with about five of them.

Source: Reprinted from *Social Forces* 36: 362–67 (1958). "The Incidence of Romanticism during Courtship" by C. W. Hobart. Copyright © the University of North Carolina Press.

it sooner (Kamin, Davidson, and Scheck 1970). In addition, women tend to end affairs, and men suffer more at the termination. Males more than females generally find it hard to accept that they are no longer loved and it appears that males may be the more romantic of the two sexes. (Rubin 1973, 200–204).

Three times as many men as women commit suicide after a love affair ends. However, the experience of love—"felt like I was floating on a cloud, felt like I wanted to jump, run, and scream, had trouble concentrating, felt giddy and carefree, was nervous before dates"—is more common among females. Although men may be more romantic, women may feel and display the experience and emotions of romance more dramatically and intensely (Walster 1978, 49).

QUESTION: Is adolescent "puppy love" genuine?

I remember at age 14 having a crush on a boy in my neighborhood. I never really came in contact with him or did anything with him, but in my mind, I liked him an awful lot. I remember feeling heartbroken and crying the day my friend told me that he had no interest in me and liked another girl. The feeling I had then, over an infatuation or imaginary relationship was every bit as real as the hurt and loss I've felt after the ending of more mature relationships in the more recent past.

Judging by the reported intensity of feelings, the adolescent in love experiences emotions just as strong and real as the adult. The love may, however, be less rational and logical. The author's opinion is that falling in love during youth is not a social convention, but has probably been a universal experience among

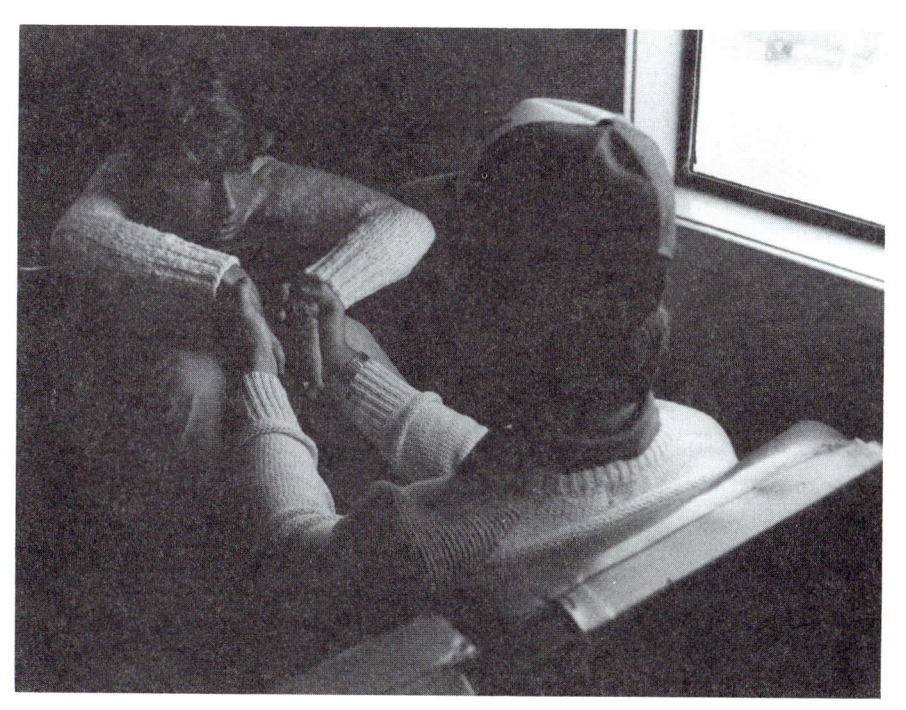

The adolescent's feelings of love are reported to be as intense as those of the adult. The love may be less rational and logical, however.

humankind from recorded history. Shakespeare's Romeo and Juliet would be called preadolescent at age thirteen. Consider the following quotes from biographies during the 1900s:

> Beth's first love affair was with a bright, fair-headed, fat-faced boy, who sat near her pew on Sundays. They looked at each other during services, and she felt a glad glow in her chest spread over her, dwelt on his image, smiled, and even the next day felt a new desire to please. She watched for him to pass from school. When he appeared. "she felt a most delightful thrill shoot through her." The first impulse to fly was conquered; she never thought a boy beautiful before. . . .
>
> Jacob Riis "fell head over heels in love with sweet Elizabeth" when he was 15 and she was 13. His "courtship proceeded at a tumultuous pace, which first made the town laugh, then put it out of patience and made some staid matrons express the desire to box my ears soundly." She played among the lumber where he worked, and he watched her so intently that he scarred his shinbone with an adze he should have been minding. He cut his forefinger with an ax when she was dancing on a beam nearby, and once fell off a roof when craning his neck to see her go round a corner. (Hall 1905, 586)

The love of youth is likely romantic and similar to the love scale rather than to the liking scale presented in Table 9–1. Regardless of the judgment that adults place on teenagers' love, for youth the experience is valid, important, and real. The youth's perception should therefore be considered the important element in making decisions about a young person's feelings of love. The importance of these love feelings in the life of an adolescent is shown by the importance and attention given to the societal activity of expressing love during adolescence. This activity is called dating.

QUESTION: How does dating influence an adolescent's social relationships?

The popular concept of the irrational nature of adolescents' love and crushes has been documented. The social custom of dating is a significant event in the life of adolescents and can influence many of their other relationships, as seen in the following case study:

> Most of my dates were typical of other teenage dates. I did not formally begin to date until I was 16 years old. However, at age 14 I began to "simulate" dating with other friends. We would casually meet girls that we associated with at social get togethers, then would attempt to pair off as if on a date. That continued until age 16 when I was allowed to formally date. My dates consisted of movies, dinners, dances, roller skating, etc. Frequently they were organized functions through school or church that required dates. I rarely went out on big, fancy dates due to lack of money.
>
> The girls I dated usually fit the same mold: popular, brunette, pretty, fun to be with, and a unique personality. It was difficult for me to date a different girl each weekend. I tended to continue dating the same girl for an extended period of time before I dated others.

The most significant aspect of dating was the feelings it produced within me. They were not all pleasant. I was accepted by girls, and that built my confidence and self-esteem. Girls seemed to be attracted to me physically and through my personality.

Other times I felt feelings of insecurity, inferiority, and conflict. I had many limitations in dating. I needed more money than I had to do the things I really wanted to, and many of my friends had enough. They also had their own car. Any time I used a car I had to ask my father for permission to use his. Internally I was striving to feel autonomous, yet I knew that he always had some degree of control over me.

Occasionally older girls made passes at me. If they were attractive I went out with them, but felt inferior due to age. Whenever I was around them I had feelings about not being mature or "cool" enough. I was very inhibited.

The greatest conflict came through my father. He was afraid of me getting sexually involved with the girls I dated. He tried to restrict me through every control he had. That "battle" put an emotional strain on me and hindered our father/son relationship. All I wanted was wholesome social interaction. Although I refused to admit it then, I knew that if I dated without his limitations, I would become sexually involved in my dating.

Dating helped me to mature and develop many good characteristics. It was an important part of my life and I will encourage my own children to date. Oddly enough, I will impose many of the same limitations that my father gave me. Hopefully, through my past feelings and experiences I can find the proper balance between teenagers' need for autonomy and the limitations I should impose on them as a parent. I think if that balance is found and properly implemented the teenage dating years will be character building for teenagers, and strengthen relationship between teenagers and parents.

QUESTION: Why do adolescents date?

One author (Rice 1984, 311–14) identifies seven reasons why adolescents date: recreation; companionship without the responsibility of marriage; status grading and achievement; socialization; sexual exploration, satisfaction, or exploitation; mate selection or sorting; and achieving intimacy. The following is a brief summary of Rice's ideas concerning each of these reasons:

Recreation. Rice first points out that dating is an intrinsically fun and rewarding activity. Sufficient grounds therefore exist for engaging in the activity for its own sake alone.

Companionship. The desire to simply be with someone of the opposite sex is a strong motivation. Dating may achieve this goal.

Status. Dating can simply be a means of raising social status. Basically, adolescents may increase their status level by increasing their dating level.

Socialization. One goal (perhaps not a conscious one) is to learn social skills by means of peer interaction during dating.

Sex. Some adolescents date for sexual exploration or satisfaction. Since sexual intercourse among teenagers has increased, sex has been a goal of dating, but sex during dating is more often an outgrowth of the relationship rather than the result of a predetermined goal.

Mate Selection. A natural outcome of dating is the development of relationships that lead to mate selection.

Intimacy. As discussed in Chapter 3, Erikson believes that achieving intimacy is the prime task of interdevelopment. Dating may, however, operate as a means to achieving this end during adolescence.

The following case study shows how significant dating was for this young man and how dating serves one or more of the previously mentioned reasons:

> In my early adolescent years I was scared to death at the prospect of interacting with girls on any more than an extraneous level. I desired to have a close sharing relationship with a member of the opposite sex but I was too afraid to open myself to possible rejection or even ridicule, as I saw it. I guess overcoming this fear became one of my earliest reasons for dating. I knew that the only way to overcome it was to jump into the water, so to speak. I also knew that it would help me to develop social skills.
>
> When I finally got up the courage to ask a girl on a date, I was petrified. When she said, "Yes," I could hardly believe it. Needless to say, my social skills on that first date were not exactly those of Don Juan. I fell flat on my face. This, of course, increased my desire to improve my social skills.
>
> Obviously, I was not Mr. Confidence after that experience. However, I still felt the need for female companionship. Over the next year I dated only a few times and gained a little experience but I was still rather naive going into my senior year in high school. I had never really had a girl friend up to this time; however, at the end of my senior year I found a girl friend.
>
> The experiences I had with this, my first girl friend, were possibly the most significant in my life in terms of learning social skills and interpersonal relations. I most likely learned more from my relationship with her than I have from all my other dates put together. I learned how to become close to a member of the opposite sex and perhaps most importantly I learned that I could do it. As a result of this experience I tasted the fulfillment and satisfaction that can come when two people open their lives to each other. After this, dating became less a means of learning social skills and more a search for a renewal of that intimacy, for most of the skills had been learned. I could now seek the evasive prize of love.
>
> As I entered college, however, I faced a setback. Many of the skills I had learned in high school did not work in a campus society. I again felt inadequate and as a result I did not date much my freshman year.
>
> During my second year of college, which came two years later, my friends did a lot of match making for me. Most of my dates were blind dates. This really helped me to work on my dating skills and after about a year I was no longer letting my friends fix me up but was using my newly developed skills to choose my dates myself. Now my motivation for dating was almost exclusively to find intimacy as well as to find a mate. These remain my primary motivations for dating. I still date simply for fun at times but my main focus is on finding a person with whom I can share my life and who can share hers with me.

Adolescents date for many reasons: dating is fun in and of itself, it is a learning experience, social status is based partly on dating, and many more. Perhaps the most significant reason for dating, however, is for the fulfillment of the human need to achieve intimacy.

QUESTION: When do adolescents begin to date?

Two researchers (Douvan and Adelson 1966) found that during the 1960s American girls began to date between the ages of fourteen and fifteen, and boys around age sixteen. A later study in the 1970s noticed a trend toward earlier dating (Cox 1974). Specific ages will vary depending on social class, racial background, and geographical area, but most adolescents apparently begin dating during their midteens or earlier.

One researcher was interested in determining the effects of early or late parental permission to begin dating (Wright 1982). By administering a questionnaire to ninety-five seniors from a middle-class community in central Texas, Wright measured the subjects' self-concepts, perceptions of their parents, reported drinking and drug abuse, delinquent behavior, suicidal thoughts, and frequency of drug use. He found that early permission to date was significantly related to feelings of being confident and independent and to a good relation-

Adolescents date for many reasons, but perhaps the most significant reason involves the fulfillment of the human need for intimacy.

ship with the mother. Early permission to date, however, was also related to reported drinking and drug abuse, and frequent use of alcohol, marijuana, downers, cocaine, and tobacco. Late permission to date was related to feelings of being insecure and dependent, to having suicidal thoughts, and to a poor relationship with the mother. These subjects perceived the mother as overly strict. Those who were in a medium group, who received permission to date at age fifteen, were in most cases better off than the early or late daters on almost all measures.

Wright concludes that the year following the fifteenth birthday may be the most appropriate time for parents to allow or to encourage their children to begin dating. Other researchers (Fernstein and Hardon 1979) believe that parents who deny their children the privilege of dating when most youngsters their age have been dating for some time may be delaying important opportunities for their children to experience normal development and growth, and to establish a positive relationship with their family and parents. The significant element is apparently not the precise age but the perception of freedom, independence, responsibility, and trust the adolescents may feel. This perception is likely established through comparison with peers.

Sexual behavior development

QUESTION: Does sexual maturation provide motivation for dating?

In their article "Sex Role and Dating Orientation," McCabe and Collins (1979) state that the development of sex roles appears to be culturally specific. Rothschild (1980) maintains that in the United States, a "romantic attachment" rather than a social one exists between the two sexes. This means that dating is for "love" rather than for "fun" or "friendship." Rothschild also contends that the American young woman learns she must act in "a so-called sex appropriate manner," to be popular with boys. The appropriate way could be defined as relative passivity, deference, low intellectuality, and cooperativeness. The female may "play dumb in exchange for popularity." Some societies, however, such as Greece, encourage a social attachment instead, which means the development of a friendship group that allows girls to achieve highly in school without the need to play less than they are. Intelligent girls have a higher status in a friendship group than less intelligent girls.

McCabe and Collins (1979) conducted an experiment involving sex roles and relationships to determine what influences if any these roles have in the dating relationship. They questioned 120 Australian males and 139 Australian females. The subjects were placed into three groups, age sixteen to seventeen, nineteen to twenty, and twenty-four to twenty-five. None of the subjects had been married. The subjects answered questions about three different stages of dating—the first date, several dates, and going steady—according to the types of activities they desired to experience at each stage. The results of the questionnaires are shown in Table 9–2.

In the sixteen to seventeen age group, the females desired light physical contact, such as holding hands, while the males preferred less of the light contact. The older subjects preferred it less than did the younger subjects (16–17: males 89 percent, females 96 percent), (19–20: males 92 percent, females 76

TABLE 9-2 Psychoaffectional Attitudes of Males and Females in Three Age Groups and at Various Stages of the Dating Relationship (Percentage)

	16–17 years						19–20 years						24–25 years					
	First Date		Several Dates		Going Steady		First Date		Several Dates		Going Steady		First Date		Several Dates		Going Steady	
Relationship	M	F	M	F	M	F	M	F	M	F	M	F	M	F	M	F	M	F
Sincerity	89	93	98	98	98	100	89	92	92	98	100	98	83	100	97	100	100	100
Compatibility	87	97	98	97	100	100	100	98	100	100	100	98	90	96	93	100	93	100
Understanding	83	88	98	100	100	100	81	88	97	98	100	100	72	100	100	100	100	100
Affection	96	82	93	98	100	100	82	73	97	96	100	98	76	79	97	100	100	100
Concern	91	93	97	97	100	100	92	96	97	96	100	98	90	92	100	100	100	100
Mutual sharing of life experiences	69	66	85	92	97	90	69	79	86	96	97	98	66	75	83	92	100	100
Relaxed relationship	87	94	98	94	94	97	94	94	97	98	94	98	93	96	100	100	100	100
Security	58	54	79	75	94	98	50	60	72	83	100	98	52	58	62	83	97	100
Trust	69	49	86	92	98	100	64	60	86	92	97	98	52	58	82	90	100	100
Mutual respect	87	85	98	97	98	97	83	94	97	98	100	98	93	96	100	100	100	100
A confidante	70	58	89	89	97	100	69	60	92	94	100	98	48	50	79	83	97	100
Reassurance	80	61	94	89	98	95	89	77	94	94	100	96	76	58	90	92	100	96
Companionship	85	89	87	95	98	98	94	96	97	94	100	98	83	87	100	100	100	100
Tenderness	76	87	98	94	100	98	92	83	94	94	100	98	90	87	100	96	100	100
Romance	38	34	53	61	89	87	33	38	56	56	89	92	21	46	55	79	93	96
Self Oneness	25	14	51	27	84	67	44	15	58	48	89	90	28	37	55	58	93	92

Source: M. P. McCabe and J. K. Collins, "Sex Role and Dating Orientation," *Journal of Youth and Adolescence* 8(4): 415 (1979).

percent), (24–25: males 90 percent, females 87 percent). As the relationship became more involved, the behavior became more physical for both males and females. Behavior also grew more physical with the increase in dating. Necking on the first date (16–17: males 67 percent, females 31 percent) increased after several dates (males 84 percent, females 79 percent), and after going steady a high percentage of females desired to neck (94 percent). Familiarity apparently encourages the desires. Regarding intercourse, however, 16 percent of the males and 0 percent of the females in the sixteen to seventeen age group desired intercourse on the first date. After going steady the male desires increased to 62 percent, compared with only 19 percent of the females. Another psychologist (McCandless 1970) also indicates that not until youth are in their twenties do uncommitted couples meet the sexual needs of one another. The McCabe and Collins study shows that as dating progresses, so does the desire for greater sexual involvement. This finding has a direct bearing on the next section dealing with the theories of sexuality.

In contrast with the progressively stronger biological role in dating, another study found the cultural, social push to be much more important. In one study (Dornsbusch et al. 1981), a sample of over seven thousand subjects in the U.S. National Health Examination Survey was analyzed. For youth age twenty to seventeen, the question investigated was whether dating was more closely linked to sexual maturation or to general social development associated with progressing through the school grades. Using advanced statistics, the authors concluded that sexual maturation (the biological development of one person relative to other same-age persons) added little to the onset and frequency of dating. The researchers found that social pressure, based on what was considered typical and appropriate for the ages, determines the onset of dating and that individual biological maturation has little impact. The following are the highlights of their conclusions:

> The peer group, usually fairly homogeneous in age, also exerts pressure on its members to engage in dating behavior that is typical for members of the age group at any time. . . .
> An adolescent who does not date when his or her friends do date may be temporarily rejected, only to be reaccepted into a group when he or she begins to date. . . .
> Our findings do not contradict the view that the sexual drives of each individual are real and sometimes urgent. But sexual behavior is an arena in which biological and social forces interact, and nowhere is their interaction more clear than in adolescence. A simple biological determinism cannot explain our findings.
> It is not the case that society ignores sexual development in the pressures that peers and family put upon adolescents. The best way to examine the situation is to think of an institutionalized set of images in which members of the society have conceptions of what is typical and appropriate behavior at various ages. It is as if people have learned to respond to the typical art to ignore individual differences among members of an age category. . . .
> Social pressures appear to overwhelm the individual whose rate of biological development deviates from the norm. (Dornsbusch et al. 1981, 184)

Dating therefore seems more of a social convention rather than a response to sexual motivation. This understanding of sexual development, however, is necessary to understand both dating and sexual behavior among adolescents.

QUESTION: What are some theories of sexual development?

The easiest way to explain sexual development is to assume a simple, uncomplicated biological explanation: "Sexual behavior is due to biochemical processes within the body that accelerate during puberty and cause the individual to become more sexual." As these physiological changes increase, the individual becomes more sexual and hereditary mechanisms determine the expression of sexuality. Using this model, the two basic questions of amount and type of sexual activity can easily be answered. Unfortunately, scholarly examinations of human sexuality find this explanation inadequate. (Hardy 1964; Byrne 1977; Miller and Simon 1980; Jessor et al. 1983). Since this text focuses on the adolescent, we will review recent studies showing the importance of including sociocultural variables to provide an adequate understanding of sexual development during adolescence.

QUESTION: How do social factors influence the type or direction of sexual motivation?

It might seem that human beings are infinitely pliable in what they can learn to associate with excitement. Common observation and clinical case studies indicate that *some* individuals clearly have learned to be aroused to such various stimuli as perfume, a back seat of an automobile, public urinals, pre-pubescent children, sheep, dead bodies, the odor of spermicidal foam, rock music and motel rooms. (Byrne 1977, 19)

Perhaps the best demonstration of social factors influencing the amount of sexuality is presented in a recent study that investigated the time of first intercourse (Jessor et al. 1983). This carefully done study involved 430 youth who were initially tested in 1969 and retested in 1979 to obtain information about the time of their first intercourse and related life factors that could be used to predict when a person would first have intercourse. The researchers concluded the following regarding the development of early sexuality or coitus:

Several important findings of the present study bear reviewing. First, the precursors of sexual onset are variables in all three of the psychosocial systems in problem-behavior theory—the personality system, the perceived environment system, and the behavior system. Among adolescent virgins, both male and female, relative earliness of subsequent onset of sexual intercourse is related to personality system variables such as higher value on and expectation for independence, lower value on and expectation for academic achievement, more socially critical beliefs about society, more tolerance of deviance, and less religiosity. In the perceived environment system, earliness of onset is linked with less compatibility between parents and friends, less parental influence relative to that of friends, and more perceived social approval and models for problem behavior, including sexual behavior. With respect to the behavior system, earliness of onset is signaled by an already greater involvement in other problem behavior and less involvement in conventional behavior such as attendance at church. The pervasiveness of these variables across the different systems of problem-behavior theory suggests that there is a general psychosocial patterning of proneness to, or readiness. (Jessor et al. 1983, 623)

To conceptualize and understand this conclusion, it should be clarified that these researchers in earlier reports (Jessor and Jessor 1977), stated that there are three basic elements that influence sexual motivation: (1) the personality system, (2) the perceived environment system, and (3) the behavior system. Of these elements they state:

Within the personality system, proneness is most clearly represented in the motivational-instigation structure by higher value on independence, lower value on academic achievement, higher value on independence relative to achievement; in the personal belief structure, proneness is represented by greater social criticism and greater alienation; and in the personal controls structure, proneness refers to a more tolerant attitude toward deviance, lesser religiosity, and greater positive relative to negative reasons for engaging in problem or transition behavior. Within the perceived environment system, proneness is most clearly represented in the distal structure by lesser parental and friends' controls, less compatibility between parents' and friends' expectations, and greater influence of friends relative to parents; in the proximal structure (those perceived environment variables that directly implicate the various problem behaviors), proneness refers to greater parents' and friends' approval of problem behavior and greater perceived prevalence of social models who engage in it. In the behavior system, proneness is reflected in greater involvement in other problem behavior and at the same time, less involvement in conventional behaviors, such as attending church and doing well in school. (Jessor et al. 1983, 609–19)

QUESTION: What are the main factors that influence development of sexuality in adolescents?

To answer this question, one might review the basic findings in a chapter on the development of adolescent sexuality found in *The Handbook of Adolescent Psychology* (Miller and Simon 1980) The authors focus on gender role expectancies:

> Much social, sexual behavior in early adolescence is motivated or facilitated by expectations concerning gender-appropriate behavior rather than in intrinsic interest in the sexual. "Falling in love" and "going steady" are essentially expressions of non-sexual, social arrangements. These experiences potentiate sexual acts almost independently of erotic interest or sexual arousal. Light and heavy petting, for example, serve the non-sexual interests of both genders by certifying gender-role adequacy. . . . Undoubtedly, gender-role expectations represent the most powerful factor shaping adolescent sexual behavior. (Miller and Simon 1980, 391–92)

In other areas the authors show that psychological motivations underlie the engagement in sexual behavior. Some of these motivations are antisocial and even pathological. This situation tends to occur when adolescents engage in sexual behavior despite severe sanctions against such behavior:

> These conditions are, of course, experienced differently according to gender, race, maturity, peer climate, and aspirations for adulthood. Nevertheless, adolescent pre-marital coital behavior is commonly viewed as rebellious, pathological, immoral, deviant or delinquent by a range of professions, clinicians, social-scientists, theologicals, law-enforcement agents concerned with the development of the young. (Miller and Simon 1980, 393)

Although differences exist among the sexes regarding motivation for sexual behavior during adolescence, a certain amount of following norms or scripts seems to occur. Affection and love are encouraged along with romance. These motivations are considered normal, healthy, and desirable, and undoubtedly spill over into sexual behavior:

> The increasing salience of the rhetoric of love among boys in conjunction with increasing sexual experimentation among girls suggest the possibility of gender convergence, not only in sexual behavior but also in the interpersonal scripts that organize adolescent sexual behavior. (Miller and Simon 1980, 401)

QUESTION: Can sexual behavior be increased or decreased?

The preceding studies clearly indicate that personality and social factors can be used to influence sexual behavior. Some more extreme examples have been reported by Mosher (1966) and Griffitt (1973), in which males used imagination, fantasy, and other materials to increase sexual excitement in females to facilitate seduction.

Sexual motivation can certainly be increased and decreased by changing the biological conditions of the person. For example, during illness, sickness, injury, stress, and other traumas, sexual motivation is expected to be lower. In a review article, one theorist (Hardy 1964) maintains that on a more permanent basis, the motivation for sexual behavior can be slowed or delayed through the following activities:

1. Participation in activities which fill one's life with abundant gratifications, so that sexual intimacies are not indulged in as an escape from boredom or emotional starvation. Athletic, intellectual, altrustic, occupational, vocational, esthetic, or social pursuits may serve this function.
2. Comprehension of the nature of sex motivation and the factors which govern it, to help the person to foresee the consequences of alternative courses of action, thus enabling him to make a knowledgeable decision in terms of his own motives and values.
3. Prevent the appetite from growing by abstinence from arousing activities until the time acceptable for sexual expression. This implies a dating-courtship pattern which is centered upon a wide variety of nonsexual activities which additionally might contribute to a more adequate prediction of marital compatibility.
4. Exposure to entertainment, reading material, companionship, etc., which have nonsexual connotations of intrinsic interest to the person. This will tend to prevent the recurrent arousal of sexuality.
5. Emphasis upon the long-term rewards of continence, and idealization of the ability to delay immediate gratification of impulse (Hardy 1964, 15).

QUESTION: What are the types and what is the extent of adolescent sexual behavior?

A research team reviewed twenty studies of adolescent sexual behavior in the United States (Diepold and Young 1979). The team attempted to summarize data accumulated over three decades by looking at the specific behaviors of dating, kissing, petting, masturbation and premarital coitus, homosexual contacts, and birth control. The following is an abridged summary of their main conclusions. (References format has been altered).

I. *Dating*
There were no data reported in the 1940s or 1950s which dealt directly with adolescent dating practices. However, when the few studies reported during the 1970s are compared to the single study reported during the 1960s, an increase of only a few percentage points is found for both sexes. . . .

There is general agreement that almost all adolescents have participated in dating at least once by the time they are 18–19 years of age.

By that age the cumulative percentages range from 77% to 100% and there is relatively little difference between males and females. What little data is available indicates that by age 14–15 roughly half of the adolescents have dated. . . .

II. *Kissing*

From the studies in the 1970s it can be speculated that there has been a slight increase (approximately 10%) for males engaged in kissing since the 1940s. There is no data on females during the previous three decades but the 1970 data suggest that the onset of experience of females is practically identical to that of males. . . . Heterosexual kissing by middle adolescence is a nearly universal phenomenon and there are few differences between males and females, blacks and whites. There is a suggestion that both black and white male homosexuals report a much lower percentage of heterosexual kissing than any other sample.

III. *Petting*

The act of petting has often been divided into "light" petting which is typically restricted to those activities above the waist and "heavy" petting which involves genital contact but not sexual intercourse. From age 16 to 19, no differences have been found in the amount of light petting reported by both sexes over the past 30 years. At age 14, however, in more recent studies there is evidence to suggest that both males and females are beginning their involvement at an earlier age. This is especially evident for females who report an increase of approximately 40% over their 1940 counterparts. The overall data for the studies indicates that approximately 60% have engaged in light petting by the age of 15, whereas about half that percentage have been involved in heavy petting. By age 18–19 nearly 90% of the males and 80% of the females reported light petting. For heavy petting there are important but gradual increases over time in the reported experience for both sexes at each age level. At age 14, the 1970s male and female samples reported an increase over the 1940 samples of 68% and 83% respectively.

IV. *Masturbation*

Overall there appears to be no marked changes in the reported practice of masturbation during the past 30 years for either sex. There is some suggestion, however, that more females are gradually beginning to engage in masturbation by age 18. . . . The data indicate that almost all males have masturbated to orgasm during their teens. Even with the old myths surrounding the feared consequences of masturbation, e.g., acne, mental retardation, insanity, weak heart, etc., there appears to be little behavioral inhibition of this behavior. Nearly 80% of the males sampled have engaged in masturbation by age 14, with an increase throughout the later adolescent years to where 90–98% report the experience by age 18. . . .

V. *Pre-marital coitus*

A great deal has been written during the past decade or so about a kind of "sexual revolution." While it may be true that attitudes and an openness to talk about sexual behaviors have occurred, there is little evidence of any sudden massive change in adolescent sexual behavior in terms of pre-marital coitus. The data indicate that while males have remained fairly stable, females have gradually increased their pre-marital involvement and have begun to close the gap between the sexes. . . .

The 1970 studies indicate that male involvement has not markedly changed since the 1940 data. For females, however, there has been a gradual and significant increase in reported pre-marital coitus over the past 30 years. By age 19, the 1940 data indicated that more males engaged in pre-marital coitus at a ratio better than 3:1 over the females. In the 1970s, however, the females are 1:1 with the males from age 16 on up. At age 15, the 1970 data show a 500% increase in engagement compared to their 1940 counterparts, and a 300% increment at age 18. For both sexes, the incidence of pre-marital coitus doubled between the ages of 17 and 18. (Diepold and Young 1979, 49–63)

QUESTION: Has a sexual revolution occurred?

Sexual behavior motivation

The empirical studies reviewed in the Kantner and Zelnik (1972) report suggest that during the last thirty to forty years a gradual change has occurred in the evolution of adolescent sexual behavior. Evidence suggests that a greater percentage of adolescents are engaging in more sexual practices and perhaps beginning them somewhat earlier than in past decades. Still the relative stability of these behaviors over several generations for males is significant. As reflected in the available literature, support for the notion of a sexual revolution is weak, at least regarding reported sexual practices. In another review of surveys (between 1930 and 1970), however, Hopkins (1977) noted a significant liberalization in adolescent sexual behavior. The apparent trend is toward earlier sexual experience for both males and females. Further, more adolescents are sexually experienced than in earlier generations, and the incidence of premarital intercourse for females has rapidly increased. Perhaps attitudes and willingness to openly discuss sexual behavior have shifted radically, and future research will reveal a corresponding but delayed effect in sexual practices (Kantner and Zelnik 1972a, 1972b, 61–62). Consider the following account of sexual behavior in a large Arizona high school. While reading this account, the reader should ask how general are the observations of the review of sexual behavior.

The perceptions of the norms of this particular high school came from two individuals—a male who graduated in 1976 and a female who graduated in 1977. As summarized, both were in positions favorable to a general knowledge of "what was going on." The male was a football star and the homecoming king, and the female was a cheerleader.

> In this particular high school most of the student body identified themselves informally with one of four groups: the "hicks" (cowboys), the "burnouts" (drug users), the "high-rollers" (upper-middle class to wealthy), and the "jocks" (athletes).
>
> The "jocks" were probably the most sexually experienced group and of course the group with which he was most familiar. The "high-rollers" were the next most experienced group. Actually many of the "jocks" were "high-rollers" also.
>
> It was a status symbol to be able to talk about their "conquests" in the halls and locker rooms. They were often very crude. More guys than girls seemed to be experienced and had a greater number of partners.
>
> It seemed that the sexual experience of the males had little to do with how good looking they were, but might have had something to do with how popular and outgoing they were. This perception could have been due to the fact that outgoing males talk more about their sexual experience.

The girls who were generally "loose" were well-known and had several distinguishing characteristics. These girls were differentiated from steady girl friends who had sex only within that one "meaningful" relationship. The blatantly wild girls were not always good looking and were often taken out (dated) by the guys for the sole purpose of getting sex. These girls were often talked and joked about among the guys. The subject could easily identify these "easy" girls by their appearance and manner. How they dressed was a good indication, but perhaps the most distinguishing factor was the amount of make-up they wore—especially around the eyes. The way they walked and carried themselves also served as a come-on, as the guys paid more attention to the girl's bodily form than her face and hair.

Many of the guys *expected* sex after a number of dates. There was never any talk about pleasing the girl in any way. The guys seemed to have more of a selfish machismo attitude. It's very interesting that the respondent never heard any talk among the guys about birth control. The possibility of getting a girl pregnant wasn't an overriding concern and any preventive measures were probably left up to the girl.

The female respondent had a slightly different perspective but her overall description was compatible with that of the male respondent. She believed that:

> The "high-rollers" were the most sexually experienced with almost all the girls that were socially popular engaging in coitus between their junior and senior years. The "burnouts" were younger at their first experience. This could be because sexual activity was always associated with drinking and often with marijuana.
>
> There was a definite status attributed to being experienced and few of them wished to graduate as a virgin. They felt like they were missing out. It was "the thing to do" and was associated, not only with popularity, but also with adulthood. Most of those who were inexperienced were so more because of lack of opportunity and possibily fear than because of moral values.
>
> It seems that the girls were much more likely than the guys to have had only one partner and that partner was usually a "steady" date. Being "in love" with the guy was an important prerequisite attaining the highest status for experience. It also seemed to make a difference how popular the guy was.
>
> Another indication that sex was associated with social acceptability was that sexual activity was the expected norm on prom night—the biggest social event of the year.
>
> Understandably, the girls were very concerned about getting pregnant. The majority of the girls that were sexually active used the pill for its effectiveness, convenience and inconspicuousness (both to their parents and to their boyfriends). Many did take their chances, however, and there were a few pregnancies. Among their friends, the pill was openly discussed and it was a popular thing for the girls to gather around and talk about the side effects they were experiencing from the pill. (Jensen 1984)

Caution is urged in drawing conclusions from this account because it represents only the perceptions of observers. It is presented to illustrate the centrality of sexual issues in the day-to-day life of many adolescents. The prevalence of sexual activity is better estimated in reports such as the one answering the following questions.

QUESTION: Are indications of a sexual revolution primarily among females?

Judging by the data reported by Diepold and Young (1979), no large changes have occurred in sexual frequency or type of activity among males. If a sexual revolution has taken place, it has basically been one of popular acceptance of sexuality and of changed behavior patterns among females. A review of the studies shows that females have primarily increased their premarital coital experience. Some evidence also suggests that the age at which sexual experience is gained is earlier than in previous years.

The sexual revolution is primarily among females. The revolution, however, is not as great as might be expected regarding conventional beliefs about sexual behavior. The Miller and Simon review article concludes:

> The studies we have discussed are exceptionally competent, reflecting the lessons of the past. Nevertheless, they necessarily provide a limited basis for evaluating sexual standards among contemporary adolescents. The data do provide some support for our earlier claim that adolescents continue to hold traditional meanings where the sexual is concerned. Strong correlations between coital experience and other forms of deviant behavior (e.g., drug use, general delinquency, etc.) are important in each study. Moreover, adolescents who have engaged in (or are about to engage in) coitus are more likely to be estranged from those institutions—the family, the church, the school—that serve to monitor and maintain commitments to conventional values. Thus

Religion can have a strong impact on adolescents' sexual behavior.

sexual experimentation during adolescence apparently continues to be imbedded in the social context of deviance. (Miller and Simon 1980, 398)

For this author, these reviews of adolescent behavior are complex enough to warrant general concern about drawing hard and fast generalizations. Overall, the appearance is that the sexual revolution is primarily among young women. Also sex is generally more visible today, and perhaps the so-called sexual revolution is primarily a more public acceptance of the visibility of sexual attitudes rather than a change in actual beliefs or values. One study of two hundred undergraduate students at the University of Arkansas (Medora and Burton 1981) focused on the acceptance of traditional sexual attitudes toward extramarital sex. In this study, both being religious and being a female were associated with less acceptance of extramarital sex. Table 9–3 displays the gender differences found, and Table 9–4 displays the religious orientation differences.

QUESTION: What is the relationship between religiosity and premarital sexual activity?

Studies have established that a strong, negative relationship exists between religiosity and sexual activity prior to marriage. Thomas (1973) found a relationship between frequency of church attendance and premarital sexuality in college students. Two-thirds of those who attended church at least once a week reported

TABLE 9–3 Gender Differences Regarding the Acceptance of Extramarital Sex

Groups	Yes	No	Totals
Males	39	61	100
Females	22	78	100
Totals	61	139	200

$x^2 = 6.81$
Chi square differences significant at .01 level.

Source: N. P. Medora and M. M. Burton, "Extramarital Sexual Attitudes and Norms of an Undergraduate Student Population," *Adolescence* 16(62): 256 (Summer 1981).

TABLE 9–4 Relationship Between Frequency of Church Attendance and Extramarital Sexual Permissiveness

Frequency of Church Attendance	Extramarital Sex Permissible Yes	No	Totals
Once a week	8	49	57
Once in two weeks	8	23	31
Once a month	13	35	48
Less than once a month	13	15	28
No church attendance	19	17	36
Totals	61	139	200

$x^2 = 17.13$
Chi square differences significant at .01 level.

Source: N. P. Medora and M. M. Burton, "Extramarital Sexual Attitudes and Norms of an Undergraduate Student Population," *Adolescence* 16(62): 259 (Summer 1981).

they had no sexual intercourse during the preceding year. Only 9.4 percent of students who had had intercourse weekly within the past year attended church weekly, while 80.8 percent never or rarely attended church.

Results of a survey by Zelnik, Kantner, and Ford (1981) measured religiosity of females between the ages of fifteen and nineteen in association with sexual activeness. Fourteen percent in 1971 and 17.4 percent in 1976 of those who indicated high religiosity were sexually experienced. Thirty-seven percent in 1971 and 52.2 percent in 1976 of those who indicated low religiosity were sexually experienced.

These and other studies (Sorenson 1972; Jessor and Jessor 1974, 1975, 1977; Rohrbaugh and Jessor 1975; Schulz et al. 1977; Mahoney 1980) support the conclusion that religiosity is a powerful influence upon premarital sexual behavior among adolescents.

QUESTION: Do parents influence the adolescent's outlook on sexual behavior?

As children progress from childhood through adolescence, a gradual change in attitude generally occurs toward who has the greatest influence on their values and behavior. Young children tend to espouse their parents' ideas, while adolescents move toward the values of their peers. Nevertheless, youth reflect their parents' views to differing degrees. The general consensus of the current research on the subject is that peers are more favorable toward sexual permissiveness than are parents.

Shah and Zelnik (1981) studied this parent and peer influence using a measure based on the subjects' perceptions of similarity of views on sex. A sample of about 2,200 women age fifteen to nineteen was used. The results of the study suggest that many youth are subject to opposing forces as the values of their friends and parents conflict. See Table 9–5.

The actual sexual experience of the subjects seemed to be relatively consistent with their reported opinions. The incidences of premarital sex were lowest for

TABLE 9–5 Percentage Distribution of Sexually Experienced 15–19-Year-Old Women, by Number of Partners Ever and by Similarity of Views on Sex to Significant Others, by Race

Number of Partners	Black Parents	Black Friends	Black Both	Black Neither	White Parents	White Friends	White Both	White Neither
1	43.1	41.3	51.2	42.2	72.9	55.7	55.7	69.6
2–3	43.1	43.3	36.6	33.7	20.8	26.8	16.4	19.6
4–5	7.8	10.4	9.8	15.2	4.2	8.2	14.8	3.9
6+	5.9	5.0	2.4	8.7	2.1	9.3	13.1	6.9
N	51	240	41	92	48	343	61	102

Source: R. Shah and M. Zelnik, "Parent and Peer Influence on Sexual Behavior, Contraceptive Use, and Pregnancy Experience of Young Women," *Journal of Marriage and the Family*: 343 (May 1981).

Note: Copyright © 1981 by the National Council on Family Relations, 1219 University Avenue Southeast, Minneapolis, Minnesota 55414. Reprinted by permission.

women with views like their parents and highest for those whose views were like their peers. The median age of first sexual experience was found to be age sixteen.

Friends and parents also affected the subjects' use of contraception. Subjects with views like their parents were more likely to have never used contraception. Those influenced by their peers were more likely to take chances; they also had intercourse with greater frequency and with a greater number of partners.

Women with values like their parents, who disapprove of premarital sex and who had had intercourse but had never used contraception, might have foregone contraception to minimize the apparent incongruity between their actions and their professed values. In this way, they tended to deny their sexual activity or at least deny forethought. Women with views like their parents, however, still have the lowest rate of premarital pregnancy because they have the lowest rate of unprotected intercourse. The pregnancy rate for women more influenced by friends is four times higher than the rate for those influenced by parents.

The proportion of sexually experienced subjects tended to increase with age. For women with more conservative parental views, however, this increase peaked at age seventeen and then declined markedly at age nineteen. Zelnik and Shah concluded that the relationships between parents and peer influence and sexual behavior is also independent of marital status, socioeconomic status, and family stability. These general findings were also reported in the Jessor et al. studies (1983, 624).

QUESTION: What is the role of peers in influencing sexual behavior?

The peer group has a strong influence on adolescent behavior. This influence holds true for sexual behavior as well, as shown by research. In a study of freshman and senior college students, Schulz et al. (1977) found that each friend, out of five, who is perceived to have had sexual intercourse increases a person's own likelihood of premarital coitus by about 12 percent. Those who perceived none of their friends as having had premarital intercourse had only a 20 percent incidence of sexual activity. Over 85 percent incidence, however, was found among those who perceived all five of their best friends to be sexually active.

DeLamater and MacCorquodale (1979) discovered that the variable that most correlated with sexual behavior of adolescents was friends' behavior. Mirande (1968) had similar findings. Jessor and Jessor (1977) offer data indicating that one variable strongly predictive of the transition into sexual activity among adolescents is the sexual activeness of the adolescent's peer group.

Schulz et al. (1977) found that adolescents tend to choose as friends and associates those whose sexual behavior is in accord with their religious values. The more religious the students, the less likely they will choose sexually permissive friends. Glass (1972) studied the premarital sexual standards of high school adolescents who were youth leaders in the United Methodist Church. Eighty percent were against premarital sexual intercourse, and 93 percent of these youth perceived their standards to be similar to those of their friends. Such a conservative standard, however, does not hold true for more general adolescent populations, as indicated in other studies. Data provided by Rohrbaugh and Jessor (1975) support this idea. Highly religious adolescents reported that their peers held stricter standards and were less involved in problem behavior than the peers of less religious adolescents.

Sex roles

The role of church, family, and peers influences not only sexual behavior and attitudes but also sexual identity. The general term for this learned cultural response pattern styled to one's self-concept is called "sex roles."

In spite of rapid and continuous changes in society, an adolescent's sex plays a leading role in producing a myriad of attitudes, perceptions, and behaviors. As a springboard to further inquiry, consider the following individuals' recollections:

> As I look at myself and analyze some ways in which my sex-role identity has been modeled throughout my life, two experiences come to mind.
>
> The first deals with the fact that I'm not a fighter physically. Though I think I'm in quite good shape, when I get wrestling around with someone, I'm almost always the weaker one—the one who ends up getting hurt or losing. In looking at my past I remember my Dad referring to me as "fragile Jeanette." He'd treat me more gently than he did my brothers and maybe was even more careful with me than with my sisters. When we'd get wrestling around he'd often say "watch out for Jeanette; she's fragile." I'm not sure if this was because I tended to "get hurt" and cry easily in the past or if because of him reinforcing this fragility in me, I never felt the need to be able to physically fight back.
>
> The second experience took place when I was in the fourth grade. My younger brother and I were playing in the woods with a couple of his friends in their "fort." After playing, we came inside and my brother and his friends began telling my Mom what we had been doing. They told her that no girls were allowed to play in it except for me. A few minutes later the boys wanted to go back outside and wanted me to come. However, my Mom said no, that she needed me to stay and help her with dinner. I remember my impression was that she didn't approve of me tomboying around with my brother and his friends. In a very mild and unforceful way, she did not reinforce this masculine behavior and at the same time did reinforce feminine behavior by having me help with dinner.

Another student reported:

> One day in seventh grade, I was talking with a friend and happened to cross my legs at the knee. As soon as I did, he decisively informed me in no uncertain terms that only girls and sissies crossed their legs like that—something I had never heard before. Stunned by his remark and determined to be a "boy," I promised myself I'd never do it again. Some fifteen years have come and gone since then and to this day, I either cross my legs at the ankles, with one ankle on the other knee, or not at all.

As the previous examples illustrate, sex roles affect a wide range of important behaviors and attitudes. Before examining these effects more closely, however, we will examine their origin, emergence, and development.

QUESTION: How do sex roles develop?

Research from a number of experiments has established that sex role development begins shortly after birth and continues through an individual's life. Although research shows that some sex role behaviors, such as aggressiveness, may be inherited, others are influenced by the way a child is treated (Maccoby and Jacklin 1974). For instance, parents play with and treat infant girls more gently than they do with boys. Girls receive dolls; boys get toy trucks. Boys tend to receive more mobility at an earlier age than do girls. A common parental correction to a girl is, "Girls don't fight"; to a boy it is, "Boys don't cry." Boys do the outdoor work; girls perform inside, "domestic" chores (Hoffman 1977; Wilson et al. 1977; Coon 1983).

Given this background, the question inevitably arises, Are sex roles innate or learned? Research seems to indicate that the answer is somewhere in between. Although innate differences exist, they can be enhanced or diminished according to an individual's conditioning.

QUESTION: What personality characteristics are associated with each sex role?

Sandra Bem of Stanford University has constructed a list of behaviors that are considered masculine, feminine, or neutral (Bem 1974, 1975a, 1975b, 1977). Sample items reflecting masculine, feminine, and neutral elements of personality are listed in Table 9–6.

A person with large numbers of both masculine and feminine behaviors is considered androgynous. Simple examples of androgynous people are the man who does not mind changing a dirty diaper or cooking dinner when necessary, and the women who feels comfortable with mathematics or changing a flat tire.

QUESTION: What is androgyny?

Androgyny is defined as attitudes and behaviors that are not solely masculine or feminine but are both masculine and feminine (Fovisha 1978). People are considered androgynous to the degree that they perform roles that society has traditionally assigned their sex, but also roles assigned to the opposite sex.

Androgyny is a learned behavior (Thornsburg 1982). Adolescents' upbringing and exposure or lack of exposure to opposite sex roles and characteristics heavily influence their ability to become androgynous, not only in career decisions and work opportunities but also in other areas, as one student's thoughts suggest:

> As an adolescent I wanted my parents to be more androgynous. My mother and father each assumed very traditional roles as parents. My mother was

TABLE 9-6 Some Masculine, Feminine, and Neutral Items from the BSRI*

Masculine Items	Feminine Items	Neutral Items
Aggressive	Affectionate	Adaptable
Ambitious	Cheerful	Conceited
Analytical	Childlike	Conscientious
Assertive	Compassionate	Conventional
Athletic	Does not use harsh language	Friendly

*Bem Sex Role Inventory

responsible for all the feminine roles such as cooking, housework, and emotional expression. My father had typical male roles with no expression of feelings or emotions. Any emotion he expressed was a mood rather than an intimate feeling he had. Love was even difficult for him to express.

Anytime my father was responsible to cook or clean house, I was anxious for my mother to take over. He was very awkward in "feminine" roles. I don't think that was due to his philosophy on parenting, nor social mores he received. That is the way he was raised, and although he does not like it, much of it has passed on to him through his father's example.

Many times I sense that he would like to share his emotions with me, but feels uneasy or embarrassed. Although I'm an adult now it continues in our relationship to some degree.

While growing up I liked the male/female uniqueness in my parents. However, as far as feelings and emotions I wanted my parents to be androgynous. I have seen many families with semi-androgynous parents and it seems to be very healthy.

When I got married I wanted to be as androgynous as possible. I did dishes, housework, cooked, and tried to openly express my emotions. It is difficult. It is hard to share emotions with my wife, and even my infant son. I've learned that when I do dishes, laundry and housework I still do it with an attitude of "I did a favor for you honey and did *your* dishes." Recently, I've noticed that I have still clung to traditional sex roles in marriage.

The concept of androgyny states that although inherent biological and emotional differences do exist between men and women, people who avoid extreme role polarization and who feel comfortable performing various roles of both sexes have a fuller, more rewarding life without giving up their innate masculinity or femininity (Bem 1975a, 1975b; Wells 1980).

QUESTION: Should a person try to become androgynous?

Bem and others believe that the more androgynous people become, the freer

Which characteristics exhibited by the women in these two photos would be considered androgynous and which would be considered traditional?

and more adaptable they feel. It is clear that Bem thinks androgynous people are freer, more adaptable, and more emotionally healthy than those maintaining traditional sex roles. Many people, some psychologists included, disagree (Coon 1983, 433). Some believe that androgyny has both positive and negative aspects or connotations.

QUESTION: As sex roles change and overlap, are there any negative aspects of becoming androgynous?

Perhaps the most prominent negative aspect involves the uncertainty of behavior that may come as an individual assumes a role traditionally ascribed to the other sex. This is particularly true when outside permission to assume that role is required. Many classic examples can be found in the business world, where legislation has supposedly opened all occupations to either sex and has forbidden discrimination therein. As an adolescent works in a nontraditional occupation, the question may arise, "Was I hired because I'm the best they could hire or because the law required them to?" Instead of greater opportunities for growth and fulfillment, adolescents may experience the opposite as doubts and uncertainty cloud their self-perception. Consequently, attempts to assume sex roles traditionally ascribed to the opposite sex, although an expanding, enlightening, and usually more fulfilling experience, are not without potential liabilities. The following description is from one student who is still struggling to successfully assume a more nontraditional sex role:

> As a child there were many forces which influenced my assimilation of the male role. First of all I realized as I was taught by my parents that I was a boy and that boys differed from girls. Although I didn't understand really how or why, I know that the difference existed. My father and older brother provided me with models of what males were to be.
>
> As I entered the peer oriented society of the schoolroom, I was bombarded with males and females who expected me to behave in a prescribed manner. I was to play boys' games at recess. I was to act tough like the other boys and to shy away from girls and girl activities. The peer group exhibited great pressure to conform to the particular role. Much of the group's acceptance was based upon successfully meeting role requirements. Athletics became an even more important avenue for proving or exhibiting one's masculinity. Those who were good at athletics were accepted as truly a good example of what a man is like. I was therefore channeled down the path of athletics because I was successful at it which consequently brought peer group reinforcement of my sex role. Thus through many different forces, I became socialized into the masculine sex role.

Since World War II, changes in sex role behavior have occurred in an unprecedented manner in the United States. Almost all behavioral scientists and social critics have welcomed the change, but the long-term effects will require a historical perspective as they interact with other social changes. Changing economic conditions have caused the stability and predictability associated with traditional sex roles to collide with the opportunity for more personal freedom and equality, especially as articulated by the women's movement of the 1970s. As noted, these changes in sex roles have been reflected most prominently in the behaviors and attitudes of women. Betty Friedan (1983), an acclaimed leader of the women's movement, now believes the second phase of the women's movement will need to include changes in men and traditional social institutions.

Conclusions

Acquaintance with the general research findings presented in this chapter may raise more questions than answers. The primary variables determining adolescent sexual behavior can, however, be identified as parents, religion, peers, and social expectations. Observations of the general culture media lead one to conclude that sexuality is highly visible in modern society, yet a review of sexual behavior does not support the belief that a large-scale sexual revolution has occurred for men. The sexual revolution has calmly taken place for women. Since sexual behavior is almost always a cooperative venture between the two sexes, future research should reveal the interaction between women's sexual revolution and males' sexual behavior. The increased visibility, salience, and openness of sexuality in today's culture should have a behavioral impact if the theories purporting a strong sociocultural emphasis are true.

Summary

Psychological and adjustment problems are associated with the powerful emotions of sex, love, and romance for adolescents encountering these emotions for the first time. This is particularly true for teenage boys, who generally find it difficult to admit to themselves or others that they are in love because of the apparent need to be manly and to be in control. Present society fails to prepare boys to freely accept and experience feelings of love, caring, and tenderness.

To understand love, distinguishing between liking and loving, as well as recognizing that some people place more value on the experience of love than do others. Romantics strongly believe in love and support statements such as, "People should marry whomever they love, regardless of social position." Nonromantics are more practical people and consider factors such as compatibility, personality, and economic security to be more important than love. Research tends to support that men are more romantic than women, but that women feel and display the emotions of romance more dramatically and intensely than do men.

Although the adolescent in love experiences emotions just as strong and real as the adult, the love may be less rational and logical. Regardless of the judgment that parents place on adolescent love, for youth the experience is valid, important, and real. The youth's perception should therefore be considered the important element in making decisions about a young person's feelings of love.

The societal activity of expressing love during adolescence is called dating. The social custom of dating is a significant event in the life of adolescents and can influence many of their other relationships. Dating can provide wholesome social interaction, can be either a positive or a negative experience, and can affect adolescents self-image and their relationships with peers and with parents.

One author gives seven reasons why adolescents date: recreation; companionship without the responsibility of marriage; status grading and achievement;

socialization; sexual exploration, satisfaction, or exploitation; mate selection or sorting; and achieving intimacy. Dating is fun as well as a learning experience. The specific ages for dating will vary depending on social class, racial background, and geographical area, but most adolescents apparently begin dating during their midteens or earlier.

Sexual maturation adds little to the onset and frequency of dating. Social pressures determine the onset of dating; individual biological maturation has little impact.

The easiest way to explain sexual development is to assume a biological explanation. Sexual behavior is due to biochemical processes within the body that accelerate during puberty and cause the individual to become more sexual. Hereditary mechanisms determine the expression of sexuality. To provide an adequate understanding of sexual development during adolescence, however, including sociocultural variables is important.

Researchers have found that the amount of sexual motivation is influenced by social factors. Development of early sexuality is related to personality system variables such as high value on independence, low value on academic achievement, tolerance of deviance, and less religiosity. In the environmental system, early sexuality is linked to less compatibility between parents and friends, less parental influence, more peer influence, and less involvement in conventional behavior. A main factor that influences development of sexuality in adolescents is gender role expectations.

In reported sexual practices, support for the notion of a sexual revolution among males is weak. Perhaps attitudes and willingness to openly discuss sexual behavior have shifted radically, and future research will reveal a corresponding but delayed effect in sexual practices. If a sexual revolution has taken place, it has basically been one of popular acceptance of sexuality and of changed behavior patterns among females. Females have primarily increased in premarital coital experience, and this experience is gained earlier than in previous years.

Researchers have found that religiosity is a powerful influence upon premarital sexual behavior of adolescents. Religiosity acts as a direct control against premarital sex. Adolescents tend to choose as friends and associates those whose sexual behavior is in accord with their parental and religious beliefs.

Changes in sexuality are perhaps most pronounced in the area of sex roles. Today, traditional gender-stereotyped behaviors are not encouraged or as common as before. Androgyny is the term used to describe people who accept behaviors and attitudes associated with both sexes.

References

Beach, F. A. 1956. Characteristics of masculine "sex drive." In *Nebraska symposium on motivation*, ed. R. Jones, 1–32. Lincoln: Univ. of Nebraska Press.

Bell, A., M. S. Weinberg, & S. Hammersmith. In progress. *Sexual orientation: Its multiple routes origins* (tentative title).

Bem, S. L. 1974. The measurement of psychological androgyny. *Journal of Consulting and Clinical Psychology* 42: 155–62.

_____. 1975a. Androgyny vs. the tight little lives of fluffy women and chesty men. *Psychology Today*: 58–62 (September).

_____. 1975b. Sex role adaptability: One consequence of psychological androgyny. *Journal of Personality and Social Psychology* 4: 634–43.

———. 1977. Psychological androgyny. In *Beyond sex roles,* ed. A. G. Sargent, 322. St. Paul: West Publishing.
Broderick, C. B. 1969. Normal social, sexual development. In *The individual sex and society,* ed. C. B. Bernard & J. Bernard. Baltimore: Johns Hopkins Univ. Press.
Byrne, D. 1977. Social psychology and the study of social psychology. *Personality and Social Psychology Bulletin,* 3: 3–30.
Coon, D. 1983. *Introduction to psychology.* 3d ed. St. Paul: West Publishing.
Cox, F. D. 1974. *Youth, marriage and the seductive society.* Dubuque, Iowa: Brown.
DeLamater, J., & P. MacCorquodale. 1979. *Premarital sexuality: Attitudes, relationships, behavior.* Madison, Wis.: Univ. of Wisconsin Press.
Diepold, J., Jr., & R. D. Young, Ph.D. 1979. Empirical studies of adolescent sexual behavior: A critical review. *Adolescence* 14(53): 45–61.
Dornsbusch, S., J. Caulsmith, R. Gross, J. Martin, P. Jennings, A. Rosenberg, & P. Duke. 1981. Sexual development, age, and dating: A comparison of biological and social influences upon one set of behaviors. *Child Development* 52: 179–85.
Douvan, E., & J. Adelson. 1966. *The adolescent experience.* New York: Wiley.
Elliot, L. 1983. Dating interview. Personal communication with author, Provo, Utah.
Fernstein, S. C., & M. S. Hardon. 1979. Trends in dating patterns and adolescent development. *Journal of Youth and Adolescence* 7: 157–66.
Fovisha, B. L. 1978. *Sex roles and personal awareness.* Morristown, N. J.: General Learning Press.
Friedan, B. 1981. *The second stage.* New York: Summit.
Glass, J. C., Jr. 1972. Premarital sexual standards among church youth leaders: An exploratory study. *Journal for the Scientific Study of Religion* 11(4): 361–67.
Goodman, E. 1983. How a boy feels when he's in love. *Seventeen,* May, 14–18.
Griffitt, W. 1973. Response to erotica and the projection of response to erotica in the opposite sex. *Journal of Experimental Research in Personality* 6: 330–38.
———. 1975. Sexual experience and sexual responsiveness: Sex differences. *Archives of Sexual Behavior* 4: 529–50.
Griffitt, W., J. May, & R. Veitch. 1974. Sexual stimulation and interpersonal behavior: Heterosexual evaluative responses, visual behavior and physical proximity. *Journal of Personality and Social Psychology* 30: 367–77.
Grinder, R. E. 1966. Relations of social dating attractions to academic orientation and peer relations. *Journal of Educational Psychology* 57: 27–34.
Hall, G. S. 1905. *Adolescence,* vol. I. New York: Appleton-Century-Crofts. Cited in Rogers, D. 1981. *Adolescence and youth.* New York: Prentice-Hall.
Hall, O. L., & N. N. Eagner. Initial heterosexual experience in Sweden and in the United States: A cross-cultural survey. *Proceedings of the 80th Annual Convention of the APA* 7: 298–394.
Hardy, K. 1964. An appititional theory of sexual motivation. *Psychological Review* 71(1): 1–18.
Hill, C. T., Z. Rubin, & A. Peplan. 1976. Breakups before marriage: The end of 103 affairs, ed. O. Moles & G. Levinger. *Journal of Social Issues* 32(1): 1997–2167.
Hobart, C. W. 1958. The incidence of romanticism during courtship. *Social Forces* 36: 364.
Hoffman, L. W. 1977. Changes in family roles, socialization and sex differences. *American Psychologist* 32: 644–57.
Hopkins, J. R. 1977. Sexual behavior in adolescence. *Journal of Social Issues* 33(2): 67–85.
Jensen, L. 1984. Report given to author as part of a survey of case studies of sexual balances.
Jessor, R., F. Costa, L. Jessor, & J. Donovan. 1983. Time of first intercourse: A perspective study. *Journal of Personality and Social Psychology* 43(3): 608–26.
Jessor, S. L., & R. Jessor. 1974. Maternal ideology and adolescent problem behavior. *Developmental Psychology* 10(2): 246–54.
———. 1975. Transition from virginity to nonvirginity among youth: A social-psychological study over time. *Developmental Psychology* 11: 473–84.
———. 1977. *Problem behavior and psychosocial development: A longitudinal study of youth.* New York: Academic Press.
Kamin, E. J., K. D. Davidson, & S. A. Scheck. 1970. A research note on male-female differentiates in the experience of heterosexual love. *Journal of Sex Research* 6: 49–72.

Kantner, J. F., & M. Zelnik. 1972a. Sexual experiences of young unmarried women in the United States. *Family Planning Perspectives* 4: 9–18.

———. 1972b. Sexuality, contraception, and pregnancy among pre-adult females in the United States. *Demographic and social aspects of population growth.* Commission on Population Growth and the American Future. Washington, D.C.: U.S. Government Printing Office.

Kinsey, A. C., W. B. Pomeroy, & C. E. Martin. 1948. *Sexual behavior in the human male.* Philadelphia: Saunders.

Maccoby, E. E., & E. Jacklin. 1974. *The psychology of sex differences.* Stanford, Calif.: Stanford Univ. Press.

Mahoney, E. R. 1980. Religiosity and sexual behavior among heterosexual college students. *Journal of Sex Research* 16(1): 97–113.

McCabe, M. P., & J. K. Collins. 1979. Sex role and dating orientation. *Journal of Youth and Adolescence* 8(4): 407–23.

McCandless, B. 1970. *Adolescence: Behavior and development.* New York: Holt, Rinehart & Winston.

Medora, N. P., & M. M. Burton. 1981. Extramarital sexual attitudes and norms of an undergraduate student population. *Adolescence* 16(62): 252–59 (Summer).

Miller, D. 1974. *Adolescence: Psychology, psychopathology and psychotherapy.* New York: Aronson.

Miller, P., & W. Simon. 1980. The development of sexuality in adolescence. In *The handbook of adolescent psychology,* ed. J. Adelson. New York: Wiley.

Mirande, A. M. 1968. Reference group theory and adolescent sexual behavior. *Journal of Marriage and the Family* 30: 572–77.

Mosher, D. L. 1966. The development and multitrait-multimethod matrix analysis of three measures of three aspects of guilt. *Journal of Consulting Psychology* 30: 25–29.

Newsweek. 1980. The science of love. 25 February, 89.

Rachman, S. 1966. Sexual fetishism: An experimental analogue. *Psychological Record* 16: 293–96.

Rice, P. 1981. *The adolescent.* Boston: Allyn & Bacon.

Rohrbaugh, J., & R. Jessor. 1975. Religiosity in youth: A personal control against deviant behavior. *Journal of Personality* 43(1): 136–55.

Rubin, Z. 1973. *Liking and loving.* New York: Holt, Rinehart & Winston.

Schulz, B., G. W. Bohrnstedt, E. F. Borgatta, & R. R. Evans. 1977. Explaining premarital sexual intercourse among college students: A causal model. *Social Forces* 56(1): 148–65.

Shah, R., & M. Zelnik. 1981. Parent and peer influence on sexual behavior, contraceptive use, and pregnancy experience of young women. *Journal of Marriage and the Family* :339–48 (May).

Sorenson, R. C. 1973. *Adolescent sexuality in contemporary America.* New York: World Publishing.

Spence, J. T., & R. L. Helmreich. 1972. Who likes competent women? Competence, sex-role congruence of interest, and subjects' attitudes toward women as determinants of interpersonal attraction. *Journal of Applied Social Psychology* 2: 197–213.

———. 1978. *Masculinity and femininity: Their psychological dimensions, correlations, and antecedents.* Austin: Univ. of Texas Press.

Thomas, L. 1973. The relationship between premarital sexual behavior and certain personal and religious background factors of a sample of university students. *American College Health Association Journal* 21(5): 460–64.

Thornburg, H. D. 1982. *Development in adolescence.* Monterey, Calif.: Brooks/Cole.

Walster, E., & G. Walster. 1978. *A new look at love.* Reading, Mass.: Addison-Wesley.

Wells, K. 1980. Gender role identity and psychological adjustment in adolescence. *Journal of Youth and Adolescence* 9: 59–73.

Wilson, S., B. Strong, L. M. Clarke, & J. Thomas. 1977. *Human sexuality.* St. Paul: West Publishing.

Wright, L. S. 1982. Parental permission to date and its relation to drug use and suicidal thoughts among adolescents. *Adolescence* 17(66): 409–18.

Zelnik, M., J. F. Kantner, & K. Ford. 1981. *Sex and pregnancy in adolescence.* Beverly Hills, Calif.: Sage.

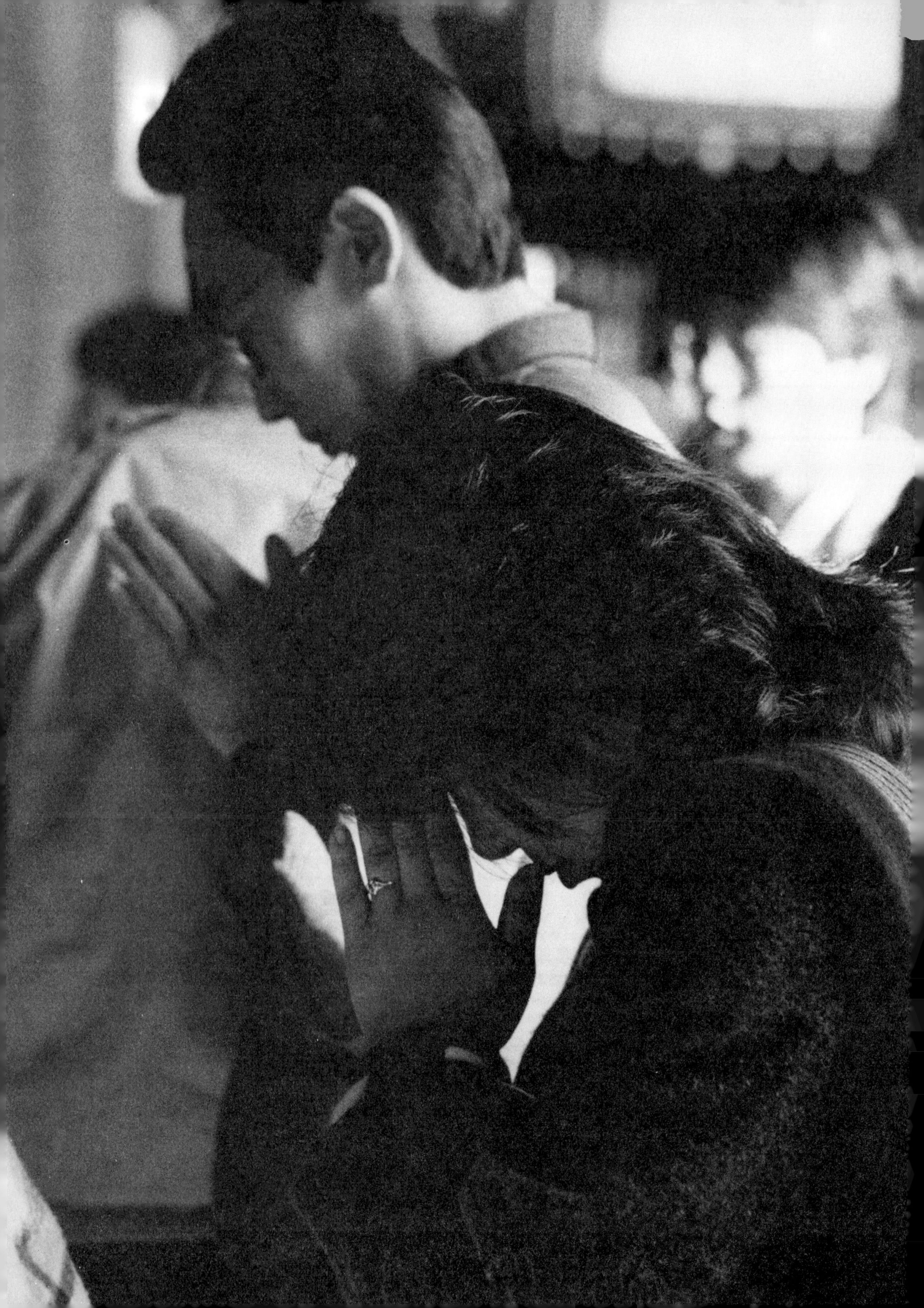

CHAPTER TEN

Morality, values, and religion

SURVEY AND QUESTIONS

This chapter covers the development of moral reasoning and its related theories. It defines values and how they are affected by age, culture, generation, and sex. Religious, parental, and peer influences on moral behavior are also discussed. Reading the chapter will provide answers to the following questions:

Development of Moral Reasoning

According to Piaget, how does one learn about rules?
What are Piaget's two moralities?
What are Kohlberg's six stages of moral development?
Is Kohlberg's theory accurate?
Do the stage theories of moral reasoning have a practical application?
Does having a high level of moral reasoning mean that one has a high level of moral behavior?

Values

How are values measured?
Does an adolescent value system exist?
What differences have been found among the values of younger and older adolescents?
What differences have been found among the values of adolescents from different cultures?
What differences have been found among adolescent values over time and across generations?
Do male and female adolescents have differing values?
Can anything be done to help adolescents acquire positive values?

Moral Behavior

Are there theories that explain moral behavior?
According to Hoffman, what motivates adolescent morality?
Is guilt a strong motivator for moral behavior?
What sort of parental discipline leads to the greatest moral development?
Do peers have a positive or a negative influence on moral development?
How does the self-concept relate to moral behavior?

Religion

Has a movement toward membership in religious cults occurred?
Is religion related to moral behavior?
What are some implications about religion during adolescence?

> You are trapped. Six hundred feet underground in a mine shaft, you and three others are trapped with no food, no blankets, and no communication with the outside. A little water is available, but there is only a limited amount of precious air. The seriousness of the situation is immediately obvious. The time required for rescue operations would be at least seven days, and the available air supply would last all four men only four or five days. Two men would, however, survive on the available air for the time required to be rescued. However, the chances for two men to be rescued diminish each day that all four continue to breathe. If two men are to survive, two men must immediately die.
>
> You know, however, that this is not the full story, because many rescue operations take up to two weeks, some even longer. So even if the two survivors have enough air and water, what about food? With that realization, the thought that should never enter the mind of a civilized person enters yours! Will you be "civilized" when faced with the prospect of starvation?
>
> To alter this situation somewhat, suppose that four men are confined in this underground prison: one is a 35-year-old bachelor; another is a conscientious citizen with a wife and three children, the third is a 23-year-old Nazi party member who is single; and the fourth is a moderately retarded middle-aged man with no family. The issue comes up for a vote: Do you decide to dispose of two men in order that two might live, or do you resolve that you will all die together? If you decide the former, which two shall die? What prospect faces the two survivors if the rescue operation is not complete before starvation sets in? Are they justified in committing cannibalism to maintain life? (Boyce and Jensen 1978, 1)

Moral dilemmas such as these are disturbing, but can result in moral learning. They force us to place ourselves in difficult situations and to examine our thinking. Moral dilemmas force us to analyze what we believe, what we desire, what we are. They force us to ask, Why one decision rather than another? Why do I think that way? Is my moral reasoning justifiable? Am I really moral? The following dialogue concerning the dilemma of the trapped men illustrates this kind of searching:

> A: I think that two of the men should be disposed of to allow at least two to survive.
> B: Why? Isn't it wrong to kill?
> A: Yes, but it's better that only two die rather than all four.
> B: Why?
> A: Because this way, at least two men will be able to go on and enjoy life and be happy. The other way, none of them will be able to.
> B: Does that make it right to kill two people?
> A: Under the circumstances, yes. That way, at least, some good and happiness will result. The other way, none will.
> B: Does the rightness of happiness outweigh the wrongness of killing?
> A: Yes.
> B: Why do you believe that's true?
> A: I don't know exactly. It just seems right. It's got to be right!
> (Boyce and Jensen 1978, 1)

Adolescence is a time when interest in deciding right from wrong is intense. New powers of moral reasoning come into play at this stage. To understand this adolescent moral reasoning, let us discuss the general origins of moral reasoning.

Development of moral reasoning

At present, the most popular theory for explaining moral development is the cognitive developmental approach of Piaget and Kohlberg. Several issues distinguish the cognitive developmental approach from other approaches. To begin, both Piaget and Kohlberg agree that basic mental structure is the result of an interaction between the organism and the outside world, rather then reflecting either one directly. In our culture, the more popular belief is apparently that our moral reasoning is entirely learned from our experience. For Piaget and Kohlberg, however, moral growth is the product of an interaction between innate mental structuring tendencies in the individual and the environment. Cognitive developmentalists also theorize that the individual proceeds through a series of fixed, qualitatively distinct stages of moral development. The high point of development is a universal sense of justice and concern for reciprocity among individuals. Each stage is designed to answer moral questions. Each new stage is a reorganization of the previous stage, but now operates from a new, higher perspective. This includes new criteria for moral evaluation. All individuals in all cultures move through the same stages in the same order, differing only in how quickly or how far they develop.

For a clear understanding of Kohlberg, becoming acquainted with Piaget's ideas is beneficial, although Piaget was basically concerned with children and

Jean Paul Piaget (1896–1980), the French developmentalist who studied the growth of intelligence and the structure of the human mind.

prepuberty. Piaget developed his theory of moral development by studying the attitudes of children toward the origin, legitimacy, and flexibility of rules in the game of marbles. He also studied children's responses to stories by asking the children to judge which of two was worse. Piaget began by studying the rules for playing marbles, because marbles is definitely a social game in which the rules are devised by the children themselves and are not usually imposed upon them by others. Piaget's findings concerning children's use of such rules give a clear picture of his theory for understanding moral development in general.

QUESTION: According to Piaget, how does one learn about rules?

Piaget noted four stages in children's use of rules. In the first stage, children exhibit a lack of organization and direction. They perform a number of different unconnected actions with the marbles. Eventually, children begin to repeat certain acts more frequently than others, producing regularity of behavior. At some point, without any instruction from adults, the marbles become symbols of other events or objects in the child's environment, such as candy, eggs, or automobiles. The development of regularity and symbolism constitutes the first stage of moral development.

Piaget calls the second stage of development, occurring somewhere between three and five years of age, "egocentrism." Children at this stage become aware that the game of marbles has rules, but they do not recognize that other children do not play the game as they play it. Children are basically attempting to imitate adults or other children, but are not interested in noting dissimilarities between their imitations and their actions. No real interaction takes place with other people. Children proceed to practice the game in almost any way that they see fit, believing that they are playing the game fully and completely.

At stage three, beginning at age seven or eight, children try to obey the common rules shared with other players. Children adhere to the rules and expect other children to do the same. Their conversations are no longer mere repetitions of expressions they have overheard. They communicate among players and define the rules that should be adhered to.

At stage four, beginning at age eleven or twelve, codes of rules are developed that apply to all games. The new element is an ability to generalize or apply the rules to more than one game or situation. The value that children place on democracy as opposed to luck begins to be reflected in their rule making.

Based on children's answers to questions such as, "How did rules begin?", "Have rules always been the same as they are today?", and "Can rules be changed?", Piaget then identified two separate moralities.

QUESTION: What are Piaget's two moralities?

Although the two moralities may overlap, Piaget asserts that a second morality replaces and follows the first. The first morality—referred to as moral realism, morality of constraint, or *heteronomous* morality—is one in which children feel obliged to comply with rules because they are viewed as sacred and unalterable.

Behaviors are viewed as either totally right or wrong, depending on their consequences, the extent to which they conform to established rules, and whether they are punished. The last criterion—whether behaviors are punished—reflects their belief in "immanent justice," the belief that wrongdoing is inevitably followed by misfortune.

Piaget's second morality, called *autonomous* morality, morality of cooperation, or reciprocity, is one in which children view rules as established through social agreement and as subject to modification in response to social needs. One's duty to follow rules is no longer defined in terms of obedience to authority, but rather in terms of respect for others.

Piaget distinguished the morality of constraint from autonomous morality in at least seven ways:

1. Younger children tend to make absolute moral judgments, not realizing that several judgments may be relative to any point of view.
2. Heteronomous children tend to judge an act to be bad if the actor is punished, not recognizing the possibility of an unjust punishment.
3. Younger children tend to have an immature conception of reciprocity, using it as an exact return of good or evil instead of considerate treatment of others as a basis.
4. Heteronomous children tend to view punishment as having only a punitive function and tend to favor severe punishments, whereas autonomous children believe that punishment is justified only if it has a reformative or restitutive function.
5. Using moral realism, children tend to base their judgment about the badness of an act solely on the consequences of the act instead of considering the intention of the person performing the act.
6. Younger children tend to believe in immanent justice, which is the belief in automatic punishment that emanates from things themselves or that flows from God's will.
7. Younger children do not consider the importance of the intentions or purpose in evaluating an action. (Kohlberg 1964, 396–97)

Clearly, adolescents and adults reason as children some of the time on some of these criteria. For example, criterion number one, which is making rigid, absolute moral judgments, can be easily observed in the often judgmental arguments of adolescents. Those whom adolescents observe are frequently considered either all bad or all good.

Piaget believes that the transformation from the morality of constraint to the morality of cooperation depends on both cognitive development and social interaction. Moral immaturity is presumed to be based on egocentrism (assuming that all others view events in the same way) and on a mixture of inferiority, dependency, affection, admiration, and fear of adults. Children feel obliged to comply with adults' commands. As children or early adolescents develop new logical skills and more experience in peer interactions, they realize that their perspective is not the only one. They realize that even the opinions of adults vary and need not be accepted unquestioningly. Interactions soon involve children in cooperative discussion that allow children to compare their motives and rules with those of others. They begin to evaluate their own and others' moral rules, eventually including those of adults. Although Piaget describes this process in relationship to children's learning, the author's opinion is that the junior high school years are the time during which the most dramatic and intense challenges to adult control are raised. Youth learn to mentally challenge rules, and thus become sensitive to the inner states that underlie the acts of others. This creates an awareness of the intentions of others, as well as a sense of the consequences of one's actions on others.

The contradiction between adolescents' perspectives and the expectations of others produces what is called a *cognitive disequilibrium,* wherein youth are motivated to resolve the dissonant mental state by reorganizing their moral thought. Piaget maintains that the stage of autonomy is achieved during later childhood, but he does not discuss moral reasoning for older ages. Kohlberg, who has focused on the stage of autonomy, finds that a substantial percentage of adolescents and young adults do not operate at the higher level.

QUESTION: What are Kohlberg's six stages of moral development?

Kohlberg has attempted to refine and extend Piaget's analysis to include young adolescents. Kohlberg formulated his six stages of moral development based on interviews with boys ranging from ten to sixteen years of age, by focusing on hypothetical moral dilemmas in which obedience to rules and authority conflicted with the needs of others. In essence, the subjects were asked how they would resolve the conflict and why they would resolve it the way proposed. Kohlberg was less interested in how they decided to resolve the dilemma than he was in the reasons given for their choices. He believed these reasons reflected the inner mental structure of moral reasoning.

Each of the six stages of moral development was defined in terms of each subject's position on thirty different moral issues. Here, for example, are six positions that could be taken on the issue of "motive given for rule obedience or moral action." For this task, the stages are:

Stage one: Obey rules to avoid punishment.

Stage two: Conform to obtain rewards, have favors returned, and so forth.

Stage three: Conform to avoid disapproval or dislike by others.

Stage four: Conform to avoid censure by legitimate authorities, and resultant guilt.

Stage five: Conform to maintain the respect of the impartial spectator judging in terms of community welfare.

Stage six: Conform to avoid self-condemnation.

By identifying each subject's answer to each dilemma as belonging to one of these six stages, Kohlberg reached an overall score that reflected the subject's dominant stage. This detailed scoring system has recently been revised to place emphasis on fewer moral issues and to place more weight on the highest stage attained by the subject on each issue rather than on the average stage. The relationship between Kohlberg and Piaget becomes clear when one realizes that

Kohlberg's first four stages are a refinement of Piaget's first stage of moral development. Box 10-1 depicts Kohlberg's six-stage model as it was first postulated.

Kohlberg concluded at that time, and still maintains, that moral development is sequential and directed. The pattern of individual development is an invariant sequence that starts with stage one and progresses sequentially until the point at which one's moral thinking culminates. He believes that the sequence is culturally universal, but that young people in various cultures develop at different rates and may not reach the same final stage.

BOX 10-1 DEFINITION OF MORAL STAGES

I. Preconventional level

The child is responsive to cultural rules and labels of good and bad, right or wrong, but interprets these either in terms of the physical or hedonistic consequences of action (punishment, reward, exchange of favors), or in terms of the physical power of those who enunciate the rules. The level is divided into two stages:

Stage 1: Punishment and obedience orientation. The physical consequences of action determine its goodness or badness regardless of the meaning or value of these consequences. Avoidance of punishment and unquestioning deference to power are valued in their own right, not in terms of respect for an underlying moral order (the latter being Stage 4).

Stage 2: Instrumental relativist orientation. Right action is that which instrumentally satisfies one's own needs and occasionally the needs of others. Human relations are viewed in terms of the marketplace. Fairness, reciprocity, and equal sharing are present, but are always interpreted in a physical, pragmatic way. Reciprocity is a matter of "you scratch my back and I'll scratch yours," not of loyalty, gratitude, nor justice.

II. Conventional level

Maintaining the expectations of the individual's family, group, or nation is perceived as valuable in its own right, regardless of consequences. The attitude is not only one of *conformity* to personal expectations and social order but also of loyalty to it, of actively *maintaining*, supporting, and justifying it, of identifying with the persons or group involved in it. This level has two stages:

Stage 3: Interpersonal concordance or "good boy-nice girl" orientation. Good behavior is that which pleases or helps others and is approved by them. There is much conformity to stereotypical images of what is majority or "natural" behavior. Behavior is frequently judged by intention—"he means well" becomes important for the first time. One earns approval by being "nice."

Stage 4: "Law and order" orientation. Orientation is toward authority, fixed rules, and the maintenance of the social order. Right behavior consists of doing one's duty, showing respect for authority, maintaining the social order for its own sake.

III. Postconventional, autonomous, or principled level

The person makes a clear effort to define moral values and principles that have validity and application apart from the authority of the groups or persons holding these principles, and apart from the individual's own identification with these groups. This level has two stages:

Stage 5: Social-contract, legalistic orientation. Generally with utilitarian overtones. Right action is defined in terms of general individual rights and standards that have been critically examined and agreed upon by society. The person is clearly aware of the relativism of values and opinions and so emphasizes procedural rules for reaching consensus. Aside from what is constitutionally and democratically agreed upon, right is a matter of personal "values" and "opinion"; emphasis is thus on the "legal point of view," but with the possibility of changing law in terms of rational considerations of social utility rather than freezing it in terms of Stage 4. Outside the legal realm, free agreement and contract is the binding element. This is the "official" morality of the American government and Constitution.

Stage 6: Universal ethical principle orientation. Right is defined by the decision of conscience in accord with self-chosen *ethical principles* appealing to logical comprehensiveness, universality, and consistency. These principles are abstract and ethical (the Golden Rule, the categorical imperative); they are not concrete moral rules like the Ten Commandments. At heart, these are universal principles of *justice of the reciprocity and equality of human rights*, and of respect for the dignity of human beings as *individual persons*.

Source: Adapted from D. Boyce and L. Jensen, *Moral Reasoning* (Lincoln: University of Nebraska Press, 1978), 100–101.

Kohlberg made the following specific points about the stages and their sequence.

1. They are qualitatively different modes of thought rather than increased knowledge of, or internalization of, adult moral beliefs and standards.
2. They form an invariant order or sequence of development. Movement through these stages is always forward and always step by step.
3. The stages form an integrated whole. A general factor of a moral stage crosscuts all dilemmas, verbal or behavioral, with which an individual is confronted.
4. The stages are hierarchical integrations. Subjects comprehend all stages below their own and not more than one above their own. Each new stage represents a synthesis between the prior stage and new elements; in this way a given stage serves as a prerequisite for a higher stage, for a later mode of thought.
5. Stages are viewed neither as the direct reflection of maturation nor as the direct reflection of learning in the sense of specific environmental exposure, reinforcements, and the like. He states that stages represent the equilibrated pattern of interaction between the organism and the environment. (Kohlberg 1973).

Lawrence Kohlberg

Kohlberg once described an even higher stage. This seventh stage involves the sense of being a part of the whole of life, not just the universal humanistic perspective of stage six. (Kohlberg 1969). Kohlberg considered Spinoza to have reached the seventh stage because he saw all finite things, even humans, as part of an infinite cosmic whole. Such a stage is more ambiguous than the other stages.

Kohlberg's theory bears a strong resemblance to Piaget's theory. Piaget emphasizes the development of an autonomous morality, characterized by an appreciation of justice developing from interpersonal relationships. People move away from a heteronomous morality characterized by dependence on external actions. Kohlberg's recent characterizations see the individual as developing from a position of blind reliance on adult and social influences to a position of self-reliance and individual commitment to self-chosen principles.

QUESTION: Is Kohlberg's theory accurate?

The great deal of research that has been generated by Kohlberg's model provides some support for his theory—that the stages are homogeneous, universal, and invariant, and that growth results from exposure to levels of moral reasoning that are higher than one's own (Hoffman 1977b). Kohlberg (1975) has suggested that the lack of empirical support for his theory (Kurtines and Grief 1974) may be due to the inadequacies of his earlier scoring procedures. Kohlberg's theory (Kohlberg 1975) has been criticized on other grounds as well. Simpson (1974) claims that Kohlberg's theory is culturally biased. Stage six, for example, requires a level of abstract thought that places moral excellence out of most people's reach. Stage five may make sense only in a constitutional democracy. Hogan (1975) believes that Kohlberg's stage six reflects a "romantic individualism," with a suspicion of the traditional mores and cultural values. Peters (1971) has said that Kohlberg's concept of cognitive disequilibrium cannot explain why a child would be motivated to be concerned for others or to change actual behavior. Nevertheless, Kohlberg can be viewed as a pioneer in introducing new ideas and theories on this aspect of human morality. In general, his views are compatible with other data in psychology, and they have an appeal to those working with youth (Kohlberg 1976, 1980).

The search for new values may lead in any one of a number of directions. Whether or not Piaget's and Kohlberg's theories are confirmed, they have made a great contribution to the area of moral development. They have illuminated the highly complex nature of moral development, as well as the important role of social experience in moral growth. Concepts such as cognitive disequilibrium may help to explain how children develop more complex moral reasoning.

QUESTION: Do the stage theories of moral reasoning have a practical application?

Yes. In a book entitled *Moral Reasoning*, the authors (Boyce and Jensen 1978) review ways to improve moral reasoning and focus on the implications of many people who have tried to develop programs to facilitate the development of moral reasoning, following theories similar to those of Piaget and Kohlberg. The following are some of the basic conclusions that were found during this review:

One such hypothesis, or guideline, is that the parents should allow the child to be exposed to a wide range of information and experience. . . . A corollary guideline is that the whole family should be exposed to a wide range of information and experience. As the child begins to individuate and assert his differentness and individuality, he must be encouraged in this process by the continued respect and acceptance of his family. This continued acceptance is facilitated if other family members are also open to new information and change. . . . This, again, appears to be positively associated with individuation and moral growth. Finally, parents can move, as much as appropriately possible, from explicit to implicit rules in the home. That is, a child in the process of being different will be more responsive to rules that are simply assumed than to those that are carved in stone and handed down. The first step for accomplishing this is to emotionally bond the child to the family and then model the desired behavior. This is done essentially by building the child's self-esteem and sense of love and belonging through horizontal family interaction. In this atmosphere appropriate discipline can be maintained while the child is simultaneously allowed a significant degree of autonomy. (Boyce and Jensen 1978, 172–73)

Accordingly, parents must also be morally mature. Parents should be able to identify moral principles and meaningfully justify them. Parents and educators cannot be content to merely spout ethical opinions, for the issues of moral reasoning lies deeper. Adolescents who hear that the El Salvador war is wrong are not confronted with a clear moral issue that they can examine meaningfully. If, however, they hear that life is inherently sacred, that war does not have a justifiable base, then they are presented with elements of moral reasoning.

The second task of parents is to justify the basic moral assumptions. Parents can demonstrate facts by meaningfully justifying them and can thus foster adolescents' search for a method of justification of their own. The method by which an adolescent's moral maturity is best stimulated is through active discussion of the fundamental issues. Such a process leads to moral autonomy (Boyce and Jensen 1978, 172–73).

Kohlberg and Piaget's theories have been applied to the schools as a model for a moral education. Two journals, the *Journal of Moral Education* and the *Moral Education Forum,* present studies showing programs to increase and facilitate moral reasoning via Kohlberg's theory. The research (Kohlberg 1976, 1980) reported in these journals generally shows a positive change in *thinking*. Kohlberg more recently has moved away from the discussion orientation to moral education and has focused more on developing a "just community" within the school. His concern is with society's recent emphasis on the self; Kohlberg emphasizes a concern for others (Minuchin and Shapiro 1983). As in any new area of research, controversy exists (Power 1979). At present, Kohlberg's theory still shows much promise as a method of moral education among adolescents.

QUESTION: Does having a high level of moral reasoning mean that one has a high level of moral behavior?

The answer to this question is complex. Although one reviewer (DeBassi 1980) shows that this question is still being debated, a reasonable conclusion is that a positive relationship exists between the way one thinks and the way one behaves. In general, people with high levels of moral reasoning apparently tend to be those who act more maturely. In an earlier review of this question, Boyce and Jensen state:

> Combining these studies, we can suggest three general conclusions. First, there is a relationship between moral judgments, beliefs, values, and behavior. Second, changes through persuasion or verbal instruction can influence behavior. Third, the stage level of the message is important in determining the amount of the behavioral change that occurs. (Boyce and Jensen 1978, 119)

Values, however, may be more closely related to moral behavior than to the more abstract moral reasoning.

Values

Although values are a popular topic of conversation and research, no generally accepted definition of a value exists. Discussion of values are found in philosophical and religious literature as well as in social scientific research. Definitions of value vary with the range of phenomena one hopes to explain. One researcher may want to know whether people view human nature as good or evil; another may want to know whether people are primarily motivated by economic, religious, social, or other values. Definitions also vary with one's theoretical bias. Those who use a complex model of human thought may view values as products of passive information processing. Others may view values as the active product of self-conscious choice.

The complexity of the concept of value is reflected in the extended definition that Rokeach provides:

> To say that a person has a value is to say that he has an enduring prescriptive or proscriptive belief that a specific mode of behavior or end-state of existence is preferred to an appositive mode of behavior or end-state. This belief transcends attitudes toward objects and toward situations; it is a standard that guides and determines action, attitude toward objects and situations, ideology, presentation of self to others, evaluations, judgments, justifications, comparisons of self with others and attempts to influence others. Values serve adjustive, ego-defensive, knowledge, and self-actualizing functions. Instrumental and terminal values are related yet are separately organized into relatively enduring hierarchical organizations along a continuum of importance. (Rokeach 1973, 35)

This definition raises some of the major issues regarding values. For Rokeach, values are transcendent, enduring beliefs (Williams 1968; Rokeach 1973). They are not associated with specific objects. For Rokeach and Williams, values are the criteria that guide human thought and action. Value systems function as general plans for making decisions and for resolving conflicts. Values are viewed as the link between culture, society, and institutions on the one hand, and all human thought and behavior on the other.

Rokeach distinguishes terminal values from instrumental values. The terminal values, or goals, are likely to be few in number for each individual. Instrumental values, or modes of conduct, are likely to be more numerous than terminal values, but still less numerous than the thousands of specific beliefs and attitudes. Terminal and instrumental value systems are somewhat independent of each other. Goals can change without changing modes of conduct, and modes of conduct can change without changing goals. However, terminal values and instrumental values function together. Rokeach has developed a value survey that includes eighteen terminal values and eighteen instrumental values.

Rokeach apparently believes that values are the ultimate standard that guides human thought and action. Other theorists agree that values provide continuity and meaning under changing environmental circumstances (Feather 1975, 249). Because values are relatively stable and enduring beliefs, they are sometimes called structures of the personality. These structural characteristics include the amount of feeling and the sense of "oughtness" that is associated with the value. The depth of our emotional commitment to our values, as well as other structural characteristics, create the continuum of importance in Rokeach's definition.

QUESTION: How are values measured?

Human values have many different measures. Rokeach's survey of terminal and instrumental values has already been mentioned. Respondents rank the values in each set in their order of importance, which results in a terminal value system and an instrumental value system for each respondent.

One of the best-known tests is the study of values developed by Allport, Vernon, and Lindsey (1951, 1960). This test measures the relative strength of six basic values: theoretical, economic, aesthetic, social, political, and religious. A more general measure of one's general philosophies of life has been developed (Kluckholm and Strodtveck 1961). These researchers compared cultures with respect to five value orientations:

1. Conceptions of the character of innate human nature: evil, neutral or mixed, good, mutable or immutable
2. Humans' subjugation, harmony, or mastery over nature and supernature
3. The temporal focus of human life, whether past, present, or future
4. The modality of human activity: being, being-in-becoming, or doing
5. Humans' relationship to other humans: linearity, colinearity, or individualism

Another researcher (Morris 1956) developed thirteen concepts, each describing a possible way of living:

1. Preserve the best that man has attained.
2. Cultivate independence of persons and things.
3. Show sympathetic concern for others.
4. Experience festivity and solitude in alternation.
5. Act and enjoy life through group participation.
6. Constantly master changing conditions.
7. Integrate action, enjoyment, and contemplation.
8. Live with wholesome carefree enjoyment.
9. Wait in quiet receptivity.

10. Control the self.
11. Meditate on the inner life.
12. Chance adventuresome deeds.
13. Obey the cosmic purposes.

Others have tried to develop measures of values that do not limit responses to a set of fixed choices. Letters, newspapers, folktales, movies, interview material, and other personal and cultural products have all been used as indirect evidence of personal and cultural values. Which categories and means of measurement will have the greatest usefulness and explanatory power is not yet clear. Although a more extended discussion of values would not be appropriate in a text on adolescence, these concepts are presented, since values are such a central aspect of personality, and the development of values is believed to be an important aspect of adolescence.

QUESTION: Does an adolescent value system exist?

We need to be cautious about generalizing to adolescent values. In general, the answer is no. The term *adolescence,* as pointed out, is ambiguous and controversial. Some theorists do not even view adolescence as a universal stage of development. For example, Keniston (1971) argues that adolescence is made possible by the prolongation of education in more affluent societies, and he would not consider it appropriate to call a set of values held by young people "adolescent values."

Other theorists would ask whether one is talking about male or female adolescents. To the extent that traditional roles hold, males may assign higher importance to values of achievement and competence, while females may place more emphasis on values of nurturance and affiliation. Differences in sex roles are discussed elsewhere and do reflect basic differences in values. According to Douvan and Adelson (1966), the key terms in adolescent development for the traditional boy in our culture are the erotic, autonomy (assertiveness, independence, achievement), and identity. For the traditional girl the comparable terms are the erotic, the interpersonal, and identity. What the girl achieves through intimate connection with others, the boy must manage by disconnecting, by separating himself and asserting his right to be distinct.

Still other theorists have discussed different adolescent prototypes. If this is true, then one might conclude that different "subspecies" of adolescents may exist, grouped according to their value systems. Peck and Havighurst (1960) define five character types: amoral, expedient, conforming, irrational-conscious, and rational-altruistic. Havighurst (1975) also distinguishes between adolescent "forerunners," "practical minded," and "left-outs." Many other classifications have been suggested. Conceiving of adolescence as a single, universal experience with one set of values is too simplistic. Speaking of adolescent values in general is therefore a mistake. Adolescent values are influenced not only by life-cycle or ontogenetic factors but also by cultural, historical, and purely personal circumstances. Nevertheless, adolescents differ in values and are active in the process of acquiring, evaluating, holding and/or discarding the values discussed in this section.

QUESTION: What differences have been found among the values of younger and older adolescents?

Although many studies have been done of teenager values generally, little research has investigated changes in values from early through late adolescence. Beech and Schoeppe (1974) have used Rokeach's value survey to study boys and girls from grades five, seven, nine, and eleven, in New York City. The most important terminal values for boys across all grades were a world at peace, freedom, family security, and equality. The most important terminal values for girls across all grades were a world at peace, and freedom. The boys' least important terminal values were salvation and social recognition; the girls' least important terminal value was salvation. The most important instrumental values for both boys and girls of all ages were being honest and being loving. The least important instrumental values for both boys and girls of all ages were being imaginative and being logical.

Signs indicated that with age, boys and girls placed greater value on achievement, open-mindedness, responsibility, and self-respect, and less value on conformity to convention and authority. These results support theoretical discussions of the importance of identity, autonomy, and fidelity in adolescence. Similar results were obtained in a study of Australian schoolchildren (Feather 1975). Similar conclusions were also reached in an Australian study by Connell et al. (1975). These researchers found that the value most universally rejected by teenagers in Australia was that of conformity to societal views on politics, war, and peace. As far as criteria of judgments are concerned, the researchers stated:

> [T]here is an overwhelming rejection of conformity and social compliance as the basis for valuing anything, and a nearly equivalent formation of a principle of personal independence and autonomy. Coercive justification and narrow self-satisfaction are also relatively disliked, while ideals, reciprocity, and expertise are more often given a high place in the rank order of categories. (Connell et al. 1975, 79)

QUESTION: What differences have been found among the values of adolescents from different cultures?

Already mentioned was the similarity between adolescents in New York and Australia. Important to remember, however, is that the United States and Australia are similar in other respects as well, such as degree of industrialization, affluence, and education. Extending the comparisons to countries different from the United States in these and other respects is important.

The following observation was made by an exchange student from a Southeast Asian country:

> It was a big adjustment for me when I first came to America. I attended the 12th grade and had a difficult time relating to my classmates. Things that were important to them were not important to me—like owning a car or a motorcycle. I didn't even know how to drive. Where I'm from, cars are a luxury not a necessity. Everyone uses the public transportation.

Differences have been found in the values of students from Israel and Papua New Guinea when compared with the United States, Canada, and Australia.

Israeli students showed a high concern for competence, peace, and national security, and a low degree of concern for salvation and being forgiving. Papua New Guinea students also ranked values such as world at peace and national security high, but also gave high priority to salvation. These results are not surprising in view of the Arab-Israeli conflict, the emergence of Papua New Guinea as a nation, and the strong influence of Christian missions in Papua New Guinea (Feather 1980, 267).

Interesting differences were present even among affluent countries. Americans appeared more materialistic, more achievement oriented, and more orthodoxly religious (salvation minded) than Australians. Australians placed more value on peace of mind, an active life and a cheerful disposition, and true friendships. These findings indicate that strong cultural forces are at work in shaping values prior to and during adolescence.

QUESTION: What differences have been found among adolescent values over time and across generations?

Adolescents in 1950 and adolescents in 1970 belong to different generations and have been influenced by different historical events and social forces. Some influences may be fairly constant across generations, some may be cyclical, and others may be unique.

Certain studies show a remarkable degree of continuity among values over successive generations. In a study that spans at least two generations, Caplow and Bahr (1979) surveyed the attitudes of high school students in a town designated "Middletown." Caplow and Bahr conclude that "some of the religious, political, and social attitudes of the post-WWI era have persisted with remarkable tenacity among Middletown's adolescents."

They did not find "any trace of the disintegration of traditional social values that is commonly described by observers who rely on their own intuitions." Middletown adolescents appeared to be as religious, patriotic, and devoted to the Protestant work ethic as their grandparents were at the same age, but they also appeared more tolerant of those with differing values.

Morris and Small (1971) also found that 1970 American students did not differ greatly from 1950 students. Using the previously mentioned "ways to live" scale developed by Morris, the researchers found that respondents in both 1950 and 1970 were most in favor of way seven ("Integrate action, enjoyment, and contemplation"). Although the researchers found a notable drop in liking for way one ("Preserve the best that man has attained"), the overall difference appeared to be one of strategy or conduct rather than one of goals or professed values.

Other shorter-term studies have found differences in adolescent values. Yankelovich (1973), the pollster discussed in Chapter 1, found a cluster of new social values emerging in the late sixties and early seventies. Yankelovich found that following the Vietnam War, the assassination of the Kennedys and of Martin Luther King, and the rise of the civil rights movement and the student protest movement, changes occurred in moral norms and in social values. These changes first appeared in a group that Yankelovich calls the "forerunners" (using Havighurst's term), but gradually diffused to other segments of the population, sometimes creating curious mixtures of new and old values. Yankelovich has found a decline in the percentage of both college and noncollege youth who believe that religion, patriotism, and a clean, moral life are important values. Fewer than 45 percent highly valued having children, religion, patriotism, money, or changing society. Yankelovich also found that noncollege youth are less likely to support the puritan ethic, traditional attitudes toward sex, war as an instrument of national policy, authority, and conformity.

Studies of several hundred thousand freshmen at UCLA during the late 1960s and 1970s also showed measurable changes in values. The freshmen generally showed declining idealism and increasing cynicism and materialism. Developing a meaningful philosophy of life, a popular goal endorsed in 1967, disappeared between 1971 and 1976. The increased concern for financial security may be viewed as a realistic response to a flagging world economy (Astin 1977a, 1977b).

Studies of adolescents in the United States, England, and Japan, reported in Chapter 1, all agree that today's college students have more liberal attitudes toward sex than those of a decade ago.

QUESTION: Do male and female adolescents have differing values?

Although an extensive overlap is present among values of female and male adolescents, which should not be ignored, some important differences are also present. One researcher (Dukes 1955) found that men score higher than women on the Allport-Vernon-Lindsey theoretical, economic, and political values, but lower on the aesthetic, religious, and social values. Block (1973) studied sex roles in terms of Bakan's distinction between agency and communion (Bakan 1966):

> Agency is concerned with the organism as an individual and manifests itself in self-protection, self-assertion, and self-expansion. Communion is descriptive of the individual organism as it exists in some larger organism of which it is a part and manifests itself in the sense of being at one with other organisms. (Block 1973)

Block found impressive cross-cultural uniformity in the self-descriptions of males and females with respect to agency and communion. Males tend to describe themselves as practical, assertive, dominating, competitive, critical, rational, and ambiguous—all adjectives reflecting *agency*. Females tend to describe themselves as loving, sympathetic, generous, sensitive, and artistic—all adjectives reflecting *communion*.

One study by Rokeach (1973) found that males value a comfortable, exciting life, mature love and pleasure, and value being ambitious, capable, independent, intellectual, logical, and self-controlled more than do females. Females value a world at peace, a world of beauty, equality, inner harmony, wisdom, cheerfulness, forgiveness, helpfulness, and honesty. These are only two studies showing that within one culture, differences exist between the sexes in basic values. Judging by changes in recent years, the women's movement will undoubtedly have a powerful impact on values, which is discussed further in the chapter on sex roles.

QUESTION: Can anything be done to help adolescents acquire positive values?

A number of programs have been developed to teach and enhance values in the schools. These programs could be applied in the home, although they are usually not. One popular program is called Values Clarification, the goals of which are stated by the author:

> We are interested in the processes that are going on. We are not much interested in identifying the values which children believe in a world that is changing as rapidly as ours. Each child must develop habits of examining his purposes, aspirations, attitudes, feelings, etc., if he is to find the most intelligent relationship between his life and the surrounding world, and if he is to make a contribution to the creation of a better world. . . . The development of values is a personal and lifelong process. It is not something that is completed by early adulthood. (Raths, Harmin, and Simon 1966, 37)

Authors Louis Raths, Merrill Harmin, and Sidney Simon advocate teaching valuing rather than teaching traditional, or even recently derived, values to youth. They propose teaching children better ways to value (value used as a verb).

The major goal proposed in this model is to develop a person capable of valuing. What does valuing mean? The model is discussed here because it is the only such program to acquire substantial support from both the public and the educational communities. The authors propose that seven basic elements characterize a person who is valuing. These elements are presented in Box 10–2.

Some researchers believe that children should be taught better ways to value instead of the traditional values themselves.

> **BOX 10-2 THE PROCESS OF VALUING**
>
> 1. **Choosing freely.** If something is in fact to guide one's life whether or not authority is watching, it must be a result of free choice. If there is coercion, the result is not likely to stay with one for long, especially when out of the range of the source of that coercion. Values must be freely selected if they are to be really valued by the individual.
> 2. **Choosing from among alternatives.** This definition of values is concerned with things that are chosen by the individual and, obviously, there can be no choice if there are no alternatives from which to choose. It makes no sense, for example, to say that one values eating. One really has no choice in the matter. What one may value is certain types of food or certain forms of eating, but not eating itself. We must all obtain nourishment to exist; there is no room for decision. Only when a choice is possible, when there is more than one alternative from which to choose, do we say a value can result.
> 3. **Choosing after thoughtful consideration of the consequences of each alternative.** Impulsive or thoughtless choices do not lead to values as we define them. For something to intelligently and meaningfully guide one's life it must emerge from a weighing and an understanding. Only when the consequences of each of the alternatives are clearly understood can one make intelligent choices. There is an important cognitive factor here. A value can emerge only with thoughtful consideration of the range of the alternatives and consequences in a choice.
> 4. **Prizing and cherishing.** When we value something, it has a positive tone. We prize it, cherish it, esteem it, respect it, hold it dear. We are happy with our values. A choice, even when we have made it freely and thoughtfully, may be a choice we are not happy to make. We may choose to fight in a war, but be sorry circumstances make that choice reasonable. In our definition, values flow from choices that we are glad to make. We prize and cherish the guides to life that we call values.
> 5. **Affirming.** When we have chosen something freely, after consideration of the alternatives, and when we are proud of our choice, glad to be associated with it, we are likely to affirm that choice when asked about it. We are willing to publicly affirm our values. We may even be willing to champion them. If we are ashamed of a choice, if we would not make our position known when appropriately asked, we would not be dealing with values but something else.
> 6. **Acting upon choices.** Where we have a value, it shows up in aspects of our living. We may do some reading about things we value. We are likely to form friendships or to be in organizations in ways that nourish our values. We may spend money on a choice we value. We budget time or energy for our values. In short, for a value to be present, life itself must be affected. Nothing can be a value that does not, in fact, give direction to actual living. The person who talks about something but never does anything about it is dealing with something other than a value.
> 7. **Repeating.** Where something reaches the stage of a value, it is very likely to reappear on a number of occasions in the life of the person who holds it. It shows up in several different situations, at several different times. We would not think of something that appeared once in a life and never again, as a value. Values tend to have a persistency, to make a pattern in a life.
>
> *Source:* L. Raths, M. Harmin, and S. Simon, *Values and Teaching: Working with Values in the Classroom* (Columbus, Ohio: Merrill, 1966).

Comprehensive and detailed instructional materials have been developed in this program for teaching value clarification. The essentials of these specific techniques are:

1. Encourage youth to make choices and to make them freely.
2. Help them discover and examine available alternatives when faced with choices.
3. Help them weigh alternatives thoughtfully, reflecting on the consequences of each.
4. Encourage consideration of what it is that they prize and cherish.
5. Give them opportunities to make public their choices.
6. Encourage them to act, behave, and live in accordance with their choices.
7. Help them to examine repeated behaviors or patterns in their life.

The purpose of these techniques is to raise questions in the minds of youth to help them examine basic issues, actions, and ideas. Basically, the program encourages youth to examine and think about their lives in a climate of trust and respect. The program is best done on an informal, face-to-face, personal basis. The basic accomplishment is that the program shifts the responsibility for valuing from the teacher to the students, who must do the examination and valuing. The program is generally nonmechanical and contains few, if any, theoretically right or wrong answers.

This approach has basically been derived from the humanistic theories of psychology prevalent and developed during the mid-twentieth century. In this approach, internal rather than external factors are deemed to be the prime motivators of human behavior. By changing a person's values, behavior is free and will inevitably change.

Moral behavior

QUESTION: Are there theories that explain moral behavior?

Yes, American psychologists have made a strong research effort to explain the origin of what is called prosocial behavior (Staub 1978). Most of their research has not been guided by a single theory but by several theories. One theory that has had some direct emphasis is the psychoanalytic explanation.

In the psychoanalytic view, the young male child is inevitably subject to many frustrations that create hostility toward the parents. Because of erotic desires, males also experience the urge to have close contact with the mother. Anxiety builds due to a fear of punishment from the father, the male child's main rival for the mother's affection. To control this anxiety, the male child represses both hostility and erotic feeling for the mother, and adopts the rules and prohibitions of the parents, especially those of the father. Because of frustration and anxiety over attraction to the opposite-sex parent, the child finds safety by identifying with the same-sex parent. Out of this general motive to emulate the parent with whom they have identified, children acquire character, values, and beliefs.

The psychoanalytic view holds that a boy uses this form of identification to resolve the Oedipal conflict (i.e., a boy falls in love with his mother and, finding that he cannot compete with his father, fears reprisals from him). To escape fear and competition engendered by the father, the male child tries to be like him. If he becomes enough like Dad, he might be able to win the affections of a girl just like Mom. An opposite attachment is said to occur for the girl and is called the Electra complex.

Certain generalizations on how identification occurs become clear and can be interpreted from other theoretical positions. First, identification is considered a basic process in socialization. Also, adults must apparently have at least some of the following attributes in their relationship with the child: warmth, mastery or power over the environment, proximity, some amount of status or esteem, and perceived similarity. Because many parents lack these characteristics, and many times the appropriate model is absent, considering how children acquire identification in disorganized families is necessary.

Certain events can result in identification when the same-sex parent is absent. First, the other parent can create images of the absent spouse. For example, if a father is absent for an extended period of time, the mother may place a picture of him in a conspicuous location and discuss him frequently with the child. Second, other substitute models are usually available. Schoolteachers are frequently aware of close attachments since they function as role models for numerous young children. Pastors, coaches, club leaders, or even older boys can serve as identification figures for boys. Even without specific individuals to model, a culture often provides numerous real or symbolic models for the child, with a not-always-subtle message that they be copied. Literature and folklore can serve this function. In our modern, impersonal society, the mass media continually present stereotyped models, the choice and effects of which may be questionable. These conclusions are not dependent upon believing the Freudian interpretation of identification and could logically occur at any age, including adolescence.

In essence, each culture emphasizes appropriate identification behavior and provides numerous means for this process to occur. O. H. Mower, a learning theorist, outlines the ideal way to learn these complex processes:

> In the ideal family constellation, a little boy finds it very natural and highly rewarding to model himself in his father's image. The father is gratified to see this recreation of his own qualities, attitudes, and masculinity; and the mother, loving the father, finds such a course of development acceptable in her son. Tentative explorations, conscious and unconscious, in the direction of being "like mother" quickly convince the boy that this is not his proper or approved destiny; and he speedily reverts to his identification with father. In the well-ordered, psychologically healthy household, much the same picture, in reverse, holds for the little girl. (Mower 1950, 596)

Nevertheless, most psychologists consider identification to be only a partial explanation for the development of morals. For a more general explanation, which is basically nontheoretical, let us consider Martin Hoffman's excellent review about the development of morals during adolescence, entitled "Moral Development and Adolescence" (Hoffman 1980).

QUESTION: According to Hoffman, what motivates adolescent morality?

Hoffman contends that empathy provides the key motive for moral action. Studies show that persons exposed to others in distress usually respond either with empathy or by helping. Evidence also suggests that subjects act more quickly the greater the victim's distress. Empathy increases prior to a helpful act and diminishes following the helpful act (Hoffman 1977a).

Human beings apparently empathize almost from birth. Hoffman lists three modes of empathic arousal that apply to adolescents. The first mode is empathy through *association*. The sight of blood and the sound of a cry, for example, remind us of our own prior experiences of pain, and revive the unpleasant emotions associated with them.

The second mode is through *motor mimicry*. Observers tend to mimic the posture and facial expressions of the people they watch. One study showed that college students blinked more frequently when observing models who were blinking their eyes (Bernal and Berger 1975). Other studies have shown that different emotions appear to be associated with different degrees of muscle tone.

The third mode of empathic arousal is *imagination*. Imagination is similar to empathy through association, except that it is more subject to conscious control and involves a cognitive restructuring of events. One views what is happening to another as though it were happening to oneself. In one study, subjects showed greater empathic distress when they were asked to imagine how they would feel if they were exposed to the same pain that another was experiencing, rather than when they were told to imagine how the other person felt when he or she was experiencing that pain (Stotland 1972). Although children are capable of recognizing happiness or sadness in others in simple situations, not until early adolescence does a child usually become aware of other persons' general plight in life. This ability is the basis for a motivator to help, to act, and to be moral in helping others. To achieve this type of moral motivation, first necessary is helping young people to empathize with others. After empathy exists, young people can be helped to acquire moral behaviors both to reduce others' distress and to produce positive feelings associated with others' joy.

QUESTION: Is guilt a strong motivator for moral behavior?

Ample evidence suggests that youth are capable of experiencing both guilt over what they have done and guilt over what they have *not* done. Guilt is not the same as empathy. Adolescents have the ability to imagine an event that might have occurred, and therefore can imagine what they might have done to help avoid another person's distress. A study by Hoffman (1975) clearly showed that children age ten to fourteen have a clear capacity for feeling guilty not only over action but also over inaction. In another study (Keniston 1970), student activists were shown to be motivated by the guilt that they were much more fortunate than others. In discussing some poor Mexican children he had known, one of Keniston's respondents described his experience in a way that clearly depicts the role of guilt in moral action:

> I was the one that lived in a place where there were fans and no flies, and they lived with the flies. And I was clearly destined for something, and they were destined for nothing. . . . Well, I sort of made a pact with these people that when I got to be powerful I might change some things. And I think I pursued that pact pretty consistently for a long time. (Keniston 1965, 50)

Guilt over circumstances beyond one's control is often called existential guilt, and may at times be a far more potent motivation than true personal guilt. Rather than requiring only a single act of restitution, existential guilt may require continued activity in the service of suffering humans. Existential guilt may also lead to a fear of success or a renunciation of privileges. A story situation of "John finds himself at the top of his medical school class" drew the following response from a male college student:

> John is perplexed upon hearing the news. He's mad that everything is so assured. Resents the fact that he's hereditarily good and others are not. (Hoffman 1980, 313)

Existential guilt such as this may be less applicable to youth today than to youth in other generations. In informal interviews, Hoffman has found that adolescents today place a high value on success and do not feel as strongly about the disadvantaged. They are worried about finding jobs themselves, and they believe that economic conditions have improved for many disadvantaged groups (Hoffman 1980). Moral action based on existential guilt may be less when adolescents are worried about meeting their own needs.

QUESTION: What sort of parental discipline leads to the greatest moral development?

A great deal of investigation has gone into the relation between parental discipline and moral internalization. The way in which children are disciplined is bound to have an effect on the way in which they balance their egoistic needs against external demands. Hoffman (1977b) has reviewed the discipline research and has organized it around three broad types of discipline: (1) power assertion, which includes physical force, deprivation of material objects or privileges, and the threat of these, (2) love withdrawal, which includes strong but nonphysical expressions of anger and disapproval, and (3) induction, which includes explanations for why children should change their behavior, appealing to children's pride, mastery, strivings, or concern for others. These approaches to discipline were evaluated based on the child's ability to make moral judgments based on moral principles, to confess and accept responsibility for a misdeed, to experience guilt (as opposed to fear of punishment), and to resist temptations.

Results of studies generally indicate that power assertive techniques create a fear of external detection and punishment, and that inductive techniques create an independence of external sanctions and a greater capacity for healthy guilt. No clear relationship exists between love withdrawal techniques and the adolescent's moral orientation. Most parents use all three techniques. Power assertion and love withdrawal are often considered necessary to get children to stop what they are doing and to listen. Once they are listening, the parents try to communicate the harm that children have done to someone else and to elicit empathy and guilt. The communication of moral instruction, however, may be obscured by overuse of power assertion and love withdrawal, as indicated by one student:

> Through my parents' actions, example and counsel I always knew exactly what they expected of me. When I went out to a social function there was no set curfew. I was simply to be home soon after it was over. If I was delayed somewhere for various reasons, I was to call and let them know when I would be home. This attitude seemed to work quite well. The responsibility for obeying my parents was totally up to me.
> One of my girl friends had parents whose philosophies seemed just the opposite to my parents. She had to be in by midnight no matter what. Dances were no exception and she would often have to leave dances early. Her attitude towards the rule was typical. Since the decision had been made by the parents and simply imposed on her, she had no respect for it and rebelled.

Hoffman believes from the research on discipline that the mother ordinarily has a more important influence on a child's moral internalization than does

The exact influence of peers on an adolescent's moral development has been disputed by different theorists. In activities such as scouting, individuals can learn from observing adult leaders, as well as from their peers.

the father. This seems odd, considering that a number of theorists, especially Freud, believe that the child acquires moral standards of society from the father. Studies of the effects of a father's absence, however, have indicated that even if the father's *particular* discipline techniques do not make much difference, fathers still play an important part in moral socialization.

QUESTION: Do peers have a positive or a negative influence on moral development?

The importance of peers is commonly said to reach a peak during adolescence, but theorists disagree as to whether the influence of peers on moral development is generally constructive. Piaget has argued that unsupervised play among peers is essential for the formation of autonomous moral thinking, and that adolescents often learn the meaning of justice in spite of adults (Piaget 1965). If moral development is always progressive, the net effect of peer interactions will be positive.

Many researchers are less optimistic about peer influences. Urie Bronfenbrenner has boldly stated, "If all children have contact only with their age mates, there is no possibility for learning culturally established patterns of cooperation and mutual concern" (Bronfenbrenner 1970, 17). The view that the voice of conscience is barely audible to unsupervised adolescents is dramatically illustrated in William Golding's *Lord of the Flies*. Experimental research seems to confirm that moral action tends towards the lowest common denominator among adolescent peer groups. Children who observe physically aggressive behavior by a model going unpunished tend to behave aggressively when given the opportunity shortly thereafter. Similarly, children who observe models yielding to temptation and cheating in a game will generally cheat when given the opportunity. In one study, children bowled with adult and peer models, who rewarded themselves alternatively for a high score or a low score by eating available candy. Children were found to employ stringent or lenient standards of self-reward, depending on what the model did. If the children saw an adult using a stringent standard and a peer using a lenient standard, however, the children tended to use the more lenient standard of self-reward (Bandura, Grusec, and Menlove 1967).

The research here is controversial. Studies cited in the chapter on peers do show that the peer group has a powerful impact upon youth, but the influence definitely needs guidance within the socialization process.

QUESTION: How does the self-concept relate to moral behavior?

Evidence to answer this question comes from an experiment. In this experiment, a change in self-perception also occurs, and with certain changes in self-perception there follows a difference in resistance to temptation behavior. Although the experiment used young children, the principle can be applied to other age groups.

Lepper (1973) forbade two groups of children from playing with attractive toys, with either a mild or a severe threat of punishment, while giving the third group no threat at all. Having done this, a second experimenter returned three weeks later and asked the subjects to play a game in which they could obtain attractive prizes only by falsifying their scores. Lepper predicted from his self-perception theory that subjects who complied in the earlier experiment under mild threat would show more resistance to temptation because they would have more positive self-evaluation ("I am good"), whereas those who received the strong threat would not be as likely to resist temptation because they would justify their original good behavior in terms of complying to the severe threat that was given them. Under the severe threat they may conclude that they are "bad" and that only the severe threat of punishment kept them from disobeying in the earlier situation. The results were as Lepper predicted. The group that had experienced the mild threat falsified their scores least. The next best group included those who had no threat; the worst were those who had been threatened severely.

Could it be that people come to perceive themselves as disposed to behave in certain ways? One popular theory of how a person forms self-perceptions is this: People attribute personality characteristics to others after observing (1) the others' overt behavior and (2) the extenuating circumstances (Bem 1965). When external forces are seen as powerful, then behavior is attributed to the environment, and when the external forces appear weak, behavior is attributed to actions of the self. If this is how people evaluate others, would they not use the same method to evaluate themselves or to form a self-concept? Aronson (1963) proposed that this is the case. He found that when subjects are induced to perform an unpleasant behavior under conditions of weak external pressure, the subjects afterward conclude that they engaged in the behavior because they wished to do so. When strong external forces are invoked, however, the subjects rarely state that they wanted to behave as they did.

This change in evaluation of the self is similar to the change of evaluations made in the experiment described earlier. When children were asked not to play with an attractive toy under mild or severe threat of punishment, children under mild threat later tended to devalue the prohibited toy more than did children who had received severe threat of punishment.

A few conclusions can be drawn from the studies presented. First, people can apparently resist temptation, and in the process they learn to devalue or derogate the incentive offered for deviation. Second, certain factors facilitate this devaluation, such as people's self-perception and the amount of freedom they perceive in a situation. A person's self-concept may therefore be one of the more salient causes of moral or immoral behavior. In contemporary U.S. society, moral behavior is often associated with religion. No logical reason supports grouping these topics, other than religions often advocate stands on moral issues. A section on religion is presented because it is an important influence on adolescent behavior independent of any association with morals.

Religion

As do most adults in the United States, the majority of adolescents believe in God; some polls report as high as 94 percent (Sigelman 1977). Even though most adolescents believe in God, and a large number are affiliated and active with a traditional religion, a question arises, Is there a trend for *more* or *less* religion? Perhaps the most extensive study to look at a long-term trend was in the Middleton studies, where a community was studied in depth in 1924 and again in 1977. In 1924 the concern was that there was a trend away from religion since 1890 and that the trend would continue. In 1977 the investigators found that the trend had not continued, and no major or substantial changes in religious behavior had occurred among adolescents between 1924 and 1977 (Caplow and Bahr 1979).

A distinction must be made between professing a religious belief and church attendance. Traditional church attendance and acceptance of conventional church beliefs are different from religion. Adolescents' nature likely predisposes them to search for answers, ideologies, and religion. Conventional churches may provide the answers, but in many cases do not. In discussing this problem, one reviewer writes:

> It seems then that what most adolescents need is understanding and guidance to help them through the period of adolescence. It is a critical time of life for youth as they try to formulate a system of beliefs which will help guide them through the rest of their life. Many have become frustrated with traditional religions and have turned to more radical forms of worship. . . . Many of the youths become disillusioned with traditional churches and shy away from them, though they still consider religion important in their lives. Perhaps if a more conscious effort were made on the part of churches to reach youth and deal with their problems, the church could provide more assurance and guidance to them at a crucial time in their lives. (Hauser 1981, 319)

QUESTION: Has a movement towards membership in religious cults occurred?

The answer appears to be yes. Movements such as Hare Krishna and the Jesus movement appear to have gained momentum, but only among a small but visible minority (Galanter 1980). These cults or religions may provide an organized structure for disillusioned youth. The actual dynamics of why some youth surrender their individuality to strong authoritarian cults are not understood. A common element seems to be a history of prior experimentation with life (e.g., drugs and sexual experimentation) that has been unsatisfactory (Bengston and Starr 1975, 224–66). Also likely is that the need to belong is an important motivation in seeking religious experiences with others in a community setting.

The issue of seeking extreme churches and cults and unorthodox mystical religious experiences is not adequately researched, but does constitute another recent phenomenon in adolescent behavior that is beginning to receive research and public attention. One researcher estimates that 2 to 3 million adolescents and young adults are members of religious cults (Swope 1980). His reasons for why youth join cults are:

1. *Idealistic*. Due to the teachings and example of family, religious leaders, peers, eduators, and others, there has developed within young people a desire to help others, to improve society, and often to know God better. The cults manipulate this idealism, convincing (their) members that only within their specialized groups can such inclinations be actualized.
2. *Innocent*. Because relationships with religious leaders in the past have been wholesome, the potential recruit naively believes that all who claim to speak in the name of God are sincere and trustworthy. Elmer Gantry and Jim Jones notwithstanding, the trappings of religion are a powerful lure here.
3. *Inquisitive*. On college and high school campuses around the country, intelligent young people, looking for interesting groups to join, are approached by enthusiastic, "together" recruiters who invite them to meetings where, they are told, they will meet other fine young people. It sounds exciting. Discussion, they are assured, will focus on ecology, world problems, religion, ethics, education—anything in which the recruit has shown some interest.
4. *Independent*. Many young people are recruited into cults when they are away from home—independent for the first time. Parents of such students are not always aware of how their children spend evenings and weekends, and often do not learn that they have left college until several weeks or months after they drop out. Backpackers are particular targets for cult recruiters. These young people are often lonely and susceptible to invitations for free meals and fellowship.
5. *Identity-seeking*. Young adults in every generation experience identity crises as they seek to determine their own strengths and weaknesses, their value systems, goals, religious and social beliefs.
6. *Insecure*. Inquisitive young people—looking for new experiences, seeking to clarify their own identities, away from the influence of family, friends, and mentors—develop uneasy feelings of insecurity. Lacking trusted counselors to whom they can turn when upset or disturbed, they are especially vulnerable to smiling, friendly people who show great interest in them and manipulate them through what one cult calls "love bombing." (Swope 1980, 20–21)

QUESTION: Is religion related to moral behavior?

Religion is apparently related to moral reasoning, behaviors, and values among devout and active members. Unknown is whether religious behavior is a cause or a result of other factors that produce both positive and negative moral action, thought, and values. Researchers indicate that religious people have more stringent and definite moral beliefs and consider a wider range of action to be wrong (Dedman 1959; Middleton and Putney 1962; Gorsuch and Aleshire 1974).

Religion may be too broad a term for classification purposes. Some researchers (Middleton and Putney 1962) differentiate ascetic morality from social morality. In ascetic morality the consequences of actions are felt mainly by the wrongdoer, but in social morality the consequences are felt by other people. These researchers believe that social morality results from group life and is equally present among people with and without religious beliefs. Ascetic morality results from religious training and traditions, and is not supported by nonbelievers. Actions such as sexual activity, gambling, smoking, and drinking are classified as ascetic morality, whereas stealing, cheating, and aggression are considered social morality. Middleton and Putney found that religion was related to ascetic morality, but was not as strongly related to social morality. Others have replicated their study (Wright and Cox 1967). These later researchers found the same results, but also discovered that religious subjects tended to be more severe in their evaluations:

> Analysis of the comments made by subjects on all items reveal a clear difference between the devout and the non-religious. The non-religious tend to argue that, if a form of behavior has no undesirable consequences for other people, it is not a legitimate matter for the moral evaluation of others; the devout claim that the individual's life is not his own, that all his behavior concerns God, and that hence there is no part of it which may not be the subject of moral evaluation on occasion. (Wright and Cox 1967, 142)

Expressing strong religious beliefs and active church attendance are apparently related to less deviant behavior, less problem behavior, and less marijuana and drug use among adolescents (Jessor and Jessor 1977).

Religion can play an important role in shaping adolescents' moral reasoning, behaviors, and values. Especially the training and traditions that are a part of many religions may lead to the development of an ascetic morality.

One author expressed the general correlation between religious affiliation and prosocial behavior by stating that church youth and others differ sharply in sense of moral responsibility; desire for meaningful life; religious participation; social action; self-regard; feelings for people; God-awareness; and family (Strommen 1974). Looking at more general areas this same researcher found that church youths identified more with their parents in the areas of values, attitudes, and life qualities, and engaged in less premarital sex, drinking, and drug use.

Another researcher found that religion was associated with enjoyment of school and a feeling of being in control of oneself within society (Gladding 1977). Other researchers have found this general attitude about self and role in society, which extends to even those who identify with more fundamental types of religion and the Jesus movement (Stones 1977).

The reason for the positive relationship between religious affiliation or motivation and general prosocial behavior or adjustment (or both) is hard to establish. Perhaps one does not cause the other, but other factors produce both religious behavior and social adjustment. A simple, parsimonious answer might be that adolescence is a time of searching for a meaning in life, as has been seen in Chapter 3, and that religion provides one answer for those adolescents, an answer that provides a way of dealing with moral and behavioral issues that result in positive behavior. Simply put, adolescents are looking for value systems and guidelines for behavior; traditional orthodox religion apparently provides both for some of these youth.

QUESTION: What are some implications about religion during adolescence?

As adolescents become more capable of abstract thought, they learn to compare and contrast ideas, and as discussed in the chapter on thinking, they then accept less and less on the basis of authority and conventionality. Not surprisingly, then, adolescents will begin to question religious beliefs and statements, and will want to formulate their own. This change often causes conflict with parents and established religious leaders. Since this process is inevitable, some consider that the wisest and only reasonable approach is to allow adolescents the freedom to question and challenge even established, cherished beliefs. Trying to prevent examination of religious beliefs by well-meaning conscientious adults will only produce rebellion, frustration, and resentment among youth. Even when cherished beliefs are rejected by adolescents, their appeal may reappear at a later time in life. This is more likely if adolescents have been granted freedom to accept or reject religious tenets. One text summarizes the problem this way:

> Adolescents confronted with their quest for religious identity ask, "Who am I? Why am I here? What is the purpose of life? What can I believe? What can I value? How should I live?"
>
> From biographies and autobiographies we can see that religious experiences in adolescents may in some individuals be deeply charged with feeling, ranging from ecstatic joy to despair and despondency.
>
> It is disquieting at any time of life to question what one has been taught by those one respects and loves. It is disturbing if one feels that one must reject what one has believed and taken for granted over a period of several

years. To question one's religion, if it has played an important role, is equivalent to questioning an important foundation to one's approach to life. When young people question their religious beliefs, it is not just a doctrine or a theory that they are questioning. They are, in a sense, calling into question their own capacity for understanding as well as the relationship with those who have taught them and in whom they have placed their trust. The fact that doubt may be uncomfortable perhaps accounts in part for the fact that a large proportion of adolescents do not doubt very seriously. (Jersild, Brook, and Brook 1978, 551)

This analysis of adolescent religious behavior may provide a basis for a compassionate understanding for the interaction of adolescents, organized religions, and the religious experience.

Although the research shows a strong positive association between professed religious beliefs and activity and positive social behavior, more research is needed to understand religion's effects. For example, the chapter on sexual behavior shows that religion is one of the best predictors of adolescent sexual activity. Therefore, although researchers in psychology have not been inclined to study religion, religion does seem to be a very powerful factor influencing human behavior.

Summary

Adolescence is a time when interest in deciding right from wrong is intense. New powers of moral reasoning come into play at this stage. The most popular theory for explaining moral development is the cognitive developmental approach of Piaget and Kohlberg. This approach views moral growth as the product of an interaction between innate mental structuring tendencies in the individual, which in turn develop by interacting with environmental contingencies. All individuals proceed through a series of distinct stages of moral development in the same order, differing only in how quickly or how far they develop.

Piaget identified two moralities. First, moral realism (morality of constraint, or heteronomous morality) is one in which children feel obliged to comply with rules because they are viewed as sacred and unalterable—either totally right or wrong, depending on whether a punishment is involved. Second, autonomous morality (morality of cooperation, or reciprocity) is one in which children view rules in terms of respect for others rather than in terms of obedience to authority. The transformation from the former to the latter morality depends on cognitive development and on social interaction. A *cognitive disequilibrium* results from contradiction between a child's perspective and the expectations of others.

Attempting to extend Piaget's analysis, Kohlberg formulated his six stages of moral development. His first four levels are classes within Piaget's stage one. In stage one, punishment and obedience orientation and the goodness or badness of an action are determined by the physical consequences. Stage two is an instrumental relativist orientation. The right action is one that satisfies one's own needs. Reciprocity is not a matter of gratitude, justice, nor loyalty. At stage three, interpersonal concordance, much conformity to stereotypical images takes place, and behavior is judged by intention (i.e., "he means well"). Stage four is the law and order orientation—toward authority, fixed rules, and maintenance of the social order. Stage five is the social-contract, legalistic orientation. This is the "official" morality of the American government and Constitution. Right action is defined in terms of individual rights that have been agreed upon by society. Stage six is the universal ethical principle orientation—abstract ethical principles (defined by the conscience) that are comprehensive, universal, and consistent.

Kohlberg maintains that moral development is sequential and directed. He sees the individual as developing self-reliance and commitment to self-chosen principles. Similarly, Piaget emphasizes the development of an autonomous morality.

One researcher claims that Kohlberg's theory is culturally biased. Another labels it "romantic individualism." Whether confirmed or not, Piaget and Kohlberg's theories have helped to develop further understanding of the highly complex nature of moral development and the role of social experience in moral growth.

These theories have practical applications to improve moral reasoning. One guideline is that parents should allow children to be exposed to a wide range of information and experience. As children begin to assert their individuality, they must be encouraged by the respect and acceptance of their family. Parents can move from explicit to implicit rules in the home. Appropriate discipline can be maintained as well as a significant degree of autonomy.

Parents' primary task is to be morally mature themselves. Their second task is justification of their basic moral assumptions. Parents can stimulate children's moral maturity by actively discussing aspects of morality and presenting moral possibilities. In general, people with higher levels of moral reasoning tend to act more mature.

Values are closely related to moral behavior. According to Rokeach, values are transcendent, enduring beliefs. He distinguishes terminal from instrumental values. Values are sometimes called structures of the personality because they are relatively stable and enduring beliefs. Values are measured in different ways—through studies, tests, and rising personal and cultural products as indirect evidence of personal and cultural values.

Since adolescence cannot be conceived of as a single, universal experience, speaking of adolescent values in general is a mistake. An adolescent's values are influenced by age. With age, boys and girls place greater emphasis or value on achievements, open-mindedness, responsibility, and self-respect, and less value on conformity to convention and authority.

Differences have been found among the values of adolescents from different cultures, due to cultural variations in degree of industrialization, affluence, and education. Different historical events and social forces also affect adolescent values, and male and female adolescents have differing values.

Programs such as Values Clarification have been developed to improve adolescent values. This program stresses teaching youth *how* to value (valuing) rather than *what* values to have.

Several theories help explain moral behavior. The first psychological theory that has had a direct emphasis is the psychoanalytic view, which involves Freud's Oedipal conflict and Electra complex. (The young son seeks the mother's attention, and the young daughter seeks the father's attention. In controlling this anxiety and frustration, the child tries to emulate the parents.) According to Hoffman, *empathy* provides the primary motive for moral action. He lists three modes of empathic arousal that apply to adolescents: empathy through association, through motor mimicry, and through imagination. Youth also experience guilt, which is a motivator for moral behavior.

The way children are disciplined has an effect on moral internalization. Hoffman organized discipline into three major types: (1) power assertion, which includes physical force, deprivation of privileges, and the threat of these, (2) love withdrawal, which includes strong but nonphysical expressions of anger and disapproval, and (3) induction, which includes explanations for why children should change their behavior.

Results of studies on these discipline types indicate that power assertive techniques create a fear of external punishment, and inductive techniques create an independence of external sanctions and a greater capacity for healthy guilt. The communication of moral instruction may be obscured by overuse of power assertion and love withdrawal. Hoffman also believes that the mother has a more important influence on a child's moral internalization than does the father.

Theorists disagree as to whether the influence of peers on moral development is generally constructive. If moral development is always progressive, the net effect of peer interactions will be positive, but experimental research seems to confirm that moral action tends toward the lowest common denominator among adolescent peer groups. The self-concept also influences moral behavior. With changes in self-perception there follows a difference in resistance to temptation behavior.

Religion is related to moral reasoning. A positive relationship exists between religious affiliation and general prosocial behavior or adjustment (or both). Adolescents are looking for value systems and behavior guidelines, which are often provided by religion.

References

Allport, G. W., P. E. Vernon, & G. Lindsey. 1951. *A study of values: A scale for measuring the dominant interests in personality*. Rev. ed. Boston: Houghton Mifflin.
———. 1960. *A study of values: Manual of directions*. Boston: Houghton Mifflin.
Aronson, E. 1966. The psychology of insufficient justification: An analysis of some conflicting data. In *Cognitive consistency,* ed. S. Feldman, 109–33. New York: Academic Press.
Astin, A. 1977a. *Four critical years*. San Francisco: Jossey-Bass.
———. 1977b. The new realists. *Psychology Today:* 50–53, 105–7 (September).
Bakan, D. 1966. *The duality of human existence*. Chicago: Rand McNally.
Bandura, A., J. E. Grusec, & F. L. Menlove. 1967. Some determinants of self-monitoring reinforcement systems. *Journal of Personality and Social Psychology* 5: 449–55.
Bandura, A., & L. Rosenthol. 1966. Vicarious classical conditioning as a function of arousal level. *Journal of Personality and Social Psychology* 3: 54–62.
Beech, R. P., & A. Schoeppe. 1974. Development of value systems in adolescence. *Developmental Psychology* 10: 644–56.
Bem, D. J. 1965. An experimental analysis of self-persuasion. *Journal of Experimental Social Psychology* 1: 199–218.
Bengston, V. L., & J. M. Starr. 1975. Contrast and consensus: A generational analysis of youth in the 1970s. In part 1 of *Youth: The seventy-fourth yearbook of the National Society for the Study of Education,* ed. R. J. Havighurst & P. H. Dreyer, 224–64. Chicago: Univ. of Chicago Press.

Bernal, G., & S. M. Berger. 1975. Some effects of a model's performance on observer electromyographic activity. *American Journal of Psychology* 88: 263–76.

Block, J. 1973. Conceptions of sex role: Some cross-cultural and longitudinal perspectives. *American Psychologist* 28: 512–26.

Boyce, D., & L. Jensen. 1978. *Moral reasoning.* Lincoln: Univ. of Nebraska Press.

Bronfenbrenner, U. 1970. *Two worlds of childhood: U.S. and U.S.S.R.* New York: Russell Sage Foundation.

Caplow, T., & H. Bahr. 1979. Half a century of change in adolescent attitudes: Replication of a Middletown survey by the Lynds. *Public Opinion Quarterly* 43: 1–18.

Connell, R. W., R. E. Stroobant, K. E. Sinclair, & K. W. Rogers. 1975. *Twelve to twenty: Studies of city youth.* Sydney, Australia: Hicks, Smith.

Dedman, J. 1959. The relationship between religious attitude and attitude towards premarital sex relation. *Marriage and Family Living* 21: 171–76.

Douvan, E., & J. Adelson. 1966. *The adolescent experience.* New York: Wiley.

Dukes, W. F. 1955. Physiological studies of values. *Psychological Bulletin* 52: 24–50.

Feather, M. T. 1975. *Values in education and society.* New York: Free Press.

_____. 1980. Values in adolescents. In *Handbook of adolescent psychology,* ed. J. Adelson. New York: Wiley.

Galanter, M. 1980. Psychological induction into the large group: Findings from a contemporary religious sect. *American Journal of Psychiatry* 137: 1574–79.

Gladding, S. T. 1977. Psychological anomie and religious identity in two adolescent populations. *Psychological Reports* 41: 419–24 (October).

Gorsuch, R. L., & D. Aleshire. 1974. Christian faith and ethnic prejudice: A review and interpretation of research. *Journal for the Scientific Study of Religion* 13: 281–307.

Hauser, J. 1981. Adolescents and religion. *Adolescence* 16(62): 311–19 (Summer).

Havighurst, R. J. 1975. Youth in social institutions. In *Youth,* ed. R. J. Havighurst & P. H. Dreyer. Chicago: Univ. of Chicago Press.

Hoffman, M. L. 1975. Sex differences in moral internalization. *Journal of Personality and Social Psychology* 32: 720–29.

_____. 1977a. Empathy, its development and pro-social implications. In *Nebraska symposium on motivation,* vol. 25, ed. C. Keasey. Lincoln: Univ. of Nebraska Press.

_____. 1977b. Moral internalization: Current theory and research. In *Advances in experimental social psychology,* vol. 10, ed. L. Berkowitz. New York: Academic Press.

_____. 1980. Moral development and adolescence. In *Handbook of adolescent psychology,* ed. J. Adelson. New York: Wiley.

Hogan, R. 1975. Theoretical egocentrism and the problem of compliance. *American Psychologist* 30: 533–40.

Jersild, A. T., J. S. Brook, & D. W. Brook. 1978. *The psychology of adolescence.* 3d ed. New York: Macmillan.

Jessor, R., & S. L. Jessor. 1977. *Problem behavior and psychosocial behavior: A longitudinal study of youth.* New York: Academic Press.

Keniston, K. 1965. *The uncommitted.* New York: Harcourt Brace Jovanovich.

_____. 1970. Student activism, moral development, and morality. *American Journal of Orthopsychiatry* 40: 577–92.

_____. 1971. *Youth and dissent: The rise of a new opposition.* New York: Harcourt Brace Jovanovich.

Kluckholm, F. R., & F. L. Strodtveck. 1961. *Variations in value orientations.* Evanston, Ill.: Row, Peterson.

Kohlberg, L. 1964. Development of moral character and moral ideology. In *Review of child development research,* vol. 1, ed. H. Hoffman & L. Hoffman. New York: Russell Sage Foundation.

_____. 1969. Stage and sequence: The cognitive-environmental approach to socialization. In *Handbook of socialization theory and research,* ed. D. Goslin. Chicago: Rand McNally.

_____. 1973. Continuities in childhood and adult moral development revisited. In *Lifespan developmental psychology: Personality and socialization,* ed. P. Baltes & K. W. Shaie. New York: Academic Press.

_____. 1975. The cognitive developmental approach: New developments and a response to criticism. Paper presented at the annual meeting of the Society for Research in Child Development, Denver, March.

———. 1976. Moral stages and moralization: The cognitive-developmental approach. In *Moral development and behavior*, ed. T. Lickona. New York: Holt, Rinehart & Winston.
———. 1980. *Recent research in moral development*. New York: Holt, Rinehart & Winston.
Kurtines, W. & E. Grief. 1974. The development of moral thought: review and evaluation of Kohlberg's approach. *Psychology Bulletin* 81: 453–70.
Laird, J. D. 1974. Self-attribution of emotion: The effects of expressive behavior on the duality of emotional experience. *Journal of Personality and Social Psychology* 29: 475–86.
Lepper, M. R. 1973. Dissonance, self-perception and honesty in children. *Journal of Personality and Social Psychology* 25 (1): 65–75.
Middleton, R., & S. Putney. 1962. Religion, normative standards and behavior. *Sociometry* 25: 141–52.
Minuchin, P. P., & E. K. Shapiro. 1983. The school as a context for social development. In *Handbook of child psychology*, 4th ed., ed. P. H. Mussen. New York: Wiley.
Morris, C. W. 1956. *Varieties of human values*. Chicago: Univ. of Chicago Press.
Morris, C. W., & L. Small. 1971. Changes in conceptions of the good life by American college students from 1950 to 1970. *Journal of Personality and Social Psychology* 20: 254–60.
Mower, C. H. 1950. *Learning theory and personality dynamics*. New York: Ronald Press.
Peck, R. F., & R. J. Havighurst. 1960. *The psychology of character development*. New York: Wiley.
Peters, R. S. 1971. Moral development: A plea for pluralism. In *Cognitive development and epistemology*, ed. T. Mischel. New York: Academic Press.
Piaget, J. 1965. *The moral judgment of the child*. New York: Free Press.
Power, C. 1979. The moral atmosphere of a just community high school: A four-year longitudinal study. Ph.D. diss., Harvard University.
Raths, L., M. Harmin, & S. Simon. 1966. *Values and teaching: Working with values in the classroom*. Columbus, Ohio: Merrill.
Rokeach, 1973. *The nature of human values*. New York: Free Press.
Sigelman, L. 1977. Review of the polls. *Journal for the Scientific Study of Religion* 16: 289–94 (September).
Simpson, E. L. 1974. Moral development research: A case study of scientific cultural bias. *Human Development* 17: 81–106.
Spinoza, B. 1927. *Ethics*, trans. W. Hale White. London: Oxford Univ. Press.
Staub, E. 1978. *Positive social behavior and morality*, vols. 1 and 2. New York: Academic Press.
Stones, C. 1977. The Jesus people: Changes in security and lifestyle as a function of nonconformist religious influence. *Journal of Psychology* 97: 123–33. (September).
Stotland, E. 1972. Exploratory investigations of empathy. In *Advances in experimental social psychology*, vol. 6, ed. L. Berkowitz. New York: Academic Press.
Strommen, N. M. P. 1974. *Five cries of youth*. New York: Harper & Row.
Swope, G. W. 1980. Kids and cults: Who joins and why? *Media and Method* 16: 18–21.
Williams, R. M., Jr. 1968. Values. In *International encyclopedia of the social sciences*, ed. D. L. Sills. New York: Crowell Collier & Macmillan.
Wright, D., & E. Cox. 1967. A study of the relationship between moral judgement and religious belief in a sample of English adolescents. *Journal of Social Psychology* 20: 135–44.
Yankelovich, D. 1972. *The changing values in campus*. New York: Washington Square Press.
———. 1974. *The new morality: A profile of American youth in the 70s*. New York: McGraw-Hill.

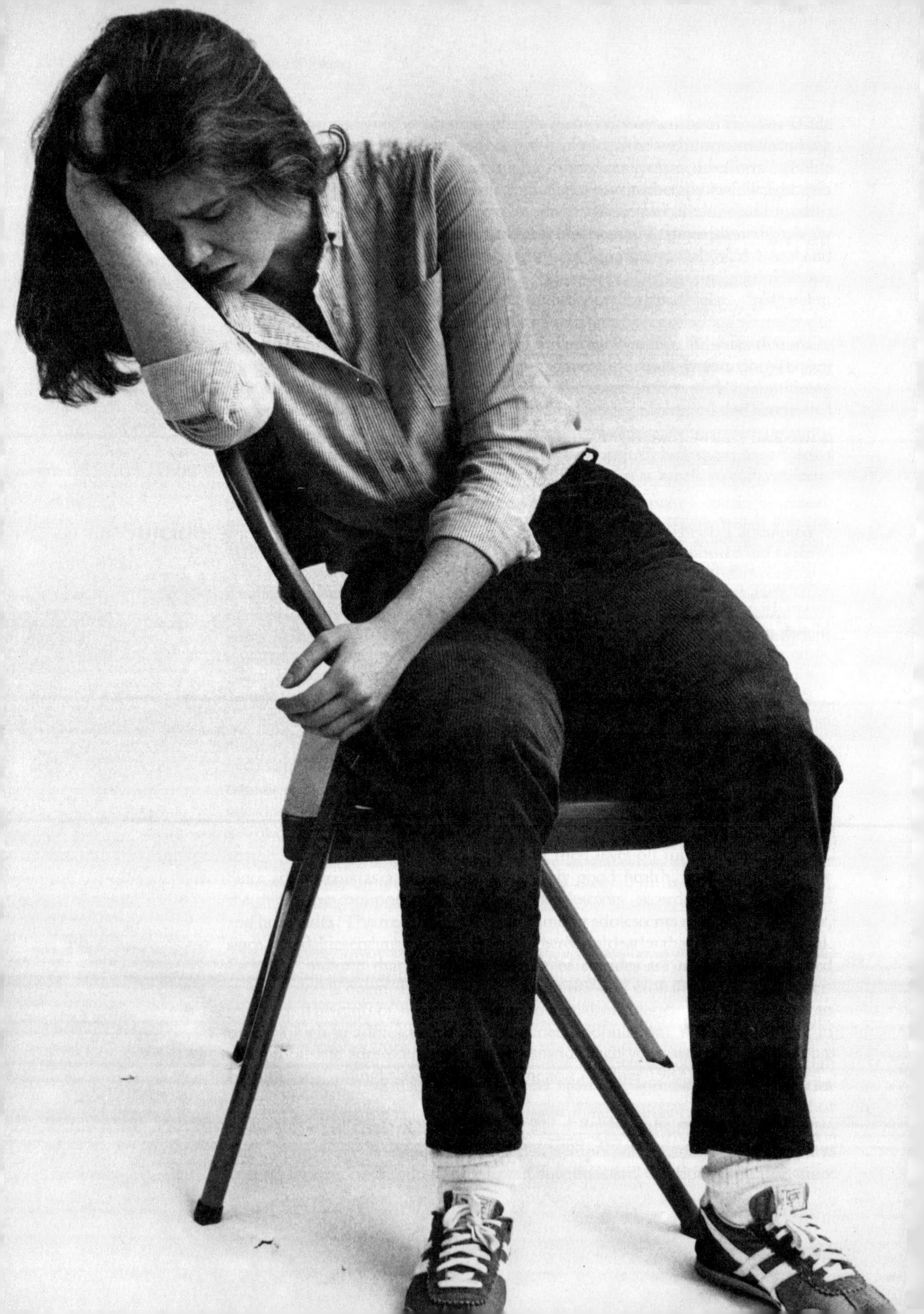

CHAPTER ELEVEN

Clinical problems in adolescence

SURVEY AND QUESTIONS

In this chapter the following topics and questions will be presented and discussed:

Mental Health and Stress

If the concept of mental health is subject to different interpretations, how can we decide which adolescents need clinical attention?
Does mental health depend on how much stress the adolescent is under?
How can one determine how much stress an adolescent is experiencing?
How can an adolescent learn to cope successfully with stress?

Hyperactivity

Are some youth "born to be bad?"
What is hyperactivity?
How common is hyperactivity?
How can adolescents with hyperactivity be identified and treated?

Depression or Affective Disorders

Are some symptoms of hyperactivity, such as depression, common among adolescents?
How common is depression among adolescents?
How can adolescents with affective disorders be identified?
Do adolescents conceal their depression?
What are the explanations for becoming depressed?
Are the causes of manic-depressive disorders different from the causes of depression?
How can adolescents with affective disorders be helped?

Neurosis

At what point does a fear become a phobia?
What are the origins of phobias?
Are particular phobias especially common among adolescents?
What is an obsessive-compulsive disorder?
At what point do preoccupations and cautiousness become obsessive compulsiveness?
What causes an adolescent to become obsessive-compulsive?

Conversion Reaction

What is a conversion reaction?
How long do conversion reactions last?

Are some adolescents more likely than others to display conversion reactions or hypochondriasis?
Is therapy necessary for adolesents who show neurotic symptoms?
What are the basic therapeutic approaches?

Schizophrenia

Are adolescents more likely to show a quick recovery from schizophrenic symptoms?
Are adolescents with schizophrenia distinguishable from those with other problems?
How can adolescent schizophrenia be prevented and treated?

Anorexia Nervosa

What is the origin and nature of anorexia nervosa?
How should adolescents with anorexia nervosa be treated?

Suicide

Are adolescent suicide attempts a call for help?
What motivates suicidal behavior in adolescents?
How should suicidal adolescents be treated?

My 20-year-old male cousin just committed suicide. I believe that peer problems were the biggest factor in his death.

When he was little he was cheerful, outgoing and happy although he had to wear a leg brace. As he grew older he became more and more withdrawn and quiet. His parents are quiet people and have a good marriage as far as I know.

When he went to school he was considered to be a slow learner and placed in with the retarded and disabled kids. He was not retarded but never spoke much and when he did it was slow and deliberate. The kids at school were really mean to him and always treated him as if he were retarded. The label stuck and he was never able to progress socially and never really had any friends except for one retarded boy. After school he stayed at home to help his dad farm. He was the youngest and therefore all alone at home. I know he was lonely and depressed and must have sent out many warning signals that we should have caught but didn't.

He should never have been placed in the school situation he was in. And those of us who were near him should have been more sensitive and helpful to his needs.

This sorrowful retrospective account illustrates only one of the many serious clinical problems that become manifest during adolescence. This chapter discusses this and other clinical problems. To provide an adequate discussion, being more precise and technical than in other chapters is necessary.

Clinical issues in adolescence include abnormal behaviors as well as those which appear unhealthy. What is meant by *abnormal* and *unhealthy?* These terms are defined in different ways by psychologists, and are often used as though they were roughly synonymous. Even in common usage, abnormality is often confused with unhealthiness, such as when we call someone "crazy" when we really mean that the person is eccentric. In this chapter, however, abnormality simply means "different from the average; unusual; irregular," as typically used in the standard college dictionary. In other words, normality is a statistical concept; a behavior is normal if it is typical of a given group of people. Psychologists use the word *normal* in this way when they say that someone has "normal intelligence." People with normal intelligence are those whose scores on intelligence tests are close to the average for their age group.

A moment's reflection will convince most that people are not necessarily unhealthy just because they are abnormal. Geniuses, for example, are quite abnormal, but are not necessarily unhealthy. Perfection of any kind is highly abnormal, and yet striving for perfection is not abnormal. The converse is also true. Just as being abnormal is not necessarily unhealthy, being normal is not necessarily healthy. When people ask questions like, "What is this world coming to?", they usually mean that unhealthy behavior seems to be the rule rather than the exception. Occasionally, psychologists have argued that normal behavior *cannot* be viewed as unhealthy behavior. Leo Canner, a leader in the field of child psychiatry, makes this kind of argument about the 65 percent of schoolchildren who bite their nails at some time or another: "It is hardly realistic to assume that two-thirds of our youth are degenerate, exquisitely psychopathic or walking around with an unresolved Oedipus complex" (Canner 1960). Canner is right that these children should not be viewed as "degenerate," since most of us do not regard nail biting as seriously unhealthy. This, however, is no reason to reject the idea that nail biting might be a reaction to some kind of problem. Mob violence is a better example of behavior that can become statistically normal, but which is regarded by most people as seriously unhealthy. Although the distinction is arbitrary, behavior that is both normal and unhealthy is often viewed as a sociological rather than a psychological problem.

Normality and abnormality can be given a precise statistical definition, but healthiness and unhealthiness cannot. Unlike normality and abnormality, the quality of an adolescent's mental health depends on one's point of view. From society's viewpoint, an adolescent's mental health is defined in terms of its conformance with sociocultural norms. From an individual viewpoint, mental health tends to be defined in terms of happiness or self-satisfaction. From the viewpoint of mental health professionals, mental health tends to be defined in terms of some ideal of personal integration or actualization (Strupp and Hadley 1977). These points of view can be at odds with one another, as when adolescents feel altogether satisfied with their membership in violent gangs or in communal religious cults. When making judgments about mental health, specifying which vantage point one is taking is therefore important.

Mental health and stress

QUESTION: If the concept of mental health is subject to different interpretations, how can we decide which adolescents need clinical attention?

As might be expected, the question of when an adolescent needs clinical attention can be complicated. Fortunately, much of the time the individual, societal, and professional viewpoints agree as to whether an adolescent has a psychological problem, as, for example, when an adolescent attempts suicide. Adolescent suicide attempts can be a call for help, and are usually (although strangely enough, not always) taken to be indications of legitimate need by parents, professionals, and government agencies. In other cases, however, disagreements may arise as in the case of so-called conduct disorders. For example, not uncommon is for young adolescent girls to be referred by their parents for treatment for promiscuity, even though the adolescents themselves may see nothing wrong with their behavior. Ethical problems often arise whenever adolescents, their parents, professionals, and society disagree as to whether an adolescent is psychologically disturbed.

QUESTION: Does mental health depend on how much stress the adolescent is under?

Another factor that complicates the question of whether an adolescent needs clinical attention is that poor mental, emotional, and physical health is often the *normal* reaction to excessive stress. This means that an adolescent who might be healthy under one set of circumstances may exhibit unhealthy behavior under another set of circumstances. Psychologists have found that any change in circumstances that requires some kind of individual adjustment involves some stress. Normal life events, even joyous events, can apparently add up to produce what psychologists call "reactive disorders." If adolescence can be viewed as a period of rapid growth and change, then adolescence should be a period of relatively high stress (Erikson 1963; Holmes and Rahe 1967).

The official *Diagnostic and Statistical Manual,* third edition (DSMIII), classification system of the American Psychiatric Association divides reactive disorders into two types: post-traumatic stress disorders and adjustment disorders. Adjustment disorders are problems that result from the cumulative stress of ordinary life. Post-traumatic stress disorders are problems that result from traumas or catastrophes of sufficient magnitude to produce symptoms of distress in most people. For example, victims of rape or of serious automobile accidents are likely to experience post-traumatic stress disorders. These two categories should be regarded as having somewhat fluid boundaries, since what is traumatic to one adolescent is not necessarily so to another (Lazarus and Launier 1979). Although the life changes involved in adjustment disorders may seem relatively insignificant, their cumulative weight seems to be an important factor, especially in suicidal inclinations, depression, and schizophrenia (Paykel 1974).

Stressors (i.e., things that bring on stress) can have several different origins. Biological stressors are conditions such as infection, fatigue, and malnutrition. Psychological stressors are conditions such as fear and guilt. Social stressors are conditions such as unemployment, overpopulation, and war. The rapid social changes such as those which Alvin Toffler desribed in his popular book *Future Shock* (Toffler 1970) are examples of social stressors, which Toffler believes increase mental illness.

QUESTION: How can one determine how much stress an adolescent is experiencing?

Since adolescents differ in their interpretation of situations and in their coping ability, predicting precisely when adolescents may be reaching their breaking point is impossible. Nevertheless, certain conditions do seem to amplify stress. Life changes are more likely to be experienced as stressful by an adolescent when many occur during the same period of time, when they are sudden or novel, when they are ambiguous or inevitable, and when the adolescent is isolated from family, friends, and outside communication. A helpful model for understanding the course of reactions to stress has been developed by Hans Selye (1956). Selye identified three stages of the general adaptation syndrome: (1) the alarm stage, when the person becomes aware of the stressor, (2) the stage of resistance, when one attempts to cope with the stressor, and (3) the stage of exhaustion, when coping behaviors fail, or when one stops attempting to cope.

QUESTION: How can an adolescent learn to cope successfully with stress?

Life changes during adolescence are not only numerous but also unfamiliar and unexpected. Add to this adolescents' uncertainty about themselves and about their relationships with others, and seeing why adolescents may be especially vulnerable to stress is easy. Resisting stress can be done through several possible methods: (1) practice, (2) preparation, (3) information, and (4) collaboration. Practice helps reduce the novelty of stressful situations and enhances adolescents' confidence that they can deal with the situation. Even mental practice can dramatically improve performance and hence confidence. Important, though, is that adolescents imagine themselves *successfully* managing the stressful situation. Studies of dart throwing, for example, have shown that mental practice can improve accuracy, but only if the subject imagined that their darts were hitting near the target center (Howell 1973).

Preparation for a stressful situation helps prevent a sense of panic or hopelessness by improving one's chances for dealing successfully with the situation. For example, adolescents may prepare for the possibility that they will not get into the college of their choice by applying to other colleges. Information helps to reduce the ambiguity of stressful situations.

Dealing with stressors by denying them is not necessarily unhealthy. This is particularly true when nothing can be done to change the factors that produce the stress, as when an adolescent experiences the death of a friend or a family member. Denial may be the only coping mechanism available for the time being (Lazarus and Launier 1979).

Social support, probably the most important coping mechanism of all, reduces adolescents' sense of loneliness and meaninglessness. At times when adolescents' entire world appears to be in flux, the most important question may be whether adolescents have an island of strong and dependable relationships with others. These relationships should be ones in which adolescents receive more encouragement than criticism, and in which they are urged to take on new challenges and to rely on themselves.

There are ways in which an adolescent can learn to cope successfully with stress. Friends and social support, for example, can provide the necessary strength and stability an adolescent may need to cope with a stressful situation.

Hyperactivity

QUESTION: Are some youth "born to be bad?"

When asked when the trouble began, parents of troubled adolescents are often heard to say, "He's been a problem since the day he was born!" Parents are often able to recall problems in feeding and sleeping that date back to their adolescent's infancy. Research has confirmed that the developmental history of some troubled youth consists of a long chain of irregularities (Thomas, Chess, and Birch 1970, 108-9). In infancy, the child may have eaten and slept poorly and cried frequently. Such children are often fitful, temperamental, and slow to acquire motor and language skills. Later, during the preschool years, these children are more excitable, impulsive, and prone to distraction than are other children. They may also be ill-tempered, aggressive, or generally restless. In elementary school, they are more likely to be learning disabled, and may fail one or more grades in school even though they may be of normal or high intelligence. In the classroom, these children are likely to daydream, make strange sounds, move about without permission, and be aggressive or negative (see Table 11-1 for examples). Not uncommonly, this behavior makes them unpopular with their peers and teachers. As a consequence of constant teasing and criticism, these children are likely to develop a low self-esteem. In an effort to make matters better, they may often make matters worse by behaving in silly ways that are intended to attract attention. This progression is so common among children that it has been labeled the "hyperactive child syndrome."

TABLE 11-1 The Stability of Temperaments Over Time

Temperamental Quality	Rating	2 Months	6 Months
Activity level	Low	Does not move when being dressed or during sleep.	Passive in bath. Plays quietly in crib and falls asleep.
	High	Moves often in sleep. Wriggles when diaper is changed.	Tries to stand in tub and splashes. Bounces in crib. Crawls after dog.
Rhythmicity	Regular	Has been on 4-hour feeding schedule since birth. Regular bowel movement.	Is asleep at 6:30 every night. Awake at 7:00 A.M. Food intake is constant.
	Irregular	Awakes at a different time each morning. Size of feeding varies.	Length of nap varies; so does food intake.
Approach/withdrawal	Positive	Smiles and licks washcloth. Has always liked bottle.	Likes new foods. Enjoyed first bath in large tub. Smiles and gurgles.
	Negative	Rejected cereal the first time. Cries when strangers appear.	Smiles and babbles at strangers. Plays with new toys immediately.
Adaptability	Adaptive	Was passive during first bath, now enjoys bathing. Smiles at nurse.	Used to dislike new foods; now accepts them well.
	Not adaptive	Still startled by sudden, sharp noises. Resists diapering.	Does not cooperate with dressing. Fusses and cries when left with sitter.

Intensity of reaction	Mild	Does not cry when diapers are wet. Whimpers instead of crying when hungry.	Does not kick often in tub. Does not smile. Screams and kicks when temperature is taken.
	Intense	Cries when diapers are wet. Rejects food vigorously when satisfied.	Cries loudly at the sound of thunder. Makes sucking movements when vitamins are administered.
Quality of mood	Positive	Smacks lips when first tasting new food. Smiles at parents.	Plays and splashes in bath. Smiles at everyone.
	Negative	Fusses after nursing. Cries when carriage is rocked.	Cries when taken from tub. Cries when given food she does not like.

Key:

	Easy Child	Slow-to-Warm-Up Child	Difficult Child
Activity level	Varies	Low to moderate	Varies
Rhythmicity	Very regular	Varies	Irregular
Approach/withdrawal	Positive approach	Initial withdrawal	Withdrawal
Adaptability	Very adaptable	Slowly adaptable	Slowly adaptable
Intensity of reaction	Low or mild	Mild	Intense
Quality of mood	Positive	Slightly negative	Negative

1 Year	2 Years	5 Years	10 Years
Finishes bottle slowly. Goes to sleep easily. Allows nail-cutting without fussing.	Enjoys quiet play with puzzles. Can listen to records for hours.	Takes a long time to dress. Sits quietly on long automobile rides.	Likes chess and reading. Eats very slowly.
Walks rapidly. Eats eagerly. Climbs into everything.	Climbs furniture. Explores. Gets in and out of bed while being put to sleep.	Leaves table often during meals. Always runs.	Plays ball and engages in other sports. Cannot sit still long enough to do homework.
Naps after lunch each day. Always drinks bottle before bed.	Eats a big lunch each day. Always has a snack before bedtime.	Falls asleep when put to bed. Bowel movement regular.	Eats only at mealtimes. Sleeps the same amount of time each night.
Will not fall asleep for an hour or more. Moves bowels at a different time each day.	Nap time changes from day to day. Toilet training is difficult because bowel movement is unpredictable.	Food intake varies; so does time of bowel movement.	Food intake varies. Falls asleep at a different time each night.
Approaches strangers readily. Sleeps well in new surroundings.	Slept well the first time he stayed overnight at grandparents' house.	Entered school building unhesitatingly. Tries new foods.	Went to camp happily. Loved to ski the first time.
Cries when placed on sled. Will not sleep in strange beds.	Avoids strange children in the playground. Whimpers first time at beach. Will not go into water.	Hid behind mother when entering school.	Severely homesick at camp during first days. Does not like new activities.
Was afraid of toy animals at first, now plays with them happily.	Obeys quickly. Stayed contentedly with grandparents for a week.	Hesitated to go to nursery school at first; now goes eagerly. Slept well on camping trip.	Likes camp, although homesick during first days. Learns enthusiastically.

Continues to reject new foods each time they are offered.	Cries and screams each time hair is cut. Disobeys persistently.	Has to be hand led into classroom each day. Bounces on bed in spite of spankings.	Does not adjust well to new school or new teacher; comes home late for dinner even when punished.
Does not fuss much when clothing is pulled on over head.	When another child hit her, she looked surprised, did not hit back.	Drops eyes and remains silent when given a firm parental "No." Does not laugh much.	When a mistake is made in a model airplane, corrects it quietly. Does not comment when reprimanded.
Laughs hard when father plays roughly. Screams and kicks when temperature is taken.	Yells if he feels excitement or delight. Cries loudly if a toy is taken away.	Rushes to greet father. Gets hiccups from laughing hard.	Tears up an entire page of homework if one mistake is made. Slams door of room when teased by younger brother.
Likes bottle; reaches for it and smiles. Laughs loudly when playing peekaboo.	Plays with sister: laughs and giggles. Smiles when he succeeds in putting shoes on.	Laughs loudly while watching television cartoons. Smiles at everyone.	Enjoys new accomplishments. Laughs when reading a funny passage aloud.
Cries when given injections. Cries when left alone.	Cries and squirms when given haircut. Cries when mother leaves.	Objects to putting boots on. Cries when frustrated.	Cries when he cannot solve a homework problem. Very "weepy" if he does not get enough sleep.

Source: Adapted from H. Thomas, S. Chess, and H. Birch, "The Origin of Personality," *Scientific American* 223(2): 108–9 (1970).

QUESTION: What is hyperactivity?

Assuming that this syndrome involved some impairment of the central nervous system, medical researchers later called it "minimal brain dysfunction (MBD)." In the DSMIII, the American Psychiatric Association has renamed it "attention deficit disorder (ADD)" to avoid the implication of brain damage, which has not been demonstrated (American Psychiatric Association 1980). For the remainder of this chapter, we refer to this condition simply as hyperactivity. Since many hyperactive children gain more self-control with age, a common belief is that hyperactive children grow out of their problem. Studies seem to confirm that about half of the hyperactive children do show moderate or marked improvement in adolescence. Without treatment, however, at least half of these children develop even more severe problems (Mendelson, Johnson, and Stewart 1971; Minde et al. 1972; Milich and Loney 1979). Since much of academic learning is cumulative in nature, hyperactive children may fall even further behind their peers in school as adolescents. Repeated failures in school and rejection by peers and teachers sometimes cause these children to become extremely withdrawn and depressed as adolescents. They may become socially isolated, or they may seek the company of younger children or of antisocial peer groups.

When an antisocial peer group becomes the basis of adolescents' identity, adolescents' delinquent behavior often draws attention away from their underlying difficulties. Follow-up studies of hyperactive children have found that anywhere from 25 percent to 60 percent of them are subsequently involved in antisocial conduct serious enough to cause conflicts with authorities. For example, consider the following case of David:

> David was 13 years old and in the eighth grade when he first came to professional attention. The occasion was a call from the school about his having scratched a mirror in the lavatory. His parents sought psychological help, since they regarded this as the last straw in a series of events that had been worrying them recently, including (a) wide variations in David's academic performance, (b) his inability to sustain any friendships, (c) his frequently getting into fights, mainly because of being highly sensitive to personal slights and easily provoked to anger, and (d) persistent bed-wetting. For years they had tended to gloss over these problems, primarily because "he was never left back in school, so things couldn't have been that bad."
>
> Now, however, having finally decided that David's problem called for attention, they were able with the psychologist's assistance to recall some diagnostically significant features of his earlier life as well. He was anoxic at birth and required emergency measures to start him breathing after he already appeared blue and lifeless. As a preschooler, he "walked funny" and sometimes was difficult to understand because of "slurred speech." When he entered school he still seemed "clumsy," and in the third grade a school psychologist described him as very poorly coordinated.
>
> David's own view of himself at age 13 was "I'm a big, stupid clod," and he felt that the only way he could avoid being mocked or taken advantage of by others was to "show them who's boss" and "make them sorry for fooling with me." In fact, he was neither stupid nor any longer clumsy. Testing indicated average intelligence, with an I.Q. of 105, and he showed only very slight difficulties in perceptual-motor coordination or in tasks requiring attention, concentration, and concept formation. Moreover, his above-average size and strength were making him respected more and teased less by his peers than before.
>
> Nevertheless, after years of struggling to preserve his self-respect with lashing out at others as his only tool, David already bore numerous personality scars. In particular, he seemed on the verge of becoming a characterologically impulsive, self-centered, aggressive individual with little consideration for the rights and needs of others. Psychotherapy was recommended in the hope of helping David avoid any further movement toward an adult impulse disorder. (Weiner 1982, 144–45)

QUESTION: How common is hyperactivity?

Estimates of the prevalence of hyperactivity vary widely, depending on how strictly the term is defined. Hyperactivity possibly affects as many as 5 percent of school-age children—at least one child in every classroom. For unknown reasons, hyperactivity is more common in boys than in girls, by a ratio of between three and seven to one. Over a third of hyperactive children fail to improve at all during adolescence (Weiner 1982, 130).

Although the number of adults who continue to suffer has not been determined, it is probably substantial. Hyperactive adults may commonly be diagnosed as having impulse disorders, depression, or other problems. In one study of the long-term consequences of ADD, twenty men who had been diagnosed as having ADD as children were interviewed twenty to twenty-five years later. Although the severity of their symptoms had decreased considerably, comparisons with their brothers showed that they were still more nervous, restless, irritable, and depressed. They were found to have fewer friends and a lower socioeconomic status than that of their brothers, even though they were of comparable intelligence. Nine of them, compared with none of their brothers, were found to have some emotional disorder (Borland and Heckman 1976). Although the idea that hyperactivity is outgrown clearly has some truth, also clear is that without treatment, many hyperactive children become troubled adolescents and adults.

QUESTION: How can adolescents with hyperactivity be identified and treated?

Since the initial manifestations become apparent to the keen observer during the preschool years, a number of books have been written recently to alert parents to the symptoms of ADD among two-to-five-year-olds. One such book is *Raising a Hyperactive Child* by Stewart and Olds (1973). A careful developmental history will help diagnose the problem. One questionnaire has been developed (Conners 1969), which asks parents and teachers to rate how frequently an adolescent shows, or has shown, the following behaviors: (1) restlessness, excitability, impulsivity, (2) provocation of other children, (3) failure to finish projects, (4) short attention span, (5) fidgeting, (6) distractibility, inattentiveness, (7) low threshold of frustration; demanding, (8) frequent crying, (9) sudden mood changes, (10) explosive and unpredictable behavior.

A hyperactive adolescent will not necessarily show all of these behaviors, and will not necessarily have shown all to the same degree. The most common problem involves controlled motor activity. As children, they are likely to have appeared tense and restless, awkward, and slow to learn tasks that involve motor coordination. Since many of the symptoms are normal for young children, making careful comparisons with age-appropriate norms is necessary. In general, the more symptomatic behaviors that are found in an adolescent's developmental history, and the more extreme the symptoms, the more likely that the adolescent is classified as hyperactive or has ADD (Weiner 1982, 131–39).

The primary behavioral and perceptual-cognitive manifestations of hyperactivity—distractibility and impulsivity—often improve with drug treatment. Sixty to 70 percent improve substantially when treated with stimulants, presumably because the stimulants arouse inhibitory centers of the nervous system. Unfortunately, stimulants have not been found to improve secondary consequences (e.g., interpersonal difficulties, low academic achievement, and low self-esteem). Stimulants have undesirable side effects, such as possible stunted growth, and the desirable effects are not maintained during adolescence and adulthood, when medication is discontinued. Most psychologists therefore prefer to use nondrug approaches (Weiner 1982, 152).

The behavioral and social learning approaches seem to be the most useful. Operant conditioning has been effectively used to reduce restlessness and to encourage a longer attention span, and seems to be especially effective when the emphasis is on positive reinforcement. The study habits of adolescents appear to improve when teachers and peers are good models of a careful, reflective manner. Finally, hyperactive adolescents achieve better results on difficult academic tasks if they learn to talk themselves through these tasks in a careful way. Adolescents can be taught to repeat instructions to themselves, such as, "Go slow," "One step at a time," and "You made it! Congratulations!"

Although traditional psychotherapy does not seem to be effective in treating the primary symptoms, it is useful in dealing with interpersonal problems, feelings of failure, and other emotional consequences (Gardener 1975). Family therapy is also helpful, since parents need to learn to have realistic expectations and to be encouraging and constructive rather than critical of these adolescents.

Depression or affective disorders

QUESTION: Are some symptoms of hyperactivity, such as depression, common among adolescents?

Many, if not most, adolescents experience many of the secondary symptoms, such as depression. A mistake, however, is to assume that adolescents who show signs of restlessness or depression (or both) are hyperactive. An adolescent who experiences frequent bouts with depression may be suffering from another clinical problem called an affective disorder. An affective disorder consists of unhealthy extremes in mood, thinking, attitudes, and physical condition. This disorder can be of two different types: unipolar affective disorder, which is characterized by extreme depression, and bipolar affective disorder, which is characterized by alternating depression and extreme elation, or mania. These two conditions are usually referred to as depression and manic-depressive disorder, respectively. For the most part, depression and manic-depressive disorder are distinct problems; fewer than one in twenty adolescents with depression ever experience manic episodes (Weiner 1982, 264).

QUESTION: How common is depression among adolescents?

As with many clinical problems, estimates of prevalence vary a great deal depending upon how they are made. Surveys that ask adolescents whether they ever feel moderately to severely depressed report that about 33 percent of seventh and eighth graders, and about 22 percent of ninth and tenth graders, have experienced depression. Although the official diagnoses of psychiatric clinics and hospitals show a much lower rate of depression among adolescents, these estimates are likely biased by the widespread view that depressive disorder is so psychologically complex that only adults are capable of developing it. Because of this bias, depression has likely been underdiagnosed in both children and adolescents. For reasons that are controversial, but which are probably both biological and sociocultural, depression is almost twice as common among females as among males (Weiner 1982, 268).

For all age groups, manic-depression is far less common than depression. Twenty-five percent of Americans will experience depressive episodes sometime during their lifetime, whereas manic episodes are experienced by only 1.2 percent of the population. Still, at least 1 in every 100 people in the United States will experience a pathological manic reaction at some point in their life, and studies of manic-depressive adults show that 20 percent to 35 percent show their first signs of disturbance during adolescence (Weiner 1982, 268-69). One study suggests that as many as 10 percent of adolescents who are hospitalized in a psychiatric unit may be diagnosed as manic-depressive (Hudgens 1974).

QUESTION: How can adolescents with affective disorders be identified?

The clinical symptoms of depression may be organized into four psychological domains: (1) the affective domain, (2) the cognitive domain, (3) the behavioral domain, and (4) the physiological domain (Mendels 1970). The cardinal characteristic of depression is severe persistent sadness. To be considered a major depression the DSMIII requires that a depressive episode last at least two weeks, but this may be misleading, since severe depressions (even leading to suicide) are often expressed as no more than a general moodiness (Mack and Hickler 1981). Depressed adolescents may weep uncontrollably, but they may also appear as simply "blue." Adolescents often believe that their feelings are unique and may not be understood by others, and therefore do not express them freely. The journal entry of a twelve-year-old girl named Vivienne, who committed suicide at age fourteen, expresses this doubt:

> Do you understand me? Do you love me? Do you know the things I know? Do you feel the way I feel? . . . I bet nobody knows the things I know or feels the things I feel. (Mack and Hickler 1981, 15)

Although sadness is the definitive characteristic of depression, depressed adolescents are often easier to identify on the basis of thoughts and ideas. Thoughts may be considered meanings that adolescents give to emotions. Although emotions seem to "come over" them or "happen to" them, adolescents have more of a sense of "controlling" their thoughts. The most common thoughts associated with depression are statements of self-deprecation and pessimism. Beck (1974) has argued that depression involves a cognitive triad, consisting of a negative view of the self, the outside world, and the future. The first elements of this triad can be seen in one of Vivienne's journal entires:

1. Negative view toward the self: "Today was about the worst day of this year. The fact that I've already got a really sore throat doesn't help because I have to keep quiet and being quiet brings on depression for me. I don't think anyone really likes me. I feel like they've all been pretending all year. I feel like crying."
2. Negative view toward the world:
   > "You are fenced in
   > it's no use to try
   > to see through;
   > you can't even
   > see out.
   >   Seeing is comprehending
   > and that you can never do
   > you need the finest of sight
   > and that you can never have
   > while you are here.
   >   Time passes slowly
   > while you are sitting here
   > there is no escape!
   >   No use climbing the steely fence;
   > the fence is higher
   > than all your life stacked up
   > for you are a prisoner
   > of your world."

3. Negative view of the future:
"And then
there are times
when I have nothing
to look forward to
in life
at all.
Like now." (Mack and Hickler 1981, 45–64)

Vivienne was an unusually gifted writer for her age. Although her sadness was more eloquently expressed than that of most adolescents, it is similar in other respects.

Severe depression can sometimes be detected through changes in the adolescent's dress, grooming, and motions. Dress and grooming may show signs of neglect. Facial expressions, speech, and bodily movements may all become dulled. The adolescent may speak less frequently and in shorter sentences. Depressed individuals sometimes behave like a windup toy that is running down; this slowing down is called psychomotor retardation (physiological symptoms). Mendels (1970) has found six somatic symptoms to be characteristic of depression: (1) loss of appetite and weight, (2) constipation, (3) insomnia, (4) a wide variety of aches and pains, (5) changes in the menstrual cycle, and (6) aversion to sexual activity. Depressed adolescents will not necessarily display all these symptoms, however, and may even display opposite symptoms (e.g., an increased appetite resulting in weight gain).

In manic-depressive adolescents, depressive episodes may alternate with periods during which all the symptoms of depression are reversed. An elated mood, enthusiastic and grandiose thoughts, animated and accelerated motions, and indefatigable energy are all characteristic of manic episodes. Manic intensity appears to have three distinct levels. In its mildest form, hypomania, adolescents will appear energetic, uninhibited, and impulsive. In its more intense form, acute mania, adolescents will become more obviously overactive. They may become irritable, irrational, and domineering, and speech may become incoherent. In its most acute form, delirious mania, adolescents will behave like the proverbial "raving maniac"—wildly loud and excited. At this point, adolescents may have hallucinations and delusions, and may be a danger to themselves or to others (Weiner 1982, 271).

QUESTION: Do adolescents conceal their depression?

Whether or not they intentionally conceal depression, in adolescents depression often seems to be masked. Instead of appearing slow and weary, depressed adolescents often appear in constant need of stimulation and excitement (Weiner 1982, 274). Rather than reveal their depression to others, adolescents may religiously avoid personal contacts, preferring to be alone or, perhaps, to be with pets. They may become involved in a number of defiant or antisocial acts, which bring them to the attention of others without having to expose their inner struggles. The following case of Steven is an example of masked depression:

Steven C is a 12-year-old sixth grader referred to your psychiatric clinic by a school psychologist because of temper tantrums, poor academic performance, and threats of suicide. He is accompanied by his mother, an anxious-looking woman who introduces herself as "Dr. C." Steven is an obese, awkward-looking boy who announced he thought this was a physical exam and refuses to talk to "a shrink." He then glares at his mother, who tearfully provides the history.

Steven has always had a difficult temper but had done well in school until about six months ago. Since then he has received failing grades in all subjects, been suspended from school twice for fighting, and alarmed the school psychologist by saying he was planning to kill himself. At home, he has been noncompliant, argumentative, and physically intimidating with Dr. C and a 15-year-old sister, the only other members of the household. In addition, he has started numerous fires, one of which burnt a hole in the living room carpet. His mother ends her monologue by telling Steven, "It's like I don't even know you anymore, you're a different person." (Tomb et al. 1983, 14)

In response to further questioning by the therapist, Steven's mother related that his grandfather had died about nine months ago and that Steven had not shown much of a reaction at the time, even though Steven was fond of his grandfather and visited him almost daily. Since the death of her father, Steven's mother had decided to move to a distant city to take advantage of a good job offer. Since that time, Steven has begun to speak about suicide, and has gained about thirty pounds due to a newly developed sweet tooth. She states, parenthetically, that Steven's father shot himself in front of the family eight years ago. Although one can reasonably assume that Steven's unusual behavior over the past six months is a depressive reaction to the death of his grandfather and to the prospect of moving away, it is easy to see how depression in adolescence can be obscured by symptoms such as fighting at school and starting fires (Tomb et al. 1983).

In early adolescence, depression is most often masked by symptoms of restlessness, withdrawal, and problem behavior. In later adolescence, however, the behavioral indices of depression take a different form. Drug abuse, sexual promiscuity, suicidal behavior, and profound apathy are common signs, or secondary reactions, to depression. None of these types of behaviors is a sure sign of depression; each of them has other possible explanations. The best approach, however, is being aware that a well-worn trail runs between depression and these problem behaviors.

QUESTION: What are the explanations for becoming depressed?

Explanations of depression based on experience have been formulated in three different ways: (1) depression results from negative views toward oneself, the world, and the future; these negative views, in turn, are caused by earlier experiences (often childhood experiences) that have sensitized a person to such losses (Beck 1974; Blatt et al. 1979); (2) depression results from learned helplessness —the belief that one has little control over one's circumstances. Learned helplessness is caused by earlier life experiences that the person was unable to do anything about (Seligman 1975); (3) depression results from a person's inability to behave in ways that will be positively reinforced; this inability is caused by the lack of earlier opportunities to learn appropriate modes of behavior (Lewinson 1974). Each of these three theories views the effect of past experience in different ways, and each of the theories has certain strengths. The strength of Lewinson's behavioral point of view is that it captures the fact that depressed adolescents often behave in ways that perpetuate their depression by depriving them of positive reinforcement. The strength of Seligman's learned helplessness theory is that it captures the fact that depressed adolescents often behave in ways that perpetuate their depression by depriving them of positive reinforcement. The strength of Seligman's learned helplessness theory is that it captures the defeatest attitude of depressed adolescents ("What's the use of trying? It's no use.") The strength of Beck's cognitive model is that it captures the pervasive negativeness of the depressed adolescent.

Depression has been defined by psychoanalysts as "the emotional correlate of a partial or complete collapse of the self-esteem of the ego since it feels unable to live up to its aspirations (ego ideal, superego) while they are strongly maintained" (Bibring 1953, 26). The understanding of adolescent depression depends, in other words, on an understanding of the way in which self-esteem develops and is sustained.

In this view, self-esteem comes from at least three important sources: of (1) the esteem of others, conveyed initially by parental love, and later by the love of siblings, peers, and others, (2) the experience of being competent or otherwise gifted, and (3) the experience of measuring up to one's ideals (Cotton, forthcoming). The first source of self-esteem is parental love. Children identify with their parents and tend to internalize their love as they grow older. The inevitable shortcomings of parental love, however, are said to bring about two important and related developments. First, to counteract the reality of their helplessness, children begin to fantasize that they possess great and magical

One of the problems that depressed adolescents may have in overcoming their depression involves the fact that they often behave in ways that perpetuate their depression by depriving themselves of positive reinforcement.

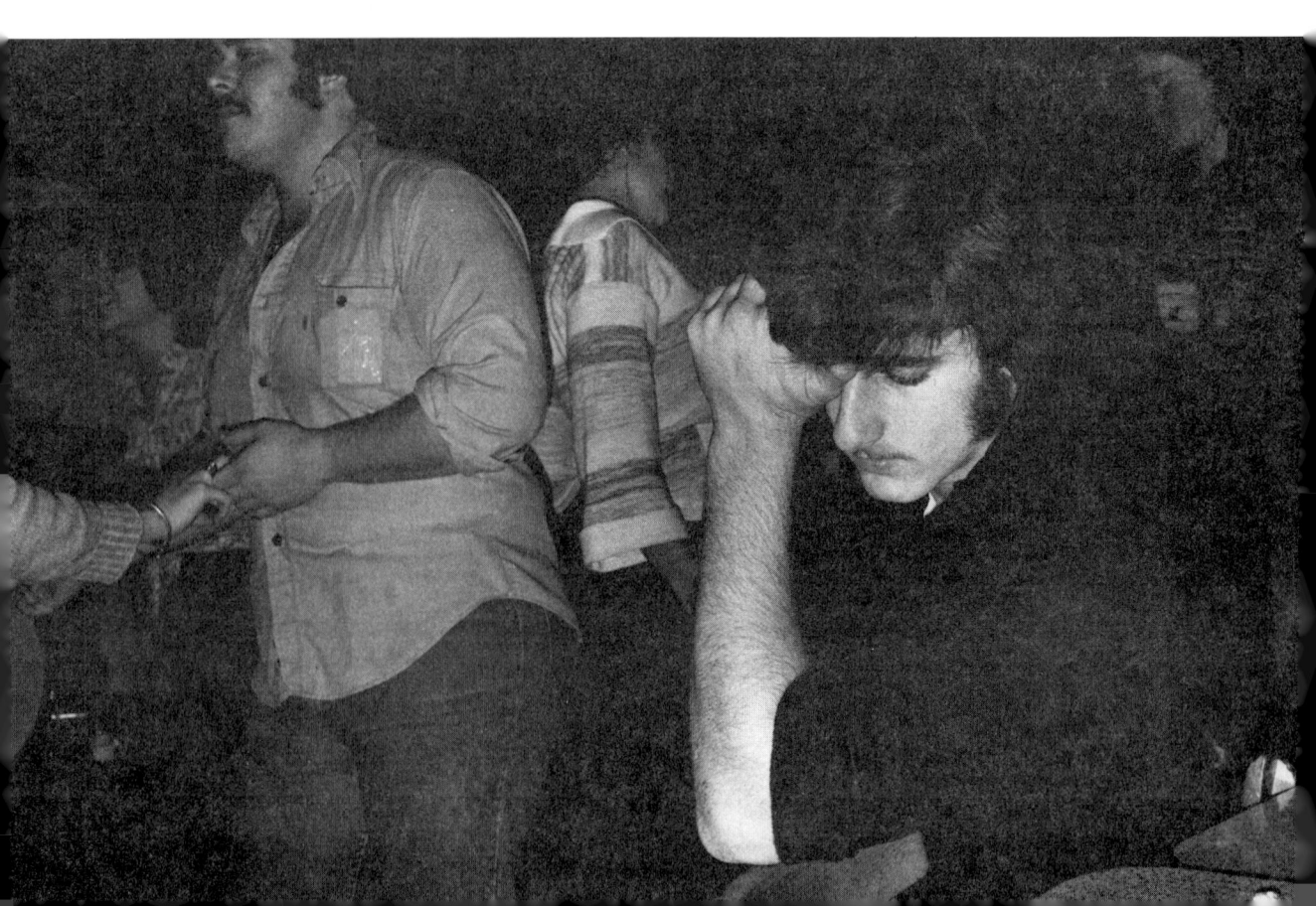

power. Second, children begin to idealize their parents as possessing extraordinary powers that they will share if only they can become like their parents. The first development is the beginning of self-love, or narcissism, and the second is the beginning of object love, or the love of others.

Although each of these formulations provides an interesting and important description of the depressed adolescent, whether they are adequate explanations of the origins of depressive personalities remains an open question.

QUESTION: Are the causes of manic-depressive disorders different from the causes of depression?

Because it is less common, considerably less attention has been paid to the experiential factors of the bipolar affective disorder. One hypothesis is that mania results from an effort to avoid depression, and depression results when the individual is no longer able to sustain manic behavior. Although this hypothesis is as yet unconfirmed, the importance of genetic factors in manic depression is relatively clear. The evidence so far suggests that manic-depressive disorder is even more dependent on genetic factors than is unipolar depression (Weiner 1982, 281).

QUESTION: How can adolescents with affective disorders be helped?

In most cases, adolescents will recover from bouts of depression and manic depression within six to eighteen months, even without treatment. Nevertheless, the prognosis for adolescents who require hospitalization for affective disorder is not nearly as good as the prognosis for adults. Current studies indicate that two-thirds of adolescents hospitalized with depression do not completely recover, and will experience recurrent depression. Nearly all adolescents who are hospitalized with manic depression continue to be disturbed as adults. Therefore, a serious mistake is to make light of the emotional problems of adolescents.

Despite the prevalence and seriousness of affective disorder among adolescents, few controlled studies have been made of the psychological treatment of affected adolescents. Weiner points out that several comprehensive reviews of research on child and adolescent psychotherapy do not even discuss depression (Weiner 1982, 287).

The effectiveness of drug therapy on adolescent depression is still debated. For some reason, drugs that are effective in treating adults are not as effective in treating adolescents. The drug most commonly used to treat adolescent depression is imipramine (Trofranil), one of the family of drugs called tricyclics. Studies with adults have shown that treatment with both drugs and psychotherapy is more effective than treatment with either one alone, but as yet no clear evidence supports that this is true with adolescents as well. Mania in adolescents, however, has been treated successfully with lithium, without dangerous side effects. Lithium is a mood-stabilizing drug that reduces impulsive or explosive behavior in adolescents, whether or not they suffer from a mania disorder (Weiner 1982, 288).

Drugs may prove to be helpful in treating adolescent depression, but they are not the solution. The principal goal of therapy is to bring about changes in the adolescent that will promote permanent emotional stability. Therapeutic techniques vary with the psychological theory. Cognitive therapists believe that the critical factor in depression is the way the adolescent thinks about things, and propose that the adolescent be taught to think in a new, more healthy way. Those who believe that helplessness is the critical element in depression propose that the adolescent's environment be arranged so that the adolescent can experience control over circumstances. The behaviorists view the critical element as a lack of adaptive behavior, and try to increase the rate of positive reinforcement as well as the repertoire of winsome behavior. Psychoanalysts believe that the critical element in depression is the painful memory of early injuries—too painful, perhaps, to be faced and resolved except in the context of a new and caring relationship in which the adolescent's worth is clearly affirmed.

Whichever approach is used, whoever assumes the task of helping an adolescent overcome depression should not become the backbone of the adolescent's recovery. However flattering it is to be the "sunshine" of an adolescent's life, this is not the goal of therapy. The goal is to go beyond immediate support and to equip the adolescent to handle disappointment and loss. As Vivienne put it,

> teach me how
> to defend my needs
> from that which is
> life. (Mack and Hickler 1981, 52)

Neurosis

The term *neurosis* has been overused and has often been used as a synonym for maladaptive behavior of any kind. Estimating the prevalence of genuine neuroses among adolescents is difficult. For our purposes, neurosis will be used as a general term for several specific disorders, including phobic disorder, obsessive-compulsive disorder, and conversion reactions. This approach is consistent with current usage in psychopathology. What the neurotic disorders have in common is that they all involve anxiety or fear. Phobias are fears that are unreasonably strong and upsetting. Obsessions and compulsions are habitual but ineffective ways of dealing with great fears. Conversion reactions involve the translation of anxiety into bodily or somatic symptoms.

For several reasons, the neurotic disorders tend to be underdiagnosed in adolescents. Many professionals wish to avoid placing the stigma of neuroses on adolescents, especially since the psychological problems of adolescence are often viewed as transient reactions to developmental hurdles. Neurotic disorders are also less incapacitating and pervasive than other disorders, and are therefore not as likely to come to the attention of mental health specialists. When diagnosing those under age eighteen, professionals prefer nonstigmatizing labels such as "transient situational disorder" and "childhood or preadolescent disorder" to categories such as depression and neurosis. Research surveys have found a high prevalence of neurosis among adolescents ranging anywhere from 5 percent to 50 percent of patients (Weiner 1982, 301).

QUESTION: At what point does a fear become a phobia?

Fears are considered phobias when they are both abnormal (statistically, for a person's age) and disproportionate to the actual danger present. Not all unreasonable fears are considered phobias. Infants, for example, frequently show a fear of strangers and of separation from parents, which normally disappears by the time they are three or four years old. In turn, preschoolers develop fears of the dark, of imaginary monsters, of reptiles, rodents, insects, and so on. These fears normally diminish with age and are not considered phobias unless they are unusually extreme. In other words, phobias consist not only of fears that are greatly exaggerated but also of even mild fears that persist longer than is normal. Experiencing some fear of sexuality may be normal for an adolescent, but an adolescent who is still afraid of the dark probably has developed a phobia. A distinction is made, however, between a phobic disorder, in which the phobia is so intense that it is experienced always and everywhere, and phobic symptoms, which arise only under special circumstance. Phobic symptoms are much more common than phobic disorders. A study of the general adult population in Burlington, Vermont, reported that as many as 7.7 percent displayed phobic symptoms, but only .22 percent of the population had a phobic disorder (Agras, Sylvester, and Oliveau 1969).

QUESTION: What are the origins of phobias?

Although phobic symptoms are more common among adults than among children, the onset (incidence) of phobia is highest among children (Weiner 1982, 305). This indicates that the relative weakness and helplessness of children makes them more vulnerable to various fears. Three theories have been formulated about the specific process that leads to the development of phobia. The first is that phobias are conditioned responses to experiences that have become associated with some truly fearful event. For example, being bitten by an unleashed dog may cause one to be afraid even of dogs on a leash or tether, when the danger of being bitten is small. Although studies have shown that phobias can result from conditioning, few phobias can be traced to a specific traumatic event. Most phobias are thought to occur either through modeling or through displacement (Marx 1977). Modeling involves the acquisition of fear by imitating others who appear afraid of something. This modeling is especially common among children, since they tend to rely on the examples and warnings of adults and older children to determine whether a threat in fact exists.

Displacement is a process by which relatively unthreatening objects or situations become a representation of something else that is feared. The fear, for example, can easily be expressed as an unreasonable fear of even minor injuries. Freud believed that displacement serves to minimize fear toward something that is unavoidable (such as death) by transferring it to something that is somewhat avoidable (such as injuries) (Freud 1955).

QUESTION: Are particular phobias especially common among adolescents?

A common neurosis in adolescence is school phobia—a reluctance to attend school, often expressed as physical complaints or as criticisms of the school.

Estimates indicate that school phobia occurs in 1 percent to 2 percent of the student population, and observations have been made that one of the peaks in the incidence of school phobia is during the transition from junior high to senior high school. School-phobic adolescents can generally be recognized by the cyclical pattern of their illnesses (healthy on weekends but unhealthy on weekdays) and by the recurrence of their complaints. New schools are considered as unsatisfactory as old ones. Interestingly, school phobia occurs equally in males and females, and bears no relation to IQ scores or levels of achievement. Like other phobias, school phobias tend to develop during the elementary school years. The older the children, the less likely they are to experience acute (short-lived) school phobia for the first time. In older students, school phobia appears more often as a chronic condition (Weiner 1982, 340–41).

School phobia could frequently be the result of maternal overprotection. Mothers of school-phobic children tend to cling to the mother-child relationship and to promote excessive dependency in their children. Such mothers may feel lonely when their children go to school and may even encourage their children to stay home because of the weather, a sniffle, or a slight cough. Fathers often contribute to this pattern by accepting flimsy excuses and by encouraging their wives to be overprotective so that they can concentrate on matters outside the family (Chotiner and Forrest 1974). This family pattern tends to produce adolescents who are dependent, manipulative, and possessed of an exaggerated and unrealistic sense of their own powers. Accustomed to governing matters in the home with their tantrums and threats, they easily become anxious in situations in which the demands of teachers and the judgments of peers are unavoidable (Jexon 1964).

QUESTION: What is an obsessive-compulsive disorder?

Despite the unfamiliarity of the term *obsessive-compulsive disorder,* the reader likely knows several people with obsessive-compulsive personality traits. Freud described the obsessive-compulsive personality style in terms of the three Ps: parsimony, pedantry, and petulance. By these terms, Freud meant that the obsessive-compulsive person is cautious, nit-picking, and rigid. These are people who have to think about all aspects of a situation before they can come to any conclusion, whose speech and writing are cluttered with qualifications and elaborations, whose expression of emotion is calculated and constrained, and whose behavior is never casual or lighthearted. As adolescents, obsessive-compulsive persons are often commended for what appears to be emotional maturity and a sense of responsibility. In actuality, obsessive-compulsive adolescents lag far behind their peers in emotional experience and overall flexibility.

QUESTION: At what point do preoccupations and cautiousness become obsessive compulsiveness?

Although obsessive-compulsive traits are not unusual, they rarely crystallize into stubborn symptoms that are clearly unhealthy. Pathological obsessions and compulsions, however, are more likely to develop in people who have an obsessive-compulsive personality style. Research indicates that of all cases of obsessive-compulsive disorder, 30 percent to 40 percent make their appearance between the ages of fifteen and twenty. Weiner has clearly expressed the difference between an obsessive-compulsive personality style and the corresponding disorder: "The essential nature of obsessive compulsive disorder is the feeling of being driven by fate to take certain actions and/or think certain thoughts, regardless of how foolish they seem, regardless of how much trouble they cause, and regardless of how desperately the person wants to act or think otherwise" (Weiner 1982, 310). Consider the following example:

> Allen was referred at the age of 14 because, in spite of an excellent scholastic record until seventh grade, he was at that time failing in mathematics. Allen was a very sensitive boy, reared in a family of low cultural and educational standard, in which the criterion of manliness was the ability not to break under brutal treatment. He had tried to fit into his family by never causing trouble; his reward for this was open rejection, particularly by his mother and oldest, much admired brother. In therapy his murderous impulses and his guilt concerning those impulses—the victims were his mother and brother—were soon verbalized. To protect his victims he had developed elaborate rituals. If he masturbated once his mother would die, twice his brother would die, three times and he would die; thus if he yielded to an impulse to masturbate he had to do it three times.
>
> Allen could not divide numbers because the larger number represented his family, and dividing the family meant separating his mother and brother from the family since the answer would be less than the original number. He could not subtract because that meant detroying by "taking away" his mother and brother. . . .
>
> His hatred and unrequited love for his mother and brother did not begin in adolescence; it had, however, been effectively repressed until that time. As a comment on unconscious learning, after he had worked through the meaning of his difficulty with numbers it was found that he had actually mastered all the mathematical tools during seventh grade and on the final examination in eighth grade he had the highest grade in his class. (Josselyn 1971, 77–78)

QUESTION: What causes an adolescent to become obsessive-compulsive?

Although some evidence suggests that neurotic disorders run in families and therefore may have a genetic component, the kinds of studies necessary to distinguish genetic from experiential factors (e.g., the cross-fostering of identical twins) have not yet been undertaken for most neurotic disorders. Most researchers believe that experiential factors are more important in the transmission of obsessive-compulsive personality traits. Obsessive-compulsive disorder, like other neurotic disorders, is commonly conceived of as a defense against anxiety. Freud believed that obsessions are a substitution for a true conflict (often sexual in nature) with an idea that symbolizes the true conflict but is less threatening. In other words, in obsession we have "the intrusion of the unwelcome thought [that] 'seeks' to prevent anxiety by serving as a more tolerable substitute for a subjectively less welcome thought or impulse" (Laughlin 1957). Freud also believed that several other types of defense mechanisms—undoing, reaction-formation, isolation—are prominent in obsessive-compulsive behavior. Repetitive hand washing may be an attempt to ritualistically undo or atone for unacceptable thoughts or impulses. Meticulousness and orderliness may be reactions that have formed against the forbidden impulse to simply let loose. The intellectualization of emotion may serve to isolate and remove aggressive or sexual impulses.

Other explanations of obsessive-compulsive behavior focus on the child-rearing practices and general examples of parents. Freud referred to the obsessive-compulsive personality as an "anal character," because he believed it resulted from parental overemphasis on bowel control during infancy (Freud 1958). Adams has suggested other parental activities that may encourage obsessive-compulsive traits:

> Advising a frightened, sleepless child to say his prayers again.
> Telling a child in the throes of a nightmare to think good thoughts.
> Sweeping feelings away with talk, instead of accepting them.
> Faming and recommending neutrality in all controversial matters.
> Following brutalities with sweet, undoing talk. (Adams 1973, 71)

These activities refer to patterns in a life-style and not to a singular, unilinear statement. In addition to directly promoting obsessive-compulsive traits, parental modeling has a powerful influence, especially on those children who strongly identify with the obsessive-compulsive parent.

Conversion reaction

QUESTION: What is a conversion reaction?

Conversion reactions consist of bodily impairments with psychological rather than organic causes. The term *conversion reaction* conveys the idea that anxiety is dealt with by being "converted" into somatic symptoms. Originally, conversion reactions were thought of as a defense against a special kind of anxiety —the anxiety caused by an instinctual drive that is pressing to become conscious. The repressed drive was usually sexual, and the somatic symptoms generally had some recognizable connections with sexuality. Now clear, however, is that conversion reactions can affect every system of the body and that they express a wide variety of anxiety types (Rangell 1959). Consistent with the somatic symptoms of conversion reactions being a protection against anxiety, the adolescent often views the symptoms in a surprisingly casual way. Other identifying features of conversion reactions include the existence of some clear precipitating event and the sometimes symbolic nature of the symptoms. Consider the following two cases from early and late adolescence:

> A 12-year-old boy suddenly became unable to speak at a time when his brother, two years younger, fell from the back of a truck on which they both had just hitched a ride. The inability to speak lasted for almost a week.
> The boy was hospitalized, but no organic cause for his muteness was found. It was subsequently discovered that the older boy had a great deal of animosity towards his younger brother, and that he frequently had "difficulty in getting rid of the brat." The truth was that the 12-year-old saw his brother "starting to slip and wanted to warn him" but found, at that very moment, that he could not speak.

A second example is that of a 22-year-old Italian athlete, who had recently started his own construction company and challenged his younger brother to a brick-laying race to prove his superiority. As he neared the end of the race and suddenly realized he was going to lose, he fainted.

The loss of consciousness for the contractor was face-saving in that he recalled a fleeting thought just before he fainted which was, "I will never be able to face him (my brother) again." As it turned out the younger brother was willing to accept the idea that his older and stronger brother would have won if he had not fainted. (Guggenheim and Nadelson 1982, 264)

QUESTION: How long do conversion reactions last?

In contrast with adults with conversion reactions, the physical symptoms of adolescents disappear fairly readily once the basic problem is identified (Josselyn 1971, 65–66). Nevertheless, the disappearance of symptoms does not mean that an adolescent no longer needs psychological help. The states of anxiety that are deflected into conversion reactions need to be fully recognized and resolved.

Adolescents who have a persistent preoccupation with their physical condition are referred to as hypochondriacal. Hypochondriasis is common in adolescents, presumably because the adolescent undergoes relatively rapid change in physical size, shape, and functioning. These bodily changes frequently become the focus of anxieties of many different origins. Matters of personal health can become a kind of lightening rod for all the diffuse anxieties of adolescents. Hypochondriasis is similar to conversion reaction in that both involve the expression of a psychological conflict by means of a medical problem. Whereas hypochondriasis is characterized by fear and complaint of bodily disease, conversion reactions actually involve the loss or disturbance of normal physical functioning.

QUESTION: Are some adolescents more likely than others to display conversion reactions or hypochondriasis?

Just as an adolescent with an obsessive-compulsive personality is more likely to develop an obsessive-compulsive disorder, conversion reactions and hypochondriasis apparently occur more frequently in adolescents with what is called a hysterical personality style. In general, the hysterical personality is just the opposite of the obsessive-compulsive personality. Hysterical adolescents are emotional, unreflective, and impulsive. Hysterical adolescents tend to make friends more easily than do obsessive-compulsive adolescents, but they also impress others as more self-centered and prone to theatrics. Whereas obsessive-compulsive adolescents may appear mature for their age, hysterical adolescents will appear immature. Most of the characteristics of hysteria are typical of young children. Although hysterical adolescents are not the only ones who develop conversion reactions and hypochondriasis, they do seem to be more likely to express their anxieties through bodily channels (Weiner 1982, 320).

QUESTION: Is therapy necessary for adolescents who show neurotic symptoms?

Neurotic disorders of adolescents tend to correct themselves in time and rarely lead to adult psychopathology. Not all adolescents, however, will recover without treatment, and even those who are bound to recover may recover more speedily with treatment. Given the high rate of success of psychotherapy with neurotic adolescents, leaving troubled adolescents to their own devices is probably not worth the risk.

The goal of psychotherapy with neurotic adolescents is twofold: to remove the neurotic symptoms and to understand the function of the neurosis. Although these goals are not truly antithetical, psychologists have often criticized one another for putting too much emphasis on one or the other. Vast literature has developed that argues the pros and cons of various therapies, but the results seem to be largely inconclusive. In the view of many professionals, the meaningful question is not whether alternative forms of therapy are effective, but whether a given form of therapy is appropriate for particular types of problems and clients (Sue, Sue, and Sue 1981, 550–58).

QUESTION: What are the basic therapeutic approaches?

A number of therapeutic approaches are used with adolescents. The most popular approach with children and adolescents is one that integrates the goals of therapy by focusing on the complex relationships in the family. The general consensus among therapists is that family members need to be involved in the psychotherapy of adolescents. Although a number of differences are present in how therapists involve the family in psychotherapy, the following principles seem to be universally agreed upon: (1) Both parents would be involved, (2) parents should be fully informed regarding the nature of their adolescent's problems, (3) parents should not be blamed for their adolescent's problems, but

Psychologists have disagreed over what the goal of psychotherapy with neurotic adolescents should be, as well as over what type of therapy is appropriate for adolescents with specific problems.

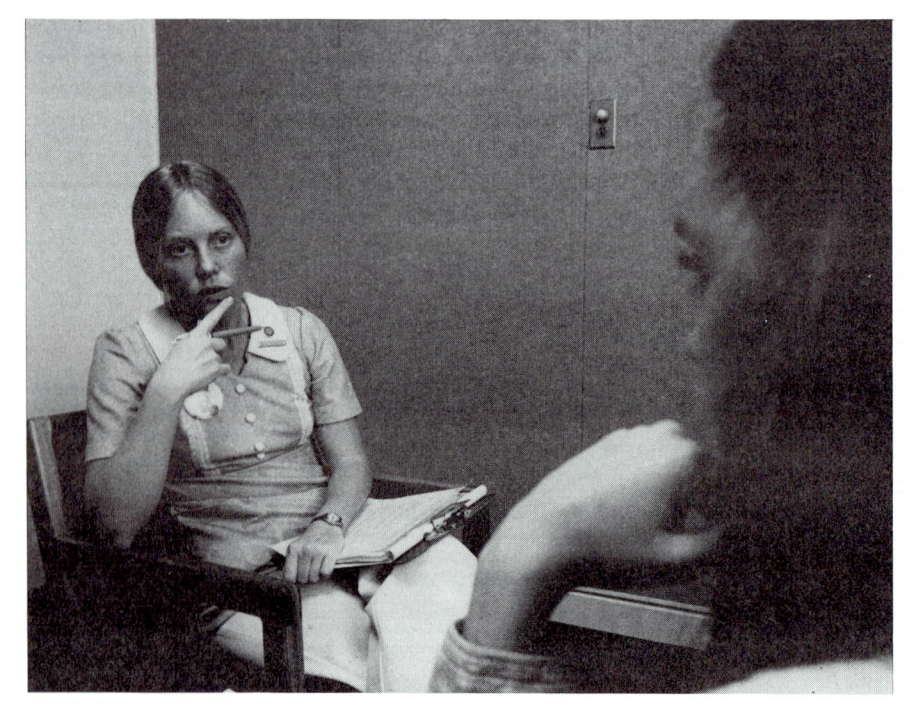

should be aware of how their behavior may aggravate or perpetuate the problem, and (4) parents should be counseled on how to be more effective with, and understanding of, their adolescents (Weiner 1982, 327).

Some forms of therapy seem to be more effective with certain neuroses than with others. Behavior therapy seems to be the simplest and most effective method for treating phobias in adolescence (Lambson 1978). The behavior therapists do not view phobias as inextricably linked or a derivative of underlying fears.

Fearful behavior can be treated directly by a process called systematic desensitization. Systematic desensitization generally involves three steps: (1) training and relaxation, (2) the formation of a fear hierarchy, and (3) the alternation of relaxation and recollection of scenes from the fear hierarchy (Sue, Sue, and Sue 1981, 564). A fear hierarchy is a list of situations that produce fear in the adolescent, ranked according to the amount of anxiety they produce. Once adolescents have been taught to relax, they imagine each scene until they are able to imagine even the most fearsome scene without anxiety. Proponents argue that systematic desensitization is more effective than traditional psychotherapy and requires fewer sessions to extinguish the fear (Wolpe 1973).

Gestalt therapy is ideally suited to obsessive-compulsive adolescents. These adolescents use intellectualization, isolation of affect, and reaction-formation (doing the opposite of what one would like to do) to put distance between themselves and their emotions. Gestalt therapy emphasizes the immediate awareness of present experiences (i.e., the experience of being in the room with the therapist) and tends to cut through the barriers between the adolescent's thoughts and feelings. Cognitive therapy can also be helpful in controlling obsessive thinking. By telling themselves to stop every time an obsessive thought comes to mind, and by countering that obsessive thought with a more positive thought, adolescents can be taught to gradually reduce the amount of time spent in obsessive thinking (Lambson 1978, 58–63).

Although many types of therapy have been used successfully to treat conversion reaction and hypochondriasis, family therapy appears to be a good beginning. Adolescents who develop conversion symptoms often come from families in which physical complaints receive much attention and sympathy (Cavenar and Caudill 1979). Second, the nature of disorders is that adolescents will frequently not admit that their physical problems have emotional origins. They may not respond positively, therefore, to traditional psychotherapy. Family therapy may, in some cases, be a way of resolving conflicts without focusing all the attention on the adolescent. In most cases, insights-oriented therapy is probably necessary to bring out the specific conflicts (such as sibling rivalry) that underlie the physical symptoms (Schmale 1982, 263–67).

Schizophrenia

Eugen Bleuler, the Swiss psychiatrist who coined the term *schizophrenia*, also commented that the adolescent age seems to offer a particular predisposition to this disease (Bleuler 1950). Subsequent research has confirmed that most forms of schizophrenic disturbance begin during adolescent (Holzman and Grinker 1974). Schizophrenia is diagnosed in 25 percent to 30 percent of adolescents admitted to public mental hospitals, in 15 percent of those admitted to psychiatric units of general hospitals, and in 6 percent to 8 percent of those seen in outpatient clinics. Transient situational disorders and depressive disorders aside, schizophrenia is the most common diagnosis among adolescents referred for inpatient psychiatric care (Weiner 1982, 224).

QUESTION: Are adolescents more likely to show a quick recovery from schizophrenic symptoms?

Unlike neurotic disorders in adolescents, which often seem to correct themselves even without therapy, schizophrenia disorder seems to be more serious the earlier it appears. More than half of the adolescents hospitalized for schizophrenia do not even partially recover. These adolescents remain social invalids and often remain permanently hospitalized (Weiner 1982, 242). Only 23 percent show full recovery without any residual symptoms or relapses. Although advances in antipsychotic medication and in community mental health practice have helped to reduce the amount of time that schizophrenics spend in the hospital, schizophrenia is far from having been eliminated as a major public health problem. Many adolescents, rather than remaining continuously hospitalized, are continually discharged and readmitted to the hospital—a phenomenon known as the "revolving door." Chronic hospitalization is twice as common among schizophrenics who are hospitalized at age fifteen to nineteen as among those who are hospitalized at age twenty or later (Kris, Schiff, and McLaughlin 1971).

Almost 50 percent of these adolescents are permanently crippled; the prospects appear better for adolescents who do not require hospitalization. In addition, numerous studies indicate that the rate of relapse depends on the stressfulness of the person's environment. If the adolescent has appropriate living arrangements and support from family, relapse is much less frequent (Veck 1978).

QUESTION: Are adolescents with schizophrenia distinguishable from those with other problems?

The question of how to distinguish schizophrenic adolescents from those with other problems raises questions about the definition of schizophrenia. The term *schizophrenic* applies to all adolescents who fit the general description of schizophrenia. In this sense, schizophrenia is characterized by the following: (1) disordered and illogical thinking, (2) inaccurate perceptions of reality, (3) ineptness in personal relationships, and (4) inadequate ability to control ideas, affects, and behavior. These four characteristics are general features of schizophrenia at all ages. In adolescence, these symptoms may be relatively unpronounced and difficult to detect.

Three guidelines can be used to distinguish adolescent schizophrenia from depression and delinquency:

1. The more persistent the schizophrenic symptoms in the overall clinical picture, the more appropriate a diagnosis of schizophrenia becomes. If a frequently depressed adolescent speaks in an incoherent way even when he is not depressed, this is very good evidence of schizophrenia.
2. The less concern an adolescent shows for age appropriate developments such as independence and heterosexual relationships, the greater the likelihood of schizophrenia. Schizophrenics are typically unequipped to cope

with the demands of their environment. This is often expressed in a striking immaturity of interests and attitudes, though in other cases it is expressed in a deceptive pseudomaturity. However, neither immaturity nor pseudomaturity conclusively demonstrates schizophrenia in adolescents.

3. The more prominent the formal irregularities of an adolescent's behavior, the greater the chances of schizophrenia. Formal manifestations of the disturbance are to be distinguished from content manifestations, those that involve *what* the person is saying or doing. An adolescent's strange obsessions or bizarre fantasies may be evidence of schizophrenia, but if an adolescent expresses even ordinary thoughts in ways that are illogical or ambiguous, the evidence of schizophrenia is far stronger. (Weiner 1982, 224–26)

Adolescents are generally as capable of close relationships as are adults. Consistent physical or emotional withdrawal from others, and an inability to engage in close relationships with others, are as suggestive of schizophrenia in adolescents as they are in adults. The following is an example of a thirteen-year-old boy whose preoccupation with fantasies and withdrawal from others may be indicative of schizophrenia:

> Don, age 13, was referred by the school he attended for a diagnostic study. He had superior intelligence but was doing poorly in school, failing to bring in homework, and seemingly daydreaming through class sessions. Furthermore, he was thoroughly disliked by faculty and students. He was arrogant, contemptuous of both his schoolmates and the faculty, and responded hostilely to anyone's slightest suggestion that implied he should be different.
>
> During the first and the beginning of the second interview he talked freely of his contempt for everyone. There was, above all, no psychiatrist who knew as much as he did; therefore, he was helping himself. He obviously was so superior that his peer group was far behind him and adults were unable to grasp his profound ideas. Of course he spent most of his time fantasizing, trying to formulate a goal for the use of his unique abilities. This was hard because there were so many possibilites.
>
> He thought about these goals when he was supposed to study. Books were so stupid it was better to think about his goals, which always, he was certain, were possible. He would become, dependent upon his final choice, the richest businessman in the world, if he decided on that career; the youngest President of the United States, if he became a politician; the greatest musician in the world, if he decided to study music; or he would, if he decided to do so, create a new philosophy that would make the other philosophers so archaic there would be no need to study them. (Josselyn 1971, 71–72)

Research indicates that adolescents do not have the same control over disturbing thoughts and images as adults (Ames, Métraux, and Walker 1971). Nevertheless, an adolescent who shows emotions that are inappropriate under the circumstances (such as inexplicable giggling or weeping), or who displays involuntary or explosive behavior, may well be expressing schizophrenic disturbance. The following is a clear example of involuntary action suggestive of schizophrenia in a sixteen-year-old high school student named Todd:

> Question: "Why did you come to the hospital?"
> Answer: "Why did I come? Why did I come to the hospital? I came to the hospital because of crazy things with my hands. Sometimes my

hands jump up like that . . . wait a minute . . . I guess it's happening . . . well, yes, see it's been happening" (making robotlike gestures with his hands).
Question: "Are you sick?"
Answer: "Am I sick? No I'm not sick . . . these fidgeting habits, these fidgeting habits. I have habits. I have fidgeting habits." (Spitzer, et al. 1983, 140)

Schizophrenia is a wide category, embracing a great variety of clinical problems. Finding two schizophrenics with a similar clinical profile is extremely rare (Carpenter 1976). The symptoms that are most suggestive of schizophrenic disorder in adolescence are distorted perceptions, social withdrawal, inappropriate emotions, and lack of self-control. The entertainment of abstract or disturbing thoughts, although possibly indicative of schizophrenia, are less conclusive in adolescents than in adults (Weiner 1982, 230).

QUESTION: How can adolescent schizophrenia be prevented and treated?

Since no general agreement exists as to the "core" of schizophrenia, probably best is to view the different approaches to treating schizophrenia in terms of the specific symptoms and deficits that each addresses. As we have noted, the symptoms of adolescent schizophrenics can be quite diverse and may in many cases suggest which forms of therapy should be used. Individual, group, and family therapies are all recommended for preschizophrenic and schizophrenic adolescents. The goals of these types of therapy are to reduce adolescents' social isolation and withdrawal by building personal relationships, and to improve adolescents' perception and judgment by helping them test the reality of their ideas. The goal of building relationships is undoubtedly the most important for the prevention and treatment of schizophrenia: "Successful psychotherapy with schizophrenic adolescents hinges on how well the therapist can impress them as a genuine, caring, empathetic, and trustworthy person" (Weiner 1982, 245). For the schizophrenic adolescent, such a relationship may constitute a unique and healing experience.

This is not to say that building relationships with schizophrenics, or even with withdrawn or antisocial adolescents, is an easy matter. Overcoming the basic distrust of an emotionally crippled adolescent takes a tenacious and enduring interest. At the same time, the schizophrenic adolescent should not be indulged or treated as an infant. Stormy adolescents, in particular, need to have strict limits placed on their behavior so that they realize that the therapist and others are strong enough to help them work through their problems.

Challenging and limiting adolescents' behavior is one way of correcting their inaccurate perceptions—of improving their reality testing. Neither poor social judgment nor delusions and hallucinations should be indulged; adolescents must know that their fears and expectations have no basis in reality, and that there are better ways of responding to stressful situations. The goals of improving reality testing and improving personal relationships often pull in opposite directions. Important is learning how to challenge and correct schizophrenic adolescents without undermining a trusting relationship with them. The effort to improve an adolescent's reality testing requires a continual assessment of the adolescent's ability to be warm and well meaning rather than cold and critical. In group and family therapy, identifying and diverting destructive comments is important, as well as teaching the group how to communicate in a more understanding way (Shapiro 1979; Weisberg 1979).

Other forms of therapy are geared to teach specific skills and to promote certain behaviors. The goal of occupational and rehabilitational therapy, for example, is to identify and provide the social and vocational skills adolescents need to have confidence in themselves. Dance and art therapy may be offered as a nonverbal way for adolescents to communicate their feelings and concerns, and as a form for interaction with other adolescents. Behavioral therapy is often used to make sure that the adolescent is not being reinforced with attention and concern only for negative behaviors. In a busy family or in a busy psychiatric ward, troubled adolescents may be ignored until they do something disruptive or aggressive. In conjunction with other therapies that emphasize durable relationships, behavior modification (to be discussed later) may be an important aid in encouraging adaptive behavior. Stress management techniques and cognitive coping strategies may help the adolescent to better manage stressful life events that often precipitate relapse.

When schizophrenia cannot be prevented or adequately treated without them, medication and milieu therapy are an effective and common form of therapy. Many different antipsychotic (neuroleptic) drugs are in use today, and seem to be as effective with adolescents as with adults. Neuroleptics reduce sensitivity to external and internal stimuli, to emotional arousal, and to impulsive tendencies (Lehmann 1975). These effects dramatically reduce the prominent symptoms of schizophrenia, such as delusions, disordered thought, and hallucinations, and thus improve the adolescent's response to other forms of therapy (Siris, Van Kammen, and Docherty 1978). In a review of the literature on drug therapy, Davis and Chang (1978) conclude that the exclusive use of medication is no more effective than the exclusive use of psychotherapy for schizophrenia. Drugs are not equally effective for all adolescents, and in any case they have a number of unpleasant side effects. Drugs alone do not enable an adolescent to form intimate relationships or to cope more successfully with life's demands and pressures (Mosher and Mann 1978). Thus, antipsychotic medication is effective for treating schizophrenia and should be complemented by other forms of therapy that are designed to build relationships and to teach skills.

The goal of milieu therapy is to provide the adolescent with a new and healthier environment. Pioneers in the treatment of schizophrenia believed that separating the schizophrenic from the family, home, and society is important, as well as creating a therapeutic environment (Simmel 1929). Overhospitalization of schizophrenics has waned recently. Residential care is necessary whenever adolescents pose a threat to themselves or to others, and when environmental stresses are clearly exacerbating the adolescents' difficulties. Research seems to indicate that severely schizophrenic adolescents respond better to treatment on mixed adolescent-adult units, but that it is important for treatment to include programs specifically tailored to an adolescent's social and recreational needs (Garber 1972; Lordi 1979). When hospitalization is required, it is important that adolescents' reentry to their own environment is graduated rather than

Anorexia nervosa

QUESTION: What is the origin and nature of anorexia nervosa?

Anorexia nervosa is a severe weight loss due to inadequate eating. Anorexia was recognized as a clinical problem more than a century ago, but has dramatically increased in frequency during the 1980s. The incidence of anorexia nervosa is not known; however, anorexia does occur mostly among adolescents. It occurs ten times more frequently among females and is increasing especially among upper-middle-class families (Bruch 1974).

To gain insight into the confused mental state of many anorexic adolescents, one might consider the following:

> As an [anorexic], I expected my body and the food I took into it to exert a "perfecting influence" on my life. The date, February 29, was created to "make up for" the cumulative imperfections of ordinary days. The books are witness to my relentless, blind pursuit of thinness. I ate a Spartan diet but lusted after rich desserts. A bone-thin body, completely under my command, could more than make up for the imperfections that did not fit my image of myself as a powerful, in-control-of-it-all person. The S on the T-shirt stands for Superwoman. I saw myself split into two equal but opposing forces. There was the me that was, if I could just get to it, perfect and beautiful. There was the me that threatened to overpower all else with its laziness, gluttony, ugliness, and general inferiority. (Ciseaux 1980, 1469)

Basically, anorexia symptoms consist of one or more of the following symptoms: an extreme loss of body weight; under twenty-five years of age; a distorted attitude toward food and weight (i.e., history of problem eating); desire for extreme thinness; enjoyment of not eating; hoarding of food; no medical or psychological disorder; and periods of overactive, self-induced vomiting (Feighner et al. 1972).

QUESTION: How should adolescents with anorexia nervosa be treated?

In the past, two predominant approaches were used to treat anorexia nervosa, each with its own advantages and disadvantages. The first, weight gain therapy, addresses the adolescent's most obvious problem—undernourishment. In weight gain therapy, the adolescent is restored to a normal body weight by increasing nutritional intake and (in case of hyperativity) decreasing activity. These basic principles have been implemented in four different ways: (1) hospital milieu, (2) pharmacotherapy, (3) hyperalimentation, and (4) behavior modification. In hospital milieu therapy, the adolescent is admitted to a supportive medical ward and is provided with a high-calorie diet under the close observation of the staff *(Nursing Times* 1980). In pharmacotherapy, the adolescent's appetite is stimulated using drugs suited to the patient's personality, bodily, and behavioral characteristics (Piazza, Piazza, and Rollins 1980). In hyperalimentation, the severely undernourished adolescent is fed intravenously (Maloney and Farrell 1980). In behavior modification, improved eating habits and weight gain are systematically reinforced with valued privileges and activities. All of these forms of weight gain therapy have proven successful in restoring the adolescent's normal body weight, nutritional balance, and, to some extent, psychic functioning.

The second traditional treatment for anorexia nervosa, psychotherapy, addresses the problem of how to maintain normal body weight and eating habits over an extended period. As it turns out, the weakness of weight gain therapy was precisely in its failure to make adolescents more able to properly control their eating habits by themselves: "The goal for treatment of anorexia nervosa includes the maintenance of normal weight and eating habits over time with a return to adequate functioning" (Vigersky 1977). Some authorities on anorexia nervosa believe that to neglect the psychological aspects of the disorder, and to provide only weight gain treatment, may actually aggravate the problem. Bruch (1974), who believes that the critical issue for anorexic adolescents is one of achieving autonomy, states that weight gain treatment alone may confirm the patient that she is not in control of her own destiny.

The goal of psychotherapy is to treat the underlying psychological causes of anorexia nervosa. These causes are generally identified as eight personal fears, such as the fear of fatness, of adulthood, or of sexuality, or as abnormal family relationships. Individual psychotherapy is best suited to treating the personal fears of adolescents, and family therapy is the most powerful tool for modifying the functional interactions within the family. Even if family abnormalities are not a fundamental reason for anorexic behavior, the family's support, which may be harnessed through family therapy, may be important. Oddly enough, not until recently were individual and family therapy used in tandem. Therapists have only recently recognized the need for the involvement of the family

The weakness of weight gain therapy alone for treatment of anorexia nervosa is that it does not help the adolescent independently sustain healthy eating habits. Psychotherapy's goal is to treat the underlying psychological causes of the problem.

in the treatment of anorexia nervosa. The growing consensus is that, as Hilde and Bruch state, "Psychotherapy does not take place in a vacuum, and disturbing interactions with family members might counteract treatment efforts" (Hilde and Bruch 1977, 105). The general advantage of psychotherapy over weight gain treatment is that individual differences can be taken into account and used to tailor a specific treatment program. In cases of severe undernourishment, weight gain therapy may initially be necessary to prevent serious physical harm and psychological complications.

A final problem associated with anorexia nervosa, particularly in females, is hormonal imbalance. The clearest manifestation of hormonal imbalance is the cessation or irregularity of the menstrual function. Evidence indicates that many adolescents with anorexia nervosa have some endocrine dysfunction (Halmi 1980). Hormone treatment is often necessary to restore a properly functioning hormonal level in the body, which is essential to good physical and emotional health. A multidimensional approach, including weight gain treatment, psychotherapy, and hormone treatment, may result in optimal treatment for anorexia nervosa in adolescents.

Suicide

While teaching 15- and 16-year-old students in Sunday School, I attempted to activate a young man who had an alcoholic father. His mother and sister (10 years) were active and were anxious for him to be also. He did start coming after many phone calls. He enjoyed the lessons and became an active attender.

However, the members of his class would not accept him. He seemed to try in every way to be a part of the group. I talked with them and also with members of the younger and older classes to try to get their support.

His family problems were so unpleasant combined with his unfriendly reception every week at church. They even ignored him during the activities we planned.

One morning I received a phone call. This boy had committed suicide.

Although actual suicide is rare among adolescents, it appears to be more common than it once was. Statistics show that adolescent suicide attempts and suicides nearly tripled in the twenty years between the late 1950s and the late 1970s (National Center for Health Statistics 1978). Suicide rates rise extremely sharply between age ten and twenty, and then level off until the mid-thirties. Since adolescents as a group enjoy relatively good health, suicide has become the third most common cause of death in adolescents, exceeded only by accidents and homicides. The frequency of suicide among adolescents may be even higher, since suicidal intent many often go undetected in deaths that appear accidental. Estimates indicate that up to 50 percent of suicides are mistakenly recorded as accidents (Toolan 1975). Suicide attempts are probably similarly underreported. The ratio of suicide attempts to actual suicides clearly runs five to ten times as high in adolescents as in the general population. With at least one in every thousand adolescents attempting suicide each year, attempted suicide has become an alarmingly common phenomenon (Weiner 1982, 435).

QUESTION: Are adolescent suicide attempts a call for help?

Although the ratio of suicides to suicide attempts among adolescents may be as low as one to one hundred, attempted suicide is still a serious indicator, since one in ten who attempt suicide will commit suicide within five years (Avery and Winokur 1978). Some evidence, however, indicates sex differences in the ratio of attempted to actual suicide. Although males are more likely than females to actually kill themselves, by a ratio of more than three to one, females account for up to 90 percent of adolescent suicide attempts (National Center for Health Statistics 1978). One reason why males more often succeed is that they frequently use more violent methods, such as shooting or hanging themselves. Females appear more likely to choose a method in which no disfigurement occurs, such as poisoning. Even though less lethal methods of attempting suicide may suggest a less serious intention to die, they are no guarantee. A much wiser approach is to assume that every suicide attempt communicates at least the contemplation of actual suicide.

QUESTION: What motivates suicidal behavior in adolescents?

Suicidal behavior in adolescents is undoubtedly precipitated and motivated by many factors. One factor that is commonly associated with suicidal behavior is family instability and discord. Suicidal adolescents frequently come from disturbed families. A study of adolescent suicide attempts in Los Angeles County, California, found that 72 percent of these adolescents had one or more parents absent from the home, 62 percent had two employed parents, and 58 percent had a parent who had been married at least twice (Teicher 1973; Corder, Shorr, and Corder 1974). A number of researchers have noted that the loss of a parent through death or divorce has commonly occurred among adolescents who commit suicide (Barter, Swaback, and Todd 1968; Haider 1968; Hendin 1975). The alienation from parents that is typical of suicidal adolescents may also be indicated by the fact that 88 percent of adolescent suicide attempts occur in the home, frequently with at least one parent nearby (Teicher and Jacobs 1966). Even in cases in which the adolescent's nuclear family is intact, suicidal adolescents frequently express that they feel unable to communicate their distress to, or to derive emotional support from, their parents (Hofmann 1975). Suicidal adolescents often do not feel close to their parents or to any adults; they feel that there is no one to turn to when they are troubled. Indeed, one researcher has concluded that "social isolation appears to be the most effective factor in distinguishing those who will kill themselves and those who will not" (Yacoubian and Lourie 1973).

From a psychodynamic point of view, the loss or absence of a warm, parental figure may make an adolescent particularly vulnerable to subsequent losses. Such an adolescent may invest a great deal of emotional energy into relationships with boyfriends and girlfriends, and may perceive these relationships as truly life sustaining. Consider a letter by Vivienne Loomis to her former teacher, John May, written approximately six months before she committed suicide:

> Dear Mr. May, how are you doing? Do you know I still miss you? Even though you have been gone a very long time. I hope that you are happy. What is California like?
>
> Will you please write, and send it airmail? My last letter to you I didn't send airmail because we didn't have enough stamps. But this time I'll try to. Otherwise, even if you answer promptly (which is a fantasy I don't even

indulge in dreaming up!), there would be approximately a month's interval of time before I received anything back from you. You don't know what joy it would afford me if you would answer my letters! (No matter how long it takes!) But really, please do! Enough of that!

. . . And now I must say something and it's not easy. You see there have been a lot of tears lately. Not where anyone would see, but just by myself. I think I'm lonely or something related to it. But there's nobody about who can help me. I was just wondering if you would please send me something encouraging, positive, anything! for me to live on for awhile. It's funny, but I've really gone to pieces. I remember my mother saying how you commented on how nice and good our family is. But sometimes the family can't help. Not with this. I've lost faith in everything. It sounds so dramatic, and yet it's true. I'm asking you as a friend to help me. I would be so grateful. Yours, Vivienne. (Mack and Hickler 1981)

Suicidal adolescents may believe that the absence of a loved object, such as the absence of Vivienne's adult friend, John May, is the result of their intrinsic worthlessness and therefore can never be replaced (Yusin 1973). This belief, according to psychodynamic theory, commonly leads to depression. The following lines from Vivienne's journal reflect the sense of worthlessness and emptiness that the loss of a loved one occasions for some adolescents:

Upon learning that her teacher was planning to move away:
"He is going to leave me.
Forever????
He is going to leave me behind as he goes on his merry way. But if he leaves me what way will I have to go? Why won't he stay? When will I die? It seems like I ought to die now while the going's good."
Later, after her teacher's departure:
"I am worthless. I am of no use to anyone, and no one is of any use to me. What good to kill myself? How can you kill nothing? . . . why live? Why die?"
Still later, in a poem:
"Are you so blind?!
You cannot see
You were given
All I had.
Now my arms
Are empty."
"It's my place to know
Consistent emptiness and loss
Within my soul.
It is my place, also
To know joy just before it vanishes
And sorrow just before it appears
Within my soul." (Mack and Hickler 1981, 99–100)

Family mobility is another factor that appears to contribute to adolescent suicidal behavior. The effect of mobility is particularly clear with respect to recent immigrants. In New York City, for example, Puerto Rican immigrants account for 22 percent of the city's suicide attempts while constituting only 11 percent of the population (Jacobziner 1965). Aside from the generally stressful nature of changed circumstances, a number of specific emotional losses are bound to occur with a change of residence. Aggravating the loss of friendships is that the family preoccupied with the business of moving is unlikely to be aware of their adolescent's great need for support. In a memorial narrative, Vivienne's mother described their home environment at the time of Vivienne's suicide as follows: "Our home had been in turmoil preparing for our move to the new church and community. Packed cartons, pictures off the walls and shrouded in sheets, rugs rolled up ready to go, created a depressing sight" (Mack and Hickler 1981, 3). Vivienne hung herself while her mother and father were attending a farewell party in their honor, a few days before their scheduled move.

The stress that precipitates suicidal behavior may also originate from the pressures of academics, vocational choice, social acceptance, and conflict over sexual activity. That suicide attempters are more likely to be the eldest child, and may consequently be subjected to the greatest pressure to succeed, suggests that stress may indeed by an important factor in suicidal behavior (Haider 1968). The role of pressure for academic achievement is also suggested by the fact that suicidal college students tend to come from more highly educated families and tend to have a high grade point average, which may drop suddenly during the semester preceding suicide (Seiden 1966; Blaine and Carmen 1968). Although the role of stress in adolescent suicidal behavior is undeniable, an interaction usually takes place between environmental stress and social isolation. If an adolescent is anxious or depressed because of overwhelming stress and is also suffering from social isolation, the probability of suicidal behavior is increased. Successful suicides are definitely more likely among those adolescents who feel isolated (Jacobs and Teicher 1967).

QUESTION: How should suicidal adolescents be treated?

Giving a recipe for the treatment of suicidal adolescents is difficult, if not impossible, since the reasons for suicidal behavior differ so greatly. As Andre Haim puts it in *Adolescent Suicide*:

> Quite obviously, there is no such thing as treatment for suicide as such, apart from its prevention at the moment, the act is taking place. There is also treatment of a medico-surgical kind for the consequences of a suicide attempt—but that is another question. What, then, of the prevention of suicide through the treatment of this suicidal tendency? But this is still too limited a point of view; the suicidal adolescent is both an adolescent and, possibly, a psychotic, a depressive, a psychopath, etc. There is therefore no treatment of the suicidal tendency, but various different treatments whose progress is influenced by the existence of a suicidal tendency. (Haim 1974, 297)

In spite of the wide variety of suicidal motivations, some general rules apply to immediate and long-term intervention. The following techniques for dealing with suicidal crises are those which have been found most successful by experts in suicide prevention:

1. Take suicidal threats seriously, even when they are voiced in a subtle form, such as, "I just can't take it anymore," or "they'll be sorry . . ." Eighty percent of suicide attempts are preceded by some form of threat or warning.

2. Move the adolescent to a safe, private area. (Offer food and other refreshments to the adolescent.)
3. Establish a rapport with the adolescent. Let him know that you would like to help, that you take his threat seriously, and that you fully sympathize with the feelings he expresses. Comments such as "I can see that your situation is really overwhelming," and "You must feel very lonely," are ways of validating the adolescent's feelings; do not denounce an adolescent for feeling the way he does. If the adolescent wishes to, be willing to talk about his suicidal schemes. These are all important ways of developing trust.
4. While gaining as much information about the adolescent as possible, try to identify and talk about aspects of the adolescent's life which he enjoys. Try not to focus on death alone.
5. Try to identify and talk about the adolescent's main problem or problems.
6. Propose alternative solutions to his problem. An adolescent who is overwhelmed by his problems often becomes very inflexible in his thinking.
7. Try to agree on a specific course of action which the adolescent may take. Be optimistic and supportive, but do not promise the impossible.
8. Locate and enlist the help of family, close friends, and professionals. (Mitchell and Resnik 1981, 151-54)

The professional treatment of suicidal adolescents is usually based on the assumption that the adolescent has somehow become cut off from the support of significant others (Teicher 1979). As one expert puts it, "The therapist makes an intense, explicit commitment to becoming, for as long as necessary, the young person's 'life line'" (Weiner 1982, 444). Once one has developed a rapport with the adolescent, the goal is to open the lines of communication between the adolescent and the family. Family sessions are used to discover how communication and trust break down in the family, and to encourage more supportive family interaction. Individual therapy is used to focus on the adolescent's motives for attempting suicide. Adolescents have little insight into their reasons for committing suicide, and attribute it entirely to a single precipitating event. Until adolescents have had an opportunity to review their life, vent their frustrations, and explore their motives for suicide, suicidal behavior remains a possibility (Weiner 1982, 445).

Summary

The quality of an adolescent's mental health depends on one's point of view. From society's viewpoint, an adolescent's mental health tends to be defined in terms of its conformance with sociocultural norms; from an individual viewpoint, it tends to be defined in terms of happiness or self-satisfaction; and from the professional viewpoint, it is defined in terms of some ideal of personal actualization. The question of when an adolescent needs clinical attention can be complicated; however, much of the time the individual, societal, and professional viewpoints agree as to whether an adolescent has a psychological problem.

Poor mental, emotional, and physical health are often the *normal* reaction to excessive stress. The two types of reactive disorders are (1) adjustment disorders, which are problems resulting from the cumulative stress of ordinary life, and (2) post-traumatic stress disorders, resulting from traumas or catastrophies.

Certain conditions amplify stress, but due to differences in coping ability, predicting precisely when an adolescent may be reaching the breaking point is impossible. Adolescents can learn to cope with stress in several ways: practice, preparation, information, and collaboration.

Some troubled youth have developmental histories that show problems in behavior and temperament from infancy on through childhood. This problem has been labeled "hyperactivity." Hyperactivity possibly affects as many as 5 percent of school-age children and is more common in boys than in girls. Behavioral and social learning approaches seem most useful in treating hyperactivity.

Many, if not most, adolescents experience many of the secondary symptoms of hyperactivity. This, however, does not necessarily mean that these adolescents are hyperactive. An adolescent who experiences frequent depression may be suffering from another clinical problem called an affective disorder.

The cardinal characteristic of depression is severe, persistent sadness. The most common thoughts associated with depression are statements of self-deprecation and pessimism. In adolescents, depression often seems to be masked. In most cases, adolescents will recover from bouts of depression and manic depression within six to eighteen months, even without treatment. Nevertheless, nearly all adolescents who are hospitalized with manic depression continue to be disturbed as adults.

Neurotic disorders all involve anxiety or fear. Fears are considered phobias when they are both abnormal and disproportionate to the actual danger present, and mild fears persist longer than is normal. The incidence of phobia is highest among children, due to their vulnerability to various fears. The three theories about the development of phobias are: (1) phobias are conditioned responses; (2) phobias occur through modelling, and (3) phobias occur through displacement. A common neurosis in adolescents is school phobia, which generally seems to be the result of maternal overprotection.

An obsessive-compulsive, according to Freud's description, is cautious, nit-picking, and rigid. Obsessive-compulsive disorder is commonly conceived of as a defense against anxiety. Some explanations focus on child-rearing practices and general examples of parents.

Conversion reactions consist of bodily impairments with psychological rather than organic causes. In contrast with adults with conversion reactions, the physical symptoms of adolescents disappear fairly readily once the basic problem is identified. This disorder occurs more frequently in adolescents with what is called hysterical personality styles. Although neurotic disorders of adolescents tend to correct themselves in time, not all adolescents will recover without treatment. The therapeutic approaches used with adolescents include behavior therapy, Gestalt therapy, cognitive therapy, and family therapy.

Schizophrenia is the most common diagnosis among adolescents referred for inpatient psychiatric care. More than half of the adolescents hospitalized for schizophrenia do not even partially recover. Schizophrenia is characterized by (1) disordered and illogical thinking, (2) inaccurate perceptions of reality, (3) ineptness in personal relationships, and (4) inadequate ability to control ideas, affects, and behavior. These symptoms may be relatively unpronounced and difficult to detect in adolescents. Symptoms that are most suggestive of schizophrenia in adolescents are distorted perceptions, social withdrawal, inappropriate emotions, and lack of self-control. The symptoms in many cases suggest which forms of therapy (individual, group, or family) should be used.

Anorexia nervosa is a severe weight loss due to inadequate eating. It occurs mostly among adolescents, especially females. The two predominant approaches to treating anorexia are weight gain therapy and psychotherapy. Recently, individual and family therapy have been used in tandem.

Suicide has become the third most common cause of death in adolescents. One in ten who attempt suicide will commit suicide within five years. One factor commonly associated with suicidal behavior is family instability and discord. Family mobility, stress, pressures of academics, social acceptance, and conflict over sexual activity are other factors. Individual therapy is needed to focus on the adolescent's motives for attempting suicide. Family sessions are used to encourage more supportive family interaction.

References

Adams, P. L. 1973. *Obsessive children.* New York: Brunner/Mazel.

Agras, W. S., D. Sylvester, & D. C. Oliveau. 1969. The epidemiology of common fears and phobia. *Comprehensive Psychiatry* 10: 151–56.

American Psychiatric Association. 1980. *Diagnostic and statistical manual of mental disorders.* 3d ed. Washington, D.C.: U.S. Government Printing Office.

Ames, L. B., R. W. Métraux, & R. N. Walker. 1971. *Adolescent Rorschach responses.* Rev. ed. New York: Brunner/Mazel.

Arieti, S. 1974. *Interpretation of schizophrenia.* 2d ed. New York: Basic Books.

Avery, D., & G. Winokur. 1978. Suicide, attempted suicide and relapse rates in depression. *Archives of General Psychiatry* 35: 749–53.

Barter, J. T., B. O. Swaback, & D. Todd. 1968. Adolescent suicide attempts: A follow-up study of hospitalized patients. *Archives of General Psychiatry* 19(5): 523–27.

Beck, A. T. 1974. The development of depression: A cognitive model. In *The psychology of depression: Contemporary theory and research,* ed. R. J. Friedman & M. M. Katz. New York: Wiley.

Bibring, E. 1953. The mechanism of depression. In *Affective disorders,* ed. P. Greenacre, 26. New York: International Univ. Press.

Blaine, G. B., Jr., & L. R. Carmen. 1968. Causal factors in suicidal attempts by male and female college students. *American Journal of Psychiatry* 125(6): 834–37.

Blatt, S. J., S. J. Wyein, E. Chevron, & D. M. Quinlan. 1979. Parental representations and depression in normal young adults. *Journal of Abnormal Psychology* 88: 388–97.

Bleuler, E. 1950. *Dementia precox or the group of schizophrenias.* New York: International Univ. Press.

Borland, B. L., & H. K. Heckman. 1976. Hyperactive boys and their brothers: A 25-year follow-up study. *Archives of General Psychology* 33: 669–75.

Bruch, H. 1974. Eating disturbances in adolescence. In Child and adolescent psychiatry sociocultural and community psychiatry. Vol. II of *Handbook of psychiatry,* ed. G. Caplan, 275–84. New York: Basic Books.

Bulletin of the Meninger Clinic. 1977. Anorexia nervosa: An overview. Vol. 41(5): 429 (September).

———. 1977. On the psychotherapy of patients with anorexia nervosa. Vol. 41(5): 439 (September).

Canner, L. 1960. Do behavior symptoms always indicate psychopathology? *Journal of Child Psychology and Psychiatry* 1: 17–25.

Carpenter, W. T. 1976. Current diagnostic concepts in schizophrenia. *American Journal of Psychiatry* 133: 172–77.

Cavenar, J. O., & L. H. Caudill. 1979. Family neurotic symptoms. *American Journal of Psychiatry* 136: 1474–75.

Chotiner, M. M., & D. U. Forrest. 1974. Adolescent school phobia: Six controlled cases studied retrospectively. *Adolescence* 9: 467–80.

Ciseaux, A. 1980. Anorexia nervosa: A view from the mirror. *American Journal of Nursing* 80: 1468–70.

Conners, C. K. 1969. A teacher rating scale for use in drug studies with children. *American Journal of Psychiatry* 126: 884–88.

Corder, B. F., W. Shorr, & R. F. Corder. 1974. A study of social and psychological characteristics of adolescent suicide attempters in an urban, disadvantaged area. *Adolescence* 9: 1–6.

Cotton, N. Forthcoming. *The development of self-esteem and self-esteem regulation*. International Univ. Press.

Davis, J. M., & S. S. Chang. 1978. A look at the data. In *Controversy in psychiatry*, ed. J. P. Brady & H. K. Brodie. Philadelphia: Saunders.

Erikson, E. 1963. *Childhood and society*. New York: Norton.

Feighner, J. P., E. Robins, S. Guze, R. Woodruff, G. Winokur, & R. Munoz. 1972. Diagnostic criteria for use in psychiatric research. *Archives of General Psychiatry* 26: 57–63.

Freud, S. 1955. *Analysis of a phobia in a five-year-old boy*. Standard ed., vol. 10. London: Hogarth.

――――. 1958. *The disposition to obsessional neurosis*. Standard ed., vol. 12. London: Hogarth.

Garber, B. 1972. *Follow-up study of hospitalized adolescents*. New York: Brunner/Mazel.

Gardener, R. A. 1975. Techniques for involving the child with MBD in meaningful psychotherapy. *Journal of Learning Disabilities* 8: 272–82.

Guggenheim, F. G., & C. Nadelson. 1982. *Major psychiatric disorders*. New York: Elsevier Biomedical.

Haider, I. 1968. Suicide attempts in children and adolescents. *British Journal of Psychiatry* 114(514): 1133–34.

Haim, A. 1974. *Adolescent suicide*, trans. A. M. Sheridan Smith. New York: International Univ. Press.

Halmi, K. A. 1980. Anorexia nervosa. In *Comprehensive textbook of psychiatry*, vol. 2, ed. H. Kaplan, K. Freedman, & B. Sadock, 1882–91. Baltimore: Williams & Wilkins.

Hendin, H. 1975. Student suicide: Death as a lifestyle. *Journal of Nervous and Mental Disorders* 160(3): 204–19.

Hilde, B. 1977. Psychotherapy in eating disorders. *Canadian Psychiatric Association Journal* 22(3): 105 (April).

Hofmann, A. D. 1975. Adolescents in distress: Suicide and out-of-control behavior. *Medical Clinics of North America* 59(6): 1429–37.

Holmes, T. H., & R. H. Rahe. 1967. The social readjustment rating scale. *Journal of Psychosomatic Research* 11: 213–18.

Holzman, P. S., & R. R. Grinker. 1974. Schizophrenia in adolescence. *Journal of Youth and Adolescence* 3: 267–79.

Howell, G. E. 1973. Negative and positive mental practice in motor skill acquisition. *Perceptual and Motor Skills* 37: 312–13.

Hudgens, R. W. 1974. *Psychiatric disorders in adolescence*. Baltimore: Williams & Wilkins.

Jacobs, J., & J. D. Teicher. 1967. Broken homes and social isolation in attempted suicides of adolescents. *International Journal of Social Psychiatry* 13: 140–48.

Jacobziner, H. 1965. Attempted suicides in adolescents. *Journal of the American Medical Association* 191: 7.

Jexon, L. 1964. Anxiety and adolescence in relation to school refusal. *Journal of Child Psychology and Psychiatry* 5: 59–73.

Josselyn, I. M. 1971. *Adolescence*. New York: Harper & Row.

Kris, A., L. Schiff, & R. McLaughlin. 1971. Susceptibility to chronic hospitalization relative to age at first admission. *Archives of General Psychiatry* 24: 346–52.

Lambson, A. 1978. *Guide for the beginning therapist*. New York: Human Sciences Press.

Laughlin, H. P. 1957. *The neuroses*. Washington, D.C.: Butterworth.

Lazarus, R. S., & R. Launier. 1979. Stress related transactions between person and environment. In *Internal and external determinants of behavior*, ed. L. Pervin & M. Lewis. New York: Plenum.

Lehmann, H. E. 1975. Psychopharmacological treatment of schizophrenia. *Schizophrenia Bulletin* 13: 27–45.

Lewinson, P. M. 1974. A behavioral approach to depression. In *The psychology of depression*, ed. R. J. Friedman & M. M. Katz. Washington, D.C.: Winston.

Lordi, W. M. 1979. Hospital and residential treatment of adolescence. In *The short course in adolescent psychiatry*, ed. J. R. Novell. New York: Brunner/Mazel.

Mack, J., & H. Hickler. 1981. *The life and suicide of an adolescent girl.* Boston: Little, Brown.

Maloney, J, & M. K. Farrell. 1980. Treatment of severe weight loss in anorexia nervosa with hyperalimentation and psychotherapy. *American Journal of Psychiatry* 137(3): 310 (March).

Marx, I. M. 1977. Phobias and obsessions: Clinical phenomena in search of laboratory models. In *Psychopathology: Experimental models*, ed. J.D. Maser & M. E. P. Seligman. San Francisco: Freeman.

Mendels, J. 1970. *Concepts of depression.* New York: Wiley.

Mendelson, W., N. Johnson, & M. A. Stewart. 1971. Hyperactive children as teenagers: A follow-up study. *Journal of Nervous and Mental Disease* 153: 273–79.

Milich, R., & J. Loney. 1979. The role of hyperactive and aggressive symptomology in predicting adolescent outcome among hyperactive children. *Journal of Pediatric Psychology* 4: 93–112.

Minde, K., et al. 1972. A five-year follow-up study of 91 hyperactive school children. *Journal of the American Academy of Child Psychiatry* 11: 595–611.

Mitchell, J. T., & H. L. P. Resnik. 1981. *Emergency response to crisis.* Bowie, Md.: Brady.

Mosher, L. R., & A. Mann. 1978. Community residential treatment for schizophrenia: Two-year follow-up data. *Hospital and Community Psychiatry* 29: 715–23.

Nameche, G. F., M. Waring, & D. F. Ricks. 1964. Early indicators of outcome in schizophrenia. *Journal of Nervous and Mental Disease* 139: 232–40.

National Center for Health Statistics. 1978. Vital statistics of the United States (1975 and 1976) *Mortality*, vol. 2, pts. A & B. Hyattsville, Md.: National Center for Health Statistics.

Nursing Times. 1980. Anorexia nervosa. February, 325.

Paykel, E. S. 1974. Life stress and psychiatric disorder. In *Stressful life events*, ed. B. S. Dohrenwend & B. P. Dohrenwend. New York: Wiley.

Piazza, E., N. Piazza, & N. Rollins. 1980. Anorexia nervosa: Controversial aspects of therapy. *Comprehensive Psychiatry* 21(3): 178 (May–June).

Psychiatry. 1978. Anorexia nervosa: Reflections on theory and practice. Vol. II: 299 (11 August).

Psychological Medicine. 1977. Present status of anorexia nervosa. Vol. 7: 366.

Psychosomatic Medicine. 1975. A functional anteriohypothalamic defect in primary anorexia nervosa? Vol. 37 (2): 104 (March–April).

Rangell, L. 1959. The nature of conversion. *Journal of American Psychiatry* 7: 632.

Richardson, T. F. 1980. Anorexia nervosa: An overview. *American Journal of Nursing* 80: 1470–71.

Rieder, R. O. 1979. Borderline schizophrenia: Evidence of its validity. *Schizophrenia Bulletin* 5: 39–46.

Robins, L. N. 1966. *Deviant children grown up.* Baltimore: Williams & Wilkins.

Schmale, A. H. 1982. Somatic expressions and consequences of conversion reactions. In *Major psychiatric disorders: overviews and selected readings*, ed. by F. G. Guggenheim and C. Nadelson, 263–67.

Seiden, R. H. 1966. Campus strategy: A study of the student suicide. *Journal of Abnormal Psychology* 71(6): 389–99.

Seligman, M. E. P. 1975. *Helplessness: On depression, development, and death.* San Francisco: Freeman.

Selye, H. 1956. *The stress of life.* New York: McGraw-Hill.

Shapiro, R. L. 1979. Adolescents in family therapy. In *The short course in adolescent psychiatry*, ed. J. R. Novello. New York: Brunner/Mazel.

Simmel, E. 1929. Psychoanalytic treatment in a sanitorium. *International Journal of Psychoanalysis* 10: 70.

Siris, S. G., D. P. Van Kammen, & J. P. Docherty. 1978. Use of anti-depressant drugs in schizophrenia. *Archives of General Psychiatry* 35: 1368–77.

Southern Medical Journal. 1977. Anorexia nervosa: A combined therapeutic approach. Vol. 70(4): 448 (April).

Spitzer, R. L. et al. 1983. *Psychopathology: A case book.* New York: McGraw-Hill.

Stewart, M. A., & S. W. Olds. 1973. *Raising a hyperactive child.* New York: Harper & Row.

Strupp, H. H., & S. W. Hadley. 1977. A tripartite model of mental health and therapeutic outcomes. *American Psychologist* 32: 187–96.

Sue, D., D. W. Sue, & S. Sue. 1981. *Understanding abnormal behavior.* Boston: Houghton Mifflin.

Teicher, J. D. 1973. A solution to the chronic problem of living: Adolescent attempted suicide. In *Current issues in adolescent psychiatry,* ed. J. C. Schooler, 129–47. New York: Brunner/Mazel.

———. 1979. Suicide and suicide attempts. In *Basic handbook of child psychiatry,* vol. 2, ed. J. D. Noshpitz. New York: Basic Books.

Teicher, J. D., & J. Jacobs. 1966. The physician and the adolescent suicide attempter. *Journal of School Health* 36(9): 406–15.

Thomas, H., S. Chess, & H. Birch. 1969. *Temperament and behavior disorders in children.* New York: International Univ. Press.

———. 1970. The origin of personality. *Scientific American* 223(2): 102–9.

Toffler, A. 1970. *Future shock.* New York: Random House.

Tomb, D. A., C. K. Berenson, R. C. Ferre, T. A. Halversen, & W. M. McMahon. 1983. *Child psychiatry and behavioral pediatrics case studies.* New Hyde Park, New York: Medical Examination Publishing.

Toolan, J. M. 1975. Suicide in children and adolescents. *American Journal of Psychotherapy* 29: 339–44.

Veck, J. C. 1978. Social influences on the prognosis of schizophrenia. *Schizophrenia Bulletin* 4: 86–101.

Vigersky, R. A., ed. 1977. Behavior therapy: Extended follow-up. In *Anorexia nervosa.* New York: Raven Press.

Weiner, I. B. 1982. *Child and adolescent psychopathology.* New York: Wiley.

Weisberg, P. S. 1979. Group therapy with adolescents. In *The short course in adolescent psychiatry,* ed. J. R. Novello. New York: Brunner/Mazel.

Weschler, H. 1960. Half-way houses for former mental patients. *Journal of Social Issues* 16: 20–26.

Wolpe, J. 1973. *The practice of behavior therapy.* New York: Pergamon.

Yacoubian, J. H., & R. S. Lourie. 1973. Suicide and attempted suicide in children and adolescents. In *Pathology of childhood and adolescence,* ed. S. L. Copel, 149–65. New York: Basic Books.

Yusin, A. S. 1973. Attempted suicide in an adolescent: The resolution of an anxiety state. *Adolescence* 8: 17–28.

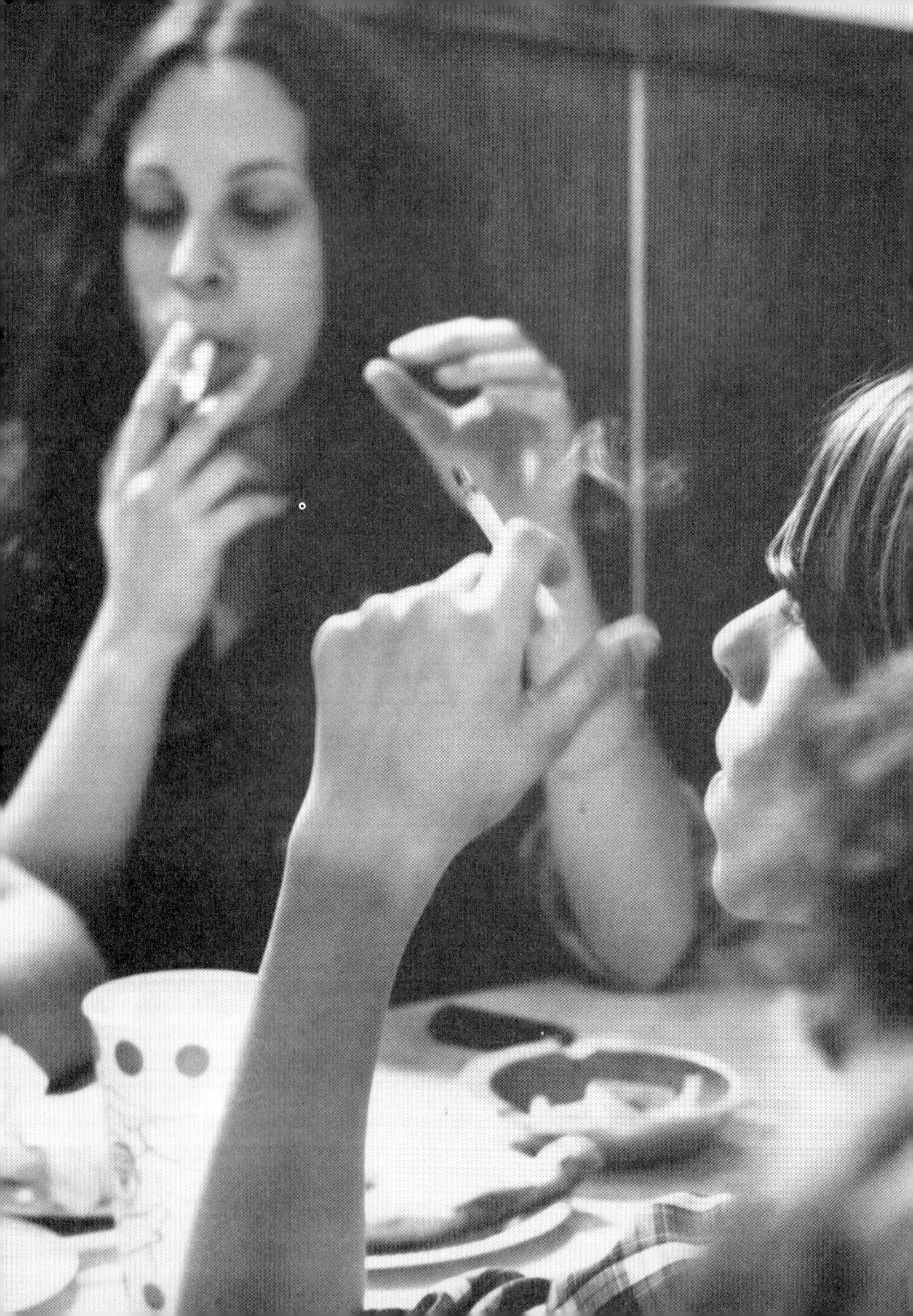

CHAPTER TWELVE
Drug use during adolescence

SURVEY AND QUESTIONS

This chapter covers the definition and types of drug usage, considers the motivations for adolescent drug use, and discusses prevention and treatment of drug abuse. Reading the chapter will provide answers to the following questions:

Adolescent Drug Use

What are the categories and characteristics of different drugs?
How widespread is the use of psychoactive drugs among adolescents today?
At what age do today's adolescents first experiment with psychoactive drugs?
Are college-bound high schoolers less experienced with drugs than those who are not bound for college?
Are males or females more likely to use drugs?
Do differences exist between adolescents living in the country and those living in the city?

Theories of Motivation for Drug Use

What are the motives for using drugs?
What are the theories concerning adolescent use of psychoactive drugs?
What other explanations have been offered for adolescent drug use?
What is the behaviorist explanation for adolescent drug abuse?
What is the social learning theory of drug use?
Do adolescents use drugs as a way of rebelling against society?

Prevention and Treatment of Drug Abuse

According to these theories, how can adolescent drug abuse best be prevented and treated?
What is the psychodynamic approach to drug prevention and treatment?
What is the behaviorist approach to treatment of drug abuse?
Can adolescent drug use be treated with the behavioral model without using punishment?
Has the cognitive social learning approach been more successful for treating adolescent drug abuse?
What is the cognitive restructuring approach in the social learning theory?
How can adolescents be helped to evaluate their attitudes and beliefs?

Adolescent drug use

A taxi driver lights a cigarette. An accountant working late drinks a cup of coffee. A politician offers friends drinks in his office. An insomniac takes a prescribed sleeping pill. Lawyers and business people pass around marijuana cigarettes at a dinner party. A sixth-grader sniffs glue in her bedroom. A teenager uses money from a stolen purse to buy heroin and "shoots up." An electronics engineer consumes three Manhattans with dinner at a restaurant; on the way home he kills two people in an auto crash.

At about the same time, a professor at a cocktail party refuses a drink. A high school student quietly leaves the room when his friends start passing a marijuana "joint." A truck driver turns down the pill his buddy offers. And a housewife decides to see whether her headache will go away without aspirin. (Fort and Cory 1975, 3)

Until recently, most people thought that the term *drug culture* referred to a small group of teenagers and college students using illegalized drugs. What has now become clear is that U.S. society as a whole is a drug culture. Millions of adults engage in the daily use of caffeine, nicotine, and alcohol. Drug taking is a ritual. For example, we associate the use of alcohol with toasting at weddings and parties, with having a beer at the ball game, with cocktails before dinner, wine with dinner, and a cordial after dinner. We also have cigarette breaks and coffee breaks. A report of the National Commission on Marijuana and Drug Abuse indicates that over 63 million Americans smoke tobacco, and over 89 million drink alcoholic beverages. Americans spend $25 billion a year for alcohol, $12 billion for cigars and cigarettes, and $2.5 billion for coffee, tea, and cocoa (containing the stimulant theobromine). These figures do not include the money spent on psychoactive prescription drugs (Fort and Cory 1975, 6).

The widespread use of drugs is not a recent development. Drugs were big business long before the discovery of the New World. When Marco Polo returned from the Far East in the fifteenth century, he brought with him the Oriental cure for psychological malaise: opium. Since alcohol was the only intoxicant known to Europeans at this time, they compared the effects of opium to drunkenness or stupor. Although opium was first used by physicians to treat diseases, it soon became a curiosity and a luxury among the ruling classes. As long as drug use was limited mainly to the ruling classes, the authorities did not worry about it. Sir Walter Raleigh later brought tobacco back to the Old World from Virginia. Tobacco gained support from the medical community, and soon began the urban panacea: "Valuable whether taken into the lungs or into the digestive system—or applied externally to wounds; effective alike against headaches, carbuncle, chilblains, worms, or venereal disease" (Inglis 1975, 37).

Raleigh successfully grew tobacco on his Irish estates and began smoking it in a pipe as the Indians did. Smoking tobacco became so fashionable among the ruling classes in Britain that King James I was powerless to ban the drug. Instead, he put a 4,000 percent tax on tobacco. The tax was aimed at prohibiting the working classes from smoking, since it encouraged them to sit and talk rather than work. Smuggling tobacco became so common, however, that King James decided to find the rate of taxation that provided the greatest tax revenues for the Crown.

Like opium and tobacco, tea and coffee were introduced to Europe as medicines. When the authorities discovered that the lower classes were using these substances for pleasure, they were prohibited or heavily taxed. Eventually, they proved too popular and too profitable to prohibit.

The historical ambivalence toward drugs is clearly seen in the policies of Britain regarding alcohol and opium. Before alcohol was clearly identified as a problem the British had invested large sums in breweries and distilleries. The government encouraged drinking because it pushed up the price of government grain and rye and increased tax revenues. When alcohol abuse created severe problems in London, Parliament passed a bill prohibiting gin sale or consumption. The new law resulted in violent rioting and black marketing of gin, and the government was forced to repeal the law. Parliament settled for a stiff sales tax on gin instead. In the opium wars with China, this same conflict over the costs and benefits of drug sales is evident—only this time the Chinese paid the costs, and the British reaped the benefits. In both Britain and China, the use of opium was restricted. A committee of the British House of Commons was established to review the affairs of the East India Company, which was smuggling large amounts of opium into China for sale. When the committee learned that the sale of opium to the Chinese resulted in over 2 million pounds in revenue to the British Crown, the committee decided that it would be unwise "to abandon so important a source of revenue as the opium trade, the duty upon opium being one which falls principally on the foreign consumer" (Cranshaw 1978, 13).

This same conflict between the profitability and the dangers of drug use can be seen in twentieth-century America. Around the turn of the century, a businessman from Atlanta, Georgia, concocted a drink that he peddled as a "remedy for headache and quick pickup" and as "the intellectual beverage and temperance drink . . . valuable brain tonic, and a cure for all nervous afflictions." The ingredients included cocaine, cola nut, and a little syrup; the drink was called Coca-Cola. By 1914, the evidence had become clear that cocaine also caused serious problems. Alcohol, however, was not prohibited as were other narcotics under the Harrison Act of 1914. Some have pointed out that alcohol was instrumental in the development of the frontier West: "Whisky was the force which impelled the American fur traders into the . . . West . . . whisky fueled the engines of the political machines and corroded their steering mechanisms: whisky oiled the escalators to political success and greased the skids to oblivion" (Grey 1972, 1–2). The sale of alcohol was prohibited under the Eighteenth Amendment in 1920, but due to extensive bootlegging and corruption, the amendment was repealed in 1933.

In studying adolescent drug use, one should keep three points in mind. The first is that drug use and abuse is a widespread social and cultural problem that is not restricted to a youth culture or subculture. The second is that drug abuse has a long history and is not confined to the present generation. The third point is that drugs is a subject about which we tend to have a double attitude. Opium, morphine, heroin, and cocaine—the wonder drugs of history—are illegal. Yet, the average American keeps about thirty drugs in the home medicine cabinet and takes the use of alcohol and tobacco for granted. This schizophrenic national attitude has been summarized in a report by the Drug Abuse Council.

> We prohibit heroin, jail [the] addicts, and employ thousands of agents to suppress the illicit traffic; yet we spend hundreds of millions of dollars to advertise

alcohol, amphetamines, barbiturates, and tranquilizers—substances which can be far more injurious to individuals and society than heroin. We support harsh criminal penalties for heroin addicts because we are afraid of the street crimes they may commit. . . . Yet we tolerate thousands of automobile deaths each year due to drunken driving. (Bergen 1974, D–1)

Is it any wonder why adolescents are confused?

QUESTION: What are the categories and characteristics of different drugs?

In the broadest sense, the term *drugs* refers to any substance that will produce a definable physical or psychological reaction in human beings. In a narrower sense, the term refers to any substances that change the minds or moods of the people who take them. Drugs in this narrower sense are called psychoactive drugs and may be grouped into eleven major categories: caffeine, marijuana, inhalants, tranquilizers and antidepressants, psychedelics, narcotics, cocaine, amphetamines, barbiturates, nicotine, and alcohol. Their effects vary widely, not only from drug to drug but also from user to user, depending on dosage, personality, and circumstances.

CAFFEINE

Caffeine is one of the most psychoactive drugs and is probably one of the safest. Caffeine acts as a stimulant to the central nervous system. It seems to make people more alert and to improve speed and accuracy at most tasks. Large doses of caffeine may cause convulsions and even death, but this is extremely rare. To consume a lethal dose, a human being would have to drink about 100 cups of coffee or over 200 cans of cola. Even in small doses, however, caffeine is apparently addictive. Doctors at Stanford University have found that people who drink only five cups of coffee a day feel jittery and nervous if they are given only decaffeinated coffee, and that these symptoms disappear immediately when they are allowed to drink caffeinated coffee (Fort and Cory 1975, 35).

MARIJUANA

Marijuana is the world's fourth most widely used psychoactive drug, after caffeine, nicotine, and alcohol. Marijuana is a preparation from the hemp plant, which grows almost everywhere in the world and is the source of hemp fibers for rope and linen fabric. Hashish is the concentrated resin from the hemp plant and is six to ten times more powerful than marijuana. The active ingredient in marijuana and hash is tetrahydrocannabinol (THC).

The effects of THC are quite variable. A small amount, perhaps half a joint, makes the user talkative, relaxed, and jovial. A joint and a half increases the intensity of sensory impressions, slows the user's perception of time, and slightly dims the memory. Two joints can relax muscles and impair coordination and judgment. Three or more may cause hallucination, and panic in inexperienced users. THC can also produce drowsiness, dizziness, tremors, dilation of pupils, nausea, and hunger. Marijuana does not appear to be physically addictive, and there is no known fatal dose.

INHALANTS

The inhalants are often called "garbage highs" and are used mostly by younger adolescents who want to get high when other drugs are either unknown or unavailable. In the late 1950s, adolescents discovered that they could get high on model airplane glue, household cement, fingernail polish remover, paint thinner, and gasoline. If ingested, the chemicals contained in these substances are poisonous. When inhaled, the vapors of these products give short highs similar to those of alcohol or barbiturates. These drugs produce dizziness, dullness, floating sensations, feelings of power, and in some users, aggressiveness. Nitrous oxide, used as an anesthetic and also as a gas to force whipped cream out of aerosol containers, produces a sense of relaxation, euphoria, and a blurring of perceptions. The body develops a tolerance to most inhalants (nitrous oxide is an exception), but does not undergo withdrawal when use of the drug is discontinued.

The many deaths associated with the use of inhalants have been caused mainly by suffocation from the plastic bags in which users squeeze the substances to concentrate the fumes. Some users have also had sudden fatal heart attacks during heavy physical activity after inhaling. Some studies have shown that inhalers may develop blood, liver, and kidney disorders, which may be fatal.

TRANQUILIZERS AND ANTIDEPRESSANTS

Tranquilizers and antidepressants are widely used in psychiatry, especially in treating schizophrenics. True tranquilizers differ from depressants (barbiturates, alcohol, and opiates) in that they can be taken in large doses without producing drowsiness or overdose. Besides inducing calmness, tranquilizers produce numbness, muscular stiffness, strange muscle relaxation and twitches, lack of initiative and slowness of thought, and damage to the liver and bone marrow. Chlorpromazine (Thorazine), triflouperazine (Stelazine) and thioxanthene (Traractan) are common tranquilizers.

Antidepressants differ from stimulants and other amphetamines in that they often take effect only after several weeks of use, and they have different effects. Antidepressants are used in psychiatry only for severe depression. Tranquilizers and antidepressants are not addicting, but neither do they have quick, intense effects. For these reasons, they are not often sought out for highs by adolescents, and no black market for these drugs seems to exist.

PSYCHEDELICS

The word *psychedelic* literally means expansion of the mind, or psyche. The most well-known psychedelic drug, LSD, was accidentally created in a Swiss lab in 1943. In effects, and to some extent in chemical makeup, LSD is related to a number of other synthetic and natural substances. The natural psychedelics, especially in ancient, Central, and South America, have a long history of use in religious ritual. Beginning in the 1950s, many intelligent and artistic people in the United States began to experiment with the psychedelic drugs. A literature grew that fervently proclaimed that the psychedelic drugs were the means to a new way of life, and which discounted the possibility of any danger (Alpert, Cowan, and Schiller 1966).

The effects of psychedelic drugs, more than any other drugs, depends on the user's expectations and circumstances. Some users enter a dreamlike, meditative state in which sensations, emotions, and thoughts are intensified and unusually connected. Bad trips seem to result if the user is anxious or afraid, or is confined in a jail, clinic, or hospital. Both good and bad trips are often so emotional that even after the drug has worn off, the memory of it will sometimes flash back into the user's mind. Under the influence of the unusual thoughts that psychedelics produce, some users have attempted to take flight from skyscrapers and to step in front of cars. Psychedelic drugs were once thought to cause birth defects, but that danger now appears negligible. A tolerance for psychedelic drugs does develop, but none of the psychedelic drugs produce physical addition.

NARCOTICS

Naroctics, along with barbiturates and alcohol, are powerful depressants. Unlike the others, narcotics are also extremely effective painkillers. Narcotics come in both natural and synthetic forms. The natural forms include opium and its derivations, morphine, heroin, and codeine. Methadone is the best known of

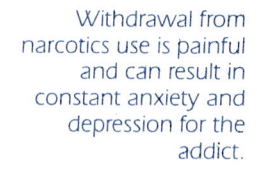

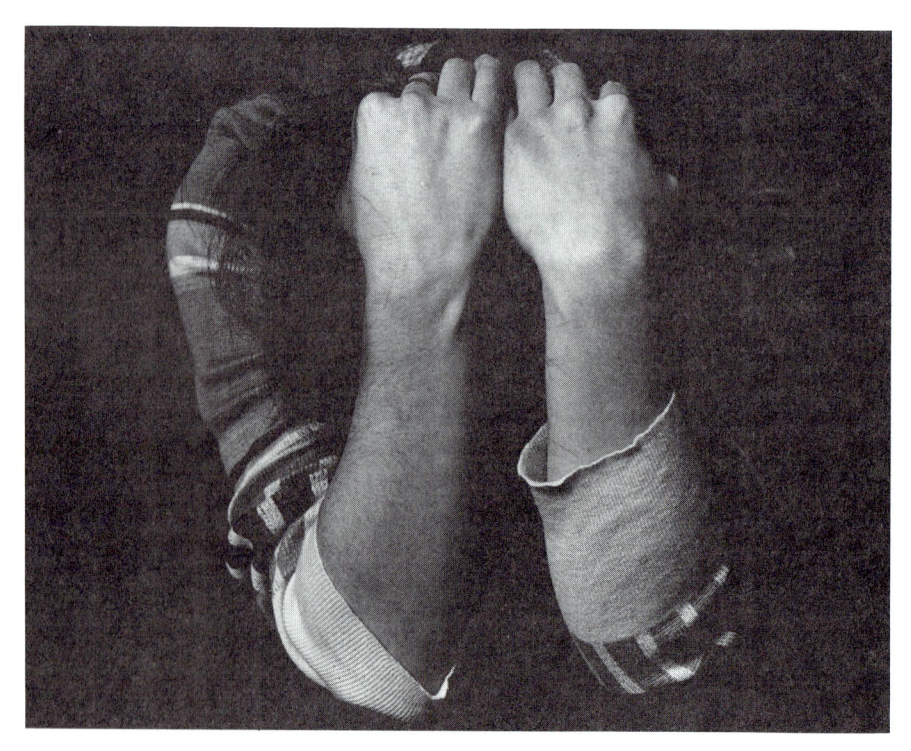

Withdrawal from narcotics use is painful and can result in constant anxiety and depression for the addict.

scores of synthetic narcotics. Heroin is the strongest natural narcotic. First-time users of heroin usually experience nausea or vomiting, but repeat users usually experience a thrilling "rush" similar to orgasm, followed by feelings of warmth, peacefulness, and increased self-esteem. As tolerance and addiction develop, these effects disappear and side effects such as impotence and sterility often occur.

Narcotics, even in large doses, do not appear to do long-term damage to the human body. Potency and fertility, for example, usually return when the drug is no longer used. Nevertheless, dirty needles, poisonous substitutes, malnutrition, and overdoses do seem to contribute to a higher death rate among narcotics users. Tolerance and addiction to narcotics develop more rapidly than with any other drug. Withdrawal from narcotics is painful, but is less dangerous than sudden withdrawal from alcohol or barbiturates. After withdrawal, addicts often suffer constant anxiety and depression, which doctors call "postwithdrawal syndrome."

COCAINE

Cocaine is a stimulant that is extracted from the coca bush. It was introduced in the 1880s to combat morphine addiction and was thought to be no more harmful than coffee or tea. Until about 1906, it was used to flavor Coca-Cola. An average dose of cocaine makes a user feel alert and extraordinarily powerful for about fifteen minutes to an hour. Although cocaine is not physically addicting, it has an extremely strong psychological appeal. Laboratory animals that are given drugs for pushing a lever will push it 250 times in a row for caffeine, 4,000 times for heroin, and 10,000 for cocaine.

The extended use of cocaine has a number of side effects. Users can become paranoid and may even have the sensation of bugs crawling under their skin. A cocaine high is sometimes followed by depression, and long-time users can easily become ill from insomnia and malnutrition. Cocaine also causes permanent damage to the mucous membranes of the nose.

AMPHETAMINES

Amphetamine was first produced in Germany in the 1880s and was originally used to treat narcolepsy. Its production was greatly increased during World War II, when it was given to soldiers on both sides because it increased their capacity to carry out strenuous tasks and to concentrate. After the war, it was illegally used by truck drivers, students, and dieters. The stimulant Ritalin was also prescribed for an estimated 1 million "hyperactive" children, often for periods of several years. Amphetamines are now one of the most widely used psychoactive drugs.

Amphetamines create alertness and a loss of appetite. Among their side effects are restlessness, headaches, dizziness, tremor, and a dry mouth. Large doses lead to fatigue, depression, high blood pressure, and respiratory failure. In rare cases, amphetamines may increase the risk of heart attack, but in general, the warning "speed kills" is not supported by evidence. The body does quickly develop a tolerance to amphetamines, and withdrawal can produce fatigue and depression that last for months.

BARBITURATES

Barbiturates were introduced into medicine by German chemists around the turn of the century, and have been prescribed for insomnia, epilepsy, and unfortunately, for a great variety of other neurotic complaints. The effects of barbiturates are so similar to alcohol that they have sometimes been called "solid alcohol." In small doses, they are called sedatives; they make users relaxed, light-headed, and uninhibited. In larger doses, barbiturates are called hypnotics; they produce drowsiness, slurred speech, and anesthetic effects. In extremely large doses, barbiturates can slow down bodily functions to the point of coma and death. Barbiturates are highly addictive, and too-rapid withdrawal can be fatal.

NICOTINE

Nicotine is a poison used in insecticides, but it is also a strong stimulant found in cigarettes. Nicotine is categorized as a stimulant because, before tolerance develops, it stimulates glands, raises blood pressure, and gives users a sense of alertness. Most smokers find smoking relaxing due to the ritual that keeps their hands and mouth busy rather than to the chemical. The first-time smoker is likely to grow dizzy and nauseous, but the smoker becomes both tolerant and addicted to nicotine with continued use. The addictive quality of nicotine is easy to overlook, since true addicts can obtain cigarettes easily.

Withdrawal from nicotine produces drowsiness, headaches, and both diarrhea and constipation. Withdrawal can be so difficult that doctors recommend that some smokers—10 percent to 15 percent—may be better off taking nicotine by mouth or using snuff than trying to quit. Nevertheless, in the last decade, 10 million Americans have stopped smoking. Studies by the American Cancer Society show that ex-smokers can recover from much of the damage caused by smoking. The longer people go without smoking, the more likely they are to live as long as people who have never smoked.

ALCOHOL

Alcohol, or ethanol, is generally a depressant, although in small amounts it may act as a stimulant. The effects of alcohol vary a great deal with the expectations and personality of the user. Alcohol is a fairly safe drug when used in moderation, but is one of the more dangerous drugs when used in excess, in combination with barbiturates, or while driving. Because alcohol slows reflexes and dulls judgment, the blood alcohol level that is allowed while driving has been steadily reduced and is as low as .05 percent to .08 percent (the equivalent of about two drinks).

Recent research indicates that even moderate drinking can have long-range harmful effects on the body. It may disturb the functioning of heart cells, increase fat deposits on the liver, and inhibit the manufacture of proteins in the brain. Alcohol can also be physically addicting. Symptoms of withdrawal include tremors, sleeplessness, nausea, and if withdrawal is untreated, hallucinations, convulsions, and even death. Alcoholics also have a tendency to develop cirrhosis of the liver, one of the ten leading causes of death in the United States.

Alcoholics also suffer from malnutrition and digestive disorders, and they have a particularly low resistance to bacteria. Alcohol users have been known to literally drink themselves to death; the lethal dose is equivalent to about twenty highballs.

QUESTION: How widespread is the use of psychoactive drugs among adolescents today?

The National Institute on Drug Abuse recently published a study of national trends in student drug use. The study focused on high school seniors between 1975 and 1982. The study showed that although the use of many illicit drugs has declined from peak levels during the late seventies, illicit drug use is still more prevalent in the United States than in any nation in the industrialized world (Johnston, Bachman, and O'Malley 1982, 14). Figure 12-1 presents the prevalence and recency of drug use among the class of 1982.

Marijuana use has declined since 1979, but is still by far the most widely used of the illicit drugs. Almost two-thirds of all seniors have at least tried marijuana; this percentage has remained fairly stable. The current level of marijuana use by seniors, however, has dropped from 30 percent in 1979 to 29 percent in 1982. The daily use of marijuana, which had risen from 6 percent to 11 percent of all seniors between 1975 and 1978, has fallen again to 6 percent in 1982. In other words, in 1982, about one percent in every sixteen seniors used marijuana on a daily basis. A related publication entitled "Student Drug Use, Attitudes, and Beliefs" (Johnston, Bachman, and O'Malley 1982) graphically describes trends for all drugs (see Figure 12-2).

Alcohol abuse is the often overlooked and underestimated drug problem in the United States today.

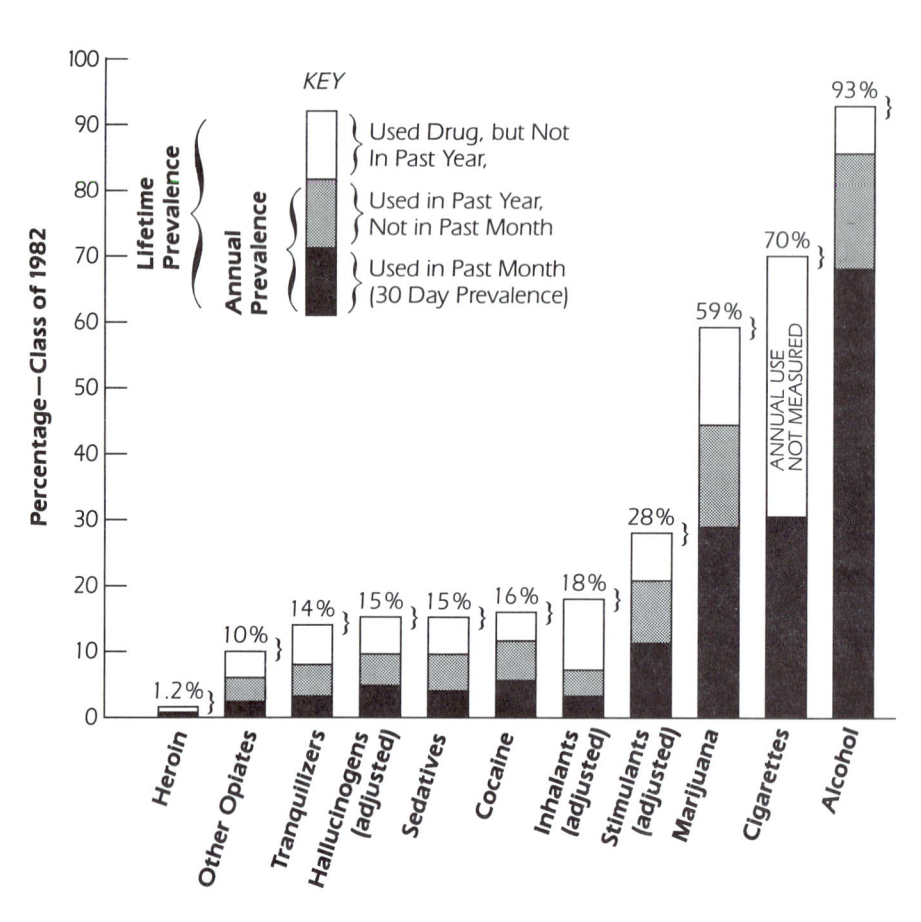

Figure 12-1 Prevalence and Recency of Use of Eleven Types of Drugs, Class of 1982

NOTE: The bracket near the top of a bar indicates the lower and upper limits of the 95% confidence interval.

Source: Johnston, Bachman, and O'Malley 1982, 17.

The second most widely used illicit drugs are amphetamines (stimulants). Between 1975 and 1979, about one in four high school seniors had tried amphetamines at least once. While most other drugs were falling in popularity, the lifetime prevalence of amphetamine usage rose to about one in three seniors. In 1982, the percentage of high school seniors who had used amphetamines at least once increased to 36 percent, the highest rate ever. Evidence suggests that the rise in amphetamine use is partially due to the aggressive marketing of over-the-counter diet pills and stay-awake pills. Over-the-counter diet pills have been used at least once by 42 percent of female seniors of the class of 1982, and stay-awake pills have been used at least once by 19 percent of the class of 1982. When the investigators revised their questions to estimate the use of amphetamines apart from diet pills and stay-awake pills, the prevalence was still high:

Chapter 12 Drug use during adolescence ■ **381**

Figure 12-2 Trends in Annual Prevalence of Fifteen Drugs by Sex

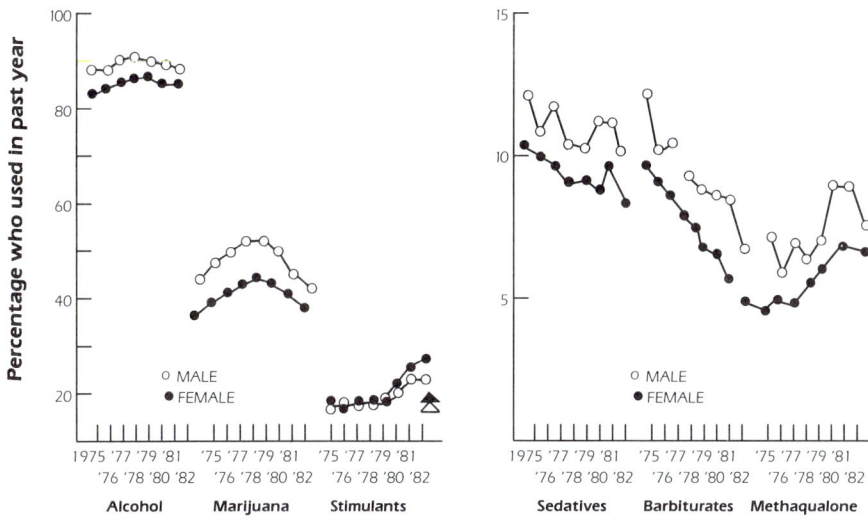

NOTE: The triangles indicate the percentage which result if non-prescription stimulates are excluded.

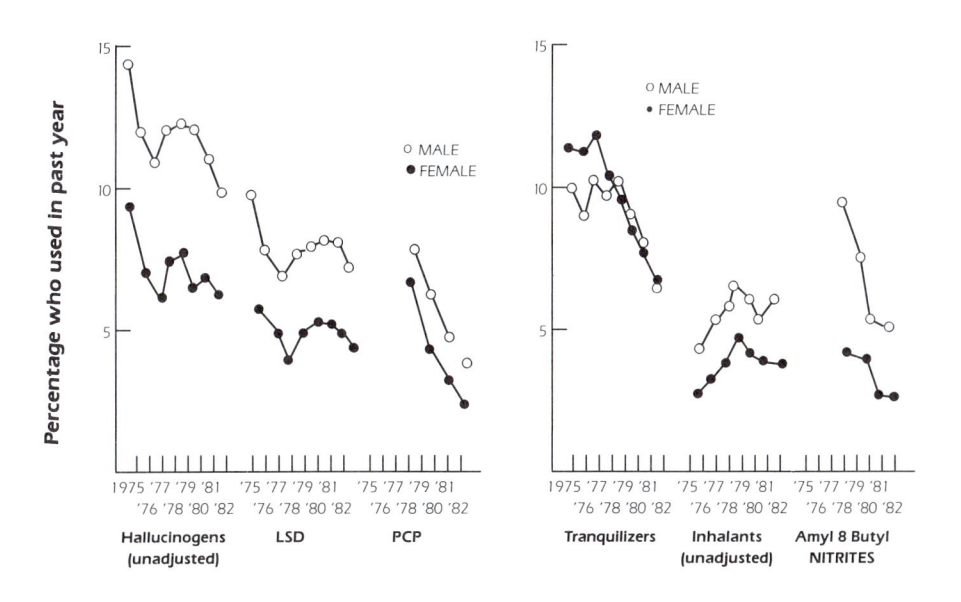

28 percent at least once, 20 percent in the last year, 11 percent in the last month. These figures indicate that although more seniors have tried amphetamines than ever before, active use has dropped slightly (Johnston, Bachman, and O'Malley 1982, 11–12).

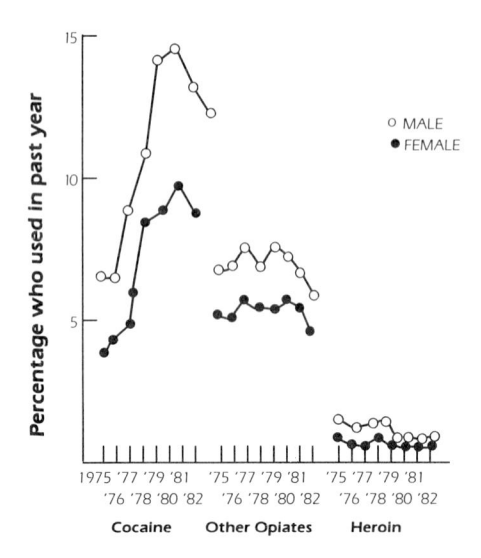

Source: Johnston, Bachman, and O'Malley 1982, 44–48.

Considering the well-publicized dangers involved in the use of inhalants, the number of seniors who have used inhalants at least once is surprisingly high (18 percent). In 1979, 9.2 percent of seniors had used inhalants during the past year. In 1982, this percentage dropped to 6.6. The relatively high percentage of seniors who have used inhalants, but who have not used them during the past year, indicates that inhalants are more popular among younger adolescents (Johnston, Bachman, and O'Malley 1982, 10–11).

The prevalence of cocaine use among high schoolers more than doubled between 1975 and 1979. This percentage began to level off between 1979 and 1981, and for the first time, began to decline in 1982. The percentage of those who had used cocaine at least once in the last year dropped from 12.4 percent in 1981 to 11.5 percent in 1982. The prevalence of cocaine use, more than that of any other drug, shows regional differences. In the western and northeastern regions of the country, the annual prevalence of cocaine use is roughly twice that of the south and north central regions (Johnston, Bachman, and O'Malley 1982, 10).

The nonmedical use of barbiturates and tranquilizers also continued to decline in 1982. Both barbiturates and tranquilizers have shown a long-term steady decline, even when the use of other drugs was still on the rise. The number of seniors who had used tranquilizers during the past year declined from a high of 10.8 percent in 1977 to 7.0 percent in 1982. The annual prevalence of barbiturate use has declined from a high of 10.7 percent in 1975 to 5.5 percent in 1982 (Johnston, Bachman, and O'Malley 1982, 10).

The use of hallucinogens presents something of a mixed picture. The annual and lifetime prevalence of LSD use has remained fairly steady since 1977, after a small decline in earlier years. The use of PCP, however, has decreased dramatically since first measured in 1979. The number of seniors who had used PCP at least once in 1979 was 7.0 percent. This number dropped to only 2.2 percent in 1982 (Johnston, Bachman, and O'Malley 1982, 11).

The use of narcotics (opiates) has also not shown uniform decreases. Although estimating the prevalence of narcotics use is difficult, since the legal penalties for its use are especially severe, the use of heroin apparently dropped by one-half between 1975 and 1979. The number of seniors who had tried heroin at least once in the past year dropped from 1 percent to .5 percent during this period. By contrast, the use of opium, morphine, and codeine has not declined much since the study began in 1975. Some signs indicate that the use of other opiates has declined over the past couple of years, from an annual prevalence of 6.3 percent in 1980 to 5.3 percent in 1982.

The prevalence of alcohol use among high schoolers, unlike that of the illicit drugs, has shown no decline since 1975. Alcohol is by far the most widely used and abused drug among high schoolers. Ninety-three percent of all high school seniors have tried alcohol at least once, and 70 percent have used alcohol during the past month. Forty-one percent of 1982 seniors said that they had had five or more drinks in a row during the prior two weeks, as compared with 37 percent in 1975. Almost 6 percent of high school seniors drink daily, about the same percentage as in 1975; thus, roughly the same number of high schoolers use alcohol daily as use marijuana daily (Johnston, Bachman, and O'Malley 1982, 13).

The most encouraging decline was in the prevalence of cigarette smoking. In 1977, 29 percent of high school seniors smoked daily. This number dropped to 20 percent by 1981, and appears to have leveled off. During the same period, the daily use of a half a pack a day or more fell from 19.4 percent to 13.5 percent. Interestingly, slightly more females than males are regular smokers (14.7 percent versus 13.1 percent). Students who do not plan to go to college are far more likely than college-bound students to be regular smokers (21 percent versus only 8 percent). Although cigarette smoking has declined, about 30 percent of high school seniors have smoked cigarettes during the last month, and many of these are likely to become regular smokers. Cigarettes are still more likely than any other drug to be used by adolescents on a daily basis (see Figure 12–3) (Johnston, Bachman, and O'Malley 1982, 13).

Although remarkable changes have occurred in the use of specific illicit drugs during the past eight years, the overall proportion of the adolescent population who have used illicit drugs at least once has risen steadily. Figure 12–4 shows that the percentage of high school seniors who have used any illicit drugs has risen from 55 percent in 1970 to 66 percent in 1982. Although the proportion of high school students who clearly abuse illicit drugs has decreased slightly over the past few years, the number who have at least used illicit substances has clearly increased. Experimentation with drugs, if not drug abuse, is extremely widespread among adolescents. This trend can be seen in Table 12–1.

QUESTION: At what age do today's adolescents first experiment with psychoactive drugs?

In today's society, it is almost impossible for a child to go through the school system without encountering the drug abuse problem. Depending on the envi-

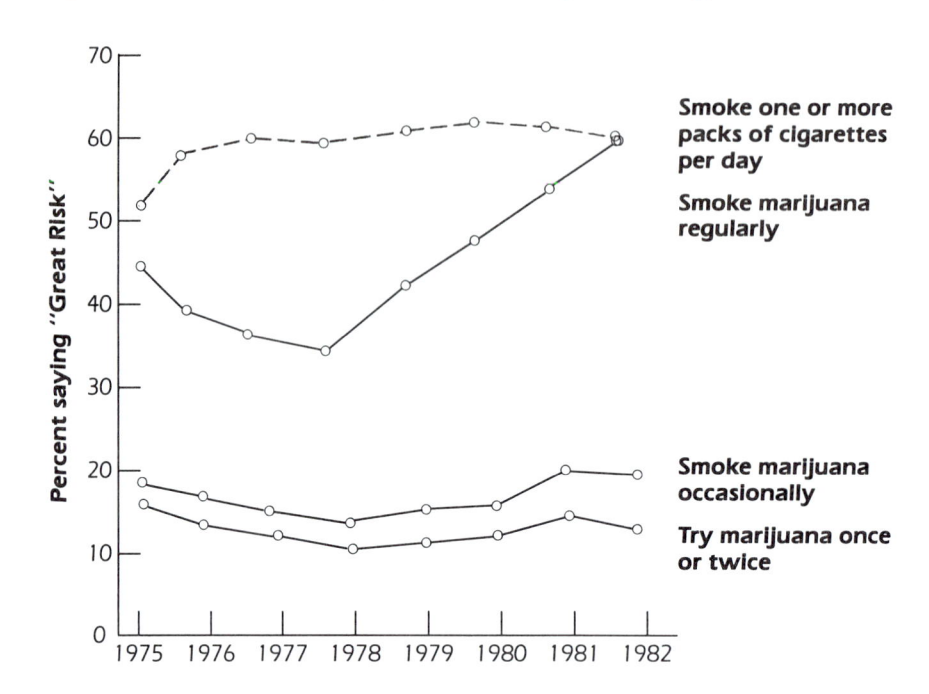

Figure 12-3 Trends in Perceived Harmfulness: Marijuana and Cigarettes

Source: Johnston, Bachman, and O'Malley 1982, 95.

ronment and location, this may happen early or late. A college student related the following experience:

> I had my first exposure to the drug culture at a young age. It was something new, and you were pretty "cool" if you knew about drugs, so I was naturally curious. It began in elementary school where I heard about two girls being sent home for possession of pep pills. In junior high, I would hear of drug busts in the girls' locker room, and inevitably, I had my first chance to buy some "pot." I resisted but rather than staying naive, I tried to find out all of the facts.
>
> In high school, I had the reputation of being pretty normal despite my failure to try out the drugs. The general feelings that existed were that if you had tried drugs, and did not want them, you were fine. But if you just refused to try, you were looked down on as being too controlled by family, religion and society.
>
> Almost all the high school kids tried drugs, normally just marijuana, but their main problem was alcohol. After trying drugs first, they would realize that they were dangerous, and only the "hard-core stoners" would stay with the stuff. But it was very common to have "keggers" every weekend in good weather, and everyone went. It was socially an important part of the high school lifestyle.

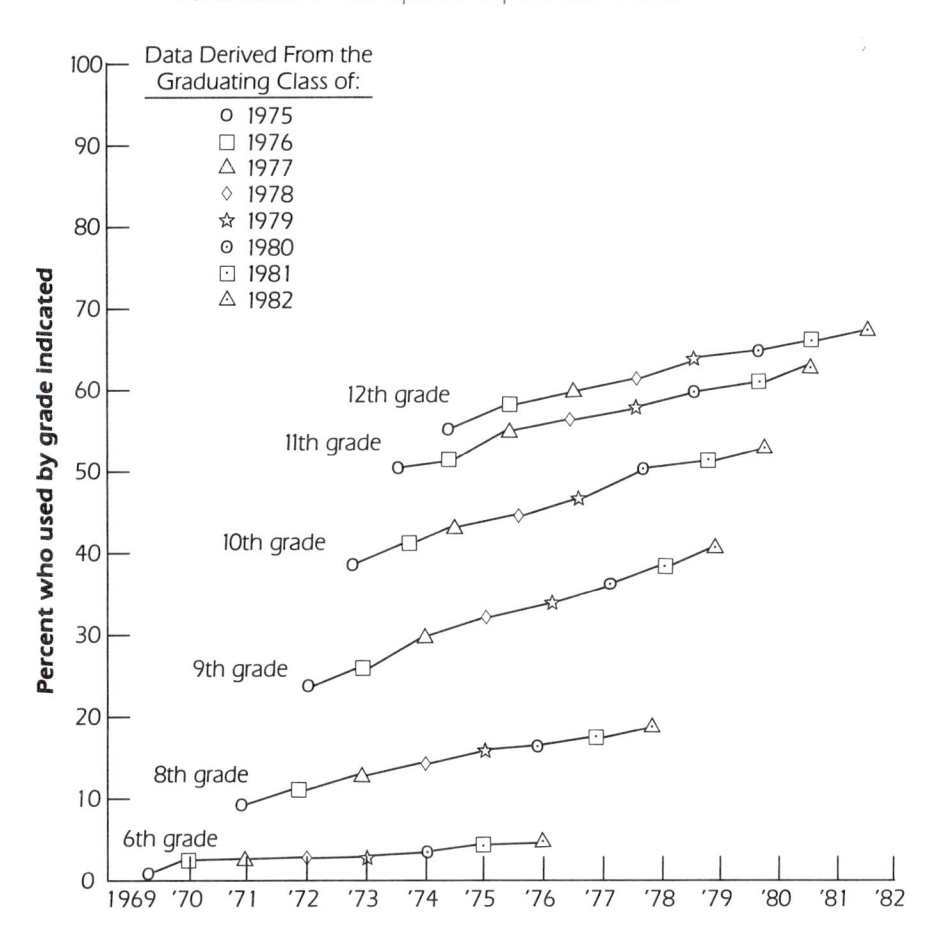

Figure 12-4 Use of Any Illicit Drug: Trends in Lifetime Prevalence for Earlier Grade Levels Based on Retrospective Reports from Seniors

Source: Johnston, Bachman, and O'Malley 1982, 64.

In their eight-year study of drug use among high school seniors, the National Institute on Drug Abuse asked high school seniors when they tried each class of drugs. The study showed that initial experimentation with most illicit drugs (i.e., drugs other than cigarettes and alcohol) occurs during the sophomore, junior, and senior years of high school. No drug except marijuana had been used by more than one out of ten of the class of 1982 at the time they entered their sophomore year. For marijuana, alcohol, and cigarettes, experimentation began much sooner. Before entering tenth grade, 35 percent had tried marijuana, 56 percent had tried alcohol, and 15 percent already smoked daily. By the seventh to eighth grade, over 15 percent had tried marijuana, over 21 percent had tried alcohol, and over 7 percent smoked cigarettes daily (these figures all apply to the seniors in the class of 1982).

These same figures indicated that the age at which illicit drugs were first tried became progressively younger for each graduating class between 1975 and 1982. Figure 12-4 presents these findings graphically. The upward curves show

TABLE 12-1 High School Senior Drug Use: 1975-1983

The following table shows the percentage of high school seniors from the classes of 1975 through 1983 who have used drugs of abuse. These numbers were gathered in annual nationwide surveys conducted for the National Institute on Drug Abuse by the University of Michigan Institute for Social Research. The 1983 survey involved more than 16,300 high school seniors from public and private schools.

Ever Used

	Class of '75	'76	'77	'78	'79	'80	'81	'82	'83
Marijuana	47%	53%	56%	59%	60%	60%	60%	59%	57%
Inhalants	NA	10	11	12	13	12	12	13	14
Amyl & Butyl Nitrites	NA	NA	NA	NA	11	11	10	10	8
Hallucinogens	16	15	14	14	14	13	13	13	12
LSD	11	11	10	10	10	9	10	10	9
PCP	NA	NA	NA	NA	13	10	8	6	6
Cocaine	9	10	11	13	15	16	17	16	16
Heroin	2	2	2	2	1	1	1	1	1
Other Opiates	9	10	10	10	10	10	10	10	9
Stimulants	22	23	23	23	24	26	32	36	35
Sedatives	18	18	17	16	15	15	16	15	14
Barbiturates	17	16	16	14	12	11	11	10	10
Methaqualone	8	8	9	8	8	10	11	11	10
Tranquilizers	17	17	18	17	16	15	15	14	13
Alcohol	90	92	93	93	93	93	93	93	93
Cigarettes	74	75	76	75	74	71	71	70	71

Daily Users

	Class of '75	'76	'77	'78	'79	'80	'81	'82	'83
Marijuana	6%	8%	9%	10.7%	10.3%	9.1%	7%	6.3%	5.5%
Inhalants	NA	0.0	0.0	0.1	0.0	0.1	0.1	0.1	0.1
Amyl & Butyl Nitrites	NA	NA	NA	NA	0.0	0.1	0.1	0.0	0.2
Hallucinogens	0.1	0.1	0.1	0.1	0.1	0.1	0.1	0.1	0.1
LSD	0.0	0.0	0.0	0.0	0.0	0.0	0.1	0.0	0.1
PCP	NA	NA	NA	NA	0.1	0.1	0.1	0.1	0.1
Cocaine	0.1	0.1	0.1	0.1	0.2	0.2	0.3	0.2	0.2
Heroin	0.1	0.0	0.0	0.0	0.0	0.0	0.0	0.0	0.1
Other Opiates	0.1	0.1	0.2	0.1	0.0	0.1	0.1	0.1	0.1
Stimulants	0.5	0.4	0.5	0.5	0.6	0.7	1.2	1.1	1.1
Sedatives	0.3	0.2	0.2	0.2	0.1	0.2	0.2	0.2	0.2
Barbiturates	0.1	0.1	0.2	0.1	0.0	0.1	0.1	0.1	0.1
Methaqualone	0.0	0.0	0.0	0.0	0.0	0.1	0.1	0.1	0.0
Tranquilizers	0.1	0.2	0.3	0.1	0.1	0.1	0.1	0.1	0.1
Alcohol	5.7	5.6	6.1	5.7	6.9	6.0	6.0	5.7	5.5
Cigarettes	26.9	28.8	28.8	27.5	25.4	21.3	20.3	21.1	21.2

Used in Past Month

	\'75	\'76	\'77	\'78	Class of \'79	\'80	\'81	\'82	\'83
Marijuana	27%	32%	35%	37%	37%	34%	32%	29%	27%
Inhalants	NA	1	1	2	2	1	2	2	2
Amyl & Butyl Nitrites	NA	NA	NA	NA	2	2	1	1	1
Hallucinogens	5	3	4	4	4	4	4	3	3
LSD	2	2	2	2	2	2	3	2	2
PCP	NA	NA	NA	NA	2	1	1	1	1
Cocaine	2	2	3	4	6	5	6	5	5
Heroin	*	*	*	*	*	*	*	*	*
Other Opiates	2	2	3	2	2	2	2	2	2
Stimulants	9	8	9	9	10	12	16	14	12
Sedatives	5	5	5	4	4	5	5	3	3
Barbiturates	5	4	4	3	3	3	3	2	2
Methaqualone	2	2	2	2	2	3	3	2	2
Tranquilizers	4	4	5	3	4	3	3	2	3
Alcohol	68	68	71	72	72	72	71	70	69
Cigarettes	37	39	38	37	34	31	29	30	30

Used in Last Year

	\'75	\'76	\'77	\'78	Class of \'79	\'80	\'81	\'82	\'83
Marijuana	40%	45%	48%	50%	51%	49%	46%	44%	42%
Inhalants	NA	3	4	4	5	5	4	5	4
Amyl & Butyl Nitrites	NA	NA	NA	NA	7	6	4	4	4
Hallucinogens	11	9	9	10	10	9	9	8	7
LSD	7	6	6	6	7	7	7	6	5
PCP	NA	NA	NA	NA	7	4	3	2	3
Cocaine	6	6	7	9	12	12	12	12	11
Heroin	1	1	1	1	1	1	1	1	1
Other Opiates	6	6	6	6	6	6	6	5	5
Stimulants	16	16	16	17	18	21	26	26	25
Sedatives	12	11	11	10	10	10	11	9	8
Barbiturates	11	10	9	8	8	7	7	6	5
Methaqualone	5	5	5	5	6	7	8	7	5
Tranquilizers	11	10	11	10	10	9	8	7	7
Alcohol	85	86	87	88	88	88	87	87	87
Cigarettes	NA	NA	NA	NA	NA	NA	NA	NA	NA

Source: *Drugs and American High School Students, 1975–1983*. National Institute on Drug Abuse.

Note: Separate questions about the use of PCP (angel dust) and amyl and butyl nitrites (poppers) were not asked until 1979.

NA indicates data not available   * indicates less than .5%

Terms: Ever Used: Used one or more times.
    Daily Users: Used 20 or more times in the month before survey.
    Used in Past Month: Used at least once in the 30 days prior to survey.
    Used in Last Year: Used in the 12 months prior to survey.

that with each successive graduating class, a greater percentage of the class had experimented with some illicit drug for each grade level. Early experimentation with marijuana accounts for most of this increase (Johnston, Bachman, and O'Malley 1982, 57–66).

QUESTION: Are college-bound high schoolers less experienced with drugs than those who are not bound for college?

In general, seniors who expect to complete college (college bound) have lower rates of illicit drug use than those without these goals. Forty-eight percent of the noncollege-bound seniors reported that they had used marijuana during the past year; 41 percent of the college-bound seniors reported that they had used marijuana during that period. The differences are even more dramatic when the frequent use of illicit drugs is compared. Almost twice as many noncollege-bound seniors use marijuana and alcohol daily as do college-bound seniors (Johnston, Bachman, and O'Malley 1982, 53).

QUESTION: Are males or females more likely to use drugs?

Although males are generally more likely than females to have used drugs, the picture changes greatly from one drug to another. Females tend to take fewer types of drugs and to use drugs with less frequency than do males. Only a 3 percent or 4 percent difference, however, exists between males and females when it comes to experimentation with some illicit drugs other than marijuana during the last year. Going beyond marijuana may be an important threshold in illicit drug use. If so, then nearly equal numbers of male and females were apparently

There have been studies done showing that the use of illicit drugs is lower in senior high school students who expect to go to college than in those who do not. Students' experiences with drugs may change once they're in college, however.

willing to cross that threshold. Still, the frequent use of alcohol is much more common among males than among females. Over twice as many males as females drink alcohol daily, and male high schoolers tend to drink in larger quantities than do females (Johnston, Bachman, and O'Malley 1982, 42ff.)

QUESTION: Do differences exist between adolescents living in the country and those living in the city?

Population density does seem to be a factor in adolescent drug use. When high school seniors were divided into three groups—those from the twelve largest cities in the United States, those from other metropolitan areas, and those from nonmetropolitan areas—the findings were that overall illicit drug use is highest in the largest cities and lowest in the nonmetropolitan areas. Fifty-five percent of adolescents from the largest cities have used some illicit drug during the past year, compared with only 44 percent in the nonmetropolitan areas. The use of certain drugs, such as cocaine, psychedelics, and inhalants, are even more strongly related to population density. Cocaine and PCP are used twice as much by adolescents living in large cities as by adolescents living in nonmetropolitan areas (Johnston, Bachman, and O'Malley 1982, 56).

Some noticeable regional differences are also present in adolescent drug use. Illicit drug use is most prevalent in the Northeast, followed by the West, the North Central region, and lastly, by the South (see Table 12–2). The western United States ranks as high as they do largely due to the use of cocaine, which is far more prevalent in the West than elsewhere. The West has a below-average ranking for all other drugs except marijuana and the milder opiates. Cigarette smoking (half a pack a day or more) is distinctly less popular in the West (7 percent) than in the South (13 percent), the Northeast (16 percent), or the North Central (17 percent) regions. Drinking alcohol, particularly daily drinking and binge drinking, is also somewhat less prevalent in the West and South than it is in the Northeast and North Central regions. The highest rates of use for many individual drugs is found in the Northeast, and the lowest rates of usage for most drugs is found in the South (Johnston, Bachman, and O'Malley 1982, 53ff.)

QUESTION: What are the motives for using drugs?

In looking for explanations for drug use among young people, we first need to recognize that there will be different reasons, different combinations of reasons, and an overlap of reasons for drug use. In trying to identify these different reasons, finding simplistic answers is easy, and as we examine one reason, the reader will find that it then contributes to a second and a third reason.

A person usually uses drugs based on several motives rather than on one. Basically ten reasons have been offered as motivations for drug use. By understanding the reasons, we can be more effective in helping adolescents either prevent or cope with and stop a drug habit. The following is a list of reasons extracted from a review of a number of textbooks on adolescent behavior:

1. Relief from stress. In our society, we relieve stress and pain through medication. This practice is popularized through the media, which portray many

Theories of motivation for drug use

TABLE 12-2 Annual Prevalence of Use of Sixteen Types of Drugs by Subgroups, Class of 1982

	Marijuana	Inhalants[a]	Amyl/Butyl Nitrites	Hallucinogens[a]	LSD	PCP	Cocaine	Heroin	Other Opiates	Stimulants[b] (adjusted)	Sedatives	Barbiturates	Methaqualone	Tranquilizers	Alcohol	Cigarettes[c]
All seniors	44.3	4.5	3.6	8.1	6.1	2.2	11.5	0.6	5.3	20.3	9.1	5.5	6.8	7.0	86.8	14.2
Sex:																
Male	47.2	5.8	5.0	9.6	7.4	2.8	13.1	0.8	6.0	19.6	10.0	5.9	7.5	6.9	88.5	13.1
Female	40.8	3.1	2.3	6.1	4.3	1.6	9.6	0.4	4.6	20.3	8.0	5.0	5.9	7.1	85.3	14.7
College Plans:																
None or under 4 yrs.	48.2	4.9	3.7	9.5	7.5	2.9	12.5	0.7	6.1	23.7	11.4	7.4	8.4	8.0	87.8	21.0
Complete 4 yrs.	40.6	4.1	3.5	6.2	4.3	1.8	9.9	0.4	4.6	16.8	7.0	3.8	5.1	6.3	86.4	7.8
Region:																
Northeast	50.9	6.2	4.6	11.4	8.0	3.6	16.9	0.9	5.6	21.5	9.5	5.6	7.2	7.8	92.3	15.6
North Central	45.6	3.6	2.8	9.1	7.3	1.5	9.0	0.5	5.5	24.1	8.9	5.4	6.5	6.2	90.7	17.3
South	36.7	3.8	3.7	4.6	3.9	2.3	6.3	0.5	4.5	16.4	10.3	6.3	7.8	7.4	80.7	13.3
West	45.5	4.4	3.2	7.8	4.8	1.6	17.9	0.3	6.2	18.7	6.5	3.9	4.5	6.4	81.9	7.1
Population Density:																
Large SMSA	50.4	5.5	3.8	10.9	7.3	3.0	17.2	0.7	5.2	21.6	9.5	5.3	7.2	7.0	89.4	15.9
Other SMSA	44.8	3.9	4.2	7.6	6.3	2.4	10.1	0.4	5.7	20.7	9.4	5.7	6.8	7.2	86.7	12.9
Non-SMSA	38.5	4.4	2.7	6.5	4.8	1.5	8.5	0.6	4.9	18.8	8.5	5.5	6.3	6.8	84.9	14.2

[a]Unadjusted for known underreporting of certain drugs.
[b]Adjusted for overreporting of the non-prescription stimulants.
[c]Based on 30-day prevalence of a half-pack-a-day of cigarettes, or more. Annual prevalence is not available.

Source: L. D. Johnston, J. G. Bachman, and P. M. O'Malley, *Student Drug Use, Attitudes, and Beliefs: National Trends 1975-1982* (Rockville, Md.: National Institute on Drug Abuse, 1982), 26.

nonprescription drugs and nondrug substances as ways to improve life and to escape boredom and stress. The substances range from prepared foods and soft drinks to tobacco and alcohol. The medical model is also one that prescribes medication for everyday stress and discomfort. The advice of taking two aspirins, drinking a lot of liquids, and going to bed suggests to young minds that pills or other substances injected through the mouth will relieve discomfort. Both medical and popular media models suggest to youth that turning to substances is one way to cope with stress and pain.

2. Curiosity and stimulation. In all cultures, children have always been curious to explore their environment. This human quality continues throughout life, but in our culture adolescents have the opportunity to experiment with tobacco, alcohol, and other drugs beyond the supervision and approval of church, school, and parents. Most children simply experiment to satisfy their curiosity; they have no serious motives. Adults who do not wish adolescents to take this initial step may find that supplying accurate information can reduce the curiosity for experimentation with alcohol, drugs and tobacco.

3. Peer expectations and pressure. America has been described as a group- and peer-oriented society. When Urie Bronfenbrenner compared adolescents of different cultures, he found that Americans were more peer oriented than were their European and Russian counterparts. Part of the peer orientation comes from the attempt to be successful in society, which is encouraged by American families. An unfortunate by-product of this focus is that the youth who seek success and achievement turn to their peers rather than to traditional social institutions and family for confirmation and approval. The peer group will often condone the use of drugs. In sometimes subtle, sometimes in forceful and direct ways, the peer group often tells adolescents to use drugs.

4. Boredom and dissatisfaction. A common experience among young people today is that their life seems empty and meaningless. They are disillusioned about the rewards they receive and are generally dissatisfied with life. Drugs offer a way out of this boredom by promising that adolescents can experience highs and thrills. Adults who are interested in preventing drug abuse of this type should keenly observe youth and note when they are restless and disenchanted with life. By correcting the problem at this state, adults may avoid having to deal with the more difficult decisions involving drug abuse.

5. Immediate self-gratification. Self-gratification is a general cultural phenomenon that is expressed via TV, movies, and our general life-style. When things are not going properly, or when boredom takes place, drugs offer immediate gratification and positive sensations. To cope with this type of motivation, adults should stress values such as service or achievement rather than personal gratification as life goals.

6. Inadequate coping and vulnerability. Because of physical, intellectual, social, or other types of handicaps, some people simply cope poorly with life. Many of these people find that they are not successful in meeting the challenges of life. Whey they fail to cope adequately, they sense they will not receive the rewards that others obtain. They seem to say, "Life is passing me by, and I'm not getting much out of it." These people become vulnerable to the equality

Drug use may provide an outlet for an adolescent's feelings of rebelliousness and desire for non-conformity. Drugs may also represent a form of power over authority for an adolescent.

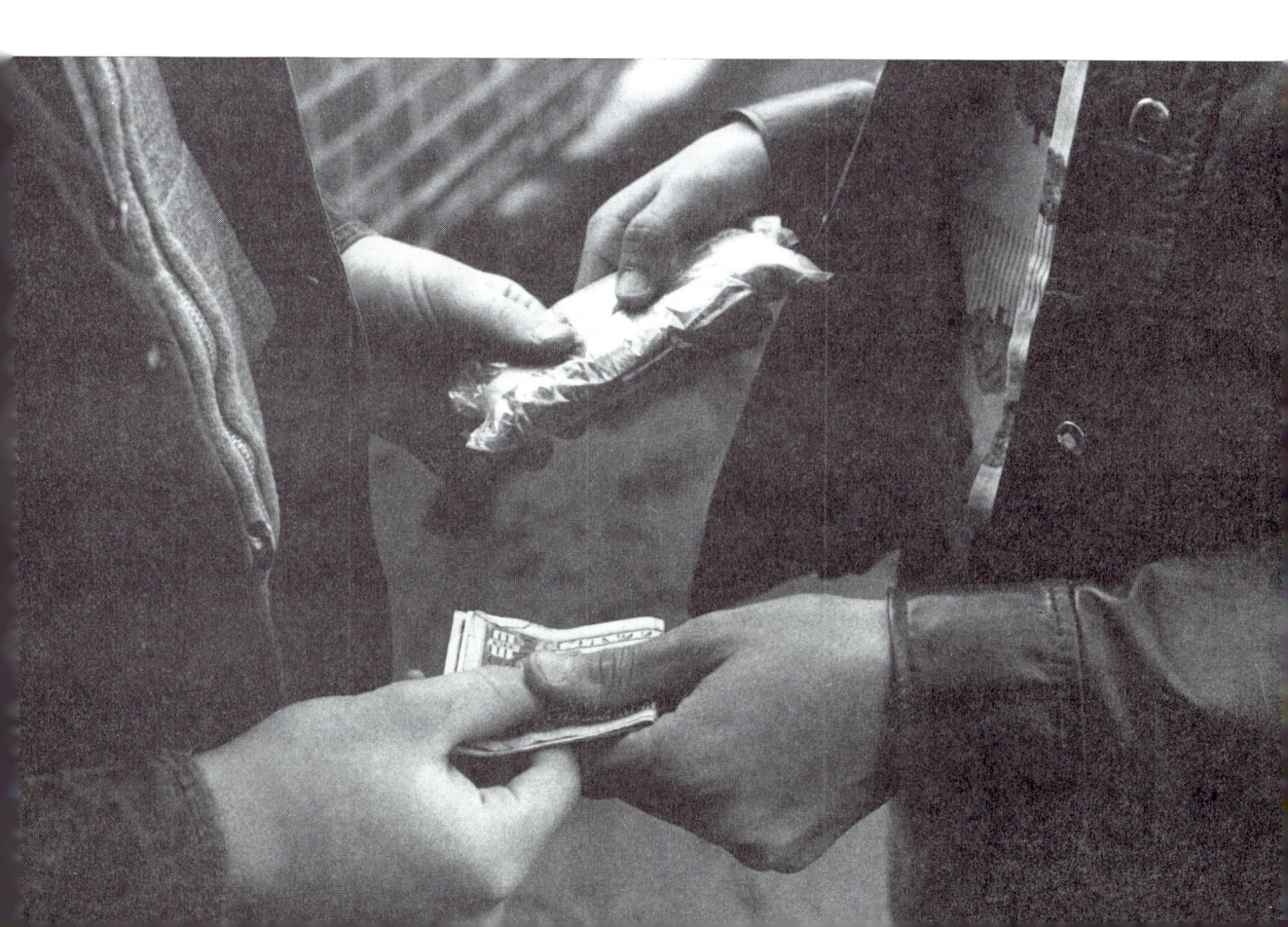

offered in drug usage. Their rationale is that even though they may fail in other activities, they, too, can experience highs and good feelings, the same as those around them.

7. Role expectations. For many adolescents, one expectation of life is to use drugs. Adolescents see their fathers, mothers, and other adult relatives using alcohol and drugs, and sometimes assume that using drugs is part of growing up. For them, drug use is an indication that they are mature and are ready to assume adult roles. Adults who detect this type of motivation in adolescents should demonstrate and point out alternative role models. For example, adults can help adolescents to see that using alcohol or cigarettes is not a sign of masculinity, femininity, or achievement.

8. Rebelliousness and nonconformity. For some adolescents, drugs represent power that they can wield over adult authorities. These youth turn to drugs to demonstrate their autonomy. When drugs are used out of the home and concealed from parents, youthful users feel they are rebelling against the rules and restrictions that authority imposes upon them. Rebelliousness and nonconformity to traditional expectations perhaps play a small role in a drug-oriented society.

9. Transcendental and mystical urges. During adolescence, youth become infatuated with religious and philosophical experiences. For some adolescents, mind-altering drugs are an easy way to have mystical experiences and to escape our materialistic society. Youth who use drugs for these reasons are commonly idealistic individuals who yearn for a new and better way of life with more personal fulfillment. Adults who wish to prevent this type of drug usage should acquaint adolescents with legitimate, socially accepted ways of obtaining emotional and spiritual highs, such as conventional religion, politics, reading, drama, and music.

10. Lack of self-esteem. A consistent finding is that drug users often have lower self-images and self-esteem than do nondrug users. The logic that connects drug usage with low self-esteem is hard to identify. Nevertheless, the relationship between self-image and drug usage indicates that drug use either minimizes the pain associated with low self-esteem or perhaps increases feelings of self-esteem and confidence.

QUESTION: What are the theories concerning adolescent use of psychoactive drugs?

The question of why anyone does anything is always complex and controversial. It is difficult to even begin to answer such a question without crossing some theoretical battle lines. Considering the superstition, wishful thinking, and unsupported "obvious answers" that surround the subject of drug abuse, one can see that any answer to the question of why adolescents use drugs is bound to be unsatisfactory to someone. A helpful point to remember that although we tend to think of a single cause, more than one specifiable cause exists for any given event. To use a simple example, a pot that has been left on a hot stove boils over not only because of the temperature of the stove but also because of the level of fluid, the shape of the pot, the nature of the fluid, and even the altitude. Since many factors affect whether something occurs, more than one way is usually available to prevent it. Perhaps the more factors we can identify, the more successful we will be in preventing drug abuse.

A logical way to begin is to ask adolescents why they use or do not use drugs. This approach produces the most colorful information. Table 12-3 shows the variety of reasons for drug use that have been given by high school students (Lettieri 1975, 66). The diversity of reasons for drug use found in such studies suggests that the pharmacological properties and clinical symptomology of drug use may not be as crucial as the way in which the user construes the drugs' effects. Even if the precise reasons for an adolescent's initial experimentation with drugs are difficult to ascertain, the idiosyncratic meaning that the drug has come to have for an adolescent may be more important. Many clinical studies support the view that adolescents' opinions about drugs are more significant than the nature of the drugs themselves. One investigator, who asked adolescent drug users to describe what they were like "on" or "off" drugs, noticed the following trends:

> (a) Persons with essentially the same clinical symptomology or psychiatric diagnosis often give very *different* descriptions, (b) persons with distinctively variant clinically syndromes often relate *similar* experiences when using or not using drugs, (c) different individuals who have preference for the same drug can give greatly different descriptions, while (d) the multiple drug user is likely to emphasize one or two core experiences *regardless* of the drug used. (Kovacs 1975, 67).

Many of the effects of drugs that adolescents describe (see Table 12-3) suggest that adolescents feel their lives lack certain important qualities without drugs. The statement that drug use relieves nervousness, depression, or boredom indicates that these adolescents feel nervous, depressed, or bored without drugs. These different reasons for experimenting with or abusing drugs are illustrated in three clinical cases that Kovacs relates:

Case 1

M. A., a tall, somewhat unattractive but friendly, 22-year old single woman from a working class family, described herself as "shy" around people and as always having been rather "nervous." She stated that although she was not "smart enough" she "pushed" herself to get an LPN degree because she likes "helping people." M. A. started to experiment with drugs at age 16 and then became a regular user of marijuana, barbiturates, and "pain pills." She stated that when she was not on drugs she "couldn't talk to people" and was "always depressed," noting that drugs somehow help her "to function." She spontaneously added that she does not like "being addicted," yet she feels that she cannot "go on living" without them.

Case 2

J. J., a 17-year-old, slender, effeminate-looking and childish young man, dropped out of the 10th grade because he was "bored." He subsequently had only one job which lasted one day. He reported that he has been "very unhappy" since his mother's death two years ago, specifically because he feels that his grandmother doesn't like "to put up" with him and because people "don't accept" him since he is "gay." For some time now, J. J. has been systematically sniffing "carbona." He stated that sniffing "makes me feel

TABLE 12-3 Reasons for and Effects of Drug Use Cited by Drug Users

Study	Taintor and D'Amanda (1973)	Robbins, Robbins, et al., (1970)	Mirin, Shapiro, et al., (1971)
Sample	multiple drug user heroin addicts	multiple drug user college students	"heavy" marijuana users—volunteers
Reasons Effects	relieve nervousness	expand consciousness	to get along in the world
	physical pain	increase insight	enhance insight
	withdrawal symptoms	enhance artistic sensitivity	increase sense of harmony
	depression		wish for union with cosmic force
	curiosity	for kicks	
	pleasure	improve condition	increase awareness
	because friends were users	relieve tension	appreciate art
	boredom	ease physical discomfort	to feel more friendly, involved, or agreeable
	physical craving	lessen depression	
		relieve insomnia	
	increase self-esteem	diminish fear of psychosis	
	to get along better		
	to escape problems		
	to relate to another	increase sociability	
	for courage	heighten sexual pleasure	
	to improve sexual relations	curiosity	
	to talk to girls		
	to destroy self		
	to hurt someone else		

Source: M. Kovacs, Ph.D., "A Phenomenological Approach toward the Meaning of Drug Use," in *Predicting Adolescent Drug Abuse: A Review of Issues, Methods, and Correlates,* edited by D. Lettieri (Rockville, Md.: National Institute on Drug Abuse, 1975), 67.

good" but then added that he also hoped that "one day, it might just happen . . . I'll sniff enough to kill me."

Case 3

R. H., an 18-year-old, slender, somewhat underweight young man, reported that he was depressed because (a) his girlfriend had left him, and (b) his relationship with his parents had gotten increasingly worse. Around the onset of puberty he started having "problems," the nature of which he could not articulate. He had had several months of training as a mechanic but had been fired from a job a few months prior to this interview. At age 15 R. H. had started to experiment with various drugs and became a regular "poly-drug" user. He would shoot heroin for a few months, then stop and "switch" to some other substance: "speed," "uppers," "downers," Valium, etc. He also stated that when *not* on drugs, or not high, he feels "uncomfortable with people" and finds that he has "nothing to say." He added, "I just want to stay high." (Kovacs 1975, 30–35)

These clinical accounts shed a good deal of light on the psychology of drug use by describing the different meanings that drugs are given and the different uses to which they are put.

Based on her studies of the phenomenology of drug use, Kovacs believes that the use of drugs may be divided into three stages: experimentation, psychological assessment, and perpetuation of positive effects. The first phase, experimentation, is the one in which social or intrapersonal factors are likely to be relevant. The initial use of drugs, in other words, may depend on factors such as the availability of drugs, peer pressure, and the individual's level of curiosity and interest in conformity. The crucial aspect of this phase is that when adolescents experience the unfamiliar sensations and changes within themselves, they assess these changes in either positive or negative terms. Experimentation therefore leads into the next phase, psychological assessment of drug effects.

During this phase, adolescents attach some meaning, value, or label to their drug experiences. The way in which adolescents assess drug experiences determines the extent of subsequent use. If a drug is assessed in positive terms, then the adolescent enters phase three, the perpetuation of positively evaluated drug effects. The positive value that the adolescent has attached to the drug is expressed in systematic or chronic drug use. As time goes on, the meanings that an adolescent originally attached to the use of a drug may become insignificant, and may be replaced by new meanings and labels. For example, the long-term user may forget what life was like without drugs, and may continue to use drugs mainly out of the fear of the unknown (Kovacs 1975, 69).

An example of the way in which psychological assessment of drugs takes place is M. A.'s statement (Case 1). M. A. says that when she is not on drugs, she (1) cannot talk to people and (2) is always depressed. Should M. A. be literally taken to mean that drugs help her to talk to people and to stay in a better mood? Probably not, since no drug has the inherent quality of helping a person to talk to people, and since the drugs that M. A. used (marijuana, barbiturates) are not truly mood-elevating drugs. The easiest way to make sense out of M. A.'s statement is to see that when M. A. experienced the relaxant or analgesic properties of the drugs, she assessed the drug experience as valuable and meaningful for her. Kovacs points out that M. A. is essentially saying, "Whatever happens to me when I use drugs is *good*, because it helps me talk to people and not be depressed, both of which are *important* to me" (Kovacs 1975, 70). Kovacs also points out that the user seems to assess drug effects along two basic dimensions: pleasure-displeasure and usefulness-uselessness. M. A. has apparently assessed her drug experience along both dimensions. Drugs are pleasurable because they help her not to be depressed, and are useful because they help her to talk to people. These two dimensions obviously overlap, since a person who uses drugs to escape problems probably views escape as both pleasurable and useful. Studying the meanings of drug use for adolescent users has obvious implications for prevention, therapy, and rehabilitation, which is explored later.

QUESTION: What other explanations have been offered for adolescent drug use?

Besides the phenomenological approach, which focuses on how adolescents consciously construe the drug experience, many investigators have tried to understand drug abuse in terms of unconscious or symbolic meanings. This is generally called the psychodynamic approach. Those who use the psychodynamic approach do not focus so much on why adolescents may initially experiment with drugs as on why adolescents use drugs systematically and chronically. Drug abuse and addiction are assumed to be attempts to remedy a weakness in the core of the adolescent personality. Individuals may not be consciously aware of this weakness or of the way in which they use drugs to compensate for it. Adolescents may crave a drug, in other words, because it has become for them a substitute for the love of a parent who has failed them early in life. Taking a drug may symbolically represent the soothing acceptance of a parent, or the drug may represent the parental powers that adolescents hope to share or control by ingesting them. Drugs may thereby give adolescents the feeling of being strong and self-confident. Drugs may also increase adolescents' feeling of being alive, and so increase their sense of a definite, certain existence (Blaine and Julius 1977, vii–ix).

From the psychodynamic point of view, the crucial questions do not necessarily involve the quality of children's toilet training or of their fathers' work identity. The important questions involve how the parents have contributed to adolescents' self-esteem during those periods when adolescents have viewed themselves mostly as extensions of their parents or vice versa. As long as children or adolescents strongly identify with their parents, it is important for parents to show approval for at least some of their children's attributes and functions. Also important is that the parents represent a kind of calmness and strength that children can admire and imitate. If parents cannot provide children with approval and with a model of personal strength, adolescents' defective self esteem and inadequate ideals may lead to reliance on poor parental substitutes.

Psychodynamic research indicates that a drug user's selection of drugs is determined by particular vulnerabilities, dispositions, and drives. Certain drugs are thought to compensate for certain personality defects. The drug of choice is thought to be whatever drug induces an ego state that is reminiscent of the stage of personality development during which the individual experienced some trauma. In one study, amphetamine and heroin addicts were given personality tests under both abstinent and intoxicated conditions. They were compared with a control group of unintoxicated nondrug users. The results appear to show that the effect of the users' drug of choice was to bolster their characteristic modes of adaptation. Amphetamine users, for example, have a significantly higher sense of confidence (based on stated feelings of adequacy) than do heroin users or nondrug users. Under the influence of amphetamines, the mean scores for the sense of confidence are even higher for amphetamine users. Certain adolescents may abuse amphetamines, then to further compensate for feelings of helplessness and inadequacy. This is consistent with clinical impressions that amphetamine users expend a great deal of energy defending against fears of passivity. These defenses are thought to be a type of regression to the stage of psychosexual development called the "practicing period," when infants try to achieve maternal approval and affection by learning to walk.

By contrast, the effect of opiates on the heroin addict was to create a state of quiet lethargy, in which even sexual drives were dampened. This feeling seems to agree with the clinical impression that heroin addicts perceive their environment as hostile and threatening, and that they tend to cope with problems by passive withdrawal. Psychoanalysts believe that this mode of defense marks a regression to an early phase of development, in which infants anxieties are smothered in a blissful union with the mother's breast. According to psychodynamic theory, lack of success in treating drug addiction is due to our lack of understanding of drug users' inner needs (Blaine and Julius 1977, 142–56; Frosch and Milkman 1977).

QUESTION: What is the behaviorist explanation for adolescent drug abuse?

The behaviorists have produced extensive literature on substance abuse, based on the principles of operant and respondent conditioning. From this point of view, behavior is thought to be dependent on two features of the person's environment: antecedents and consequence. The link between antecedents (stimuli) and behavior (responses) is the basic unit of study for respondent conditioning. The relationship between behavior and its consequence is the fundamental unit of study for operant conditioning. The behaviorists do not attempt to study the conscious or unconscious meanings that persons may attach to their behaviors. A behavioral analysis of substance abuse begins by conceiving of drugs as powerful reinforcers. The research is not so concerned with why drugs are powerful reinforcers for some adolescents as it is with the problem of intervention and treatment. McFall has called the dominant research strategy of the behaviorists a "horse race." Different treatments are lined up, hopefully without handicaps, and the investigator waits at the finish line (McFall 1978, 707–12). As Lichtenstein (1979) has pointed out, such studies are largely atheoretical and are little concerned with the processes involved in behavior change, even when the outcomes are successful. A more theoretical behavioral approach is the social learning model.

QUESTION: What is the social learning theory of drug use?

When the behavioral approach is expanded to take account of the individual's cognitive processes, it is generally referred to as social learning theory (Bandura 1977). One of the interesting explanations for adolescent drug use offered by social learning theorists has to do with the example that is set for an adolescent by others. The idea is that adolescents model their behavior after that of parents, peers, and others in the community. Parents who use alcohol or drugs as a means of coping with life's problems set an example for their adolescents. If both parents use psychoactive drugs, their adolescent children are even more likely to follow suit (Smart and Fejer 1972). A survey of 1,400 high school students in a suburb of New York City showed that of those students who had seen their mother drunk, 44 percent were drug users; only 28 percent of those who had never seen their mother drunk used drugs (Wyden 1970).

Teenage drinking, in particular, is likely to follow the patterns and variations of the adult community. The abstinent adolescent is likely to have parents who do not drink, the moderate drinker is likely to have parents who drink moderately, and the adolescent who abuses alcohol is likely to have parents who drink heavily (Maddox 1964). This pattern is illustrated in the following account by one college student:

> There is a family from my hometown where the father is an alcoholic. This has caused many problems for the family. As I entered junior high, the wife began drinking heavily with her husband. I guess she believed "if you can't beat them, join them."
>
> Also, during these years, the children of the family were caught many times breaking in houses, clubs, and schools. But they always managed to escape jail. Soon my friends began sniffing glue, smoking marijuana, and drinking beer. Their drinking, at first, was mainly social. Soon they were drunk at school during different occasions. As a result, they were released from school. Only one of the three brothers completed high school and nearly all are now confirmed alcoholics. It is rare not to see them high or drunk.

The relationship of adult example to adolescent behavior is not always a simple one, however. Two studies suggest that drunkenness is less common among Jewish students (over 90 percent of whom have drank alcohol most commonly during religious holidays, sabbath, dinners, and so on, in moderation since childhood) than among ascetic Protestant and Mormon students, whose

Studies have shown that excessive drinking is sometimes more of a problem with adolescents who are used to a strict ascetic environment than with those who have associated drinking with many traditional family gatherings.

religious philosophies forbid drinking (Skolnick 1958; Snyder 1958). Sociologist Jerome Skolnick has suggested that drinker adolescents from teetotaling subcultures may be living up to the expectations of their religious leaders who portray drinking in decadent terms. Perhaps adolescents with ascetic backgrounds drink to excess because they have never been shown how to drink in moderation. The wisdom of teaching children to drink in moderation is difficult to access. In both France and in Greece, children are often given a little wine with meals from an early age. Yet France has one of the highest alcoholism rates of any country that keeps statistics on drinking behavior, while drunkenness is fairly uncommon in Greek villages. Although modeling seems to be a factor in adolescent drug use, it is probably only one of many factors.

One study considered the effects of social norms or expectation on drinking and drug behavior (Krohn et al, 1982). Through a questionnaire, the researchers studied seventh- through twelfth-grade adolescents and identified four norms: (1) proscriptive—totally prohibiting use, (2) prescriptive—permitting use but setting standards of what is acceptable (3) permissive—allowing use without guidelines or limits, and (4) ascriptive—vague and unclear positions taken by reference groups of family, religion, peers, and so on. The most powerful norm group is peers, followed by family, and then religion. The family, however, possibly influences the selection of both peers and religion.

Tables 12–4 and 12–5 display the findings showing the normative groups and the use of alcohol and marijuana.

The researchers concluded that permissive norms generate the highest use and abuse of drugs, and the proscriptive norms produce the lowest use and abuse. Peer group norms have the most important influence. Parents and religions that want to reduce drug usage should realize that education programs, advice, counseling, and so on, will likely fail if a youth continues membership in a peer culture that encourages drug use. Stated more positively, the first step to managing drug use should focus on the membership and normative orientation of the peer culture. Krohn et al, state:

> The process whereby the various primary groups' norm qualities affect substance use is supposedly through the groups' norms being taken on as the

TABLE 12–4 Influence of Reference Groups on Drug Use

Reference Group	Permissive	Prescriptive	Ascriptive	Proscriptive
Alcohol				
Adults (N = 2981)	70.7	69.8	60.2	51.0
Teens (N = 2986)	79.5	57.2	53.0	15.9
Religion (N = 2640)	72.7	69.1	66.1	59.1
Marijuana				
Adults (N = 2985)	49.3	58.9	37.8	24.8
Teens (N = 2968)	54.0	30.0	17.0	2.4
Religion (N = 2932)	47.6	40.5	35.2	25.2

Source: M. D. Krohn, R. L. Akers, M. J. Radosevich, and L. Lanza-Kaduce, "Norm Qualities and Adolescent Drinking and Drug Behavior: The Effects of Norm Quality and Reference Groups on Using and Abusing Alcohol and Marijuana," *Journal of Drug Issues* 12(4): 352 (1982).

TABLE 12-5 Influence of Reference Groups on Drug Use

Alcohol

Reference Group	Permissive	Prescriptive	Ascriptive	Proscriptive
Adults (N = 2427)	26.1	18.1	11.8	12.6
Teens (N = 2431)	25.3	10.9	10.2	1.4
Religion (N = 2135)	28.0	15.1	20.0	15.5

Marijuana

	Permissive	Prescriptive	Ascriptive	Proscriptive
Adults (N = 1260)	30.4	28.5	27.7	19.2
Teens (N = 1256)	29.6	12.2	19.5	4.1
Religion (N = 1054)	42.9	34.8	24.7	19.0

Source: M. D. Krohn, R. L. Akers, M. J. Radosevich, and L. Lanza-Kaduce, "Norm Qualities and Adolescent Drinking and Drug Behavior: The Effects of Norm Quality and Reference Groups on Using and Abusing Alcohol and Marijuana," *Journal of Drug Issues* 12(4): 354 (1982).

individual's own normative attitudes toward the substance; that is, if teenagers' friends, family, and religion disapprove of alcohol or marijuana, they will learn to think the same way and act accordingly. The literature also suggests that people who use these substances in the face of either nonscriptive or proscriptive norms should be more likely to go on to abuse them than users in prescriptive environments. Our findings contradict this assertion in that we found the highest percentage of abuse within the permissive and prescriptive normative environments. Proscriptive environments are not only conducive to total abstinence from both alcohol and marijuana but are also conducive to moderation among those who do begin to use in violation of the norms. (Krohn et al, 1982, 355)

QUESTION: Do adolescents use drugs as a way of rebelling against society?

Rebellion is a common explanation for adolescent drinking and drug use. The theory is that adolescents resent the authority of their parents and the conventions of their society, and that using forbidden substances is their way of expressing their autonomy. The "imitation" theory is that since drug use is an integral part of our society, learning to use drugs is part of an adolescent's socialization. These two views are not necessarily contradictory. First, some adolescents may use drugs rebelliously, and others may use them imitatively. Second, learning to drink alcohol and to smoke cigarettes may largely be imitative behavior, and using illicit drugs may mostly be rebellious behavior. Since alcohol and cigarettes are openly advertised and widely used by adults, they easily become a symbol of adult status, of coming of age. Since the use of other drugs is not socially approved even for adults, the imitation theory may explain drinking and smoking better than it does illicit drug use. Third, even when adolescents are rebelling against adults, they may be imitating their peers. Adolescents model their peers' behavior just as they model their parents' behavior. Some studies suggest that parents have a greater effect on young adolescents, while peers have a greater effect on older adolescents. One researcher believes that four out of five high school students prefer spending their spare time with their peers, and that high school students are as afraid of their friends' disapproval as they are of their parents' (Coleman 1961). Sociologist Alfred Lindesmith has said, "If a kid goes to college these days and never develops an interest in marijuana, he's got a problem and you should worry. He may be a loner and not accepted by his peers' (Lindesmith 1969, 69). The case is probably that neither imitation and the need for conformity, nor rebellion and the need for autonomy, are capable of explaining all adolescent behavior. The types of motivation probably operate in different ways, even in the same adolescents.

The phenomenological, psychodynamic, behavioral, and social learning theories approach the problem of adolescent drug use from different perspectives. The behaviorists tend to accept that drugs are a powerful reinforcer for some adolescents, and focus more on identifying successful treatments than on searching for explanations. The social learning theorists differ from the behaviorists not so much in the use of concepts such as social pressure or modeling, since these can be described in terms of behavioral cues and reinforcers, but rather in the cognitive processes of addiction-prone individuals. By studying, for example, adolescents' perceptions of themselves and expectations about drugs, social learning theory gives us some idea of why adolescents use drugs. The phenomenological approach, such as that of Maria Kovacs, differs from the behavioral and social learning theories in that it focuses more on the way the individual adolescent construes drug effects. This approach assumes that although cultural similarities may be present in the meanings adolescents give to drugs, idiosyncratic differences are just as important. The approach also assumes that most adolescents are capable of expressing how they construe the drug experience. The psychodynamic approach resembles the phenomenological approach in that it also looks for the meanings that drugs have for individual adolescents. The psychodynamic theorists differ from the phenomenological theorists in that they do not assume that adolescents are able to admit or express the true significance of their drug use. According to psychodynamic theory, the function of drug abuse may be partly to help individuals hide certain things from themselves.

Prevention and treatment of drug abuse

QUESTION: According to these theories, how can adolescent drug abuse best be prevented and treated?

Each of the theories mentioned implies a distinct approach to treatment, although a possibility is for treatment programs to follow a combined, eclectic approach. Phenomenological theory suggests that understanding the significance of drugs for adolescents may provide a basis for differential treatment. That adolescents have a logical, systematic explanation for their own drug use is not necessary. It is necessary to realize that adolescents do make some type of evaluation of the drug experience, and that this evaluation has a great deal to do with their subsequent behavior. Consider Kovacs's case of M. A. as an example. Since M. A. uses drugs in order *not* to feel something (i.e., depression), rather than to get high or have a good time, she apparently construes drugs as being, above all, useful to her. She believes that drugs help her to avoid depression and to talk to people.

Kovacs believes that the instrumental value of drugs (i.e., their usefulness) more often leads to systematic drug use than the pleasurable value. Those who construe drugs as useful to them often feel that drugs are the only way to achieve something that is important to them. From a clinical point of view, Kovacs has distinguished four types of instrumental values: (1) positive self-directed, (2) negative self-directed, (3) positive other-directed, and (4) negative other-directed. Positive instrumental value is involved when adolescents believe that a drug will help them to overcome shortcomings and to improve themselves. Negative instrumental value is involved if adolescents feel that a drug will help them to avoid emotional experiences or to escape unpleasant situations. Although the adolescent may view avoidance or escape as positive, helpful for purposes of treatment is distinguishing an evasive use of drugs from the use of drugs for growth and change. Also helpful is distinguishing drug effects that relate to intrapersonal problems (self-directed) from drug effects that relate to interpersonal problems (other-directed). M. A.'s use of drugs to avoid depression can be classified as negative self-directed. Her use of drugs to be able to talk to people can be classified as positive other-directed.

The therapeutic value of this type of classification lies in the fact that once the instrumental values of drug use have been identified, a therapist may be able to offer alternate, preferable means of achieving them. Adolescents who believe that drugs help them to talk to people or to relate better (positive other-directed) may need to be helped to discover why relationships with others are difficult for them. A program can then be devised in which adolescents learn to better communicate with others without the use of drugs.

Adolescents who use drugs in order not to be bored, however, (negative self-directed) may respond well to a structured program in which they are required to participate in activities and to take on responsibilities. They are revealing, in other words, that they lack the psychological resources necessary to engage themselves in interesting activities. When adolescents are given a clear alternative to the instrumental use of drugs, the value of drugs themselves often diminishes. In any case, the phenomenological approach seems to offer an easy, practical way of categorizing drug users so that treatment programs can be tailored to the individual adolescent. This approach may also prove to be useful in determining which adolescents are likely to become habitual drug users and which are in most need of therapeutic attention.

QUESTION: What is the psychodynamic approach to drug prevention and treatment?

Although the psychodynamic approach appears to have generated a great many insights into the nature of drug dependency, psychoanalysts agree that the psychodynamic treatment of drug addicts has not been successful (Krystal 1977). Henry Krystal, a psychoanalyst who has had extensive experience with drug-addicted patients, has concluded that the difficulties involved in the psychoanalysis of drug addicts "determines that successful psychoanalytic psychotherapy will continue to be the exception" (Krystal 1977, 98). To understand why psychoanalysis is unsuccessful for many drug addicts, we need to take a closer look at both the psychodynamics of the drug addict and the process of psychoanalysis.

In the psychodynamic view, the kind of people who become drug dependent are those for whom drugs have become a representation of a loved mother or of a rival father. As children develop, they normally take over certain functions from their mother and father through identification with them. If all goes well, these children are gradually able to take care of themselves in the same ways that their parents took care of them and of themselves. A variety of traumatic conflicts, however, can occur in childhood, which may cause children not to identify with their parents, to deny themselves permission to take over parental functions, and to wall off the powerful but mixed emotions that they feel toward their parents. For example, if otherwise good mothers become jealous or show disapproval when their children attempt to care for themselves—perhaps by thumb sucking or masturbation—the children may feel that they are not permitted to exercise these self-comforting functions. These children may begin to deprive themselves of any self-help and may eventually lose any capacity to nurse themselves when tired, ill, or hurt. When children feel that they are not permitted to exercise these functions, they grow envious of their mothers (as well as of others who care for the children and for themselves), and they attempt to obtain their forbidden powers in roundabout, symbolic ways.

Briefly stated, people who take drugs to obtain comfort do so to gain access to maternal functions that they do not feel they can openly assume. They long to recreate and to be united with the good mother of their fantasies, and at the same time they dread being united with the maternal love that they have been taught to repress and which they therefore secretly resent. These people idealize their mothers as loving symbols, yet also deeply hate their mothers for having deprived them of part of themselves. Having learned to repress their anger toward their mothers, lest they lose the much-needed maternal love and affection, these people go through life with a profound, yet largely unconscious, ambivalence toward anything or anyone resembling their mothers.

The ambivalence of this type of drug addict creates a serious problem for therapy. Since the goal of reuniting these patients with the maternal and paternal functions that they have walled off requires that the patients become aware of the repressed feelings of rage and aggression toward parents, healing takes place in psychoanalysis when patients go through what has been called "effective grieving"—a process analogous to mourning (Wetmore 1963). In effect, these patients need to grieve the "death" of their idealized mothers whom they have looked to from infancy to take care of them. Beyond this, patients need to be faced with their own infantile rage, which is the true source of their self-destructive life-style. A great deal of caution is needed to make sure that these patients are not overwhelmed by their aggressive feelings or guilt.

An unusual patient is one who is able to experience these feelings of repressed rage without becoming terrified and leaving treatment. Addicts who continue in therapy will eventually give up the treasured view of themselves as helpless and innocent victims, and will be able to acknowledge that both parental functions and their aggressive impulses are truly a part of themselves. In other words, they will be reunited both with their long-lost self-love and with their deeply repressed emotional life. As Krystal has put it, "The objective of therapy is to permit the patient to extend his conscious self-recognition to all of himself, thereby freeing him from the need for the placebo effect of the drug as a means of gaining access to his alienated parts and functions" (Krystal 1977, 98).

Despite the dismal prognosis, a number of severely chronic drug abusers have been helped through intensive psychotherapy. "Intensive" may mean as many as three to seven sessions a week, often for longer than one hour, for periods of several years. Dr. Leon Wurmser has made a number of recommendations regarding the treatment of chronic drug abusers. Although these recommendations are meant primarily for the psychoanalyst, they apply as well to concerned friends and family:

First, the concerned person needs to be very nurturing, supportive, and persevering. The adolescent needs to be shown the kind of human warmth which he deeply longs for, but also distrusts and fears. Don't give up on the adolescent. The rehabilitation of drug abusers usually involves many relapses and disappointments. Many people who have quit smoking tobacco, for example, have failed many times before they finally gained control of their habit.

Secondly, it is just as important to maintain a certain distance and attitude of detachment from the drug abuser. The concerned person must try to be warm and personally involved, without becoming intrusive, as the adolescent's mother very likely was or still is. Be concerned, but lead an independent life. In this way, the drug abuser's very deep seated fear that he is bound to destroy the one that cares for him will be put to rest. If a drug abuser has a way of spoiling important plans or occasions, for example, let him know that you can and will go without him. The point is not to abandon the adolescent, but rather is to create an atmosphere of respect for the adolescent's separateness and individuality.

Thirdly, it is important to set limits for the adolescent without condemning or preaching to him. The focus could be on the self-destructive potential of the adolescent's behavior, rather than on its prosocial or antisocial nature. A punishing or scornful attitude is likely to confirm the adolescent's sense that, as Wurmser puts it, "no one can ever be trusted, I am suffering again betrayal and degradation, and thus I prove the basic unworth of human relationships; I can rely on my actions and on nonhuman substances."

Fourthly, don't indulge the adolescent or minimize his problems. Trying to satisfy an adolescent's every whim and demand perpetuates the idea that he cannot care for himself; since the adolescent's demands are often impossible and insatiable, he is likely to become enraged at the person who tries but fails to satisfy them. In order to prevent the adolescent from placing all his demands, and directing all his anger towards one person, it is often best to have a team of therapists working with the patient. It is must easier for a group of concerned individuals to maintain perspective than for a single individual.

Finally, Wurmser urges that we avoid "many of the current faddish 'shortcuts' and fashionable new 'simplistic' techniques." In spite of its mixed results with drug addicts, Wurmser feels that the psychodynamic approach is the only one which has "set itself the goals of a deeper systematic understanding of the human mind." (Wurmser 1977, 60–71)

QUESTION: What is the behaviorist approach to treatment of drug abuse?

According to the behaviorists, meanings that an adolescent attaches to drug use—be they conscious or unconscious—do not need to be explored to affect the adolescent's drug-taking behavior. In other words, drug use may be influenced in two ways: (1) indirectly—by focusing on the social, personal, and emotional adjustment of the adolescent, and (2) directly—by focusing treatment directly on drug-taking behavior. Far from being a "simplistic shortcut," the behaviorists believe that theirs is the most direct approach to the treatment of drug abuse.

The behaviorist alters behavior by changing the environmental circumstances that somehow reinforce the behavior. Behavioral techniques may be divided into two general types—those that are designed to weaken undesirable behavior and those that are designed to strengthen desirable behaviors (Blackham and Silverman 1975). The most common technique for weakening undesirable, drug-related behavior is to punish it (i.e., to consistently attach negative consequences to it). Depending on the type of punishment used, this technique is called either aversion therapy or covert sensitization. In aversion therapy, punishment is usually in the form of some painful stimulus, such as an electric shock or antagonistic drugs. In covert sensitization, the punishment is usually in the form of unpleasant scenes or experiences that the patient is asked to imagine. The idea in either case is to countercondition the undesirable behavior, which is supposed to have been conditioned by the drugs' inherently reinforcing properties.

An example of aversion therapy for alcoholism involves the use of an antagonistic drug called Antabuse. Antabuse is an inexpensive drug, introduced in Denmark in 1948, that reacts with alcohol to produce nausea. After taking Antabuse, patients help themselves to their favorite liquor. The sickness that follows causes the patient to have unpleasant associations with alcohol. This type of therapy can be successful, but its success often depends on the patients' willingness to continue to take Antabuse whenever they are tempted to consume alcohol. Other antagonistic drugs, such as naltrexone, are available for the treatment of heroin addiction, but have met with mixed results (Rewson et al 1979).

Covert sensitization has been found to be effective in some cases of adolescent drug abuse. Kolvin (1967) used covert sensitization to treat a fourteen-year-old who had habitually used inhalants for seven years. Kolvin used the adolescent's fear of heights and of falling as aversive images in the counterconditioning process. The boy was first encouraged to relax and to imagine sniffing inhalants. Once he had a vivid image of petrol sniffing, he was asked to imagine himself teetering or falling from a great height. This process was repeated for twenty half-hour sessions, five days a week, and proved effective. A thirteen-month follow-up showed that the boy had not resumed the use of inhalants. Follow-up sessions, however, are often necessary to permanently suppress drug-related behavior. Aversion therapy and covert sensitization seem most effective in eliminating undesirable behaviors when desirable behaviors are simultaneously reinforced (Blackham and Silverman 1975, 83).

QUESTION: Can adolescent drug use by treated with the behavioral model without using punishment?

Adolescent drug abuse can also be treated by using positive reinforcement to promote abstinence from, or reductions in, drug use. These techniques are usually called contingency management procedures, since the technique involves making certain reinforcers contingent on changes in drug-related behavior. Alcohol consumption, for example, has been significantly reduced in controlled laboratory settings by rewarding reduced consumption with money and with other personal and social privileges (Stitzer, Bigelow, and Liebson 1979, 70). Contingent management procedures have also been used to help people stop smoking. Several studies show that if a monetary deposit is made contingent on reductions in smoking, a high rate of abstinence (84 percent of smokers in one study) can be achieved (Stitzer, Bigelow, and Liebson 1979, 70).

Cases of reductions in drug use have also been recorded based on the use of contingent reinforcers. In one study of heroin addicts, the individuals were rewarded for morphine-free urine samples with $7.50 in cash. The results indicate that the incentive had no effect on drug-taking behavior of the six heroin addicts. In a second study, however, the cash reinforcer was increased to $15. The results show that all four of those participating in this second study had reduced levels of opiate use, as measured by urinalysis (Stitzer, Bigelow, and Liebson 1979). This study suggests that the success of contingency management procedures depends to a great extent on the value of the reinforcers that are used. This aspect may help explain why few reports have been made of the successful use of nonaversive behavioral treatment of drug addiction (Fischer and Gochros 1975). The use of drugs appears to be so highly reinforcing to individuals that it is difficult to find competing reinforcers that are potent enough to be used for discouraging drug use.

QUESTION: Has the cognitive social learning approach been more successful for treating adolescent drug abuse?

Besides contingency management procedures, the social learning approach includes techniques that are geared to change the adolescent's personal values, environment, and decision-making ability. This approach places more emphasis on the adolescent's perception of and expectations about a drug's effects, and on the way in which these perceptions are affected by personal models in the adolescent's social environment.

Social learning theorists frequently believe that aversion therapy is useful for reducing drug use, but that maintaining lower levels of drug use requires three other strategies: social support, coping skills, and cognitive restructuring (Lichtenstein 1979, 121–22). Social support refers to the influence of parents, peers, and significant others on the adolescent's ability to sustain the motivation necessary to keep from using drugs. Programs such as Alcoholics Anonymous have used the social support strategy for a long time, yet little systematic study of the approach has been done. Coping skills are the strategies and tactics necessary to develop self-control, such as learning to deprive oneself of drugs, to find substitutes, and to recognize and avoid high-risk situations. Cognitive restructuring refers specifically to the process of changing the attitudes and self-perceptions that are associated with drug use.

The importance of social support can be seen at every level of prevention and treatment. Peer pressure has often been identified by students as the most important factor in their decision to smoke. Social learning theorists believe that one of the reasons why attempts to prevent adolescent smoking have not been effective is that they have failed to counter the social pressures to smoke during adolescence. One highly successful prevention program based on social learning principles consisted of teams of high school students, who gave a series of lectures on the health hazards of smoking to junior high school students. In all, the junior high students were given ten hours of instruction on how to identify and resist the pressures to smoke. During the program, the junior high students were asked (1) to commit themselves publicly to be nonsmokers, (2) to hear testimonials from high school students who had been habitual smokers, (3) to challenge themselves to successfully resist pressures to smoke, (4) to identify the pressures to smoke in the media and in their family and peer relationships, (5) to rehearse methods for resisting these pressures, and (6) to role play situations in which they surmount the pressures to smoke. The researchers also note that they carefully selected nonsmoking, extroverted, ''Fonzie-type'' students as peer teachers. The encouraging results of a follow-up survey (verified by breath tests) found major reductions in smoking (Perry 1980).

Positive peer models have been shown to be important not only in prevention programs but also in recruiting students for smoking cessation programs. In one study, the effectiveness of a standard recruitment procedure, using posters, public address system announcements, and announcements in a daily bulletin, was compared with that of an active recruitment procedure, in which peers distributed leaflets to students and announcements were made in class. Recruiters tried to be as friendly, informal, and nonjudgmental as possible. At the school at which the standard recruitment procedure was used, only one subject volunteered for the smoking cessation program. At the school where the personal recruitment procedures were used, there were thirty-one program volunteers. When personal recruitment procedures were used at the former school, there were an additional twenty-one volunteers. Although the number of volunteers totaled only about 6 percent of the estimated smokers in the schools, the results are encouraging. The researchers suggest that personal recruitment procedures are most effective because (1) they provide detailed information in a personalized manner, (2) they reduce student fears about confidentiality, and (3) they provide credible nonsmoking models.

Another indication of the value of social support is the success of buddy systems in drug abuse programs. Smokers, for example, who are paired with a buddy during a treatment program, have been found in follow-up studies to smoke significantly less than those without buddies (even though contact with buddies was not maintained after the treatment was over) (Lichtenstein 1979, 123).

Coping skills are the skills that are required for self-control, such as identifying and avoiding the cues that often lead to drug use, finding substitutes for drug use, learning to relax, and learning to assert oneself in the face of social pressures. Social learning theory suggests that the reason why drug users are not able to maintain abstinence is that they lack the necessary coping skills. Studies in which aversion techniques were supplemented by coping skills training, however, did not support this theory. The rate of relapse among persons who were given coping skills training is just as great as the rate of relapse among groups that were given only aversion therapy (Lichtenstein 1979, 122).

QUESTION: What is the cognitive restructuring approach in the social learning theory?

The problem with motivation suggests that the third approach, the cognitive restructuring approach to maintenance, ought to be more effective. Unfortunately, the cognitive restructuring approach is the newest and least developed approach of social learning theory. Nevertheless, studies of adolescent attitudes and beliefs about drugs show strong parallels between how adolescents think about a drug and how commonly they use the drug. For example, among illicit drugs, marijuana is the most frequently used and is also the least likely to be seen as risky to use. Since 1979, adolescents have tended to view marijuana use as more hazardous, and this shift in attitude coincides with a downward trend in the actual use of marijuana:

> From 1975 through 1978 there had been a decline in the harmfulness perceived to be associated with all levels of marijuana use; but in 1979, for the first time, there was an increase in these proportions—an increase which has continued fairly steadily since then. By far the most impressive increase has occurred for *regular marijuana use,* where there has been a full 25 percent jump in just four years in the proportion perceiving it as involving great risk—i.e., from 35 percent in 1978 to 60 percent in 1982. This is a dramatic change, and it has occurred during a period in which a substantial amount of scientific and media attention has been devoted to the potential dangers of heavy marijuana use. There is evidence, however, of this trend ending—perhaps in 1983—judging by the decelerated rate of increase this year. (Johnston, Bachman, and O'Malley 1982, 94)

A coincidence in the perceived harmfulness of a drug and its actual use can also be seen in the figures regarding the occasional or experimental use of marijuana. The perceived harmfulness of occasional or experimental use of marijuana, unlike that of the regular use of marijuana, has remained fairly constant. This is consistent with the fact that although regular marijuana use has declined significantly from a high point in the late 1970s, the lifetime prevalence of marijuana use among high school seniors has remained relatively unchanged. This suggests that an important relationship exists between adolescents' attitudes toward drugs and their drug-related behavior, and also that the various attempts that have been made to educate adolescents regarding the risks of drug use are effective.

Besides the perceived risks, many other beliefs and attitudes affect an adolescent's drug-related behavior. Cognitive restructuring involves identifying and modifying all the psychological states that underlie drug abuse (Emery, Hollon, and Bedrosian 1981). These underlying problems may be characterized as depression, anxiety, nonassertiveness, apathy, or other symptoms. These cognitive undercurrents of drug abuse are sometimes generalized, as in Mendel's hypothesis that drinking serves as a defense against depression (Mendels 1970).

The most critical stage of cognitive restructuring involves helping adolescents to observe their own thinking. Once the determination is made that an adolescent's drug use is connected with depression, for example, the next step is finding out what kinds of thoughts bring on depression. This subject is explored in the following conversation between a college student and his therapist:

> Patient: I agree with the descriptions of me but I guess I don't agree that the way I think makes me depressed.
> Therapist: How do you understand it?
> Patient: I get depressed when things go wrong. Like when I fail a test.
> Therapist: How can failing a test make you depressed?

Patient: Well, if I fail I'll never get into law school.
Therapist: So failing tests means a lot to you. But if failing a test could drive people into clinical depression, wouldn't you expect everyone who failed the test to have a depression? . . . Did everyone who failed get depressed enough to require treatment?
Patient: No, but it depends on how important the test was to the person.
Therapist: Right, and who decides the importance?
Patient: I do.
Therapist: And so, what we have to examine is your way of viewing the test (or the way that you *think* about the test) and how it affects your chances of getting into law school. Do you agree?
Patient: Right. (Beck, et al. 1979, 145)

The therapist trains patients to identify patterns of thought that are distorted and that lead to self-defeat. Once adolescents' self-defeating cognitive patterns are well-defined, adolescents can be shown how alternative patterns of thinking will help them to avoid depression and consequent drug use.

QUESTION: How can adolescents be helped to evaluate their attitudes and beliefs?

To help adolescents evaluate their attitudes and beliefs, it is often useful to show them how to record their responses to events. In one column, adolescents should describe the events that led to their feelings or beliefs. In the next column, adolescents should list the feelings that these events brought about. In the third column, adolescents should list the cognitions, or thoughts that went with these feelings. In the last column, adolescents should try to think of other possible interpretations of the events.

In all of these treatment approaches, granting freedom and giving responsibility to the adolescent are important. In general, a social or group context is desirable. The author's opinion is that all of these approaches can be helpful, and optimal use depends upon the personality of helper and adolescent.

Summary

Drugs have been used and abused long before the discovery of the New World. In a broad sense, the term *drugs* refers to any substance that will produce a definable physical or psychological reaction in human beings. In a narrow sense, the term refers to any substances that change the minds or moods of those who take them. Psychoactive drugs are grouped into the following categories: caffeine, marijuana, inhalants, tranquilizers and antidepressants, psychedelics, narcotics, cocaine, amphetamines, barbiturates, nicotine, and alcohol.

Caffeine is a stimulant to the central nervous system, causing alertness and improved speed and accuracy at most tasks. Even in small doses, caffeine is apparently addictive.

Marijuana is from the hemp plant. Hashish, concentrated resin from the hemp plant, is six to ten times more powerful than marijuana. Both contain tetrahydrocannabinol (THC), which causes various effects depending on dosage. Marijuana does not appear to be physically addictive.

Inhalants, or "garbage highs," are used mostly by younger adolescents. Inhalants include model airplane glue, household cement, fingernail polish remover, paint thinner, and gasoline. These drugs give short highs similar to those of alcohol or barbiturates, and are not addictive. Deaths have been caused mainly by suffocation from plastic bags used to contain the fumes. Some users have had fatal heart attacks, and some have developed blood, liver, and kidney disorders, which may also be fatal.

Tranquilizers and antidepressants are widely used in psychiatry, especially in treating schizophrenics. They often take effect only after several weeks of use, and are not addicting. Tranquilizers induce calmness but also produce numbness, muscular stiffness and twitches, slowness of thought, and damage to the liver and bone marrow. They are not sought out for highs by adolescents because they do not have quick intense effects.

Psychedelic literally means expansion of the mind, or psyche. LSD is the most well-known psychedelic drug. Different effects occur depending on the user's expectations. Both good and bad trips are so intensely emotional that later the memory will sometimes flash back into the user's mind. These drugs are not physically addictive.

Narcotics are effective painkillers as well as powerful depressants. Natural forms include opium, morphine, heroin, and codeine. Of the scores of synthetic narcotics, the most common is methadone. Narcotics do not appear to do long-term damage, but dirty needles, poisonous substitutes, malnutrition, and overdoses contribute to a higher death rate among users. Addictions develop faster than with any other drug.

Cocaine, extracted from the coca bush, has an extremely strong psychological appeal, though it is not physically addicting. Users can become paranoid. A high is sometimes followed by depression and illness from insomnia and malnutrition. Cocaine causes permanent damage to the mucous membranes of the nose.

Amphetamines create alertness and loss of appetite, as well as restlessness, headaches, dizziness, tremor, and a dry mouth. Large doses lead to fatigue, depression, high blood pressure, and respiratory failure. Withdrawal can produce fatigue and depression that lasts for months.

Barbiturates create effects similar to alcohol. In small doses they are called sedatives; in large doses they are called hypnotics. In extremely large doses, they can slow down bodily functions to the point of coma and death. Barbiturates are highly addictive.

Nicotine is a stimulant found in cigarettes, and is addictive. Studies by the American Cancer Society show that the longer people go without smoking, the more likely they are to live as long as people who have never smoked.

Alcohol drinking, even in moderation, can have long-range harmful effects. Alcohol is not only addicting but may also disturb the functioning of heart cells, increasing fat deposits on the liver, and inhibit the manufacture of proteins in the brain.

According to research, the use of psychoactive drugs among adolescents has declined since 1975, except for alcohol use. Alcohol is the most widely abused drug among high schoolers. The overall proportion of the adolescent population who have used illicit drugs at least once has risen steadily. Experimentation, if not drug abuse, is extremely widespread among adolescents.

The age at which illicit drugs are tried is becoming progressively younger for each class, according to studies. Initial experimentation occurs during the sophomore, junior, and senior years of high school. In general, college-bound seniors have lower rates of illicit drug use than do those who are noncollege-bound. Females tend to take fewer types of drugs and to use drugs with less frequency than do males.

Population density, as well as regional differences, seem to be factors in adolescent drug use. Drug use is less prevalent among adolescents living in the country than those living in the city.

Motivation for drug use includes the following: relief from stress, curiosity and stimulation, peer expectations and pressure, boredom and dissatisfaction, immediate self-gratification, inadequate coping and vulnerability, role expectations, rebelliousness and nonconformity, transcendental and mystical urges, and lack of self-esteem.

A number of theories deal with the use of psychoactive drugs. Kovacs divided the use of drugs into three stages: experimentation, psychological assessment, and perpetuation of positive effects. The user seems to assess drug effects along two basic dimensions: pleasure-displeasure and usefulness-uselessness. This is the phenomenological approach.

The psychodynamic approach seeks to understand drug abuse in terms of unconscious or symbolic meanings. Drug abuse is assumed to be an attempt to remedy a weakness in the core of an adolescent's personality. Behaviorists, however, are more concerned with finding successful treatments than with searching for explanations for drug use.

Social learning theory, an expansion of the behavioral approach, follows the idea that adolescents model their behavior after that of parents, peers, and others in the community. Some adolescents may use drugs rebelliously, and others may use them imitatively. Also possible is that even when adolescents are rebelling against adults, they may be imitating peers.

Each of the theories suggests distinct approaches to treatment. Phenomenological theory offers a practical way of categorizing drug users so that treatment programs can be tailored to the individual adolescent. Psychodynamic treatment has not been successful, due to ambivalence in types of drug addicts. This approach assumes that drugs have become to the addict a representation of a loved mother or of a rival father. The behaviorists alters behavior by changing the environmental circumstances that somehow reinforce the behavior. The most common technique is by punishment—attaching negative consequences to drug-related behavior. Another treatment is by using positive reinforcement to promote abstinence from drug use.

The social learning approach uses techniques geared to change the adolescent's personal values, environment, and decision-making ability. This approach uses three strategies: social support, coping skills, and cognitive restructuring. The cognitive restructuring approach deals with educating adolescents regarding the risks of drug use. It involves identifying and modifying all the psychological states that underlie drug abuse, and helping adolescents to observe their own thinking. This approach appears to be the most effective.

References

Alpert, R., S. Cowan, & L. Schiller. 1966 *LSD.* New York: New American Library.
Bandura, A. 1977. *Social learning theory.* Englewood Cliffs, N. J.: Prentice-Hall.
Beck, A. T., L. Rush, J. Shaw, & A. Emery. 1979. *Cognitive therapy of depression.* New York: Guilford Press.
Bergen, N. J. 1974. *Evening record,* 15 September, D–1.
Blackham, G. J., & A. Silverman. 1975. *Modification of child and adolescent behavior.* Belmont, Calif.: Wadsworth.
Blaine, J. D., M.D., & D. A. Julius. 1977. *Psychodynamics of drug dependence.* NIDA Research Monograph 12. Rockville, Md.: National Institute on Drug Abuse.
Coleman, J. S. 1961. *The adolescent society.* Glencoe, Ill.: Free Press.
Cranshaw, P. 1978. *Core knowledge in the drug field,* vol. 1. Ottawa, Canada: Minister of Supply and Services.
Emery, G., S. D. Hollan, & R. C. Bedrosian. 1981. *New directions in cognitive therapy.* New York: Guilford Press.
Fischer, J., & H. Gochros. 1975. *Planned behavior change.* New York: Free Press.
Fort, J., & C. T. Cory. 1975. *American drugstore A (alcohol) to V (Valium).* Boston: Little, Brown.
Frosch, W. A., M.D., & H. Milkman, Ph.D. 1977. Ego functions in drug use. In *Psychodynamics of drug dependence,* ed. J. Blaine & D. A. Julius, 142–56. NIDA Research Monograph 12. Rockville, Md.: National Institute on Drug Abuse.
Grey, J. 1972. *Booze.* Toronto: Macmillan.
Inglis, B. 1975. *The forbidden game.* London: Scribner.
Johnston, L. D., J. G. Bachman, & P. M. O'Malley. 1982. *Student drug use, attitudes, and beliefs: National trends 1975–1982.* Rockville, Md.: National Institute on Drug Abuse.
Kolvin, I. 1967. Aversive imagery treatment in adolescents. *Behavior Research and Therapy* 5: 245–48.
Kovacs, M. 1975. A phenomenological approach toward the meaning of drug use. In *Predicting adolescent drug abuse: A review of issues, methods, and correlates,* ed. D. Lettieri. Rockville, Md.: National Institute on Drug Abuse.
Krohn, M. D., R. L. Akers, M. J. Radosevich, & L. Lanza-Kaduce. 1982. Norm qualities and adolescent drinking and drug behavior: The effects of norm quality and reference group on using and abusing alcohol and marijuana. *Journal of Drug Issues* 12(4): 343–56.
Krystal, H., M.D. 1977. Self- and object-representation in alcoholism and other drug dependence: Implications for therapy. In *Psychodynamics of drug dependence,* ed. J. Blaine & D. A. Julius, 88. NIDA Research Monograph 12. Rockville, Md.: Institute on Drug Abuse.
Lettieri, D. J. 1975. *Predicting adolescent drug abuse: A review of issues, methods, and correlates.* Rockville, Md.: National Institute on Drug Abuse.
Lichtenstein, E. 1979. Social learning, smoking, and substance abuse. In *Behavioral analysis and treatment of substance abuse.* NIDA Research Monograph 25, 114–27. Rockville, Md.: National Institute on Drug Abuse.
Lindesmith, A. 1969. Pop drugs: the high as a way of life. *Time* 26 September, 69.
Maddox, G. L. 1964. High school student drinking behavior: Incidental information from two national surveys. *Quarterly Journal on Alcohol* 25: 339–47.
———. 1970. Drinking prior to college. In *The domesticated drug: Drinking among collegians,* ed. G. Maddox. New Haven, Conn.: College & University Press.
Marlatt, G. A., & D. M. Donovan. 1970. Behavior modification. In *The domesticated drug: Drinking among collegians,* ed. G. Maddox, 265–69. New Haven, Conn.: College & University Press.
McFall, R. M. 1978. Smoking—cessation research. *Journal of Consulting and Clinical Psychology* 46: 707–12.
Mendels, J. 1970. *Concepts of Depression.* New York: Wiley.
Perry, C. L., J. Killen, L. Slinkard, & A. L. McAlister. 1980. Peer teaching and smoking prevention among junior high students. *Adolescence* 15(58): 277–81 (Summer).
Rawson, R. A., M. Glazer, E. J. Callahan, & R. P. Liberman. 1979. Naltrexone and behavior therapy for heroin addiction. In *Behavioral analysis and treatment of substance abuse,* ed. N. A. Krasnegor, 26–43. NIDA Research Monograph 25. Rockville, Md.: National Institute on Drug Abuse.

See, E. G. 1970. Status configurations and cigarette smoking in a junior high school. *Journal of School Health* 40: 23–31.

Simmel, E. 1948. Alcoholism and addiction. *Psychoanalytic Quarterly* 17: 6–31.

Skolnick, J. H. 1958. Religious affiliation and drinking behavior. *Quarterly Journal of Studies on Alcohol* 19: 452–70 (September).

Smart, R. G., & D. Fejer. 1972. Drug use among adolescents and their parents: Closing the generation gap in mood modification. *Journal of Abnormal Psychology* 79(2): 153–60.

Snyder, C. R. 1958. *Alcohol and the Jews*. Glencoe, Ill.: Free Press.

Stitzer, M., G. Bigelow, & I. Liebson. 1979. Reinforcement of drug abstinence: A behavioral approach to drug abuse treatment. In *Behavioral analysis and treatment of substance abuse*, ed. N. Krasnegor, 70. NIDA Research Monograph 25. Rockville, Md.: National Institute on Drug Abuse.

———. 1979. Student drug use, attitudes, and beliefs. In *Behavioral analysis and treatment of substance abuse*, ed. N. Krasnegor, 91. NIDA Research Monograph 25. Rockville, Md.: National Institute on Drug Abuse.

Wetmore, R. J. 1963. The role of grief in psychoanalysis. *International Journal of Psychoanalysis* 44: 97–103.

Wurmser, L. 1977. Mr. Pecksnitt's horse? In *Psychodynamics in compulsive drug use*, ed. J. Blaine & D. A. Julius, 36–72. NIDA Research Monograph 12. Rockville, Md.: National Institute on Drug Abuse.

Wyden, B. 1970. Report of an anonymous study. *New York Times News Service*, 1 November, 32.

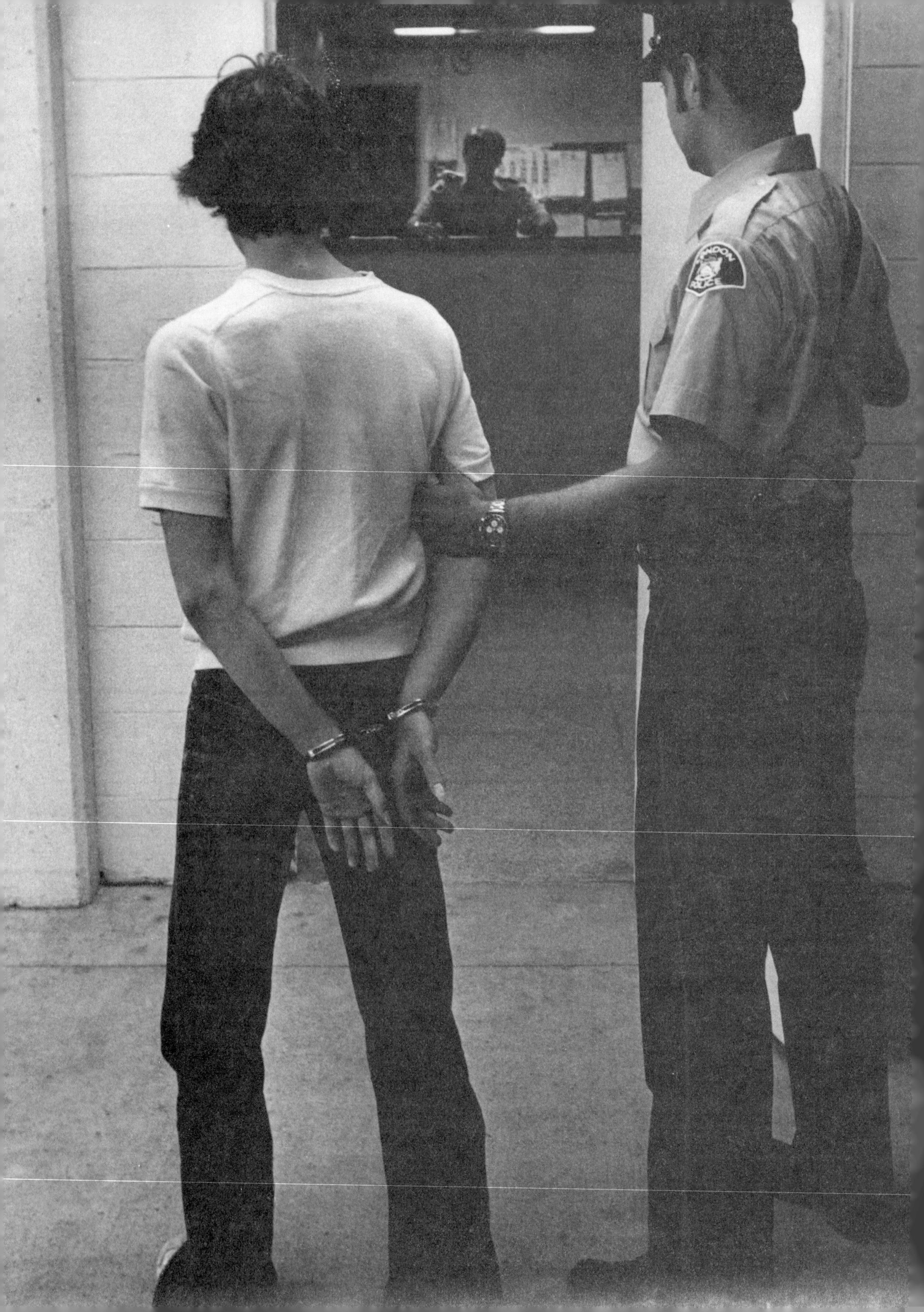

CHAPTER THIRTEEN

Juvenile delinquency

SURVEY AND QUESTIONS

This chapter serves as an overview of the problem of juvenile delinquency in our society. The chapter defines juvenile delinquency, identifies its possible origins, discusses common behavior patterns associated with juvenile delinquency, and examines methods of prevention and treatment. Reading the chapter will provide answers to the following questions:

Defining the Problem

What is a juvenile delinquent?
What constitutes a delinquent act?
How widespread is juvenile delinquency?
Do statistics tell the truth?

Causes of Juvenile Delinquency

What are the origins of juvenile delinquency?
What kind of family is likely to produce delinquents?
What kind of society produces delinquents?
What is social control?
What is the strain theory?
What is the subculture theory?
What causes delinquency among affluent youth?
How does psychoanalytic theory fit in?
Why does the personality theory fail?
Are there biological reasons for delinquency?

Behavior Patterns

Why do young people run away?
Is there a sexual dichotomy in juvenile justice?
How big a problem is property crime?
Is adolescent violence a serious problem?

Prevention and Treatment

Where did the juvenile justice system come from?
What are the alternatives to the juvenile courts?

Defining the problem

Part of being twelve years old is belonging to a "gang," having a secluded treehouse in a vacant lot, and spending idyllic hours high in the branches, drinking soda pop, reading comic books, and planning various adventures. Now, as I recall those times it seems most of our "fun" consisted of petty vandalism and technical trespass: breaking Christmas tree bulbs to hear them pop, touching off illegal fireworks, scavenging the local dump for treasures, and "cutting across" anyone's property that happened to be in our path. One summer day, however, we transcended those petty offenses and destroyed the local tennis courts.

It had rained the previous night and the clay surface was saturated. The gates were locked, so we climbed over the fifteen-foot fence and dropped to the courts, sinking to our knees in the quagmire. Before we were through, we had obliterated four tennis courts with our feet. Woven in with other intricate designs, we had even stomped our names in the clay to sign our handiwork. It had been a fun morning.

When the police arrived, I remember being surprised. It hadn't occurred to me that what we were doing was vandalism. I didn't even know what it meant. I was taken to the police station, questioned, fingerprinted, and finally after two hours, I was driven home in a squad car.

On June 28, 1969, I became a juvenile delinquent without even realizing it. As far as I had known, I was only being twelve years old.

Huckleberry Finn was a juvenile delinquent according to the standards of his society; yet members of the Hitler youth corps were not. A group of boys who trespass on private property are committing a delinquent act; yet their behavior will likely go unreported, viewed only as an example of "boys being boys." If other factors are involved, however—a different racial or ethnic heritage, for example—that perception may be altered and the police summoned. The technical standard of juvenile delinquency is subject to enormous perceptual leeway. A delinquent is only a delinquent when perceived as one.

From the prodigal son and Billy the Kid to yesterday's hippies and today's runaway subculture, juvenile delinquents have been with us as long as there have been juveniles. Juvenile delinquency continues to escalate nationwide in both perceptions and statistics. Like an egalitarian epidemic, it strikes both rich and poor, both upper social strata and lower castes, both healthy families and broken homes. The best efforts of professional and lay workers have not checked the advance; from the tenements of the south Bronx to the swimming pools of southern California, juvenile delinquents are a ubiquitous presence and a cross-cultural phenomenon.

This chapter discusses the following questions: What is a juvenile delinquent? What is a delinquent act? Is delinquency a natural outgrowth of adolescence or another symptom of societal disintegration?. How is it caused? Is it a sociological, familial, psychological, or biological phenomenon? How does delinquency express itself? Can it be predicted or prevented? Can it be treated? Do we compound the problem through efforts to cure it? What are the best ways to deal with delinquency?

QUESTION: What is a juvenile delinquent?

Since this question is more difficult than it appears on face value, a useful first step might be to define *juvenile* in legal terms.

In thirty-two states, a juvenile is defined by statute as being any child younger than eighteen years old. In twelve states, the age limit is seventeen, and in the remaining six states, the cutoff is sixteen years old. A juvenile delinquent in one state could be treated as an adult criminal in a neighboring state. In Florida, a juvenile delinquent is defined in this way:

(11) "A child in need of supervision" means a child under the age of 18 years who:
   a) Being subject to compulsory school attendance, is truant from school.
   b) Persistently disobeys the reasonable and lawful demands of his parents or other custodians and is beyond their control.
   c) Has run away from his parent or other custodian.
(12) "Delinquent child" means a child who commits a violation of law, regardless of where the violation occurs, except a child who commits a juvenile traffic offense and whose case has not been transferred to the circuit court by the court having jurisdiction. *(Florida States Annotated* 1974)

According to William Sanders in *Juvenile Delinquency,* a juvenile delinquent is a juvenile who has been given the social identity of a delinquent (Sanders 1981, 10). Admittedly, this definition is self-serving and circular, but the term *juvenile delinquent* is extremely malleable in society's hands. Juveniles who commit crimes are not necessarily juvenile delinquents as long as they are not discovered. Conversely, the element of criminal conduct is unimportant if society chooses to assume that someone is a juvenile delinquent simply because of appearance, attitude, or demeanor.

Classification as a juvenile delinquent varies from community to community. The different definitions of a juvenile between states can cause incongruities when it comes to criminal prosecution in the courts.

QUESTION: What constitutes a delinquent act?

Delinquent acts can be divided into four categories: crimes against a person, crimes against property, crimes against society, and status offenses.

Crimes against a person include the violent crimes that tantalize the media: rape, murder, assault, and robbery. Crimes against property include vandalism, shoplifting, auto theft, burglary, and the like. Crimes against society are the so-called victimless crimes (prostitution and drug use, for example). Any of the acts in the prior three categories are inherently criminal whether committed by an adult or by a juvenile.

Status offenses, however, are acts that would not be offenses if committed by an adult. They include truancy (missing school), running away from home, disobeying parents or school authorities, or simply being "incorrigible" (an undefined catchall). For these offenses, youth and only youth can be handled by the juvenile justice system. Since more categories of crime exist for youth than for adults, children have a greater chance of getting into trouble with the law then their parents. Some have suggested that punishment for violation of a status law may be unconstitutional. The Fourteenth Amendment requires that states may not deprive an individual of "liberty" without due process of law. The amendment does not distinguish between adults and juveniles in this protection. Since a juvenile could be jailed (sent to a detention center) for a status offense, this may be a violation of both due process and equal protection under the law. The Supreme Court has yet to address the issue.

QUESTION: How widespread is juvenile delinquency?

This question can be answered by offering another definition of the juvenile delinquent—practically all of *us* who are reading these words. The President's Commission on Law Enforcement and Administration of Justice (1967) has estimated that 90 percent of all people have committed at least one act as a juvenile that could have brought them under the jurisdiction of the juvenile justice system. This study was conducted using a self-reporting survey that allowed juveniles to tattle (anonymously) on themselves. Readers who answer the following questionnaire may begin to recognize the widespread nature of juvenile delinquency:

> The following questions pertain to activities you did when you were a juvenile, before 18 years of age in most states. It is a general set of questions to be used in estimating the presence of juvenile delinquency. Take the test. Keep in mind that the questions refer only to what you did as a juvenile.
> Current Age_____   Sex: Male_____ Female_____
> 1. Disobeyed your parents, defying them to their face.
>   Yes___ No___
> 2. Stole something from a store (shoplift).
>   Yes___ No___
> 3. Ran away from home overnight without your parents' permission.
>   Yes___ No___
> 4. Stole a car, even if you just drove it around and abandoned it.
>   Yes___ No___
> 5. Drove a car before you had a license or learner's permit.
>   Yes___ No___

6. Took money or other valuables from a person by using force or the threat of force.
     Yes___ No___
7. Broke into a building and stole something.
     Yes___ No___
8. Defaced, damaged, or destroyed property that did not belong to you or your family.
     Yes___ No___
9. Drank alcoholic beverages without your parents' knowledge or permission.
     Yes___ No___
10. Had sexual intercourse with someone of the opposite sex (if not married at the time).
     Yes___ No___
11. Used illegal drugs, such as marijuana, LSD, cocaine.
     Yes___ No___
12. Skipped school without a valid or legitimate excuse.
     Yes___ No___

(Sanders 1981, 300)

Admittedly, a self-reporting survey is subject to some limitations (e.g., poor memory and exaggeration), but on the whole, it illustrates that there are many more juvenile delinquents than official records indicate.

QUESTION: Do statistics tell the truth?

If most of us have committed an occasional delinquent act, it is clear that official records greatly underestimate the amount of juvenile delinquency in our society. Society does not insist on a strict interpretation and enforcement of statutory delinquency. In practical terms, this leniency is often translated as a tendency to apprehend high-visibility minority group members for juvenile offenses more often than their white middle-class counterparts. This is partly a result of subtle (or not-so-subtle) bias in the police officer's exercise of judgment, and partly due to police being more active in the inner city. A study by Goldman (1976) found that only 33.6 percent of white youth were likely to be referred to a juvenile court after a crime, as opposed to 64.8 percent of black youth.

Official records, then, may be inherently suspect. They tend to be biased in favor of privileged youth and against disadvantaged youth. Affluent parents have the resources and the knowledge to keep their children out of the juvenile justice system. Disadvantaged parents may have neither. Consider this example:

> Al had always been an active, upper-middle-class boy. . . . At age 16, Al and several of his friends broke into a local swimming pool for after hours swimming and fun. . . . No police complaints or court referrals were initiated following police detection of the incident. It had just been a prank.
>
> In the same year, Al was caught purchasing liquor from a package store. The owner of the store got into trouble with the police for selling liquor to minors. No action was taken against Al or his friends. . . .
>
> The next year, Al was caught driving while under the influence of alcohol. . . . The police stopped the car and were ready to take the whole group to the station when one officer recognized Al—who happened to be the son of the local school board president and a prominent businessman. The other kids

were also recognized as children of prominent townspeople—the local doctor, lawyer, and so on. The police took the kids straight home to their parents and took no further action.

Al's pranks continued in college. He and several friends "borrowed" a 6-foot alligator from a city park during the winter hibernation period. . . . When Al and his buddies were caught, their parents intervened to prevent police action. . . .

After graduation, Al became a respected member of his community. Through all his pranks, he never acquired a police record. (Griffin and Griffin 1978, 279–80)

The inference is that if Al had been a black youth from a poor home, he might not have gotten away with so much and would now be committing his pranks in a detention center.

To obtain a more accurate appraisal of juvenile crime than can be found in police or court records, self-reporting surveys and victimization surveys are used (the latter are filled out by residents in a given area to track down unreported crime). These methods probably provide a more accurate picture of juvenile crime, although they are still subject to certain limitations.

In summary, any definition of a juvenile delinquent must be cast in society's terms, according to its perception of the youth. A juvenile delinquent is only a juvenile delinquent when perceived as such. Official records tend to be biased, both in the nature of the offense (lesser offenses are not as often reported as more serious offenses) and in the nature of the offender (disadvantaged youth are disproportionately represented).

Causes of juvenile delinquency

QUESTION: What are the origins of juvenile delinquency?

At the outset, admitting that no one really knows the definite origins of juvenile delinquency might be helpful. Some generalizations can be drawn, but they are rife with exceptions. The search for the magic bullet goes on, but more and more sociologists and psychologists are viewing juvenile delinquency as a phenomenon with multiple origins. The lure of a simpler theory is that therapy and prevention would then be simpler, but as the situation exists today, no completely effective predictors can help to prevent or identify delinquency.

A minority of researchers view delinquency among youth as a perfectly normal manifestation, neither correctable nor preventable. Emile Durkheim (1958) observed that society needs antisocial behavior, from both young and old, to better define its goals. Libertoff (1980) theorized that delinquent behavior such as running away from home could be construed as a perfectly rational action under certain circumstances. Settlement of the American West was due in large part to the migration of those who might be called "juvenile delinquents" today.

The predominant view, however, is that juvenile delinquency is a social ill that needs to be understood and corrected. The theories on the origins of juvenile delinquency can be grouped into three categories: Sociogenic (familial and societal influences), psychogenic (originating in the psyche), and biogenic (caused by physiological or genetic abnormality).

SOCIOGENIC THEORY

QUESTION: What kind of family is likely to produce delinquents?

Studies have indicated a correlation between certain family environments and juvenile delinquency. We would probably assume that broken homes, child abuse, and a lack of communication and discipline in the home might be factors in the formation of the delinquent youth. Would we suppose, however, that corporal punishment in the home can encourage delinquency, or that marital tension alone is more predictive of delinquency than divorce?

BROKEN HOMES

Broken homes are frequently reported in the case histories of juvenile delinquents. McCord, McCord, and Zda (1959) demonstrated, however, that "quarrelsome, neglecting homes" were more predictive of delinquent behavior than homes where an outright parental break had occurred. In addition, Douglas, et al. (1966) showed that homes broken by the death of either parent were only half as likely to produce a juvenile delinquent as homes broken through divorce or separation. The hostility and tension associated with marital discord are seemingly more predictive of delinquency than the simple absence of a parent in the home.

A potential pitfall should be avoided in considering the influence of broken homes on delinquency. Children from incomplete familes are far more likely to be referred to the juvenile court in the first place by the recommending officer. They "appear" to need more help than children from complete families. This likelihood may lead to a misleading representation in official statistics.

CHILD ABUSE

"There is a common assumption that violence begets violence" (Shanok 1981, 223). In medical histories of abused delinquents, Shelly Shanok gave the following case histories of several children incarcerated in detention centers:

> One child who burned down an entire building at a school where he was placed, had a history of being wetted down, held by the arms and legs by male relatives, and beaten on the back by a psychotic mother. Another child who threatened others with dangerous weapons on several occasions, had, as an infant, been thrown across the room by a father who was recently discharged from a psychiatric hospital. His legs were subsequently broken with a broomstick, wielded by his mother. Another youngster who beat up a young girl and then stood guard while his friend raped the girl, had fractured his skull in a car accident when his mother deliberately crashed into a pole in an attempt to kill herself and her children. Yet another boy who committed sexual assault had a history of having had his genitals tied with string by his father who wished to teach him a lesson for wetting the bed. Another child who, among many offenses, threatened others with knives, had been thrown down the stairs by his father. He also had a well-documented history of having been chained to his bed and beaten sequentially by his father and then his mother. (Shanok 1981, 222)

A high proportion of children in detention centers have a history of having been abused by their families. Violent delinquency, in particular, seems to correlate positively with once having been the target of abuse (Lewis et al. 1979). In one study, 75 percent of extremely violent children had been severely abused by their families (Shanok 1981). A study by Rogers and Leunes (1979) demonstrated that delinquents who had been abused as children were characterized by poorer home adjustment, intolerance and suspicion, inflexibility, and deficient socialization. In short, they had become afraid of establishing relationships.

Child abuse is not normally a one-shot proposition. If it were, perhaps children would recover more readily from the trauma. Abuse is usually long lasting, an ongoing practice inflicted on children until they are either capable of leaving home or resisting. Clearly, physical abuse of a child may promote delinquency. The growing number of abusive parents may bode ill as a juvenile delinquent baby boom may soon be under way.

CORPORAL PUNISHMENT

According to Neapolitan (1981), a connection exists between a parent's physical discipline of a child and the child's future aggressive behavior. After studying 212 boys age fourteen to nineteen, Neapolitan concluded that physical punishment from parents served as a model for the juvenile's own aggression and violent delinquency. This was found to be particularly true when the child "desired to be like" the punishing parent. Interestingly, punishment by mothers seemed to push the boys into aggressive behavior, perhaps in an attempt to regain the masculinity that had been ignored. Snider and Murphy (1975) proposed essentially the same social learning theory (that violence is learned through modeling), although they dealt primarily with corporal punishment in the school system. They give this example:

> A seventh-grade girl was whipped by a teacher. When the child walked out of the whipping room, she had a look of triumph on her face. The look was not understood until the girl remarked that she had been whipped for fighting. She had scored a victory in compelling the teacher to demonstrate that the thing to do when one has a problem is to strike out in violence. Later, in history class this girl will study about negotiations, peace conferences, collective bargaining, and will be told that Henry Clay is a hero because of his ability to bring about compromise. But no amount of teaching in history can refute the lesson taught by the paddle. (Snider and Murphy 1975, 300)

Another example of the power of the parental model can be found in the following experience, described by a young parent:

> Bringing this down to a personal level, I see the action of my own two-year-old son, upon whom I have used corporal punishment as a means to control his behavior. He is smart; he observes and learns well and now I'm fighting to prevent him from "disciplining" his little sister in the same manner he has been disciplined. Once that behavior has been started it appears very difficult to stop.

Although spanking children will not automatically sentence them to a life of delinquency, enough evidence encourages alternate methods of discipline.

SATELLIZATION

Ausubel and Sullivan's (1970) theory of "satellization" explains the personality development of the adolescent through a study of interaction in the family. The authors particularly focus on the parent-child relationship and its mediation in the adolescent's struggle to achieve an independent identity. Acceptance is the key to a successful passage into adulthood, and Ausubel and Sullivan describe acceptance in terms of satellization. In a satellizing relationship, children revolve around the nuclear family and are accorded unqualified status and acceptance. They are endowed with "derived status." The status is not earned or acquired, but freely given to children because of what they are: children. In a nonsatellization relationship, children will experience either "rejection" or "qualified acceptance." Qualified acceptance means children are viewed as burdens and will only be accepted if they "deserve" it in the parents' view. These children feel undervalued and seek self-esteem in external values, having no confidence in their inherent self-worth.

According to Ausubel and Sullivan, children initially feel "omnipotent." They recognize that they are catered to and that every whim is satisfied by their "parent-slaves." When this illusion is shattered and the children's weakness is revealed, they will retreat to dependence on their family and find comfort in satellization.

Children will feel love and support with a guaranteed source of unconditional status. They will identify with their parents and with parental values, and as their consciences develop, they will see the world morally through their parents' eyes. This is how society perpetuates itself and its values.

If, however, children are nonsatellized and are rejected, they will seek status elsewhere. They will examine parental values carefully and critically, and will adapt only those which will serve their self-interest. Nonsatellization can lead to alienation from societal norms. A desperate need to please others and compensate for a lack of intrinsic self-esteem may make children more susceptible to delinquent influences. This can be especially true if a paucity of legitimate opportunity is available to children. Less advantaged youth may not turn to the socially accepted symbols for status, because they may lack the skills necessary for academic success; instead, they may turn to the streets (Deitz 1969).

QUESTION: What kind of society produces delinquents?

Many perceptions of juvenile delinquency are imbued with the almost hallowed idea that delinquency is a sickness of the poor. The general assumption has been that delinquency and poverty go hand in hand. Although the poor are over-represented in delinquency statistics, inherent bias in the system may be responsible for incarcerating the poor and releasing the rich. For example, a disturbed youth from a poor background will be institutionalized and receive state-funded treatment, while an equally troubled youth from an affluent background will be permitted to seek private, but expensive, counseling.

The first real concern with juvenile delinquency arose as millions of impoverished immigrants and their children arrive in the United States in the nineteenth century. Poverty was seen as the root of delinquency, and philanthropic efforts were made to rescue the impoverished youth. A more cynical view is that the concern for delinquency was more a concern for maintaining the established social order in the face of a flood of immigration. Uncontrolled youth could upset the status quo. Treatment of delinquents, then, became a method of social control.

QUESTION: What is social control?

Social control theorists maintain that juvenile delinquency would not be a major problem if society would "control" youth more effectively, either externally (through legal and quasi-legal systems) or internally (though instilling a values system).

An important component of social control is "bonding." Loyalty and attachment are created whenever the youth has a positive experience. Like a duckling imprinted to follow its mother, youth can be bonded to parents, symbols, jobs, country, and social organizations. Involvement within these social parameters causes the youth to conform to, be loyal to, and identify with the values and ethics society wishes to promote. Sutherland and Cressey (1978) have pointed out that youths' associations will dictate what they consider normal, proper, and justified behavior.

A logical dilemma, however, is associated with social control. Where do the values come from in the first place? Unless one believes, as John Locke did, in universal natural law, one has to fear the inculcation of values on a programmatic scale. Values could be dictated, and social control theory could be used to achieve a certain mind-set. Consider the following example of eminently successful social control and bonding:

> In no country in the world had there been a youth movement of such vitality and numbers as in republican Germany. Hitler, realizing this, was determined to take over and Nazify it.
>
> On December 1, 1936, Hitler decreed a law outlawing all non-Nazi organizations for young people.... From the age of six to eighteen, when conscription for the Labor Service and the Army began, girls as well as boys were organized in the various cadres of the Hitler Youth. Parents found guilty of trying to keep their children from joining the organization were subject to heavy prison sentences.... From the age of six to ten, a boy served a sort of apprenticeship for the Hitler Youth as a *Pimpf*.... At ten, after passing suitable tests in athletics, camping, and Nazi field history, he graduated into the *Jungvolk* ("Young Folk")....
>
> At fourteen the boy entered the Hitler Youth proper and remained there until he was eighteen, when he passed into the Labor Service and the Army. It was a vast organization organized on paramilitary lines similar to the S.A. and in which the youngsters approaching manhood received systematic training not only in camping, sports, and Nazi ideology but in soldiering....
>
> From ten to fourteen, German girls were enrolled as *Jungmaedel*—literally, "young maidens"—and they too had a uniform, made up of a white blouse, full blue skirt, socks, and heavy—and most unfeminine—marching shoes. Their training was much like that of the boys of the same age ... but emphasis was put on the role of women in the Third Reich—to be, above all, healthy mothers of healthy children.... (Shirer 1959, 252–56)

Juvenile delinquency was not a problem in the Third Reich. Delinquency is much less widespread in authoritarian countries than it is in the United States. Prosocial behavior, for example, was found to be much better internalized among Soviet youth than among American youth (Bronfenbrenner 1968).

Could delinquency be one of the prices we pay for a free society? Another view of the dichotomy between Soviet and American youth could be more Marxist in nature. Perhaps delinquency is engendered, at least in part, by the economic inequality endemic to a capitalistic system and the frustration that must surely exist among the lower socioeconomic masses. Robert Merton is a chief proponent of this so-called strain theory.

QUESTION: What is the strain theory?

According to Merton (1957), delinquency is created by the frustration of not being able to achieve, through legitimate activities, internalized middle-class American goals. Success and happiness are defined as the acquisition of "culturally prescribed goods"—a home, a car, all the ideals of consumer America.

Few are able to attain all culturally prescribed goals. Not everyone can be a successful businessperson; there are not enough businesses to go around. Still most Americans can *try* to achieve these goals. For the members of the lower socioeconomic class, however, equal opportunity may exist only as a myth. They do not have the education, the money, or the connections for upward mobility. They may be blocked by racial or ethnic prejudice.

> Frequently, the lower-class child does not get adequate training for job placement. One ex-delinquent articulated his problem in the following way:
> "What kind of school program were you doing? Vocational education?"
> "Yeah, vocational training."
> "Did that prepare you for a job?"
> "It was supposed to prepare me for a job but it didn't."
> "Did you try to get a job?"
> "Yeah, I tried to get a job. The men said I wasn't qualified."
> "Did you think while you were in school that you would get a job?"
> "That's right—that's why I stayed in school so I could get a job upon completion of high school because they put so much emphasis on getting a high school diploma. 'If you get a high school diploma, you can do this and you can do this, without it you can't do this.' And I got one and I still can't do nothing. I can't get a job or nothing after I got one." (Griffin and Griffin 1978, 258)

According to Merton, individuals faced with this dilemma have five choices. They can (1) *conform*, despite it all, and keep trying, (2) *innovate* by turning to crime to circumvent the road to success, (3) *live by ritual* and reduce goals to more realistic expectations, (4) *retreat* by using drugs as an escape and giving up completely, or (5) *rebel* by replacing society's imposed cultural goals with opposing goals.

The strain theory has been modified somewhat by Cloward and Ohlin (1960), who call it the "subculture theory."

QUESTION: What is the subculture theory?

The subculture theory explains the social dynamics of gang formation among youth who share a collective frustration. They bond together and seek status through illegitimate means. Risk taking, violence, and crime are seen as symbols of daring, of strength, and of status. Role models may be available to provide a pattern for success.

The role model is admired and almost venerated by youth as the paradigm of success. This example leads to a stable social organization called a *criminal subculture*. Sutherland and Cressey's (1978) "differential association" theory comes into play as members of the gang accept the standard of the group and form loyalties to one another.

If no successful role model exists to pave the way and teach, a more anarchistic subculture will be formed. The *conflicts subculture* is overt violence. Bravery, the one recognizable virtue, becomes the tool of the status seeker. Until opportunity is available in other areas, criminal or legitimate, gang violence will continue unabated. A Marxian model of struggle forms between the warring gangs, creating cohesion among the members and extreme polarization and antagonism against the opponent.

A *retreatist subculture* is available to those who either cannot achieve status in the other subcultures or do not wish to. Drug use and drug traffic are predominant features of this group, as is contempt for society at large.

Generally, the strain and subculture theories are limited in application to lower socioeconomic groups. They do little to explain widespread delinquency among the affluent.

QUESTION: What causes delinquency among affluent youth?

Seemingly, affluent youth have little reason to turn to delinquency, for they have access to the legitimate goals that are denied disadvantaged youth. A historical view of postwar America, however, shows a consumer boom unsurpassed in history. The baby-boom generation experienced reappraisal of traditional ethics of hard work. Many adults ironically behaved like adolescents. The youth, in turn, have exaggerated these behaviors. Unfortunately, most adult behaviors that the youth enjoy modeling—autophilia, sex, drinking, drug use, self-indulgence, instant gratification—turn out to be contrary to the juvenile code as status offenses. Youth are then punished for adult "virtues" and become alienated from their society, labeling it hypocritical. The youth are then prepared to join a retreatist subculture and seek values of their own.

PSYCHOGENIC THEORY

QUESTION: How does psychoanalytic theory fit in?

According to Freudian theory, delinquent behavior is the result of unresolved drives and instincts buried deep in the unconscious. When conflict arises, so do behavior problems. When one behaves improperly vis-à-vis society, crime results. These deep-rooted conflicts can be resolved only with professional help.

According to Freud, infants enter the world as "criminals" of sorts. They are socially maladjusted and can adjust properly only through the passage of critical life stages; children must learn to bring the id (pleasure), and ego (personality), and the superego (conscience) into balance. Their Oedipal (male) or Electra (female) complex will be resolved through an appeal to the superego. The same-sex parent will no longer be mistrusted, and the opposite-sex parent no longer sexually desired.

If, however, these conflicts are not resolved, behavior problems may arise. If the Oedipal complex is not resolved, the boy, unable to attack his father because of his superego, may attack authority figures as surrogates. A pistol or a rifle used in a criminal act could represent a fear of impotence. Breaking and entering could be symbolic of a violation of the mother (Griffin and Griffin 1978, 170–73). Teenage girls may run away from home to avoid the unconscious incestuous tension of an Electra complex (Robey et al, 1964).

The main criticism leveled at psychoanalysis is that it is not empirically testable and cannot be proved. One psychogenic theory that is testable is the personality theory.

QUESTION: Why does the personality theory fail?

Personality theory approaches delinquency with a battery of tests—MMPI, IQ, and Rorschach—and attempts to define the delinquent personality through empirical testing. These tests, however, may not be helpful in providing a profile of the delinquent.

A known delinquent is given a test to discover what a delinquent personality encompasses. The Minnesota Multiphasic Personality Inventory (MMPI), for example, includes fourteen questions dealing with aspects of delinquency (one reads, "Have you ever been in trouble with the law?"). One criticism is that the test may show nothing more than that adolescents who have been in trouble with the law are more likely than those who have not been in trouble with the law to indicate that they have been in trouble with the law (Jensen and Rojek 1980, 146).

The trauma of detention and exposure to the court system may also be manifest on the test, and a difficulty would be establishing which personality traits were the *cause* of delinquency and which were the *results* of delinquency. In addition, an early study (Healy and Bronner 1936) of 113 juveniles revealed that the control group—the nondelinquents—looked significantly more abnormal on paper than did the delinquents themselves.

A corollary to the personality theory is the sociopathic theory, which postulates that juvenile delinquents have no moral constraints and act as they please. In most cases, this reasoning is clearly inaccurate, since delinquents generally have a sense of what can and cannot be done within their group. They feel the need to justify their behavior and operate under moral restraint—though the standard of morality may not be the same as in mainstream society. They have different morals, but are not amoral or antimoral (Sanders 1981, 34–35).

BIOGENIC THEORY

QUESTION: Are there biological reasons for delinquency?

Early theories of criminality were concerned with the physical appearance of the criminal, assuming that physiognomy could be the cause of criminal behavior. Cesare Lambroso conducted a study in 1876 that has been enshrined in history. The study measured cranial capacity, the size of ears, facial asymmetry, and other anatomical features of criminals, in an attempt to prove that criminals were examples of "atavism"—genetic throwbacks to more primitive, aggressive forms of humankind.

A few years ago, with the discovery in some criminals of a chromosomal observation, XYY, a resurgence occurred in the biogenic theory of criminality. This anomaly was thought to promote aggressiveness and criminal behavior, but a latter study by Fox (1971) demonstrated that the XYY inmates were not as violent as their normal XY counterparts in the prison.

William Sheldon (1940) demonstrated that biological theories were not dead. In a more recent study two hundred boys were traced through their lives for thirty years and evaluated in terms of somatotypes (general body shape) and personality. The following is an example of the description of one of these men:

> Comment—with this somatotype pattern, life is lived for the muscles. He shows one kind of mesotonia with a continuous somatic demand and a need for almost constant muscular exercise. A high level of somatic drive and physical competence enabled him to do well through the years in this modified athletic pattern in spite of the importunities of a nagging wife, and some loss of coordination and agility as he aged. Now that he is growing older we wonder whether he will be able to accept retirement gracefully and find another way to expend his prodigious energies and keep up with his need for physical activity. Dominant mesomorphs with a need for action sometimes find retirement difficult. (Hartl, Monnelly, and Elderkins 1982, 269)

Although this description reads like a horoscope, we should not dismiss all biological considerations from our minds. Organic dysfunction has an effect on human behavior. Brain tumors, spinal and nerve damage (common in abused children), hypoglycemia, and hormonal imbalance have all been shown to induce abnormal behavior. In addition, all personalities are influenced to some degree by physical appearance. Racial discrimination can affect a personality, and unattractive or handicapped individuals may have difficult emotional problems to surmount. People are often treated according to their physical appearance, but this treatment is not due to their physiognomy as much as to society's intolerance of them. This approach, then, is more of a sociogenic theory of delinquency, not biogenic.

Behavior patterns

Some common delinquent behaviors include running away, truancy, prostitution, vandalism, shoplifting and auto theft. Most violent crimes committed by adolescents are either robberies or assaults.

QUESTION: Why do young people run away?

Between 500,000 and 1,000,000 teenagers run away each year. Running away from home is a status offense in most states and can lead to judicial action.

No single feature distinguishes the "runner" from the "nonrunner." Theories about motivations are legion. A feeling of rejection at home and in

Many factors may lead an adolescent to run away from home. However, most runaways do not run far, do not stay away long, and are not traumatized by the experience.

school plays an important part, and the home, internal conflict, divorce, beatings, and a lack of parental communication are all considered factors. If school is also unsatisfactory, the juvenile may commit the scholastic equivalent of running away and be truant.

As many classification schemes exist for runaways as there are researchers. Homer (1973) maintains that runaways can be divided into two categories: those who run *from* something and those who run *to* something. Roberts (1982) contends that runaways can be grouped as *explorers* (who seek adventure), *manipulators* (who wish to change the home situation through emotional blackmail), *retreatists* (who escape into a drug or alcohol subculture), and *endangered runaways* (who leave home to escape physical or sexual abuse).

A conflicting and stressful situation is likely to exist before a child runs. Running may even be a rational alternative (Libertoff 1980). In nearly every case, the run is preceded by months of tension and strained family relations.

According to Johnson and Carter (1980), the adolescent search for meaning has been impeded by a modern society that does not consider its youth "functional." To a large extent, all youth, whether poor or wealthy, black or white, are considered impatient, irrelevant, and generally anonymous. The hope is that they will quietly endure the role society has assigned to them, but that is a task youth are most reluctant to perform. In a primitive society, the rites of passage are distinct and well organized; in our society, they are delayed and take the forms of college, work, the armed services, or a trip to Europe for the summer. In a primitive society, a boy of fourteen may have a wife, a house, and status. In our society, he plays video games.

For many youth, running away may be a rite of passage. Most runaways do not run far, do not stay away long, and are not traumatized by the experience. Unfortunately, a minority feel compelled to leave an intolerable home situation and are victimized in the adult world. Some of these runaways are discussed in the next section dealing with prostitution.

PROSTITUTION

Female adolescents who run away sometimes find themselves entrapped in a prostitution racket. When a young girl leaves home with little or no money, no friends, and no marketable skills, she may have to exchange sex for room and board. Within that context, it hardly seems unreasonable for her to become a prostitute and make some money from a behavior that she would be pursuing in any case.

Consider these examples of adolescent prostitution:

> Karen, 14, met a pimp in downtown Minneapolis one day at 9 a.m. He bought her breakfast and took her to his apartment and bedded her. Next day she quarreled with her parents over having stayed out most of the night, so she ran off to see her new friend. He said she would have to work the street to stay with him and steal money from her customers so she could get the bus fare to Chicago. Once there, she earned another $800 in three weeks. The two moved to Manhattan, where she picked up men around luxury hotels, robbing them when she could. Sick of the life after six weeks, she tried to leave her pimp, but he broke her jaw. After hospitalization, she was forced back on the streets by him with her jaw wired shut. When an attempt to kill herself failed, she phoned her parents and fled New York. In ten weeks she had provided her pimp with some $4,000.
>
> Clare, 16, having run away from home, met a pimp along Minneapolis' Hennepin Avenue and moved in with him. He persuaded her to hit the streets. "He wouldn't let me come into the house unless I brought him $150 a day," she recalled. After she was arrested for prostitution, she and her pimp flew to New York, where she collected at least $100,000, of which she saved only $800. She was arrested 42 times for prostitution and once for grand larceny ("It was a trick who wanted his money back"), but never served a day in jail. When she tried to return home the pimp beat her so badly that she was hospitalized. *(Time* 1977, 23)

> Pimp offered to care for the baby. I needed money for the baby (the girl was 13 years old). I wanted a straight job real bad when he first started to talk me into working the street. . . . I said no and tried every single way I could to get a job. . . . I knew I would have to go home and my brother would either kill me or do something. . . . so I gave in.
>
> I was very lonely, being a young girl and not knowing nothing. No jobs. What else was I going to do? (Silbert and Pines 1982, 488)

A study in San Francisco involving two hundred young prostitutes (Silbert and Pines 1982) revealed that in their previous home life, 67 percent had been beaten, 59 percent had been abused, and—perhaps the most revealing statistic of all—60 percent had been victims of sexual abuse or incest in the home.

Studies have shown that young prostitutes are very often victims of sexual and/or physical abuse in their previous home lives before becoming prostitutes.

QUESTION: Is there a sexual dichotomy in juvenile justice?

One of the profound hypocrisies of our culture is our predilection toward condemning young women for engaging in sexual relations before marriage while applauding (secretly) the young man who has done the same. The perception is this: The young woman has lost something (her virtue), while the young man has gained something (his manhood).

Seventy percent of young women referred to juvenile courts are there for either running away or promiscuity—or both. Chesney-Lind (1974) has noted that girls are far more likely to be arrested for sexual offenses than are boys, although, presumably, the numbers were originally compatible. In New York City, young women must undergo a vaginal smear test even if arrested for shoplifting, while young men are subject to no similar sexual abuse (Sanders 1981, 103). The assumption in the juvenile justice system is that the young woman has been sleeping around and must be stopped.

In contrast, two recent Supreme Court cases have defended the right of an unmarried female minor to have an abortion in the first trimester of her pregnancy. State statutes forcing her to obtain her parents' permission were struck down as unconstitutional *(Planned Parenthood of Missouri* v. *Danforth* and *Bellotti* v. *Baird)*. It is ironic that the same young woman who has the constitutional right to seek an abortion as an adult is still subject to the juvenile justice system for her sexual behavior as a juvenile.

A recent study (McClelland 1982), using statistics from the United States and England, shows how gender, ethnicity, and class play their part in adolescent female delinquency. Female delinquency peaks at two age periods: during the teen years and after the age of thirty. In a twenty year study (1957–1977), female delinquency steadily rose. Not only have the numbers increased but also the types of crimes committed are beginning to resemble male delinquency more and more. (McClelland 1982)

The difficult task of assessment by the courts is complicated by two considerations peculiar to females, the first being that of stereotypes. Nurturance, passivity, dependency, and nonaggressiveness are seen as female traits and positive indices of mental health. Because of this perception, the possible range for behavior is much more restricted for the female before transgression occurs.

The second complicating factor is the effect of theories of female delinquency, which affects official response and the training of professionals. As viewed by professionals, female delinquency is an individual trait not a social force, with a central theme of sexuality. Professionals show marked leniency toward women involved in property crimes, and deal severely with sexual offenses. Sexual offenses account for 60 percent to 72 percent of all female referrals while only accounting for 27 percent of all male referrals.

Girls are more likely to be arrested for trivial offenses and remanded for less reason than males. In the United States, 71 percent of all girls remanded are remanded for status offenses, whereas only 29 percent of remanded males are status related.

Thirty percent of crimes committed by adolescent females are observed or discovered by police: the remaining 70 percent are reported by the public. Lower-class and black offenders are dealt with more severely than middle-class white offenders. Lower-class white girls' offenses, however, are recorded more often than lower-class black girls' offenses, most likely reflecting a more paternal attitude taken by police toward white girls. The nature of the crime also differs. Black girls are more likely to be involved in fistfighting, while white girls are most likely to be involved in property and automobile offenses.

Our society has moved closer to an androgynous state in the last few decades, and so have adolescent gangs. Females, age seventeen or less, commit crimes in the company of others. Seventy-two percent of all female adolescent crimes occur in groups. Our stereotype of the delinquent being poorly socialized and unaccepted by peers is not true. Delinquent females are highly socialized and popular among their own peers.

The discovery has been made that the ethnic group of Latin origin stands out with low percentages of female delinquency. These families seem to be closer and have better supervision. In female delinquency, psychological relationship with parents and school expectations are said to be strong indicators of delinquency. McClelland concludes that for females, less parental supervision enhances the risk of delinquency. (McClelland 1982)

QUESTION: How big a problem is property crime?

More than 50 percent of property-related crime is committed by 13.2 percent of the population—youth age eleven to seventeen (President's Commission on Law Enforcement and Administration of Justice 1967, 56). Lest this seem like an area exclusively controlled by the young, we should note that much more property crime in dollars is committed by white-collar America (Sanders 1981, 127). When juveniles steal, it is rarely to make money.

Stealing is a group activity and a test of bravery. Shoplifting is seen as an attempt to gain economic independence. Interestingly, shoplifting drops off enormously as youth grow up and find legitimate ways to obtain goods.

Vandalism is another activity relegated to the youth, but adults vandalize, too—and in much more damaging ways. When youth destroy property it is called vandalism. When adults destroy property it is called pollution (Sanders 1981, 138). Here is one area in which a distinction can be drawn along a socioeconomic class line. Affluent youth are most likely to be involved in property-related crimes while disadvantaged youth are most likely to be involved in violent crimes.

QUESTION: Is adolescent violence a serious problem?

All violence is a serious problem, but the problem of teenage murder and rape seems to be exaggerated. In 1979, about 4 percent of all juvenile arrests were for violent crimes. Of that number, only a small percentage of the arrests were for murder and rape. Robbery and assault together constituted almost 93 percent of adolescent violence (U.S. Department of Justice 1982, 4–9). Some of the conclusions are reported in Box 13-1.

Almost all violent crime is committed by recidivists (repeat offenders), and the juvenile courts are examining ways to end that cycle. Almost all states allow criminal courts to try children age fifteen and older for serious violent crimes. The state will usually leave the decision of jurisdiction up to the juvenile court judge unless the act is particularly serious, in which case the juvenile will be tried in criminal court.

QUESTION: Where did the juvenile justice system come from?

Prevention and treatment

According to common law, children under age seven could not be found guilty of any offense. Children age seven to fourteen were responsible only if they understood the nature of their crime. Children age fourteen and older were tried as adults in criminal court.

In 1899, the first juvenile court was established in Cook County, Illinois. This was perceived as an attempt to keep children out of jail, where they would be corrupted by unhealthy contact with adult prisoners, while still providing detention facilities for those children who should not be on the streets (Adams and Gullotta 1983, 400–401). The acceptance of juvenile criminals' conduct can be seen in Figures 13–1 and 13–2, which show the number of states that provide criminal trials for youth of different ages.

> **BOX 13-1   QUESTIONS AND ANSWERS ABOUT JUVENILE CRIME**
>
> 1. *What proportion of all arrests for serious and violent crimes do juveniles account for?*
>
>   In 1979, juveniles accounted for about 20 percent of all violent crime arrests, 44 percent of all serious property crime arrests, and 39 percent of all serious crime arrests.
>
>   Young persons accounted for 17 percent of all violent crime arrests; 19 percent, serious property; and 18 percent, overall serious.
>
>   Adults accounted for 63 percent of all violent crime arrests; 38 percent, serious property; and 43 percent, overall serious.
>
> 2. *What proportions of juvenile arrests are for serious and violent crimes?*
>
>   In 1979, about 4 percent of all juvenile arrests were for violent crimes, 35 percent for serious property crimes, and 39 percent for serious crimes overall. About 10 percent of all juvenile arrests for serious crimes were for violence; about 90 percent were for serious property crimes.
>
>   These data make it clear that juveniles are disproportionately involved in serious crimes, especially when one considers that in 1979, youths age ten to seventeen represented about 14 percent of the total U.S. population.
>
> 3. *What proportion of each violent crime do juveniles account for?*
>
>   In 1979, juvenile arrests represented about 9 percent of all arrests for murder, 16 percent of all arrests for robbery, and 16 percent of all arrests for aggravated assault.
>
>   These data indicate juvenile involvement in violent crime to be most disproportionate in robbery offenses.
>
> 4. *What proportion of each serious property crime do juveniles account for?*
>
>   In 1979, juvenile arrests represented about 49 percent of all arrests for arson, 49 percent for auto theft, 49 percent for burglary, and 40 percent for larceny.
>
>   These arrest data clearly document the disproportionate involvement of juveniles in serious property crimes.
>
> 5. *What is the proportion of violent juvenile arrests for each such offense?*
>
>   In 1979, 2 percent of all violent juvenile arrests were for murder, 5 percent for rape, 47 percent for robbery, and 46 percent for aggravated assault.
>
>   These data show that among violent crimes arrests of juveniles, robbery and aggravated assault are more predominant.
>
> 6. *What is the peak age of arrests of juveniles for serious and violent crimes?*
>
>   For serious property crimes, age sixteen; for violent crime, age seventeen to eighteen.
>
> *Source:* U.S. Department of Justice, *Dealing with Serious Repeat Juvenile Offenders,* Office of Juvenile Justice and Delinquency Prevention (Washington, D.C.: U.S. Government Printing Office, 1982), 5.

Certain major problems exist within the juvenile court system that would not be permitted in adult criminal courts. One problem is the presumption of guilt. No need would exist for rehabilitating and protecting a youngster who was not involved in some wrong. Indeed, this process would be a waste of the court's time. If a juvenile is before the judge, then, the assumption is that the juvenile is guilty of some offense. This attitude is quite the opposite from the approach in normal criminal law, which maintains that one is presumed innocent until proven guilty (Sanders 1981, 235–36).

Another problem is the lack of the traditional adversarial relationship between prosecutor and defender to ensure that the juvenile's best interests are protected. The judge as "parental surrogate" has an enormous amount of power over the juvenile with no checks to balance it.

Because of the heavy burden on these courts, procedural due process is also suspect. Some surveys have found judges taking less than three minutes on each case when the juvenile's future was at stake. If cases are rushed, mistakes will be made.

Perhaps most importantly, some have suggested (McCord, McCord, and Zda 1959) that the worst thing that can be done to first-time juvenile offenders is to label them as juvenile delinquents. The "labeling theory" suggests that we will perceive ourselves as others see us. If juveniles are brought to court,

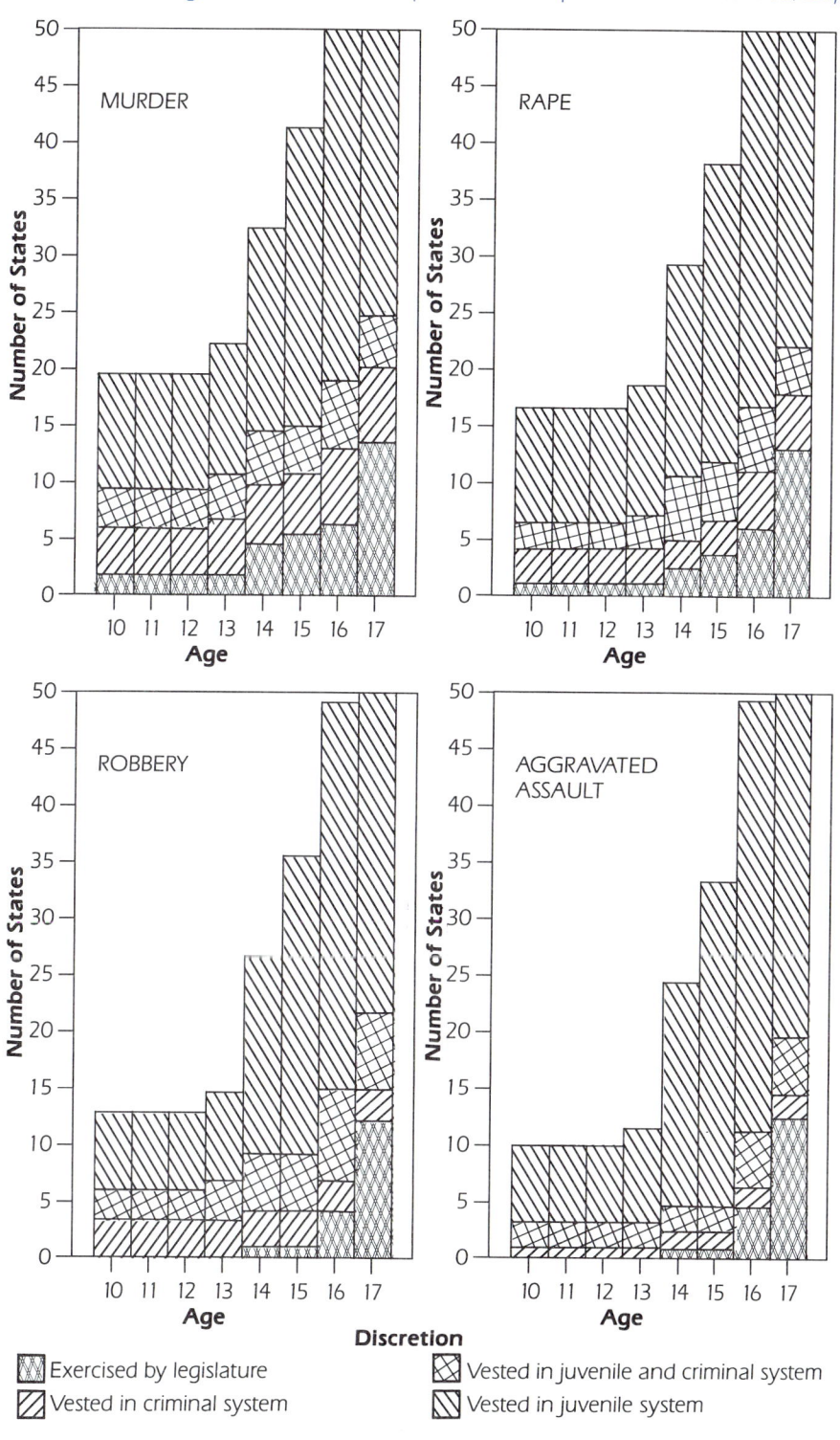

Chapter 13 Juvenile delinquency   **435**

Figure 13-1 Number of States Providing Criminal Trials for Persons Age Ten to Eighteen Charged with Violent Crime *(Source:* U.S. Department of Justice 1982, 25.)

Discretion

- Exercised by legislature
- Vested in criminal system
- Vested in juvenile and criminal system
- Vested in juvenile system

436 ■ Section 3 Behaviors and thinking

Figure 13-2 Number of States Providing Criminal Trials for Persons Age Ten to Eighteen Charged with Violent Crime *(Source:* U.S. Department of Justice 1982, 26.)

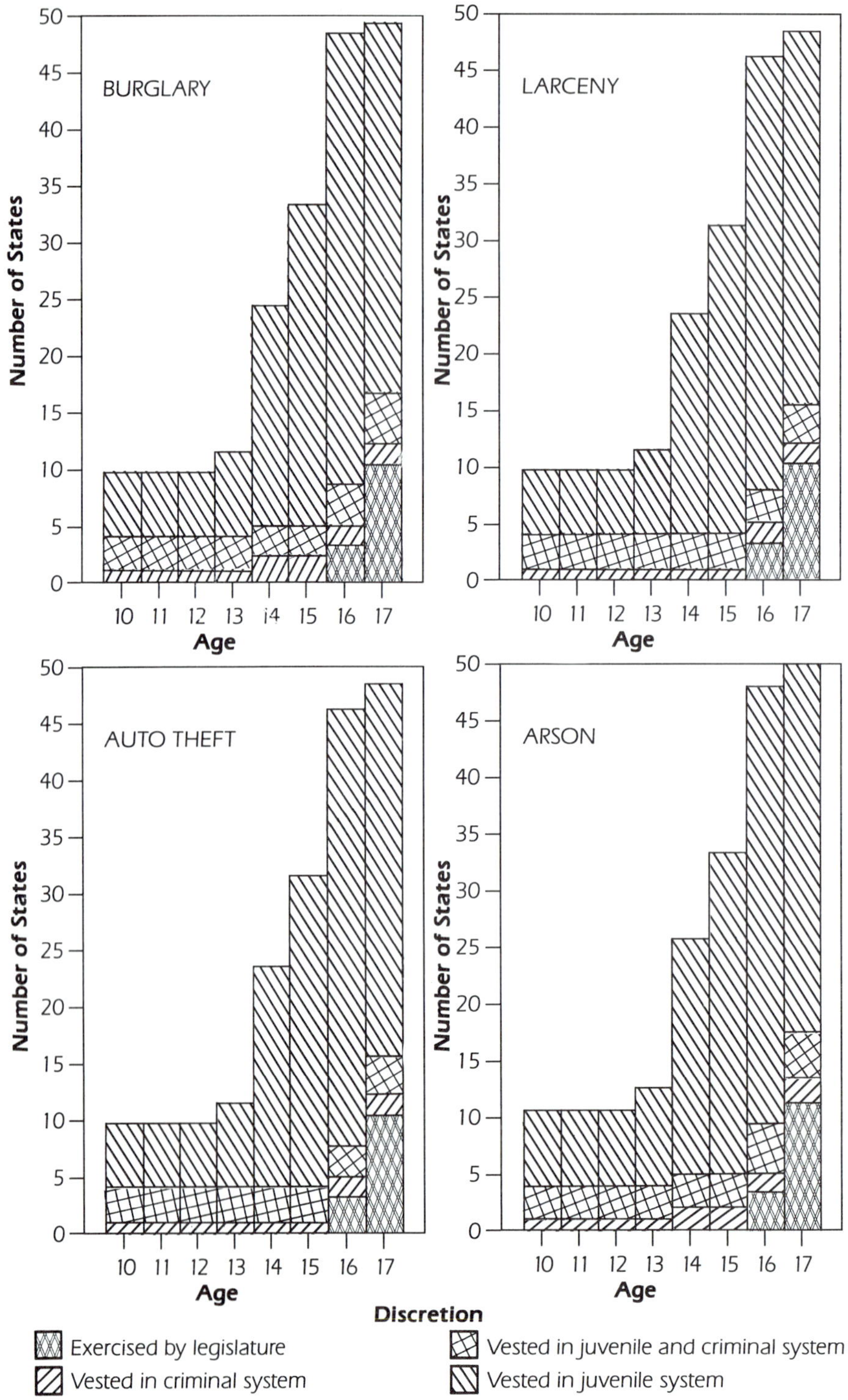

they will see themselves as juvenile delinquents. If they are not brought to court, neither they, nor their friends, nor their families are likely to consider them delinquent.

Though the number of incarcerated delinquents has been reduced considerably since the 1950s, the problem of juvenile detention is still of major concern. These centers are designed for rehabilitation but are often run strictly as prisons.

The *Gault* (1967) decision by the U.S. Supreme Court addresses some of the blatant violations of basic constitutional rights inherent in the juvenile justice system:

> Gerald Francis Gault was adjudicated delinquent in 1964 and sentenced to the state industrial school. Gault was 15 and was given a disposition which could result in incarceration for as many as six years. The charge against Gault was "lewd phone calls"—an act prohibited by the Arizona Criminal Code, which specified that anyone who used vulgar, abusive, or obscene language was guilty of a misdemeanor. The penalty for adults was a fine of 5 to 50 dollars or imprisonment for a few months.
>
> When Gault was taken into custody his working parents were not at home. No attempt was made to inform the parents that their son had been arrested and taken to a detention home. A petition was filed in juvenile court, but it was not served to the Gault family.

The juvenile courts were established to help youth and they have become an important element in our justice system. However, a heavy burden of cases on these courts threatens to cramp their effectiveness.

When the hearing was held, the complaining witness was not present. Gerald Gault did not have a lawyer and no court transcript or recording of the hearing was made. Gault was questioned by the juvenile judge and admitted to making the call and some of the lewd remarks. Gault was returned to the detention home. The Gault family was notified of further hearings by a letter. At the new hearing Gerald Gault was committed to the state training school.

On May 15, 1967, the Supreme Court considered the Gault case. Justice Abe Fortas in writing the majority opinion, said:

> Neither the fourteenth amendment nor the Bill of Rights is for adults only. Under our constitution, the condition of being a boy does not justify a kangaroo court.

The Gault decision gave rights to juveniles accused of criminal offenses. Among the rights were the right to receive notice of charges against them, the right to be represented by counsel, the right to face witnesses and accusers while cross-examining them, the right to remain silent and refuse to answer questions that might result in self-incrimination, and the right to a transcript of all proceedings. (Griffin and Griffin 1978, 310)

In this case, the juvenile justice system had to be rescued from itself. Partly because of the furor over this case, alternatives are being suggested and implemented in the juvenile justice system, both as prophylactic measures to prevent delinquency and as alternative treatments for delinquency after the fact.

QUESTION: What are the alternatives to the juvenile courts?

The traditional procedure of arrest or warning, hearing or dismissal, and incarceration or probation may soon be modified by ideas that are more related to modern concepts of the origins of juvenile delinquency.

Dennis Stott, author of *Delinquency: The Problem and Its Prevention* (1982), claims that the best way to cure delinquency is not to "punish" delinquents but to redirect these youth and their energies in progressive and responsible ways that will neither degrade the offenders nor stigmatize them. Stott's principles include: restitution to the community through labor on civic projects, financial restitution to the victim when possible, and face-to-face reconciliation between the victim and offender to determine damages and restitution.

By requiring juveniles to work on community projects, social bonding may occur, and juveniles may begin to identify with the community and its values. Because they would be providing a service to the community, they would not be labeled as delinquents but would be seen in a more favorable light, therefore increasing their self-esteem.

Another proposal for modification of the juvenile justice system entails removing status offenses entirely from the court's jurisdiction and ceding them to public agencies, clinics, and schools. This proposal serves the dual purpose of reducing both the court's work load and the stigmatization inherent in the juvenile justice system.

Where will the juvenile justice system go from here? The juvenile courts no longer enjoy the unqualified support they once did. More and more juveniles will likely be diverted from the courts into community programs.

PREVENTION

The prevention and rehabilitation of juvenile delinquents has not been dramatically successful. Perhaps the most credible approach has involved behavioral principles. Theory and a sample program are described in Chapter 15, "Applying Behavior Theory to Adolescents."

One interesting program to prevent juvenile delinquency enjoyed nationwide attention in 1979. Mildly delinquent boys were brought to Rahway State Prison in New Jersey, where they glimpsed their terrifying future. For hours, inmates harangued, threatened, and told the truth about life in prison. This incident occurred toward the end of one session:

> The last speaker was tall, thin, unsmiling, and his blue eyes blazed like laser beams. He told the boys he'd give anything to change places with them. They could go home at the end of the morning. He had to stay at least 20 more years.
>
> Without a word, the boys got up and filed out one by one—through the seven steel doors, through the room where the invisible ink on their wrists was checked with black light to make sure it matched the day's code, through the corridor past the riot-equipment room. Finally, they emerged into blinding sunlight.
>
> There were green trees in front of the prison—a sight some convicts hadn't seen in decades. A 12-year-old impulsively threw his arms around the juvenile officer who'd brought them. "Don't ever let them take me back there!" he pleaded. (Tunley 1978, 98)

Sadly, later studies showed that the boys who had experienced Rahway were more likely to engage in delinquent activity than boys who had not. (Finckenauer 1982)

If this example points out anything, it should be that no panaceas are in sight. Any positive treatment or prevention of juvenile delinquency will be the result of thorough research and program testing.

The origins of delinquency have been sought, at various times, in the physique, in the mind, in the personality, in the genes, in the family, and in the society of the juvenile. Delinquency is endemic to adolescents, to one degree or another. Few of us have never committed an act during our youth that could have been classified as delinquent. Confronted with this realization, some have suggested diverting less serious offenses to community resources and reserving the juvenile justice system for more serious offenders.

That appears to be the thinking of many professionals today when faced with juvenile delinquency and a somewhat discredited—and overworked—juvenile justice system. The juvenile courts, born of good intentions, have acquitted themselves less than honorably. By attaching a criminal stigma to juvenile offenders, the courts may even have reinforced the concepts of delinquency by ostracizing the youth from their communities. The juvenile justice system came into being in 1899 to rescue the juvenile from an adult criminal justice system. In 1967, the U.S. Supreme Court had to rescue the juvenile from the juvenile justice system.

Movement from the courts to community programs now appears to be the course to take for less serious offenses (Farrington, Biron, and LeBlanc 1982). Although the problem of juvenile delinquency has no quick-fix solutions, recent research and creative theory have at least pointed directions in which the search may continue.

Although the content of this chapter has a negative connotation, some encouraging program developments have occurred. These authors, in describing these developments, present a vigorous take-charge attitude:

> At the moment we are witnessing an explosion of trial and error techniques to replace traditional therapy and large scale institutionalization. Programs run the full range: Forestry camps, outward bound programs, walk abouts, special summer camps, halfway houses, group homes, and alternative schools are just some of the current diversion techniques being tried. Some, such as forestry camps, have long histories while others, such as halfway houses or group homes, are quite new.
>
> Obviously, we are still in an exploratory stage in treating delinquency. (Sprinthall and Collins 1982, 359)

This observation may have focused on the key element: social experimentation. One approach that may prove successful is the family-parent education program. Courts in at least two states, Texas and New Jersey, have in some instances required parents of delinquents to attend parent education programs. In some cases, the expense is borne by the state; in others the program cost is required instead of a fine.

Juvenile program experimentation, a better understanding of the nature and causes of juvenile delinquency, and the willingness of society to commit resources to prevention and treatment are necessary to reverse the trend of growth in juvenile crime statistics.

Summary

Depending on the state, a juvenile is any child younger than age sixteen, seventeen, or eighteen. Children are delinquent when they commit a violation of law. Delinquent acts include crimes against a person, crimes against property, crimes against society, and status offenses. Since most people have committed an occasional delinquent act, official records greatly underestimate the amount of juvenile delinquency in our society. Any definition of a juvenile delinquent must be cast in society's terms, according to its perception of the youth. Official records tend to be biased.

No completely effective predictors can help to prevent or identify delinquency. Studies have indicated a correlation between certain family environments and juvenile delinquency (e.g., broken homes, child abuse, and corporal punishment). Many perceptions are imbued with the idea that delinquency is a sickness of the poor.

Social control theorists maintain that juvenile delinquency would not be a major problem if society would "control" youth more effectively, either externally or internally. According to Merton's strain theory, delinquency is created by the frustration of not being able to achieve, through legitimate activities, internalized middle-class American goals.

Subculture theory explains the social dynamics of gang formation among youth who share a collective frustration. Role models may be available to provide a pattern for success.

According to Freudian theory, delinquent behavior is the result of unresolved desires and instincts buried deep in the unconscious. The main criticism leveled at psychoanalysis is that it is not empirically testable and cannot be proved.

Personality theories approach delinquency with empirical tests, but they may not be helpful in providing a profile of the delinquent. Biological theories on delinquency also exist.

Some common delinquent behaviors include running away, truancy, prostitution, vandalism, shoplifting, and auto theft. More violent crimes are robberies and assaults.

Many theories explain why young people run away, which include rejection at home and in school. Female adolescent runaways may be trapped into prostitution. However, most runaways do not run far, do not stay away long, and are not traumatized by the experience.

A sexual dichotomy is apparently inherent in the juvenile system. Girls are more likely to be arrested for trivial offenses and remanded for less reason than males, especially in regard to sexual offenses.

More than 50 percent of property-related crimes are committed by 13.2 percent of the population—youth age eleven to seventeen. Juvenile stealing, however, is more a test of bravery than it is an attempt to make money. The problem of teenage murder and rape also seems to be exaggerated.

The first juvenile court was established in 1899 in Cook County, Illinois, in an attempt to keep children out of jail and to provide detention facilities for those who should not be on the streets. Certain major problems exist with the juvenile court system, such as presumption of guilt, lack of the traditional adversarial relationship between prosecutor and defender, and rushed procedural processes. Because of these problems, alternatives are being considered that use modern concepts of the origins of juvenile delinquency. Some of these ideas include restitution through labor on civic projects and the removal of status offenses from the court's jurisdiction, ceding them to public agencies, clinics, and schools. Some have suggested reserving the juvenile justice system for more serious offenders.

References

Adams, G. R., & T. Gullotta. 1983. *Adolescent life experiences.* Monterey, Calif.: Brooks/Cole.
Ausubel, D. P., & E. V. Sullivan. 1970. *Theory and problems of child development.* 2d ed. New York: Grune & Stratton.
Bellotti v. Baird, 443 U.S. 622 (1979).
Bronfenbrenner, U. 1968. Response to pressure from peers versus adults among Soviet and American school children. *International Journal of Psychology* 2: 199–207.
Chesney-Lind, M. 1974. Juvenile delinquency: The sexualization of female crime. *Psychology Today:* 43–66 (July).
Cloward, R. A., & L. E. Ohlin. 1960. *Delinquency and opportunity: A theory of delinquent gangs.* New York: Free Press.
Deitz, G. E. 1969. A comparison of delinquents with nondelinquents on self-concept, self-acceptance, and parental identification. *Journal of Genetic Psychology* 115(2): 285.
Douglas, J. W. B., J. M. Ross, W. A. Hammond, & D. G. Mulligan. 1966. Delinquency and social class. *British Journal of Criminology* 6: 294–302.

Durkheim, E. 1958. *The rules of sociological method*. Trans. S. A. Solovay & J. M. Mueller, New York: Free Press.
Farrington, D. P., L. Biron, & M. LeBlanc. 1982. Personality and delinquency in London and Montreal. In *Abnormal offenders: delinquency and the criminal justice system*. Ed. by J. C. Grunn and D. P. Farrington. New York: Wiley.
Finckenauer, J. O. 1982. *Juvenile awareness project*. Englewood Cliffs, N.J.: Prentice-Hall.
Florida States Annotated. 1974. Chap. 39, sec. 11 and 12.
Fox, R. 1971. The XYY offender: A modern myth? *Journal of Criminal Law, Criminology, and Police Science* 62: 59–73.
In Re Gault, 387 U. S. 1 (1967).
Goldman, N. 1976. The differential selection of juvenile offenders for court appearances. In *The ambivalent force*, ed. A. Niederhoffer & A. S. Blumber, 183–87. New York: Holt, Rinehart & Winston.
Griffin, B. S., & C. T. Griffin. 1978. *Juvenile delinquency in perspective*. New York: Harper & Row.
Hartl, E. M., E. P. Monnelly, & R. D. Elderkins. 1982. *Physique and delinquent behavior*. New York: Academic Press.
Healy, W., & A. Bronner. 1936. *New light on delinquency and its treatment*. New Haven, Conn.: Yale Univ. Press.
Homer, L. 1973. Community-based resources for runaway girls. *Social Casework* 54(8): 473–79.
Jensen, G., & D. Rojek. 1980. *Delinquency: A sociological view*. Lexington: Heath.
Johnson, R., & M. Carter. 1980. Flight of the young—Why children run away from their homes. *Adolescence* 15(58): 483–89.
Lambroso, C. 1876. *L'uamo delinquente*. Milan: Hoepi.
Lewis, D. O., S. S. Shanok, & D. A. Balla. 1979. Perinatal difficulties, head and face trauma and child abuse in the medical history of serious youthful offenders. *American Journal of Psychiatry* 136: 288–92.
Lewis, D. O., S. S. Shanok, J. H. Pincus, & G. H. Glaser. 1979. Violent juvenile delinquents: Psychiatric, neurological, psychological, and abuse factors. *Journal of American Academy of Child Psychiatry* 18: 307–19.
Libertoff, K. 1980. The runaway child in America: A social history. *Journal of Family Issues* 1: 151-64.
McClelland, A. M. 1982. Changing rates of changing roles—adolescent female delinquency reassessed. *Adolescence* 5: 85–98.
McCord, W., J. McCord, & I. K. Zda. 1959. *Origins of crime*. New York: Columbia Univ. Press.
McCune, S., & D. L. Stodder. 1965. Juvenile court judges in the United States. *Crime and Delinquency* 11: 121–31.
Merton, R. K. 1957. *Social theory and social structure*. New York: Free Press.
Neapolitan, J. 1981. Parental influences on aggressive behavior: A social learning approach. *Adolescence* 16 (64): 831–39.
Planned Parenthood of Missouri v. *Danforth*, 428 U.S. 52(1976).
President's Commission on Law Enforcement and Administration of Justice. 1967. *The challenge of crime in a free society*. Washington, D.C.: U.S. Government Printing Office.
Proverbs 22:6.
Roberts, A. R. 1982. Adolescent runaways in suburbia: A new typology. *Adolescence* 17(66): 387–95.
Robey, A., R. Rosenwald, J. E. Shell, & R. E. Lee. 1964. The runaway girl. A reaction to family stress. *American Journal of Orthopsychiatry* 34: 762–66.
Rogers, S., & A. Leunes. 1979. A psychometric and behavioral comparison of delinquents who were abused as children with their non-abused peers. *Journal of Clinical Psychology* 35(2): 470–72.
Sanders, W. B. 1981. *Juvenile delinquency: Causes, patterns, and reactions*. New York: Holt, Rinehart & Winston.
Shanok, S. S. 1981. Medical histories of abused delinquents. *Child Psychiatry and Human Development* 2(4): 222–31.

Sheldon, W. H., S. S. Stevens, & W. B. Tucker. 1940. *The varieties of human physique*. New York: Harper & Row.

Shirer, W. L. 1959. *The rise and fall of the Third Reich*. New York: Simon & Schuster.

Silbert, M. H., & A. M. Pines. 1982. Entrance into prostitution. *Youth and Society* 13(4): 478–500.

Snider, S. J., & W. C. Murphy. 1975. Discipline—What can it teach? *Elementary School Journal* 75: 299–303.

Sprinthall, N. A., & A. W. Collins. 1982. *Adolescent psychology: readings*. Mass: Addison-Wesley.

Stott, D. 1982. *Delinquency: The problem and its prevention*. New York: Spectrum.

Sutherland, E. M., & D. R. Cressey. 1978. *Criminology*. 5th ed. Philadelphia: Lippincott.

Time. 1977. Youth for sale on the streets. 28 November, 23.

Trojanowitz, R. 1978. *Juvenile delinquency—Concepts and control*. New York: Prentice-Hall.

Tunley, R. 1978. Don't let them take me back! *Reader's Digest,* January, 96–100.

U. S. Department of Justice. 1982. *Dealing with serious repeat juvenile offenders*. Office of Juvenile Justice and Delinquency Prevention. Washington, D.C.: U.S. Government Printing Office.

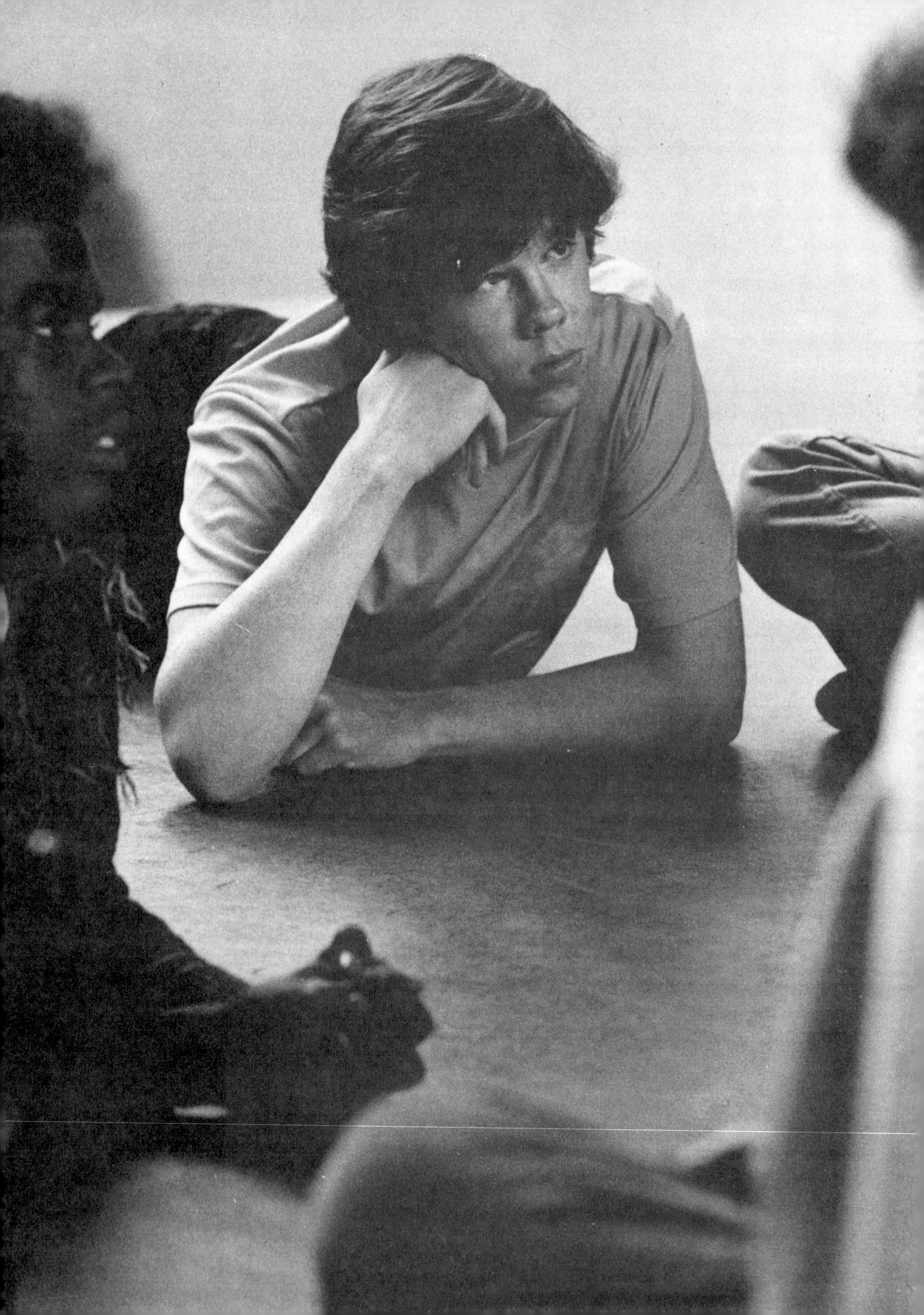

CHAPTER FOURTEEN

Thinking and intelligence

SURVEY AND QUESTIONS

In this chapter the student will find the following topics discussed and the associated questions answered:

Piaget's Theory of Learning

How is Piaget's theory different from those of American psychologists?
How can a person act upon the environment and reconstruct reality?
How does one acquire a knowledge of the external world?
How does a person interact with the external world?
What are physical experiences and logical-mathematical experiences?

Adolescent Thinking

What does Piaget believe about the importance of age factors in individual development and learning?
What are the characteristics of Piaget's developmental stages?

Change in Cognitive Development and Formal Operations

Is it possible to speed up the progression through the stages of development?
How does the formal operations stage influence an adolescent's education?
How can Piaget's ideas be specifically applied?
What is equilibration?
Do the writings of Piaget apply to social relationships in a practical way?
How does the movement into formal operations influence adolescents' thinking about themselves?

The Concept of Intelligence and Intelligence Testing

What is intelligence?
Are intelligence tests reliable, valid, and valuable?
What are the criticisms of intelligence tests?
Can a person be highly intelligent in some areas and less intelligent in others?
What is the significance of believing that intelligence consists of separate factors?
Is intelligence inherited or learned?
Are there racial differences in intelligence?
What is the practical implication of use and discussion of IQ tests?

> But all of these specific attitudes pale into insignificance compared with something else I have learned of: the astounding level of ignorance of the Southern California teenager. No amount of preparation could possibly cushion the blows of unawareness of even the most elementary current events, history, politics, economics, or just what goes on each day in the world outside of Los Angeles which lurks in the cheerful minds of these children.
>
> Of the (at least) twelve whom I have asked, none has known within forty million what the population of the United States is. Only two could tell me where Chicago is, even in the vaguest terms. (My particularly favorite geography lesson was the junior at the University of California at Los Angeles (UCLA) who thought that Toronto must be in Italy. . . .
>
> Within the last week, I watched a television news show about the so-called "lifting" of martial law in Poland. On the screen were pictures of Poles in large pen-like enclosures rounded up after martial law began. One of my assistants, a junior at USC, stared at the screen open-mouthed.
>
> "What's going on there?" she asked. "Why are those people in that big cage?"
>
> I explained that they had been imprisoned as the result of a crackdown by the Communist government. "Why don't they just leave and come to L.A.?" she asked. (Stein 1983, 19)

These humorous observations made by Benjamin J. Stein have some data backing from the National Assessment of Educational Progress (1977). Using a national sample of 3,500, the NAEP concluded that at age seventeen, youth still cannot deal with many problems. For example, few are able to determine among different-sized boxes of rice which is the best buy. Most automatically choose the large size without calculating. Only one-third can make conversions with measures geometry or solve word problems with more than one step. Only half can understand the fine print obligations in many contracts, such as joining a book club. Less than half can identify the author's point of view in a first-year college textbook or write a clear essay.

Locating specific information gaps among youth and using these deficiencies as a general criticism of youth today is not difficult. In the chapter on education, the fallacy of concluding that today's youth are intellectually inferior to the same-age cohorts of previous generations was discussed. One way to understand some of these seeming discrepancies of fact is to separate quantity from quality when discussing intelligence or thinking. Quantity refers to the amount that has been learned or can be learned per unit of time. Quality refers to the kind or way of thinking. During adolescence a qualitative change occurs in the type of thinking employed (Elkind 1968).

To fully understand this change in qualitative differences, we need to understand Piaget's theory. Piaget proposed a radically different theory about the development of the mind, which has had the most significant impact on the study of cognitive development in the latter half of this century (Piaget 1952, 1954, 1955). Turning now to this serious scholar-researcher, we will first look at a theory of the mind.

Piaget's theory of learning

For over fifty years, Jean Paul Piaget (1896–1980), a French developmentalist, studied the growth of intelligence and the structure of the human mind. He began his work on cognitive functioning in Alfred Binet's Paris laboratory, where the beginning of modern intelligence testing originated. Piaget disagreed with Binet's insistence that intelligence is a fixed phenomenon, and began to explore the possibility of acquiring higher-level thought processes (Piaget and Inhelder 1958).

A prolific writer, Piaget reported many provocative discoveries regarding the structure of cognitive thought processes. His original works, however, were often unavailable or laborious to read; many students and researchers rely on various summary sources and interpretive writings, such as Flavell's *The Developmental Psychology of Jean Piaget* (1963) and Furth's *Piaget and Knowledge* (1969).

Only in the last decade have American psychologists given Piaget the attention he has merited in the area of developmental psychology, partially because his works were at first not translated into English. The major obstacle to acceptance by American psychologists, however, was Piaget's departure from American assumptions about the development of the mind.

QUESTION: How is Piaget's theory different from those of American psychologists?

Piaget's conception of knowledge is different from the associationistic and seemingly commonsense point of view of Western culture. The associationistic point of view is that people at birth have empty minds. They soon become surrounded by external stimuli that subsequently form the mind. These external stimuli are made up of the world one knows and understands. Human knowledge is simply an imperfect copy of the external world and is made up of individual perceptions, images, and understanding. The learning goal of each individual is to somehow accurately symbolize the content of the external world within the mind. This task is often accomplished through the use of language. Associationism claims that almost anything can be taught to any child if it is presented on an appropriate level. Piaget, however, maintained that all individuals have to actually act upon the external world; they must personally reconstruct that world to truly know it. Without this constant action and reconstruction, a person remains stationary and undeveloped.

QUESTION: How can a person act upon the environment and reconstruct reality?

People act upon their environment and reconstruct reality by forming schemata that enable them to find complex solutions to everyday occurrences. The human mind comes to know the external world through individual mental constructs, cognitive structures, and mental operations. An example of a schema is the idea of "object permanency." Prior to about the age of ten months, children have the notion that if any object is not in their immediate field of vision, it does not exist. After the age of ten months, children become aware that an object exists in spite of various perceptions. Once children realize that objects can reappear after they disappear, they have made a major step in learning about object permanency. Although this fundamental notion of the permanence of objects seems extremely simple, object permanence is a prerequisite schema for further, more advanced operations. Piaget explained that only through interaction between the child and objects can this knowledge come about. Not possible is acquiring this knowledge by mere copying and passive imitation of the external world. Piaget maintained that children must personally reconstruct (learn or make) their own schema regarding the permanence of objects in order to make it part of their own respective reality.

A series of schemes is called "schemata," and an act of the mind is called a "construct." The totality of these interrelated substructures is called the "cognitive structure." Different schemata can be created at different points in development. The schema of object permanance is achieved during the first year of an infant's life. Another example of a schema that occurs later in the child's life is the schema of "conservation of volume." When children are presented with two glasses filled with equal amounts of liquid, they correctly perceive that the amount of liquid is the same in the two containers. If the contents of one container are poured into a short, wide jar, and the contents of the other glass are poured into a tall, narrow jar, children will maintain that more liquid is in the tall, narrow jar than in the short, wide jar. Children are seemingly unable to consider perceptual distortions and do not have the rudimentary logic required to understand the conservation of volume. The conservation of volume is a fundamental property of matter and must be understood to acquire more advanced knowledge of the related external world.

QUESTION: How does one acquire a knowledge of the external world?

According to Piaget, a knowledge of the external world is not merely a learned response, but is also brought about by active interaction with the environment

Solving problems is probably the most fundamental method of learning about the external world for individuals.

and also by physiological and psychological maturation. To create a correct schema, active interaction must be accompanied by accurate reasoning. If people make a decision only on the basis of what appears to their senses, they will be mistaken. To achieve a schema about the conservation of volume, one must logically reason that nothing is added or taken away from equal amounts of liquid, and that the amounts will remain the same even though their appearance might change. Piaget therefore argued that all schemata come about not by passive experiences, but by the force of logic and interaction with the external world.

QUESTION: How does a person interact with the external world?

Piaget used the terms *assimilation* and *accommodation* to explain the processes of interaction. Assimilation is used much as it is in biology. For example, the assimilation of food includes both ingestion and digestion as the food is transformed into a form useful to the organism; in other words, the food is changed. Correspondingly, when a child interacts with the environment, assimilation refers to the changing of raw sensory experiences into a form that fits into the existing structure system or schemata of the child. People assimilate new experiences, such as tasting, touching, and perception, to fit their existing schemata. Older youth assimilate external information into existing words or mental categories. The person therefore changes the external world.

Accommodation refers to a process of changing existing schemata or constructing new cognitive structures to be more compatible with current experiences. Accommodation is an active process usually involving such acts as questioning, manipulation, doing things differently, and so on. As individuals solve problems and inconsistencies through these activities, they often create new schemata for acting upon the external world.

Cognitive structures and schemata constitute knowledge of the external world, that is, how an individual fits into the real world. The acts of assimilation and accommodation occur simultaneously. In any new situation, experiences are either assimilated into existing structures or accommodated by changing existing structures. This interplay is called *adaptation,* and a *state of equilibrium* is reached when the processes function normally. An inaccurately assimilated bit of information elicits a cognitive state called *centration,* where one centers on one aspect of a perceived event to the disregard of other salient aspects. Piaget called this naive state *egocentrism*. The growth of intelligence requires individuals to change their egocentric view of the world and to develop a more mature accommodation of other perspectives.

QUESTION: What are physical experiences and logical-mathematical experiences?

Piaget's beliefs regarding physical experiences and logical-mathematical experiences are closely related to the concepts of assimilation and accomodation. Essentially, physical experiences require continual processes of abstracting and identifying properties in objects and events. Physical experiences act upon individuals; the individuals themselves are relatively passive in the process. This passiveness is exemplified as a younger person learns about object properties such as shape, color, and so on. No logical reasons can explain most of an object's attributes. For example, a banana is elongated and yellow, but an apple is round and red. In summary, physical learning is similar to what is ordinarily called "rote learning," and includes both classical and operant conditioning. Conversely, in logical-mathematical experiences, a person acts upon things, and this includes such concepts as direction, movement, causality, and quantity. The interaction not only is motor or manual manipulation (or both), but also is mental or perceptual manipulation as well. A single, long row of five pennies may look longer than two short rows totaling five pennies, yet older children learn that five pennies remain five pennies even though they are arranged in different patterns. The conservation of five pennies is the same no matter how the pennies are arranged; this illustrates a simple logical-mathematical operation. In the example of the conservation of volumes of liquid in different containers, a person also imposes a logical-mathematical operation to learn that the quantity of the object does not change when the shape is altered. What the person learns is a new relationship, sometimes called "insight" by other psychologists.

Adolescent thinking

QUESTION: What does Piaget believe about the importance of age factors in individual development and learning?

Piaget believed that age is an important factor in the capacity for learning. The chronological age is not the critical element of maturational development, but age is associated with progression through the stages. For example, physical experiences are more simple by nature than are logical-mathematical experiences. Maturity into adolescence increases the capacity to learn through logical-mathematical experiences. The age sequence is displayed in Table 14–1.

TABLE 14–1 Piaget's Stages in Mental Development

Stage	Typical Activities
1. Sensorimotor (birth–age 1½)	Perception, recognition, and coordination
2. Preoperational (age 1½–6) Preconceptual Intuitive thinking	Comprehension of simple functional relations; symbolic play
3. Concrete operations (age 6–11)	Invariant structures of operations, class, relations, conservations, and seriation
4. Formal operational (puberty and adolescence)	Propositional and hypothetical thinking

Essentially, Piaget's stage theory proposes that mental structures are developed in sequential directions; that is, mental structures occur in a sequence of increasing complexity. The later stages are dependent upon completion of the previous stages. A progressive integration of the lower stages into higher stages occurs by actually incorporating the lower-level accomplishments into increasingly abstract logical-mathematical patterns of thinking. Mental development is therefore orderly and follows basic time schedules. Developmental changes (learning) are highly influenced by maturation. Although environments can influence the acquisition of thought processes, the person is largely subject to natural development maintained through self-regulations.

QUESTION: What are the characteristics of Piaget's developmental stages?

During each of the developmental stages, certain learning processes are achieved. The sensorimotor stage begins with the reflexes that exist at birth and last through the motor manipulations that are achieved toward the end of the year. The basic quest for a child in this stage is to gain the ability to deal with objects.

As children leave the sensorimotor stage and enter the stage of operational thought, they gain the ability to manipulate symbols that represent the environment. In simple terms, an operation is a mental action. Children are only able to evaluate or synthesize actual events. For example, they first have the ability to imitate the actions and speech of people around them (concrete entities), but do not have the capacity to comprehend another person's point of view, because a point of view is not tangible.

When children pass to the concrete operational stage of development around the age of six, they become capable of elementary logical thought. Logical thought can exist only after children have sufficient experience with their environment, have gathered a store of relevant concepts, and have mentally organized these thoughts. The thoughts at this stage are called "concrete operations" because they have grown out of the overt actions of the sensorimotor period.

During the period of formal operations (11–15 years), adolescents become capable of performing operations upon operations. Piaget described these operations upon operations as "second-order operations." For example, as weight and volume become operational for adolescents, they can then perform the operation of proportion, which allows them to place the two other operations in a logical relationship to each other. Adolescents in the formal operations stage also become capable of formulating hypotheses and working out the results of these hypotheses without manipulating concrete objects. Adolescents in this stage can also follow an argument by form, and yet disregard its content.

Formal operations include four basic logical abilities. The first is the ability to make hypotheses and to use deductive thinking, such as is used in the scientific method or in problem solving. The second ability is inductive thinking, which is the ability to form conclusions based on data or information. These two abilities, deductive and inductive thinking, are usually used simultaneously. The third ability is reflective thinking, which is the ability to think about thoughts so as to reflect on individual mental processes or to analyze the thoughts of another person. This skill is necessary for analyzing and criticizing in logical arguments and debates and for understanding other people's points of view. Reflective thinking would include the ability to answer the question, "Should there be mandatory arms control?" or "Should the sale of handguns be regulated?" The fourth ability is interpropositional logic. This is the same as the ability to analyze logical arguments. For example, analyze the following:

Proposition 1: All women are reckless drivers.

Proposition 2: Reckless drivers should be put in jail.

Conclusion: All women should be put in jail.

Adolescents should be able to analyze that the conclusion does follow from the two propositions. If they do not want to accept conclusions, they should then have the ability to question the validity of the propositions. This is what Piaget called "formal propositional logic," the ability to combine and validate propositions.

Even though these four types of thinking commonly occur in adolescents, not all children obtain the skills that would classify their thinking as formal operations. In most studies, approximately 50 percent of adult subjects perform at the formal operational level (Neimark 1975; Keating 1980).

Change in cognitive development and formal operations

QUESTION: Is it possible to speed up the progression through the stages of development?

Piaget considered this question typically American. He felt it was a product of the American temperament and did not think the question was useful. Modern Piagetians feel that little or nothing can be gained by trying to accelerate the natural development pattern. They propose that time, repetition, and self-discovery produce a stronger, more enduring qualitative change than formal training to master a given concept.

Piagetians agree, however, that early experience can be beneficial. A promising and comprehensive study combined the research on effects of twelve different investigations of infant and preschool programs. The study found that this early intervention had a number of long-term effects. Children who had progressed through these programs were less likely to be assigned to special education classes or to fail promotion. They did better on IQ tests for several years after the program, but this effect eventually diminished. The effect was more permanent on achievement tests. Children who had attended the early programs were more likely to have positive attitudes in values about themselves, school achievement, and work (Lazer and Darlington 1984).

QUESTION: How does the formal operations stage influence an adolescent's education?

During the stage of formal operations, adolescents are able to think about thinking or to perform operations upon operations. In other words, they can deal with hypothetical situations and abstractions, and can understand the basic elements of the scientific method.

Although Piaget himself did not attempt to apply his theory specifically to parenting or education, voluminous literature has since developed that focuses on the applications of Piaget's theory. In review, Piaget's theory presents ideas on how a child progresses from one stage of intellectual development to the next. Many adults feel that the purpose of education is to help a child reach higher levels of intelligence. If this goal is accepted, Piaget's theory has relevance for educators. Piaget viewed intellectual development as a continuous progression through a series of invariant stages. This concept has been interpreted by educators to mean that here is an optimum time and manner for curricula to be presented.

Perhaps an even more important contribution that Piaget has made is that of drawing attention to the need for activity in the learning process. For example, to the naive observer, play and the manipulation of objects seem to have little importance and impact upon development. Piaget, however, considered the stimulation received through interactions such as these to be a crucial determinant in the development of intelligence. Adequate opportunities to receive stimulation and to interact with objects are the most important requirements for effective learning. Although this is true of both children and adolescents, it is particularly important during the preoperational stages of an individual's life.

According to some Piagetian educators, introducing conceptual tasks such as arithmetic too early may be harmful because the youth will develop negative reactions. Children that are too young are unable to conceptually handle the concepts required for appropriate mathematical operations. Instead, they learn verbal names and patterns of speech that suggest difficult concepts when in fact they do not. To ascertain children's actual understanding, parents or teachers can probe children in ways similar to those which Piaget used.

In school systems that focus on verbal skills and memorization, children may actually be kept from learning basic elements and important logical-mathematical operations by being required to memorize by rote verbal or numerical operations. For example, children may learn multiplication tables, but may not understand the logical processes for which they have verbal skills. Because schools

Most youth have the necessary motivation if the learning task is presented properly. Personal computers may offer new and more interesting ways for students to learn.

and parents frequently evaluate a child's achievement in terms of verbal ability, a number of errors in assessing the child's development are often made. Some children may have acquired fluent verbal skills and yet may not be able to reason clearly or understand conceptual matter. Other children may understand important and necessary concepts, but may be unable to verbally describe these concepts to the satisfaction of their teachers. Both situations produce errors in the evaluation of a child's true developmental progress. This result suggests that there should be a de-emphasis on language and verbal learning with an accompanying emphasis on *learning to think*.

Perhaps one of the strongest spokespersons for de-emphasizing verbal skills and languages is Hans Furth (1970). He encourages educators to use curricula that are oriented toward development according to a Piagetian stage sequence. For example, in teaching new concepts, Furth argues that a better approach is teaching the common property or relationship first, and then *later* teaching the ability to describe it.

Piaget also made applicable assumptions about the nature of motivation. He assumed that motivation is an integral and internal aspect of development. Young people continually act and move in an effort to achieve equilibrium between their own processes of assimilation and accommodation. An unnecessary or superfluous process is for adults to introduce to children additional motivation such as external rewards, and so on.

People are not passive learners; they are not sponges that passively soak up liquidlike knowledge. Young people are busy, active participants in life. Although books, lectures, and television can assist in the quest for knowledge, the processes of manipulating and experimenting with real objects in their immediate world teach faster, and have a greater impact with longer-lasting effects. These and other major applications of Piaget's theory are summarized in Box 14–1.

BOX 14–1 APPLICATIONS OF PIAGET'S THEORY

1. The basic purpose of education is to teach people how to think and how to develop their minds, not to simply give them knowledge.
2. For maximum learning to occur, children must be taught on the basis of their dominant mode of thinking and stage of development.
3. Playing and manipulating objects are critical elements of learning during the early childhood years.
4. Trying to accelerate specific patterns of children's thinking processes is inadvisable.
5. Providing a stimulating environment and freedom of experience are the most important elements in effective teaching.
6. Formal language training is less important than development of thought and should preferably be delayed.
7. Mental growth can be better ascertained by analyzing the ability to think rather than by judging their performance on standardized IQ tests.
8. Fluent verbal skills are not an indicator of a person's ability to conceptualize matter.
9. Errors on a test are not always appropriate evaluations of development. Rather, persons should be evaluated from the perspective of the dominant type of mental operations and structures that are appropriate for their age.
10. There is no such thing as "wrong" thinking.
11. A communication gap exists between adults and children because of differences in their respective reasoning abilities, not because of differences in their language abilities.
12. Motivation is a natural part of human growth and need not be compelled from without (e.g., by introducing external rewards).
13. The best way to facilitate development is to present youth with problems that are appropriate to their developmental growth level.
14. Dilemmas and problems facilitate learning processes because they create disequilibrium, which then causes the mind to form new operations, structures, and schemata to bring about equilibrium.

QUESTION: How can Piaget's ideas be specifically applied?

An important application for educators emerges from Piaget's analysis: The basis of education must be to help a child learn to form appropriate operations. An advisable procedure is to present situations that require the child to construct or form mental structures. This process promotes accommodation. Although the importance of assimilating already developed structures is not to be minimized, developing new structures out of accommodation is the most essential task necessary for growth. Operations can be understood only when one actually performs the operations. This implies that during the early stages of development, one should be allowed to make operations on concrete objects. During the later stages of formal operations, adolescents should be presented with situations in which they can manipulate previously held ideas or knowledge to obtain or develop new, mature structures and operations.

QUESTION: What is equilibration?

Equilibration is a self-regulatory mechanism similar to the biological concept of homeostasis. Homeostasis means "balance." For Piaget, intellectual structures function as a total system that seeks balance, although the structures can be modified by the intrusion of sensory information. New sensory experiences cause disequilibration (an imbalance), which in turn causes a process of construction resulting in new structures or schemata. During the early stages, mental structures are not in a stable state of equilibrium, and are frequently modified and added upon as one moves from lower to higher stages of development. These structures are in higher states of equilibrium as the child progresses toward the more advanced stages. For example, at the stage of formal operations, the basic structures are relatively stable and will undergo less modification than they did in earlier stages. Equilibrium at the highest stage of formal operations is achieved by moving between one structure and another, or by focusing on more than one element (decentering). Disequilibration between two or more focuses provides motivation for the adolescent. Practically speaking, to effect a structural change during the formal operations stage, a problem-solving activity is initiated, which in turn causes disequilibrium and movement toward equilibrium. Most students of Piaget base their concept of motivation upon the principle of equilibrium, and feel that providing an individual with a problem (i.e., a discrepancy between what the person believes and external information) is the optimal way to increase human motivation.

QUESTION: Do the writings of Piaget apply to social relationships in a practical way?

Elkind, a follower of Piaget, applies the Piagetian theory to interpersonal relationships (Elkind 1981). During the stage of formal operations, an adolescent becomes able to formulate hypotheses or plans of ways to respond to adult pressures. Sometimes the plans are congruent with those of adults, and sometimes they are directly opposite to adult expectations, which helps to explain why adolescent rebelliousness seems to be of a different nature than childhood rebelliousness. Adolescents are able to perceive a gap between the ideal world that some adults verbally espouse and the real world that adolescents know.

They may see for the first time that some adults are hypocrites—living one way yet stating ideals to the contrary. The first stage of the consequent rebelliousness is often to criticize existing institutions and people, rather than to try to change the institutions or to understand the reasons for the discrepancy between thoughts and actions in some individuals. Adolescents believe that they can see possible alternatives to adult life-styles, which causes them to rebel against and criticize adults. From early experience, however, adolescents come to understand the real world from a more seasoned perspective, and to see the different roles, responsibilities, and discrepancies of the world in a different light. Adolescents' rebelliousness therefore lessens as they mature and see other points of view including those of people who are in authority.

QUESTION: How does the movement into formal operations influence adolescents' thinking about themselves?

When adolescents enter the formal operational stage, they become capable of thinking both introspectively and theoretically. They are therefore able to observe and think about themselves in an objective way for the first time. Adolescents can now understand the reactions of others toward them and the discrepancy between the theoretical ideal self and the real self. Adolescents themselves become capable of deceptively thinking one thing and saying another. They lose that pure innocence so typical of childhood. They can hide their thoughts from others. With this ability, they can interact in new ways with parents and with others. This newly discovered sense of self then moves them to experiment with various roles and ways of behavior.

Speaking about the changes resulting from formal operation, one writer observes:

> It has appeared that intellectual transformations bring the youngster to ask himself questions about himself, to understand himself, to acknowledge himself, just as much as do the physical transformations and just about the same time. The values that the adolescent is "trying out," not without paradoxes and sophisms, the opinions that he defends sometimes with as much fire as thoughtlessness, are these not just so many ways of looking for himself, of defining himself, so many attempts to be and become himself (Osterrieth 1969, 15–16)

The concept of intelligence and intelligence testing

When Gregory Ochoa was a high school student in California, he and his classmates were given an IQ test. Gregory and the other students were told that the results would enable the school to place them in classes commensurate with their skills. It seemed like a fair thing to do; after all, they were all being given the same chance, the same test.

But, after looking at the test questions, Gregory discovered that he just didn't understand many of the words, and he couldn't understand exactly what he was supposed to do.

Spanish was the language spoken in his home, and his English skills were not quite equal to those of most of his classmates. Gregory, and a few others who were having the same trouble, pointed out their difficulty to the person administering the test. They were told, "Do the best you can."

A few weeks after taking the test, Gregory found himself in a "special" class. Most of the other students in the class also had Spanish surnames . . . Gregory didn't fully realize what had happened. He never understood the term "educable mentally retarded" which was written on the teacher's letterhead and on the bulletin board in the classroom. All Gregory knew was that his special class didn't do regular school work. Gregory's teacher was sort of a coach, and they played a lot of soccer. Any class member interested in intellectual pursuits, such as going to the school library, found that such activities were out of bounds.

Gregory soon dropped out of school. He drifted about and got into trouble. He was sent to a reform school where he received some remedial reading. After reform school he joined the navy. He scored well on the navy tests. They never told him what his IQ was on retesting, but they seemed pleased that a retarded person could do so well. While in the navy Gregory earned high school credits, which eventually enabled him to attend college as a student on probation. His first quarter in college he received all A's. His second quarter he again received all A's, but he was kept on probation. Gregory finally graduated from San Jose City College on the dean's list as an honor student—on probation! The college was apparently unable to think of him as no longer "mentally retarded." By the age of forty, Gregory Ochoa was an assistant professor at the University of Washington in Seattle, where he taught classes in social casework.

When asked whether he thinks IQ tests should still be given, Gregory Ochoa said:

> I think first of all, one would have to ask why you want to know what this person's intellectual capacity is. Are you using it in order to make sure that every horizon available to him is reached, or are you using it to diminish his opportunities or to prove to him, or to oneself, that Blacks, or Chicanos, or other minorities are inherently inferior to others. I think that is the critical issue—what is it being used for? (Dworetzky 1981, 347–48)

This example is extreme, but illustrates another way to look at intelligence. Piaget focuses on mental development, but American and British research typically jump right into the quest to measure intelligence.

QUESTION: What is intelligence?

Was Mozart brilliant when one considers that he handled his money so poorly that he was always running away from creditors? Was Einstein intelligent when we consider his academic record was mediocre as a young man? For centuries we have tried to specify what is meant by the words *genius, bright, dull,* and so on. To date, no acceptable definitions have emerged.

The word *intelligence* has no exact definition, but generally it refers to the ability of individuals to act purposefully, to think rationally, and to deal effectively with their environment. To avoid confusion about the meaning of the phrases "dealing effectively with the environment" and "purposeful and rational behavior," psychologists have relied heavily upon an operational definition of intelligence to measure high and low intelligence. An operational definition means that a method or operation of measurement has been established that is objective and public. For the concept of intelligence this means that intelligence is defined as what a specific intelligence test measures.

QUESTION: Are intelligence tests reliable, valid, and valuable?

Of all psychological testing procedures, none are based on a more solid research base than are intelligence tests. Both individual and group-administered intelligence tests are reliable. Reliability refers to measuring consistently over a time period. Whether intelligence tests actually measure "real intelligence" is more questionable. This question is one of validity. To further understand validity, let us consider the origin of intelligence testing.

The first informal intelligence test was made by Alfred Binet in 1904. He was commissioned by the French government to develop a test that would predict which youngsters would do well in school and which would not do well. Binet found he could predict how youngsters would do in school by examining their answers to different types of questions. The questions requested general information about vocabulary, arithmetic, culture, and science, and presented situations that required problem-solving skills. Subsequent tests developed by other researchers have fairly well followed the general pattern that Binet devised. They have been validated principally upon successful prediction of school success. Although school success is not always an accurate indicator of intelligence, it is a fairly useful concept in student evaluation, student placement, and other areas in which decisions must be made regarding student behaviors. In general, IQ tests are good predictors of school success and are probably the most sophisticated, reliable, and valid tests psychologists have yet developed (Wayne and Wallace 1971; Feldhusen et al. 1974).

IQ scores, however, have not been very successful in predicting achievement or success in other areas (Berg 1970) or achievement in later life (Wallace 1976). Researchers have stated, "A person can obtain a very high IQ score and still not behave very admirably in the real world" (Zigler and Trickett 1978).

Nevertheless, predicting success in academic pursuits, such as school, on-the-job training, and university graduation, is a significant achievement. Perhaps the most impressive study comes from a follow-up of 1,500 California schoolchildren who were having IQs of 140 or more, qualified as mentally gifted. The study traced the subjects from childhood to their middle-age years. The surprising finding was that these geniuses did not match the popular stereotype. They were above average in height, weight, and appearance, and were superior in social activity, leadership, and personal adjustment. A large portion of these subjects went to college, had high academic records, and made important contributions (Terman 1925). In reviewing the results of this long-term study of geniuses, one reviewer stated:

> Findings such as these establish beyond a doubt that IQ tests measure characteristics that are obviously of considerable importance in our present technological society. To say that the kind of ability measured by intelligence tests is irrelevant or unimportant would be tanamount to repudiating civilization as we know it. (Jensen 1972, 9)

QUESTION: What are the criticisms of intelligence tests?

One major criticism is that factors other than innate intelligence influence intelligence test scores. For example, adolescents with high anxiety do not do as well on IQ tests as do people who have more emotional security. Another example is that some children, especially middle-class children, are much more motivated than children from other socioeconomic classes to perform well on school-based assessments such as IQ tests (Stennet 1969; and Cavalli-Sforza 1970; Scarr-Salatapek 1971). In addition, children from some low socioeconomic classes may grow up in an environment in which words are not as important or significant as they are in the middle-class family. These children therefore tend to perform poorly on the high-verbal IQ tests. Children from families whose primary language is one other than English tend to experience some first-language retardation, which negatively influences their IQ scores.

Perhaps the biggest popular criticism of intelligence testing is the classification or labeling that often results following testing. One student writes:

> My little sister had taken I.Q. tests in junior high because she was having problems with school. She has trouble functioning or dealing on a symbolic or abstract level. She scored quite low on the I.Q. tests and the counselor was afraid she would not be able to graduate from high school. Heidi was not told the results of the I.Q. scores, she did have difficulty in her schoolwork but mother and dad really pushed her and gave her extra help. They employed tutors and talked to her teachers and did all that they could to help her. Heidi is graduating from high school this year. She has done much better than any of us expected, which shows how much environment makes a difference. Because Heidi was slower in school the kids gave her a hard time in jr. high and also some in high school. This has made her feel that she was not accepted or part of the crowd. Recently Heidi has started dating which has really helped her self-confidence. Also Heidi has always come to the family for strength and encouragement. It is great to watch her overcome so much to feel success in her life! The I.Q. scores have affected the way the family and others have treated Heidi be it positive or negative.

Test scores are commonly interpreted with numbers, and labels such as *genius, dull, average,* and *superior* can have positive or negative connotations and can represent overgeneralizations. In some cases, children are assigned to classes for the mentally retarded on the basis of erroneous test scores. One mother related:

> We had moved four times in six years, meaning that we had changed schools four times. When my son was beginning junior high, he had some problems with math and English. The school tested him, found him lacking in some of the basic skills, and placed him in a special education class. This was a devastating experience for him. He was labeled "a retard," and it stayed with him until we moved again in his junior year in high school. Even though he was only in the special ed. class for a few months, his record followed him, and what was most difficult was the friends and associates who didn't expect him to achieve a great deal. It is interesting to note that when he was in a new environment, where he was expected to accomplish the same as his peers, he did just that and even excelled in some areas. He became editor of his high

school paper and received an academic scholarship to college. According to my son, being placed in that special ed. class was the lowest point in his life.

Unfortunately, children sometimes live up to the labels applied to them. In one popular study, which has not been successfully replicated, teachers were told that a certain 20 percent of the children in their classrooms would have marked academic growth during the school year. Eight months later, these 20 percent were found to have changed much more than other children in the class, even though they had been randomly selected. The only things that could account for the differences in academic growth were the labels given to the 20 percent (Rosenthal and Jacobson 1968).

Still another criticism of intelligence tests is that fluctuations tend to occur in an individual's IQ scores over time. In general, although researchers have found that the average fluctuations are less than ten points over twelve years, some individuals *do* change much more drastically (Pinneau 1961). Part of the problem in accounting for these fluctuations over time is the age at which the first testing is done. The correlation between adult intelligence and infant intelligence is zero (Anderson 1939). The older children are when tested, however, the more stable and reliable will be their test scores. In general, not until approximately age ten can reliable predictions be made of adult intelligence from the child's IQ score (Bloom 1964). Even at this age, however, studies have shown

Different ability levels are common amongst adolescents of the same age group. These varying levels reflect both experience and innate differences that may exist.

that considerable variations occur, and in a few exceptional cases, they fluctuate by as many as twenty IQ points. (Bayley 1970)

QUESTION: Can a person be highly intelligent in some areas and less intelligent in others?

Yes, and the following extreme example illustrates this notion, although the principle does apply to persons in the normal range of intelligence.

> Ask George in which recent years April 21 fell on a Sunday. Without hesitation he will answer: "1968, 1963, 1957, 1946." Surprisingly, this gives only the slightest hint of his skill. George will go back as far as 1700 with complete accuracy! He has "calendar calculations" covering a range of at least 6,000 years, extending centuries beyond present perceptual calendars. With equal ease he can identify February 15, 2002, [or] August 28, 1591 as a Wednesday. . . . George's abilities are all the more amazing in view of the fact he is mentally retarded and cannot add, subtract, multiply, or divide even simple numbers. (Coon 1983, 392)

George's case is unusual but exemplifies a research finding that people can vary substantially in different areas or aspects of intelligence. Early psychological theories tended to stress the concept that each person had an intelligence level that was consistent over a large number of subject areas and skills (Spearman 1927). More recent theories, however, stress that a person's intelligence may be high in some areas and low in others (Thurstone 1938; Guilford 1959, 1966, 1967).

Gardner (1983) recently identified six intelligences, each of which is controlled by a specific region of the brain. Two of them—the ability to use language and to reason logically or mathematically—are familiar. Gardner also includes musical ability, spatial skill to analyze the visual world (diagram), bodily talents like dance, and personal abilities such as access to one's own feelings and a capacity to perceive those of others. Although the intelligences can cooperate, each works in "splendid isolation." Studies of amnesiacs, for instance, suggest that each intelligence has its own memory bank. These patients might not remember conversations, but they can learn new songs and new faces.

> Each intelligence has its own life history, blooming and then fading at a certain time of life. Musical intelligence is the first to emerge . . . one can excel at music without having lived life very fully, but to excell at personal intelligence one must have experienced such emotions as love, anger and jealousy. (Gardner 1983).

J. P. Guilford (1972) also proposes a theory of intelligence which depicts specific areas of ability. He defines intelligence in terms of the type of *content* one is dealing with. The content may be, for example, words, behavior, patterns, or symbols. For each specific content, people use different *mental operations*. These mental operations may include memory, divergent production, evaluation, cognition, and convergent production. Finally, the interaction of the contents with the mental operations produces different types of mental *products,* called classes, relations, systems, units, transformations, and implications. These three components of the mind are displayed in Figure 14-1. Guilford identified these patterns from research using a statistical technique called factor analysis. Every individual has a specific combination of all three components that work together in unison. Guilford believes that at least one hundred abilities can be identified from combinations of these factors.

Figure 14-1 Guilford's Model Depicting the Structure of the Intellect

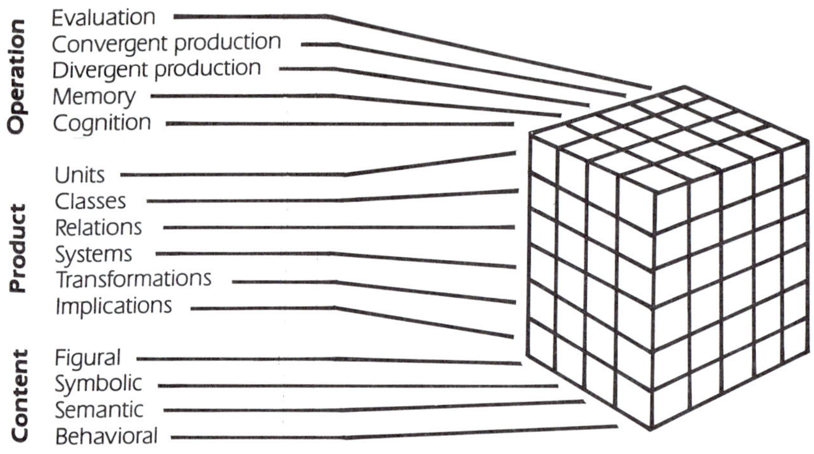

Operation
- Evaluation
- Convergent production
- Divergent production
- Memory
- Cognition

Product
- Units
- Classes
- Relations
- Systems
- Transformations
- Implications

Content
- Figural
- Symbolic
- Semantic
- Behavioral

Source: Guilford 1967, 63.

QUESTION: What is the significance of believing that intelligence consists of separate factors?

This type of theory demonstrates how some of the criticisms against intelligence testing can be ameliorated. For example, if intelligence comprises separate abilities that work together in unison, and one is aware of this, one would be less likely to label or classify someone (e.g., "slow") on the basis of a single aspect of intelligence. Even less likely is that a person would be classified as wholly smart, intelligent, or dumb, but would be considered as having a combination of strengths and weaknesses in each of the areas. Some people have an excellent ability to think logically and yet are not exceptional memorizers. Some people have great musical talent or verbal fluency, but do not do well at abstract reasoning. The concept of multiple abilities seems a more positive approach for evaluating intelligence.

The multiple-factors approach can be applied to vocational guidance because of its hypothesis that different types of intelligence exist. Individuals in occupational professions, such as carpentry, engineering, and architectural work, use mostly figure information; the ability to read diagrams, patterns, and shapes is essential. In academic research and study, however, lawyers and college professors must often use symbolic, semantic, abstract reasoning. Individuals in the helping professions, such as nurses and teachers, require a type of "human intelligence" to work with the underlying behavioral patterns of patients and students. These differences in the ability to excel in one or more vocational areas conform more with general experience than does the concept that a person has only one all-encompassing intellectual level.

QUESTION: Is intelligence inherited or learned?

A close analysis of the research leads to the conclusion that intelligence is both inherited and learned. Some of the evidence for a hereditary basis in intelligence comes from research findings on identical twins who were reared apart. These twins have IQs that are more similar than the IQs of fraternal twins who were reared together. Intelligence correlation coefficients of adopted children and their natural parents are higher than the coefficients of the same children paired with the foster parents with whom they had been raised. (Anastasi 1972). The data in Table 14–2 illustrate some of these findings.

TABLE 14–2 Correlations of Intelligence Test Scores

Correlations Between Individuals	Median Value
UNRELATED PERSONS	
Children reared apart	−.01
Children reared together	+.20
RELATED PERSONS	
Siblings, reared apart	+.46
Siblings, reared together	+.52
Fraternal twins, same sex	+.56
Identical twins, reared apart	+.75
Identical twins, reared together	+.87
Parent (as adult) and child	+.50
Parent (as child) and child	+.56

Source: Adapted from J. P. Dworetzky, *Psychology* (St. Paul: West Publishing, 1984), 383. [For discussion see Jensen 1969.]

Reviews show that environmental factors have a strong influence on IQ scores (Kamin 1974, 1975, 1977), but isolating the exact degree of influence is difficult. The closest estimates have been given by researchers using complicated statistical procedures. One researcher, Christopher Jencks (1972), believes that 45 percent of a person's intelligence is due to heredity, 35 percent to environment, and 20 percent to gene-environment covariance. Another study of intelligence estimated 60 percent from heredity, 25 percent from environment, and 15 percent from covariance (Lowhlin, Lindzey, and Spuhler 1975).

QUESTION: Are there racial differences in intelligence?

This question has often been asked. Even Cicero in ancient Rome supposedly advised his fellow Romans not to obtain slaves from Britain, because British individuals were so stupid and dull that they were not fit to be slaves. More recently, the controversy over racial differences in IQs has flared anew because of a claim by psychologist Arthur Jensen. He maintained that the observed IQ differences of approximately fifteen points between blacks and whites was due more to genetic variables than to environmental factors (Jensen 1969). His projection that the low IQ scores of blacks are due to genetic differences was immediately criticized by the findings of another researcher, J. S. Kagan (1969).

The most telling criticism of Jensen's claim is a logical argument. Differences that do appear between racial IQs can be attributed to differences in the environment. Until evidence shows that the environment for blacks as a group is comparable to that of whites, including school facilities, family structure, culture, and motivation, then differences that are found can still be attributed to environmental differences. The question of racial differences in IQs will apparently not be fully answered until environmental differences are eradicated. As a conclusion to this controversial question, an interesting observation made by Thomas Sowell, a black economist, is presented:

> History shows that there is nothing unique about the black I.Q. level . . . Group I.Q. averages at or below 85 have been common in history and currently. . . . Numerous studies show these kinds of I.Q. averages for such American ethnic groups as the Italians, Greeks, Poles, Hispanics, Slovaks, and Portuguese. More recent studies show Mexican/Americans with lower average I.Q.s than Blacks in the 1940s, 1950s, and 1960s, and Puerto [Ricans] with lower I.Q.s than Blacks in the 1970s. . . .
>
> These groups often are recent immigrants and have yet to be assimilated into the culture and thus will be unable to respond as efficiently in testing

Group differences in intelligence are not explainable and may disappear when social and learning opportunities are more equal between individuals.

situations. In addition, these groups all experience different levels of poverty. Poverty can influence intellectual functioning in a number of ways including pre- and post-natal nutrition, health, motivation, [and] school. (Sowell 1981, 753).

To show how culture can influence intelligence, one research team gathered data on IQ scores of black children who were adopted and raised by white families, and found that if the children were adopted at a young age, their scores were similar to white IQ averages (Scarr and Weinberg 1976).

One could say that both biology and environment are not fair. Some individuals within all racial groups benefit from a superior genetic inheritance and a more facilitative environment. Intelligence differences found between racial groupings can clearly be associated with the environmental deficit.

QUESTION: What is the practical implication of use and discussion of IQ tests?

In addition to individually administered IQ tests, millions of group-administered IQ aptitude, and achievement tests are given in schools and workplaces each year. Many of these, like the Scholastic Aptitude Test (SAT), determine important decisions such as whether a person will be admitted to college. Others influence whether a person will be employed, receive a license or gain a certification. These tests affect the way thousands of people live and identify many people who would not substantially benefit from educational programs and training. These concerns warrant their use from the economical perspective of institutions. These institutional economical benefits, however, need to be weighted with the consideration that some people who would excel in educational programs may be excluded solely on the basis of tests.

On the positive side, tests do provide an equality of opportunities. The disadvantaged and the racial minorities who score high on IQ tests have objectively based criteria upon which to argue their merits or ability. Nevertheless, caution must always be used in employing and interpreting test results.

It has been successfully argued in the courts that placing students at a young age in different track systems on the basis of IQ scores is discriminatory against certain racial groups who habitually score lower on IQ tests. One such study found that a disproportionate number of blacks and Mexican-American children were being placed, on the basis of their IQ scores, in classes for the mentally retarded. A psychologist (Mercer 1971, 1972) then developed a test which all the Anglo-American children assigned to the program failed, but 90 percent of the blacks and 60 percent of the Chicanos passed. California later passed a law making it illegal to assign a child to a program for the mentally retarded based solely on the results of an IQ test.

Even though IQ tests can predict school performance, there are those who believe they cannot predict anything else very well (McClelland 1973). In predicting academic, school, or training success, however, intelligence and achievement tests have accomplished a significant feat and will accordingly continue to be used. The importance of these tests in influencing the present and future lives of adolescents is obvious. By understanding the problems and limitations of the tests, adults can intelligently interpret and apply these powerful assessment instruments.

Summary

For over fifty years, Jean Paul Piaget, a French developmentalist, studied the structure of the human mind. He reported many provocative discoveries regarding cognitive thought processes. Although many American psychologists believed that mental knowledge was simply an imperfect copy—acquired through one's perceptions—of the external world, Piaget thought that everyone must *act* upon their environment and actually reconstruct it within their own minds to gain knowledge.

People act upon their environment by forming schema that allow them to identify and organize environmental patterns. Assimilation is the process whereby people change and modify raw perceptual experiences into forms that are consistent with their existing structure system (their schemata). Accommodation is the process of changing an existing structure system in order to be more compatible with current experiences. The former process alters the meaning of experience to match existing schemata, and the latter process alters the existing schemata to match the perceived meaning of current experiences.

Adolescents learn more through logical-mathematical experiences. Logical-mathematical experiences require people to act upon their environment through motor, manual, and mental manipulations. Concepts such as direction, movement, causality, and quantity are often involved in logical-mathematical experiences.

Piaget divided maturational and biological development into a series of stages. His stage theory proposes that mental structures are developed in sequential directions; that is, mental structures occur in a sequence of increasing complexity. The later stages are dependent upon completion of the previous stages. A progressive integration of the lower stages into higher stages occurs by actually incorporating the lower-level accomplishments into increasingly abstract logical-mathematical patterns of thinking.

The formal operations stage is characterized by an adolescent's ability to perform operations upon operations, or in Piaget's terminology, "second-order operations." During this stage, an adolescent also becomes capable of formulating hypotheses and working out the results of these hypotheses without manipulating concrete objects.

Intelligence generally refers to the ability of individuals to act purposefully, to think rationally, and to deal effectively with their environment. Intelligence tests used as predictors of scholastic success are probably the most sophisticated, reliable, and valid tests that psychologist have yet developed.

Intelligence test scores are often influenced by several factors that are not necessarily related to intelligence. For example, different levels of anxiety, motivation, and homelife verbalization all influence individual test scores.

Some psychologists emphasize that individuals may be highly intelligent in one area and less intelligent in other areas. Guilford defined intelligence in terms of the type of *content* one is dealing with, the mental *operations* involved, and the mental *products* (classes, relations, units, and so on) that are created as a result of the interaction between content and operation.

Intelligence levels are both inherited and learned from the environment. Some researchers estimate that intelligence is composed of 45 percent hereditary factors, 35 percent environmental factors, and 20 percent gene-environment covariance factors.

Differences in average racial intelligence levels can be attributed to differences in the environment. The validity of different intelligence levels cannot be accurately tested until environmental differences are eradicated.

References

Anastasi, A. 1965. *Individual differences*. New York: Wiley.
Anderson, L. D. 1939. The predictive value of infant tests in relationship to intelligence at age 5 years. *Child Development* 10: 203–12.
Bayley, N. 1970. Development of mental abilities. In *Carmichael's manual of child psychology,* ed. P. H. Mussen. New York: Wiley.
Berg, I. 1970. *Education and jobs*. New York: Praeger.
Berlyne, D. E. 1964. Recent developments in Piaget's work. In *The cognitive processes: Readings,* ed. R. J. Harper, et al. Englewood Cliffs, N.J.: Prentice-Hall.
Bloom, B. S. 1964. *The stability and change in human characteristics*. New York: Wiley.
Bodmer, W. F., & L. L. Cavalli-Sforza. 1970. Intelligence and race. *Scientific American* 4: 19–29.
Coon, D. 1983. *Introduction to psychology, exploration and application*. St. Paul: West Publishing.
Dworetzky, J. P. 1984. *Psychology*. St. Paul: West Publishing.
Elkind, D. 1968. In Cognitive development in adolescence. In *Understanding adolescence,* ed. J. F. Adams, 128–58. Boston: Allyn & Bacon.
───. 1981. *The hurried child, growing up too fast, too soon*. Reading, Mass.: Addison-Wesley.
Erikson, E. 1950. *Childhood and society*. New York: Norton.
Feldhusen, J., W. Kryspin, & J. R. Thurston. Prediction of achievement with measures of learning, social behavior, sex, and intelligence. *Psychology in the Schools* 11: 59–65.
Flavell, J. H. 1963. *The developmental psychology of Jean Piaget*. Princeton, N.J.: Van Nostrand.
Furth, H. 1969. *Piaget and knowledge: Theoretical foundations*. Englewood Cliffs, N.J.: Prentice Hall.
───. 1970. *Piaget for teachers*. Englewood Cliffs, N.J.: Prentice Hall.
Gardner, H. 1983. *Frames of mind: The theory of multiple intelligences*. New York: Basic Books.
Guilford, J. P. 1959. Three faces of intellect. *American Psychologist* 14: 469–79.
───. 1966. Intelligence: 1965 model. *American Psychologist* 21: 20–26.
───. 1967. *The nature of human intelligence*. New York: McGraw-Hill.
───. 1972. Thurstone's primary mental abilities and structure of intellect abilities. *Psychological Bulletin* 77: 129–43.
Jencks, C. 1972. *Inequality: A reassessment of the effects of family and schooling in America*. New York: Basic Books.
Jensen, A. 1969. How much can we boost I.Q. and achievement? *Harvard Educational Review* 39: 123.
Jensen, A. R. 1972. The hereditability of intelligence. *Saturday Evening Post* 244: 9.
Kagan, J. S. 1969. Inadequate evidence and illogical conclusions. *Harvard Educational Review* 39: 274–77.
Kamin, L. J. 1974. *The science and politics of I.Q.* Hillsdale, N.J.: Erlbaum.
───. 1975. Is I.Q. heritable? *Contemporary Psychology* 20: 545-47.
───. 1977. Burt's I.Q. data. *Science* 19: 245–48.
Keating, D. P. 1980. Thinking processes in adolescence. In *Handbook of adolescent psychology,* ed. J. Adelson. New York: Wiley.
Lazer, I., & R. Darlington. 1984. Lasting effects of early education: A report from the consortium for longitudinal studies. *Monographs of the Society for Research in Child Development*. In press.
Lowhlin, J. C., G. Lindzey, & J. N. Spuhler. 1975. *Race differences and intelligence*. San Francisco: Freeman.
Maier, H. W. 1965. *Three theories of child development*. New York: Harper & Row.
McClelland, D. C. 1973. Testing for competence rather than intelligence. *American Psychologist* 28: 1–14.

Mercer, J. R. 1971. Social cultural factors in labeling mentally retardants. *Peabody Journal of Education* 48: 188–203.

———. 1972. IQ: The lethal label. *Psychology Today* (September).

National Assessment of Educational Progress. 1977. *What students know and can do: Profiles of three age groups.* Denver, Colo.: Educational Commission of the United States.

Neimark, E. D. 1975. Longitudinal development of formal operation thought. *Genetic Psychology Monographs* 91: 171–225.

Osterrieth, P. A. 1969. The effects of early childhood education on adolescents: Some psychological aspects. In *Adolescence: Psychosocial perspectives,* ed. G. Caplan and S. Levovici. New York: Basic Books

Phillips, J. L. 1969. *The origins of intellect: Piaget's theory.* San Francisco: Freeman.

Piaget, J. 1952. *The origins of intelligence in children.* New York: International Univ. Press.

———. 1954. *The construction of reality in the child.* New York: Basic Books.

———. 1955. *The language and thought of the child.* New York: Meridan Books.

———. 1970. Piaget's theory. *Carmichael's manual of child psychology,* ed. P. H. Mussen. New York: Wiley.

Piaget, J., & B. Inhelder. 1958. *The growth of logical thinking.* New York: Basic Books.

Pinneau, S. R. 1961. *Changes in intelligence quotient.* Boston: Houghton Mifflin.

Rosenthal, R., & L. Jacobson. 1968. *Pygmalion in the classroom: Teachers' expectations and pupils' intellectual development.* New York: Holt, Rinehart & Winston.

Sawrey, J., & C. Telford. 1968. *The psychology of adjustment.* Boston: Allyn & Bacon.

Scarr, S., & R. A. Weinberg. 1976. IQ test performance of black children adopted by white families. *American Psychologist* 31: 726–39.

Scarr-Salatapek, S. 1971. Environment, heredity, and intelligence: The I.Q. argument. *Science* 174: 1223–28.

Sowell, T. 1981. Historical data show black/white I.Q. gap neither unique nor related to segregation. *Phi Delta Kappan* 62: 753.

Spearman, C. 1927. *The abilities of man.* New York: Macmillan.

Spock, B. 1968. *Baby and child care.* New York: Pocket Books.

Stein B. J. 1983. Valley girls view the world. *Public Opinion Quarterly:* 18–19 (August–September).

Stennet, R. G. 1969. Relationship of sex and social economic status to I.Q. change. *Psychology in the Schools* 6: 385–90.

Terman, L. M. 1925. *Genetic studies of genius.* Vol. 1 of *Mental and physical traits of a thousand gifted children.* Stanford, Calif.: Stanford Univ. Press.

Thurstone, L. L. 1938. Primary mental abilities. *Psychometric Monographs* 1.

Wallace, N. A. 1976. Tests tell us little about talent. *American Scientist* 64: 57–63.

Wayne, C. W., & N. A. Wallace. 1971. *College admissions and the psychology of talent.* New York: Holt, Rinehart & Winston.

Zigler, E., & P. K. Trickett. 1978. IQ, social competence and evaluation of early childhood intervention programs. *American Psychologist* 33: 789–98.

SECTION FOUR

theories for application

15 Applying Behavioral Theory to Adolescents

16 Phenomenological Theory: Application for Building Relationship Skills

17 Phenomenological Theory: Application for Building Helping Skills

These last chapters depart in purpose from the preceding chapters. They are written to provide skills for helping adolescents. Accordingly, this section contains some style change and less documentation. The chapters are a direct application of the two most basic theoretical positions in modern psychology. The position in Chapter 15 is behaviorism, and Chapters 16 and 17 cover the skills derived from phenomenological theory.

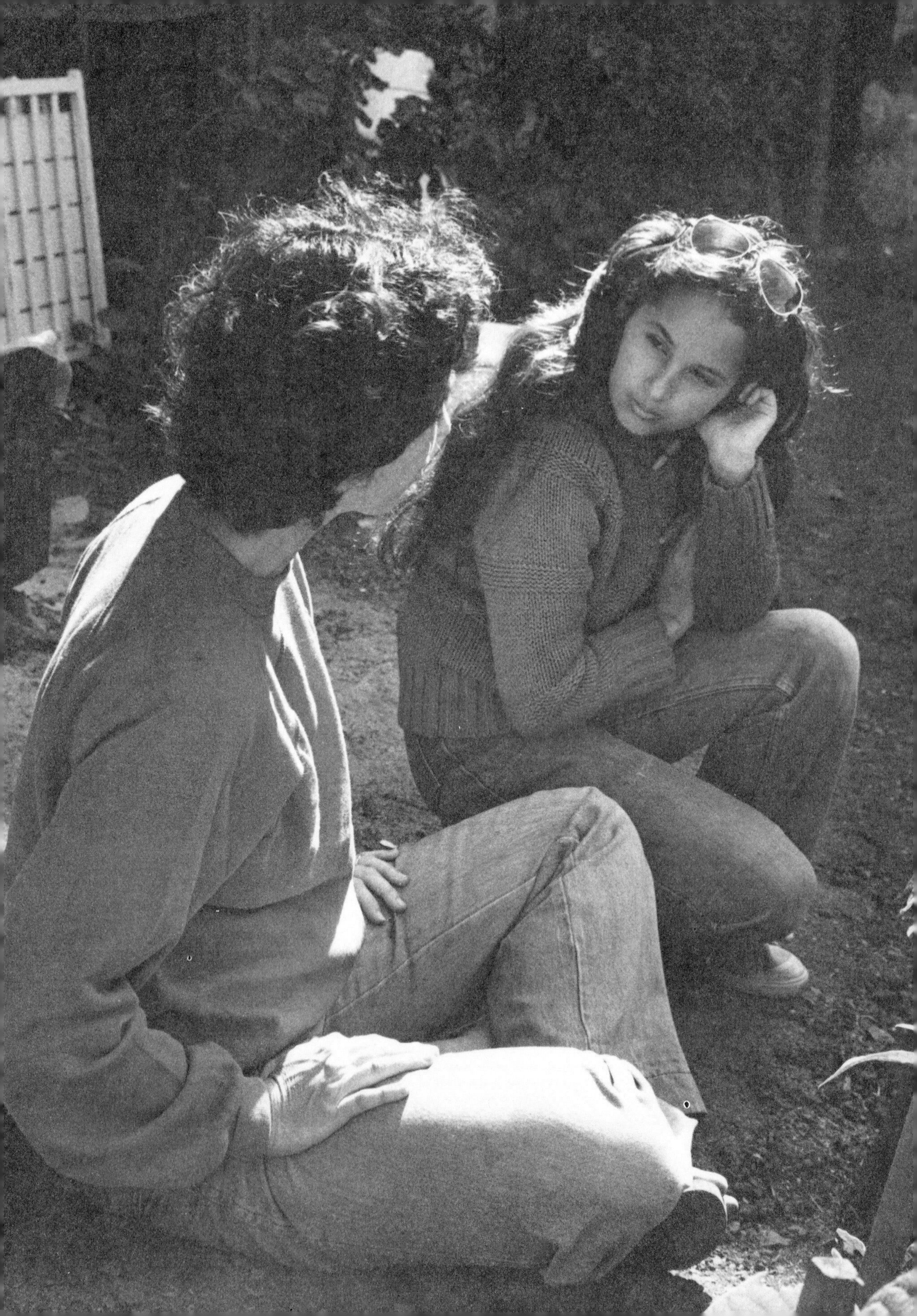

CHAPTER FIFTEEN

Applying behavioral theory to adolescents

SURVEY AND QUESTIONS

This chapter will first present a brief, straightforward description of behavioral theory. The conceptual basis of behaviorism is not difficult and it is possible to then discuss application of this powerful theory. Success in using behavior modification with adolescents will depend on how it is presented and perceived. The latter part of the chapter will describe several approaches.

Behavior Modification Theory

According to behaviorists, what determines behavior?
What is behavior modification?
Why do behaviorists use technical language?
What are the other types of consequences besides positive reinforcement?
Does behavior modification theory contend that adolescent behavior is totally determined by the environment?
Does the theory imply that free will does not exist?

Shaping

If people can increase or decrease existing behaviors, can they develop a new behavior?
To reinforce a behavior, do people have to wait for the behavior to occur?
Can people simply be told what to do to get the reinforcer?

Token Economies

Behavior modification sounds practical in theory, but can adolescents be treated using behavior modification?
How does a token economy operate?
By what sorts of behavior can adolescents earn points?
What if adolescents do not care about their point totals?
What if adolescents feel they have been unfairly penalized?
The token economy sounds satisfactory for treating delinquent adolescents, but how can it be used to treat adolescents with other problems?
What are the specific guidelines needed to set up a behavioral change program?
How enduring are the changes produced by a token economy program?

Positive Reinforcement and Punishment

Which is more effective for changing behavior: positive reinforcement or punishment?
In which cases can punishment be successfully used in combination with positive reinforcement?
What are effective substitutes for punishment, and how can they be employed?

Special Concerns When Using Behavior Modification with Adolescents

What is a practical example of using behavior modification with a large group of adolescents?
Will adolescents object to having to earn reinforcers that they feel belong to them anyway?

Other Approaches

What is the systems approach?
What is the positive relationship approach of using behavior modification?
How can one make behavior modification work without being either impersonal or charismatic?
How can the contract approach be used to change such a general characteristic as personality?
What is the self-directed approach?

Behavior modification theory

Do instincts, motives, personality, spirits, willpower, and intentions cause behavior? When the civil law asks whether the criminal had willful intentions, the assumption is that an inner cause of behavior exists. One concept of law even assumes that to be punishable, behavior *must* follow from inner causes. Our whole notion of being blameworthy is based on the belief that inner causes are responsible for people's actions.

The traditional view of abnormal behavior has relied on inner causes. This view, called the medical model, assumes that problems in adjustment are analogous to problems in physical health. Just as a high fever might prevent a person from going to school, truancy might be viewed as caused by inner mental or emotional disturbances. Those who use the traditional medical approach try to find the inner cause that has produced the undesired behavior. Freud, for example, looked for conflicts over sexual and aggressive impulses. Other theorists look for other kinds of causes, such as the self-concept, feelings of inferiority, and so on. All these theories have one thing in common: They assume that observable behavior is the result of inner causes.

Although the medical model has been popular, psychologists of the behaviorist school believe that explaining human behavior by reference to inner causes does not increase understanding or provide solutions. For example, terms such as *peer pressure* and *low self-esteem* are often used to explain poor academic performance or antisocial behaviors. The question is, does low self-esteem produce antisocial behaviors, or does it simply accompany them? Are people with low self-concept necessarily poor students, or may they be excellent students? Behaviorists feel that a concept as difficult to measure as self-esteem is not very useful for understanding or changing behavior and provides only a pseudo explanation.

QUESTION: According to behaviorists, what determines behavior?

Behaviorists believe that behavior is caused by a person's environment. Instead of looking for inner causes, behaviorists look for elements in the environment that produce behavior. When they find a relationship between external events and behavior, the behaviorists say that the event determines the behavior or that the behavior is learned. For example, if a teenager has been denied the use of the family car, and then throws a temper tantrum, the teenager's parents may change their minds. If they do change their minds and give the teenager the keys, a relationship exists between throwing a temper tantrum and being given the car keys. A behaviorist might describe this relationship in terms of causation or learning. The teenager's temper tantrum caused the parents to change their minds. The teenager has learned that temper tantrums are an effective means of getting the car keys. This is a two-way street. If the parents had not changed their minds, then the teenager would have learned that a temper tantrum is not an effective means of getting the car keys, and the parents would have caused a change in their teenager's behavior.

The point is, the particular behavior that a person shows in one situation is influenced by past experiences in similar situations. The effect of the past is to bring out a set of successful behaviors when similar conditions reappear. What happens in the present situation will therefore either strengthen or weaken our tendency to behave the same way under similar circumstances in the future. One might say that these tendencies to behave in certain ways are inner causes, but the behaviorists' reply is that naming these tendencies does not help us. Instead, what we need to know is what elements in the environment will produce desirable behaviors. From this point of view, behavioral problems are symptoms of an unhealthy environment. To change behavior, behaviorists use a technique called behavior modification.

QUESTION: What is behavior modification?

The most popular theorist and spokesperson for behavior modification is still B. F. Skinner (1948, 1953). His early writings are clear, succinct, and congruent with subsequent research. Behavior modification is based on the principles of operant conditioning, which describe the relationship between a person's behavior and environmental events. When a behavior is followed by an event in the environment, the behavior is called the antecedent. The event that follows the antecedent is called a consequence. In the example given, the teenager's temper tantrum was an antecedent, and the parents' decision to lend the car was its consequence. If an event occurs only after a certain behavior, it is said to be contingent upon performance of the behavior. The concept is important, because behavior is changed by altering the contingencies that control a particular behavior. If our teenager's parents decided to lend the car only after the teenager waxed it, and to ignore any temper tantrums, they then would alter the contingency on which the use of the car depends. The use of the car would be contingent on waxing it rather than on having a temper tantrum.

Four basic types of contingent relationships exist between antecedent behaviors and their consequences: positive reinforcement, negative reinforcement, punishment, and extinction. A consequence that follows a certain behavior and then increases the frequency of that behavior is called a *positive reinforcer*. People typically refer to these reinforcers as rewards. Rewards can be positive reinforcers, but distinguishing them is best, since an event is a positive reinforcer only if it leads to an increase in the frequency of behavior. The difference can be made clear by a few examples. If the class clown is being disruptive, and the teacher responds with a verbal reprimand, the reprimand may actually strengthen the disruptive behavior. If the reprimand does lead to an increase in disruptive behavior, then the reprimand is a positive reinforcer. On the other hand, a parent might reward an adolescent with fifty dollars for every A received, but if this does not result in a higher frequency of A's, then the money is not a positive reinforcer.

QUESTION: Why do behaviorists use technical language?

Since technical language can be confusing, this question is legitimate. Ironically, psychologists use technical language to avoid confusion and imprecision. From the distinctions made between rewards and positive reinforcers one can already see that concluding that all rewards are effective means of increasing behavior can sometimes be misleading. Psychologists have coined terms that they hope will express their exact meaning.

Much of the early research done by behaviorists relied heavily on animal experimentation and much of the current terminology has its roots in this early reliance. Mazes are still sometimes used to test theories of positive and negative reinforcement.

QUESTION: What are the other types of consequences besides positive reinforcement?

The removal of something unpleasant also leads to an increase in behavior. This consequence is called a *negative reinforcer*. A negative reinforcer, like a positive reinforcer, is defined solely by the effect it has on behavior. An adolescent may find many conditions in life annoying. These conditions are negative reinforcers only if their *removal* results in an increase in the strength of the behavior that precedes the removal. Reinforcement, whether positive or negative, always results in an increase in the behavior.

The third consequence that may follow a behavior is *punishment*. Punishment, in everyday language, is a penalty imposed for some action. Punishment in operant conditioning, however, is an operation that is the opposite of a reinforcement. Punishment refers to removing a positive reinforcer or adding a negative reinforcer. Punishment can also be called positive or negative, depending on whether a favorable condition is ended or an unfavorable condition is begun.

Figure 15–1 should help to distinguish between the three types of consequences already mentioned. Reinforcement refers to procedures that *increase* a response, and punishment refers to the opposite procedures that may or may not have similar outcomes. Punishment and negative reinforcement are easily confused. In punishment, either something desirable is taken away or something undesirable is given (boxes 1 and 4). In negative reinforcement, something undesirable is taken away (box 2). In positive reinforcement, something desirable which strengthens behavior is given after the behavior (box 3).

The fourth type of consequence, which is not illustrated in Figure 15–1, is called *extinction*. In extinction a behavior is simply ignored. The idea is that a behavior that has previously been reinforced will gradually disappear if it is no

Figure 15-1 Value of Consequence

	Desirable	Undesirable
Remove	Punishment (negative)	Negative Reinforcement
	1 2	
	3 4	
Add	Positive Reinforcement	Punishment (positive)

Illustration of the relationship between three of the principles of operant conditioning. *Source:* Adapted from Kazdin 1975, 35.

longer reinforced. In the example of our teenage driver, the teenager's temper tantrum has been reinforced by the parents' consequent decision to lend the family car. If, in the future, the parents consistently ignore their teenager's temper tantrums, behavioral theory predicts that the teenager will stop having tantrums in this situation. The parents, however, may need to ignore many tantrums before this behavior is totally extinguished.

Most important to remember is that both positive and negative reinforcement is used to strengthen desirable behaviors. Punishment and extinction are ways of weakening undesirable behaviors. Behaviorists believe that behavior is learned, either to terminate a condition that is distressing or painful, or to produce positive sensations. Behavior can be modified by altering its consequences in systematic ways. If the environment is arranged so that an adolescent must behave in a certain way to end an unpleasant condition or to produce a pleasant consequence, then that behavior is said to be reinforced. If an environment is arranged so that an adolescent's behavior, which may have previously been reinforced, is consistently ignored, then the behavior is said to be extinguished.

QUESTION: Does behavior modification theory contend that adolescent behavior is totally determined by the environment? Does the theory imply that free will does not exist?

These questions are extremely important. Many leading behaviorists believe that because behavior can be modified by changing its consequences, behavior is therefore determined by the environment. Behaviorists make this assumption because they want to be able to study human behavior in the same way, and with the same accuracy, that Newton studied falling objects. Just as a falling object is presumed not to have any "say" in how it falls, humans are presumed not to have any say in how they behave. Even if someone appears to have two alternatives, the behaviorist would say that the person will choose to behave in the way that has been most heavily reinforced in the past. The behaviorist does not take into serious account that people consciously believe that they make free choices. Even if adolescents decide not to do what they were told to do, the behaviorist would say that this is because adolescents have learned to disobey from past reinforcement. The view that human beings do nothing but what they are "trained" to do was expressed in 1913 by John Watson, the founder of American behaviorism:

> Psychology as the behaviorist views it is a purely objective branch of natural science. Its theoretical goal is the prediction and control of behavior. Introspection [i.e., a study of human thought] forms no essential part of its methods, nor is the scientific value of its data dependent upon the readiness with which they lend themselves to interpretations in terms of consciousness. The behaviorist, in his efforts to get a unitary scheme of animal response, recognizes no dividing line between man and brute. (Watson 1913, 158)

Joseph Rychlak (1981), a leading personality theorist, has pointed out that when behaviorists say that a person's behavior is determined by the environment, they confuse their experimental method with their theory. That behaviorists have decided to rule consciousness out of their experimental method places them in a poor position to judge the effect of consciousness on behavior. A different theory, one that describes behavior in terms of a person's choices, is entirely compatible with the results of behavioral experiments. After all, no evidence supports that children disobey their parents because they have been trained to do so. A theory of human behavior in which people actively and consciously conceive of alternatives is compatible with the findings of behavioral studies. In a survey of the behavioral literature, Brewer has concluded that there is no convincing evidence that the behavior of adult humans is automatically conditioned by the environment (Brewer 1974).

Shaping

QUESTION: If people can increase or decrease existing behaviors, can they develop a new behavior?

When trying to modify adolescent behavior, one must first decide whether the desired behavior is in the adolescent's behavioral repertoire. No one can simply reinforce a behavior that never occurs; yet pigeons have been taught to play Ping-Pong and to guide military missiles. These behaviors are accomplished by *shaping*. In shaping, the behavior is achieved by reinforcing small steps or approximations toward the final response, rather than by reinforcing the final response itself. By reinforcing successive approximations of the desired behavior, the behavior is achieved gradually.

A well-known example of shaping is training animals to perform tricks. If an elephant trainer waited for an elephant to stand on its hind legs before reinforcing the behavior, the trainer would wait forever. By shaping the response, however, the trainer can achieve the goal relatively quickly. First, the trainer may reinforce the lifting of one leg a few inches off the ground. Later, the trainer may reinforce the elephant's lifting backward, and so on. Steps closer to the final goal are reinforced in sequence. Eventually, only the elephant's standing on its hind legs will be reinforced.

Suppose that someone wishes to increase the social participation of a shy adolescent. Suppose also that the adolescent is a computer lover. Using computer time can then be used as a reinforcer. The adolescent may be successfully reinforced for the following:

1. Glancing at a group of adolescents involved in some activity
2. Standing in the same room with them
3. Standing in the same side of the room
4. Sitting with a group
5. Performing the same activity as the group
6. Responding to a question
7. Initiating a conversation
8. Initiating an activity
9. Playing cooperatively

Although shaping is a simple procedure, success depends on certain requirements. To be successively reinforced, the behaviors must carefully be defined, must immediately be reinforced, and must not be reinforced for too long. If shaping proceeds too rapidly, the earlier behaviors may be extinguished, but if shaping proceeds too slowly, intermediate behaviors may become too well established. Practically speaking, if the process is too slow, one will become bored and will refuse to cooperate.

QUESTION: To reinforce a behavior, do people have to wait for the behavior to occur? Can people simply be told what to do to get the reinforcer?

A number of ways can make approximations of the final response more rapid. Simply instructing an adolescent is one way to begin the response. Another way is to allow an adolescent to observe another person perform the behavior, such as watching someone else play a game. A third way is to physically guide the behavior, as one might when teaching someone to swing a golf club. All these ways assist a person to begin a behavior so that the behavior may be reinforced. They are called "prompts."

Token economies

QUESTION: Behavior modification sounds practical in theory, but can adolescents be treated using behavior modification?

Behavioral principles naturally lend themselves to implementation in structured, institutional settings. Inpatient behavior programs have been demonstrated to be effective with a wide variety of behavioral problems, ranging from weight control to the changing of sex role behaviors. They have been used to develop self-care behaviors among chronically institutionalized psychotic patients, to improve academic performance of children in special education, to help adolescents learn self-control, and to generate numerous other changes in a wide variety of behaviors by controlling the consequences of those behaviors. The early years of behavior therapy have been described as the "whoopee" phase, because the behaviorists eagerly scooped up the most difficult cases to prove that behavior therapy works (Patterson 1971).

One of the appeals of token economy systems is that they offer 24-hour learning environments where changes in behavior can be measured. Desirable behaviors, such as completing homework, are rewarded with points.

One of the important, early demonstrations of the effectiveness of behavioral therapy came out of the National Training School for Boys in Washington, D.C., where token economy systems were developed for use in institutions for delinquents. The directors first converted an old cottage at the National Training School into a "24-hour learning environment" for forty-one delinquents. Their treatment philosophy emphasized using positive reinforcement rather than the usual "do what we say or be punished." They found that within a year's time, the adolescents became better disciplined, developed a pride of ownership in their belongings and living quarters, and even showed an increase of over twelve points in their IQs. The work at the National Training School, along with Ayllon and Azrin's work with chronic schizophrenics in 1968, became the model for token economies throughout the country (Ayllon and Azrin 1968).

Token economy systems are popular for many reasons. The behavioral problems of adolescents are often of such major proportions that adolescents can no longer remain in the community; the degree of behavioral control that is required can be achieved only in an institutional setting. A token economy is a "24-hour learning environment" rather than a few hours of therapy in an office or at school. Token economies involve a tight structure that permits measurable progress in behavior change. Despite the tight structure of the token economy, it is easily adapted to treat different types of behavioral problems, even within the same treatment program.

QUESTION: How does a token economy operate?

The point system provides the foundation for a token economy. Points are the coinage of the token economy program. Desirable behaviors are reinforced by the addition of points to a patient's point total, and undesirable behaviors result in point fines. Patients can exchange their points for various goods and services. The economy is designed in such a way that if patients perform most of the specified behaviors and do not receive too many fines, they can afford to purchase most of the privileges. Adolescents are not given extended credit; they must earn their way. Privileges to be purchased with points include the use of television, stereo, and radio, as well as smoking, game room use, outings, and passes with parents. Table 15–1 displays the expenses for activities. Tables 15–1, 15–2, and 15–3 contain the point system as is actually used in a southern California residential treatment center for emotionally disturbed adolescent males, and can be used as a guide to setting up any token economy. Behaviors and consequences will be different, but the approach will be the same.

QUESTION: By what sorts of behavior can adolescents earn points?

When token economies are described as being tightly structured, this means that the token economy is designed to reinforce with points as many desirable behaviors as possible. Adolescents can earn points from almost the minute they wake in the morning until they go to sleep at night. Adolescents earn points for being punctual for breakfast, for room inspection, and school, and for most of the organized activities of the day. They earn points for not being disruptive during activities (proper behavior) and for fully participating in the activities (performance). During room inspection, they earn points for having made their beds, cleaned their bathrooms, ordered their closets, and for being well groomed. Adolescents may earn points for not smoking and for eating nutritiously. Every important aspect of the adolescent treatment program can be point reinforced (see Table 15–2).

Just as any clearly described behavior can be point reinforced, any well-defined undesirable behaviors can be fined. The amount of the fine is designed

TABLE 15–1 Expenses for Activities

Item	Cost
Room and board (includes snacks)	10
Game room	
Electronic items	15 per item
Pool/Ping-Pong	10 per game
Table games	5 per game
Late-night TV	25 per hour
Smoking	15
Radio	10
Passes	
4 hr (return by 8:00 P.M.)	25
10 hr (return by 8:00 P.M.)	40
Overnight (return by 9:00 P.M.)	60
Weekend (return by 10:00 P.M.)	80
Extra hours	10 per hour
Special event	35
Open unit transfer	60

TABLE 15-2 Credits for Activities

Activity	Points Per Day	Weekly Consistency Points
Breakfast		
Punctuality (1 min leeway)	1	1
Proper behavior	1	1
Room inspection		
Punctuality	1	1
Bed made	1	1
Clothes put away	1	1
Closet in order	1	1
Bathroom clean	1	1
Personal hygiene		
Clean clothes	1	1
Clean hair	1	1
Clean body	1	1
School		
First session		
Punctuality	1	1
Performance	2	2
Proper behavior	2	2
Second session		
Punctuality	1	1
Performance	2	2
Proper behavior	2	2
Third Session		
Punctuality	1	1
Performance	2	2
Proper behavior	2	2
Homework		
Math	3	3
English	3	3
History	3	3
Other	3	3
Physical Education		
Punctuality	2	2
Performance	2	2
Proper behavior	2	2
Community meeting/grievance hearing		
Punctuality	1	1
Proper behavior	1	1
Occupational therapy		
Punctuality	2	2
Performance	2	2
Proper behavior	2	2
Housekeeping skills	2	2
Long-term project	2-5	2
Group therapy		
Punctuality	2	
Performance	2	
Proper behavior	2	
Study hall		
Punctuality	1	1
Performance	2	2
Proper behavior	2	2

Multifamily workshop		
Punctuality	3	
Performance	3	
Proper behavior	3	
Evening social activity (Sing-along, charades, indoor volleyball, etc.)		
Punctuality	1	1
Performance	1	1
Proper behavior	1	1
Peer feedback session		
Punctuality	1	1
Performance	1	1
Proper behavior	1	1
Nutrition	3	3
No smoking	3	3
Medication	2	2
Bed check		
Punctuality	1	1
Proper behavior	1	1
Punctual return from pass	1	1
Individual program	7 points maximum	
Daily consistency award		
1. All possible points earned	5	
2. No penalties	5	
Remain on open unit—Monday–Friday		5

to reflect the seriousness of the inappropriate behavior (see Table 15–3). In this way, eating in one's room might carry a ten-point fine, profane language a twenty-point fine, smoking in one's room a thirty-point fine, and so on. The point earnings and losses of each adolescent are recorded in a bankbook, and whenever an adolescent receives a fine, the point total is revised.

QUESTION: What if adolescents do not care about their point totals?

As one might expect, the positive reinforcement of the token economy is not always enough to discourage undesirable behavior. If some adolescents' behaviors were easily changed, they would probably never have been placed in a treatment program in the first place. For such adolescents only two treatment possibilities are available. The therapist either must identify a positive reinforcer that is adequate to change the behavior or must conceive of a punishment that is effective without being unnecessarily cruel. The first possibility seems preferable, especially since positive reinforcers do not have the possible undesirable side effects of punishment. In practice, both positive reinforcement and punishment are used—punishment to suppress the undesirable behavior, and positive reinforcers to reinforce the opposite, desired behavior (Bandura 1969).

The punishment most often used in behavioral treatment programs exploits adolescents' dislike for boredom. Common is for a treatment program to have an open unit and a closed or locked unit. The open unit offers numerous positive reinforcers in the form of games and activities, and the closed unit offers

TABLE 15–3 Fines

Behavior	Fine
Physical aggression	125 points, 48 hr in C.U., 24 hr in room isolation
Property damage	100 points, 24 hr in C.U., 12 hr in room isolation
Possession of illegal or dangerous items	80 points, 24 hr in C.U.
Possession of potentially dangerous items	30 points
Verbal threats or gestures	80 points, 24 hr in C.U., 12 hr in room isolation
Substance abuse	75 points, 24 hr in C.U.
Stealing	60 points, 24 hr in C.U.
Sexual behavior	50 points, 24 hr in C.U.
Refusal to follow staff orders	50 points, 24 hr in C.U.
Out of bed after bedtime	40 points
Smoking in room	30 points
Smoking without purchase	25 points
Inappropriate language	20 points
Inappropriate use of items	10 points
Food or drink in room	10 points
Violation of unit rules	10 points
Absent without authorization	First hour—20 points Second hour—40 points 24 hr—24 hr in C.U., 300 points
Absent without accountability	15 points
Cost response program	40 points
Interfering with staff procedures	40 points
Encouraging major inappropriate behavior	40 points
Staff manipulation	40 points
Out of room during point-reinforced activity	40 points

Source: Adapted from worksheets supplied and used by Vern Lewis who, as a staff worker, implemented behavior treatment in a residential treatment facility in southern California.

few positive reinforcers. If adolescents' point totals drop below zero, they are sent to the closed unit until they are able to accumulate enough points to purchase a transfer back to the open unit. Seriously inappropriate behaviors, such as stealing and drug and substance abuse, may carry mandatory closed unit time as well as a point fine. The most seriously inappropriate behaviors, such as property damage and physical aggression, may also carry room isolation time. In room isolation, the adolescents are confined to a room, and so are deprived not only of the positive reinforcers of the open unit, but also of the positive reinforcement of interaction with peers in the closed unit.

QUESTION: What if adolescents feel they have been unfairly penalized?

One of the general goals of a token economy system is to teach adolescents to anticipate and to accept the consequences of their behaviors. By providing an environment in which socially desirable behaviors are consistently reinforced, and in which socially undesirable behaviors are consistently punished, adolescents learn to exercise self-control and to take responsibility. The need for self-control and responsible action is just as great when adolescents feel they have been unfairly penalized. In the community at large, individuals who feel that they did not deserve traffic tickets can express their objections in court. Since the token economy system is meant to be a micromodel of the community, the adolescents are provided with a form for appropriate expression of grievances. The grievance procedure requires adolescents to respond in a mature fashion rather than by losing their temper, becoming destructive, or choosing some other undesirable means of dealing with their anger.

QUESTION: The token economy sounds satisfactory for treating delinquent adolescents, but how can it be used to treat adolescents with other problems?

Adolescent problems can be reduced to either behavioral excesses or behavioral deficits in the adolescent's repertoire (Mann 1976). That is, adolescents tend to perform a specific behavior either much more often or much less often than is "normal." Simply a failure to conform to the expectations of society is often what brings adolescents into problems. This means that in addition to the general structure created by the token economy, a behavioral treatment program for adolescents must have special programs that are designed to treat individual excesses and deficits. Adolescents need to be made aware of inappropriate behaviors and to be given an opportunity to learn more socially appropriate behaviors.

Adolescents expressing a wide range of behavioral excesses or deficits can all benefit from the tight structure of the token economy. However, special programs within the economy are often necessary to treat specific problems in individuals.

QUESTION: What are the specific guidelines needed to set up a behavioral change program?

At least six basic procedures are essential for an individualized adolescent treatment program (Rees 1966):

1. Identify and define the behavior to be changed. The behavior to be changed is usually called the target behavior. The target behavior needs to be described in terms of the observable behavior the subject is to perform and the conditions under which the behavior must occur. Suppose that the adolescent is being treated for anorexia nervosa and is literally starving herself. The target behavior might be that the patient must weigh at least one hundred pounds when weighed every morning before breakfast. This definition of the target behavior leaves no doubt about what the adolescent must do or about how progress will be measured.

2. Obtain a baseline of the target behavior. A baseline is a measure of the frequency or magnitude of a target behavior before the behavior has been reinforced or treated. By obtaining a baseline, determining which contingencies are the most effective reinforcers is possible. In our example of the adolescent with anorexia, we might simply ask her parents for a record of her weight loss over the previous month, or we might weigh her every morning for a week. If her weight had dropped from 120 to 90 pounds during the last month (a weight loss that is not uncommon among anorexics), we would know that any treatment that stopped this downward trend and maintained her weight at 90 pounds is effective.

3. Determine whether the individual can perform the desired response. One of the most important initial judgments that a behavior therapist must make is whether the desired response is in the subject's current repertoire of behaviors. In the case of our anorexic adolescent, assuming there are no medical complications, we know that she is capable of weighing 100 pounds, since she weighed 120 pounds only a month ago. If, however, our target behavior is for a student to pass algebra tests, while in fact she is stuck on fractions, then we need to revise our target behavior so that it can be performed and reinforced. In such a case, we might redefine the target behavior to be one hour's study of fractions each night. The student's behavior would need to be gradually shaped until capable of studying algebra.

4. Identify potential reinforcers. A possible approach is to punish the failure to perform the target behavior, and to negatively reinforce the target behavior by removing the punishment when it has been performed. School systems use this strategy when they bar a student from extracurricular activities until grades are improved. The behaviorists, however, believe that it is more effective to use positive reinforcers, since by repeatedly pairing a behavior with a reinforcer, the behavior itself becomes a reinforcer (Locke 1969). That is, a behavior that is paired with positive reinforcers may eventually no longer need to be reinforced. Perhaps the easiest way of identifying reinforcers is to observe an adolescent during free time. What an adolescent does most frequently during free time is likely to be a behavior that has strong reinforcing properties. Reinforcers can be material (money), an activity (playing basketball), or social (receiving attention). If an adolescent smokes, for example, at every available chance, then smoking is a potential activity reinforcer. If smoking is not the target behavior, then another reinforcer will have to be found, perhaps listening to the radio or watching TV.

5. Shape and reinforce the desired behavior. This is the point at which treatment begins. Every time the adolescent performs the target behavior, it should be followed by the positive reinforcer. A frequency count of the target behavior is maintained and is compared with the baseline measures. Once the target behavior is being performed at a high frequency, the amount of reinforcement should be diminished so that the adolescent is not reinforced after every performance. It may also be necessary to use a variety of reinforcers, since the value of some reinforcers seems to fade.

6. Maintain records of the target behavior to determine whether the frequency increases and is maintained. Comparing the frequency of the behavior under treatment with its frequency before treatment quickly reveals whether the reinforcement is successful.

QUESTION: How enduring are the changes produced by a token economy program?

Some evidence suggests that without some kind of follow-up, the effects of token economy programs are short-lived. Follow-up studies of a token economy program developed by the California Youth Authority showed that almost as many adolescents failed parole during the next twelve months as had failed parole under previous institutional programs (Jesness and DeRisi 1973). Some contend there is little "generalization" (i.e., maintenance) of behavior learned in a token economy system once the adolescent is returned to the community.

Behavior therapists are attempting to deal with the problem of generalization in many ways. The most obvious solution is that when feasible, the adolescent should not be removed from the community in the first place. The trend is toward applying behavior modification principles directly in the adolescent's natural environment (Fo and O'Donnell 1974). Many schools, churches, and neighborhood groups are developing behavior modification programs, sometimes with the help of a behavioral consultant. One neighborhood group in Los Angeles used behavioral principles to keep adolescents in school and off drugs. Using a big brother system, they rewarded school attendance and drug avoidance with attention and tangible rewards. Besides beating the problem of generalization, this community approach avoided the implication that the adolescents were "sick" and needed to "get treated" (Los Angeles Federation of Community Coordinating Councils 1973).

Unfortunately, institutionalization is often necessary and is at any rate common. How, then, can the improvements made in an institution be maintained? One answer is the so-called halfway house. In a halfway house, adolescents only gradually return to their natural environment. The technical word for this procedure is *fading*. In fading, the environment of adolescents is gradually changed until a behavior performed in one environment is performed in another. Another way of maintaining the behaviors learned in a token economy system is through the use of behavioral contracts. The behavior therapist helps adolescents and their parents to develop an agreement that extends the contingencies of the token economy into the home environment. These behavioral contracts are discussed later.

Positive reinforcement and punishment

QUESTION: Which is more effective for changing behavior: positive reinforcement or punishment?

In his fictional utopia, Walden II (1948), B. F. Skinner decided that punishment would not exist. Skinner later wrote:

> In the long run, punishment, unlike reinforcement, works to the disadvantage of both the punished organism and the punishing agency. The aversive stimuli which are needed generate emotions, including predispositions to escape or retaliate, are disabling anxieties. For thousands of years men have asked whether this method could not be improved or whether some alternative practice would not be better. (Skinner 1953, 183)

Skinner (1953) believes that although punishment might produce a temporary suppression of a behavior, the temporary advantages are not worth the side effects, such as fear, neurosis, and psychosis. His position was later summarized in this way:

> Civilized man has made some progress in turning from punishment to alternative forms of control. Avenging gods and hell-fire have given way to an emphasis upon heaven and the positive consequences of the good life. In agriculture and industry, fair wages are recognized as an improvement over slavery. The birch rod has made way for the reinforcements naturally accorded the educated man. Even in politics and government the power to punish has been supplemented by a more positive support of the behavior which conforms to the interests of the governing agency. But we are still a long way from exploiting the alternatives. (Skinner 1953, 192)

Punishment seems to have undesirable side effects. Repeated punishment of aggressive behavior may inhibit not only the aggressiveness but also desirable assertiveness. Punishment may result in the avoidance of the punisher altogether, and thus the loss of an opportunity to be positively reinforcing. A common problem with teenagers is that punishment may result in escape and avoidance behaviors, such as lying or running away. Another problem is that parents who are punitive may turn out to be models of aggressive behavior; boys with punitive fathers may become combative in activities with their peers. Even when punishment for one behavior is quickly followed by reward for another positive behavior, a logical possibility is that following punishment with reward may lead to masochistic tendencies. In view of the possible side effects, should punishment be used at all?

More recent studies of the effects of punishment seem to show that punishment can effectively discourage certain types of behavior, and if used properly, can do so without undesirable side effects. Blackham and Silberman have summarized some guidelines for the safe and effective use of punishment: (1) Use punishment sparingly and never as the only means of eliminating undesirable behavior. (2) Clearly communicate the acceptable and unacceptable behaviors and the consequences for each. When adolescents are punished, they should know the reasons for the punishment. (3) Punish undesirable behaviors as soon as they occur, and do not mix positive reinforcers with punishment. (4) Make adolescents aware of desirable behavioral alternatives. (5) Positively reinforce the behavior you wish to promote. (6) Be consistent. Inconsistent punishment may entrench the undesirable behavior (Blackham and Silberman 1975, 71).

Even when punishment is properly used as just described, it is often difficult to distinguish the positive reinforcement elements from the punishment. If a teenager is verbally reprimanded for disrupting the class, is this positive reinforcement or punishment? Getting reprimanded is one way of getting attention, and although attention may be punishing to a few adolescents, it is positive reinforcement for many. Mischievous behavior is often performed precisely for the sake of attention.

Some feel that teaching is as effective when correct responses are rewarded and incorrect responses ignored as it is when correct responses are rewarded and incorrect punished. In short, both punishment and positive reinforcement can be useful and effective means of changing behavior. However positive reinforcement is effective even without the use of punishment, and does not seem to have harmful side effects. Punishment on the other hand seems to be temporary when used within existing social constraints, is ineffective without positive reinforcement, and has some undesirable side effects when misused.

QUESTION: In which cases can punishment be successfully used in combination with positive reinforcement?

Punishment is frequently used to eliminate behavior that has undesirable long-term effects, such as smoking, overeating, drug abuse, and sexual deviancy. The type of punishment used in treating these cases is called aversive therapy because it involves pairing an aversive, or painful, stimulus with the undesired behavior. Homosexual adolescents have been treated by administering electric shocks while viewing photographs of nude persons of the same sex. The patient avoids the shock by operating a switch that removes the picture within eight seconds of its appearance. To enhance the sexual attractiveness of the opposite sex, slides of nude members of the opposite sex are presented immediately after those of the same sex are removed. Initially, the least attractive male members of the same sex are paired with the most attractive members of the opposite sex. Gradually, as the adolescent grows indifferent to the member of the same sex and removes the picture quickly, more attractive members of the same sex and less attractive members of the opposite sex are paired. This procedure is continued until unattractive members of the opposite sex are preferred to attractive members of the same sex. The entire process takes approximately fifteen sessions and must be followed up by "booster shots." Homosexual practices tend to disappear, and heterosexual interest is greatly increased (Bandura 1969, 7).

Administering a painful or otherwise noxious stimulus is not the only way to punish a behavior. Another type of punishment is referred to as response cost. As its name suggests, the undesirable behavior costs the individual something in that some desirable object or condition is removed. When an athlete, whose grades are not passing, is denied the privilege of playing in after-school sports, the suspension is a response cost. In general, the more positive the reinforcer that is removed, the more likely it is to change the undesirable behavior. As with all punishments, however, too great a punishment may provoke anger and make the effects less predictable. One must not forget that adolescents, unlike laboratory animals, make judgments about the fairness of rewards and punishments. Assuming that the punishment is not too severe for the behavior, the response cost type of punishment has been found to be more effective than aversive therapy (Berrett 1965, 255–63). During the years of using behavior modification techniques, psychologists have developed alternatives to the use of punishment that appear to be as effective in eliminating unwanted behavior.

QUESTION: What are effective substitutes for punishment, and how can they be employed?

As substitutes for punishment, at least five preferable methods can be used to weaken undesirable behavior.

Time Out. The first alternative method of time out has been proven effective. When used properly, it will not produce the stressful negative emotions and unpredictable behaviors associated with punishment. The method can be introduced with an explanation that typically in games, a player or an official can call a time out. A time out is necessary when things are not going well. The players sit down and think about what is going on and have time to cool off. In some games like hockey, officials ask players to leave the game when they break the rules or play too rough. Time out helps the adolescent to understand that there is nothing personal in asking a player to leave the action for a while. The official who asks a player to leave the game may like the player very much. Life is like a game, and when players do not play according to the rules, they will hear the words "time out." In the future, and without any discussion, the adolescent will be expected to sit in another room for a short time. After a short period of cooling off and recognizing what mistake has been made, the adolescent will be allowed to return to the action.

Some consider the time out technique as punishment, but the effects are different. The adolescent will more willingly accept this method because it is simply part of a rule system and not a personal criticism. Time out is short, and the adolescent knows how to avoid and prevent it. A wise approach is to let adolescents participate in setting up the time out agreement, for they will then accept it better. Adolescents should know that nothing vindictive, willful, or painful is involved in using time out.

Parents of large families, where fights, small conflicts, and quarrels are expected, often use this method. The parents explain to their children that they do not have time to referee each fight. Instead, they tell the children in advance that a mandatory fifteen-minute time out will be called whenever a quarrel disrupts. The parents will not spend time talking, listening to excuses, or trying to find out who started the quarrel. Children soon learn that it takes less time for them to settle things quickly among themselves than to sit out for fifteen minutes, and that working out their problems is their responsibility.

Extinction. In the psychological laboratory, extinction is the most dependable method of weakening behavior. Extinction simply means removing rewards. No behavior will endure if it does not produce positive consequences. People who continue to lose their tempers, fight, argue, cheat, or withdraw are actually receiving rewards for these actions. To weaken these undesirable behaviors, one should determine what rewards are maintaining the behavior. Attention is the most common reward for most unwanted behavior in adolescents. If the attention is removed, the behavior will gradually weaken. One need not threaten, warn, or admonish. Adolescents will soon discern that unacceptable behavior has no payoff. If the reward is something that adolescents should have anyway—such as attention, freetime, or money—they should receive it before, not after, the misbehavior starts. In this way, adolescents lack an incentive for misbehaving.

Satiation. One can have too much of a good thing. We become sick of sweets at Christmas, the new toy eventually loses appeal, and the favorite album becomes tedious after too much repetition. Similarly, adolescents can become satiated with repeated exposure to the same stimulus. In satiation a stimulus that is actively sought is presented so many times that the adolescent later wants to avoid it. In twentieth-century folklore, the same story is repeatedly retold of a father who forever stopped his child from smoking by taking him out to the barn to smoke cigars.

Negative Practice. Negative practice is similar to satiation, except the undesirable response is repeated instead of the stimulus. This technique works when a stimulus or activity is initially attractive. In these cases, adolescents should be instructed to perform the unwanted activity and to continue without stopping until they become bored or thoroughly turned off. One youth with a swearing problem was asked to spend fifteen minutes each morning and afternoon in forced swearing practice. After a few days, swearing did not seem much fun anymore.

Incompatible Response. The most effective way to permanently weaken a behavior is to strengthen an incompatible response. Simultaneously performing opposite actions is impossible. The secret of success in using this method is to find an action that is the opposite of the undesirable behavior. Once one or more of these undesirable responses have been identified, a reward should be given constantly when adolescents perform the desired opposite action. For example, crankiness can be eliminated by rewarding pleasant smiles. Aggressive people can be rewarded for cooperation, kindness, or patience. Lazy adolescents should not be nagged. Instead, they should be watched closely and rewarded for small actions. A simple thanks can be the reward.

These methods—time out, extinction, satiation, negative practice, and rewarding the incompatible response—can weaken undesirable behaviors without producing the many problems encountered when using punishment. These preferable methods can be effectively combined and used simultaneously. They will require less time and policing, will provoke less resistance and emotion, and will allow new behaviors to be learned. Instead of saying, "Spare the rod and spoil the child," it is more practical to say, "Spare the rod and teach the child."

Special concerns when using behavior modification with adolescents

Adolescence is a period of development during which autonomy and self-direction are most important. Young children may take it for granted that their parents, teachers, and other adults have the power to reward or punish, but adolescents object to being controlled by someone who gives them the equivalent of an M&M for good behavior. Adolescents value their newfound freedoms and their personal identity, and they are often rebellious against authority. When a parent, teacher or other authority figure seems to say, "If you will be good, I'll give you some candy," adolescents may make a special point of not being "good." To adolescents, behavior modification can seem insulting and too manipulative, and condescending. Adolescents would rather go without candy and have personal freedom. How then can the principles of behavior modification be applied without running into this type of problem?

Let us assume the validity of the behavioral theory. Humans perform responses to bring about positive consequences to themselves or to remove negative conditions in their lives. Can this knowledge be put into some type of program where it will be usable with adolescents, particularly for adolescents who are deliberately rebellious?

Perhaps an answer lies in understanding the role of power in personal relationships. Social psychologists have found that the exercise of power can result in good relationships if (1) the power is used for the benefit of others, not exclusively for the pleasure of the authority, (2) criteria to earn the rewards are clearly spelled out, (3) the rewards are consistently delivered when these criteria have been met, (4) the person, as much as possible, is given freedom to either pursue or reject the rewards, and (5) the distribution of rewards is fair and impartial (i.e., the authority does not play favorites). These methods can prevent resentment toward authority figures who use behavior modification (Higbee and Jensen 1978).

QUESTION: What is a practical example of using behavior modification with a large group of adolescents?

A common challenge for high school teachers is maintaining order in the classroom. High school students tend to be gregarious, loud, and somewhat suspicious

Behavior modification programs are best when adapted to meet the special concerns of each adolescent. It is important that adolescents feel that their opinions and ideas are being respected by those authority figures using behavior modification.

of their teachers. Since teachers naturally hope to be accepted by their students, they often either ignore their students' misbehavior or will try to develop a rapport with their students through rap sessions, outside activities, and personal counseling. If this fails, the teacher may turn color and give the students a harsh lecture. What, then, is the behavioral solution to the problem of disruptive class behavior?

A study of twenty-five students in a low-track eleventh- and twelfth-grade English class shows how the systematic use of praise and reprimands can have a dramatic effect on classroom behavior. The first step that was taken was to carefully define the behavior to be changed. In this case, "talking out" and "inappropriate turning" were selected as target behaviors. "Talking out" was defined as vocal behavior, except during group discussions, without teacher permission. "Inappropriate turning" was defined to be turning more than ninety degrees from the position facing the front of the room. The second step was to obtain a measurement of the frequency of the inappropriate behaviors before the teacher was given any instructions on behavior modification. During twenty-seven days of baseline measurements, talking out occurred during an average of 25 percent of the time intervals, and inappropriate turning occurred during an average of 15 percent of the one-minute intervals. Since the positive reinforcer (praise) and the punishment (reprimands) were already identified, the third step was to begin reinforcement. To dramatize the effects of reinforcement, the teacher was instructed to begin by treating only the talking out behavior. From Day 28 on, whenever a student talked out, the teacher would respond by identifying and reprimanding the student. The teacher might, for example, say, "Doug, shut up!" When all the students became quiet, the teacher would praise the entire class, saying something like, "Thank you very much for not talking!" The graph shows that from Day 28 on, the frequency of talking out decreased steadily and finally reached an average of 5 percent. Meanwhile, the frequency of inappropriate turning remained the same. Beginning on Day 53, when the teacher likewise began to treat inappropriate turning, the frequency of that behavior also rapidly decreased and reached an average of about 4 percent.

Several important comments should be made about this successful procedure. First, the teacher concentrated praise and reprimands during the first two minutes of the class period, since the baseline indicated that most of the inappropriate behavior occurred during this period. Without this emphasis on the first few minutes of class, the procedure may have been far less effective. Second, perhaps the best approach is to begin by using only positive reinforcement and to use punishment only if necessary. Third, an essential element is that the teacher did not make threats that could not be carried out. Praise and reprimands were all that were necessary; idle threats would have probably decreased the teacher's effectiveness (McAllister et al. 1969).

> **QUESTION: Will adolescents object to having to earn reinforcers that they feel belong to them anyway?**

To answer this question, distinguishing between appropriate and inappropriate contingencies is necessary. Reinforcers can be considered in three general categories: (1) survival entitlements (e.g., food, shelter, and safety), (2) nature entitlements (e.g., love, dignity, and respect), and (3) discretionary entitlements (e.g., those not crucial to adolescents' survival or self-respect. Reinforcements that relate to the survival or self-respect of adolescents should ordinarily be given without any strings attached. Adolescents' physical and emotional safety should be protected even if they do not do what an authority wants them to do. They should also not be made contingent on good behavior, except in extreme cases. The problem is trying to decide which entitlements are discretionary. Adolescents may insist that they simply cannot survive without a new surfboard. The judgment about which contingencies are appropriate is largely at the discretion of the authority.

Once again, consider the problem that teenagers do not want to be manipulated by an authority. How can this theory be applied with these adolescents? One way of looking at this problem is to realize that as long as adolescents feel that power is being used for the authority's benefit, or believe that the authority can be successfully outwitted or ignored, adolescents will continue to rebel. As long as adolescents feel personally affronted and challenged by the authority, they will not see that certain behavioral changes are actually to their own advantage. Presented next are some ways to handle this problem through some adaptions called the systems, my-rights, positive relationship, contract, and self-directed approaches.

Other approaches

QUESTION: What is the systems approach?

The idea in a *systems approach* is to devise a nonpersonal system of behavior modification—a program that cannot arbitrarily be altered. The most popular kind of systems application is the token economy already described. If adolescents do not earn points or tokens, they can blame only the program or themselves. A program instituted on an impersonal basis and justified beforehand should not evoke resentment toward the authority by adolescents. Adolescents could not feel that an authority figure is arbitrarily manipulating; rather, their life is being controlled by the economy of the system. The hope is that adolescents will eventually see that how they survive in the token economy does not depend on another person; it depends on themselves.

QUESTION: What is the positive relationship approach of using behavior modification?

Another approach, which is the opposite of the systems approach, is the *positive relationship approach*. The systems approach is necessarily impersonal, but the positive relationship approach depends on a positive personal relationship between the authority figure and the teenager. This approach can be seen in the positive relationship between coaches and their teams. These coaches have a great deal of power at their disposal. They tell the teams what they want, and the teams work hard to get the coaches' attention and approval. The key to this approach is to become liked and respected. Authority figures who have managed to attain this goal find that adolescents will almost worship them. With these people, adolescents go to great lengths to get compliments and praise, even during the so-called rebellious teenage years.

QUESTION: How can one make behavior modification work without being either impersonal or charismatic?

Some find that the systems approach does not appeal to them because of its impersonal nature. Others are not sure they are charismatic enough to use the positive relationship approach. For these people, three other approaches are possible. The first is called the *my-rights approach*. People who use this approach openly assert a legitimate authority role over adolescents. Adolescents are not confronted by an impersonal system, nor are they motivated by idolized adults. Instead, adolescents deal with authority figures who definitely relate to adolescents from a leadership role. Rather than being manipulative, authority figures mince no words with adolescents when it comes to standards of behavior and rewards. They display the reinforcements at their disposal, and explain rights and privileges as parents, teachers, or other authorities. They point out that parents' rights include the right to preside in their own home, to decide matters that affect the family, to make final decisions, to set the standards for the family, and so on. The second step in this approach is for authority figures to state exactly what their expectations are, as well as to state exactly how adolescents will be rewarded for complying. The third step is to reward adolescents, as promised, for complying. Authority figures may back up their statements with as much argument, logic, and example as they can, but they always make it clear that they are the final arbitrators and will administer the rewards as they see fit (Robinson 1982).

Another method is called the *contract approach*. In contrast to the my-rights approach, adults are willing to bargain with adolescents. Adults follow five steps:

1. They state what they want.
2. They state what they will give in return for what they want from adolescents.
3. They bargain with adolescents until they agree on expectations and rewards.
4. They write up a binding agreement, which both adult and adolescent sign.
5. They monitor adolescents' behavior, and they reward according to the contract. The contract approach has been widely and creatively applied. Although the approach is often used to change specific behaviors and to settle specific disputes, it has even been used to address adolescents' general personality styles.

QUESTION: How can the contract approach be used to change such a general characteristic as personality?

In one study, the contract included a description of the adolescent's self-image, patterns of relating to others, and methods of handling life experiences. Each contract contained two images or labels, one positive and one negative. For example, a contract for Laura, an older adolescent girl, used the images "lofty rattlesnake" and "blue-ribbon horse." These images may be used with a wide variety of patients. For lower-functioning patients, more concrete contracts are written. Psychotic patients may get a contract such as "tuned-in Sam versus tuned-out Sam." The adolescent's peers are often a source of such positive and negative images.

This type of contract has several advantages over those which only specify certain behaviors. By treating adolescents as special enough to deserve individualized contracts that describe their uniqueness, adolescents are encouraged to take an active interest in change. The general images tend to discourage adolescents from making sport of finding loopholes in the contract. Finally, the use of a positive image, especially one suggested by the adolescent's peers, helps to take the dark, courtroom quality out of the contract process.

The contracts used in this approach seldom have any legal implications and can be written in almost any form or order. The wording of the contract should be simple and clear, and should not contain jargon. Most adults, let alone adolescents, cannot make sense of legal documents. Important, though, is including all of the following items:

1. The date the agreement begins and ends
2. A clear, precise description of the behavior to be changed
3. The type and amount of reward to be used
4. The schedule on which the rewards will be delivered
5. The signatures of the adolescent, parents or others, and the mediator, if there is one
6. A scheduled review or renegotiation date

In the self-directed approach to behavior modification adolescents are involved in and responsible for monitoring their own progress. Reasons for the rewards that parents provide, such as use of the family car, are explained to the adolescent so that he has full knowledge of the behavior modification process.

Besides these six items, often helpful is including a bonus clause for exceptional performance and a penalty clause in case the behavior is not performed (DeRisi and Butz 1975, 45).

QUESTION: What is the self-directed approach?

The last approach to using behavior modification with adolescents is different from the first four. Although the *self-directed approach* requires more adolescent initiative, it also requires adult involvement in at least four ways. First, adults should discuss goals with adolescents. What do adolescents want out of life? Why have they not been able to achieve what they want from life? Once adolescents' goals and their obstacles are defined, the second step is to outline the principles of behavior modification. The adult should make sure adolescents understand how contingent reinforcers are used and how behavior change can be measured. The third step is to help adolescents implement a program. What behavior would they like to reinforce? If the behavior requires shaping, what are the successive steps? How will adolescents measure their progress? The fourth and final step is to provide encouragement, support, and rewards.

The great advantage of the self-directed approach is that it does not provoke resistance or rebellion in adolescents. Although adults usually supply the rewards, adolescents are responsible for monitoring their own progress. Because adolescents are involved in every stage of the process, they have a growing, satisfying sense of autonomy and responsibility. *Self-directed Behavior* (Watson and Tharp 1972) is an excellent book on how to implement the approach.

Summary

Behaviorists believe that behavior is caused by a person's environment. When behaviorists attempt to resolve problem behavior, they attempt to locate and eliminate environmental factors that cause the behavior; they do not look for internal causes as do the psychotherapists. The external events are said to determine the behavior, and the individual is said to have learned the behavior. Individuals learn various behaviors over time, and current experiences either weaken or strengthen those behaviors. In a sense, behavioral problems are simply manifestations of an unhealthy environment. Behavior problems should be dealt with through a process of behavior modification, which is based upon the principles of operant conditioning, a philosophy forcefully espoused by B. F. Skinner. The principles of operant conditioning describe the relationship between a person's behavior and environmental events. If an environmental event occurs only after a certain behavior, then the event, or consequence, is said to be contingent upon the performance of the behavior.

The following are the four basic types of contingent relationships:

1. Positive reinforcement
2. Negative reinforcement
3. Punishment
4. Extinction

Rewards are positive reinforcements. The removal of an unpleasant consequence is a negative reinforcement. A penalty imposed for some action is a punishment. Ignoring certain behaviors is the process of extinction. Positive and negative reinforcements are used to strengthen certain behaviors, and punishment and extinction are used to weaken undesirable behavior.

Shaping is the process of reinforcing small changes in behavior that match a desired overall behavioral goal. For example, to shape shy individuals' behavior into more gregarious behavior, a behaviorist might reward them for the smallest behavioral movements toward sociability, such as allowing the individuals to have a favorite dessert for simply smiling at someone.

For shaping to be a successful process, the behaviors to be reinforced must carefully be defined, must immediately be reinforced, and must not be reinforced for too long.

Behavioral principles naturally lend themselves to implementation in structured, institutional settings. Inpatient behavior programs have been demonstrated to be effective with a wide variety of behavioral problems, from weight control to sex role changes. Token economy systems are behavior programs that heavily stress positive reinforcement. A token economy is a "24-hour learning environment," has substantial behavioral control over its participants (which makes it useful for dealing with delinquents), and permits measurable progress for a variety of behavioral problems.

The point system forms the basis for token economies. Desirable behaviors are rewarded with points, and undesirable behaviors are punished by point fines. Patients can exchange their points for various goods and services. The following are the six basic steps in setting up an individualized adolescent treatment program:

1. Identify and define the behavior to be changed.
2. Obtain a baseline of the target behavior.
3. Determine whether the individual can perform the desired response.
4. Identify potential reinforcers.
5. Shape and reinforce the desired behavior.
6. Maintain records of the target behavior to determine whether the frequency of the desired behavior increases and is maintained.

To be effective, punishment must be used with extreme caution. B. F. Skinner believes that even when punishment is used with caution to temporarily suppress a behavior, the temporary advantages are not worth the side effects, such as fear, neurosis, and psychosis. Blackham and Silberman, however, believe that punishment can be effective under certain conditions:

1. Use punishment sparingly and never as the only means of eliminating undesirable behavior.
2. Clearly communicate the acceptable and unacceptable behaviors and the respective consequences for each.
3. Punish undesirable behaviors as soon as they occur, and do not mix positive reinforcers with punishment.
4. Make adolescents aware of desirable behavioral alternatives.
5. Positively reinforce the behavior you wish to promote.
6. Be consistent.

At least five preferable alternatives to punishment can be used to weaken undesirable behavior: time-out, extinction, satiation, negative practice, and incompatible response.

Authority figures—those who administer behavior modification programs—are often viewed by adolescents with distrust. The following are five ways to prevent resentment toward authority figures and behavioral programs:

1. Make sure the power of the authority figure is used for the benefit of others and not exclusively for the pleasure of the authority.
2. Clearly explain the criteria to earn rewards.
3. Consistently deliver the rewards when the criteria have been met.
4. Give adolescents freedom to either pursue or reject the rewards.
5. Distribute the rewards fairly and impartially.

The following are five effective behavior modification approaches:

1. The systems approach emphasizes impartial, nonpersonal programs that participants can trust. It rejects arbitrary or subjective program orientations.
2. The positive relationship approach depends upon a close, intimate relationship between authority figures and participants.
3. The my-rights approach encourages authority figures to openly assert their rights and roles.
4. The contract approach emphasizes the role of bargaining between authority figures and participants.
5. The self-directed approach emphasizes the role of participants in the modification process and provides participants with a growing, satisfying sense of autonomy and responsibility.

References

Ayllon, T., & N. Azrin. 1968. *The token economy.* New York: Appleton-Century-Crofts.

Bandura, A. 1969. *Principles of behavior modification.* New York: Holt, Rinehart & Winston.

Beitel, A., P. Everts, B. Boile, E. Nagel, C. Bragdon, & B. MacKesson. 1983. Hub group: An innovative approach to group therapy in a short term in-patient unit. *Adolescence* 18(69): 1–15 (Spring).

Berrett, B. H. 1965. Reduction in rate of multiple text by free operant conditioning methods. In *Case studies in behavior modification,* ed. L. P. Ullmann & L. Krasner, 255–63. New York: Holt, Rinehart & Winston.

Blackham, G., & A. Silberman. 1975. *Modification of child and adolescent behavior.* 2d ed. Belmont, Calif.: Wadsworth.

Brewer, W. F. 1974. There is no convincing evidence for operant or classical conditioning in adult humans. In *Cognition and the symbolic process,* ed. W. B. Weimer & D. S. Palermo, 1–42. New York: Wiley.

DeRisi, W. J., & G. Butz. 1975. *Writing behavioral contracts: A case simulation practice manual.* Champaign, Ill.: Research Press.

Fo, W. S., & C. R. O'Donnell. 1974. The buddy system: Relationships and contingency conditions in a community intervention program for youth with nonprofessionals as behavior-change agents. *Journal of Consulting and Clinical Psychology* 42: 163–69.

Higbee, K., & L. Jensen. 1978. *Influence: what it is and how to use it.* Provo, Utah: Brigham Young University Press.

Jesness, C. F., & W. J. DeRisi. 1973. Some variations in techniques of contingency management in a school for delinquents. In *Behavior therapy with delinquents,* ed. J. S. Stumphauser, 196–235. Springfield, Ill.: Thomas.

Kazdin, A. 1975. *Behavior modification in applied settings*. Homewood, Ill.; Dorsey Press.
Los Angeles Federation of Community Coordinating Councils: The Community Acts for Delinquency Prevention. 1973. Fortieth Annual Meeting, April, Los Angeles.
Mann, R. A. 1976. Assessment of behavioral excesses in children. In *Behavioral assessment: A practical handbook,* ed. M. Hersen & A. S. Bellack. New York: Pergamon Press.
McAllister, L. W., J. G. Stachowiak, D. M. Baer, & L. Conderman. 1969. The application of operant conditioning techniques in a secondary school classroom. *Journal of Applied Behavior Analysis* 2(4): 277–85.
Patterson, G. R. 1971. Recent trends in behavior modification with children. Paper presented at the Western Psychological Association Convention, April, San Francisco.
Rees, E. P. 1966. *The analysis of human operant behavior*. Dubuque, Iowa: Brown.
Robinson, P. 1982. *Manipulating parents*. New York: Prentice-Hall.
Rychlak, J. 1981. *A philosophy of science for personality theory*. Melbourne, Fla.: Krieger.
Skinner, B. F. 1948. *Walden II*. New York: Macmillan.
_____. 1953. *Science and human behavior*. New York: Macmillan.
_____. 1961. *Cumulative record*. New York: Appleton-Century-Crofts.
Watson, D. L., & R. G. Tharp. 1972. *Self-directed behavior: Self-modification for personal adjustment*. Monterey, Calif.: Brooks/Cole.
Watson, J. B. 1913. Psychology as the behaviorist views it. *Psychological Review* 20: 158.

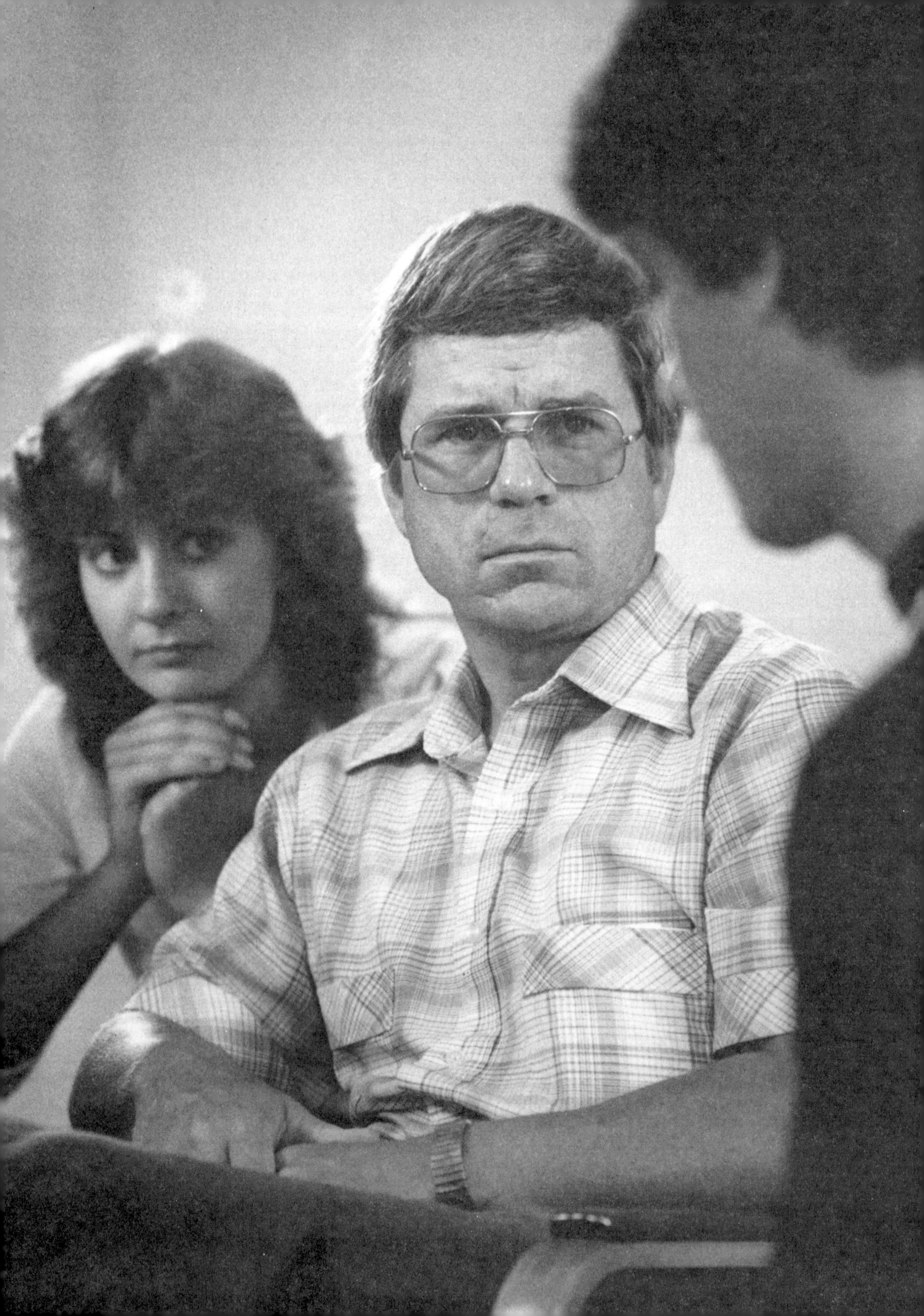

CHAPTER SIXTEEN

Phenomenological theory: application for building relationship skills

SURVEY AND QUESTIONS

This chapter discusses how phenomenological theory helps in developing effective relationship and communication skills. Reading the chapter will provide answers to the following questions:

Phenomenological Theory and Its Application

If society were to allow all people to grow as they "will," would chaos result?
Are some people well adjusted and others maladjusted?

Relationship Skills

Why do nonprofessionals do well with patients?
What does the nonprofessional, paraprofessional, or lay person do that is so beneficial?
What does Carkhuff propose should happen in his training program?
How does Carkhuff's theory apply to adolescents?
What are the major helping conditions?
What are authoritarian behaviors?
What are blaming behaviors?
What are opinionated behaviors?
What is tuned-out behavior?

Communication Skills

What are the key elements of effective communication?
What is an example of clarifying?
What kinds of communication responses are helpful?
What is a supportive response?
What is an advice-giving response?
What is an interpretative response?
What is a questioning response?
What is a sympathizing response?
What is an active-listening response?

Listening

What is active listening?
When should a person use active listening?

Owning Feelings

What does it mean to own feelings?
What are the effects of owning and disowning feelings?

Empathy

What is empathy?
How does empathy directly help communication?
Can levels of empathy be categorized?

Phenomenological theory and its application

A traveler approached an old gentleman sitting in front of a general store on the outskirts of a small midwestern town. The traveler inquired, "Could you tell me what the people of this town are like? I'm considering moving here."

"Well," the old gentleman replied, "first tell me what the people were like in the town you came from."

The traveler answered, "The people there were insincere, given to gossip, could not be trusted, and well, they just weren't good neighbors."

After a short pause the old man warned, "You'd best travel on. The people here are the same way."

A short time after, another traveler arrived and asked the same question. Again, the old gentleman asked, "What were the people like where you came from?"

The second traveler stated, "Very gracious, excellent neighbors. They were kind and good to us. Our family hated to leave them."

"Well," the old gentleman replied, "you are fortunate. Here you will find the same kind of people."

The theoretical approach presented in this chapter assumes that reality is based on what people perceive. Accordingly, all people have their own reality because all people have their unique and private perceptions of the world. Although differences exist among people's realities, similarities are still present because of common elements in human perceptual experience. The differences among perceptions result in individual behavior.

Besides questioning the fundamental assumptions about human reality, phenomenological theorists usually take a definite position on the issue of human nature. These theorists believe that a positive growth force leads humans toward mental health and desired social behavior. The two basic tenets or assumptions presented in this chapter are: (1) perception is the basis of reality and behavior, and (2) within each individual there exists a positive growth force toward health.

The theorist who holds the perceptual or phenomenological point of view almost always ascribes to these two assumptions. Abraham Maslow (1954, 1968), Coombs and Snygg (1959), Carl Rogers (1961, 1969), and Sidney Jourard (1971) are referenced in this chapter because they are popular spokespeople for this position. These theorists generally believe that a growth tendency exists in all people that directs them toward self-fulfillment or, in Abraham Maslow's words, "self-actualization."

In *Motivation and Personality* (1954), Maslow describes this characteristic. Self-actualized people are reality oriented, and have an accurate view of reality. They also accept themselves and other people for what they are, both emotionally and behaviorally. They devote their attention to duties, making themselves problem centered rather than self-centered. These people seek privacy, but also enjoy other people. They concentrate on developing rich and deep relationships with a limited number of people. They are self-directing and independent, being autonomous in the face of rejection or unpopularity. They have the capacity to see the simple beauties and purposes of life—for example an early morning sunrise, the smiles on children's faces when they do well in school, beautiful music, and so on. They frequently have mystical, spiritual, and rich emotional experiences. They identify with all humankind rather than just with a small family, state, or country. They feel a belongingness with people in general.

Self-actualized people evaluate others as individuals and not on the basis of race, social status, or other artificial distinctions. They have basic ethics and values upon which they govern their behavior. Their sense of humor is not hostile, but more philosophical.

Maslow developed this description after studying a group of eminent men. The self-actualizing tendency assumes that people have a basic inherent growth force that leads them to accomplish and obtain these characteristics, and recognizes that these characteristics can be expressed in many ways.

QUESTION: If society were to allow all people to grow as they "will," would chaos result?

Rogers (1961) believes that what is consistent with the maintenance and enhancement of an individual is also consistent with the maintenance and enhancement of society in general. This conception encourages the giving of freedom, because the growth of an individual is entirely consistent with the welfare and general promotion of humankind as a whole. Rogers rejects the notion that humans are selfish, negative, and potentially destructive. Rogers also maintains that behavior that is destructive to others is destructive to oneself and vice versa. When humans are allowed to express their natural potential, they will live a reasonably ordered, constructive life without the necessity of being held in check by social institutions and controls.

The phenomenologist believes that perception is the basis of reality and that each person has a positive growth tendency. What can get in the way of this positive growth, however, is an individual's inaccurate concept of themselves.

QUESTION: Why are some people well adjusted and others maladjusted?

Although all living matter is said to have a growth force, only in humans does it take a form that can find expression in the self-concept. Rogers considers the self the most important part of psychological growth. He therefore focuses on the growth of a healthy self-concept. Healthy people develop positive self-concepts from experiencing *positive regard* from significant other people, such as mothers, fathers, close friends, wives, husbands, and so on. This positive regard later becomes a positive self-regard. Positive self-regard refers to people first receiving approving evaluations of themselves. When some thoughts and behaviors are approved and others are rejected, especially by significant others, people are said to have experienced "conditional positive regard." Under these conditions, people develop a self-concept that distorts or denies these aspects of behavior or thought that have been rejected or attacked. Without complete and accurate information about themselves, people then have an inaccurate or unrealistic concept of themselves. This results in defensiveness. Because of the self-restriction imposed on incoming information, people are unable to accept themselves for what they are. When people deny incoming information about themselves, which is typical of people who experience conditional self-regard, they then become psychologically crippled. They are unable to know their true self because of their defensiveness or because of their denial and distortion of new information. We call these people maladjusted, neurotic, and in extreme cases, psychopathic. Those individuals fortunate enough to have experienced unconditional positive regard, however, rapidly grow toward becoming fully functioning people.

Unconditional positive regard basically means that significant people respect others' thoughts and behaviors even when they are sometimes disagreeable or different from their own.

Relationship skills

A number of theorists and writers have developed some specific approaches to help translate these concepts into practical application for working with adolescents. Perhaps the best beginning is the following statement by Carl Rogers:

> [S]elected housewives can be given training in a year's time which enables them to try on therapy with disturbed individuals—therapy, which in its quality is indistinguishable from the work of experienced professionals. (Rogers 1969, 319)

Today the number of adolescents who need help far surpasses the number of available professionals in the helping professions. To alleviate this shortage of highly trained, specialized psychotherapists, counselors, and social workers, volunteers and lay people have been introduced into the social mechanisms for helping troubled youth.

To meet the need to train lay people as well as others who are designated as paraprofessionals, a number of books and approaches for short-term training have emerged (Goodman 1972; Gazda 1973; Egan 1975; Johnson 1981). Reported research and theory support the assertion that paraprofessionals or lay people (or both) can be effective in the helping process (Carkhuff and Truax 1965; Hurvitz 1970; Goldstein 1973; Kopita 1973; Lamb and Clack 1974).

Researchers (Poser 1966; Ellsworth and Ellsworth 1970) have even found that male patients with chronic schizophrenia showed more improvement when treated by lay therapists than similar patients treated by professional therapists. In one rehabilitation program, clients seen by nonprofessionals had better rehabilitation outcomes than those seen by professional counselors (Truax 1969). These studies were cited in an article describing how volunteers can be trained to work with troubled boys. The author (Schaefer 1981, 728–29) states:

> In recent years there has been a growing recognition that mental health services cannot adequately be provided by a small, specially trained group of professionals. There are simply too many people in need of help and too few therapists. One proposed solution is to use nonprofessionals for certain tasks that do not necessitate highly specialized training or experience. . . .
>
> The success that volunteers have experienced with adult mental patients has also been reported in projects involving children. Functioning as friends and companions, volunteer college students have achieved therapeutic success in working with emotionally disturbed children in elementary school settings (Cowen, Zax, and Laird 1966), severely disturbed, institutionalized children (Girona 1972), children with learning problems at a rural outpatient clinic (Mitchell 1966), children experiencing difficulty relating to others (Goodman 1967), and disturbed, withdrawn adolescents (Hilgard and Moore 1969). In addition, mature men have long been used effectively as a "big brother" substitute for children from fatherless homes. (Litchenburg 1956).

QUESTION: Why do nonprofessionals do well with patients?

One answer was given by Carkhuff and Truax (1965), who reported that training in clinical psychology decreased the amount of warmth, openness, and genuineness that students had with their patients. This may be an overstatement, but does bring into focus a key element in working with adolescents: the positive relationship. Another reason for the success of lay therapists is that patients may see the nonprofessionals as more similar to themselves (Goodman 1972). In many cases, the volunteer also serves as a model, as in the "big brother" programs. Some research indicates that people who do not receive therapy often do as well as people who receive treatment. One explanation for this improvement is that those who do not receive treatment are helped by others such as friends, clergy, Alcoholics Anonymous, and so on. This type of help may not be received by people who undergo professional counseling.

QUESTION: What does the nonprofessional, paraprofessional, or lay person do that is so beneficial?

The key elements seem to be genuine caring and the development of positive relationships between the volunteers and the patients. Carkhuff and others developed a popular theory that focuses on these elements (Carkhuff and Truax 1965; Carkhuff 1969a, 1969b, 1971, 1972a, 1972b, 1972c). Carkhuff and Berenson (1967) found that the essential characteristics of the successful helpers were accurate empathy and genuineness. Carkhuff's basic theory was developed by borrowing concepts from the phenomenological theory and by examining what happens when people are helped in nonprofessional helping relationships.

Carkhuff refers to the person receiving help as the "helpee" (instead of the "patient"), and refers to the therapist as the "helper." Carkhuff felt that he could best develop training techniques in a small-group setting and that the person seeking help (the helpee) could best benefit from learning how to help others. An example of this type of person or relationship can be seen in the following:

> I remember having a good relationship with my mother as a teenager and being able to talk with her about almost anything. I remember coming home from junior high and she would either be baking something or lying down (because of her illnesses) and I would go into her room, flop down beside her on the bed, and relate the happenings of the day.
>
> She always wanted to know everything about me and my friends—especially in our sports and social lives. Also, for some time she was a good friend with the mother of my girlfriend and she would often have much needed information about what the "girls" were doing, who they liked, and why they liked who they did. So we would generally have these little talks and she seemed to enjoy being involved in my world.
>
> Later on in high school, she would often be waiting up after a date and when I got home we would sometimes sit down and talk about my date. Usually my older sister or brothers had a date the same night and we would all be home around the same time—so we would often sit and talk until two or three in the morning.
>
> I think we were able to have such a good relationship because she would talk to me on my level and was very interested in my life—and that was important to me. Furthermore, I always felt totally loved and accepted by my mother and I know that this made a difference in my being able to open up.

QUESTION: What does Carkhuff propose should happen in his training program?

Carkhuff believes that the helping process has three basic stages. The first stage is *self-exploration*, during which helpees and helpers come to know each other better. This stage involves development of empathy and a deep understanding for one another. It also involves learning to respect and believe in each other, and to give warmth in the form of caring love. Before helpers can be of assistance, they must understand helpees in depth. Helpees must also be able to know themselves and must feel that they can trust and believe in the helpers.

The next stage is *understanding*. Here the role of the helpers is to assist the helpees in seeing and understanding their situation better. As helpees look at their life more accurately and clearly, with the assistance of the helpers, they begin to understand why they have problems.

The third stage is helpee *action*. In this stage, helpers provide confrontation and immediacy. Immediacy means looking at what is now happening between helpers and helpees. Helpees use immediacy as an illustration of what is going on in other areas of their life. Helpers and helpees then take chances in considering plans of action. The helpees devise a plan to resolve their problems. During this third stage, helpees and helpers must be capable of mutual problem solving to develop a program or actions that will result in a better life for the

The ability to relate well with adolescents is the key to a successful helping relationship. The professional helper, such as a school guidance counselor, as well as the para-professional and lay person, can all improve their effectiveness with adolescents by developing genuine caring relationships with them.

helpees. This phase is the most important, and the skills learned during this time should be of assistance to helpees in solving future problems.

QUESTION: How does Carkhuff's theory apply to adolescents?

In the remainder of the chapter, readers are given a program to enable them to work more successfully with troubled adolescents. The program is based on the Carkhuff model. The third phase, or action phase, is not presented, however, because the behavior modification chapter can serve as a substitute for Carkhuff's third phase. The action stage in the Carkhuff model is basically a problem-solving approach in which helpers ask helpees to go through the following steps:

1. Define the problem areas.
2. Describe the goals in the problem areas.
3. Analyze the critical dimensions and directions.
4. Consider the alternative courses of action.
5. Consider the advantages and disadvantages of alternative courses of action.

6. Develop physical, emotional, or intellectual programs that could be successful.
7. Develop progressive gradations of the programs (Carkhuff 1969a, 242).

The steps in behavior modification basically accomplish the previous steps in a slightly altered form.

This chapter uses a program developed by Vern H. Jensen (1978) to accomplish training in the first two stages. The program that follows, presented in two phases, uses Professor Jensen's materials with permission. This program has been revised with many improvements (Jensen, Heaps, Nelson, and Shingleton 1983), and has been modified and condensed in the following pages. Because readers do not have the benefit of group training with a leader, as is required in the Jensen et al. program, the primary modification is to present the content of the program with self-instructional activities. These activities are to be completed by readers to assist them in developing helping skills. The term helper is used in the remainder of the chapter and the helpee is referred to as the adolescent.

Completion of this program is not meant to prepare readers to take the place of professional therapists or counselors. Helpers should be aware of their limitations, and should be sensitive to and aware of the need to refer some adolescents to professionals and helping agencies. Nevertheless, in most avenues of life people are called upon to help one another, either in relationship to their work or as a friend. Table 16–1 lists lay people who are often called upon to help adolescents.

One writer classified the types of helpers into the categories of structured and unstructured. After considering Table 16–2 one can see that even if an individual does not at some time find that he or she is in a structured helping role, he or she most likely will function in an unstructured helping role.

QUESTION: What are the major helping conditions?

My mother just never stopped talking to me and my brothers and sisters. The communication lines were always open and she was always very interested in anything we had to say.

TABLE 16–1 Lay People Frequently Called Upon to Counsel and Help Adolescents

Chaplains	Organizational-developmental consultants
Child-care workers	Parents
Church workers	Peer helpers
Community-development workers	Physicians
Counselors	Police
Correctional-system workers	Probation officers
Family members	Psychiatrists
Friends	Psychologists
Group leaders	Rehabilitation workers
Hospital workers	Residence-hall directors, counselors, and assistants
Human-relations specialists	Social workers
Interviewers	Teachers
Marriage partners	Trainers
Mental-health workers and aids	Tutors
Ministers	Volunteers in human-service programs
Nurses	Youth workers

Source: Adapted from *The Skilled Helper,* by G. Egan. Copyright © 1984, 1975 by Wadsworth, Inc. Reprinted by permission of Brooks/Cole Publishing Company, Monterey, California 93940.

TABLE 16-2 Structured and Unstructured Helping

Helping affiliations can be classified into various levels, from formal and structured to informal and unstructured as illustrated below.

Structured

Professional helpers. (Examples: social workers, ministers, psychologists, teachers, school counselors, physicians, nurses, psychiatrists, legal counselors with specialized training and legal responsibility.)
Paraprofessional helpers. (Examples: trained interviewers, receptionists, aides in mental health and rehabilitation, and persons in correctional, educational, employment, and social agency settings.)
Volunteers. (Nonpaid persons with short-term training in basic helping skill and agency orientation.)

Unstructured

Friendships. (Informal, mutual, and unstructured helping relationships over time.)
Family. (Informal mutual helping system, interdependent in variables degrees.)
Community and general human concern. (Informal, unstructured, ad hoc helping acts to alleviate danger, suffering, or deprivation.)

Source: Brammer, 1979, 12.

My father, on the other hand, found it harder and harder to really talk to us as we got older. For quite a while only the normal everyday things were said to one another. I think this really started when my sister and I started to cry more often over things he thought were silly and he would leave us and send in Mom to make us feel better. What did help us grow closer to Dad again were our family outings and vacations, I feel. When Dad worked he had too many things to fix around the house or was too tired to communicate but when he took a day or a week off for a family outing we really learned to communicate with him again. It started with impersonal things that we did like playing frisbee or football, etc., and just having so much fun together at those times made it easier to communicate about many things with him. The lines were re-opened. Now I can talk about anything with my father and this has brought us closer than ever before.

The personal relationship a helper establishes is paramount to helping. A climate in which adolescents feel free to express their attitudes and explore their problems will be more effective than one in which they feel restrained or misunderstood.

The purpose of Phase I is to focus on the basic helping conditions that are essential to providing an effective helping relationship. An important ingredient in establishing and maintaining a helping relationship is the ability to communicate effectively with others. The goal is for communication to flow freely and understandably between helper and adolescent. The helper, however, sets the stage by responding appropriately to the adolescent to open lines of communication and to establish a working relationship. The helper therefore needs to be the more skillful person. Four skills are taught in this chapter: (1) positive versus negative communication, (2) active listening, (3) owning feelings, and (4) empathy.

As a result of conditioning during the early years of life, and through tradition, we have a tendency to pick up faulty communication patterns that we use in our relationships with others. At least four types of faulty patterns are readily identifiable. Although they are treated separately here, a good deal of interrelatedness exists among the four behaviors. They are authoritarian behaviors, blaming behaviors, opinionated behaviors, and tuned-out behaviors.

QUESTION: What are authoritarian behaviors?

Authoritarian behaviors include advising, directing, urging, forbidding, warning, moralizing, ordering, and commanding, which often create roadblocks to communication. This is not to say that authoritarian behaviors are faulty in all cases, but they do need to be reevaluated as to the frequency and appropriateness of their use. When people use such behaviors, they should be conscious that they are using them, that they are intentionally using them, and that they have a particular purpose in mind. Ordering, forbidding, commanding, and so forth may be appropriate at times. If a small child, for example, is heading toward a busy street, we may not only give a command, but we may also physically carry the child to safety. Such an emergency situation may not allow for other types of communication, but only action. In examining authoritarian behaviors, we might consider the following three drawbacks in their use:

1. They tend to be overused.
2. They are often used inappropriately.
3. There may be more effective ways of behaving when working with particular people and under certain situations.

QUESTION: What are blaming behaviors?

Two forms of blaming behavior are considered here. In the first, people simply blame others for their problems. A department staff, for example, may infer

Authoritarian behaviors include advising, directing, urging, as well as forbidding, moralizing, and commanding. These types of behaviors may be appropriate in some instances, but they should be used consciously, with regard to their effectiveness.

that they would have no problems if it were not for the central administration. Students may contend that they would have received higher grades if the teachers had been more capable. Blaming behavior is a defense mechanism whereby individuals have a need to shift the blame to others and thus deny themselves the responsibility for dealing directly with the real problem.

In the second form of blaming behavior, individuals fail to recognize or admit their own feelings and frustrations, and project them onto others through accusative behavior. Parents, for example, may react to their teenagers who have come home late from a date by lashing out at them in an accusative manner. Parents in their frustration may tell their children that they are no good, that they cannot trust them, and that they need to grow up. At the same time, parents fail to own up to their feelings that they became frustrated when their children did not come home on time. Both of these forms of blaming behavior tend to block communication and create locked-in communication cycles.

QUESTION: What are opinionated behaviors?

Opinionated behaviors, like blaming behaviors, take two different forms. In the first form, vague, general statements are made without being substantiated by evidence to back them up. Such statements as, "Women are bad drivers," "Buses never arrive on time," and "Executives are too busy," are good examples. These irrational statements often lead to mistrust and overgeneralization, which tend to frustrate communication.

In the second form, which is closely related to the first, statements are made as though they were facts, when in reality they are only personal opinion and sometimes even fallacies. In this form, statements may be specific, but they are still opinion rather than fact. Some examples are as follows: "While in public, you should never run across the street." "A wife's duty is to bring her husband his paper and slippers." "People will rise in the organization only if they take paperwork home each night." "One should never end a sentence with a preposition." Old wifes' tales often fall in this category: "Remember to buy an apple for your dinner—an apple a day keeps the doctor away." Opinions stated as facts have a tendency to either turn off communication or create a locked-in communication cycle, which in essence leads to, "I am right, you are wrong."

QUESTION: What is tuned-out behavior?

People who exemplify tuned-out behavior simply do not listen. These people may have such little interest in what others have to say that they intentionally tune them out. Other people may be so engrossed in their own thoughts or what they are going to say that they fail to listen to what the speaker is saying. Still others may hear the words or phrases the other person is saying, but they may be insensitive to the real message or feeling the person is trying to convey. A person, for example, may say, "I have so many things coming at me all at once that it is just one big series of frustrations," only to get a response like, "Why don't you just relax a bit and forget it?" Another person might say, "I just don't seem to be getting along with my boss. I can't seem to do anything to please him—it just seems too hopeless." The response may be something like, "I would like you to meet my boss. She is a great person. She has even promised me a raise next month." To practice recognizing these behaviors, the reader should take the Self-Test for Communication Blocks on the next page.

Communication skills

QUESTION: What are the key elements of effective communication?

Sharing and listening are the key elements of effective communication. Listening helps us respond appropriately to what another person shares. To communicate, however, listening must be more than remaining passive. Listening leads to a further step called clarifying. This step is to make certain that a message a person shares is received or perceived correctly and that the sender's message is understood. To make sure the message has been sent and received as intended, the listener or receiver can clarify the message that was shared. Clarifying brings the sender and receiver closer together in that they can now understand one another. Sharing, listening, and clarifying all solidify a common bind between the sender and the receiver, and put both on the same wavelength.

QUESTION: What is an example of clarifying?

Let us suppose that a person shares his feelings about a book he is reading. He may say, "This is really a poor book, and it irritates me that a publisher would even put it out for sale." The receiver of the message may clarify the message by responding, "You mean that you get irritated because a publisher would put out reading material that is so boring?" The sender may say, "No, what I mean is that the book has a poor cover, and it keeps falling off when

Effective communication skills can be taught and learned in group activities, such as a group counseling session. In this setting the key elements of sharing and listening can be developed and lead to clarification.

514 ◾ Section 4 Theories for application

◾ SELF-TEST FOR COMMUNICATION BLOCKS

By filling in the blanks, indicate whether the following statements illustrate (1) authoritarian, (2) blaming, (3) opinionated, or (4) tuned-out behavior:

Type of Behavior

Younger sister: "I had a miserable time at the dance last night. I didn't get to dance even once. It was terrible. I don't think I ever want to go to another dance as long as I live."

Older sister: "Well, I'm not a bit surprised. I told you yesterday that you should have had a different hairstyle. And look at that dress. You should have worn blue, not red. Besides, you shouldn't be so negative."
_____

Person A: "Aren't you ready yet? We're always late for parties. I wish for once you would get ready on time."

Person B: "You really make me boil. The last time I tried to get you to a wedding reception so we wouldn't have to stand and wait, we got there ten minutes after the line had broken up."
_____

Person A: "All my life I have wanted to have a birthday party, but no one has ever seemed to care enough to give me one."

Person B: "You should have been to the birthday party I had last year. Ten of my best friends showed up, and I received all kinds of gifts."
_____

Adolescent: "I couldn't help it. I just brushed by the lamp and it fell off the table."

Parent: "Why don't you watch where you are going? I don't know how on earth you can be so clumsy."
_____

Person A: "But I just don't feel like eating spinach today. It just does not appeal to me."

Type of Behavior

Person B: "You really ought to eat it. It has the vitamins you need. Not only will you get weak, but your energy will slow down."
_____

Student: "I wanted to talk to you about my test. I guess I really blew it—I feel awful!"

Teacher: "As I told the class last week—and you were there—everyone would have to burn some midnight oil. I presume you were not listening."
_____

Person A: "Here you are making us late for class again. I wonder if we will ever be able to get here on time."

Person B: "Why me? If you would get up when your alarm goes off we would get here on time."
_____

Person A: "I have not brought work home from the office for a whole month. Isn't that great?"

Person B: "I'm not so sure about that. It's really people who bring work home that get ahead in life."
_____

Employee: "I feel that I am doing the best I can on the project. It's just that we ran into some complications, and it's taking longer than I thought."

Supervisor: "I warned you about that two weeks ago. If you had been on time there would have been no complications. I've done it a hundred times myself, and I know how long it takes to do it."
_____

Key: Self-Test for Communication Blocks
3, 2, 4, 2, 1, 4, 2, 3, 1

I read it." Had the receiver failed to listen and clarify through this two-way feedback system, this communication would have been distorted.

We might speculate on how many different interpretations we would list if someone were to say, "I really went out on the town last night." Unless we clarify the message, we may interpret it in terms of our own experience or value system. Listening and clarifying therefore help us to understand what other people mean from their frame of reference.

QUESTION: What kinds of communication responses are helpful?

Several specific skills are helpful: supporting, advice giving, interpreting, questioning, sympathizing, and active listening. Let us consider each separately as a response to the following statement:

> I get so fed up with my job. No one seems to notice the time and effort I put in, and I never seem to get anywhere. One of these days I'm just going to up and quit.

QUESTION: What is a supportive response?

A supportive response suggests that the helper agrees with the adolescent and supports her in whatever she intends to do. This response is helpful where the emotional support is for the good of the adolescent. If, however, the helper agrees to some unsubstantiated opinion that the adolescent has communicated, or if he assumes responsibility that the adolescent should assume, the response may be detrimental. Some supportive responses are:

> "I can see what you mean. It is an unrewarding place to work. I don't blame you for wanting to quit."

QUESTION: What is an advice-giving response?

The helper who uses an advice-giving response tells the adolescent what he should do or how to solve his problem. Advice is perhaps the easiest to give, and nearly everyone is eager to give it. The advice-giving response may be useful if the helper understands the adolescent's problem, but it often amounts to "what is good enough for me is good enough for you." The advice-giving response is often overused. In an emotional situation, advice is easily rejected. Some examples are:

> "I really think you should talk to your boss. It also might be a good idea to look at what you're doing. You really should stick with it."

QUESTION: What is an interpretative response?

The helper who uses an interpretative response attempts to explain to the adolescent why she behaves and feels the way she does. At times the interpretative response may be helpful to the adolescent in giving her reasons for her feelings or behavior, but it often does not help her to change her feelings. Some examples of interpretative responses are:

> "I suppose we have to expect to put in long hours. Look at my job. Sometimes after working all day, I even get called out in the evenings. Seldom do I ever get a word of appreciation."

QUESTION: What is a questioning response?

A questioning response is useful in getting information and in helping to clarify situations. Although a questioning response is sometimes helpful, it can often be taken as probing, and the adolescent may feel he is being put on the spot. Another disadvantage is that questions are asked at times when other techniques would be more helpful. Furthermore, the questions themselves are not necessarily inappropriate, but they tend to be overused. Examples of questioning responses are:

> "What has made you feel this way? Is it something about the work or the people? Do you get along with your boss? What have you done about it?"

QUESTION: What is a sympathizing response?

A sympathizing response is an expression of sorrow or regret for a tragedy or misfortune that has happened in another person's life. In most social situations and even in some counseling situations, the offering of sympathy is appropriate. In most helping situations, however, people are not looking for sympathy but are seeking to be understood. In other words, they are looking for empathy rather than sympathy. Examples of sympathizing responses are:

> "I regret that you have to work where you do, and I feel sorry for you. It is too bad that this has happened to such a nice person."

QUESTION: What is an active-listening response?

An active-listening response shows that the helper understands both the content of the message and the feelings of the adolescent. She makes an effort to reflect and clarify what the adolescent is saying. The active-listening response is perhaps the most difficult to use, but is the most helpful to the person in an emotional situation. Because of its importance and the skill required, considerable attention is given to this response. Examples of active-listening responses are:

> "I sense that you feel pretty discouraged about your work. What you do goes unappreciated, and you wonder whether it's worth staying with it."

To practice identifying the various communication responses, the reader should take the following Self-Test for Positive Helping Responses.

SELF-TEST FOR POSITIVE HELPING RESPONSES

Identifying Responses

Read the adolescent statements, then label the following helper responses. Each of the response labels should be used for the eight helper responses.

Response Labels

1. Supportive response
2. Advice-giving response
3. Interpretative response
4. Questioning response
5. Sympathizing response
6. Active-listening response

Adolescent Statement 1

"What seems to be bothering me most is a problem with my boss. We used to get along real well, but now I just feel all tensed up when I go to work. It's almost as though he doesn't like me anymore. I've even thought of quitting."

Helper Responses

____ Helper A: "What makes you think he doesn't like you? Are you doing a good job? Have you talked to him?"

____ Helper E: "I don't blame you for feeling that way. It would be frustrating to work for a guy like him. I kind of like the idea of your thinking about quitting.

___ Helper B: "Now and then we can all expect to have trouble with our bosses. We do have our ups and downs you know. You are likely at one of those low points now. Give it a while and everything will be all right."

___ Helper C: "If you will analyze your own behavior a little, you'll likely discover that it is not so much your boss, it is you. I know your boss and I doubt if he could dislike anyone."

___ Helper D: "What I seem to hear you say is that your relationship with your boss is confusing and frustrating, particularly when you are not sure where you stand."

___ Helper F: "I've been through what you're going through myself. I had a boss once who I know didn't like me and there was just no way that we could come to terms."

___ Helper G: "I suggest you go talk to your boss. Let him know how you feel. Before you get serious about quitting, you better be sure you have prospects for another job."

___ Helper H: "That's really too bad. I hate to see a good person like you confronted with something like this. You must be going through a lot right now."

Adolescent Statement 2

"I feel pretty low today. I took that test this morning, and I'm sure I really blew it. It is just one more thing that has shattered my confidence. I feel really sure now that I want to drop the class."

Helper Responses

___ Helper A: "I think you should try to study harder so you won't get in this bind. Now that it's over, maybe you ought to go to a movie to get things off your mind."

___ Helper B: "That class is a hard one, so I can see why the test would be hard. I would go along with you in dropping the class."

___ Helper C: "It is pretty natural to feel down after you take a test. It was bound to blow your confidence for a time. Like the rest of us your body and spirit can take a lot, so you will be back on top again soon."

___ Helper D: "I really feel for you. That teacher has put you through a lot. I think it's terrible that you should be confronted with such a situation."

___ Helper E: "Did you study before the test? What was in the test that made it so hard? Are you sure you really blew it? Do you really want to drop the class?"

___ Helper F: "I just don't think you gave it all you could. You have got your priorities mixed up. You spend too much time socializing. I warned you about that last week."

___ Helper G: "I know just how you feel. When I went through college I had to drop a class because I failed at least three tests. You can imagine what I went through—a lot!"

___ Helper H: "It is not only blowing the test that makes you feel bad, but it is also a blow to your confidence, and it makes you want to get out of it altogether."

Key: Self-Test for Positive Helping Responses
4, 2, 2, 6, 1, 3, 2, 5,
2, 1, 3, 5, 4, 2, 5, 6

Listening

QUESTION: What is active listening?

Active listening is an art. People learn it with practice and experience. With practice people become able to listen not only for facts, words, and content but also for understanding, attitudes, and feelings. In other words, active listening means listening for the total meaning of what the other person has to communicate. Furthermore, active listening means responding to others appropriately. Only when people grasp the full significance of the speaker's statement are they in a position to respond appropriately. Active listening also goes beyond what the speaker has to say verbally. An active listener also watches for such nonverbal cues as body movements or gestures, facial expression, breathing, eye movements, and so forth.

Mastering active listening is not an easy task. Sometimes it means a change in people's basic attitudes as well as in their behavior. For example, meeting a hostile remark by replying with an active-listening response takes courage. The typical way of behaving is to become defensive and sometimes to retaliate. While people are learning the art of active listening, they may feel embarrassed, awkward, and even phony, as some people feel while learning to dance. People may have their attention focused so much on their own responses that they may miss the relationship entirely. Like dancers, however, who may eventually learn the skill, focus their attention on the music, and forget their feet, people who become skilled in active listening give attention to the relationship as the new skill becomes natural.

QUESTION: When should a person use active listening?

The helper need not use all of the elements of active listening in every contact, but the concept alone will help set a tone that will enhance the relationship. Furthermore, active listening will serve as a valuable tool whenever the occasion calls for it. Helpers will have obtained an additional skill that they can add to their repertoire.

The skill of active listening will help keep the lines of communication open and will break down defensive behavior. The helper will find that active listening is one of the basic elements for demonstrating empathy. A major reason for the considerable amount of attention given here is because active listening indicates an accepting attitude and opens the door to further communication.

To provide further understanding, the reader should take the Self-Test for Active Listening on the following page.

Owning feelings

QUESTION: What does it mean to own feelings?

To own feelings means to acknowledge one's feelings and to take responsibility for these feelings. Owning feelings means honesty, genuineness, and openness in a relationship. It helps to create an atmosphere in which communication can flow freely and understandably. If people feel frustrated, they can admit that they feel frustrated. If they feel excited, they can admit that they feel excited. Through owning feelings people allow others to know where they stand. Owning feelings therefore promotes trust and confidence.

Disowning feelings, however, is to cover up or to deny that they exist. To disown feelings may mean that people cover up by acting out their frustrations in an accusative manner, or it may mean that they blame someone else for the way they feel. In both instances, they refuse to acknowledge or to take responsibility for their own feelings. For example, assume that a parent is upset when an adolescent stays away from home later than expected. The parent feels worried and concerned about the adolescent, and even angry for being inconvenienced. When the teenager returns, the parent is apt to disown his real feelings and lash out at the teenager in an accusative manner. Rather than owning his feelings by saying, "I was worried; I was concerned; I was even angry," the parent acts out his frustration by saying, "Where have you been? How can you be so irresponsible and inconsiderate?" These accusations are labels that tend to belittle the adolescent and put him on the defensive, thus creating a communication roadblock.

A person who blames another for the way she feels may make such statements as, "You make me angry; you irritate me; you upset me." No one, however, *makes* another person angry. She makes herself angry because she is the one who owns the feelings. Rather than blame the other person, the person would best own her feelings if she were to say, "I feel angry; I feel irritated; I feel upset." She then takes the responsibility for how she feels rather than putting the other person on the defensive to protect her ego.

When people fail to own their feelings, innocent disagreements sometimes move from a content level to an ego protection level. Disagreements over politics, religion, and the like are areas in which this sometimes occurs. This happens, for example, when the disagreement becomes a struggle of, "I am right; you are wrong" rather than, "This is the way I feel about it, and I can respect the way you feel about it, even though I may disagree with you."

As a result of disowning feelings, helper and an adolescent may find themselves locked in a power struggle. For example, the adolescent may be a silent,

SELF-TEST FOR ACTIVE LISTENING

Listening for words alone is not really hearing or understanding, but is a first step toward that goal. To practice this first step, read the following statements and identify them as either (1) parroting, (2) paraphrasing (listening for content), or (3) listening for feelings.

Type of Response

Adolescent: "I wanted to go on that trip so badly; then I came down with a miserable cold."

_____ Helper: "You wanted to go on that trip so badly; then you came down with a miserable cold."

Adolescent: "I really studied hard all the time, and here it is at the end of the year and my grades are simply awful."

_____ Helper: "What you are saying is that even though you put a lot of effort into your studies, it does not really seem to pay off in the end."

Adolescent: "At first I did not want to go to the party, because I thought it would be a bore, but after I got there, I had a good time."

_____ Helper: "In other words, you were not too eager to go to a party that might be boring, but after you got there you were glad you went."

Adolescent: "It's not that I didn't study. I put in hours and hours. I thought I was prepared, and I thought I did well, but it was a real letdown when my grade came out."

_____ Helper: "With all of the effort and time you put into your studies, you really feel disappointed about the grade you received."

Adolescent: "I get so uptight because I don't ever seem to make the right decision. No matter what I do, I get criticized for doing it the wrong way. Sometimes I get to the point that I'm afraid to do anything."

_____ Helper: "Sometimes you feel frustrated and even trapped because you can't move in any direction without being criticized for what you do."

Key: Self-Test for Active Listening
1, 2, 3, 3, 3

resistant individual. The helper might act out his frustrations by saying, "I can see you are a stubborn person. Your silence will not get us anywhere. You are just defeating your own purpose." The helper might, however, own his feelings by saying something like, "I am beginning to feel uncomfortable and frustrated about our relationship. I do want to be of help, but wonder if there is something about me that is turning you off. Could it be that you don't feel you can trust me?"

When we own our feelings, we send what are called "I" messages, and when we disown our feelings, we send "you" messages. In all of the prior examples, a distinct difference can be noted between the "I" and the "you" messages. The "I" messages begin with "I feel concerned, upset, worried, uncomfortable, frustrated, and so on." The "you" messages begin with such accusations as, "You are inconsiderate; you are irresponsible; you make me angry; you are stubborn, you are wrong, and so on. One difficulty we may encounter in our attempt to send "I" messages is that we may cancel out the "I" message by attaching a "you" message at the end. For example, a person may say, "I feel bad because you are stupid."

QUESTION: What are the effects of owning and disowning feelings?

The extent to which we own or disown our feelings may create any one of at least three different types of relationships. Disowning feelings may create either a flight or fight relationship, and owning feelings tend to create a leveling relationship. In a flight relationship, one or both parties may flee physically or psychologically. In a fight relationship, the parties engage in verbal conflict that brings not only feelings into the open but also accusative statements that are often destructive.

Both flight and fight relationships can lead to a locked-in-cycle syndrome. A more desirable relationship is maintained by owning feelings or by sending "I" messages that help to keep the lines of communication open without destroying a relationship. One way that almost assures breaking out of a locked-in cycle is to own a feeling and to reflect a feeling. Owning a feeling helps to let the other person know where one stands, and reflecting a feeling shows that one can be concerned for the other person.

Some people go for years holding resentments and grudges because they are unable or unwilling to own their feelings. The person who supposedly created the initial offense may even be unaware of the problem. Helpers many times have to ask themselves, "Is it the one being accused or the one feeling offended who has the problem?"

To further understand owning feelings and "I" messages, the reader should take the following self-test.

SELF-TEST FOR OWNING FEELINGS AND "I" MESSAGES

The following are four situations in which a message is sent in two different ways. After reading each set of statements, place an "I" in the blank if the person is owning feelings and a "Y" if the person is denying feelings.

Situation A

___ 1. "I saw you go around that corner. You haven't got a lick of sense to drive that fast. Didn't anyone ever teach you anything?"

___ 2. "I get worried when I see you turn corners that fast. I'm afraid you will have an accident, and I would really feel terrible."

Situation B

___ 1. "You are the most inconsiderate person I have ever seen. It seems like every time I want to talk to you you've got that newspaper covering your face. I wish just once you would think of someone else besides yourself."

___ 2. "I get a left-out feeling when you read the newspaper in my presence. There are times that I love to talk to you, and It's a real let down when I can't. I guess the truth of the matter is, I just feel plain rejected."

Situation C

___ 1. "I am really concerned about your leaving school. I even begin to panic a bit as I think of trying to find another roommate who could take your place. I think you are beginning to see how much you will be missed."

___ 2. "You must be clear out of your mind to even consider leaving school. Right now the grass just looks greener back East. I doubt if you really realize how nice you have had it here. My hunch is that you will live to regret the day you ever dropped out."

Situation D

___ 1. "You were supposed to roll the toothpaste, stupid, not squeeze it. Can't you ever do anything right?"

___ 2. "I get upset when someone squeezes the tube of toothpaste rather than rolling it. I guess I was taught not to be wasteful."

Note: When we own our feelings, we send "I" messages, and when we deny our feelings, we send "you" messages, which are accusative in nature. Review the four situations and note how easy it is to select the "I" and "you" messages.

Key: Self-Test for Owning Feelings and "I" Messages
Y, I, Y, I, I, Y, Y, I

Empathy

QUESTION: What is empathy?

The first task is to discover what empathy is and what it does. First, what is empathy? Accurate empathy is sensing how another person feels, getting inside the other person, and looking through that person's eyes. Empathy is understanding the other person's world and having genuine concern, caring, and respect for another person.

Second, let us look at what empathy does. Accurate empathy helps us to better understand the other person. It helps us to gain the confidence and trust of the other person and to establish rapport. Empathy also helps to open a two-way communication channel with another person. Empathy reinforces the self-exploratory behavior of another person and enables the helper to be sensitive.

QUESTION: How does empathy directly help communication?

Through accurate empathy, helpers become sensitive to adolescents' feelings and are thus able to communicate this in such a way that adolescents feel accepted and understood. Helpers are able to put themselves into the world of adolescents and can sense how adolescents feel. In effect, helpers look through the eyes of adolescents and help them to see more clearly.

In communicating empathy, helpers make an effort to accurately reflect adolescents' feelings. Through this process, helpers look for the affective meanings behind the content and the words adolescents are saying. This in turn conveys to adolescents that helpers really do understand.

Some helpers may be more effective than others in communicating empathic understanding, and even the same helper may communicate more empathically at one time than at another. In other words, there are different degrees or levels of empathic communication. The higher the level of empathic understanding, the greater the likelihood of the relationship being helpful. Read the following statement, and consider the possible responses.

> Everything has been going pretty well except for that new guy I got stuck with. He's a heel! He thinks he knows everything—a big shot—but I'll figure out some way to handle him all right, and he'll know he's been handled, too. I'm not taking any guff from a peanut like that.

The possible empathic helper responses include:

1. Come on, Joe, get off it. I don't like your attitude. You're a big boy now.
2. Why don't you just stand up to him and let him know you are as important as he is?
3. You feel pretty angry with him and would somehow like to put him in his place.
4. I see what you mean; that guy must be a real pain in the neck.
5. If he doesn't straighten out, tell him he had better see me. I'll put him in his place.

These five responses vary greatly in the sort of empathy given. The reader will likely find they can be rated.

QUESTION: Can levels of empathy be categorized?

The following are five levels of empathy. The reader should review each and then use them when taking the Self-Test for Empathy that will follow.

LEVEL 1 (LOWEST LEVEL) NO EMPATHY—SELF-CENTERED

The lowest level of empathy not only lacks helpfulness but also prevents adolescents from moving toward better self-understanding. Helpers who use this level have no sense of awareness of adolescents' most obvious feelings. Helpers may be so engrossed in intellectualizing, judging, or advising that they are far from being tuned in to what adolescents are trying to say. Helpers who use this approach are not only insensitive to the feelings expressed by adolescents but also miss much of the content. Such an approach tends to turn off adolescents.

LEVEL 2 (LOW LEVEL) FOCUS ON CONTENT ONLY

At Level 2, helpers may be aware of the content of the message and some of the most obvious feelings, but they may not yet be tuned into the nature of these feelings. They may even misinterpret the conspicuous feelings that they do recognize. Helpers who use this approach, however, are beginning to make an effort to recognize feelings, but they tend to miss establishing relationships with adolescents. Even at this point, helpers are still more apt to hinder adolescents than to help them.

LEVEL 3 (MIDPOINT) PARTIAL EMPATHY

At Level 3, helpers begin to tune into adolescents' feelings. They not only recognize the obvious feelings but also are beginning to recognize those which are less apparent. Helpers are therefore able to communicate to adolescents what adolescents are communicating to them. At times helpers may respond understandingly to adolescents' statements, and at other times they may miss the cues. Further, helpers may respond accurately to part of adolescents' statements and inaccurately to other parts. Nevertheless, adolescents perceive helpers at this level as people who are making every effort to understand them. The major point is, at this level the door has been opened for promoting more communication.

LEVEL 4 (HIGH LEVEL) ACCURATE EMPATHY

Helpers at Level 4 are able to recognize not only obvious feelings of adolescents but also those which are less conspicuous. Helpers are also able to more accurately pick up affective meanings underlying adolescents' statements. Seldom do these helpers misinterpret what adolescents are saying, and their responses show considerable understanding of adolescents' feelings and emotions.

LEVEL 5 (HIGHEST LEVEL) INSIGHTFUL EMPATHY

Helpers at Level 5 recognize most, if not all, of both the obvious feelings of adolescents and the less apparent feelings and underlying emotions. Helpers not only respond to the feeling and emotions expressed by adolescents, but also initiate communication that may be beyond adolescent awareness. Helpers respond in such a way that adolescents understand themselves. As helpers expand the underlying affective meanings, adolescents are assured that the helpers are thoroughly in tune with what adolescents are attempting to communicate.

To further understand the skill of empathy, the reader should take the following Self-Test for Empathy.

SELF-TEST FOR EMPATHY

Read the adolescent statements, then label the following helper responses according to their level of empathy (1–5).

Adolescent Statement 1

"I get so fed up with the way he treats me, sometimes I feel just like leaving him and getting out of the whole thing. Why should I have to live with him if he is going to belittle me and criticize everything I do? I get so tired of being slapped around when I don't do what he wants me to do. He thinks he owns me, and I just can't take that."

Helper Responses

____ 1. "It sounds like you have grounds to leave if you choose to do so."

____ 2. "Things are not going well between the two

____ 4. "Maybe you ought to take a look at some of the things you are doing that may be causing him to behave that way."

of you, and you are wondering what will happen to your relationship."

___ 3. "You are really upset with the way he treats you and have considered leaving him so you don't have to take it anymore."

___ 5. "You really resent the abuse you have taken from him and his treating you like his personal property, and are now struggling with the decision of leaving him if he can't start treating you with some consideration and respect."

Adolescent Statement 2

"My Mom and Dad said I should come and talk to you. They said maybe you could give me some suggestions. I guess I have been goofing off. You see, my grades are pretty bad and they are getting pretty upset. But really, if it had not been for two of my teachers, everything would have been all right. They were too busy to even talk to. I guess I could study more, but I can't help it when my friends keep calling me. I would like to do better, but I guess I'm just a born loser."

Helper Responses

___ 1. "It looks like you are trying to blame everybody for your own actions."

___ 2. "You are really on a spot. Maybe you should still try to talk to your teachers and just tell your friends you do not have time to talk."

___ 3. "Listen, I know you are not a born loser. I know that if you get a hold on yourself you could conquer these things in spite of your friends, teachers, or anybody else."

___ 4. "Everything seems to be against you and you wish you could find a way out."

___ 5. "At times it feels pretty discouraging when no one really seems to care how you come out, and what's more, some even seem to stand in your way."

Adolescent Statement 3

"We've always had problems with her doing the dishes. You can't talk to her because she so sweet—you know. She's like an angel—like she can't do anything wrong. When she is not there and the dishes pile up, you get really mad at her, but when she comes home you can't say anything because she is as sweet as can be."

Helper Responses

___ 1. "I can't understand why she is unwilling to do her share. She knows someone else will have to do the dishes if she doesn't."

___ 2. "It gets to be frustrating to you when she does not carry her share of the responsibility on the one hand and then turns on all her charm on the other."

___ 3. "Perhaps you should just tell her she is trying to manipulate you by turning on the charm to get out of doing the dishes."

___ 4. "I guess you sort of feel caught in a bind; you really want to lay down the law, but she's just too nice to confront."

___ 5. "You may want to have a good talk with her and let her know that she is fouling things up for the rest of you."

Adolescent Statement 4

"I'd like to transfer away from here. I just don't like my new boss. It seems like I can't do anything around here without him calling me on the carpet. You'd think I didn't know anything. It seems like as much time as I have spent here, I would be due a little respect. It seems like every time I turn around, something is wrong. It seems to me that he really has it in for me. Don't you think so?"

Helper Responses

___ 1. "Yes, I really agree with you. He really doesn't know what is going on around here."

___ 2. "I know your boss and he seems to be a fine person. I think if you would go talk to him, you could probably work things out."

___ 3. "By this time you should know how to deal with new bosses. I suggest you get with it."

___ 4. "You kind of feel like he has it in for you. You just can't seem to do things right."

___ 5. "I think you should give yourself a little more time. I'll talk to your boss myself and see if he might be a little more considerate."

Key: Self-Test for Empathy
2, 3, 2, 1, 5
1, 3, 4, 2, 5
2, 5, 3, 4, 1
3, 1, 1, 4, 2

The preceding discussion in the chapter focused on developing positive relationship skills. Once these skills have been established, the next phase is oriented to developing direct helping skills. These skills are discussed in the next chapter.

Summary

Phenomenological theory assumes that reality is based on what people perceive. All people have their own reality because of the uniqueness of their perceptions. Phenomenological theorists believe that a growth force exists within all individuals that can motivate and guide them to mental health and desirable social behavior. Some of the most popular phenomenological theorists are Abraham Maslow and Carl Rogers. Abraham Maslow describes certain characteristics of individuals whose growth force has led them to fulfillment and self-actualization, such as being reality oriented, spontaneous, problem centered, and so on.

Carl Rogers believes that the self (self-concept, self-esteem, and so on) is the most important part of psychological growth. Healthy people develop positive self-concept after experiencing positive regard from significant other people, such as parents, spouses, and close friends. This positive regard later develops into positive self-regard. Part of people's acceptance of their true nature is their acceptance of themselves as trustworthy individuals.

Lay people can be trained within a relatively short period of time to be effective therapists in some situations. Nonprofessional therapists have often been as successful as—or more successful than—professional therapists in providing services to certain types of clients.

The following are three basic stages in Carkhuff's helping program:

1. *Self-exploration.* In this stage, nonprofessional therapists ("helpers") and clients ("helpees") develop a sense of empathy and understanding for one another.
2. *Understanding.* In this stage, helpers assist helpees to understand their situation and their problems more clearly.
3. *Action.* In this stage, helpers use the skills of confrontation and immediacy. They guide helpees as they consider possible behavioral alternatives and a concrete program of action designed to implement one of the alternatives. The following are the seven basic steps to the action stage.

  a. Define the problem areas.
  b. Describe the goals in the problem areas.
  c. Analyze the critical dimensions and directions.
  d. Consider the alternative courses of action.
  e. Consider the advantages and disadvantages of alternative courses of action.
  f. Develop physical, emotional, or intellectual programs that could be successful.
  g. Develop progressive gradations of the program.

The personal relationship between helpers and helpees is essential to the helping process. The lack of a warm, honest relationship will certainly hinder the successful resolution of clients' problems. Helpers can learn four essential skills that will facilitate the development of a genuine helper-helpee relationship:

1. Positive versus negative communication
2. Active listening
3. Owning feelings
4. Empathy

Listening is a vital part of communication, and being a good listener allows helpers to respond appropriately to what helpees communicate. Clarifying is also an important part of effective communication, and occurs when helpers confirm that they have accurately understood what the helpees intended to communicate. Several faulty communication patterns are fairly common:

1. *Authoritarian behaviors* include advising, directing, urging, forbidding, warning, moralizing, ordering, and commanding. Although authoritarian behaviors are sometimes appropriate, they are generally overused, used inappropriately, and used in situations in which other behavioral patterns would be more appropriate.

2. *Blaming behaviors* occur when individuals either make others responsible for their problems or project their own frustrations onto others through the use of accusative behaviors.

3. *Opinionated behaviors* involve making vague, general statements that are not substantiated by evidence, or by making specific statements as though they were facts when in reality they are only opinions and sometimes fallacies.

4. *Tuned-out behaviors* are exhibited when people simply do not listen to what others say. They may be too engrossed in their own thoughts to listen to others, or they may hear what others say but are insensitive to the underlying messages behind the words.

Several helpful communication patterns can be learned by individuals:

1. *A supportive response* is appropriate in some situations and occurs when helpers agree with helpees and support them in whatever they intend to do.

2. *An advice-giving response* may be helpful when helpers understand helpees' problems and can tell them how to solve the problem.

3. *An interpretive response* occurs when helpers attempt to explain to helpees why the helpees behave or feel as they do.

4. *A questioning response* may be appropriate in isolated situations in which questions may be useful in getting information or in clarifying situations.

5. *A sympathizing response* exists when a helper expresses sorrow or regret for a tragedy or misfortune that has occurred in a helpee's life.

6. *An active-listening response* shows that helpers understand both the content of the message and the feelings of the helpee.

Active listening is a skill that is perhaps the most difficult for helpers to acquire, but is usually the most helpful to a helpee in an emotional situation. Active listening is the ability to listen not only for a helpee's facts, words, and content but also for understanding, attitudes, and feelings. Active listening is the ability to listen to the total meaning of the helpee's message and to respond to it appropriately. Listening to the total meaning of a message requires an awareness of both verbal and nonverbal expressions.

To own feelings means to acknowledge one's feelings and to take responsibility for those feelings. It reflects honesty, genuineness, and openness in a relationship, and helps to create an atmosphere in which communication can flow freely. Disowning feelings occurs when individuals cover up their feelings or deny that they exist; they refuse to acknowledge or take responsibility for their own feelings. Helpers who own feelings frequently send "I" messages. "I" messages often begin with phrases like, "I feel concerned," "I feel upset," "I feel worried," and so on. "I" messages have the effect of giving people responsibility for their own feelings.

Accurate empathy is sensing how another person feels and looking at the world through that person's eyes. Empathy enables a person to understand another person's perspective and to gain trust and confidence. One important result of empathy is the reinforcement of the helpee's self-exploratory behavior. Through empathy, helpers are also able to communicate to helpees that they truly understand what the helpees are experiencing, and they make the helpees feel accepted and understood. In communicating empathy, helpers make an effort to reflect the helpees' feelings as accurately as possible. Helpers also look for the affective meanings behind the content of the helpees' messages.

Empathic responses can be categorized in five levels, from little empathic content to insightful and effective empathic reflections:

1. No empathy—self-centered
2. Superficial empathy—focus on content only
3. Partial empathy
4. Accurate empathy
5. Insightful empathy

References

Brammer, L. M. 1979. *The Helping Relationship: Process and Skills.* Englewood Cliffs, N.J.: Prentice-Hall.
Carkhuff, R. R. 1969a. *Helping and human relations vol. I: Selection and training.* New York: Holt, Rinehart & Winston.
_____. 1969b. *Helping and human relations vol. II: Selection and training.* New York: Holt, Rinehart & Winston.
_____. 1971. *The development of human resources.* New York: Holt, Rinehart & Winston.
_____. 1972a. *The art of helping.* Amherst Mass.: Human Resource Development Press.
_____. 1972b. The development of a systematic human resource development model. *Counseling Psychologist* 3: 4–30.
_____. 1972c. New directions in training for the helping professions: Towards a technology for human and community resource development. *Counseling Psychologist* 3: 12–20.
Carkhuff, R. R., & B. G. Berenson. 1967. *Beyond counseling and therapy.* New York: Holt, Rinehart & Winston.
Carkhuff, R. R., & C. B. Truax. 1965. Lay mental health counseling. *Journal of Counseling Psychology* 29: 426–31.
Coombs, A., & D. Snygg. 1959. A perceptual approach to behavior. In *Individual behavior.* 2d ed. New York: Harper & Row.
Cowen, E. L., M. Zax, & J. D. Laird. 1966. A college student volunteer program in the elementary school setting. *Community Mental Health Journal* 2: 319–28.
Egan, G. 1975. *The skilled helper.* Belmont, Calif.: Wadsworth.
Ellsworth, R. B., & J. J. Ellsworth. 1970. The psychiatric aid: Therapeutic agent or lost potential? *Journal of Psychiatric Nursing and Mental Health* 8 (5).
Gazda, G. 1973. *Human relationship development.* Boston: Allyn & Bacon.

Girona, R. 1972. Changes operated in institutionalized children as a result of controlled interaction with a "significant adult." *Journal of Educational Research* 65 (8).

Goldstein, A. P. 1973. *Structural learning therapy: Towards a psychotherapy for the peer*. New York: Academic Press.

Goodman, G. 1967. An experiment with companionship therapy: College students and troubled boys—Assumption, selection, and design. *American Journal of Public Health* 57: 1771–77.

_____. 1972. *Companionship therapy*. San Francisco: Jossey-Bass.

Grosser, C., W. E. Henry, & J. G. Kelly. 1969. *Nonprofessionals in the human services*. San Francisco: Jossey-Bass.

Hilgard, J. R., & V. S. Moore. 1969. Affiliative therapy with young adolescents. *Journal of child psychiatry* 8: 577–605.

Hurvitz, N. 1970. Peer self-help in psychotherapy groups and their implications for psychotherapy. *Psychotherapy: Theory, Research, and Practice* 7: 41–49.

Jensen, V. 1978. *Helping relationships: Skills development manual for training professional, paraprofessional, and lay counselors*. Provo, Utah: Brigham Young Univ. Press.

Jensen, V., R. Heaps, B. Nelson, & R. Shingleton. 1983. *Interviewing skills workshop*. Provo, Utah: Brigham Young Univ. Press.

Johnson, D. 1981. *Reaching out*. Englewood Cliffs, N.J.: Prentice-Hall.

Jourard, S. 1971. *The transparent self*. New York: Van Nostrand.

Kopita, R. R. 1973. Preparing peer counselors. *Impact* 2(6): 59–62.

Lamb, D. H., & R. J. Clack. 1974. Professional vs. paraprofessional approaches to orientation and subsequent counseling contacts. *Journal of Counseling Psychology* 21: 61–65.

Litchenburg, B. 1956. On the selection and preparation of the big brother volunteer. *Social Casework* 137: 396–400.

Maslow, A. 1954. *Motivation and personality*. New York: Harper & Row.

_____. 1968. *Toward a psychology of being*. 2d ed. New York: Van Nostrand.

Mitchell, W. E. 1966. Amicatherapy: Theoretical perspectives and an example of practice. *Community Mental Health Journal* 2: 307–14.

Poser, E. G. 1966. The effects of therapists training on group therapy outcome. *Journal of Consulting Psychology* 30: 283–89.

Rogers, C. R. 1961. *On becoming a person*. Boston: Houghton Mifflin.

_____. 1969. *Freedom to learn*. Columbus, Ohio: Merrill.

Schaefer, C. 1981. Relationship therapy for troubled boys: Guidelines for volunteers. *Adolescence* 16(63): 728–41 (Fall).

Truax, C. B. 1966. Therapist empathy, genuineness, and warmth and patient therapeutic outcome. *Journal of Consulting Psychology* 30: 395–401.

_____. 1969. The use of trained practical counselors or therapists and the evolving understanding of counseling and psychotherapy. Unpublished manuscript, Arkansas Rehabilitation Research and Training Center, University of Arkansas.

_____. 1972. The meaning and reliability of accurate empathy: A rejoinder. *Psychological Bulletin* 77: 397–99.

Truax, C. B., & R. R. Carkhuff. 1965. Client and therapist transparency in the psychotherapeutic encounter. *Journal of Counseling Psychology* 12: 3–9.

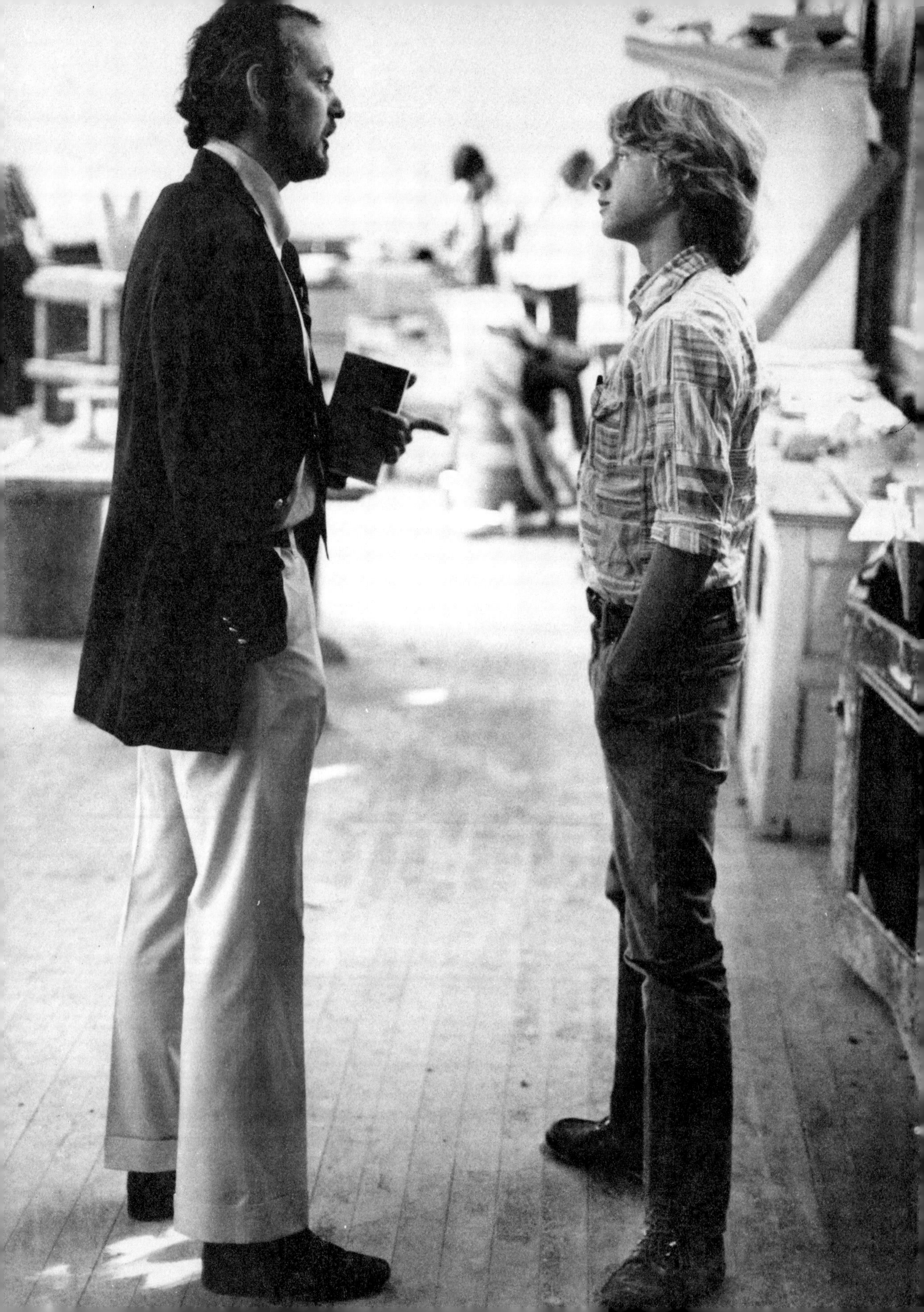

CHAPTER SEVENTEEN

Phenomenological theory: application for building helping skills

SURVEY AND QUESTIONS

This chapter continues the discussion of Vern Jensen's program for helping adolescents, which began in the last chapter. Phase II is presented here, as well as further phenomenological practices with regard to self-development. Reading the chapter will provide answers to the following questions:

Dealing with Conflict

Will providing trust, acceptance, and unconditional love produce youth who are spoiled, inconsistent, insensitive to others, and without limits?
Do genuine differences exist between adults and adolescents that result in unhealthy conflict?
How can one distinguish between positive and negative conflict?
Do adults sometimes have to be more directive?
What if the negative cycle is set up?

Skills for Helping

What are the major helping techniques?
What is concreteness?
What are the five levels of concreteness?
What is confrontation?
When should confrontation be used?
What is immediacy?
How does immediacy help?
When should immediacy responses be used?
What are the five levels of immediacy?
What is reassurance?
What is the difference between the two types of reassurance situations?
What are the five levels of reassurance?

Phenomenological Practices in Self-Development

What can significant others do to help adolescents develop a healthy self-concept?
What kind of atmosphere will promote self-development?

The first time I had a good parent talk with an adult was when I was 14 and I talked with my mother. The occasion was just after Christmas and my grandmother had had a stroke. My mom wanted to go to Germany to be with her before she died and she wanted me to be with her.

So, for the months of January and February I stayed in Germany at the hospital or the little room we rented. At first it was very boring and not being able to speak the language I was getting very restless.

My mom started talking to me then about when she was my age and about what my grandmother was like then. We grew very close, because I knew she needed me then to be strong and I saw that she was the same way I was at that age. I was finally able to relate and be open with her, because I knew she understood.

The last chapter focused on the helping conditions from Carkhuff's theory. The helping conditions covered in Phase I were geared to creating a relationship by providing a climate that fosters freedom to express feelings and explore problems. This chapter focuses on an adaption of Phase II. First, however, a discussion of conflict is needed.

Dealing with conflict

As was discussed in the previous chapter, phenomenological theorists believe that behavior is determined by perceptions, which in turn are influenced by culture and environment. In general, the ideal environment contains a minimum of conflict and negative feelings, and is characterized by unconditional love, ample trust, and acceptance.

QUESTION: Will providing trust, acceptance, and unconditional love produce youth who are spoiled, inconsistent, insensitive to others, and without limits?

No, for phenomenological theory certainly implies boundaries and limits. Boundaries and limits, however, are self-imposed, develop naturally out of the experience of the child, and are not based on an externally imposed set of constraints.

Parents and teachers must initially provide limits. This job is not difficult because society has given parents and teachers a great deal of control and power, and producing definite limits is easily within the capabilities of parents and teachers. Parents, for example, have great verbal, intellectual, and interpersonal skills, as well as control over food, shelter, clothing, physical force, affections, and so on. Growth, however, is seen as a movement away from using external controls and away from the use of power to impose additional limits. Limits should be developed by adolescents rather than imposed from without.

As youth develop toward a healthy self-concept, they become sensitive to the needs of others and begin to identify with others. The welfare of others becomes important to adolescents. Out of this type of growth—sensitivity and awareness of others—awareness and the basis of limits and self-control materialize. Adolescents soon find that they cannot engage in certain behaviors without hurting others. They usually find that certain statements or activities hurt their friends, siblings, parents, and so on. Adolescents then voluntarily impose restraints upon themselves, and their interpersonal relationships and the welfare of others are enhanced. Parents need not reward or punish certain actions, since appropriate social behavior will naturally follow when adolescents see and understand the problems caused by certain actions, and understand the implications of their actions on other people's well-being. These types of ethics, which are based on a more mature foundation of concern for others, are not expected to result from the reward and punishment type of experience.

As can be seen in the work of researchers discussed in the chapter on moral development, such as Lawrence Kohlberg of Harvard University (1978), a morality based on rewards and punishments is more characteristic of less developed people. A more mature type of morality is based on concern for the welfare of others. When a morality based on a concern for the welfare of others is developed, it is more rewarding to the people adolescents love because it becomes a part of youths' self-concept. The permanence or stability in youths behavior transcends pleasure seeking or a morality based on rewards or fear.

QUESTION: Do genuine differences exist between adults and adolescents that result in unhealthy conflict?

Is it true that at times the immediate interests of adults and adolescents are in direct opposition? Although the assumption is that the self-growth tendency and society's needs are compatible, they do not always grow in the same direction, and conflict sometimes results.

Sidney Jourard (1967) stated that conflicts (personal adjustment) can be welcomed rather than feared and approached rather than avoided, because they can provide a source of growth that enriches and develops human relationships. The following case humorously illustrates one such encounter that fortunately resulted in a positive experience:

> As a freshman in high school I was 14 and discovered that most adults aren't interested in what teenagers have to say. Other than my parents, few adults really listened out of sincere interest. One exception to this generalization was my English teacher who taught American Literature. He was a tyrant and a bore and spent day after day showing us slides of birth places and death places and places where famous American writers had once sat momentarily on a park bench. All of his slides had one thing in common—his fat little daughter was always standing right in front of—and obscuring— anything of the slightest interest.
>
> Shortly thereafter, Mr. C, the English teacher, assigned us to write the perfect one-page paragraph. I was happy to oblige and wrote a biting one-page parody of Mr. C., his travels to famous literary landmarks, and his fat little daughter. He was, of course, outraged. He ranted and raved and threatened and called me 16½ or 17 vile names . . . but then he asked me why I wrote it. Thinking he would continue his attack, I replied, "I only did what you said— I wrote a literarily perfect paragraph and you have no alternative but to give me an A—it's your 'moral and patriotic duty'. . ." (those were his words). Expecting a second explosion from him I resigned myself to the eminent attack.
>
> He caught me completely off guard by acknowledging that I was correct and asking how I had chosen my subject. Hesitantly I explained. I was amazed when he listened without condemnation and with genuine interest. He ac-

knowledged my valid points and diplomatically corrected my misconceptions. He *really* listened. It made a difference.

The mature handling of conflicts helps people to see and understand the perceptions of others, and demonstrates that many problems do not result from a conflict of needs, but from faulty communication, misconceptions, or lack of correct information. Sometimes a conflict does not even belong to someone and the other person is capable of handling it without the other's assistance. Most important, conflict between adolescents and adults provides experience in conflict resolution that is essential to other interpersonal relationships throughout life. Conflicts can therefore be a source of growth and should not be avoided or eliminated. How then are they to be handled?

A statement on this issue is found in Sidney Jourard's book *Personal Adjustment* (1967). Jourard provides an excellent analysis of a conflict situation:

> The simplest case of an interpersonal impasse consists of one person expressing an opinion or demand which the other person refuses openly. The simplest case of impasse resolution consists of either (a) the person withdrawing the demand, or (b) the other person complying with the demand, or (c) some compromise between a and b. (Jourard 1967, 344)

QUESTION: How can one distinguish between positive and negative conflict?

According to Jourard, the handling of conflict can be judged by its effects on growth. If the solution results in a valued change in the behavior repertoire of the person, or if it results in a healthy self-structure, then we can regard the solution as growth producing. If the solution simply crystallizes the behavior, however, or if it interferes with growth or produces regression, then it is unhealthy. Compulsive avoidance of impasses and interpersonal conflict is also unhealthy. In a healthy relationship, each partner feels free to express personal likes, dislikes, wants, wishes, and feelings. Conflicts create tears, laughter, centrality, irritation, anger, fear, and babylike behavior, and an occasion for growth arises when conflicts between people are acknowledged. The solution to these problems results in the growth of personality either towards health or away from health (Jourard 1967).

Jourard's analysis of conflict includes (1) the need for communication, (2) the desirability of conflict, (3) the growth potential of conflict, and (4) the ability to evaluate conflict in terms of its growth-producing elements. Through such an approach, parents and teachers can guide and facilitate the self-growth of youth in developing standards, morals, values, and other kinds of limits necessary for the preservation and welfare of human life. The methods for facilitating growth involve giving adolescents warmth, acceptance, and freedom, and letting them know that they are adequate. The focus must be on the youth and not on things that give them free access to information.

QUESTION: Do adults sometimes have to be more directive?

In some conflict situations, parents or teachers must clearly and accurately present their beliefs or positions. This presentation is best done without demand

There are some situations in which adults need to be directive and provide adolescents with a specific problem on which they can focus.

so that adolescents can share the problem that is common to both adults and adolescents. With this information, plus receiving and feeling the communication from adults, adolescents will have a problem on which they can focus. If the problem is in the realm of adolescents' personal interests, they will likely present a resolution to the conflict. The resolution will frequently be a compromise between the adolescents' position and the adults'. If the resolution is not a compromise or a concession but a descriptive form of adult needs or wishes, then the other factors, which were discussed earlier (trusting, giving of freedom, giving the experience for growth, and so on), become feasible at this point. The solution should be judged according to whether it is growth producing for one or both of the participants.

A wise approach is for adults to present only demands that adolescents are able to meet. No demand should be presented when accomplishing the expectation is impossible. One should use consideration with adolescents as well as with adults. In most cases, development of the demand should result from the communication between youth and adults. In this way, the demand comes from both adolescents and adults rather than from adults alone.

Adults should take an active role in facilitating growth. The importance of this role is seen in the circular nature of youths' environmental interaction. In general terms, youth who perceive themselves as inadequate meet their environment with less ability then they would if they perceived themselves as adequate. This perception in turn increases their chances for failure. The failure then reinforces or further strengthens their perception of themselves as inadequate. A vicious cycle is therefore set up. Healthy people are more successful, but unhealthy people are less successful, and the resulting failure confirms their belief that they are less successful, therefore producing a lower self-concept. The opposite is true for healthy people, whose success in turn promotes subsequent feelings of adequacy. This type of event is true for all aspects of the self-concept. When adolescents identify with others, they are more likely to meet others in an appropriate and successful manner. Their manner encourages others to respond to them in kind, resulting in a successful experience for adolescents. Adolescents are then more likely to identify with other people who have had successful experiences. Adolescents who are alienated from other people, however, approach others with misgivings and are unsure, hesitant, and self-conscious in manner. This type of general awkwardness increases the likelihood of more poor experiences. These adolescents will then be less likely to engage in interpersonal activities, and in the future they will become more alienated than before.

QUESTION: What if the negative cycle is set up?

Breaking a negative cycle is difficult, but it must be broken. Adults must at some point be willing to accept, identify, and trust these adolescents. In these cases, no immediate satisfaction of basic needs will occur for the helping adults. Adults must be willing to continue to accept these youth, even though the youth may give nothing to the relationship. They will perhaps even attack the adults. If parents repeatedly accept adolescents, these youth will eventually come to see that they are valued and that they are regarded as positive, at least by these particular adults. They can then begin acting positively or competently, become less defensive, and move toward healthy growth.

As adolescents break the cycle, a larger part of their world will respond to them positively, thus leading them to more successful experiences. Soon they will be less dependent upon facilitating adults to provide unconditional acceptance, trust, and faith. Adults will no longer be necessary as props or supports in breaking the vicious cycle. These youth will have obtained the independence and autonomy desired.

Before adults can perform this crucial helping task, they must have some degree of growth toward self-actualization so that they can defer their immediate well-being to the welfare of adolescents. Unhealthy adults cannot provide this type of acceptance and trust. They are reluctant to give the kind of honest freedom needed to accept mistakes and to live with the associated problems that will result from incompetence in handling problems.

Skills for helping

Continuing the modified program of Vern Jensen that began in the last chapter, the helping techniques in Phase II build upon and expand the helping conditions through various skills. The skills or techniques in this chapter enable adolescents to move toward more self-understanding and to find more effective courses of action. Helping conditions set the stage, and once the stage has been set, helpers can move out in many directions by using a variety of helping techniques. Helpers can now be more specific, frank, and even confrontive, because adolescents know that the helpers have the adolescents' interests at heart.

QUESTION: What are the major helping techniques?

The purpose of Phase II of the program is to become acquainted with a variety of helping techniques that may prove useful in the helper-adolescent relationship. The intent of this phase is not to cover every technique but to discuss some of those which are most frequently used. The helping techniques considered in this phase of the program include (1) concreteness, (2) confrontation, (3) immediacy, and (4) reassurance.

CONCRETENESS

QUESTION: What is concreteness?

Characteristics of adolescents is generalizing problems to the extent that they later need help in even identifying the problems. The task for helpers is to assist adolescents to be specific and concrete about the problems they are facing. One adolescent, for example, may say he is upset all the time because he does not get along with his boss. The helper should help him to see exactly what is causing the conflict between him and his boss. Another adolescent may say that her difficulty is that of procrastination. The helper needs to call the adolescent's attention to the meaning of procrastination. In both instances, an inappropriate position is to simply gloss over these statements without pinning these adolescents down as to what they mean. In either case, a more helpful position is for the helper to say something like, "Can you tell me a little bit more about it?" or "Could you be more specific about what you mean?" Generalizations tend to cloud problems and situations. If helpers are concrete in their responses to adolescents, adolescents will in turn be more concrete in identifying and solving the problems.

To illustrate concreteness, assume that an adolescent says, "From time to time I get this peculiar sensation." In this short statement are two vague terms. The first is "from time to time," and the second one is "peculiar sensation." The helper either may gloss over these generalities with no comment, or may reflect them by responding with something like, "Now and then you seem to be having some real strange experiences." Although this is a good reflective response, it may leave the adolescent as vague as when he began. The helper could, however, help the adolescent to be more concrete by such a response as, "I feel a little confused about what you mean by 'from time to time' and by 'peculiar sensation'."

A general reflective response may or may not help adolescents move toward concreteness. For some adolescents, this may be all that is needed, but for others the response may reinforce them to maintain their stance of vague generalities. Concreteness is particularly valuable as a skill if adolescents have a tendency to ramble on about irrelevant material. At times, however, such as during an interview, allowing adolescents to go off on a tangent may be helpful. This may be particularly helpful at the outset of a relationship, as was indicated in Phase I. Reflecting feelings without concreteness may be important for creating a climate in which adolescents can feel free to express themselves and can enjoy a certain amount of catharsis. Once the relationship is under way, however, concreteness is a valuable tool for getting to the heart of the problem.

QUESTION: What are the five levels of concreteness?

To practice giving concrete responses, the reader should study the five levels of concreteness that follow, then take the Self-Test for Concreteness. The following adolescent statement will serve as an example:

> "I'm trying to make it in school, but then there are all of the interferences. They just won't let me alone. How do they expect a person to concentrate?"

Level 1 (Lowest Level) Does Not See Problem and Has No Concreteness The helper's response at Level 1 may not only be vague and general, but may also be unrelated to the basic problem that the adolescent is presenting. The helper completely misses both the specific content of the message and the feelings of the adolescent. Since the response detracts from concreteness, it is considered a minus or a negative. An example of a Level 1 response to the previous adolescent statement is, "I don't blame you one bit for complaining. This school is really a rat race." By responding with the words "rat race," the helper's response not only reinforces vagueness but also misses the unrelated problem of the disadvantages of the school.

Level 2 (Low Level) Sees Problem but Has No Concreteness The helper at Level 2 may indicate that he recognizes the problem, but he still tends to be vague and general in his response to the adolescent statement. The helper's response detracts from concreteness and tends to lead the adolescent toward further vague generalizations. For example, a Level 2 response to the previous adolescent statement is, "It's too bad they don't leave you alone so you can concentrate on your schoolwork." The helper's response does focus on the interferences in school, but no reinforcement is given for the adolescent to get down to the specifics of the problem, which leads to further ambiguity.

Level 3 (Neutral) No Movement The helper's response at Level 3 not only indicates that she recognizes the problem, but also reinforces some type of response regarding the problem. In getting down to specifics, however, the helper's response is neutral, meaning that it could cause the adolescent to move to either a higher level or a lower level of concreteness, or even remain the same. Reflections and paraphrasing will tend toward neutrality if the helper uses the same or synonymous general terms that the adolescent uses in his statement. An example of a Level 3 response is, "You are wondering just how you are going to get your schoolwork accomplished with all the interferences you have." This response reinforces the adolescent to respond to the problem, but it may or may not cause him to be specific.

Level 4 (High Level) Specific and Concrete At Level 4, the helper's response is positively directed to assist the adolescent to be more specific and concrete. The helper not only responds directly to the content of the message and to the important feelings of the adolescent but also narrows some of them down to where the helper and adolescent can begin to deal with the problem specifically. The helper identifies and responds to at least one specific feeling, situation, or event that is part of the adolescent's statement. Although the helper may respond

Participating together in some recreational activity may foster the necessary trust underlying the major helping techniques in the helper-adolescent relationship.

to other parts of the adolescent's statement in a general way, he responds in such a manner that he is helping the adolescent to move in the direction of concreteness. At Level 4 a helper might respond to the previous adolescent statement by saying, "I can understand how frustrating it is for you to make an effort in school and then have so many interferences that it is hard to succeed, but I am not sure I know what or who it is that won't let you alone."

Level 5 (Highest Level) Encourages Higher Level of Concreteness Like Level 4, the helper's response at the highest level is positively geared toward assisting the adolescent to be concrete. The helper again responds directly to the adolescent's essential feelings and experiences. The difference between Level 4 and Level 5 is one of degree. The helper's response simply encourages a higher level of concreteness; the helper goes beyond Level 4. She recognizes most, if not all, of the generalities that the adolescent conveys, and responds in such a manner that helps the adolescent to move even further toward concreteness. An example of a Level 5 response to the previous adolescent statement is, "What I understand from your statement is that you are trying in school, but someone is keeping you from it. However, I'm not clear who 'they' refers to and what you mean by 'interferences' and 'concentrate.' Maybe we could look at each of these words one at a time."

For a further understanding of concreteness, the reader should take the following self-test.

SELF-TEST FOR CONCRETENESS

Read the following adolescent statements and then rate the helper responses according to the level of concreteness (1–5).

Adolescent Statement 1

"I think the thing I need to do is to get down to business and study. I guess I'm beginning to let my social life interfere, or maybe getting involved socially is a way out or an excuse to get away from the drudgery of studying. It is really nothing more than procrastination. Everything seems to be going to pot. I really want to succeed, but it is really discouraging when things don't work out the way you want them to."

Helper Responses

____ 1. "It seems to me that it might be well to re-examine your values to see whether it is really school or your social life that is important."

____ 2. "You feel discouraged because you really want to discipline yourself so that you can get down to studying, but it takes more effort and sacrifice than you are willing to give at the moment."

____ 3. "I can sense the discouragement you are feeling, but I'm just not quite sure what you mean by getting down to the business of study, how your social life might be interfering with your study, and what it is that is going to pot."

____ 4. "Why don't you work out a plan where you have time for your social life and time for your study. Get yourself a good schedule."

____ 5. "Could you tell me a little more about what you mean by 'everything seems to be going to pot?'"

Adolescent Statement 2

"You were wondering how I would like my life to be different. Well, let me tell you. First of all, I would like to get out of this rut I'm in. I get so fed up and wonder when it will ever come to an end. I just want to be a somebody, and not a thing to be trampled on. I'm tired of being outside the circle all the time. I want so much to get in, but how? You want to put your best foot forward—do something—but then you know if you do, you'll pull some big blunder and put yourself right back in it further than you were before."

Helper Responses

____ 1. "I guess when you get in that kind of rut, it's hard to get out because if you try to get out it might backfire, and you will find yourself in a deeper rut."

____ 2. "If I get what you mean, the rut you want to get out of is that of not being accepted by others, because it really hurts to be left out. Yet, at the same time, it is really risky to become involved."

____ 3. Perhaps the best thing we could do would be to help you to build your self-esteem; then you would be able to take risks and not be afraid of making blunders.

____ 4. "This leaves me just a little confused about what it is that you really want to do—what your goal really is. It may be helpful to you to state just what is meant by 'being in a rut,' 'a somebody outside the circle,' and 'pulling a big blunder.'"

____ 5. "Maybe we could take each of the concerns that you have mentioned one at a time and see how we might formulate some goals. Let's first look at what you mean by 'being in a rut'; then we can move onto the rest of them step by step."

Adolescent Statement 3

"I can't understand why I keep doing these stupid things that keep getting me in trouble. I really want to be straight, but no matter how hard I try, I seem to mess things up. I'm almost to the point that I don't even care."

Helper Responses

____ 1. "You feel pretty frustrated because you want to be good, but regardless of how hard you try, things don't seem to work out."

____ 2. "I'm not sure what you mean by 'stupid things' that get you into trouble."

____ 3. "If you would use a little willpower, I'm sure you could change your behavior."

____ 4. "I guess I feel just a little confused by what 'these stupid things' has reference to, how you are messing things up, and what you mean by being 'straight.'"

____ 5. "I guess we all do stupid things and mess things up now and then. None of us is really perfect."

Key: Self-Test for Concreteness
4, 5, 3, 1, 2
3, 4, 2, 1, 5
5, 1, 2, 1, 3

CONFRONTATION

QUESTION: What is confrontation?

Adolescents sometimes face problems in which they are so emotionally involved that they are unaware of the inconsistencies and discrepancies that may exist in their behavior and experiences. They therefore have little way of knowing what is happening unless the inconsistencies are called to their attention. The process that gives feedback to adolescents about their inconsistencies and contradictions is called confrontation. To be of most help, helpers must require adolescents to face up to these contradictions. Even more important than confronting adolescents is the way in which they are confronted. Confrontation can be destructive as well as helpful. The helpers' best approach is to describe their own reactions to what adolescents say or do, rather than to be accusative or judgmental. Less threatening is, "Even though you smile and say nice things, I get the feeling that you may be angry by the way you clench your fist" rather than, "You smile and talk like an angel, but your behavior tells me you are not." Confrontation is therefore more helpful and less threatening when it is accompanied by empathy and is void of accusations.

QUESTION: When should confrontation be used?

Although confrontation may be helpful in many situations, the following situations serve as examples in using this technique:

1. Adolescents may need to be confronted with discrepancies between *what they say and what they do*. In their present frame of mind, adolescents may be unaware of this inconsistency. A young man, for example, may say he has great affection for his fiancée, but indications are that he spends little time with her. An appropriate confronting response might be, "You say you love your fiancée, but I seem to keep hearing you say that you spend little time with her" rather than, "Your actions prove that you do not love her."

2. Discrepancies may exist in adolescents' *perceptions of reality*. For example, suppose a secretary says, "I'm really basically honest, but I can see taking a few office supplies home now and then, especially since the firm has more money than they know what to do with." A likely helping response might be, "Perhaps I don't quite get the picture; you say you are basically honest, but you say you take things that do not belong to you"

rather than, "How can you possibly think that way? You are just as much of a thief as you would be if you robbed a bank."

3. Adolescents' *goals* and *ambition* in attaining goals are sometimes inconsistent. An adolescent might say, "I want to succeed. I've always wanted to be a physician, and I'll be one someday. Right now I'm just tired of school. The more I go the more I get fed up." An appropriate helper response might be, "You tell me that your goal is to be a physician, which takes a lot of schooling, yet you are always fed up" rather than, "You'll never make it with that attitude about school."

4. Without being aware of it, adolescents may *make contradictory statements*. A young woman, for example, might say she is "uptight" about the failure of a love affair because she was dropped by her boyfriend, and almost in the same breath may state how relieved she is that it is over. A helpful response might be, "You tell me you are really upset because your boyfriend left you."

To help evaluate confrontation, five levels are now identified, which are followed by a self-test.

Level 1 (Lowest Level) Put-Down The helper's response at Level 1 not only lacks empathy but also may be judgmental or accusative. The adolescent may feel put down or even attacked. The adolescent may therefore be put on the defensive to the point where he is unable to deal rationally with inconsistencies or distortions that may exist in his problem. This type of response detracts from helping the adolescent to deal with inconsistencies. A Level 1 response to the previous adolescent statement might be, "You'll likely never get a date with the attitude you have toward men."

Level 2 (Low Level) Misdirected The helper's response at Level 2 detracts from the distortions and contradictions, although it may not be taken as an attack or a put-down. The response not only lacks empathy but also may lead the adolescent into channels where the inconsistencies are obscured. Levels 1 and 2 are therefore alike in that they both lack empathy and concreteness, and they both detract from clearing up distortions and inconsistencies. The levels are different in that a Level 2 response is less accusative and judgmental than Level 1. A Level 2 response to the previous adolescent statement might be, "I wouldn't be too concerned about dating. After all, there are a lot of women who don't date in this community."

Level 3 (Neutral) A response in Level 3 may or may not be empathic; it puts the situation in a neutral position. A neutral empathy response, for example, may reflect back to the adolescent what she has said and how she feels, but the impact may be too low for her to discern discrepancies or inconsistencies. Although the response indicates that the helper recognizes the discrepancy, it is usually either too general or ignores the dynamics of the discrepancy. Since such vagueness is left to the adolescent, she may or may not gain insight into the inconsistency. A Level 3 response to the previous adolescent statement might be, "You would like to date and are pretty disappointed because you are not. You see the men as being conceited and undependable to the point where you may not trust the relationship."

Level 4 (High Level) At Level 4, the helper's response attends directly to the adolescent's inconsistencies or distortions. Sufficient attention is given to the discrepancy for the adolescent to begin to deal with. The levels of concreteness and specificity may be only moderately high, but at least sufficient feedback is given for the adolescent to recognize and begin to deal with the discrepancy. A Level 4 response might be, "You really want to date and have a relationship with men, but has it ever occurred to you that your hostile feelings toward them may be keeping them away?"

Level 5 (Highest Level) At Level 5, the helper's response not only attends directly to the adolescent's inconsistencies and distortions but also indicates a high degree of empathy and concreteness. At this level, a helper response might be, "I can sense the frustration you are experiencing when you are not dating, especially when guys are all around, but I also wonder if the guys may be sensing some of the negative feelings you have toward them, such as their playing games and being conceited." This response not only recognizes the discrepancies but also focuses on some of the specifics and responds to the adolescent's feelings.

For a further understanding of confrontation, the reader should take the following self-test.

SELF-TEST FOR CONFRONTATION

Read the following adolescent statements and then rate the helper responses according to the level of confrontation (1–5).

Adolescent Statement 1

"One thing I know is, I'm really getting discouraged. I'm at the point where I don't know whether to stay in school or not. I can't even start to count the problems. First there is the problem of getting my homework done. I don't seem to be able to concentrate. I've had five assignments and only turned in two. I'm not prepared for tests. Then, there are two of my instructors. They are sad! I guess this is the thing that bugs me the most. One's class bores me to tears. I can't seem to please the other one. His tests and assignments are stupid. I don't do well on them either."

Helper Responses

____ 1. "One of the things that seems to be bothering you most is what you say your instructors are doing to create problems for you, but yet you say you have difficulty concentrating and turning in assignments. Perhaps it would be helpful if you could clarify this for me."

____ 2. "It is really discouraging to have problems concentrating and studying and at the same time have contrary instructors to deal with."

____ 3. "I don't blame you for feeling discouraged with all the problems you are facing. I can readily see why you would like to leave school."

____ 4. "It is obvious that you are blaming your instructor for your own problems and irresponsibility."

____ 5. "You might try to get a tutor to help you, or maybe the help sections in the classes where you are having trouble could help you get on your feet."

Adolescent Statement 2

"I would like to have more friends, but I guess I'm what you would call the quiet type. I don't really mix very well with people either. Even when I meet somebody I know on the street, I seldom speak to them. I suppose in one way it's because people around here are not very friendly. If I spoke to them and they did not speak back, I'd feel real silly; so I guess I sort of wait for them to say hello first, but that would probably be just too much to expect."

Helper Responses

____ 1. "I have lived around here a long time, and I know people are friendly. If you would quit feeling sorry for yourself and change your timid behavior you wouldn't have to worry about friends."

____ 2. "It might be helpful for us to start working on raising your self-esteem so you will have more confidence in making friends."

____ 3. "You would really like to make friends, but it feels just a little risky to put your best foot forward to make a friend, because they may not reciprocate."

____ 4. "What I hear you saying is that you would like to have more friends, yet you expect them to take all of the initiative to get things going."

____ 5. "It comes across to me that you feel somewhat trapped. You would like to make friends, but you're caught between being alone or taking the risk to make friends for fear of being ignored or rejected. Yet at the same time I am wondering if it might have something to do with your own reluctance to be friendly. In other words, is it possible that to see people as being friendly or to have a friend you may need to take the risk of being friendly or being a friend yourself?"

Key: Self-Test for Confrontation
5, 3, 2, 1, 4
1, 2, 4, 3, 5

IMMEDIACY

QUESTION: What is immediacy?

Often helpful is for adolescents to focus on the immediate experience in their relationship with helpers. What is happening at the moment between them may be more significant than what has happened to adolescents in the past or even what they are currently experiencing outside the relationship. Regardless of the type of problem adolescents may present, they will almost invariably be having some difficulty with interpersonal relationships. The helper-adolescent relationship itself therefore gives an opportunity to experiment with improving inter-

Many of the positive elements of a helping relationship emerge spontaneously between friends.

personal relationships in a safe and secure atmosphere. At times, focusing directly on their relationship is helpful for helpers and adolescents. This process is called immediacy or focusing on the here and now.

QUESTION: How does immediacy help?

Immediacy responses in the relationship help adolescents to better understand their own behavior in relating to other people. They learn how they come across to people by the modeling and the feedback they get from the helpers. As adolescents begin to feel more comfortable with immediacy responses in the relationship, they also begin to generalize their new learned behaviors with other people outside the relationship. Assume, for example, that a young man has been having difficulty on his job. He has little trouble with his skills, but he feels discouraged primarily because he does not seem to get ahead, and no one seems to care even when he does a good job. He has had several different supervisors during the years he has been working, and he feels none of them have treated him kindly. He says, "I'm reluctant to have a talk with my supervisor, because I just don't think she likes me and it would make matters worse. All my life I've had difficulty talking to people who are in authority and even people who are older than I am." An appropriate immediacy response might be, "It puts you in a bind when you want to have a good relationship with your supervisor, but at the same time it is hard for you to talk to people in authority. I guess you may even feel uncomfortable here with me, since I fall into the category of 'older people.'"

In the previous situation, the problem shows difficulty in interpersonal relationships. The helper therefore finds an opportunity to focus on the immediacy of the relationship. The helper is now able to assist the young man in experiencing a new, safe, here-and-now relationship with him, which may generalize to his relationships with his supervisor and with other people.

Immediacy responses need to be used cautiously and wisely. Since they are generally at a higher level than other responses previously discussed, a good rapport needs to exist between the helper and adolescent. The immediacy response should be used to improve interpersonal relationships with others or to alleviate whatever may be getting in the way of the helping relationship itself. Both rapport and timing are important considerations in determining how and when to use immediacy responses. On occasions, timing may be a more appropriate consideration than rapport. At the beginning of a meeting, for example, before a relationship has been established, immediacy responses may be helpful for reluctant adolescents to help break down their resistance. In a situation such as this, an appropriate immediacy response might be, "You hesitate to tell me about it because you are not quite sure you can trust me." Whether the time is before or after a relationship has been established, the helper needs to be cautious in the use of immediacy responses. Without the appropriate conditions, helper immediacy response may frighten adolescents or may pose other kinds of threats.

QUESTION: When should immediacy responses be used?

Immediacy response may be helpful in a number of specific situations. The following are a few of these situations:

1. Adolescents are reluctant to talk, or they avoid the real problem.
   Helper response: "You seem to be hesitant to talk about the problem. Could it be that you really don't trust me?"
2. Either the helper or the adolescent seems to feel nervous or uncomfortable.
   Adolescent statement: "I guess I just feel a little nervous here. Maybe I don't know quite what to expect."
   Helper response: "I suppose it does put you in an awkward position to find yourself here with me when you didn't want to come anyway. I feel just a little uncomfortable myself."
3. Adolescents resist carrying their share of the responsibility.
   Helper response: "It just occurred to me that even though you say you are willing to try out a new skill or technique, I seem to wind up doing it for you. Maybe I'm just not quite sure where we both stand."
4. Adolescents would benefit by practicing and experiencing immediacy in a safe relationship with the helpers.
   Helper response: "I keep getting the message that you have difficulty expressing your feelings in your relationship with people. Maybe it would be helpful if you could express, from time to time, the feelings you have toward me in our relationship."
5. Adolescents depend on the helpers to do all the working and talking.
   Helper response: "Sometimes I get the feeling that I am doing the work for both of us. I seem to be the one who decides what we are going to talk about, and I seem to get caught up in firing questions at you. Could it be that I don't give you enough time to think and to respond, or do you like the comfort of sitting back and being passive?"
6. Either helpers or adolescents do not feel they are getting anywhere.
   Helper response: "At first we seemed to be making real progress, but now I am wondering if we are just going around in circles. I sense also that you are beginning to feel uncomfortable, too. Maybe we ought to take a look at what's going on between the two of us."
7. The helper or adolescent has a strong attraction for the other, or for each other, which may be interfering with progress.
   Helper response: "From what we have both said, it seems obvious that we like each other. Maybe we are afraid to say the things that would be most helpful because we are afraid of hurting each other's feelings. Perhaps we are caught up with giving each other "strokes," rather than dealing directly with what is bothering you. Do you think we could just be realistic and admit how we feel about each other and then get on with it, or do you see it differently than the way I do?"
8. The helper and adolescent seem to be on different wavelengths and are having difficulty communicating.
   Helper response: "I keep getting the feeling that we are coming from different angles. You seem to be talking about one thing, and I'm talking about another. I keep trying to focus on your personal behavior, and you seem to want to bring up how people have treated you in the past. Maybe our messages to each other tend to get garbled along the way. You're not sure what I'm after, and I'm not quite sure what you want. I think I would feel more comfortable if we could take time out to synchronize our watches."

9. The adolescent's statement circumvents directness by referring to "other people" rather than by referring directly to the helper.
   Adolescent statement: "I guess I'm concerned because I don't seem to relate well with people, especially older people and people in authority."
   Helper response: "Perhaps you are also concerned about our relationship, whether you will be able to relate to me, or whether we will be able to relate to each other."

The following are the five levels of immediacy. The reader should review each and then use them to take the Self-Test for Immediacy that will follow.

QUESTION: What are the five levels of immediacy?

Consider the five levels of immediacy in response to the following adolescent statement:

> "I guess I feel just a little embarrassed about bringing up the subject. People either seem to turn off before you get to it or else they think you are a real creep. I thought of mentioning it to you last time, but then I thought, 'Well, maybe it's not that important.'"

Level 1 (Lowest Level) The helper's response at Level 1 not only detracts the adolescent from moving toward immediacy but also completely misses the crux of the problem. An example of a Level 1 response to the previous adolescent statement might be, "If it's important to you, it should be important enough to someone else. If they think you are a creep, that's their problem." The real crux of the problem seems to be a matter of trust rather than a matter of the importance of the problem. Furthermore, nothing is implied in the response that will lead to a focus in immediacy.

Level 2 (Low Level) The helper's response at Level 2 may indicate a recognition of the problem, but it still leads the adolescent away from immediacy. A helper response at Level 2 might be, "You should learn to trust people more. Most people are really understanding. You have just had a bad experience by running into the wrong people." In this situation, the helper refers to the crux of the problem by bringing up the matter of trust, but the response leads toward a focus on other people rather than on the here and now.

Level 3 (Neutral) The helper's response at Level 3 recognizes the problem but leaves the adolescent in neutral position. In other words, the adolescent is reinforced to respond, but is left to move either toward or away from immediacy. Reflective listening and paraphrasing often tend to put the adolescent in this position. A Level 3 response might be, "You would really like to bring up the subject, but you're embarrassed to mention it for fear you will be misunderstood or even put down." Here the helper examines the trust problem and reflects the feeling of the adolescent. The response, however, still leaves the adolescent in a neutral position. The adolescent may move to the here-and-now relationship between himself and the helper, or he may focus his statements on his relationships with other people.

Level 4 (High Level) The response at Level 4 begins to lead the adolescent toward the immediacy of the relationship and also gets at the crux of the problem. Part of the response focuses on other people, and part also focuses on the here and now of the relationship. A helper response at Level 4 might be, "You seem to have had some experiences that make it hard for you to trust other people, and you are not quite sure you can trust me." Here we see a turn from other people to the immediacy of the relationship involving the issue of trusting the helper.

Level 5 (Highest Level) The response at Level 5 focuses almost entirely on the immediacy of the situation. The response also deals with the crux of the problem and usually carries with it a high level of empathy. Level 5 therefore focuses more on the here and now of the relationship than does Level 4 and also has a higher level of empathy. The difference between the two levels is strictly one of degree rather than kind. A Level 5 response to the previous adolescent statement might be, "You are wondering whether to take the risk in bringing up the subject here with me. You say you feel embarrassed. Could it be that you are just not quite sure I would really understand? Or perhaps you are wondering whether I might also turn off or think you are a creep." The helper deals with three of the criteria essential to a high-level immediacy response. She focuses almost entirely on the immediacy of the relationship, gets to the crux of the problem involving the issue of trusting the helper, and responds with a high level of empathy.

To further understand immediacy, the reader should take the following self-test.

SELF-TEST FOR IMMEDIACY

Read the following adolescent statements and then rate the helper responses according to the level of immediacy (1–5).

Adolescent Statement 1 (Female, Age Fourteen)

"I've been here for a whole school year now, and I still find people to be unfriendly. I walk around school, and no one even knows I'm around. My teachers could care less that I even exist. Maybe if I stay here long enough I'll eventually run into a friendly face."

Helper Responses

____ 1. "People in this school are really friendly once you get to know them."

____ 2. "You have found people in this school to be unfriendly, including students, teachers, and perhaps others. You are even wondering if I will turn out to be a friendly person."

____ 3. "I suppose after a year it is pretty tough to be without friends. Maybe you should learn some skills for making friends."

____ 4. "You would really like to have friends, and sometimes it gets pretty lonely without them."

____ 5. "I can sense some of the loneliness you have been feeling all this time, and I suppose it is even more frustrating when you begin to wonder about our friendship and whether I really care."

Adolescent Statement 2 (Male, Age Eighteen)

"I guess I'm not sure just where to start. It's really complicated. I thought once of talking the problem over with my parents; then I thought, what's the use? It would be a waste of my time and their time. What could they do to help? It would just be letting them know that they have a rotten son. When it boils right down to it, I'm not sure anybody can help."

Helper Responses

___ 1. "I think it would be good to have a relationship with your parents. You ought to tell them."

___ 2. "It seems to be pretty hard to share something so personal with me, and you are wondering whether I could understand or whether I might judge you and perhaps even reject you."

___ 3. "I get the feeling that you have a difficult time sharing your feelings with others, and you question whether you can share them here with me."

___ 4. "Why don't you just tell me why you decided to come in today. That might help you to get started."

___ 5. "It is really important to you to talk over your problems and express your feelings, but you are not quite sure anyone could help or understand."

Adolescent Statement 3 (Female, Age Nineteen)

"I can't understand why I am so weak. Why do I have to come here to see you? I should be able to solve my own problems. It hurts deeply to think that I do not have the strength to stand on my own. How humiliating it is to have to be here. I would just die if my friends knew I was here. Just count me in as another of your little weak, wretched creatures who need help."

Helper Responses

___ 1. "I don't think you are a weak person, and I doubt if your friends would think that if they knew you were here. I think it took strength to be brave enough to come."

___ 2. "You feel pretty helpless and defeated by not being able to solve your own problems, and it is humiliating to be here with me and to ask for my help. You are wondering whether I can accept you as a person because you came to me, or whether I might look down on you as just another adolescent with problems."

___ 3. "I'm really glad that you decided to come to see me and to stick with it as you have. It takes real strength to swallow your pride and to do something about your problem, even though it hurts and is humiliating."

___ 4. "You seem to have a lot of real pride, and it is humiliating to you to have problems that you feel you cannot solve and to find yourself seeking help from someone else."

___ 5. "You shouldn't feel that way. We all need help now and then when the going gets rough. It may be a little threatening to you now, but with a little more time you will get over it."

Adolescent Statement 4 (Male, Age Fifteen)

"Every time I come in here I get this uncomfortable feeling that I'll not have enough to say and we'll just sit here and stare at each other. That would be awful. After we once get started, everything seems to turn out all right, but it's in the beginning, well, a kind of feeling that I get around people who seem to be superior to me."

Helper Responses

___ 1. "Right now I get the feeling that you are just a bit tense and anxious. You are wondering if I might let you down and if I did, whether you could handle the situation. I also get the feeling that you see me as being one of these superior people who seem to leave you kind of helpless."

___ 2. "I hope I have not given you the idea that I'm superior to you. I may have a few more skills than you do, but certainly don't feel superior to you."

___ 3. "I suppose it is a little difficult right at the beginning before the ice is really broken and we get into it. It's kind of like getting acquainted all over again each time we start. I guess I feel a little uncomfortable myself until we get under way."

___ 4. "You feel pretty uncomfortable at the outset just like you do around people who appear to be superior to you, and even though things eventually seem to work out all right, it is a bit frightening until you feel more assured."

___ 5. "You won't have to worry about it. If we get in a tight spot I won't let you down. I'll see to it that things move along."

Key: Self-Test for Immediacy
1, 4, 2, 3, 5
2, 5, 4, 1, 3
2, 5, 4, 3, 1
5, 2, 4, 3, 1

REASSURANCE

QUESTION: What is reassurance?

Reassuring responses may be helpful in at least two general types of situations. The first type is that of reassuring adolescents that they are respected and their concerns are important. The second type is the reassurance that might be offered when adolescents are apprehensive or fearful about the probable outcome of a future event. These events might include the loss of a job, failure in school, abandonment by a spouse, advancement on the job, losing control, and so on. In either situation, genuineness is the key to a high-level reassuring response.

In the first situation, expressing concern for adolescents when the helpers' behavior indicates otherwise would be fruitless. The helper might say, "I'm really interested and want to help you," but at the same time may resent having to see the adolescent. This insincerity may manifest itself by such helper behavior as unconsciously cutting the time of the interview, demonstrating ineffective attending behavior, inappropriate responses, and so on. Caution also needs to be taken in attempting to build up adolescents by saying, "You are a terrific person" or "You are a nice guy." Adolescents may feel that they would be letting helpers down if they were to express feelings that would destroy the helpers' image of the adolescents.

In the second situation, genuineness is equally important. If, for example, it is certain that an adolescent who is concerned about getting ahead will soon receive a promotion, his anxiety may be relieved by responding reassuringly that the promotion is likely to happen. If the promotion is uncertain, however, a statement such as, "Everything will turn out all right" is not only inappropriate but also might promote distrust if the promotion does not happen. In this context, the response is considered at a low level.

Unless supportive data can confirm the outcome of such statements as, "You have no reason to be concerned" or "You are the kind of person who will really go places," the helper may be more harmful than helpful. The tendency of helpers is to try to cheer up adolescents with dubious reassurance, but supposedly pleasant responses or statements without substantiation tend to create further frustration and hopelessness in adolescents. This response often causes adolescents to think, "If you really understood my situation, you would not be so sure of what you are saying." Even in situations in which the probable outcome seems certain, talking about probabilities is better than talking about certainties. The helper should use statistical probabilities if such information is available. One prospective engineering student, for example, was attempting to make a decision whether to apply to a certain college of engineering. The helper was being genuine when he pointed out to the adolescent that based on his tests and academic record, his chances for success were 90 out of 100. Such a forthright response not only reassured the adolescent but also reinforced the adolescent's trust in the helper. Much greater caution needs to be taken when such statistical data are not available.

QUESTION: What is the difference between the two types of reassurance situations?

In the first type of situation, through effective attending behavior, active listening, and genuineness, adolescents are reassured that they are respected and that their concerns are important. In the second type of situation, in which adolescents are apprehensive about the outcome of a future event, the same techniques used in the first type of situation may be helpful, but may only partly fulfill adolescents' needs. In addition to focusing on adolescents' feelings, helpers may need to assist adolescents in handling their behavior more effectively when they are eventually confronted with the event. This may mean exploring alternative ways of handling the situation during the event, and even giving adolescents an opportunity to practice through role-playing techniques. In either of the two types of situations discussed, the helper response should not create false hopes for the adolescent.

The following are the five levels of reassurance. The reader should review each and then use them in the Self-Test for Reassurance.

QUESTION: What are the five levels of reassurance?

Consider the five levels of reassurance in response to the following adolescent statement:

> "I would like to tell my parents about our engagement and get it over with. I don't know how they'll take it. They've never come right out and said anything against my fiancé, but I've gotten these little insinuations ever since I started going with him. I guess that's why I never did let them know that we were getting serious. I didn't want anything to spoil it. Now I've got to let them know, and I'm frightened."

Level 1 (Lowest Level)   A helper response at Level 1 tends to either turn off the adolescent or create false hope. A low-level response to the previous adolescent statement might be, "I don't think you need to worry about telling your parents. Parents are pretty accepting, even if they do seem surprised at first, they will get over it." This response is apt to turn off the adolescent because she would likely question the sincerity of such a positively overstated response. If, however, the adolescent did accept the response as being genuine, but later found that her parents did oppose the engagement, the adolescent would lose confidence in the helper. In either case, such an unsubstantiated response creates a lack of trust.

Level 2 (Low Level)   A helper response at Level 2 is a little less positively overstated than in Level 1 and focuses more on reassuring the adolescent that she has the ability to handle the situation than on predicting the outcome of the situation. Regardless of the difference between Level 1 and Level 2, both types of responses lack genuineness unless validating circumstances are known to the helper. A Level 2 response to the previous adolescent statement might be, "From what I know about you, I think you can handle the situation regardless of what your parents have to say. I suggest you try to relax and don't cross that bridge until you get there."

Level 3 (Neutral Level)   A helper response at Level 3 tends to paraphrase or clarify the adolescent's statement. This puts the helper in a neutral position;

the adolescent could move either toward exploration and encouragement or toward further despair. A Level 3 response to the previous adolescent statement might be, "From what I hear, you say your parents may or may not approve of your engagement. You really don't know where you stand."

Level 4 (High Level) A helper response at Level 4 is directed toward assisting the adolescent to handle the situation more effectively. No attempt is made to make the adolescent feel good with unfounded predictions or insincere compliments. Rather, the focus is geared toward an approach that is genuine and realistic. Level 4 response to the previous adolescent statement might be, "Perhaps we could examine a little more thoroughly your relationship with your parents. Then maybe we could work out a plan together on how you might approach them more effectively in letting them know about your engagement."

Level 5 (Highest Level) At Level 5, a helper response not only focuses on assisting the adolescent to handle the situation but also recognizes the feelings of the adolescent and, when necessary, assists the adolescent in accepting or adjusting to a possible adverse situation. A Level 5 response to the previous adolescent statement might be, "I can readily understand the real concern you must have in telling your parents, because you are not sure they will accept your fiancé, and you're not sure how they may react or whether they might interfere with your engagement. Perhaps at this point we should explore a bit further the relationship you have with your parents, and then perhaps we could consider some alternative ways in which you might approach your parents." A Level 5 response opens lines of communication by reflecting feelings, and creates further hope and encouragement by suggesting that the helper and adolescent work on ways to handle the situation.

To further understand reassurance, the reader should take the following self-test.

SELF-TEST FOR REASSURANCE

Read the following adolescent statements and then rate the helper responses according to the level of reassurance (1–5).

Adolescent Statement 1

"I have been looking forward to dating this guy. Now the big chance has come. He has asked me out, and you can imagine I'm scared pink. It will turn out to be another flop just like all the rest. I'll put on a show just to try to impress him. I'll be as nervous as a kitten and do those stupid idiotic little things. Why can't I just relax —be myself. I hate myself for being this way."

Helper Responses

____ 1. "I have a strong hunch that everything will work out for you. A guy could not help liking a girl like you, so I don't think you need to be as concerned as you are. There is usually a good deal of anxiety when we are anticipating something like you are facing, but once you go out together, things will be different."

____ 3. "I really don't feel you have to be too concerned. I have observed you here while we have been together, and I know you are the kind of person who can handle yourself very well. If you can handle it here, you can handle it there. You might try relaxing a little from time to time before your date; then you will be relaxed with him."

___ 2. "You really have been looking forward to this, but now that the opportunity has come, you feel that you are not prepared for it. You are now scared because you are wondering just how to handle the situation—to get a relationship going with a guy you like. Perhaps we could explore some of these stupid things you say you do and look at ways that you could be more relaxed and perhaps be more yourself."

___ 4. "You did not think your chance would come, but now it has come and you are not sure what to do about it. You really want him to like you, but don't know just how to act or to be yourself so he will like you."

___ 5. "Why don't we try a few things. Let me be your date and you be yourself. As we interact together, perhaps we can discover ways that you may be coming across; then maybe we could try some new ways that would be helpful to you."

Adolescent Statement 2

"I can't help but worry about my job. For months things were going just fine; then suddenly, things have taken a downward spin. Just last week, my supervisor called me in. She accused me of spending too much time talking to the men in the office. I went into a tailspin. We have always had a good relationship. It was just a month ago that she sent in a letter of commendation about me. I can't understand. I'm not different than I was then. I told her that she had the wrong idea about me. Then she went into every little detail. I was dumbfounded! I can't communicate with her anymore. I feel insecure, and I can't function the way I used to. I'm really frightened. I just know the next time she calls me in, it will be to give me notice."

Helper Responses

___ 1. "It is likely that your supervisor had a bad day, or maybe she got a little jealous when she saw you talking to someone. Perhaps you should give it a little time until she is in a better mood. I really don't think you have anything to worry about."

___ 2. "Could it be that your supervisor doesn't really understand your side of the situation? Perhaps we could look at some ways that you might communicate with her more effectively so that she can better understand your position and you can understand hers."

___ 3. "It is pretty frustrating to not know where you stand with your supervisor, particularly when you can't even communicate with her. Could there be some way that you could approach her differently so that the lines of communication can be opened? Maybe we could talk about it and even practice a little."

___ 4. "I've known you for some time now, and you have been in some pretty rough situations. Perhaps you should take this as another challenge. It will be a growth situation. I know you can handle this one just like you have handled all the rest."

___ 5. "I guess you feel pretty trapped right now. On the one hand, you can't communicate with your supervisor, and on the other hand, your work is beginning to suffer as a result of your feeling insecure and anxious."

Key: Self-Test for Reassurance
1, 4, 2, 3, 5
2, 4, 5, 1, 3

Reassurance is the last of the four major helping techniques discussed in Phase II. Both Phases I and II reflect a phenomenological approach to dealing with adolescents. The following section provides additional phenomenological practices. These practices foster self-development because the self is the central concern in phenomenological theory.

Phenomenological practices in self-development

QUESTION: What can significant others do to help adolescents develop a healthy self-concept?

Some general practices can now be summarized, highlighted, and identified. Trust will help people perceive themselves as trustworthy. Trust goes beyond simply expecting a person to have a certain behavior; it is a genuine faith in verbal statements, values, actions, and beliefs. Trust is believing adolescents when they say, "I need your help" or "I am afraid." People often reject these simple statements, believing that they are inaccurate. How adolescents perceive themselves (or their present state) is basically more important than what others conclude based on observations of external circumstances. Even if the adult view is more accurate, however, the rejection of youths' communication will likely produce negative consequences for growth.

When significant others do not trust adolescents' statements or actions, adolescents then conclude, "Why should I trust myself?" They begin to doubt themselves—particularly the validity of their feelings, emotions, or thoughts—and they therefore lose or ignore this source of valuable information about themselves. If adolescents' basic motivation is a tendency toward good health, and if this good health is the goal of adults, then both youth and adults are on the same team. Adolescents' basic motivations, beliefs, values, and actions should then be viewed as something congruent with, not as something antagonistic to, the goals of adults.

Trust includes the encouragement and acceptance of individuality, or the avoidance of recommending that everyone choose the same goals, and leads to healthy self-growth. Many motivations, such as rewards, punishments, grades, honors, achievements, charts, and so on, often direct youth into prescribed or conforming behaviors that actually move adolescents away from natural, spontaneous, and desired growth. Healthy self-growth comes from the unhampered facilitation of individuality. The climate from which spontaneous growth develops is difficult to describe, but the word *love,* an unconditional acceptance, is probably the best description available. The climate is one of warmth, acceptance,

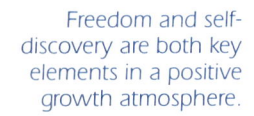

Freedom and self-discovery are both key elements in a positive growth atmosphere.

and trust, and is devoid of such practices as ridicule or sarcasm. In such an atmosphere of affection and caring, adolescents feel accepted and genuinely liked.

Acceptance does not mean that adults must behave as adolescents or even condone adolescent behavior. Adolescents, however, are free to hold values without having to continually defend them. The absence of continued defense allows youth to examine their own values and beliefs more critically and honestly. As a result of this examination, adolescents are more likely to experience growth toward a healthy set of values.

QUESTION: What kind of atmosphere will promote self-development?

Freedom logically follows the preceding recommendation. For adolescents to change or to grow toward a more healthy self-concept, they must have freedom. Freedom allows them to examine themselves and to test new behavior. If youth are not allowed freedom of behavior, evaluating and subsequently changing the behavior is impossible. Change that occurs in a nonfree atmosphere is artificial and temporary, and is known as social conformity or expediency. This change is not genuine; it results from rewards and punishments rather than from internal self-control, and is unrelated to the basic self-concept. Changes that result from the previous practices do not occur immediately—not in one day, one week, or even in one year. Self-discovery is a slow process that evolves only through the process of living.

Adolescents must discover their own unique and highly personal ways of dealing with the world and with other people. Others, such as parents or teachers, cannot tell youth exactly who they are and how they should behave; this belief must grow out of the interaction between youth and their surroundings. Particularly difficult for adults is to watch adolescents performing tasks with a great deal of clumsiness and inefficiency. Especially frustrating is when adults know how to perform the tasks and could easily teach a better method of handling them. From the growth point of view, however, adolescents must have experience in accomplishing tasks. Adolescents should have freedom to try both efficient and inefficient methods so that they can evaluate them.

Closely related to the practice of freedom is a general atmosphere that creates the feeling of adequacy. Significant people can let adolescents know that they are adequate. Out of this feeling of adequacy comes adolescents' motivation or willingness to perform and interact with the important tasks of life. Although providing information about what youth can and cannot successfully complete is important, creating self-perception of inadequacy is easily possible. Inadequacy comes about through adolescents' comparison with others who are more competent. In many cases, adolescents are directly told that they are incompetent or inadequate. A little reflection by parents or teachers will show that *every* human being adequately performs a large number of complex and difficult tasks. These complex tasks are found in even the routine functions of daily living, and simply being told that one is adequate can improve competency in a wider range of tasks.

Providing information is another practice that facilitates healthy self-growth. Information about oneself is of particular importance. With trust and additional information about themselves, adolescents have a much richer field upon which to base their beliefs and perceptions.

When adults use the perceptual self-growth approach in relating with adolescents, more genuine enjoyment often results from the personal contact between adults and adolescents. The pleasure derived from such relationships results not from the efficiency or the excellence of the psychological theory but from the emotional and personal feelings that seem to result naturally from such a personal approach. The task of raising adolescents and teaching them can become a genuine human experience inseparable from living with adolescents' hopes, aspirations, and growth.

Summary

Phenomenological theorists believe that providing trust, freedom, acceptance, information, and unconditional love will not produce spoiled, unprincipled adolescents, but will develop a morality based on a concern for the welfare of others. The mature resolution of conflict can also help individuals to better understand the perceptions of others and to learn that problems often do not result from conflicting needs but from faulty communication, misconceptions, and a lack of accurate information. Conflicts between adolescents and parents can be especially beneficial because they provide experience in conflict resolution that can be used in other interpersonal relationships throughout life. Jourard's analysis of conflict stresses the following:

1. The need for communication
2. The desirability of conflict
3. The growth potential of conflict
4. The ability to evaluate conflict in terms of its growth-producing elements

Significant others can best help adolescents learn how to resolve conflicts by giving them unconditional warmth, acceptance, love, and responsible freedom. This approach will allow adolescents' growth force to direct them to success.

The four major helping techniques in Phase II are concreteness, confrontation, immediacy, and reassurance.

Concreteness involves assisting adolescents to be specific and concrete about the problems they are facing. Concreteness has five levels: Level 1 does not see the problem and has no concreteness; Level 2 sees the problem but has no concreteness; Level 3 is neutral, no movement; Level 4 is specific and concrete; and Level 5 encourages a higher level of concreteness.

Confrontation is the process that gives feedback to adolescents about their inconsistencies, such as discrepancies between what they say and what they do, discrepancies in perceptions of reality, and contradictory statements. Confrontation has five levels with Level 1 as the lowest (put-down) and Level 5 as the highest.

Immediacy involves focusing directly on the helper-adolescent relationship. Immediacy responses are helpful when youth are reluctant to talk, feel nervous or uncomfortable, resist taking responsibility, and so on.

Reassurance may be used to reassure adolescents that they are respected and important, and to allay fears and apprehensions about future events. The skill is done through effective attending behavior, active listening, and genuineness.

The most important step in facilitating adolescents' development is to improve their self-perceptions and to help their self-concept become more accurate, realistic, and positive. Self-concept provides the motivation for all growth. If adolescents' self-concepts are healthy and undistorted, their innate growth force will direct them to mental health and self-actualization. Significant others have the most profound and positive influence when they give adolescents unconditional love, acceptance, warmth, trust, and responsible freedom.

References

Boyce, D., & L. Jensen. 1978. *Moral reasoning.* Lincoln: Univ. of Nebraska Press.
Jensen, V. 1978. *Helping relationships: Skills development manual for training professional, paraprofessional, and lay counselors.* Provo, Utah: Brigham Young Univ. Press.
_____. 1983.
Jourard, S. 1967. *Personal adjustment.* 2d ed. New York: Macmillan.
Sullivan, H. 1958. *The interpersonal theory of psychiatry.* New York: Norton.

NAME INDEX

Abramson, M., 222, 223
Adams, B. R. 128
Adams, G., 57, 60, 131
Adams, G. R., 76, 216, 433
Adams, P. L., 350
Adelson, J., 76, 111, 113, 271, 307
Agras, W. S., 347
Akers, R. L., 399–400
Aleshire, D., 321
Allport, G. W., 306
Alpert, R., 376
Ames, L. B., 41
Anastasi, A., 463
Andersen, G. S., 131
Anderson, H. W., 131
Anderson, L. D., 460
Andison, F. S., 243
Anthony, R. C., 219
Apter, D., 204
Arensberg, C., 12
Arhardt, A., 222
Aries, P., 6
Armour, R., 5
Aronson, E., 107, 318
Asch, M., 222, 223
Astin, A., 310
Asubel, B. P., 98
Athamasiou, R., 185
Atkin, C., 242
Austin, B. A., 249
Ausubel, D., 39, 60, 181, 423
Avery, D., 361
Bachman, J., 126, 168, 379–388, 408
Baer, D. M., 492
Bahr, H., 28, 309, 319
Bailey, N., 207
Bakan, D., 7, 10
Baker, M., 111
Ball, S., 245
Balla, D. A., 422
Ballswick, J., 23
Ballswick, J. K., 23
Bandura, A., 244, 397
Barter, J. T., 361
Bayley, N., 461
Bealer, R. C., 128
Beck, A. T., 341, 343, 409
Becker, W. L., 150–152
Beckman, L., 37
Bedrosian, R. C., 408
Beech, R. P., 308
Bell, R., 8
Beloff, H., 110
Bem, D. J., 318
Bem, S. L., 286, 287

Bendette, F., 174
Benedict, R., 48, 49
Bengston, V. L., 319
Bereiter, C., 180, 181
Berenson, B. G., 506
Berenson, C. K., 343
Berg, I., 458
Bergen, N. J., 374
Berger, S. M., 315
Berkowitz, L., 110, 235
Bernal, G., 315
Berne, P. H., 84
Bernstein, A. C., 85
Berrett, B. H., 489
Berscheid, E., 104, 217
Bettelheim, B., 185, 247
Bibring, E., 344
Bigelow, B. J., 112
Bigelow, G., 406
Birch, H., 335–337
Biron, L., 439
Blackham, G., 488
Blackham, G. J., 405
Blaine, J. D., 396, 397
Blatt, S. J., 343
Bleuler, E., 353
Block, J., 76, 310
Block, J. H., 155
Blood, R., 242
Bloom, B. S., 460
Blos, P., 54, 56, 57
Blum, R. H., 76
Bogatz, G. H., 245
Bohrnstedt, G. W., 283, 284
Bols, P., 201
Borgatta, E. F., 283, 284
Borland, B. L., 339
Bottoms, J., 181
Boyce, D., 109, 296, 301, 303
Brammer, L. M., 510
Brandon, T., 203, 205, 206
Brandwein, R., 130
Bremner, R. H., 45–48
Brewer, W. F., 477
Brick, P., 185
Bronfenbrenner, U., 101, 109, 110, 317, 425
Bronner, A., 427
Brook, D. W., 323
Brook, J. S., 323
Brown, C., 130
Brown, D. L., 222
Brown, J., 115
Brown, J. K., 220
Bruch, H., 358–359

Bryan, J., 244
Bueche, N., 128
Bullough, V. L., 215
Burchinal, L., 131
Burnett, J. H., 179
Burton, C. R., 45–48
Burton, M. M., 282
Butz, G., 489
Byrne, D., 274, 275
Cabior, M., 102
Calder, J., 218
Cambell, J. B., 98
Cameron, R., 167
Canner, L., 331–332
Canter, F. N., 101
Canter, L., 192
Canter, M., 192
Caplow, T., 309, 319
Carkhuff, R. R., 505, 506
Carter, M., 429
Caudill, L. H., 353
Caulsmith, J., 273–274
Cavenar, J. O., 353
Cavior, N., 104, 216
Chadwick, B., 28
Chaffee, S. H., 242
Chang, S. S., 357
Char, E., 141–142
Chesney-Lind, M., 431
Chess, S., 335–337
Chevron, E., 343
Christensen, B., 224
Ciseaux, A., 358
Clack, R. J., 505
Clark, A., 135
Clarke, L. M., 286
Clausen, J. A., 207, 209
Clor, H. M., 252
Cohen, J., 179
Coleman, J., 173, 178–180, 183, 233
Coleman, J. C., 98, 101, 113
Coleman, J. S., 45–48, 102, 400
Collins, A. W., 440
Collins, J. K., 272, 273
Comstock, G. A., 241
Conderman, L., 492
Condry, W. W., 102
Conger, J. J., 101, 106, 111
Congor, J., 128
Connell, R. W., 308
Constantian, R. D., 17
Constantinople, A., 73
Coon, D., 81, 286, 288, 461
Coopersmith, S., 78, 80, 81
Coplen, R. D., 86, 88

559

Cortes, J. B., 210, 211
Cory, C. T., 373, 374
Costa, F., 274, 284
Costanzo, P. R., 38, 98
Cotton, N., 344
Cowan, S., 376
Cowen, E. L., 506
Cox, E., 321
Cox, M., 131
Cox, R., 131
Cranshaw, P., 373
Cressey, D. R., 426
Crossman, S. M., 216
Crowley, J., 19, 20
Culp, M. B. W., 250
Curran, B. F., 131
Darlington, R., 452
Darwin, C., 37
Davidson, E. S., 243
Davis, A., 42
Davis, J. B., 45–48
Davis, J. M., 357
de Mause, L., 6
DeAzevedo, L., 236
DeBlassie, 224
Dececco, J. P., 189
Dedman, J., 321
DeFrain, J., 135
Deitz, G. E., 423
DeLamater, J., 284
Dellas, M., 128
Derbyshire, R. L., 149
DeRisi, W. J., 489
Diepold, J., Jr., 277–279, 281
Dion, K. K., 104
Docherty, J. P., 357
Doering, Z. B., 45–48
Dokecki, P., 216
Dokecki, P. R., 102
Donnerstein, E., 253
Donnerstein, M., 253
Donovan, J., 274, 284
Dopra, P., 181
Dornsbusch, S., 273–274
Dostal, J., 131
Douglas, J. W. B., 421
Douvan, E., 76, 111, 113, 271, 307
Dreikurs, R., 192
Duke, P., 273–274
Dukes, W. F., 310
Durkheim, E., 420
Durphy, D. C., 106
Dusek, J. B., 204
Dworetzky, J. P., 457, 463
Egan, G., 505, 509
Egelund, R., 85
Ehling, M., 144, 146

Eichorn, P. H., 45–48
Elder, G. H., 9
Elderkins, R. D., 428
Elkind, D., 176, 446, 455
Elliot, L., 264
Ellis, G., 238
Ellsworth, J. J., 506
Ellsworth, R. B., 506
Emergy, G., 408
Emery, A., 409
English, R., 184
Enihobich, C., 128
Erikson, E., 38, 39, 68–72, 76, 333
Evans, R., 253
Evans, R. R., 283, 284
Farr, R., 168
Farrell, M. K., 359
Farrington, D. P., 439
Farris, E., 138–140
Farris, L., 138–140
Faust, M. S., 217
Feather, M. T., 308, 309
Feighner, J. P., 358
Fejer, D., 397
Feldhusen, J., 458
Fendrich, J. M., 22
Fernstein, S. C., 272
Ferre, R. C., 343
Fischer, J., 406
Fitch, S. A., 76
Fitts, W., 78
Flavell, J. H., 447
Ford, K., 283
Fort, J., 373, 374
Fovisha, B. L., 286
Fox, D., 130
Freeman, W. H., 78, 80, 81
French, V., 7
Freud, A., 5, 55, 56
Freud, S., 51, 52, 53, 54, 55, 201, 347, 350
Fried, R., 235
Friedan, B., 289
Friedenberg, E. Z., 183
Friedrich, L. K., 241
Frier, P., 23
Furstenberg, F. F., 118
Furstenberg, F. F., Jr., 9
Furth, H., 454
Galanter, M., 319
Garbarino, J., 109
Garber, B., 357
Gardener, R. A., 340
Gardner, H., 461
Gatti, F. M., 210, 211
Gazda, G., 505
Gerbner, G., 245

Gesell, A., 41, 42
Gillies, P., 216
Ginnott, H., 191
Girona, R., 506
Gladding, S. T., 322
Glasser, W., 190, 191
Glueck, E., 129
Glueck, S., 129
Gochros, H., 406
Goldman, N., 176, 419
Goldman, N. N., 114
Goldstein, A. P., 505
Goode, E., 76
Goodman, E., 262
Goodman, G., 505, 506
Gordon, C., 180
Gordon, T., 192
Gorsuch, R. L., 321
Gray, S., 253
Greathouse, B., 136
Greven, P. J., 9
Grey, J., 373
Grey, L., 192
Griffin, B. S., 420, 425, 427, 438
Griffin, C. T., 420, 425, 427, 438
Griffitt, W., 277
Grilichos, Z., 45, 46, 47, 48
Grinker, R. R., 353
Gross, R., 273–274
Grossman, S. M., 131
Guggenheim, F. G., 351
Guilford, J. P., 461
Gullotta, T., 57, 60, 433
Guze, S., 358
Hadley, W., 332
Haider, I., 361
Haim, A., 363
Hall, G. S., 8, 14, 39, 40, 41, 268
Hallam, J., 253
Halmi, K. A., 360
Halversen, T. A., 343
Hammer, R., 29
Hammond, W. A., 421
Handzo, S., 247
Hardon, M. S., 272
Hardy, J., 98
Hardy, K., 274, 277
Harmin, M., 184, 311
Harris, M., 21, 126
Hartl, E., 428
Harvey, O. J., 100
Hauser, J., 319
Havighurst, R. J., 12, 43–45, 307
Heald, F. P., 204
Healy, W., 427
Heaps, R., 509
Heckman, H. K., 339

Hendin, H., 361
Hendry, L. D., 216
Hershberg, T., 9
Hetherington, E., 130, 131
Hickler, H., 341, 342, 346, 362
Higbee, K., 491
Hilde, B., 360
Hilgard, F. R., 72, 506
Hill, J. M., 244
Hobart, C. W., 266
Hobart, T. Y., 168
Hoffman, H. R., 242
Hoffman, L., 128, 130
Hoffman, L. W., 286
Hoffman, M. L., 314–316
Hofmann, 361
Hollan, S. D., 408
Hollander, E. P., 109
Hollingshead, A. B., 105
Holmes, T. H., 333
Holzman, P. S., 353
Homer, L., 429
Hopkins, J. R., 279
Horrocks, J. E., 111
Howell, G. E., 334
Huber, J., 222
Hudgens, R. W., 340
Huff, F. L., 244
Hung, W., 204
Hunt, M., 185
Hurvitz, N., 505
Inglis, B., 373
Iscoe, I., 98
Jacklin, C., 221
Jacklin, E., 286
Jacobs, J., 361, 363
Jacobson, L., 460
Jacobziner, H., 362
Jencks, C., 463
Jennings, P., 273–274
Jensen, A., 464
Jensen, A. R., 215, 458
Jensen, L., 109, 183, 184, 281, 296, 301, 303, 491
Jensen, V., 509
Jersild, A. T., 323
Jessor, L., 274, 284
Jessor, R., 273–276, 283, 284, 321
Jessor, S. L., 273–276, 283, 321
Johnson, D., 505
Johnson, N., 337
Johnson, 429
Johnston, L. D., 338, 379–388, 408
Johnston, 126
Jones, M. C., 207, 209
Josselyn, I. M., 349, 351, 355
Jourard, S., 535

Julius, D. A., 396, 397
Kamin, L. J., 463
Kandel, D. B., 18
Kantner, J. F., 279, 283
Katz, M. B., 9
Kazdin, A., 477
Keating, D. P., 452
Kelly, G. A., 37
Kelly, J., 131
Keniston, K., 307, 315
Kenting, K., 126
Kesson, H., 28
Kestemburg, J. S., 217
Kett, J. F., 45–48
Killen, J., 407
King, M. F., 22, 23
Kleck, R. E., 104
Kluckhohn, R., 219
Kluckholm, F. R., 306
Knight, R., 183, 184
Koff, E., 217
Kohen, B., 218
Kohlberg, L., 39, 60, 184, 299–305, 533
Kohn, M. L., 76
Kolvin, I., 405
Konner, M., 221
Kopita, R. R., 505
Kovacs, M., 393–395, 401
Krista, S., 131, 132
Krohn, M. D., 399–400
Kryspin, W., 458
Krystal, H., 402, 403
Kubey, R., 233
Lacay, G., 142–144
LaGaiqa, J. J., 112
Laird, J. D., 506
Lamb, D. H., 505
Lambson, A., 353
Lang, S. S., 249
Langlois, J. E., 104
Langlois, J. H., 104
Lanza-Kaduce, L., 399–400
Larkins, A. G., 184
Larsen, L. E., 101
Larson, R., 233
Lasser, I. M., 76
Laufer, R. S., 76
Laughlin, H. P., 349
Launier, R., 333, 334
Lazarus, R. S., 333, 334
Lazer, I., 452
LeBlanc, M., 439
Lee, R. E., 427
LeFrancois, G., 82
Lehmann, H. E., 357
LeMasters, E., 135

LeMasters, E. E., 116
Leonard, R. N., 19, 101
Lepper, M. R., 317
Lerner, J. V., 104
Lerner, R. M., 104, 212
Lettieri, D. J., 393
Leunes, A., 422
Lewinson, P. M., 343
Lewis, D. O., 422
Lewis, H. R., 116
Lewis, M., 250
Lewis, M. E., 116
Libertoff, K., 420
Lichtenstein, E., 397, 406, 407
Liebert, R. M., 243, 244
Liebson, I., 406
Ligsett, J. S., 15
Lind, D., 130
Lindesmith, A., 401
Lindey, A., 247
Lindsey, G., 306, 463
Linn, M., 131, 132
Lipset, S. M., 128
Litchenburg, B., 506
Logan, D. D., 218
Logan, M., 240
Lombardi, D. A., 104
Loney, J., 337
Lourie, R. S., 361
Lowhlin, J. C., 463
Luchterhand, 130
Lukenbill, W. B., 250
Lupenitz, D., 132
Lyly, J., 242
MacArthur, J. D., 86, 88
MacCoby, E., 152, 155, 221
Maccoby, E. E., 133, 134, 286
MacCorquodale, P., 284
Mack, J., 242, 262, 341, 346
Mackey, J., 173
Maddox, G. L., 398
Mahoney, E. R., 283
Mahoney, M. J., 224
Maida, P. R., 128
Maier, H. W., 70
Maloney, J., 359
Mann, A., 357
Mao Tse-tung, 108
Marcia, J. E., 73–78
Marotz-Badden, R., 128
Martin, J., 273–274
Marx, I. M., 347
Mash, W., 222, 223
Maslow, A. H., 87, 533
Masters, S. H., 172
Mays, J. M., 45–48
McAlister, A. L., 407

Name index

McAllister, L. W., 492
McCabe, A. E., 246
McCabe, M. P., 272, 273
McCandless, B., 183
McCandless, B. R., 29, 30
McClelland, A. M., 432
McClelland, D. A., 17
McClelland, D. C., 465
McDermott, D. J., 131
McFall, R. M., 397
McGovern, J. D., 105
McLeod, M., 242
McMahon, W. M., 343
Mead, M., 14, 49, 50, 51
Medora, N. P., 282
Meisels, M., 101
Mendels, J., 341
Mendelson, W., 337
Menlove, F. L., 244
Mercer, J. R., 465
Middleton, R., 128, 321
Milich, R., 337
Miller, A. G., 104
Miller, D. D., 169
Miller, P., 274, 276, 281
Minde, K., 337
Mischel, W., 244
Mitchell, J. T., 364
Mitchell, W. E., 506
Modell, J., 9
Money, J., 222
Monnelly, E. P., 428
Montemayor, 181
Moore, K. A., 172
Moore, V. S., 506
Moriarity, R., 246
Morris, C. W., 306, 309
Morrison, J., 131
Mosher, D. L., 277
Mosher, L. R., 357
Mott, D. E., 244
Mower, C. H., 314
Mulligan, D. G., 421
Munoz, R., 358
Munro, B., 128
Munro, C., 128
Murphy, W. C., 422
Muss, R. E., 213
Mussen, P. H., 207, 209
Nadelson, C., 351
Nawy, H., 253
Neale, J. M., 244
Neapolitan, J., 422
Neimark, E. D., 452
Nelson, B., 509
Newman, B. M., 75
Newman, P. R., 75

Nilsen, A. P., 251
Nilsen, D. L. F., 251
Norback, C., 126, 185
Norman, J., 21, 126
Odom, R. D., 244
Offer, D., 5
Offer, J. B., 5
Oliveau, D. C., 347
Olson, T. D., 186
O'Malley, P., 126
O'Malley, P. M., 379–388, 408
Orlofsky, J. L., 76
Osterrieth, P. A., 456
Ostlund, L. A., 126
Panelas, T., 237
Parish, T., 131
Patterson, G. R., 478
Paykel, E. S., 333
Peck, R. F., 307
Pendarf, J., 101
Perry, C. L., 407
Peskin, H., 209, 210
Petersen, A. C., 101, 106, 111
Peterson, A., 128, 203, 205, 206
Piaget, J., 39, 60, 296–299, 446–452, 454–456
Piazza, E., 358
Piazza, N., 358
Pines, A. M., 430
Pinneau, S. R., 460
Podd, M. H., 76
Porter, J., 23
Poser, E. G., 506
Presser, H. B., 117
Purnell, R. F., 102
Putney, S., 128, 321
Quinland, D. M., 343
Radoscvich, M. J., 399–400
Rahe, R. H., 333
Ramey, J., 128
Rangell, L., 350
Raths, L., 311
Rees, E. P., 485
Regalado, 17
Rehberg, R. A., 179
Reinhard, P., 131
Resnik, H. L. P., 364
Rice, F. P., 115
Rice, P., 18, 78, 84, 173, 269
Richards, A. K., 189
Richardson, S. A., 104
Rierdan, J., 217
Riester, A. E., 106
Ritvo, S., 217
Roberts, A. R., 429
Robey, A., 427
Robins, E., 358

Robinson, J. P., 78
Rogers, C. R., 504, 505
Rogers, D., 15, 82, 157
Rogers, K. W., 308
Rogers, S., 422
Rokeach, 305, 310
Rollins, N., 358
Ronald, L., 104
Roof, N., 114
Rosenberg, A., 273–274
Rosenhan, D., 244
Rosenthal, R., 460
Rosenwald, 427
Rosmussen, J. E., 73
Ross, J. M., 421
Rotberg, I., 175
Roths, L. E., 184
Rubin, A. M., 242
Rubin, Z., 265
Rumberger, R. W., 169, 172
Rush, L., 409
Rutherford, J., 100
Ryder, N. B., 45–48
Sanders, W. B., 427, 431, 433, 434
Santrock, J. W., 78
Savary, L. M., 84
Sawrey, J. M., 223
Scarr-Salatapek, 459, 465
Schaefer, C., 506
Schaeffer, E. S., 152
Schenkel, S., 76
Schiller, L., 376
Schiller, P., 254
Schmale, A. H., 363
Schmiedeck, R. A., 177
Schoeppe, A., 308
Schultz, J., 98
Schulz, B., 283, 284
Schwartz, M., 241
Sebald, H., 102, 103
Seizaburo, S., 26, 28
Seligman, M. E. P., 343, 344
Sells, S. B., 114
Selye, H., 333
Senbrook, 7
Shah, R., 283
Shanok, S. S., 421–422
Shakespeare, W., 268
Shapiro, D., 19, 20
Shapiro, R. L., 357
Shaver, J. P., 184
Shaver, P. R., 78
Shaw, J., 409
Shaw, M. E., 38, 98
Shaycoft, N. F., 167
Shea, J., 131
Sheingold, K., 217

Sheldon, W. H., 428
Shell, J. E., 427
Sherif, C. W., 108
Sherif, M., 108
Shine, W. A., 176
Shingleton, R., 509
Shirer, W. L., 424
Sigelman, L., 319
Silberman, A., 488
Silbert, M. H., 430
Silverman, A., 405
Silverman, L. T., 243
Silverman, R. A., 253
Simmel, E., 357
Simmons, D. D., 73
Simon, M. L., 102
Simon, S., 311
Simon, S. B., 184
Simon, W., 274, 276, 281
Sinclair, K. E., 308
Siris, S. G., 357
Sirotnik, K., 176
Skinner, B. F., 39, 60, 474, 487
Slater, E., 131, 132
Slinkard, L., 407
Small, L., 309
Smart, R. G., 397
Smith, E., 129, 130
Smith, P., 240
Smith, T., 154–155
Snider, S. J., 422
Snyder, M., 89
Snyder, M. E., 217
Sodetani-Shibata, A. E., 146–149
Solberg, J. R., 179
Sorenson, R. C., 18, 185, 283
Sowell, T., 464–465
Spearman, C., 461
Spencer, P., 15
Sprafkin, J. N., 243
Sprinthall, N. A., 440
Spuhler, J. N., 463
Stachowiak, J. G., 492
Standler, 48
Stang, D., 222
Stark, P. H., 74
Starr, J. M., 319
Staub, E., 82, 313
Stein, A. H., 241
Stein, B. J., 446
Stennet, R. G., 459
Stephan, C., 104
Stevens, S. S., 428
Stewart, M. A., 337
Stitzer, M., 406
Stone, C., 17
Stone, L. J., 98

Stones, C., 322
Stotland, E., 315
Stott, D., 438
Strauss, J., 28
Strodtveck, F. L., 306
Strommen, N. M. P., 322
Strong, P., 286
Stroobant, R. E., 308
Strupp, H. H., 332
Styczymski, L. E., 104
Sue, D., 352
Sue, D. W., 352
Sue, S., 352
Sugar, N., 131
Sullivan, E. V., 423
Sussman, N. B., 128
Sutherland, E. M., 426
Svajian, 181
Swaback, B. O., 361
Swope, G. W., 319
Sylvester, D., 347
Tanke, E., 217
Tanner, J., 234
Tanner, J. M., 208, 214
Teicher, J. D., 361, 363, 364
Telford, C. W., 223
Temperley, K., 110
Terman, L. M., 458
Thomas, H., 335–337
Thomas, J., 286
Thomas, L., 282
Thompson, G. G., 111
Thornberry, T. P., 253
Thornburg, H., 135, 150
Thornburg, H. D., 286
Thurston, J. R., 458
Thurstone, L. L., 461
Todd, D., 361
Toffler, A., 333
Tomb, D. A., 343
Toolan, J. M., 360
Traxler, A. H., 74
Trickett, P. K., 458
Truax, C. B., 506
Tucker, W. B., 428
Tunley, R., 439
Turner, R. H., 78
Vaier, E., 128
Van Kammen, D. P., 357
Vance, J., 85
Veck, J. C., 354
Vernon, P. E., 306
Vigersky, R. A., 369
Vihko, R., 204
Walbeck, N., 244
Walker, K., 129
Walker, N., 110

Wallace, N. A., 458
Wallerstein, J., 131
Wallston, B., 128
Walster, E., 267
Walters, G., 267
Waterman, A. S., 73–78
Waterman, C. K., 73–78
Watson, J. B., 8, 9, 477
Wayne, C. W., 458
Weideger, P., 218
Weight, L. J., 172
Weiner, I. B., 338–340, 342, 345–349, 351, 353–356, 360, 364
Weinstock, A., 101
Weisberg, A., 181, 182
Weisberg, P. S., 357
Weller, L., 130
Wells, K., 287
Weschler, H., 358
White, G. M., 244
Whiting, J. M., 219
Wilcox, R. T., 190–192
Williams, M., 98
Williams, R. M., Jr., 305
Willis, R. H., 109
Willits, F. K., 128
Wilson, S. B., 286
Winokur, G., 358, 361
Wolpe, J., 353
Wooden, J., 184
Woodruff, R., 358
Woods, M., 129
Wright, D., 321
Wright, L. S., 271
Wurmser, L., 403–404
Wyden, B., 397
Wyein, S. J., 343
Yacoubian, J. H., 361
Yankelovich, D., 22–25, 168, 309
Young, R. D., 277–279, 281
Yusin, A. S., 362
Zax, M., 506
Zelnik, M., 279, 283
Zigler, E., 458
Zucker, R. H., 106

SUBJECT INDEX

AA, 406, 506
abnormality, 331, 332
abortion, 25, 185
academics, 106
   achievement in, 47
acceptance, 142, 223, 423, 532
   needs for, 103
accidents, 360
accommodation, 449
acculturation, 41
acting out, 140
adaptation, 449
adolescence, 6, 15, 40, 51, 57, 109
   contradictions about, 6
   definitions of, 11–14
   as a disease, 5
   early, 57, 188
   late, 57, 99, 189
   middle, 57, 101
   as new concept, 8
   societal effects on, 9
   three stages of, 56–58
   viewpoints on, 5
Adolescent Society, The (Coleman), 233
adolescent treatment program, 496, 497
adolescents, 5, 17, 40, 101, 108
   Mexican-American, 144–146
   American, 18
   attitudes of, 101
   attitudes of college, 101
   black, 136–138, 234
   early-maturing, 207–210
   late-maturing, 207–210
   minority group, 29
   parents significance to, 128
   perceptions of, 14–16
   Puerto Rican-American, 142–144
   relating to others, 113
   relating to, 110
   speech differences of, 106
   value system, 307
adulthood, 10, 48, 102, 139
   transition to, 115
   young, 131
adults, 103, 104
   as authorities, 113
   awareness of pressure, 111
   independence from, 106
   language of, 106
   young, 99
Affect Balance Scale, 156
affective disorders. *See* disorders
Afro-Americans, 29
   see also blacks

aggression, 30, 51, 54, 58, 221, 222, 487
   and pornography, 253
alcohol, 21, 77, 140, 272, 372, 378, 405 *see also* drinking
alcoholism, 24, 139, 140, 250
American Association of School Administrators, 166, 167
American Graffiti, 21
American Indians. *See* family
American Psychiatric Association, 333, 337
Americans, 20, 100, 106
amphetamines, 377
anal stage, 53, 54
anarchists, 108
androgens, 204
androgyny, 286–289
anger, 131, 155
anorexia nervosa, 358–360
antabuse, 405
Antecedents of Self-Esteem, The (Coopersmith), 80
anticonformity, 107, 108, 109
   see also conformity
antidepressants, 375
anxiety, 42, 52–54, 58, 206, 216, 313, 487
Apache Indians. *See* family, American-Indian
appearance, 21, 47, 83, 89, 103, 106, 206, 211, 279, 427
   hormonal effects on, 201
   and physical attractiveness, 103, 215–217
approval, 106
asceticism, 55, 56
assault, 24, 173, 418, 421, 422, 433
assertive discipline, 192
assimilation, 449
associationism, 447
athletic ability, 102
athletics, 17, 18, 44–47, 53, 77–84, 137, 166, 168, 177–179, 208–216, 222, 237, 245, 250, 277, 279, 288, 488
attitudes, 101–103
   dating, 272
   evaluation of, 409
   see also adolescents
attractiveness, 104
   see also appearance
authoritarian behaviors, 511
the Azande, 15

barbiturates, 378
   see also drugs
beauty, 104
   see also appearance
behavior, 75, 106, 138, 139, 147, 169, 235, 275, 316
   adolescent, 205
   affect of social class on, 29
   aggressive, 222, 422
   antiestablishment, 103
   antisocial, 112, 473
   approval, 110
   biologically determined, 41
   causes for, 473
   change in, 485
   codes of, 18
   conforming, 109
   criminal, 5, 428
   delinquent, 131
   determination of, 473
   harmful, 185
   hormonal effects on, 201, 206
   identification of, 314
   in-school, 173
   inappropriate, 483
   literature's influence on, 250, 251
   managing, 17
   moral, 76, 78
   nonconforming, 107, 108, 109
   outside controls, 140
   parental, 150
   patterns of, 53
   physical, 273
   political, 22
   prosocial, 245
   proximity-seeking, 131
   psychotic, 114
   reality, 503
   religious, 321
   role, 146
   sex roles, 136, 286–289
   sexual, 30, 185, 206, 277
      see also sex
   sexual, types, 277
   social class differences, 28–30
   social, 112
   success, 82
   television, 242
   undesired, 141
   wide ranges of, 210
behavior modification, 192, 474, 491
belonging, 71, 85, 111, 142, 148, 503
Berkeley Guidance Study, 210
BIA. *See* Bureau of Indian Affairs

565

566 ■ Subject index

birth control, 185
birth rates, 134
blacks, 22, 136–138, 149
   see also children; family
blaming behaviors, 511, 512
blindness, 222
body types, 210
Boy Scouts, 132
Boy's Day, 147
boyhood, 12
Britain. *See* youth, European
Brown v. *Board of Education*, 174
Bureau of Indian Affairs, 139

caffeine, 374
California Personality Inventory Scale, 209
cars, 47, 86, 250, 269, 473
career, 44, 68, 250
caring, 103
casino, 237
centration, 449
character, 103
chastity, 138, 143
Childhood and Society (Erikson), 68
childhood, 5, 15
   middle, 99
   period of, 39
children, 29, 40, 104
   alternate, 148
   American Indian, 138, 139, 140
   attractive, 104
   black, 136
   caring for, 119
   Chinese, 141, 142
   conformity in, 101
   delinquent, 130
   emotional effects of working mothers on, 129
   employment of, 10
   hyperactive. *See* hyperactivity
   illegitimate, 115
   intelligence and, 463
   Japanese-American, 146–149
   lower-class, 43
   Mexican-American, 144–146
   parental effects on, 152
   peer-oriented, 110
   playing and, 142
   popular, 110
   poverty groups and, 135
   preschool, 130
   raising in America, 127
   rearing of, 116, 135, 148
   responsibilities of, 142
   Scottish, 110
   unattractive, 104
   United States, 109
   USSR, 109, 110
Chinese, 141, 142
Chinese-Americans, 142
church, 145
   influences of, 130
   see also religion
circumcision, 219
clarifying, 513
cliques, 100, 109
   characteristics of, 106
   definition of, 105
clothes, 82, 83, 86, 100, 102, 107, 111, 180, 201, 219
   western, 24
   see also dress
Coca-Cola, 373, 377
cocaine, 377
coffee. *See* drugs
cognitive disequilibrium, 300
cognitive structure, 448
coitus. *See* sex
college, 19, 74, 75, 141, 142, 146, 180
college adolescents. *See* adolescents
collegiates, 106
communication blocks, 514
communication:
   effective, 513
   empathy, 521, 522
   helpful, 514
   verbal, 141
companionship, 269
compliance, 109
computers, 182, 240
concreteness, 537–541
confidence, 114, 208, 269
conflict, 108
   dealing with, 532
   positive and negative, 534
   unhealthy, 533
conformist, 109
conformists. *See* conformity
conformity, 98–106
   anti, 107
   conformists, 107
   negative connotations of, 107
   nonconformists, 107, 108
   other-conformity, 107
   peer group, 107
   personality, 111
   see also children
confrontation, 541–544
conscience. *See* superego
continuity, 48
contract approach, 494
control, 15, 154

conversion reaction, 350, 351
coping, 133, 146
   drugs and, 391
   with handicap, 223
   skills, 56, 406
Counseling with Parents of Handicapped Adolescents, 224
counselors, 506
   lay, 509
couples, 106
   see also relationships
court, 484
   juvenile, 438, 439
   New Jersey, 440
   Texas, 440
CPI. *See* California Personality Inventory Scale
creativity, 133
crime, 10, 86, 127, 173, 417, 418, 426, 432
   juvenile, 433–435
   prevention, 433, 439
   property, 433
   treatment, 433
   violent, 428, 433
criminals, 108, 428
crowds, 47, 105, 106, 109
Cuba, 58
cults, 249, 332
   religion and, 319, 320
culture, 101
   adult, 106
   distinctions in, 106
   high school, 178
   matriarchal, 220
   middle class, 43, 105, 106
   peer, 113
   U.S., 213
   Western, 44
   youth, 45, 107, 233

dances, 268
dancing, 47
dating, 50, 53, 114, 139, 143, 180, 250, 262–278
   blacks and, 137
   dates and, 106
   interracial, 149
   reasons for, 269
daughters:
   divorced mother and, 131
   widowed mother and, 131
death, 51, 72, 128, 360
defense mechanisms, 52, 53, 56
defensiveness, 505

Subject index

delinquency, 76–79, 129, 220, 234, 271, 281, 416, 422, 425, 439
  causes for, 420–423, 427
  and child abuse, 421, 422
  definition of, 418
  female, 432
  results of, 427
  widespread, 418, 419
delinquents, 72, 100, 108, 211, 221, 479
  definition of, 417
  production of, 423
  see also children, poverty groups
dependence, 100
depression, 131, 156, 340–346
  explanations for, 343
Depression, Great, 9, 10
desegregation, 174
development, 5, 201
  adolescent, 43, 109
  adult influence on, 71
  biological, 48
  cognitive, 446
  maturational, 450
  mental, 450
  moral, 54, 313–319
  personality, 54, 423
  sex roles, 285, 286
  sexual, 274
  social, 173, 183
  television effects on, 245
  tranquil period of, 55
developmental tasks, 43–45
deviance, 100
  adolescent, 109
  see also anticonformity
diffusion, 74–77
discipline, 18, 27, 48, 75, 80, 102, 138, 139, 148, 150, 172, 173, 183, 189–192, 422
  parental, 18, 316
discontinuity, 48
discouragement, 102
disorders, 333
  affective, 340–346
  conversion reaction, 350, 351
  manic-depressive, 345
  neurotic, 346
  obsessive-compulsive, 348–350
  treatment, 345
divorce, 58, 117, 128, 130–133, 429
  affects on males and females, 131
  coping with, 132
  effects on development, 131
  emotional strains and, 131
dolls, 142
draft card burnings, 25

dress, 21, 37, 71, 101, 103, 108, 280
drinking, 10, 18, 21, 180
  see also alcohol
dropouts, 79
  see also school
drug abuse. *See* drugs
drugs, 21, 14, 86, 131, 139, 140, 173, 201, 250, 271, 272, 281, 343, 488
  behaviorist approach and, 397, 404–406
  characteristics of, 374
  city vs. country, 389
  cognitive social learning approach, 406
  effects of, 394
  high school and, 388
  motives for use of, 389
  problems, 131
  psychoactive, 379–409
  psychodynamic approach to prevention, 402–404
  reasons for use of, 394
  rebellion and, 400
  selling, 173
  sex differences and, 389
  social learning theory and, 397
  theories, 392
  treatment for abuse of, 345, 346, 401

Early Window, The (Liebert, Spraklin, and Davidson), 243
economic aid, 117
ectomorph, 210–213
education, 19, 20, 50, 117, 146, 175, 241, 425, 446
  adequateness of, 168
  Chinese, 141
  college, 137
  continued, 119
  effectiveness of vocational, 181, 183
  equal, 174
  family-parent, 440
  inadequate parental, 134
  lack of, 117
  methods of, 176
  moral, 183
  parental, 19
  public, 166
  quality of, 174
  sex, 145, 183–189
  special, 478
Educational Amendments Acts, 1972, Title IX, 179
educational system, 166
Educational Testing Service, 245
ego, 51–57, 76, 263, 344, 427

Ego Identity Scales, 73
egocentrism, 449
ejaculation, 11
Electra complex, 54, 427
emotion, 156, 235
emotional balance, 157
emotional learning, 157
emotions, 101
  sharing of, 157
empathy, 57, 221, 314, 315, 506, 510
  communication and, 521, 522
  definition of, 521
  levels of, 522, 523
  self-test for, 523, 524
employment, 19, 21, 134, 140
  lack of, 137
encouragement, 102
endocrine glands, 201
endomorph, 210–213
equilibration, 455
erogenous zones, 52
estrogen, 204
ethnic groups. *See* groups
Europe, medieval, 8
extinction, 474, 475, 489

fading, 486
family, 9, 19, 20, 46, 72, 75, 101, 113, 155, 172, 263
  absence of religion in the, 127
  allegiance to, 140
  American-Indian, 138–140
  black, 136
  broken, 84
  Chinese, 28, 141–142
  conflict within the, 44
  differences in racial groups, 133, 135
  differences in socioeconomic groups, 133
  drugs and the, 399
  effectiveness of, 128
  extended, 130, 142
  father-absent, 130
  hardships and the, 10
  immigrant, 141
  importance of the, 127, 128
  Japanese, 26
  Japanese-American, 146–149
  large, 148
  life, changes in, 128, 156
  Mexican-American, 144, 146
  nuclear, 149
  obligations to, 140
  patriarchal, 149
  power of, 126
  problems and, 27

rejected values of, 26
relationships, 130
role of black woman, 137
single-parent, 126, 130, 131
stressful environments, 115
threats to the, 127
traditional models in the, 131
fantasy, 57, 247
fashion, 103
    long hair, 108
    see also clothes, dress
father,
    American-Indian, 140
    competition with, 131
    Mexican-American, 145
fear, 52, 54
feedback, negative, 102
feelings, 157
    owning. See owning feelings
    recognizing, 522
femininity, 44
fetish, 142
films. See movies
First Amendment, 184
fitting in. See conformity
fixation, 54
food, 141, 146
foreclosure, 74–77
Forerunners, 24
formal operations, 452
foster homes, 6, 58, 126
free will, 476
freedom, 69, 103, 109, 113, 144, 147, 169, 264, 272, 308, 319, 490, 504, 555
    adolescent's, 107
    personal, 100
friend,
    role of, 115
friendliness, 103
friends, 27, 44, 81, 100, 104, 109, 112, 132, 169, 180, 263
    importance of having, 112, 128
friendships, 28, 55, 57, 68, 112, 177
    boys and, 113
    fluctuation of, 112
    genuine, 113
    girls and, 113
    healthy adjustment and, 115
    importance in later development, 114
    stability of, 112
    stages of, 111
    see also dating
frustration, 177

"Gahns," 139

Gallup Youth Survey, 18
Gamblers Anonymous, 237
gangs, 105, 113, 332, 426
Gault, Gerald, 437–438
gay, 103
generation gap, 14, 15, 18, 25, 27, 98, 101
genes, 215
genital stage, 53, 54
Germany. *See* youth, European
Gilber Islands, 49, 50
giri, 146
Girl Scouts, 132
Girl's Day, 147
goals, 70, 73–76, 100, 306, 425, 554
    unrealistic, 17, 18
grades, 47
    see also school
groups:
    counterculture, 173
    differences in ethnic, 149
    ethnic, 133
    gangs, 144
    names of various, 106
    palomillas, 144, 145
    peer, 177
    pressures of, 107
    racial, 166, 172
    socioeconomic, 135
    see also cliques
Growing Up in New Guinea (Mead), 49
guidance, 103
guilt, 70, 225

hair, 86, 107, 137, 201–204, 233, 280
Handbook of Adolescent Psychology, (Peterson and Brandon), 205
handicaps, 83, 222, 225
    coping with, 223
Happy Days, 21
hazards, 109
health, 20
    care, 137, 144, 215
    poor, 134
    services, 182
hedonism, 55
helper, therapist as, 507
helping responses, 516, 517
    see also responses
helping, 510, 522, 523
    skills, 536–556
heroes, 248
heroin. *See* drugs; narcotics
high school, 19, 48, 74, 99, 100, 103, 106, 109, 115, 146, 169
    American, 189

Canadian, 234
culture, 178
middle-class, 234
Midwestern, 46
Minnesota, 128
hippies, 108
History of Childhood, The (de Mause), 6
Hitler youth, 416, 424
home life, 101, 126, 156
    in broken home, 173
    climate of, 131
    delinquency and, 421
    importance of, 127
    Puerto Rican, 143
    unhappy, 173
homosexuality, 25, 185
honesty, 30, 103
hormones, 201, 205, 221, 222
    in males and females, 204
    imbalance of, 360
    sex, 204
horoscope, 428
horror, 248, 249
hostility, 106
Huckleberry Finn, (Twain), 416
humility, 141
humor, 103
Hurried Child, The (Elkind), 176
hyperactivity, 335–340
    definition of, 337
    symptoms of, 339, 340
    treatment of, 339, 340
hypochondriasis, 351
hypothalamus, 201

I messages, 191, 522, 523
id, 51, 55, 201, 427
ideals, 100
identity, 78, 100, 136, 137, 143, 264
    achievement, 73, 75
    crisis, 116
    crystallization of, 113
    deprivation of, 72
    ego, 71
    negative, 72
    personal, 38, 490
    sense of, 68–80
    sex, 221
    sexual, 58
    states, 75, 76, 78
Identity Achievement Scale, 73
illiteracy, 166
immediacy, 507, 544–549
immorality, 110
impotence, 185, 427
imprinting, 424

incest, 139, 220
incompatible response, 490
independence. *See* conformity
individualist, 109
infancy, period of, 39
infants, 40
infatuation, 113
influence, peer, 110
inhalants, 374
initiation rites, 219–221
    female, 220
intellect, structure of, 462
intelligence, 103, 104, 331, 446, 452, 460
    definition of, 457
    development of, 453
    factors of, 462
    television, 242
    tests, 463
intercourse. *See* sex
interests, 103
intimacy, 270
Inventory of Psychosocial Development, 73
IQ, 47, 59, 129, 130, 172, 215, 338, 348, 427, 452, 464, 479
    criticisms, 459
    testing, 456, 458
    tests, 464
    see also intelligence
isolation, 192

Japanese-Americans, 146–149
Jews, 398
job security, 9
junior high school, 50, 86, 99, 100, 201
    smoking in, 407
justice, 299, 433
juvenile delinquent. *See* delinquent
juvenile, 10
    definition of, 417

kissing, 278
knowledge, 448, 449

language, 37, 85, 101, 106, 107, 133, 136, 335, 447, 454
    unusual, 107
    changing, 106
    clean, 30
    foreign, 172
    profane, 482
LaScala Opera House, 213
latency stage, 53–55

law, knowledge of, 110
leaders, 18, 108, 209, 210
    informal, 110
leadership, 222, 237, 458
learned helplessness, 343, 344
learning, 450, 454
legal services, 135
liberty, 418
libido, 53, 55
life-style, 109
like. *See* love
listening, 510
    active, 516–519
    effective communication, 513
literature, 233, 314
    adolescent, 250, 252
logic, 452
love scale, 265
love, 17, 20, 27, 42, 44, 55, 57, 59, 71, 80, 81, 86, 87, 262–266, 272, 276, 308, 316, 345, 532, 554
    parental, 344
    withdrawal of, 153
love-support, 152–154
LSD. *See* psychedelics

magic, 50, 233
manhood, 14, 220
mania, 342
Mao Tse-tung, 108
marijuana, 18, 233, 272, 280, 374, 375
    see also pot
marriage, 9, 12, 27, 44, 45, 49, 50, 55, 172, 173, 180, 224, 431
    adolescent, 115
    American-Indian, 139
    attitudes toward early, 116
    early, 113
    interracial, 149
    intertribal, 140
    Japanese-American, 148
    parental support in, 119
    problems in, 116
    Puerto Rican, 143
    teenage, 115, 119
    unstable, 134
masculinity, 44
masturbation, 185, 278
mate selection, 270
maturation, 41, 206, 213
    effects of, 207–210
    sexual, 272, 274
maturity, 101, 201
    biological, 56
    emotional, 45
    moral, 304

physical, 43
media, 233
memory, 461
menarche, 11, 204, 214, 217
menstruation, 50, 146, 185, 202, 213, 215, 220, 342
    American-Indian, 49, 50
    anorexia nervosa and, 360
    information on, 218
    preparation for, 218
    relief of cramps, 146
    start of, 137
    see also menarche
mental health, 332, 334
mesomorph, 210–213
Mexican-Americans, 144–146, 149
minorities, 24, 25, 29, 173, 181, 182, 419
    see also groups
MMPI, 427
model, adult, 129, 223
money, 12, 24, 46, 86, 103, 110, 117, 141, 237, 268, 425
    as reinforcer, 474
moral behavior, 313–319
    and religion, 320–322
    and guilt, 315
    and self-concept, 318
moral development, 296–305
    influences on, 317, 318
moral dilemmas, 296
moral reasoning, 109, 296
moral stages, 301–303
moralities, dual, 298, 299
morality, 43, 110, 533
morals, 17, 25, 45, 99, 127, 184, 250, 534
moratorium, 73, 75, 76, 78
Mormons, 398
mothers,
    American-Indian, 139
    assistance of unwed, 117, 119
    Chinese, 141
    daughters of divorced, 131
    emotional effects on children of working, 129
    employed, 128–130
    middle-class, 129
    upper-class, 129
    widowed, 130, 131
motivation, 43, 46, 53, 129, 221, 454
    biological, 57
    sexual, 275
    sexual behavior, 279
movies, 233, 247, 254, 268, 391
moxa, 148
murder, 72, 418

Subject index

music, 18, 46, 77, 100, 234, 254, 503
   aversive, 235
   behavior, effect on, 235
   economic base, 235
   heavy metal, 234
   pop, 233, 234
   preferences, 234, 235
   rhythm and blues, 234
   rock, 24, 233
   soul, 234
my-rights approach, 494

narcissism, 345
narcotics, 376
National Commission on Excellence in Education, 166
National Commission on Marijuana and Drug Abuse, 372
National Institute of Mental Health, 156
National Longitudinal Survey of Youth Labor Market Experience, 169
National Opinion Research Center, 156
NCEE, 166
necking, 273
needs, 44, 102, 169
   approval, 113
   belonging, 111
   child care, 225
   conflict of, 534
   fulfillment of by friends, 112
   female emotional, 113
   individual, 43
   peer interaction, 113
   personal, 70
   psychological, 112
   satisfaction of, 54
   satisfying by marriage, 115
   security, 113
   sensitivity to, 110
   support, 113
   understanding adolescents', 138
negative practice, 490
negative reinforcement, 474–476
negative reinforcers. *See* reinforcers
Negro Scholarship Program, 22
neurosis, 346
neurotic anxiety, 42
New Morality, The (Yankelovich), 23
Newsweek, 169
nicknames, 82
nicotine, 378
   see also drugs
Nobel Prize, 5
nonconformity, 108, 109
   see also conformity

normality, 331, 332
norms, 42, 45, 106, 108, 113
   adult, 108
   peer group, 108, 109
   rejecting adult, 109
   societal, 423
   see also conformity
nuclear war, 20
nutrition, 215

Oakland Growth Study, 207
occult, 233
occupation, 133
Oedipal complex, 54, 332, 427
Oedipal conflict, 313
operant conditioning, 474
opinionated behaviors, 512
oral stage, 53, 54
organs, reproductive, 202
orgasm, 185, 377
other-conformity, 107–109
   see also conformity
ovulation, 204
owning feelings, 518, 519
   effects of, 520

palomilla, 144, 145
paraprofessionals, 505, 506
parental:
   control, 138, 154, 155
   disregard, 101, *see also* youth
   interest, 83
   relationships, 140
parenting, 102, 134, 150–157
parents, 6, 17, 21, 40, 57, 68, 71, 72, 77, 78, 81, 101, 102, 109, 110, 206
   anxiety in, 152
   approval of, 20
   as teachers, 85
   attitudes of Japanese, 149
   black, 136, 137
   Chinese, 141
   defensive, 225
   dependence on, 142
   foster, 126
   Japanese-American, 148
   language of, 107
   low-income, 135
   perceptions of, 271
   positive influence of, 173
   problems of teenage, 115, 116,
   Puerto Rican, 142–144
   relationship with teenagers, 269
   sex, outlook on, 283, 284
   significance of, 128

   single, 128, 130
   types of, 151–154
   of handicapped children, 225
   working, 128
Patterns of Culture, (Benedict), 48
peer domination. *See* youth
peer group, 100, 105, 109
   acceptance of, 102
   black, 137, 138
   conforming to, 111
   conformity, 102, 107
   experience, 109
   interaction, 99, 115
   orientation. *See* youth
   popularity and, 104
   pressure, 98, 99, 110, 111, 136, 391, 473
   relations, 103, 104, 173
   status, 100
peers, 18, 21, 46, 58, 70–72, 79, 81, 101, 141, 201, 206, 210, 289
   academics and, 47
   drugs and, 399
   healthy adjustment of, 115
   language of, 106
   relationships with, 12
   sex and, 283, 284
   values of, 47
penis-envy, 5
perceptions, 503
personality identity, 99
personality, 70, 72, 76, 89, 101–103, 111, 130, 211, 212, 233, 266, 275, 473
   adult, 73
   conforming, 111, 113
   contract approach, 494
   delinquent, 427
   development of, 68, 69
   hormonal effects on, 206
   somatotypes, 428
pessimism, 102
petting, 53, 276, 278
phallic stage, 53, 54
Phi Delta Kappan, 170, 171
phobias, 346–348
   common, 348
   origins of, 347
physical attractiveness, 102, 104
   see also appearance
pituitary gland, 201
pleasure principle. *See* id
popularity, 46
   needs for, 103
   role of athletics and, 179
   teenage, 103
pornography, 102, 233, 252–255

positive regard, 505
positive reinforcement, 474–476, 487
positive reinforcers. *See* reinforcers
positive relationship approach, 493
pot, 25, 77, 233
   see also marijuana
poverty, 140, 150, 464
   delinquency and, 423
praise, 191
preadolescence. *See* youth, period of
preadolescent tasks, 69
pregnancy, 115, 138, 172, 173, 185, 250, 280, 284
   in U.S., 115
   parental support in teenage, 119
prejudice, 106, 425
Premack principle, 191
prison, 221
privacy, 503
projection, 53
propinquity, 112
prostitution, 430
Protestants, 19, 398
psychedelics, 375
   see also drugs
psychological:
   adjustment, 130
   benefits of video games, 239
psychosocial moratorium, 109
psychotherapy, 356, 359
   goal of, 352
puberty, 11, 13, 14, 21, 139, 188, 201, 202, 205, 206, 210, 213, 214
   Mexican-American, 144
   onset of, 217
   sequence of, 203
pubescence, 10, 13, 14, 99
Puerto Rican-Americans, 142–144
punishment, 39, 81, 148, 219, 300, 318, 474–476, 487–489
   corporal, 138, 422
   drugs, 405
   physical, 153
punks, 24

Quinceanera, 145

race, 19
racial differences,
   intelligence and, 463, 464
   television viewing and, 242
racism, 136, 250
rape, 189, 250, 333, 418
rationalization, 53
reaction formation, 53

reality,
   behavior, 503
   reconstruction of, 447
reality principle. *See* ego
reasoning, moral, 109
reassurance, 550–553
rebellion, 21, 25, 29, 40, 77, 84, 107, 108, 113, 276, 392, 455
   drugs and, 400
   see also nonconformity
rebels, 108
recreation, 233, 269
regression, 53
reinforcers, 492, 496
   see also reinforcers
relationships, 38, 503, 506, 510
   dating, 268
   heterosexual, 113
   interpersonal, 41, 84
   intimate, 105
   mature, 44
religion, 15, 19, 20, 23, 70–77, 184, 281, 289, 309, 319–323, 398, 399
   absence of in family, 127
   adolescence and, 322, 323
   behavior and, 322
   moral behavior and, 320–322
   sex and, 282, 283, 284, 285
repression, 52
reputation, 103
responses,
   active-listening, 516
   advice-giving, 515
   interpretative, 515
   questioning, 515, 516
   supportive, 515
   sympathizing, 516
retardation, 173
rewards, 141, 300, 474, 488, 496
robbery, 173, 189, 418, 433
role diffusion, 72
role models, 140, 426
role playing, 223
roles, 392
   occupational, 116
   sex, 116
romance, 262, 266, 267, 272
romanticism scale, 266
rules, 20, 45, 108, 113, 146, 298
   involvement in making, 191
running away, 428, 429

safety, 52, 192
Samoa, 14, 48–50
SAT, 464
   see also Scholastic Aptitude Tests

satellization, 423
satiation, 492
schemata, 448
schizophrenia, 333, 353, 354, 506
   prevention of, 356
   recovery from, 354
   treatment of, 356
Scholastic Aptitude Tests, 166–168, 464
schools, 10, 21, 43, 83, 110, 114, 116, 143, 176
   achievement in, 129
   American, 167, 175, 176, 181
   Asian, 28
   athletics in, 179
   attitudes toward public, 170
   Catholic, 102, 173, 174
   courses in, 172
   desegregation of, 174
   discipline in, 189–192
   dropout rate in, 176
   dropping out in, 172, 173
   influences of, 130
   private, 166, 173, 174
   public, 166, 173, 174, 180
   religious, 174
   role of, 45
   satisfaction with, 169
   secondary, 168
   sex education in, 184–189
   size of, 177
   Soviet, 175
   subcultures in, 179, 180
   success in, 143
   underachievement, 139
   violence in, 189–192
   vocational, 181
secular trends, 215
security, 112, 126
   economic, 117
   emotional, 129
self, 78
self-acceptance, 73
self-actualization, 503, 504, 534
self-appraisal, 82
self-assertion, 143
self-centered, 23
self-centeredness, 133, 522
self-concept, 73, 78–89, 213, 223, 319, 505, 553–555
   development of, 38
self-confidence, 102, 103
   video games and, 239
self-consciousness, 9, 69
self-control, 133, 484
self-deception, 53
self-definition, 73
self-development,

promoting, 555
self-directed approach, 497
self-discipline, 30, 143
self-esteem, 69, 78–89, 99, 103, 131, 208, 213, 221, 269, 335, 344, 438, 473
  drugs and, 392
  parents', 81
  pseudo-esteem, 87
self-evaluation, 101
self-exploration, 507
self-fulfillment, 25
self-gratification, 55, 391
self-guidance, 223
self-image, 78–89
self-importance, 99
self-instruction, 223, 224, 509
self-love, 87, 345
self-monitoring, 89
self-perception, 46
self-presentation, 89
self-regard, positive, 505
self-reliance, 84, 128
self-reservation, 39
self-sufficiency, 13, 140
self-support,
  economic, 116
self-worth, 87
Senate Subcommittee on Science, Technology, and Space, 175
sense of autonomy, 69
sense of identity, 70
sense of industry, 70
sense of initiative, 69
sense of trust, 69
SES. *See* family; socioeconomic status; status
sex, 19, 21, 44, 48–50, 55, 86, 139, 206, 243, 250, 253, 262, 269, 273–281, 284, 288, 426, 430, 431, 488
  attitudes toward, 144
  characteristics, 202, 210
  contact with members of opposite, 131
  crimes and, 253
  dating and, 269
  desire and, 54
  drives, 14
  feelings about, 185
  instinct and, 51
  premarital, 21, 25, 138, 140, 185
  religion and, 282, 283
  taboos, 220
sex differences, 74, 100, 146, 147, 221, 389
sex education, 136, 145, 146, 148, 187

sex role, 12, 20, 54, 76, 222, 285–289
  development of, 69
sexual activity, 131
sexual behavior, television and, 243
sexual development,
  stages of, 204
sexual deviancy, 488
sexual energy, 55
sexual immorality, 10
sexual impulses, 21
sexual morality, 27
sexual revolution, 279–282
  females and the, 280
sexual stimulation,
  female, 254
sexuality, 48, 52, 53, 56
  black, 137
  development of, 276
shaping, 477
shoplifting. *See* crime, property
siblings, 147
  foster, 126
  relationships of, 140
single parent. *See* family
skills, 113
  personal, 166
slang, 106
  see also language; speech
slavery, 6, 150, 464
slums, 134
smoking, 18, 180, 488
  programs, 407
  see also drugs
soaps, 247–249
sociability, 102, 104, 106, 109, 112
social action, 110
social adjustment, 129
social class, 133
  differences, 149
  in behavior, 28
social competence, 99
social disorder, 127
social experience, 109
social interaction,
  Chinese, 142
social interaction, 109
social worker, 59
socialization, 269
socialized anxiety, 42
socioeconomic status, 133, 134
SOS room, 192
Soviet Union, 175
spanking, 141
  see also punishment
Special Olympics, 83
speech, 102, 103, 108
  Chinese, 141

  see also language
sperm, 204
sports, 132
  see also athletics
Sputnik, 166
stages, developmental, 450, 451
  Erikson and, 68
  Freud, S. and, 53–55
stages of development, 298
standard of living, 141
standards, 29, 111, 145, 534
  adult, 110
  American-Indian, 138
  educational, 175
  peer, 110
status offenses, 418
status, 43, 48, 112, 140, 207, 221, 238, 269, 423
  financial, 117
  grown-up, 9
  identity, 76
  intelligence, 272
  minority, 10
  sex and, 187
  socioeconomic, 133, 173, 241, 242, 339
stereotypes, 15, 18, 71, 101, 106, 126, 136, 212, 213, 221, 223, 432
storm and stress, 14, 40, 55, 222
stress, 53, 56, 103, 114, 224, 332–334 389
  coping with, 333, 334
  stages of, 333
  stressors and, 333
  youth and, 111
strum and drang. See storm and stress
students, 28, 106, 168
  American, 175
  assaults on, 189
  college, 25
  gifted, 166
  high achievement, 180
  Japanese college, 27, 28
  medical, 12
  Negro, 22
  Soviet, 175
  working-class, 234
sublimation, 53
success, 141
suicide, 24, 58, 87, 110, 271, 331, 332, 343, 360–366
  American-Indians and, 139
  motivation for, 361
superego, 51, 52, 344, 427
suppression, 52
Supreme Court, 174
surrogate, father, 140

swimming, 137
Switzerland. *See* youth, European
systematic desensitization, 353
systems approach, 493

teachers, 42, 58, 59, 71, 78, 81, 110, 115, 141, 148, 168, 173, 492
  assault on, 189
  conflict with, 532
  creative, 176
  language and, 107
  praise by, 191
  safety of, 172
  television, 233, 238, 241–247, 254, 391, 486
  effects of, 243–247
temperament, 212, 335
terrorism, 22
testosterone, 204, 221
theory,
  biogenic, 427, 428
  formulating a, 37
  learning, 447
  normative, 41
  personality, 427
  phenomenological, 503
  practicality of, 38
  psychoanalytic, 426
  psychogenic, 426
  social learning, 47, 407, 408
  sociopathic, 427
  strain, 425
  subculture, 425, 426
  use of, 58–60
  value of, 37
therapy, 507,
  aversion, 405
  aversive, 489
  behavior, 353
  behavioral, 357
  cognitive, 346, 353
  dance and art, 357
  drug, 357
  family, 353
  Gestalt, 353
  milieu, 357
  necessity of, 351
  occupational and rehabilitational, 357
  problem-solving, 508
  psychoanalysis and, 346
  success in, 506
  weight gain, 359
time out, 489
tobacco, 372
  see also drugs; smoking
toilet-training, 54

token economy, 479–484, 486
traditions, 113, 149
tranquilizers, 375
Transcendental Meditation, 23
trends, 98
tribes. *See* American-Indian
Trofranil, 345
truancy, 140, 428
trustworthiness, 103
tuned-out behavior, 512

U.S. Office of Education, 177
U.S. Senate Labor, Health, and Human Services Subcommittee, 186
unemployment. *See* employment
UNESCO, 18
United States, 50, 108, 166, 183
  political changes, 22
USSR, 175

values, 25, 42, 45, 47, 54, 73, 74, 77, 106, 113, 149, 184, 250, 305–313, 424, 504, 534, 554
  adolescents and, 101
  antisocial, 180
  core, 18
  cultural differences and, 308, 309
  instrumental, 402
  measurement of, 306, 307
  parental, 101, 128
  sex differences and, 310
  social, 110
  society's, 110
  traditional, 128
  youth and, 128
valuing, 312
vandalism, 24, 173
verbal ability, 453, 454
vid-kids. *See* video, games
video, 237, 238
video games, 237–241
  addiction to, 239
  elements of, 240
Vietnam War, 12, 21–23
violence, 25, 144, 422
  adolescent, 433
  mob, 332
  personal, 24
  television and, 243, 244
virginity, 144
Vivienne (Mack and Hickler), 341, 342, 346, 362, 363

war, 21

weight, 215, 216
widows, daughters of, 131
witchcraft, 233
withdrawal, 101
womanhood, 217
  anticipation of, 137
women's liberation, 25
work, 20, 30, 48, 141
World Press Review, 24, 26
World War I, 309
World War II, 149, 288
worth, feelings of, 85

XYY, 428

youth, 14, 46, 98, 99, 101, 106, 107
  affluent, 426
  alarming facts about, 21
  American, 18, 22, 45, 110, 128
  American-Indian, 138–140
  background of, 21
  black, 137
  Canadian, 26
  Chinese, 28, 141–142
  Chinese-American, 142
  college, 180
  definition of, 10
  deprived, 9
  of the eighties, 26
  European, 24, 25, 26
  of the fifties, 21
  high-school age, 167
  Japanese, 26
  Japanese-American, 146–149
  parents of adult-oriented, 102
  peer-dominated, 101
  peer-oriented, 101
    see also parental, disregard
  period of, 39
  of the seventies, 23–25
  of the sixties, 21–25
  societal effects on, 9
  values of Asian, 28
  working-class, 25
Youth and Adolescence, 13
Youth and Society, 13
Youth: The Years from Ten to Sixteen (Gesell and Ames), 41

PHOTO CREDITS *(continued from page iv)*

FPG. **379** Jeroboam: © 1982 Frank D. Smith. **388** Jeroboam: © 1982 Tom Carter. **391** Woodfin Camp & Associates: © Jim Anderson 1980. **398** Jeroboam: © Kit Hedman. **414** © Carolyn A. McKeone/FPG. **417** © Carolyn A. McKeone/FPG. **429** Jeroboam: Hank Lebo. **431** EKM-Nepenthe: © MCMLXXXII Robert V. Eckert, Jr. **437** James L. Shaffer. **444** Jeroboam: © Michael Rothstein. **448** Jeroboam: © Jane Scherr. **453** Jeroboam: © Laimute Druskis. **460** Jeroboam: © 1978 Suzanne Arms. **464** Stock, Boston: © Ellis Herwig. **470** Jeroboam: © Michael Rothstein. **475** Jeroboam: © Don Ivers. **479** Frost Publishing: © 1982 Bill Powers. **484** Stock, Boston: © Rick Smolan. **491** Jeroboam: © 1980 Anne Dorfman. **495** Woodfin Camp & Associates: © 1980 Arthur Tress. **500** Jeffrey Grosscup. **504** Stock, Boston: © Karen Rosenthal. **508** Stock, Boston: © Peter Vandermark. **511** Jeroboam: © Kit Hedman. **513** Jeroboam: © Peeter Vilms. **530** Stock, Boston: Peter Vandermark. **535** Frost Publishing: Future Farmers of America. **539** Frost Publishing: Tony O'Brien. **544** Frost Publishing: Helena Frost. **554** Jeroboam: © Michelle Vignes.